CW00537042

Contents

GEORGE PADMORE INSTITUTE

George Padmore is one of the major figures of the 20th century. He demonstrated an independent intellectual and organisational position in the anti-colonial and international movements for change in the 1930s and 1940s. His was the vision of a world unburdened from the arrogance and tribulation of empires and dedicated to equality, solidarity and hope. We have named our Institute after George Padmore as we see it continuing the traditions which shaped his life - **independent, radical vision, outlook and activities, connecting the Caribbean, Africa, Europe, North America and Asia.**

The George Padmore Institute is a library, educational and research centre housing materials relating to the black community of Caribbean, African and Asian descent in Britain and continental Europe. It is a charity that was set up in 1991 by a group of people connected with New Beacon Books Ltd and it occupies the three floors above the New Beacon bookshop, the freehold of the building having been donated to the Institute. **New Beacon Books** is the specialist bookshop, international bookservice and publishing house, that has also worked closely with and supported many educational, cultural and political initiatives in Britain and continental Europe since its founding in 1966.

The George Padmore Institute is catering for the organisation of:

(1) a library, educational resource and research centre, that will allow the materials in its care to be available for use by interested individuals and groups, both in person at the Institute and through the use of modern storage, retrieval and communication methods;

(2) educational and cultural activities, including conferences, courses, seminars, talks and readings;

(3) the publication of relevant materials.

The George Padmore Institute already possesses a collection of books, journals and materials that have been donated to it by some of its trustees, many of whom have been active in Britain in a variety of fields - for example education, publishing, the law, legal rights, cultural and political activities, and the development of the Notting Hill Carnival - over the past 20 to 30 years. The Institute's work will continue the method of working which every trustee of the organisation has developed over this period. Through their professional practice, as well as their rootedness in leading community based activities in pursuit of the rights of minorities and of social change, the trustees have made a significant contribution to the sense of confidence with which those communities now project themselves and seek to give expression to their cultural creativity, influence policy and effect change in the interest of social justice.

Introduction by John La Rose

This introduction is based on excerpts from the introductions by John La Rose for the seven talks in the *Life Experience With Britain* Series.

The George Padmore Institute has always been one of the essential objectives of the work in which we have been engaged over the years through New Beacon Books, the International Book Fair of Radical Black and Third World Books, and all the organisations and institutions which we have established. And for those of you who don't know, the George Padmore Institute is a follow-up from the George Padmore Supplementary School, which we started in 1969 around the same time that the Supplementary School Movement was beginning. Who was Padmore, why Padmore and what is the George Padmore Institute?

George Padmore was a contemporary of C.L.R. James. They grew up together as boys in Trinidad between Tunapuna and Arima. They were friends. Padmore, on leaving school, worked as a journalist in Trinidad before leaving to study in the United States. First, he went to study agriculture and then he ended up with law at Howard University. But his main interest was in social, political and cultural change. While James became a Trotskyist here in England, Padmore became a communist in the United States. Then they met here in Britain, when Padmore was on his way to attend a conference in the Soviet Union and they became friends again - one the Trotskyist and the other the communist. Padmore eventually broke with the Comintern and Stalin. He was in Hamburg, and almost got killed there. So Padmore broke with international Communism and James broke with international Trotskyism. They both broke with these international movements.

Padmore eventually returned to Britain and he was here from 1935, until almost the end of his life. He was one of the principal organisers in the struggle for independence in Africa and Asia and of the famous Fifth Pan African Congress, which took place in Manchester in 1945. He was the principal inspiration for that conference and along with others from America, Africa and the Caribbean, helped to organise it.

After that came the struggle for the Independence of Ghana, led by Kwame Nkrumah, in which he participated as an advisor to Nkrumah. When Nkrumah came to power with the Convention People's Party in 1957, ten years after the independence of India, Padmore went to Ghana and became Nkrumah's Advisor on African affairs. He was largely responsible for the organisation of the All Africa People's Conference in 1958 which had an enormous impact on the whole of Africa at that time. The Conference brought together all the movements in Sub-Saharan Africa fighting for their independence and the events of Africa took off from that period in 1957 into the 1960s. Padmore died just one year later in England and his ashes were returned to Ghana.

The Institute was named the George Padmore Institute after Padmore, and the Supplementary School which I founded in 1969, was also called the George Padmore Supplementary School. The Institute was something we planned that would be organized further down the road so that we would have an institution devoted to archives, research, policy proposals and all of that. That is something still to come. We have begun with the Education and Public Programme Committee's work and these series of talks called *Life Experience with Britain: lectures and conversations*.

But the foundation for this series began with the formation of New Beacon Books - our publishing house, bookshop and international bookservice - in 1966, so we have been 30 years at it, and we are proud of our achievements. I think I have said before that we are not flash and dash. We are slow builders and consolidators. And, I think that is the way that we have approached our work over the years and that is the way in which we continue to approach the work of the George Padmore Institute. This is the beginning. We have a number of ideas. For example, this will be an archive and we shall have computers, which will give us access to other people's archives and allow other people to access our archives. Then there will be educational training sessions here and research and policy planning, consultancy and special events. These are our basic objectives.

We have talked at the various sessions about George Padmore to give you some idea about why we call it the George Padmore Institute,

vi

and why George Padmore has meant so much. I began by explaining that the supplementary school, which we established in 1969, was called the George Padmore Supplementary School. It was the beginning of the supplementary schools movement. The only other school at that moment was the school that Bishop Wilfred Wood organised in Shepherds Bush, where he worked at the time as the Assistant Rector of St. Stephens. We were linked and we were associated.

With each of the sessions of this series which we call *Life Experience with Britain* we have a biography of the person who's speaking because many of us think we know the people who are involved and we don't. In the course of this series we shall be informing ourselves, and through us the entire society, of who these people are, what they have done and how important is the contribution they have made to our presence in this country.

I want to say something in connection with the 'heroic generation'. It's a term I've always used about the early immigrants who came here in the 1950s and their children, because some of us who are here belong to that generation. I came here in 1961. I came here at the age of 33, almost the same age as when C.L.R. James came to this country. The heroic generation made enormous sacrifices for their children and their families in all kinds of ways, but I know that the things they did not think about were the possibilities of sport, music and art. They were too concerned about the problems of daily living. But nevertheless, what we have seen is an enormous creativity in all the institutions of popular culture into which we have inserted ourselves in this society. For where we are, what we live at present is, has been, the past, and what we shall now live will be the future and further transformations which we shall influence in Britain and Europe.

Pearl Connor-Mogotsi

Pearl Connor-Mogotsi
First Talk in the Life Experience With Britain series at the George Padmore Institute, London (20.1.97)

I am very honoured to be here, on what I consider an auspicious occasion, celebrating the contribution of George Padmore, the birthday of Martin Luther King, and such friends as we all honour today and remember. John wanted me to relate about myself really, to go into the nitty gritty, so I'm going to give you all the treatment, right? [laughter].

I was born into a very large cosmopolitan family in Trinidad. My father, Alfred Nunez, was a headmaster in Arouca, and my mother Georgiana Nunez, was a teacher also, before they moved to Diego Martin in north Trinidad; father to take up a post as ward officer of the district, mother as registrar of births and deaths as well as running the post office. There was always a lot of coming and going from the villagers and much activity around our home.

There were twelve of us in the family of which I was number nine, but we were left alone to get on with our lives, although the older brothers and sisters bossed us around. But there were rivers to swim in before going to school and I never wore shoes at home. I was the tomboy, climbing trees in the tropical forest behind our house. Snakes and frogs often came into the house and you could hear their calls at night in the air, as fireflies danced against the dark trees. There was an abundance of fresh fruit from our estate in Cumoto, which was managed by an overseer. We needed no encouragement to lead a natural life; we lived an abandoned sort of existence, wandering in the mud and screaming with excitement. We played games with our brothers and sisters and with our close relatives because my father never allowed strangers into our midst, he was a very protective old fellow. He edited all of our reading material as he did everything that entered the house. He owned an old Austin car in which he took us to and from school every day, he was so strict about punctuality that we were left at home crying our eyes out if we were late, and had to find our way to school in Port of Spain; then we were punished.

1

There was no electricity in Diego Martin at that time. We used gas, candles and large pitch-oil lamps for light. When we were left to go to sleep at night we thought we could hear all the old frightening folklore characters coming to play. We would jump up and scream and howl in fear. We had that kind of life: a lovely, magical, folklore-based existence.

My upbringing was conservative, but I was very, very rebellious. My mother was rebellious, my father was the opposite. He controlled us with a very firm grip. My mother was a white woman with red hair, but she had some Carib blood in her. In Trinidad she was considered white. Father was a Portuguese of African origin. His mother was the daughter of a freed slave. She had been educated by the family with whom her father worked and made certain that all her children were educated. Father's two sisters also became teachers. He was a powerful little gentleman, about five foot five in height, always impeccably dressed in a three-piece suit, even in that great tropical heat. Mother was tall and an outstanding woman. She had a fine stature, she commanded respect, she was amazing for a woman in those days. She was an entrepreneur. She invested in a fleet of cars and hired drivers to drive them. She also bought cattle and brought her favourite cow 'Latchmina' from Princes Town tied to the back of a lorry, when they moved to Diego Martin

Opposite our home in Diamond Village there was a green field where the cattle grazed. Mother hired Indian farm workers to look after the cows and milk them. Most of the milk was used by the family and some of it was sold. She spoke Hindustani and communicated with the Indian workers and our Indian neighbours. She got a great deal done because she was considered white and received special privileges from the powerful high-brown people who represented colonial Trinidad. Father did not want us to mix with the villagers in Congo village, which was a short distance away from our home, because he said we would talk 'congo'. At that time I did not even know that the Congo was a country. Mind you, nothing at all about Africa ever came into our home, because under colonialism Africa was backward. Father was upwardly mobile and did not want us to speak badly. We had to speak the King's English. Hence we were

2

deprived of learning patois. He imported sheet music from England and had us singing *Green Grow the Rushes Oh!*, and other English ditties around the piano, especially on Sundays. We had to go to church on Sunday morning, and attend Sunday school in the afternoons. No smoking or card-playing was allowed in our home. Most of us were taught the piano or violin. Whenever calypsonians went past our house, minstrels singing their songs, father would call us in, and shut the shutters. We could not associate with these as they were considered a bit rude – he had something there. He had no feeling for the folklore or the patois. Mother was more liberal, hence her interest in Beryl McBurnie's work. Father's blackness was never a problem, it was more a matter of class. There was a great mixture of colours in my family, some black like ebony, others white with curly locks, some red and orangey like me with bushy hair like fibre. Yet there was never any difference between us. Father was very proud that he was the grandson of a freed slave. But in my family there were not many like that.

I received my secondary education in St Joseph's convent in Port of Spain, run by nuns, from Ireland, I believe, although I was not a Catholic myself. I was immediately aware of the different treatment of the students in my class. The French creoles and the light-skinned ones, the blondes and the golden-haired girls, were put in the front of my class; and all the black children were at the back. But the Indians were even behind us, because they were 'coolies'. The black children often forgot that they had been called 'niggers' in the recent past - but such is the nature of racism. At that time I could not understand what was going on around me, and I was in revolt. I was driving all the black children and Indians to the courtyard to protest. I could not understand why they were being treated differently. I used to visit their homes and enjoy their way of life. Trinidad Indians and Negroes suffered a lot of discrimination because of colour. I was soon aware of the colour bar. The Chinese were more elitist; they kept apart because they passed as white and dealt in business, keeping to their own exclusive clubs. That is Trinidad for you.

I vividly remember the day on which war was declared. I was standing in the long living room in front of a large mirror on the wall

3

and rain was pelting down outside when the news was broadcast. The real significance was that my eldest brother, George Nunez, was on a cycling tour of England, and my mother was very worried that he was caught up out there. He was very adventurous. He joined the Air Force and trained as a pilot. He flew a Lancaster bomber, and unfortunately was killed over Essen in Germany in 1943. There is no such memory about our people and the contributions made from little islands like Trinidad in the Caribbean. We have to remind the people in this country that we gave our best, we gave the best that we had, into that kind of struggle, which should be remembered. Remember a lot of other things but that should be remembered also.

Meanwhile, Trinidad had a lend-lease agreement with the Americans for a base at Chaguaramas, which meant an influx of American soldiers and sailors. They threw their weight about, and they used to push black people off the pavements when they walked by. But this was a two-edged sword, because the women sought their favours, and they always had the goods; stockings, chocolates and other nice things that were then unobtainable in Trinidad. So, some of the calypsonians, they caught up with the thing and they started singing, 'Rum and Coca Cola, go down Point Cumana, the mothers and their daughters, working for the yankee dollar'. The yankee dollar was very powerful and corrupted our community, who lost sight of the reason for the American presence in Trinidad. Their music could be heard all over the island, and you could hear people singing, 'I'll be with you in apple blossom time, I'll be with you to change your name to mine'. And some of the girls went up to America - they took several of them up to live with them. So, we who were there in Trinidad, we were not really close in the sense of mixing up with it, but we saw what was happening. The calypsonians, who are the historians of our culture, they were making a note of that.

The British Fleet Air Arm were also in our waters, and their sailors came ashore on leave. But they had a very different attitude to our people, and showed some respect for our customs. As a result my sister Lois was courted by an English officer whom she married, and later came to live with him in Lancashire, after the war ended.

4

Pearl Connor-Mogotsi

Now Beryl McBurnie, 'La Belle Rosette' - the Carmen Miranda of the West Indies - was most famous for having established the Little Carib Theatre, and projecting the culture and arts of Trinidad and Tobago in the dance. She was my role model and one of the greatest influences of my life. Her associates were Jack Kelshall and Lennox Pierre, two solicitors dedicated to the independence of Trinidad and Tobago. Both had a tremendous influence on my political thinking and development. There was also Wilson Minshall, father of Peter of carnival fame, and Colin Laird. They both gave Beryl much-needed support. Lennox and Jack founded the Trinidad and Tobago Youth Movement and held a conference on Caribbean Federation in 1947, which I participated in. Afterwards I travelled to other islands to establish a Federal Youth Movement.

In that same year I travelled up the islands by schooner. I mean, which was very revolutionary for that time. My father let his daughter go on a schooner - a boat with only men on it. I also established contact with Keith Alleyne who was then Attorney General of St Lucia, and who hosted my talks, and Cecil Kelsick of Dominica, later Attorney General of Trinidad and Tobago under Dr Eric Williams. And then I went to St Lucia, Castries, and I met Derek Walcott for the first time, and Derek and his friends decided that I must come and talk to them in their school. So I went to the school. The head of the college was a priest, and he asked to see me. He wanted to know why the boys wanted to hear what I had to say, so I was questioned by him whether I was a communist. I told him that I was a nationalist, working for the independence of Trinidad and Tobago and for the Caribbean Federation. I must have satisfied him, because he allowed me to address the class. I also visited the French islands of Martinique and Guadeloupe.

On my return to Trinidad, I got on a research programme for Radio Trinidad about distinguished sons of the soil. I presented biographies of famous personalities like Arthur Cipriani, Quintin O'Connor, W.J. Alexander and others. Beryl was already grooming me for greater things. It was she who arranged for me to represent youth at the West Indian National Party convention at the Princes Building, Port of Spain, under the chairmanship of Dr David Pitt, who was still in

5

Trinidad at that time. At the same time I was very much aware of the work being done for the underprivileged in our society by Audrey Jeffers, and Olive Walke's *La Petite Musicale* in immortalising our folk songs for future generations.

In 1948 Edric Connor returned to Trinidad having enjoyed great success in England, singing traditional Trinidad folk songs and appearing on stage in plays and musicals and so on. Beryl attached Barney Morris, a great friend no longer with us, and myself, to be his escort around Trinidad. This is when I first met Edric. We discussed my plans for going abroad, possibly to university in America to study journalism. Although my uncle was a doctor, practicing medicine in Manhattan, father considered America to be the devil's playground. Edric suggested I would do well to come to England, where there were many seats of learning of equal standing.

In the summer of 1948 I arrived in London and was met by Edric's secretary who took me to a hotel in Cromwell Road. Later that evening I went to see the sights, and the next morning I was put on a train at Euston, to visit my sister who was living in Blackburn, Lancashire. I found the place grey cold and forbidding, the cotton mills were still active and my brother-in-law Jack Simpson managed one of them. I felt completely cut off from civilisation as I knew it. I saw no black or coloured people, and there was no contact with the locals. Having young children meant that my sister could not take me out. You were never greeted as you walked along the street. It was completely different from the Caribbean. It was just three years after the end of the war and the country was very depressed. There were dark satanic skies over Blackburn, and I wanted to get back to London to organise my university entrance to study law. I made contact with Edric from whom I sought advice. I applied to King's College, London University, requesting the entrance requirements and soon learned that I would need to take a university entrance examination because I had no Latin. So I had a struggle, I had to register with Regent Street Polytechnic for one year in order to get the necessary qualifications. During this time I began to see more and more of Edric, whom I later married.

By 1950 I enrolled for the LL.B course at King's College and settled down to becoming a full-time student. Together with other students like Ansel Wong, Barbara Joseph, Dossy Carberry, Rawle Farley, Elsa Goveia, Hilda Bynoe and others, we established the West Indian Students' Centre, at Collingham Gardens, Earls Court, which became a meeting place for discussions, dances, plays, lectures and many other activities. It would take another 12 years before we were truly independent and could claim to have our own High Commission in London.

Edric's position in the community was well established and we made our home available to visiting dignitaries and politicians from the West Indies, like Norman Manley of Jamaica, T. A. Marryshow of Grenada, Grantley Adams from Barbados, Forbes Burnham from Guyana, Dr Eric Williams of Trinidad and Tobago. And from Africa, Tom Mboya from Kenya, Dr Azikiwe from Nigeria, Julius Nyerere from Tanzania and Joshua Nkomo from Rhodesia. In the struggle for liberation from racism we met with Seretse Khama and Chief Luthuli the first President of the ANC, and Paul Robeson, Martin Luther King and Claudia Jones. They organised fund-raising events for political ends and mobilised our artists in these efforts. We put on fashion shows and soirees at the Commonwealth Institute, and we were assisted in this effort by Sarah Carter who was the wife of the then High Commissioner, John Carter, and Genevieve Marais a South African activist.

When I left Trinidad I carried letters of introduction to C.L.R. James and George Padmore. George already had a reputation for his work in Africa, with Nkrumah in Ghana, and C.L.R. James for his efforts in assisting Haile Selassie in the struggle against Mussolini. He was also closely associated with Dr David Pitt, whose surgery in Gower street became a meeting place for consultation and discussion by potential leaders of Afro-Caribbean and Indian descent. I was invited to meet George Padmore at his home near the Unity Theatre in Mornington Crescent. His wife, Dorothy, welcomed me, and took me to meet him. He was a small, quiet man, and asked me after Beryl and others in Trinidad. After reading the letter which Beryl had sent him, he asked me about my plans for the future. I told him that I was studying law and was interested in working for the liberation of our people. He said, 'we need young people with ideas and conviction to carry on the struggle'. George was working toward the independence of Ghana and was advising Nkrumah on strategy to achieve this goal. He suggested that I should keep in touch with him when he went out to Ghana after independence.

In 1952 my education was interrupted by the birth of my first child Geraldine, and family considerations took over. I later became more and more involved with the arts, broadcasting with the BBC, and taking part in West Indian dialect and American plays. After the birth of my son, Peter, I went home for a visit with my husband Edric, who was filming *Fire Down Below* on location in Trinidad and Tobago in 1956. Local artists were recruited for this film and many of them were planning to come to England to seek their fortunes. Edric and I were asked for advice and this is how we decided to get into working with and representing artists. This was how the idea of our Theatre, Stage and Film Agency was mooted in 1956.

Edric had a strong sense of national identity, which made him a pioneer of our folk art in Britain. He was constantly promoting our songs, music and folk dances, and we often performed these at social events. We used to dance the bongo, and the doption (body movement used by Baptists) and so on and I used to dress up in traditional dress, and we used to give the people great thrilling times. He knew all these dances but I didn't, because as I told you my father kept us away from all these things. But in two two's Edric got me coached. I was absolutely on the ball, and I learnt all those dances, and I really enjoyed them, you know. I don't know what would have happened if father had had his way. So we sang the songs and performed. We worked closely with other Commonwealth artists who were in London at the time, like the Southlanders, the Jamaican quartet, with whom Edric recorded the *Songs of Jamaica* and the *Songs of Trinidad*. We maintained close ties with fellow West Indians who were working towards a federated West Indies.

The established theatre sought Edric's advice on casting roles for non-white subjects. He was often asked to recommend African, Asian and Afro-Caribbean artists for films, stage plays and documentaries.

8

For many years he helped his friends out as a favour, but his own work absorbed him more and more, and that is when I came into the frame. Coming as I did from a Caribbean cultural background, and with my legal training, I looked at the situation and realised that our people needed representation. They needed Equity, the actors' union, to tell them their rights.

By 1958, when Edric was invited to perform in *Pericles* at the Shakespeare Memorial Theatre in Stratford, I became more and more involved in running the agency. The agency provided a backup support for artists and our home became a centre. Then as we grew we moved to other premises. We struggled along for many years under difficult conditions and poor wages. We were not in a position to make demands because we had no 'name' artists on our books. We were building reputations. That was our pioneering work. We were breaking the ground and it was hard graft. We had difficulty getting Equity memberships for our artists who needed 40 weeks work in the West End of London to qualify. Even now this is an impossible criterion. Some artists joined repertory companies or did understudy roles for American plays like *A Raisin in the Sun*, *Jazz Train* and *Showboat*. But this was a rarity and did not satisfy the need for experience. Publicity was also lacking, as we were of little interest to the national press. So we created our own spotlight, with a photograph, vital statistics and resumé of work experience and training, which we circulated far and wide.

Now, those who arrived in London in the early 1950's, from Africa, India and the Caribbean, seeking education and work, came upon a situation they had not envisaged. They saw very few black people in London, apart from ex-servicemen. They had no idea what the Mother Country was really like. Britain was still recovering from the ravages of the Second World War. It showed a big heart, which soon shrunk with lack of enthusiasm for our efforts in the theatre.

Edric and Cy Grant made a significant impact with their music with the BBC. Cy did calypso on the BBC Tonight programme. Edric did Caribbean folk songs and spirituals as part of his repertoire. Louise Bennett - 'Miss Lou' - presented our folk poetry on stage and the BBC; and Nadia Cattouse, an ex-servicewoman, made a significant impact singing calypsoes and folk songs. She toured with established English groups, appearing on television, and later developing her acting talents in black theatre productions like Genet's *Blacks*.

The theatre establishment had no room for us, so early comers like Earl Cameron, Thomas Baptiste, Robert Adams, Errol John, Errol Hill, Pauline Henriques, Carmen Munroe, Nadia Cattouse and Joan Hooley began to infiltrate the system and formed the beginnings of a black theatre movement. Very few of the black caucus of actors and musicians in London were considered as professionals, not having been trained here, and consequently were relegated to understudying. When the brilliant play *Anna Lucasta* came to the West End from America, Pauline Henriques and Errol John were cast as understudies. We were an unknown factor and this was one of the problems which had to be remedied. The lack of professional representation restricted the recognition of black artists, and although Edric provided advice and information whenever it was needed, this was not enough to project Commonwealth artists onto the professional scene. The British people had their icons, like Olivier, Richardson and Gielgud. We had a hidden colonial history, quite unknown to the producers and directors. There was no level of recognition. We belonged to the colonial past as second class citizens, nevertheless we knew more about their playwrights like Shakespeare, Dickens and Sheridan than they knew about us. The Royal Court Theatre and the Theatre Royal Stratford East, Joan Littlewood's theatre, opened their doors to innovative and experimental work and provided a solid base for our efforts. The Royal Court even gave us the theatre upstairs to do experimental theatre on political situations like the Hola massacre in Kenya during Mau Mau. And we went in there and we were able to have a theatre and have an audience without having any interference.

Errol John's prizewinning play, *Moon on a Rainbow Shawl*, was premiered at the Royal Court in 1958, as was Wole Soyinka's *The Lion and the Jewel*. In that same year Barry Reckord had his play *Flesh to a Tiger* produced there, directed by Tony Richardson, co-starring his brother Lloyd Reckord, with Cleo Laine in her first drama role. Later John Bird agreed to direct another play by Barry Reckord, *You in Your Small Corner*, at the Arts Theatre in the West

End in 1962, and during the Commonwealth Festival in 1965 the Theatre Royal Stratford East put on *The Road* by Soyinka. There were not that many dramatists writing for black performers, and certainly not about the Afro-Caribbean experience in the UK. Mittelholzer, Naipaul, Lamming, Selvon, Soyinka, C.L.R. James all wrote about their own societies, and the Caribbean and world service of the BBC adapted and broadcast these novels, giving work opportunities to black artists, who had few other outlets. Selvon, alone at that time, wrote about the immigrant experience in the UK, but he was not a playwright, though some of his works were dramatised for radio broadcast.

In the struggle to create openings for black artists, Lloyd Reckord and I founded the Caribbean Theatre Trust, aided by Nigel Fischer of the British Caribbean Association, and set up a theatre workshop in a house in Hampstead, where we tried out Barry's plays. We also worked in a little theatre in Hans Crescent in a student hostel there, where Errol Hill directed C.L.R. James's *Toussaint L'Ouverture* and *Henri Christophe*, two plays based on the slave uprisings and the defeat of the French in Haiti. Errol Hill also directed Marina Maxwell's political drama, *Man Better Man*. He later went to the newly established Department of Theatre Arts at the University of Ibadan in Nigeria, and then to Dartmouth College in the USA, where he is now Emeritus Professor of Drama and Oratory.

At the same time dancers and choreographers like Boscoe Holder, Elroy Joseph, Evrol Puckering, Raymond McClean, Stretch Cox (the original limbo dancer), Stanley Jack, Corinne Skinner and Ena Babb, arrived here, having trained in their homebase. They got together in rehearsal, waiting on any opportunity which might come along, and several of them joined the cast of the film *Cleopatra* in Rome. They provided the exotic, erotic dances required by the director. They were very good at that. It is worth mentioning that amongst these dancers were many trained singers and actors. Meanwhile artists like Carmen Munroe, Horace James, Charles Hyatt and Leonie Forbes decided to keep their hand in, and adapted plays from established playwrights like Chekhov and Ibsen, and toured all around the country in town halls and other venues. They struggled to become part of the British

11

theatre, but it seemed that the powers that be did not think that the British public were ready to accept black people as part of the landscape. Many of our people worked on the buses, in hospitals, on the railways and as teachers and black professionals. There was no integrated casting at that time; no one thought black people could play roles they occupied in real life.

Then the World Theatre Season brought the cream of theatre to the Aldwych in the 1960s. We saw black actors who had perfected their art and realised that with opportunity and training we could achieve the same expertise. 1960 saw the arrival of Norman Beaton, one of the finest black talents to reach London and he soon began leaving his mark in theatre. He played repertory theatres, the Tricycle, the Cochrane, and the National Theatre. He became a director of the Black Theatre of Brixton and the Dark and Light Theatre. Also arriving on the scene was Ramjohn Holder, who is now better known as 'Porkpie' - the character in the British sitcom *Desmonds*. He entered the arena performing with his guitar in nightclubs and restaurants around the country. He was writing and recording his compositions and produced over three LPs, but he was waiting in the wings for the right opportunity in theatre, for which he had trained, and eventually entered with great success.

Horace Ove, the film director, entered the film industry and produced successful films on Carnival in Trinidad, but in his film *Pressure*, he upset the British community and establishment by criticising the police and focusing on the deprivation of young blacks. He later successfully filmed the Bhopal disaster in India, and the television film, *The Orchid House*, in Dominica. But he was a very disappointed man; he tried to do what a lot of film makers do, to focus attention on the struggle in all of us, but he got blackballed, black listed. He had to get out, to form up somewhere else.

1961 saw the arrival of 70 black performers from South Africa, in a musical drama *King Kong* about a black boxing champion who could not get a fight with the white champion, and who was driven to suicide by his frustration. We had heard about apartheid and about the struggle of black people against oppression, but we knew nothing about their musicality and their theatre. The cast showed us the life

12

in the townships and the hardships faced by the people living there. They were so professional that they were compared with Americans. Through this production more eyes were opened to the possibility of using black and Asian artists in principal roles.

By 1963 the scene was so barren, that I together with several others including Horace James, Bari Jonson, George Brown, Bobby Naidoo, Nina Baden-Semper, Tony Cyrus and Ena Cabayo came together and formed the Negro Theatre Workshop. There were about 30 of us involved. We began by presenting productions in churches and town halls, those that were available to us. We rehearsed and previewed at the Africa Centre, and at the West Indian Students' Centre. We were supported by Christian Simpson, a BBC producer/director, who made it possible to have our production *The Dark Disciples*, a jazz version of the St. Luke's Passion, with music composed by Mike McKenzie, televised by the BBC.

In 1966 we were invited to the First World Festival of Black and African Arts in Dakar, Senegal. This production was co-directed by Bari Jonson, and scored a resounding success. Another group of actors, the Pan African Players, produced Obi Egbuna's play, *Wind versus Polygamy*, and Pearl Prescod and Earl Cameron headed that cast, at the festival. Now that was an absolutely marvellous experience, because there on the pavement, sitting drinking coffee was Langston Hughes, Marpessa Dawn of Black Orpheus and all kinds of people we had only heard about but never met. And they were at our disposal. Everybody was thrilled and inspired by meeting people of that calibre in this festival. That was very good for everybody.

Then, in 1968, the owner of the Ambiance restaurant in Queensway decided to have a live lunchtime theatre and featured among others Ed Bullins' *The Electronic Nigger*, which had excellent reviews. Another development was the Caribbean Artists Movement, established by John La Rose, Andrew Salkey and Edward Kamau Brathwaite in 1966. Through CAM, artists, musicians and poets got an opportunity to exchange ideas, and arrange performances of poetry and play readings which filled a need in the artistic development of our community.

By 1970, Alton Kumalo, one of the South Africans who had remained in the UK to study drama, formed his own theatre company Temba. With some Arts Council funding he undertook successful provincial tours but was unable to expand or hold the company together as there was only work for about three months in the year. Eventually he gave up in frustration after beating his head against the establishment. Alby James took over from him but later Temba fell by the wayside. Around this time Frank Cousins formed the Dark and Light Theatre of Brixton, hoping that this would provide a vehicle for his professional colleagues. They struggled along but suffered many setbacks, because the actors had to keep themselves available for remunerative work, and there was an understanding that they could leave if the opportunity arose. That was the underlying insecurity of the company. Frank himself gave up, never having found a permanent base upon which to build.

The Keskidee Centre in Islington, provided space for playwrights, sculptors and theatre practitioners, presented West Indian and African plays, and was very supportive of the efforts of aspiring artists. By 1965 Cy Grant had gone through many changes and left London to work with the Phoenix Theatre in Leicester, where he played Othello. He later met with John Mapandero, and together they founded the Drum Black Arts Centre in London. This was shortlived because the founders began going their separate ways. By 1970 Mustapha Matura presented his play *Three Black Pieces* at the ICA, followed, in 1971, by *As Time Goes By*. By 1974 the Royal Court presented *Play Mas*, one of Matura's most successful plays. Tunde Ikoli writing about life amongst black people in England, staged his plays at the Theatre Royal, Stratford East, and Michael Abbensetts' *Sweet Talk* was premiered in 1973, at the Royal Court where he was writer in residence, as Wole Soyinka had been before him.

One of the most innovative productions to reach London was Galt McDermott's *Hair* which explored the experimentation of young people. There was nakedness, free love and wild wild living. This show gave opportunities to many young people because there was no professional criteria, simply youth, and the ability to follow a song, and move well. It was like an advanced workshop, with aspiring artists getting their first taste of the real thing. Among the artists who graduated into professionals, and became famous were, Joan Armatrading, Patti Boulaye, and Floella Benjamin. Others like George Harris, who was brought over from Sweden, Earlene Bentley and Walter Loate, scored in this production. But probably its most beneficial contribution was in allowing most of the cast to move from amateur to professional status, and become full members of Equity. *Hair* was followed by Andrew Lloyd Webber's *Jesus Christ Superstar* where a new policy was adopted by the Stigwood management, that one third of each cast should be of Afro, Asian or Caribbean descent. And that meant that we were certain if there were thirty in the cast that we had ten. That was really something.

By 1973 we had another input of black South African actors presenting two plays, *Sizwe Banzi is Dead* and *The Island* at the Royal Court Theatre, starring John Kani and Winston Ntshona. These plays riveted our attention because of their content, and the realistic performances, which conveyed the tragedy of South Africa's political prisoners on Robben Island, where Mandela and his friends were pining away. These plays did a lot to stimulate interest in the contribution black actors could make provided they had the right vehicle. For many years black actors banged on the doors of Equity alerting them to the problems facing us, and by 1965 a committee was set up to advise the Equity Council regarding work permits for coloured actors applying to enter the UK. By 1970 the committee's efforts waned but were revived in 1975, when the Association of Afro-Asian Artists alerted Equity to the reality that their members were under-employed in all sectors of the industry. They proved that they obtained about half the amount of work which they might be expected to receive. The committee pressed hard for Equity to advocate integrated casting, as the only way to stop the rot. From the 1950's the UK had traditionally hosted US exports of black musicals like *Showboat*, *Porgy and Bess*, *Carmen Jones*, *The Jazz Train* and *Bubbling Brown Sugar* in all of which British black artists were offered understudy roles. This was later improved when the Afro-Asian Committee persuaded Equity to limit contracts to six months, when local black performers could get an opportunity to take

15

over principal roles. That was how Johnny Sekka, originally from Senegal, was able to understudy Sidney Poitier, in Lorraine Hansberry's *A Raisin in the Sun* and later take over the role from him successfully.

The 1970s was a dry season for most of the black artists, and there was an absence of black representation in quality drama. Fortunately, black writers were beginning to get their teeth into the problem, and at the same time black publishers like John La Rose of New Beacon Books, Jessica Huntley of Bogle L'Ouverture, and Margaret Busby of Allison & Busby actively published literature, plays, and books relating to the struggle and survival of our people, and the societies from which they came, as well as contemporary themes. Television brought something new to the scene with sitcoms like *Love Thy Neighbour* (1972-75), starring Nina Baden-Semper and Rudolph Walker, who soon became household names throughout the UK. All their successes on the stage and in drama receded before the onslaught of television exposure. This was to affect the future of black performers' careers. The bread and butter aspect was amply satisfied, as was the fame, but there was still too little for too many. The financial implications of staging productions with little media interest, did not tempt producers to take risks without star names to aid the box office. And what a struggle there was to find British names nationally known. By 1975 most of the black theatre companies had faltered and died. There were no permanent premises and insufficient funding to keep them going. Our community were not traditionally theatre goers, and mostly functioned through their churches and community groups. Most of them were working people who had to rise up early and work late. We had not yet developed a middle class society to whom the theatre would have been an event in their social calendar.

We must praise the indomitable spirit of the Afro-Asian Caribbean artists who arrived in the no-go area of British theatre, and survived its stresses and strains, putting their markers down for posterity. We need to be aware of our history so that 'Newcomers to the Joys' can learn about the struggle of the pioneers, in altering the face of British theatre.

Pearl Connor-Mogotsi

Pearl Connor-Mogotsi is best known for her pioneering and campaigning work in the area of arts, particularly theatre. She was born in Diego Martin, Trinidad, the ninth of twelve children. Her father was a headmaster and her mother, who encouraged her interest in Trinidad's arts and culture, was a teacher. In the 1940s she joined the Trinidad & Tobago Youth Movement at the invitation of Lennox Pierre and Jack Kelshall, two solicitors involved in the struggle for independence. She was asked to recruit young people for a West Indian Federation of Youth and, after a Conference organized in 1947, she toured the islands to speak about the benefits of a united federated West Indies. Pearl came to Britain in the 1950s to study law. She married Trinidadian singer, actor and film-maker Edric Connor (1915-68) and in 1956 they started the Edric Connor Agency. Through Pearl's efforts it later became known as the Afro-Asian Caribbean Agency, representing artists, writers and performers in all areas of the arts. Her clients included actors and actresses: Carmen Munroe, Ida Shepley, Corinne Skinner, Ram John Holder, Alistair Bain, George Harris, Patti Boulaye, Johnny Sekka. Malcolm Fredricks, Yemi Ajibade, Bari Jonson, Lloyd Reckord, Nina Baden-Semper; dancers: Stretch Cox and Evrol Pickering; as well as acclaimed musicians and bands: Joan Armatrading, Osibisa, Maatata, Ginger Johnson, Black Faith, Batti Mamzelle and The Manhattan Brothers and The Woodpeckers, the last two being South African vocal quartets. The Agency was also responsible for the co-production of several films which are today considered to be milestones in British black film history: *Carnival Fantastique* (1959) and the cricket series *West Indies vs England* (1963) are probably the best known. Additionally they distributed prominent third world films such as *Pressure* (London), *Bim* (Trinidad), *Smile Orange* (Jamaica), *The Harder They Come* (Jamaica) and *King Carnival* (Trinidad) In 1963 Pearl was instrumental in establishing the Negro Theatre Workshop (a company of 30 black actors) probably best known for their productions of Wole Soyinka's *The Road* at the Theatre Royal, London, (September 1965) and *The Dark Disciples*, a jazz version of the St. Luke Passion, which apart from being chosen to represent Britain at the First World Festival of Negro Arts in Senegal, Dakar 1966, was produced for BBC television during that same year.

In 1971 Pearl married Joseph Mogotsi, leader of the prestigious black South African singing group The Manhattan Brothers. Together they planned and organised tours throughout the world for singers, dancers, musicians and actors. However, in 1976, for personal reasons, Pearl elected to close the agency, thus bringing to an abrupt close one of the most formative eras of black theatrical history in Britain. She has continued to work in the field, currently running her literary agency and black music publishing as well as acting as a consultant in all areas of the arts. Beryl McBurnie and The Little Carib Theatre in Trinidad provided Pearl's initial training in the performing arts, which she later consolidated in Britain at the Rose Bruford School of Speech and Drama. She is an accomplished actress having performed many cameo roles under her maiden name Pearl Nunez, such as in Lindsay Anderson's film *O Lucky Man* (1973). During 1987-88 she was invited to sit on the Drama Panel of the Arts Council of Great Britain. In 1955, Pearl undertook an intensive course in broadcasting at the BBC and from this base has worked for many years as a freelance broadcaster and journalist, often pursuing her special interest in and knowledge of Caribbean affairs. Pearl, as a supporter of and campaigner for black artists and the black arts has voluntarily devoted much of her time and talent to promoting the rights of the visible minority communities in Britain. She was a co-founder of the West Indian Theatre Trust and of the West Indian Students' Union based in Earls Court, London; she was also a member of the Caribbean Artists Movement and the Committee Against

Pearl Connor-Mogotsi

Racial Discrimination (CARD). Most recently she has served on the Notting Hill Carnival Committee. She chaired the first University of the West Indies Appeal Fund (London) and the Little Carib Theatre Appeal (London). In 1972, the government of Trinidad and Tobago acknowledged Pearl's contribution by awarding her the Humming Bird Silver Medal for outstanding services to the immigrant community in the United Kingdom. In 1989 she was honoured again with the Scarlet Ibis Award for outstanding and meritorious service. In Britain in 1992 she was awarded the National Black Women's Achievement Award for Entertainment and Arts.

Garth Crooks
in Conversation with Roxy Harris (18.2.97)

John La Rose introduced Garth Crooks and Roxy Harris to the audience.

Roxy Harris: Good evening. I'm glad that John did the introductions in case people thought I was Garth Crooks ... but I'm still surprised that Arsenal haven't called on me but I'm still waiting. Well, it's the local team isn't it? John said in the first talk in the series something he said a long time ago in an article 'We did not come alive in Britain'. One of the spirits in all the talks in the series is the sense that we are people living in this society but we also have present connections and antecedents from somewhere else. And I came across, as an introduction to tonight, a statement in a publication of C.L.R James', published in 1984. I think it's interesting and relevant. This is what C.L.R. James said:

> What is important to me is that there are now 3 million black people or more in Britain today. In 10 or 15 years there will be a whole generation of black people who are born in Britain, who are educated in Britain and who grew up in Britain. They will be intimately related to the British people but they cannot be fully part of the English environment because they're black. Everyone including their parents is aware that they are different. Now, that is not a negative statement. Those people who are in a Western civilisation, who have grown up in it but yet are not yet completely a part, made to feel, and themselves feeling, that they are outside, have a unique insight into their society. That, I think, is important - the black man or woman who is born here and grows up here has something special to contribute to Western civilisation. He or she will participate in it, see it from birth, but will never be quite completely in it. What such persons have to say, therefore, will give a new vision, a deeper and stronger insight, into both Western civilisation and the black people in it.

Garth Crooks in his Charlton Athletic kit in 1988   *photo: Tom Morris*

Garth Crooks

Even if we don't agree with this total sentiment of not being part, I think people like Garth Crooks are people who inserted themselves into an area of British society at a period when it was extremely difficult, and survived in it and made their mark, and so it's important for us and the wider community to get a sense of some of the things that they've experienced and been through.

So what we're going to do tonight is have a conversation in which Garth will share with us some of his perspectives on his life in and out of football, and I'd like to start off by asking Garth a question in relation to where in Britain he was located, because the first thing I remember about Garth was the fact that he came from Stoke-on-Trent and was very proud of it and always put that up front, and yet I was aware that I don't know very much about Stoke-on-Trent. So the first question to Garth is: how did your family come to be in Stoke-on-Trent?

Garth Crooks: Well, first of all, John who first addressed everyone apologised for the late start. I have to say the apology is mine. It is in no way a reflection on this group, this gathering, or indeed the George Padmore Institute, it's more a reflection on me. I apologise for that.

In terms of Stoke-on-Trent, my father found himself in the Potteries, as it's called, for the simple reason that there was work there. We're talking round 1957, he's left St. Elizabeth, he comes to England looking for work, and Stoke-on-Trent is where he finds it. The Michelin tyre company, a well-known European-based tyre company, is looking for manual workers. My father has always prided himself on telling his son - the only son he has - that he was a worker, a rural worker: cows, chickens and ploughing the fields was what he knew, but he wasn't afraid of work and, as I got older, I could see he wasn't afraid of work, almost to the detriment of his relationship with his wife. He almost submerged himself in his work and he stayed and was at the same factory for 25 years.

He has a pension, he's now returned to Jamaica having qualified for a pension, a state pension. I remember going to his retirement party at the time I was the Chairman of the Professional Footballers' Association. I had to leave the House of Commons - it was during the time of the proposed identity card scheme by Mrs Thatcher, that wonderful scheme that she was proposing and that football was fighting against - and I shot down with my sisters to be a part of his retirement function, and the opening line in his speech was, 'I've waited 25 years for this day', and it never dawned on me that, although he submerged himself in his work, that really what he wanted to do was to acquire a business of his own where he could have a control of his own destiny and do what he really wanted to do. But, in short, in answer to your question, it was the opportunity to work that brought my father to Stoke-on-Trent.

Roxy Harris: And what was it like growing up in Stoke-on-Trent? You were born in 1958 so we're talking about 1960s, 1970s. What was it like there?

Garth Crooks: Well, first, the recollections I have of Stoke-on-Trent. In the charts was Sandie Shaw, the Beatles, Herman's Hermits - you remember all those groups, don't you? And I remember just having a great desire, because our house backed onto the Victoria Ground. So I suppose it was not dissimilar from the situation here in Finsbury Park where you've got a prominent football club, the centre of the community for some people, the place right in an inner city area surrounded by homes, and it's almost impossible for those homes not to be affected by what goes on in that football ground. Well, mine was exactly the same because it made me - I was the person who was affected by what was going on. My mother and my father weren't affected. They were interested in cricket and, apart from cricket, they wanted me to be an academic - a doctor or a teacher or a lawyer. And at that time I wasn't interested and, as a consequence of that lack of interest, I think, it brought about problems for me.

I was interested in football, I played it morning, noon and night, and I remember often, growing up in Stoke and hearing the roar of the crowd. I could hear the roar of the crowd on a Saturday afternoon and I knew, and I'd learned pretty much who was winning, what the score was, by the roars of the crowd. You know, I could tell. And in those days it wasn't thought of as being unhealthy for kids to go unaccompanied by an adult to a football ground, and they were treated very well. The grown-ups would pass them down to the front. We're talking about the 1960s.

The first game I ever saw was 1965 when Sir Stanley Matthews played in his testimonial match. It was a World Eleven and Lev Yashin played, Puskas and di Stefano played and I can remember the excitement and I'd got in for the last 20 minutes of the game and there was still a magnificent buzz amongst the crowd, around the stadium and I wanted to be a part of that. And I had no real understanding of colour or culture - I was just a kid who wanted to play football. But I can remember that even in those early days that I was made to feel different. I couldn't understand why, but I was made to feel different. And the reality was, and I found out maybe about 13 or 14, that my parents were immigrants i.e. they were foreigners and I was made to feel foreign. There wasn't anything particular, there wasn't any one day that made me think I was different, but it was over a period of time.

Roxy Harris: Were there a lot of other black kids around or were there not many?

Garth Crooks: There was a black community starting to develop, as I remember. I suppose when a black man or woman or a family settle in a particular area where there's work and where black people can get work, then I think it's probable that more black people who are coming to this country will go and locate in that area because there's work there, and the whole purpose of coming to this country, as I understand it, was to improve their living standards. So it was reasonable to assume that if you got a reasonable income that your standard of living will improve and what happened was there was a growing black community located in the particular area within the Potteries that was finding work. So, it was a small community.

Roxy Harris: So what was the particular area of the Potteries?

Garth Crooks: Well, there's five towns. The Potteries are made up of five towns. Stoke is a town itself, but one of the five and many of the black people congregated in Stoke and also then moved away to the northern part of the city to Burslem, which was the part of the city. I didn't particularly like Burslem because Port Vale played there and they played in black and white and my team played in red and white and I wanted nothing to do with them and it's strange, that's stayed with me till this very day. They once asked me to play for them. I was coming towards the end of my career and they asked me to play for them. It was just purely that my team were Stoke City and I didn't want to play for them, even though I hadn't played for Stoke City for many, many years.

But in the 1970s, in the late 1970s there were pockets of the black community that were settling in Stoke, Burslem and Cobridge in particular. In Cobridge in particular there was a very distinct cultural identity growing in that area, and I remember growing up in the Potteries and thinking to myself, why is it that a lot of white people, some of them my friends, take such a dislike to black people sticking together and sharing their experiences?

Roxy Harris: So what do you remember of your schooldays? You said you weren't particularly academic, but what do you remember about it?

Garth Crooks: Just the continuation of my love for sport and playing sport, and playing football and playing cricket and being pushed into sport because that's where teachers, and you've all heard this before, but teachers thought that's where I was going to excel and, if I was going to do anything in life, that's where I was going to succeed, and I gravitated to sport because I got attention in sport. I got a tremendous buzz when I would go into the assembly the following day, having played for my school team or for my city or my county, or I'd won in athletics and I'd come back to the school and my name was read out in front of the school that I'd featured in that particular event whatever that was and it stayed with me. So it was an opportunity for me to find recognition. I identified with that very very quickly, I locked on to that.

Roxy Harris: So how did you come to know you were any good? Every boy wants to play football, but how did you realise that you were actually way above the normal?

Garth Crooks: Like everybody else - people tell you you're good, and if people tell you you're good long enough, you believe it, and I started to believe it. My problem was when people said I was rubbish I didn't believe them, I wouldn't have it. I remember when I was playing one of my first few games for Stoke City, the captain came up to me and said 'You don't think you have a bad game, do you?' and I suddenly thought 'Bad game? You people have bad games, I don't have bad games'. I mean, I soon lost that notion, that soon evaporated in the harsh realities of professional soccer or the 'winning business' as I like to call it.

It wasn't until I hit 13 or 14 that school represented an environment for real hard core education and that meant I had to work as hard with the books as I did with the ball. At first that horrified me because I got pleasure out of playing with a football and being able to pit my wits against other players who were often older and stronger than me, but I wasn't too happy about the book situation, the academic situation, because I wasn't that gifted and I wasn't that sharp and I was going to have to work very very hard. All the teachers thought that I had it and I became very unpopular with teachers because I was lazy and I wasn't prepared to apply myself. And it was only until a wonderful headmaster named Mr Moss, Edward Moss, a wonderful old man, brought me in one day to his office. He was tired of giving me the cane, tired, and sat me down and said, 'You've got to understand, if you're going to have a chance of being what you want to be, you're going to have to learn to conform'. And I remember those days, I remember those words to this day but at the time I didn't fully understand what he meant, but I remember the expression on his face. It was an expression of desperation mixed in with fear and evaporating hope, and I'd never seen him like that before. And I went away and I just remember he said 'If you want to achieve, if you want to be what you really want to be, you're going to have to apply yourself'. And I remember asking my teacher, 'What did he mean, apply yourself?' and it came back to that old adage: work, you're going to have to work, and I couldn't get out of it. I couldn't get away from this thing of work.

It was strange because that dogged me right throughout my football career. When I joined Stoke City at 16 years of age and Gordon Banks, who sadly had a car accident and lost the use of one of his eyes, it was his left eye, and he suffered this terrible trauma in his life that one day. Everything that he had and worked for was gone. And he took over the youth team at Stoke City. I was one of those youth members. So I was working with a great, someone that I'd seen play, and I loved the man, identified with him, because he was a great footballer. And he said to me as Mr Edward Moss said, 'Garth, you've got a lot of talent, but you're going to have to work'. But it was watching him work, day in, day out, whether it was sun shining, raining or snow on the ground, it didn't matter, he was always putting in, always putting in, always putting in his work, putting in time, putting in effort and I think it was he more than anyone that finally convinced me, that if I was going to have any career in the modern professional game, it was going to be playing the English way, not the French way or the Brazilian way or the Italian way, the English way. I was born in England, I was schooled in England, if I wanted to have a career in professional football in England, I was going to have to play their way. For I had no intention of going to play in Paris. I had no one-way ticket to Paris or anywhere else for that matter.

Roxy Harris: And with that choice of going into professional football, you hinted that you were good at other sports ...?

Garth Crooks: Yeah, I was but I loved football and that's what I wanted to do, and there was an attraction to football, there was a glamour attached to football. More important than anything, I'd seen other black people be successful at it.

Roxy Harris: Like who?

Garth Crooks: Clyde Best, Ade Coker, the Charles brothers at West Ham. I mean, I remember the situation at West Ham one Saturday afternoon, when three black players turned out in the West Ham team, the two Charles brothers and Ade Coker. Coker scored! And that was at the time, no real overt racism came from the terraces because there wasn't enough, I suppose, threatening black footballers posing a threat to the opposition and the mob element hadn't gripped that yet, that was to come. But what I saw was the home team embracing these players because they were a part of their team. I'm not suggesting that there were any other great motives, but they were a part of their team, and that still works today. I remember Howard Wilkinson saying when he was Leeds United's manager, when there was a particular problem at Elland Road with racism, that one way of attacking racism in a football club is bringing black players in and making them a part of that team and the morons recognising that, if they are going to support that team, they're going to have to embrace the black players in that team, and he was very brave and he did it, and it worked. So, I at a very early age saw what happened at West Ham and I believed that there was a chance for me.

Roxy Harris: So how did you get in, because getting in to be a professional football player is not easy?

Garth Crooks: Still isn't.

RoxyHarris:I mean, how did you get into Stoke City?

Garth Crooks: Well, I was spotted and everybody told my parents that they were crazy because the chances of any individual becoming a professional footballer was very very slim - I think the ratio is something like one in a thousand that make it. So there's a lot of people get turned away. But I've always had a fair amount of determination and I just played and started to play well for my town, my city, represented my country, all those and in all those situations.

And Stoke City, Sheffield United who were interested at the time, Everton interestingly enough also wanted to sign me, and Derby County and, at the time, Derby County were quite an up-and-coming side. Clough had just arrived and things were happening there. I just thought that I wanted to stay at home, I wanted to be with my Mum, my sisters and I was comfortable with that situation and it suited me. I know what I'm comfortable with, I also know what I'm uncomfortable with, you know. I've always sort of known what my limitations are and stayed away from the things that I've tended to be out of my depth with a bit.

Roxy Harris: So what was the reaction of your family to the idea that you weren't going to be an academic, you were going to be a football player?

Garth Crooks: I suppose they sort of resigned themselves to the fact that in two or three years I might be signed as a professional footballer. They didn't give me any support throughout my 'growing into' football, if I can put it quite like that, which helped in many ways. The only sad thing was when I actually started to play first team football I didn't want them there. One, because I wasn't used to them being there, and secondly I didn't want them to hear the abuse. I didn't want them to be a part of the abuse or party to that abuse that I was receiving because I was black. I don't know if any, many of you probably do remember that scene when there's the boxer, the black guy fighting the white guy in the ring, and I can't remember the names of the two fighters, but the black guy was being beaten by the white guy and the mother comes in the ring with the shoe and hits the guy with it? Well, I sat and watched that in horror, not because of what happened, but because that is my mother. She is capable of doing that and, when I was playing football, I always feared at the back of my mind, that if someone took a liberty with me, that there was going to be an embarrassment, and it was something that I just couldn't articulate and just completely talk out. So, there was always that at the back of my mind.

28

But my mother and my father, regardless of what you might hear from me and regardless of what you might see in me, are very black and very Jamaican. That's the term, they're very Jamaican. My father's command of the English language is as bad today as it was 25 years ago, yet my mother had this enormous capacity to adapt to almost anything. And of course she was a nurse when she first came here, so it's hardly surprising that she was capable of adapting, bearing in mind the things that they asked her to do, and many people like her.

So I suppose that for me, growing up in Stoke represented a number of firsts in terms of experiences. You become part of their community. What does that mean? I open supermarkets. I have to go and do articles in the press, but am I really a part of their community? I'm from Stoke, but a few years ago I wasn't welcome. When I decided I wanted to move on from Stoke and go to a bigger club to try and find out just how good I was as a professional footballer, suddenly, there was a backlash. Many people in Stoke were asking 'who's this little upstart who was born in Butler Street? How dare he?' I found that very interesting. I couldn't believe that the very people who yesterday were celebrating me, were saying these things about my colour and what or who I now was or had become, because I wanted to better myself and not just my situation, but my family's situation. And these were working-class people, people that I grew up with, I understood these people. There was nothing middle-class about me at that time. Some people say there's not very much that's middle-class about me now. But certainly at that time and I became very upset with people who came from that background and had those attitudes, and to this day I still have a distrust of certain sections of the working-class community.

Roxy Harris: What was, what is the difference between say, between a black, a young black professional footballer when you were starting out and a young white football player? You must have been in a team with some. What was the difference for you?

Garth Crooks: Well, I sit now and I get paid to sit and pontificate and theorise about the game. I'm no longer at the sharp end but I can sit and I can theorise. It's safe where I sit. It's not safe where Ian Wright sits, it's not safe where John Barnes sits. I mean, they're on the cutting edge. They're on the cutting edge of not only the white community, but the black community. You know whatever they do is magnified by both sections of the community. But the great problem I had to cope with was racial abuse. In those days there was no possibility of someone coming on the football field and attacking a player, or indeed a player attacking the fans and that's not out of the question as you well know these days.

But I remember going to Anfield in 1978. Keegan was running things at the time. John Toshack, Emlyn Hughes, Tommy Smith, Steve Heighway, fantastic side. And what I wanted to do was to play. Peter Shilton was in goal for Stoke and I played with Alan Hudson - he'd arrived in Stoke and was doing very well, but we were never in the Liverpool class. We had one or two internationals who played for the Home Countries but very few played football that often for England, not even Hudson and he was, in my view, a great player. I remember going to Anfield, about 1978 I think it was, and *King Kong* the movie had just come out, and Scousers are renowned for their wit. There was nothing funny about this because the entire Kop for some reason, as I walked on to Anfield for the very first time in my life, thinking, 'This is Anfield, this is one of the temples of football', - the entire Kop started to cry 'King Kong! King Kong!'. And I was on that part of the field, the only black player on that field. They couldn't have been talking to anybody else. Well, it would have been strange if they had. It's funny the things that stay with you. I'm sure if I was to walk into a group of Scousers and I relayed that experience, they'd think 'Of all the things that you've done Garth, what a strange thing for you to remember and recall'. But when someone hits you across the back with a stick it marks you, and their sentiments that afternoon were across my back like a stick.

The position that I find myself in now, an ex-professional footballer, an ex-professional black footballer who seems to have forced his way into the debate as far as sport is concerned, where racism in sport is concerned, if I have any value at all, it has to be from the area of saying to people who I've worked with, white people, liberal people I've worked with all my life, 'It can't be right when people going into an enclosed area are racially abused and nothing is done about it. You're supposed to be a sophisticated, civilised society, that cannot be right and I'm using the logic that you've taught me'. I don't suppose that reasoning has a lot of value to a lot of people who are being locked up as we speak, to Stephen Lawrence's parents right now. But all I can do is try and apply reason and logic and if that helps, then I'm quite happy to do it.

Roxy Harris: But when you went into the game, that's one side of being a black player. But you also said something earlier about 'If I was going to succeed, then I was going to have to play the British way'. I remember in football for many years, always talking to friends about this issue: can you explain to people what you mean by being made to play 'the British way'?

Garth Crooks: When I was growing up, as a 16, 17-year-old, I always wanted to embellish the game, always to elaborate. I wasn't just happy doing the job well, I wanted to try extra things, if you like and, without being unfair to black players, it's always very difficult to generalise. The British game by and large is not interested in elaboration. It's interested in getting the job done as efficiently as possible and going home. Well, the way I'd been brought up, we don't. We like to enjoy doing it, whatever we're doing, and when we've finished doing it, we like to then celebrate having done it, and it took me quite some time to recognise that that is a part of our culture. It took someone to sit me down and say, 'Don't be ashamed of that, you have identified with much of what your parents have'. And there's something very rich and very welcoming about that aspect of their culture and, it was only when I used to go to Lords when I started to venture down south and meet people and get even more interesting insights into my culture - and indeed Linton Kwesi Johnson, I hope he's not disappeared, still here is he? He's over there. He knows I'm coming to the era where I met Linton and was very fascinated about his life experience - but I started to recognise how important that aspect of my culture was.

Roxy Harris: But some people claim that a lot of black people of your generation, when they were playing up in North London, didn't get anywhere because they were, let's say, wanting to demonstrate their talent.

Garth Crooks: Yeah, absolutely. I have to tell you that I nearly went the same way that they went. I nearly gave it all up. I couldn't cope with it.

Roxy Harris: Why? What was happening?

Garth Crooks: Because it seemed that all the fun had been sucked out of the game, they'd dragged and ripped it out of you and suddenly it was this dull, uninteresting game that I was involved in. The only analogy I could draw was, I mean, there you had this wonderful dish of, well, this variety of food which you can select from and someone takes that away and sticks down boiled chicken, tomato and boiled potatoes with no salt, can you imagine? Bland, boring, uninteresting. It's a poor analogy but I can tell with your response that you can understand what I'm trying to say. And I thought, 'Do I really want this?'

One of the reasons that I went to Tottenham was because it was one of the few clubs along with Liverpool and Manchester United who played football as I thought it should be played and, as Pele said, 'It is a beautiful game'. It is a beautiful game and it makes me laugh now when I see coaches in this country playing systems that the continentals were playing 25 years ago, and we still can't play it very well, because people have to understand that you can't mimic people. If you don't believe it, you'll eventually get found out. I think that in their heart of hearts they don't believe this way. They try to, and Ruud Gullit knows it, he grew up with it. Glenn Hoddle knows it but again he hasn't grown up with it. You know he really came into contact with it when he went abroad. Whether or not our kids at six or seven, those are the ones that we have to teach and they have to grow up so that when they come into world-class football and the pressure cooker is turned up, it doesn't frighten them, they can still, they don't resort to the way they used to play.

So, I wanted to embellish, I wanted to improvise and when I found that I couldn't I got very upset. Players today, like John Barnes who has really captured the two elements well, the English game and the continental game where he doesn't, if I say to you, you all write so you'll understand this, you don't put exclamation marks where they're not needed do you? You put exclamation marks where they're supposed to go. Well, football's exactly the same. You call on your ability and your skill in the areas it's needed. The great problem with a lot of players coming through - black players coming from New Cross, Lewisham, North and South London, and I try to explain to them that you've got lots of ability, call on it when you need it, don't abuse it, don't start to dress the game in fancy garments. Keep it simple. You need not show me anything tremendously difficult. And I think that message is starting to come through. I think John Barnes is one of the greatest exponents of that. So is Ian Wright.

Ian Wright is clear-cut, he knows exactly what his job is, he does it probably more effectively and efficiently than any other striker in the country at the moment. And he's a black man who has worked very very hard to get where he has and he doesn't mess about. A friend of mine was talking to him recently and he was playing in the North London Derby at Spurs last Saturday and Dean Austin, the Spurs full back, put his hand on Ian. It's not an unusual thing for a defender to do to a striker you know. And Ian gave Dean Austin the worst look I've ever seen. It was 'Take you hands ...' sort of attitude. One of Ian's best friends saw it too. I told him 'Alan Shearer wouldn't have done that'. To which he replied, 'You know, it's something that Ian's developed. He got it off Garth Crooks, you know'. If that's all I've left Ian Wright, then I'm delighted. We paid our dues. We're not to be messed about.

Roxy Harris: What was it like for you coming up here now, coming to Tottenham from a small town to one of the biggest teams in the world? What was it like?

Garth Crooks: Well, it was fascinating because it helped me to put my mother in a situation that helped her because financially it helped everybody. While I'm a little frugal, as my mother likes to say - of course she doesn't quite use those words - it was something that we all benefited from, the financial aspect of moving into London.

Roxy Harris: Who was there at the club when you joined? I mean, who were some of the names?

Garth Crooks: Well. Ossie Ardiles was there and Ricky Villa, who were world-class players. I'd never worked with world-class players before. It's wonderful to work with greats, isn't it, whether they're writers or whether they're footballers, because there's so much to learn from them if you're prepared to. And real 'greats' for me are those people who know they're at the top of their industry but they're prepared to share what they have with you and they know you're not as good as them. And Ossie Ardiles in particular was one of those human beings. His house was an open house and although he was a big star, he was very welcoming. He was quite happy with you becoming a part of his family. Rather like my Nigerian wife. She's rather like that. I saw a white person with a similar culture. It was very interesting actually. I hadn't seen that before and when I travelled to Ireland I also discovered that the Irish were a bit like that as well. It wasn't long before I realised the only people who were not like that were the English! So that was all very interesting, coming to London, working with great players and pitting my wits with them and seeing how good I was. But what I found was that I had to work harder than I've ever had to work in my life, and after two or three years I found that I couldn't keep it together. There were too many factors that I was battling against.

Roxy Harris: Like what?

34

Garth Crooks: Like competition. Like politics and jealousies, things that we all have to cope with. Some black people deal with them badly, some black people deal with them very very well. John Barnes has risen above, his attitude transcends an awful lot of the problems that I couldn't cope with. I mean, goodness, he's in Liverpool of all places. I mean, that is a dreadful place for black people. I've had some of my worst experiences in Liverpool as a black person. I remember being run out of Liverpool at 14, chased out. I remember speaking to John Conteh and he was born in Kirkby, grew up in Kirkby. I remember saying to him, 'How did you cope?' He looked at me and said 'How did you think I became world champion?' But John Barnes is doing it in Liverpool and I remember, as I said, in 1977 going to Liverpool and having that awful experience with the fans. Of course, gradually things have changed. The impact black soccer players have had in this country on the game has been enormous. I remember speaking to John Barnes when he was coming to the end of his contract with Watford and I'm begging him to go and play for Liverpool because at the time Liverpool had a fantastic side and I knew that by slotting into that side, he'd be hugely successful, and he was. But now he's their captain. Now, I can't impress on you how important that was. They generally have captains that are born in Liverpool, not in Jamaica and they're grooming him, from what I can understand and Roy Evans, their manager, has told me this, if he wants to be the manager of Liverpool in the future it's there for him. Now, I never thought that would happen in my lifetime and it just shows you can click your fingers and change, and that's the impact black players, not any one individual, but all those players, have made.

Roxy Harris: So, one thing that I want just to show people a little bit is the incredible success you had when you were at Spurs, because when I look back at the records, I mean, you got two Cup Winners' medals, UEFA Cup, you got the scoring record there. You seem to have had incredible success in a few seasons one after the other.

Garth Crooks: Well, whatever I did, whatever I've done isn't even significant if you look at what Ian Wright has done. I suppose that many of the intimidations that we suffered Ian will not have to deal with. I remember going into a dressing-room as a 16-year-old with my toilet bag and what was in my toilet bag was far different from what was in my team-mates' toilets bags. An Afro comb in those days was an illegal instrument, it was an offensive weapon as far as they were concerned. Suffice to say, two years later it became a fashion item, which was very interesting. You know, and once I'd had a shower or a bath and, trust me to be offended by, to not get in the communal bath they found very offensive, because that's something you just have to deal with, just get on with it and, believe me, when you've got twelve guys in a bath, whatever's swimming in that bath, just stays swimming in that bath! However, even when - this is serious, I mean now things are changing - but even in those days, if you wanted to cream your skin there was a huge debate as to why you needed it. Now, I have to tell you, when I speak to guys like Ian Wright and Michael Thomas and all these guys, the things I hear are hilarious, what goes on in dressing-rooms. What I hear, the white boys are putting their hands in their cream, so I hear Paul Merson is creaming his hands after the game and you know, creaming their face and all that and the things the black guys say to these fellas is just unbelievable, much of it I can't share with you, but it's very funny.

Roxy Harris: When you look back at your actual playing career, what's your biggest memories, the best memories, are there striking memories of actual success?

Garth Crooks: Well, I suppose playing in Cup Finals. It's something at the time. I'm told I'm the first black player ever to score in a Wembley Cup Final. It's great. I was the first player, as you mentioned earlier, to score the winning goal at Anfield in over 70 years, for Spurs which was great because it writes you into the club's history books. When I go back to Spurs, they treat me very well. That's great and I'm very appreciative and then, of course, people invite you to functions like this and you try very hard not to arrive late! But Cup Finals, what can I tell you about Cup Finals? They are just very intense and they're just great occasions, they're a part of this country's heritage and to see the British sporting institutions come out as they do. On your first Cup Final they come to your hotel the day before and they tell you all about protocol. Protocol? What you can and can't do in front of royalty. It's a lot of nonsense but that's what you have to do. But no-one adheres to it, no-one takes any notice. You get players talking to royalty, not waiting to be asked. The Secretary at the time, the late Ted Croker, said 'Oh and by the way, gentlemen, just to warn you that we will not tolerate players celebrating goals in the Cup Final.' Can you imagine what the players said to him? I scored a goal in the replay. Ted Croker was the last person on my mind - I was away. But they're great, they're almost like footballing state occasions. Everything and everybody comes out. But you do see, and this is what interested me and still does, you see the power brokers, you see the people who run things, and I still believe to a certain degree that, unfortunately, the sporting institutions are probably still the most racist institutions along with the armed forces in this country. I mean, I'm sure you all have various ideas as to why that is, but that's my view and when you actually look around the Long Room, at the Grand National, the FA Cup Final, all the people who are there, if there's two black people you might be really lucky, Paul Boateng and possibly his wife.

Roxy Harris: Well, I mean, that bit of your career so far is interesting because interestingly, and this is another thing that makes Garth striking, when you were still playing and then more so when you finished playing, you were somebody who moved into another area. I think you still played and talked, it was very unusual in your era for a football player to talk, to be interviewed, to comment. You seem to be able to do it. How did you?

Garth Crooks: You may have noticed that I enjoy talking, and the great problem is doing it effectively and properly. Someone once said to me that you find things interesting, why don't you go back to school and, you know, recapture your education, get an education. It seemed like a good idea at the time, so I did, and my Association, the Players' Association helped me to do that. They paid for all my books and my tutorials, they paid all my school fees for six years. It was a part-time Bachelor of Science degree in Politics - Political Science.

Roxy Harris: Whereabouts did you study?

Garth Crooks: Just round the corner, Highbury Grove, at North London University. Great place and suddenly, you know, I thought, well this brain of mine does really work after all. I thought, I must be one of millions of people who suddenly discovered education at 29, 30, and that's what it was. The great problem - and a lot of professional sportsmen find this problem, particularly high profile professional sportsmen, - is that when they leave sport, they spend their life in the dressing-room and many of the things that they've been taught in their early years have become very rusty. Their grammar has become very rusty, their spelling's become atrocious, and to go back into an academic environment and to bare your all is difficult. Now I had to go through that. I'm mathematically illiterate until it comes to my money and then, for some reason, I remember everything. I've no problems counting then. When I got married - my wife is a lawyer, she had a Masters in Law - I thought 'I'm blowed if she's going to lord it over me with her education'. My wife is wonderful, she's terrific, but she comes from a socio-economic background that's very different, it's a very middle-class background, a very privileged background - her father was a diplomat who travelled everywhere - but in certain situations she's hopeless. And I thought, 'Yeah, I'm sure. I'm going back to school. I'm convinced that I can get a degree'. And of course I did. I'd like to continue but work doesn't allow me to. But going back to school was a great chapter in my life.

Roxy Harris: Another interesting thing about you is that you played a prominent part in the Professional Footballers' Association, which again was an important move, particularly for a black player. So what made you do that, to represent your fellow professionals?

Garth Crooks:I thought this was a fantastic organisation, one that I'm proud to be a part of. I learned an awful lot. The opportunity came for me to be its Chairman in 1985. I'd been on the Executive Management Committee for three years and I honestly felt, and I say it quite unashamedly, that not only was I not ready to lead this organisation. Football wasn't ready for me to be there. I instinctively knew that and when the job came up I didn't even consider it. I waited and it came around again when Steve Coppell resigned and I was the most experienced player on there. Again, I knew things were better, but the time wasn't right. So when Brian Talbot resigned and I felt that if I was asked, I was ready and I could deal with it, I wanted to see how it would pass round the Board. I remember thinking to myself, 'Can you do this, Garth?' I don't want to sound cautious in any way but it was a situation; it would be the first black Chairman they'd ever had and I knew I couldn't think of failing. I had to do it and do the job exceptionally well and that seems to be the butt of our lives, I'm afraid. But it happened. There was a vote and I won it, but it took some persuasion, not from me but from the bench. I don't need to go into the details but it's something that I'd never raised with Gordon Taylor before. He was a great friend of mine and it was he that invited me to join the Management Committee eight years before I became its Chairman. He did it, he's one of these men in football that believes that the industry has to reflect its participants, and he took on Brendon Batson as a paid employee of the Association because he was bright enough to do the job. And Brendon has proved that he's more than capable. And when the opportunity came for me to be Chairman, I think I'd be fair in saying that he had to reassure one or two members of my Executive that I was the right man for the job. And only once in my life since I retired from football have I had to remind Gordon what he did and why he did it, because there's a lot of good about our national game, but there's a lot wrong with it. I hope that's not too cryptic.

Roxy Harris: You're a master of diplomacy. You've got to be, I suppose. How did you get into journalism, because not only have you been on GLR interviewing people, when I listen to Match of the Day you're there. How did you get this range of journalism?

Garth Crooks: By refusing to go away. I remember, after a programme I did some years ago called Great Britain United, it caused a bit of a kerfuffle because one English chairman thought, by speaking to a group of women who knew nothing about football, you'd get away with talking total rot. But during that time of Great Britain United, I discovered the fact that I enjoyed many aspects of journalism, and I made it quite clear to a lot of people after that programme, regardless of what they thought I could or couldn't do, that I wasn't going to go away. I really had something to say and I was going to say it. The only great problems I have, and I think a lot of people have, is: when do they say what they feel? When does it have the greatest impact, when sometimes just saying nothing can have an even greater impact than what you feel? So, it really is a very difficult situation for many people, myself included. But the most important thing, in answer to your question, refusing to go away, just sticking at it and believing that you've got something to offer. I wanted to improve. As a footballer, I never wanted to be the best footballer, I wanted to be a good footballer. I'm interested to find out what Garth Crooks would be like if he was the best journalist he could be. I'm interested, I'm fascinated. What would that be like? It might not be very good, but I'd be interested to find out.

Roxy Harris: Have you got any stories you can share with us about what's happening at the moment. I mean, England have just played last week and lost against Italy?

Garth Crooks: Well, I still think, the great thing about my job is that many of the people I used to work with a few years ago are now running football clubs, many as managers. Many of them, those that were very fiery and aggressive, are not so fiery and aggressive. I remember speaking to Graeme Souness, who I used to have many battles with as players. My first question to him was 'What's happened? You've mellowed'. To which his reply was 'So have you'. And that's nice, you know, when you're working, you're battling with people and you're trying to come into contact with them and not very pleasant words are said, and years go by and things happen to you.

40

You come back and you shake hands, have a drink and you say 'That was an interesting chapter in our lives, wasn't it?'. And I think that's magnificent when you can do that. One of the great things about my game is that there's so many people I can share those moments with.When I compare the generation today to our generation I think maybe things that are going on today are much better, the players are much fitter. I'm not one of those players who thinks 'Oh, it was much better in my day'. People say to me 'Do you think Ian Wright's a better player than you?' I say 'Infinitely better than me. He's a much better player' and I just wonder whether or not that, as a community, the players we have today, because of nostalgia, are not as celebrated, not as players of yesterday... I don't know, it's a question I pose.

Roxy Harris:I just want to finish my part by asking you questions about your work for Sickle Cell Anaemia Relief (SCAR). One of my relatives first told me that you were involved in this years ago. You seem to have stuck with it. There's got to be a reason, a good reason why.

Garth Crooks:I'll tell you why I've stuck with it: because they won't let me out. I can't get out and I've tried to get out. It's one of those things that, and maybe this is common experience. You start something and it becomes successful, you think, 'Well, thank you very much, I've done my bit'. They say 'You can't leave now, we've just started. You can't leave now, we've done this, we've done this, we've got all this to do. You can't leave now'. And it doesn't help if you go home and your wife says 'Well, what are we doing all this for anyway?' You know, she takes you down that route.

So, we've made some horrendous mistakes but it probably brought me in contact with my community more than anything else that I've ever done, because football in this country is still not embraced by the black community for very good reasons. I don't see why any black person should go in an enclosed environment to hear their heroes abused. So, football perhaps isn't the entity for black people, that it should be and that they would like it to be. But in SCAR we raise money in one of the best ways our Committee knows, and that's by having a party, and a bloody good party. I just thought it was quite strange that, when very good mainstream charities like cancer and cystic fibrosis were tapping into our community and raising huge sums of money for their organisations, I thought I'd quite like to help and I was quite justified in asking them if they could spend a bit of time in Sickle Cell and they were more than happy to do so. Plus the fact I got quite irritated with members of our community saying that people who've taken an awful lot out of our community don't put anything back. I don't think that's true. I don't agree. They put more than their fair share back. It's personal and Sickle Cell for me has been a great testing-ground for that. At a moment's notice they're prepared to drop stuff and help out or make donations and sponsor a child's education at a minute's notice.

So, I've been heartened by a lot that's gone on in Sickle Cell. At the moment, we've got sufficient money to sponsor 30-odd kids for further education and prepare for private teaching those who have to be in hospital for eight weeks or more, having blood washed as they say, to come back to school and go to Saturday schools and have their education supplemented. We pay for that. It's expensive but it's paid for and we think it's worth it. The children benefit, the parents benefit and the particular school and children in the classroom benefit. You haven't got a disruptive child who's losing interest, with low self-esteem. The parents are often at their wits end because they see all of those things that I've just explained but feel good because something is being done about their child, and their child is understood. The teacher understands now because someone's helping the child and it's not just an element that she doesn't quite understand. He or she's prone to say 'Well, is it as serious as you say it is?'. But, because we've identified an area that is useful i.e. it's almost like short-term research as opposed to looking down a microscope. That's all excellent work, but we're told that the best breakthrough for sickle cell will come from bone marrow transplants and all that sort of genetic research. So we felt justified, when we spoke to top consultants and professionals in the field, that we should try and help the community now. That isn't as easy as it sounds. But, by getting kids who are sick, who've got sickle cell, back into school, back where

42

they live and given their life-chances back - and that might sound melodramatic but it's as important as that - then I feel that all the disadvantages, the social and economic disadvantages that that child may have, might be reduced. So I feel I should carry on.

Roxy Harris: Well, thanks very much Garth Crooks. If Garth wouldn't mind, we've got time for just a few questions from people who are in the audience.

Garth Crooks: Fine, no problems at all. As long as Linton doesn't ask any, he knows far too much about me already.

Additional points made by Garth Crooks, in response to questions from the audience

On black sportsmen in Britain as role models

'They're all very conscious of what you say. I talk to them in pubs and clubs and environments where they're prepared to express themselves about these things. However, I think that if they thought about it too long and too hard, it would overpower them, it would start to detract from what they do. It's a huge responsibility that we're talking about and I just wonder whether or not this thing, the role model which is conveniently placed on the shoulders of professional sportsmen and women around the country, black and white, is it fair to do that? I think it's something that happens but I think a lot of people are all too happy to place their responsibilities for their child onto someone else.'

On whether black sportsmen pay any attention to the black community

'Ian Wright does, Ian does definitely. I think he lives on it, thrives on it, and if it was to disappear it would crush him. I think that the others find it very difficult, how to cope with it. Ian is unique because he has this image of being what one on the street might term as 'ragga' and I think he's very comfortable with that and prides himself on being himself. I'm just trying to think of someone else who thrives off the affection, I suppose, of the community, certain aspects of the community, and I can't. No-one else springs to mind and probably that's because I'm part of that group of players. The black community are a very very unique community. There's no grey areas within it. They're definite about what they like and definite about what they don't like, and many professional sportspeople I've worked and come into contact with are so consumed by what they do, they don't have time to think about all those other elements of their existence. Professional sport often does that to professional people, whether it's Frank Bruno or it's Lennox Lewis or it's Ian Wright or it's anybody else for that matter. The demands placed on them are enormous, particularly if they're going to be as successful as some of those guys I've mentioned.'

On the potential exploitation of black sportsmen

'I get concerned that more and more white agents, in soccer at least, are targeting black players to represent. I'm concerned because it just smacks of all those old colonial horrors that I don't want to think about, of just sapping the talent for what it is, no real interest in development of the individual, that the individual has something when that immediate talent has evaporated. So I'm talking about developing their mind. I'm talking about developing their interests. I'm talking about developing their sense of community. I'm talking about developing the individual. I work with a number of black players, albeit through my church, and that's all we do. We develop each other's minds, thoughts, thinking, and we spend more time doing that than perhaps talking about football.'

On his most memorable match

'Memorable match? I think the first of anything is always the most memorable, you know. I remember running out at Stoke City on my debut as an 18-year-old, just after my 18th birthday and looking out onto the pitch and not being able to cope with it all, and just being on the edge of myself, and looking to my right-hand side and looking to exactly the same spot I used to stand, week in, week out, watching the players, who I'd suddenly become one of, and that was a wacky weird feeling, and I thought 'You can be what you really want to be, can't you? You can actually be what you really want to be, provided you stick at it'. And also putting on the lily-white shirt of Spurs because I suddenly became a part of a great club and Ian Wright's club is too. I've interviewed Ian and talked to him about it, and Ian is written into the history of Highbury. No matter what happens to Ian, that black man for generations will be talked about, and that's something that no-one can take away from him. For what it's worth, I don't even have my medals at home, I've put them in a museum. It's about my memories, that's what I share with my children. My son's now beginning to understand that I used to play football and football touches everybody's lives. He goes to a school, a prep school, and the dinner lady is teaching him to say 'Arsenal', it's his first words! 'Say Arsenal', so I'm now having to say 'Say Tottenham, not Arsenal'! But it touches everybody's lives, so there's no way of getting away from football.'

On his failure to mention Laurie Cunningham

'You're quite right. It was an oversight more than anything else. You see, when you talk about Laurie Cunningham in the manner that you just have, a buzz goes right the way through my body, because Laurie Cunningham gave every player the inspiration that I just felt. I don't think I've come across another black British player, and I include John Barnes in this, who had such raw natural ability. Now, you're talking to someone who, when Laurie signed for West Brom, I would leave my home after training sessions, and I would race down to West Brom, and I would get my own ticket, and I would sit and I would watch Laurie play. Laurie Cunningham is the only person I've ever seen who had the same sort of impact on the football public as George Best. When George was playing for Manchester United against West Bromwich Albion in a league game, it was at the Victoria Ground. Old Trafford had been closed due to violence. Alex Stepney would throw the ball to George on the edge of his own box, the crowd to a man would go 'Woo', out of sheer expectation.

Garth Crooks

I remember Laurie playing against Valencia in the quarter-final of the UEFA Cup. I remember they had a great German midfield player called Reiner Bohnhof - he's now a part of the German international coaching scene - and Mario Kempes was playing for this team too, and Laurie ripped them to shreds. He was unplayable, one of the greatest footballing nights I've ever experienced, and I became great friends with Laurie, particularly towards the end of his career. Yeah, it was an oversight, a great oversight.'

On black children, sport and education

'I'm sad that your son gave up sport, I really am. He might live to regret it, I'm sad, but then, maybe not. I always say to youngsters who want to have a crack at sport 'Have a go', and there's no reason why you can't bolt on your education along with it as you're going along, you can, you have so much time on your hands. I mean, one of the problems that professional footballers have is that they have too much time on their hands so, you know, doing something with your education is welcome as far as I'm concerned.'

On the origins of his determination, strength and perseverance

'When John La Rose was talking earlier he said I'm one of the many accomplishments black people had made. The greatest accomplishment in my life is really my mother's success. The fact that she could hold together five kids, bringing them up as a family is the greatest success story. I'm not that successful in comparison to her and it's broken her. She'll never ever be the same woman again but it was her decision. She stuck at it to get her kids through. So, whatever you see here in front of you is all down to her and this is something that I feel very strongly about. I'm really really worried that parents of our mothers' and fathers' generation may lose their passion for life because much of that passion has been scorched of them by sheer survival in Britain. They mustn't lose what they have to offer, what they've given us, because I think we're in danger of being caught between two stools: our community and our culture and replaced by the British influence and I'm not convinced that it's all that it's cracked up to be frankly.

So I'm just really concerned that you've come here to listen to me and I hope that all I'm doing is proving my mother right. Perhaps she's not heard me say this, but she was right. I'm living proof that she was right, and thousands of kids around Britain, that parents should be proud, because they have been proved to be right. They suffered the nonsense of the 1950s and 1960s, came through all that and they've got good kids out there. Yes, we hear the horror stories, we know all about that, we hear of the injustices but there's so much that's so positive about our community and I just don't want to lose that. So if you're looking to me as a success story, don't. Behind every man they say there's a woman, and she's often a great one.'

On the absence of Asian professional footballers

'I've looked at it and I've talked about it and I've been to Leicester and I've been in councils and various places. And the only thing I have to say about Asian footballers is this, 'You can't sow peas and reap corn'. Asians, have put so much effort into academia, into education and have got their rewards in business and commerce. Now if they just think they can turn it around and produce footballers with no investment it's a bit rich, if I can use those terms. If they invest the time, as many Afro-Caribbeans did in sport, they'll get the rewards. There might be many injustices that they have to face, but I've seen the successes they've had in badminton and I've seen the successes they have in squash. There's no doubt that they have the ability and the focus, but in this country at least, from the time that there's been the influx of the Asian community into the country, they've focused their attention on their kids' education and culture, on professional aspects of society and in my view, quite rightly, and they've got their benefits there. When they start investing their time in sport, I'm sure they'll get their rewards.'

Roxy Harris: Garth Crooks, thank you very much!

Garth Crooks

Journalist and regular contributor to television and radio, ex-footballer **Garth Crooks** has become one of the most familiar black people in the UK. Garth Crooks was born in Stoke-on-Trent in 1958. His parents came from Jamaica. He became a professional footballer at the age of 19 for Stoke City. He is perhaps most associated with playing for Tottenham Hotspur where he won two FA Cup Winners' Medals (1981, 1982), a League Cup Runners-Up Medal (1982) and a UEFA Cup Winners' Medal (1984). In 1985 Garth scored the only goal in the Liverpool vs. Spurs match, breaking the club's 75-year taboo at Anfield. After leaving Spurs, he played for Manchester United, West Bromwich Albion and Charlton before retiring from the game in 1990. During his 13-year career in football, Garth scored over 200 league goals and was capped four times for the England Under-21 team. Off the field, he devoted time to the Professional Footballers' Association as an Executive Member of the Management Committee (1982-88) and then as Chair (1988-1990).

Whilst still a footballer, Garth Crooks began to take on work in the media and has since carved out a great reputation for himself as a broadcaster and journalist. His television credits include working for the BBC on a range of sports programmes: he appears regularly on *Grandstand, Sportsnight* and *Match of the Day* and has also covered the World Cup (in 1982, 1990, 1994 and 1998), Euro '96 and the 1996 Atlanta Olympics. His work on sports programmes varies from reporting to being a member of the discussion panel to commentating and conducting interviews.

Garth was an Associate Producer-Presenter for the Channel 4 series in 1991 *Great Britain United*, interviewing a number of football players such as John Barnes, Ian Wright and Luther Blissett. Away from sport, Garth has been seen on many different types of television programmes: he has been a guest on *Wogan, Going Live, Kilroy* and *Blue Peter* amongst others; was the 'Gotcha' on *Noel's House Party* in 1993; and was the first non-music celebrity to host *Top of the Pops* in 1982. Garth co-hosted *Sunday Supplement* with Edwina Currie in 1993 and had an acting role in the BBC2 series *Crime and Punishment* in the same year. His appearance on these programmes and others as diverse as *World in Action, Ebony, Newsnight, Newman & Baddiel In Pieces* and *Littlejohn Live and Uncut* confirm Garth's versatility as a TV personality.

Since 1982 Garth has also been involved in radio work, reporting for the BBC (all national stations and the World Service), Capital Radio, LBC and GLR. His outside broadcasts have covered the London Marathon and the Notting Hill Carnival and in 1986 he was the BBC Radio 1 Spokesperson for the Radio 1 Young Achievers Project. Between 1990-1995 Garth worked on BBC Radio 5, presenting *Sporting Albums* (and interviewing sports celebrities from Frank Bruno to Linford Christie) and *Go!*, the Saturday morning show. Most recently he has been working at GLR where he has interviewed a range of prominent black people on his show *In Conversation With ...* Guests have included singer *Alexander O'Neal, politician Diane Abbott and poet Linton Kwesi Johnson.*

Garth Crooks has been writing for newspapers and magazines since 1989 as well as contributing chapters to various football books. He has written articles for *The Guardian, The Sunday Correspondent, The Independent, The Observer, The Evening Standard* and *The Sunday Times Literary Supplement.* He was a columnist for *90 Minutes* (1990-1993) and *The Sunday Times* (1991-1994) and since 1995 has been editor of *The Fixture.* At the moment he also contributes regularly to the black newspaper *New Nation.*

Outside the world of the media Garth Crooks has made important contributions to various organisations. He has been Chairman of the Institute of Professional Sport since

Garth Crooks

1991, an association made up of the union bodies of all major UK sports. On a more personal level, Garth founded the Sickle Cell Anaemia Relief (SCAR) in 1985 and continues to chair this charity to promote awareness about and raise funds for medical research and care for sufferers.

Linton Kwesi Johnson

photo: Deo Persaud

Linton Kwesi Johnson
in Conversation with John La Rose (17.3.97)

John La Rose: George Padmore and C.L.R. James were two contemporaries in Trinidad with different trajectories. Padmore came to London in 1935 and remained in the UK for most of the time until he went to Ghana under Nkrumah in 1957. He helped organise the 1945 Pan African Congress in Manchester. He also produced a large body of writings including *Africa: Britain's Third Empire* which was banned in Trinidad. Linton Kwesi Johnson is in that tradition - one of the most distinguished writers in this generation. He is someone I have known over a very long period since Linton was in his teens. The important aspect is that he was an activist and a writer. He has had an influence in Europe and even in Japan which seemed almost impossible at the time that I first met him - the realities of which dreams are made. Linton and I shall be conversing and you will have the chance of asking questions at some stage - we hope you will enjoy this conversation. Linton was born in Jamaica and arrived in the UK at the age of eleven. The first question is, what was it like growing up in Jamaica?

Linton Kwesi Johnson: Well, time has taken its toll on my memory. I have some very vivid memories of my childhood in Jamaica and a little bit about my family background. I never had the opportunity to meet either of my grandfathers. One died before I was born and the other for some reason or another I didn't get to meet. But I understand that my maternal grandfather was a peasant farmer with a substantial landholding and a forester; a very mean man from what my mother told me. My other grandfather was a peasant farmer. My maternal grandfather was from a place called Croft's Hill in Clarendon and my paternal grandfather was from a place called Coleyville in Manchester, so called because it is so cold there. My father was born in Peckham in Clarendon. They settled in Peckham because my grandmother says that her best friend fancied my grandfather and used obeah against them so they had to move. So that's how my father grew up in Peckham in Clarendon. My father met my mother in Chapelton where I was born. My mother was a domestic worker and my father did odd jobs. During the sugar harvest he would go and work on a sugar estate but he was a baker by trade. They both belonged to that generation of Jamaicans whom the land couldn't sustain any more. They went to the town in search of a better life.

I was born in 1952, August 1952, and my first school was a kindergarten type school run by Aggrey Burke's grandmother called Miss Watts, Miss Emily Watts. And I think it was a thruppence a week job in those days and you got the basics there - the alphabet, how to spell, and so on. Then I went to Chapelton School, an all-age school, and my teacher there was a woman called Miss Thompson who was the secretary of Donald Burke Sangster who became, briefly, Prime Minister of Jamaica. My mother and my father separated. She went off to Kingston and shipped my sister and myself off to our grandmother in a place called Sandy River. Between the ages of about seven and eleven, I was living in Sandy River - deep, deep rural Jamaica, no street lighting. We would run out to the street when we saw a car coming by just to wave at them and so on. And it was the happiest time of my life. I was the man of the yard and my grandmother would send me on all kinds of errands and of course I had responsibilities like fetching the firewood, tying out the goat, helping with the sugar cane harvest. In fact I had my own little plot where I planted yams and sweet potatoes and cassava and that kind of thing.

I got most of my folk culture from my grandmother. In the kind of environment we lived in there, there was no entertainment. No radio, no television, no books in the house. I didn't grow up with books. The only book we had in the house was the Bible. And so for entertainment, my grandmother, especially on a full moon night, would tell us stories, duppy stories, ghost stories, and she would make us guess riddles and that sort of thing and that was our entertainment.

John La Rose: You came at a time when Norman Manley was changing the Jamaican public school system. Jamaica's always had highly educated people from the elite classes who went to public school like in England, but who didn't have at the time the same kind of scholarships, but Manley introduced that ...

Linton Kwesi Johnson:I took the scholarship in fact, and I got the results when I came to England. - I think I either passed or I half-passed. I was put down to go to Excelsior, Kingston College, Clarendon College or one of those, but unfortunately I was in England. I was considered very bright as a child. In the elementary school system the class you were in would be dependent on how well you were doing. So by the time I was leaving Jamaica I was in fifth class. All my contemporaries were 14 and 15 year olds and I was 11, and I used to get lots of sweets from guys for doing their homework and stuff like that.

John La Rose: And when you got here, what was your first feeling about this new experience?

Linton Kwesi Johnson:I didn't know hardly anything about England. We had these little books in school, stories about an Eskimo boy from Canada, a boy from Borneo, a boy from Canada, a boy from London. And you know, as a child I used to think literally the streets of London were paved with gold. So I was in for a rude awakening when we arrived and I saw all these grey buildings with smoke coming out of the chimneys and so on. It was a November day, the 8th of November, and it was grey and cold and horrible and I just wanted to get back on the plane and get back to Jamaica.

School was initially a traumatic experience for me because that was my first confrontation with racism. You know, kids would be calling me 'black bastard', ' you people live in trees', and all kinds of racial abuse. At the time, the thing that was being said about us was that black people eat kit-e-kat. I don't know how that story got around. At school, the comprehensive system had three streams. You had an A stream, a B stream and a C stream and myself, and 95% of all the other black kids, were in the C stream. I gradually worked my way up into the B stream but for all intents and purposes we weren't supposed to be having any academic aspirations and so on. We were supposed to leave at 14 and go and do an apprenticeship or go and join our fathers and mothers in the hospitals or on the buses or whatever. I remember when I was 14, Mr F. Harris, our careers teacher, called me in for an interview and he said, 'Johnson, you'll be leaving school in a couple of years, what do you intend to do?' So I said, 'I want to become an accountant, Sir', because at that time my best subjects at school were accounts, commerce and economics. He said 'Accountant! A big, strong lad like you! We need lads like you in the forces. Do you realise you have to serve a five years articleship. You have to get two A levels and then you have to serve five years articles', and bla, bla, bla. 'And anyway, you people are always complaining about the police. Have you ever considered joining the police?'

Mind you, there were at least two or three teachers I had tremendous respect for. My first form tutor was a guy called Chris Harbon who had taught at the Royal Academy for Dramatic Arts and he used to take us up to the BBC, all kinds of things, to the radio and stuff. And my Sixth Form tutor was a man called Mr Winkler and he thought I had great potential. He kept on telling me about Michael Manley and how he had been to the London School of Economics and how I could do the same thing. And then there was one other teacher called Mr Woods, a Jamaican teacher, and he was excellent. I did CSE English and it was because of him I got Grade One. I didn't have to bother with the O level afterwards. So that was schooling for me.

At school I became involved in the Black Panther Movement. As a youth, growing up in Brixton I would see these people on the streets every Saturday with their newspaper *Black People's News,* or something it was called, I can't remember. And then one of the leaders of the organisation, Althea Jones, had come to our school to take part in a debate. I can't remember what the debate was about but I was very impressed by her, and I decided to go to one of their meetings. And I eventually became a member of the Black Panther Youth League and then a member of the Black Panther Movement.

John La Rose: Althea Jones became the leader of the Black Panther Movement here. I knew her when she came. She came to study chemistry, her brother came to study physics; and she knew the Caribbean Artists Movement. She came to us, and then she joined the UCPA. It split, and she formed the Black Panther Movement of which Linton became a member, and that Black Panther Youth Movement. She was a great orator. Althea spoke beautifully, very strong emotionally. And she wrote a PhD in chemistry. She was in brain research with Steven Rose at the Open University. And so she was their leader, a very powerful spokesperson. And Linton, they did lots of other things besides ...

Linton Kwesi Johnson: It was in the Panthers, John, that I discovered literature, black literature, because we were encouraged to read. In fact there were books that we studied, chapter and verse, going through them systematically. One of them was *Capitalism and Slavery* by Dr Eric Williams, the other was Frantz Fanon's *The Wretched of the Earth.* And the third one was *The Black Reconstruction* by W.E.B. Du Bois. We had a little library and we were allowed to borrow books, and one of books that I borrowed was a book called *The Souls of Black Folk* by W.E.B. Du Bois. That was a book. It was one of the most beautiful things I ever read. It just, it just blew my mind. It was about the experiences of blacks in America after slavery had been abolished; and the language, I was struck by the language, the poetic language of Du Bois' writing. I remember one phrase from that book. He talked about 'The Colour Line'; the problem of the 20th century was the problem of the colour line. And after I read that book I just wanted to read more and to write and to express my own ideas and my own feelings and my experiences about growing up in England.

John La Rose: You began to write songs and to sing to yourself quite early. Was that a beginning of your desire to become a writer and artist?

Linton Kwesi Johnson: Well no, not really. That happened in the Panthers. Writing a song and that, that was a bit trivial. I was in my early teens, 13, 14, and I was a big fan of the Heptones, a Jamaican Rock Steady Reggae Group, and I used to imagine that I was the lead singer, Leroy Sibbles. And I would go in front of the mirror and I would try to be him but I didn't harbour any dreams of becoming an entertainer or anything like that. That happened in the Panthers.

John La Rose: And in the Panthers, was this when you had Rasta Love?

Linton Kwesi Johnson: That came after. I think it was while I was in the Panthers, around the same time, that about three or four of us started something called The Black Literary Society. A little group of us, a guy called Owen Babb from Barbados, who is now a banker, a guy called Cecil Chung who is now a teacher, and Wesley Dick who was one of the people in the Spaghetti Siege. He did about 15 years in prison for his part in the Spaghetti Siege robbery. People remember the Spaghetti Siege, when they held up this place and asked for a plane to go to Libya or something. Wesley was one of these people. And what we would do is basically write our short stories and poems and have little discussions among ourselves about them. And it was around that time that I met a man called Tony Ottey who was a Jamaican Anglican priest who had just been posted to Brixton and who wanted to get to know the black youth and all that. And he came to my local youth club and I told him about what we were doing and he said, 'Oh, well, you should go and see a man called John La Rose. He has a bookshop in Finsbury Park.' And I went to number 2 Albert Road and I think I must have arrived about one o'clock in the afternoon and never left until about seven in the night. And it was a whole new world opening up to me. John introduced me to poetry by Aimé Césaire. He introduced me to the other poets of negritude like Senghor, some of the black American writers like Sonia Sanchez, Gwendolyn Brooks, some people like that. I think it was through John also that I met Andrew Salkey who took a keen interest in whatever I was doing at the time and certainly encouraged me. I used to send

56

both him and John whatever I had written for them to give me their feedback. John was a little bit more severe than Andrew. Andrew was a little over generous with his compliments. It was around that time also I discovered the Caribbean Artists Movement. I think it was about the last phase of the Caribbean Artists Movement and I was invited to things they did at the Keskidee Centre and it was the perfect ambience for a young black growing up in England with literary aspirations.

John La Rose:1973 seemed to be an important year for you. I remember I did a programme called Full House, a 90 minute TV programme, which I produced for the BBC. Althea McNish was part of it. She did some of the work for that programme which was called 'Caribbean Artists'. I produced it with a man called Nigel Williams, the internal producer, who is now quite well known but wasn't then. And I designed a reading which started with Sam Selvon and ended with Linton. I was part of it reading myself. And it was the biggest exposure we had all had at that time on television. And at the same time too Linton was writing his famous classic poem called 'Five Nights Of Bleeding'.

Linton Kwesi Johnson: Yes, remind me about that. Just before that, the programme was in March 1973 and gave me the break that made me what I am today, but the previous year, in November 1972, I was walking through Brixton Market one Saturday afternoon and saw a white man with a black youth in a stranglehold. So I went up to inquire what was going on and two other white men came and said they were police officers and this youth was under arrest. So I asked the youth for his name and address, because we were trained in the Black Panthers when you saw a black youth being arrested, you should find out his name and address and inform his parents. Because often what used to happen in those days, they would keep black people in Ashford Remand Centre for weeks without informing their parents and their parents would be out of their minds with worry. So this guy told me his name and his address and I wrote it down on a piece of paper, as we were trained to do. I was writing down the policemen's numbers and the number of the police van and all that, when I was grabbed by these officers, thrown into the black maria and given a good kicking. And I was charged with two counts of assault, and one count of GBH, (Grievous Bodily Harm).

Within an hour of my arrest there was a demonstration outside of Brixton Police Station because some people had seen me being arrested and I had managed to slip the piece of paper, that I had written all the details onto, to somebody, I can't remember who it was. Initially they charged me with two assaults and by the time of the demonstration they had increased it to the third charge of GBH. After about three hours they let me out and the case was tried in June of the following year and there was a black man and an Asian man on the jury and if it wasn't for them I would have been found guilty; myself, the youth and two girls, all four of us were charged. They were charged with various things including 'sus' and we were all acquitted. And the policemen, Farr, Leavers and Bloom, were transferred from Brixton police station because Lewis Nkosi, a South African writer and journalist, had written an article about it in *The Observer*, and they were transferred. I made an official complaint against the police and it was investigated by Sergeant Kelly of Brixton Police Station. Nothing came of it. So when John did this Full House programme, I took the opportunity of mentioning what had happened to me and talked about Farr, Leavers and Bloom.

That programme was very important to me because, of course, it gave me a national platform. What I recited on that programme was completely untypical of the kind of poetry I've been known for over the years. It was a poem called 'Two Sides Of Silence'. John particularly liked that one and that was the reason why I did that one. If I had had my way I would have done something else. But it made people take note of me and soon after that, I had written something called *Voices Of The Living And The Dead* which was a plain verse really. And Oscar Abrams, who was running the Keskidee Centre at the time, invited me to come and perform it there and we did it with a group of drummers, some Rasta drummers who I had been to school with in Brixton. They were called Rasta Love. And that's how I became involved with Rasta Love.

Linton Kwesi Johnson

And then, I do remember doing a reading there, at the Keskidee also, it was Jamal Ali, T-Bone Wilson, because those were the poets around at the time, Rudi Kizermann, T-Bone Wilson, Jamal Ali and an Asian poet whose name I can never remember, he writes plays as well, Frank John from Trinidad, and Sebastian Clarke who's since changed his name. And in the audience was George Lamming, and I remember George, I remember him sitting down like this throughout the reading and I was very perturbed and I went to ask Andrew Salkey afterwards and I said to Andrew, 'Why was George Lamming making up his face like that?' and Andrew said, 'Don't worry, man, he was just concentrating.' And after that, I got together with Rasta Love and we had a kind of a workshop situation where we would improvise on different kinds of drums and I would make up words to go along with the rhythms. Some of the poems that were eventually published in *Dread, Beat and Blood* came out of that situation - poems like 'Dread, Beat and Blood', 'All wi doin is defendin' and some others. We used to do a few gigs in various places like community and youth centres in Brixton and we got one gig at the Brixton Library. I was invited to put on an evening of poetry, through Janet Hill and Alexander McIntosh, if my memory serves me well. I think Andrew Salkey was there and yourself, John. It was the first time anything like that was ever done in Brixton. It impressed a lot of people and the rest is history, really ...

John La Rose: Andrew and I were the closest friends. We had both founded the Caribbean Artists Movement along with Kamau Brathwaite. And he was the closest friend I had at the time in London. So at one stage he began to perform with Linton at schools and in libraries, like the one we just spoke about. But he was doing much more of that than I was doing with Linton and he told me how impressed he was with the work Linton was doing, trying to give me some idea of that. And then I saw Linton subsequently and he mentioned the names U-Roy and Big Youth. If you know the sound systems and that music that came from Jamaica you know those names, DJ's. And Linton asked me if I noticed what they were doing in poetry, this was the important thing, and I told him, 'No' because

59

I had no time to follow the reggae, which I had done before with the early Judge Dread and the others - but not in this particular phase of U-Roy and Big Youth - and I think that's an important ...

Linton Kwesi Johnson: Well, that was during my time when I was a student of reggae music. I mean I had always been a student of Jamaican popular music since the days of rock steady and some of my literary influences, some of my poetic influences, came from some of the lyricists and the DJs like Big Youth and U-Roy. Between 1973 and 1976 I was at university at Goldsmith's College doing sociology and I was trying to formulate a kind of sociology of reggae music by doing some textual analysis of the lyricism of the reggae DJ's. And it was then that I coined the term 'dub lyricism' and spoke about the reggae DJ's as poets, because I saw them in a similar light to the griots, being people doing oral poetry, spontaneous oral poetry, documenting what was happening in a society at a particular time. Of course, later on, Oku Onuora in Jamaica popularised the term 'dub poetry' as a kind of generic term to describe the kind of verse that I myself, him, Mutabaruka and Jean Binta Breeze and others, a group of young writers, were doing at the Jamaica School of Drama at the time. Michael Smith, too, of course.

My first poem was published in 1973 in *Race Today.* That was the *Race Today* before Darcus Howe took it over, that was the *Race Today* edited by Alexander Kirby, an English clergyman. I got to know Alexander Kirby through a white American friend of mine called Bob Stewart who was an old Jesuit who went to Jamaica to study history to do his PhD under Kamau Brathwaite. Then they subsequently published *Voices of the Living and the Dead* which I performed at the Keskidee. By that time, by 1974, I had enough poems. I thought I was ready for publication. Everybody thinks they are ready for publication when they just start writing and I submitted it at that time to Bogle L'Ouverture and Jessica Huntley took an enormous amount of persuasion to publish it, I must say, because people like Cecil Rajendra from Malaysia, who had some years before invited me to recite at the Troubadours which he used to run with an African guy in Earls Court - it's a basement café where people used to do poetry readings - had told Jessica that it wasn't poetry. I think it took Andrew Salkey and Gus John to persuade Jessica that it was worth publishing. She herself found it very violent. She thought it was too violent. And that's how came it to be published. Errol Lloyd did a very nice cover for it which was spot on with a black youth standing on a street corner and when that book came out, when *Voices* came out I was excited, but when *Dread, Beat and Blood* came out my head was as big as this room.

John La Rose: And became very famous because *Dread, Beat and Blood* became the book by which he became well known but also Franco Rosso made a film.

Linton Kwesi Johnson: Oh, yes, I forgot about that. Franco, I don't know how Franco knew about me but anyway, he'd made a film with John, it's through John again, in 1971 about the Mangrove Nine. The Mangrove Nine were nine black people who were arrested and charged with riot, and incitement to riot, and affray over a demonstration in Ladbroke Grove. Althea Jones was one of the defendants, and Darcus Howe was another. Whatever happened to the film? It was never shown because Franco used BBC footage which he didn't get BBC permission for. Anyway Franco approached me and said that he had raised money from the Arts Council to make this film about me and about my work and if I was up for it and I said 'yes, of course'. And he made a film. I didn't get any money out of it. I think I must have got about £400. In those days I was a down and out student with wife and children and all that and a freelance journalist and every penny counted. Anyway, the film was made and in 1979 when it was supposed to be shown on television the Director General said that it couldn't be shown because the election campaign was coming up, elections were coming up. Simply because in one of the verses there was a reference to Maggie Thatcher. I think it was in the George Lindo poem - 'Maggie Tatcha on di go wid a racist show' - anyway I was a bit pissed off at the time but in the end it just gave me more attention and it was very well received.

Linton Kwesi Johnson

So during my student days, I was a freelancer. I used to interview all these musicians coming up from Jamaica, through Bob Stewart again, in Jamaica. I was there in 1974, in Jamaica, and I had read some poems on JBC and got to meet Jeremy Verity who was in charge of the radio station at that time. He gave me the name of some contacts of his at Bush House and said maybe I could get some work doing some freelance. I used to see Andrew down there all the time and quite a few other people, and Alex Pascall I met around that time as well. And I remember one of the people I interviewed for the BBC was Bob Andy in 1976. He brought out a song called 'Fire Burning' which sort of prophesied an up-rising on the part of the masses against the oppressive government of the day who were the PNP government of Michael Manley and they banned the song. And the Heptones who I had always been a big fan of, I got a chance to interview them and people like that.

It was during this time when I was at the university I wrote a paper, an article called 'Jamaican Rebel Music' and it was published in *Race & Class*. And around the same time, Ricky Cambridge and Cecil Gutzmore used to edit something called *The Black Liberator* and they published one of my poems in there and asked me to write a piece and the piece was called 'The Politics of the Poetry of Reggae Music'. That was in 1977.

Anyway, after Franco Rosso's film, while I was doing my freelance, I met a guy, a teacher in Brixton, called John Varnum. John Varnum was working for Virgin Records because Virgin Records had just gotten involved in exploiting reggae music. He used to read my poetry with the kids at school and he thought I would be the right person to help him with the marketing of it. So he got me to write copy for the radio ads and the newspaper ads, and also to write biographical details on the various artistes and the occasional sleeve note.

So one day I said to John, I said, 'Listen, man, I've got these poems that I do and people tell me that they are very musical and very rhythmic, you know, why don't I make a record?' And he said, all right then, I'll ask Richard Branson. In those days Virgin Records wasn't half as big as what it became. So, he said 'yes' and they gave me £300 and I went to this little recording 4-track studio in Wimbledon and did a demo and brought it back and they liked it. And I made my first album *Dread, Beat and Blood* in 1977. I recorded it in 1977, it came out in 1978 and was voted 'Album of the Year' in the *Melody Maker*.

And then the following year I was headhunted by Chris Blackwell from Island Records via a photographer called Dennis Morris who introduced me to Chris and they offered me a deal to do two albums. The first one was *Forces of Victory* and that was followed by *Bass Culture*. Then after the two albums he wanted to sign me up for another six. But when I got my royalty statements, my royalty statements always showed me owing the record company money. So I said, 'No, man, when my royalty statements is in the black then I'll do another record for you'. And of course, in those days nobody said 'no' to Chris Blackwell because people were kind of falling over themselves trying to get deals with Island Records, and there was this man offering me a deal for six albums and I said no. So the relationship between myself and Blackwell was soured, became a little uneasy over the years until I did *Making History* which I thought was my most overtly political album because it had on it 'Di Great Insohreckshan' about the Brixton riots, it had the 'New Cross Massacre' and things like that. And they suppressed it in this country, I don't know why, and then they re-mixed it, sent it to America, re-mixed it, and the Americans were not buying the American version, they were buying the British version. Eventually they deleted the album and took tracks from it and put them on all kinds of compilation albums and that was the end of the relationship between me and Island Records.

It was around that time I decided I was going to form my own record company and formed LKJ Records. And the first thing we put out was a 12-inch 45 by my friend Michael Smith reciting 'Me Cyaan Believe It' and 'Roots' and on the B side I had an instrumental by Rico Rodriguez called 'Solitude' or something. Nothing happened with LKJ Records again for five years until I did something with Jean Binta Breeze.

John La Rose: Now the movement of the Black Panthers, led by Althea Jones, this unique figure, both highly intellectual and very active, very commanding as a speaker, as an orator - when she spoke, the youth and people in their twenties were shouting 'Right On! Right On!', and they would go to big demonstrations. People were surprised when they heard she was writing a PhD. They didn't know she was writing a PhD. They thought she was just an ordinary girl from the street, as they say, or from the ghetto, who was leading this movement, but she was really quite a powerful figure and it was really the only mass black youth movement ever in this country which she led and they were the people who said 'Come What May, We're Here to Stay' and organised a massive conference at Alexandra Palace. Do you remember this?

Linton Kwesi Johnson: Yes - I think that was the time I first heard about Butler and the Oilfield Workers' Trade Union and how all that movement got started. The main speaker was a man called 'Blind Man Mack' I think his name was.

John La Rose: MacDonald Stanley was his name.

Linton Kwesi Johnson: Blind Man Mack - yes, I remember it very well. The Panthers was important in terms of shaping my own consciousness. That's where I became politically alive. That's where I was blooded in politics. We were an organisation that was concerned with the fight against racism, and our slogan was 'Black Power, People's Power'. We weren't anti-white and we didn't believe in separation and all this kind of thing. We had a class perspective. But we were anti-Soviet. At one time we were flirting with the ideas of Mao and all of that. But I don't think I would be the kind of person I am today if it wasn't for having been through the Black Panther Movement.

John La Rose: And that also was the period when your work was being known all over Europe.

Linton Kwesi Johnson

Linton Kwesi Johnson: That came after, with recording - because, of course, you can reach a much wider audience with a record than you can do with a book. And after the success of *Dread, Beat and Blood,* I was working at the Keskidee Centre at the time because, to go back to 1977, there was a writer's award going in Lambeth, called the C. Day Lewis Fellowship, and they would give £2000 or £3000, I can't remember how much it was, for six months. You would be in the library once or twice a week and your job would be to stimulate creative writing within the borough. I was short-listed out of 60 applicants or something, and in the finals it was me and James Berry and some other people, and I was lucky enough to get it. And, after my stint at Brixton Library, as writer-in-residence, I got a job at the Keskidee Centre. Oscar Abrams offered me a job at the Keskidee Centre, and my job at the Keskidee Centre was to help develop the library which they were building up at the time and to organise programmes for black school children in North London on Caribbean history and culture.

Oscar was a very likeable man but a very difficult person to deal with and after a while I became a little bit frustrated and a guy called Frantz De Haan offered me a gig in Holland. In those days, I didn't have a band. What I would do, I would get the backing tracks of my records, take the voice off, and just have the backing tracks on tape and I and some of my friends from Brixton, three guys - the bass player and the drummer, Vivian Weathers and Winston Curniffe, who died a few years ago from a heart attack, and another one of my friends called Percy - they were the three wise men - would be dancing on stage while I would be talking over this taped music. We did it in Holland and it worked and I thought ... mmm ... and the money was good and subsequently, soon after that, I was invited to Sweden by a guy called Tommy Appeldorn, or something, at a music festival in Uppsala, or somewhere like that, and then, after that, a guy called Kenneth Overson invited me to come and do some more, a tour in fact. It was Scandinavia, Sweden, Denmark, Finland and Norway. And so I was on the road touring and I was making reasonable money so I resigned from the Keskidee and I've been self-employed ever since, apart from three years between 1985 and 1988 when I worked in television with Tariq Ali and Darcus Howe in the Bandung File.

I started working with musicians in 1982, with Dennis Bovell, who was very well known as a sound system operator in the early days. He used to operate a sound system called Sufferers HiFi, and his sound was one of the top sounds because they had more exclusive dub plays than any other sound system, because Dennis was a musician himself and would do exclusive versions of the latest reggae tunes from Jamaica and therefore he had the edge on all the other sound systems around. Then he formed a band called Matumbi and they became the premier reggae band in this country. In the late 1970's they had a top ten hit with a tune called 'Point of View'. Matumbi had broken up and Dennis and I decided to get together and he formed a band, called The Dub Band. We decided to get together and go on the road and our first concert was at the Lyceum in London. It was promoted, I think it was Wilf Walker had something to do with it, but we were on stage with a band called Chalice from Jamaica, and they came on first and we were to come on second and, of course, they blew us away, completely blew us away. But Robin Denselow in *The Guardian* wrote a most generous review and I was able to live with that particular disastrous experience. Soon after that we went off on tour in America. A guy called John Blackwood, a Jamaican psychiatrist based in San Francisco, put together a tour for us and we did the East Coast and the West Coast and, by the end of it, the band was very tight. We subsequently toured all over Europe, everywhere, and England of course.

Of course during all of this time I was involved in the Race Today Collective and the Black Parents Movement participating in demonstrations and organising all kinds of different things, the George Lindo campaign, numerous campaigns, too numerous to mention. And then I became the Arts Editor of *Race Today* after Akua Rugg had resigned. And then I think there was a view within *Race Today* that I was too much of a high flyer, and that my wings needed to be clipped. So various people within the Alliance [of the Black Parents Movement, Black Youth Movement and Race Today Collective] were lobbied to tell Linton to stop all this travelling around the world because he was needed in Brixton to do organisational work. Of course my political commitment had always been very serious to me so I stopped touring and I 'retired' in 1985 and came off the road and spent my time with *Race Today's* business until Darcus went into television and decided he needed somebody like me to help him out up at the Bandung File. I was a researcher, a reporter, a very badly paid one, and by 1988 I frankly had had enough of it and I met Dennis one day and he said, 'Johnson let's go back on the road and tour, man', and I said, 'Yeh, I'm ready for that', and that's what I've been doing ever since and concentrating on building up LKJ Records.

John La Rose: I remember going to Paris for a conference and I met these 'beurs' as they called themselves, young Arabs, born in France. They call them the 'beurs'. We had connection with them, politically, through the Alliance that we had, and they had come to London and they were talking in meetings in Manchester and in various campaigns and so on. They were led by a man called Mogniss Abdallah, very well known in France now. But when I met them in Paris I was astonished. They were reciting Linton's poetry as though they knew the language. But it was the feeling and the emotion that carried them. And then I discovered that when Linton went to Paris, 10,000 people, he never tell me this, I'm discovering this in Paris, 10,000 people, 5,000 people at these gigs can you tell us more about this?

Linton Kwesi Johnson: Well, the first time I performed in Paris, it was a disaster. It was an unprecedented disaster. It was the second or the third major disaster I've had. People who perform on the stage know about dying on the stage. It was one of the nights when I died on the stage. The first time I died on the stage, incidentally, was in December 1977 when I did a gig at the Rainbow up here in North London. I had gotten to know Johnny Rotten who had a group called the Sex Pistols. The Sex Pistols had broken up and he'd formed a band called Public Image Ltd, PIL, and he wanted me to be one of several performers who was performing with him on two nights at

Linton Kwesi Johnson

The Rainbow. I think I'd had a little too much to drink anyway, and I came out there and I saw this sea of punk rockers, and the show was running late and I was the penultimate act and all I could hear was 'We want John. We want John', and all kinds of abuse. So I abused them back in my Jamaican style. I was using backing tapes and of course, I always used to cue myself with the drum beat at the beginning, you know, like a drum roll or something to cue me in to say my words and the idiot, some idiot, started the tape about five or six bars into the first number and I didn't know where I was. My voice was completely out of synch with the music. The same thing happened in 1979, at the Palace in Paris. I was the opening act for the film, *Rockers*. It was a big night. They had the film, *Rockers* and they had Linton Kwesi Johnson, and Chris Blackwell was there in the audience. And, for some reason or the other, they started the tape about five or six bars in and I didn't know where I was. And there was I struggling until about the second or third number when you got everything back on cue.

Then I didn't go back to France again until 1983. I'd been doing some readings in Milan and in Amsterdam and in Rome with some of the beat poets, like Allen Ginsburg, Ferlinghetti and all these people, and through them I met this French sound poet who was also an anarchist who was part of that 1968 revolution in France. He was the one who tried to burn down the French stock exchange. His name is Jean Jacques Lebel. And Jean Jacques said, if you really want to tour France, this is the man you should work with and he introduced me to a guy called George Leton.

We toured France with our band, no tapes or nothing so there was no chance of anything like the backing tape problem happening to me again. And the following year he invited us back for another tour. And we found that we were playing in places with 5,000 to 10,000 people. We ended up playing in festivals. In the end, I played by myself in the Zenith to 6,000 people. Last year we played the Zenith in Paris. It was a big reggae festival. And to show you how much the French think of me, they had Buju Banton, they had the Mighty Diamonds, they had Culture and some other reggae group, and we were the headliners, Linton Kwesi Johnson and the Dennis Bovell

Linton Kwesi Johnson

Dub Band. One time we played to 10,000 people in a place called La Villette. I think it was an old meat factory or something they converted. And I was always wondering why, why these French people liked my stuff so much. And then, one day George said to me, 'Linton, you know why these French people like you so much?' He said, 'You're very good at making them believe they understand English'.

But it only goes to show you the power of reggae music, you know. Since those days when I played my first record, we've played all over the world, all over Europe, we've been to places as diverse as Japan, Brazil, South Africa, though ... no, we haven't been to Russia.

John La Rose:I remember you telling me Linton, about your visit to South Africa not long ago and your going through Soweto, and this youngster said, 'Look at Linton Kwesi Johnson'.

Linton Kwesi Johnson: Oh, yes that was the first time I went there in 1994. Yes, because we played with the band in 1995 and I went there by myself in 1994 for poetry readings and they took us to Soweto. And as I got out of the car and looked around, a guy, a young black guy, a rasta guy, red, gold and green hat on, he says ,'Hey, Linton Kwesi Johnson'. So, I said, 'Yeh, hello man, nice to meet you'. He says, 'Ah, go away, you only look like him.' Like he couldn't believe that I would be there in Soweto.

And then, the following year I went back with the Dennis Bovell Dub Band and we had three gigs but they were all in Johannesburg in a club and the audience was 60% white, so I also insisted on playing to a black audience so they had a gig in a big football stadium, in Alexandra township. And, on our way to the airport back to England, we stopped off and did about a 40 minute set and most of the audience were like ... but there was a group of about 20 or 30 rastas who were like fanatical LKJ fans and they were running around the place, toi-toing, trying to climb up onto the stage and security had to hold them away but the rest of the people was like ... 'What's this?'

John La Rose: This was a period of great influence which the black presence in Britain had all over Europe, especially in France, Holland, Germany ...

Linton Kwesi Johnson: You know, I think the reason why I've been able to find such an audience in those countries is that I think a lot of the black population in France, in Holland, in Germany, and all that, they look to England for leadership and I think they're very impressed with what blacks have done and with what blacks have achieved in this country and I'm seen as a kind of a person who sort of represents that through music and poetry and I suppose that would account for my popularity in those countries.

John La Rose: We can talk a bit more but we want to allow you to ask questions and make comments if you wish. So Linton thank you very much for this lecture and conversation.

Additional points made by Linton Kwesi Johnson, in response to questions from the audience

On whether or not he has been a British artist

I don't think in those days ... definitely not, I wouldn't have been seen as a British poet or ... I was Caribbean. I was seen as a Caribbean poet, a West Indian poet, a Jamaican. Nowadays, I'm being sponsored by the British Council to go abroad and do readings so I suppose that means something ...

Just to add one little thing - somebody told me - some guy I drink with in the pub, told me that he heard my name mentioned on Radio 4 the other day. He said that Brian Patten, one of the Liverpudlian poets was being interviewed and he said that he talked about the Liverpudlian poets, from the late 1960s, early 1970s, himself and Roger McGough and Adrian Henri, and then according to this guy, my name was mentioned as the source of the next thing that happened in British poetry after that.

On his musical influences

I was definitely into jazz. I mean, reggae was always my first music, Jamaican music. But by the time I was about 19, 20, I was into jazz in a big way listening to people like Pharaoh Saunders, John Coltrane, all the happening musicians of the period, and when I did *Bass Culture* I wanted to sort of break out of the reggae thing and sort of experiment with other musical forms. And I thought 'Two Sides of Silence' was never written as a reggae poem anyway. So I used a Bajan horn player, James Danton, and a drummer playing free form while I was reciting in the background. Subsequently, I've done other things. In fact, my next project is to start a new label, which I'm going to call Jazz Reggae and put out strictly that kind of a music on it.

On Dennis Bovell

In my view, Dennis is like the Quincy Jones of reggae music. He's one of the greatest arrangers I've ever had the pleasure to work with. Initially, how I got to work with him was when I was a freelance journalist doing freelancing for BBC World Service and I went to interview his band, Matumbi, and they were playing at Phoebe's Club in North London, or some club like that. Vivian Weathers, my bass player, told me that Dennis Bovell is the only engineer that could give you the authentic reggae sound, because in the early days of reggae, British reggae was looked upon as a sort of sub-species of reggae if you like, and when reggae bands would play, they would be the support act for the sound system. And if people didn't pelt bottles at you, then you knew you had done a good show.

Well, Dennis had a reputation of being the recording engineer, he was also a recording engineer, who could record the drum and the bass in the way it's supposed to be recorded. So, he was playing with Matumbi and I interviewed him. And I said, after the interview, 'Listen, one of these days I'm going to make a record and I want you to be the engineer'. He said, 'Fine, whenever you're ready, come and check me'. So I went and checked him.

In those days, we used a little basement studio, in Gerrard Street in Soho, called Gooseberry. And, initially, what I used to do in the old days, I used to tell him what kind of a drum beat I want and just simply mouth the bass pattern to him and he would go 'Do you mean, like this?' and I said 'No, man, like that' and that's how we did it. And we would collaborate with each other in terms of what kind of embellishment we were going to put on top of the drum and the bass in terms of arrangement, instrumentation.

And then, later on, I reached the stage where I was able to compose my own bass lines on the bass myself so that when we come to make a record nowadays, what I would do, I would go into the studio with the drummer and I would play the guide bass while the drummer's laying down his tracks and then after that he would erase my bass and replay it properly and then, you know, I decide what kind of instrumentation I want and we decide how it's going to be arranged and how it's going to be done. Sometimes we argue. I say 'No, man, I don't like this', and he says, 'No, man, Johnson, try this, man'. In the end, he always wins out because of course I have to be humble to his musical expertise.

We're completely different people. I tend to be very serious and he can't keep a straight face for one minute. The band members, they call us 'Laurel and Hardy'. I think we're a good team. Certainly, he is one of the greatest arrangers in reggae music I've ever worked with and I would say at least 50% if not more of my success has been due to Dennis Bovell, as a recording artist.

On the relationship between his work and schools

Much later on, some years later I found out that some schools were using it, and I was a bit cynical at the time when I got this information. I thought maybe it was some left-wing, leftist teacher trying to keep his black unruly students in order by giving them some black poetry. I used to do an awful lot of schools. In fact, for about three months I did a stint up in Peterborough in a school with some 5th and 6th form black girls. And, during the latter half of the 1970s, up to the early 1980s, I did a lot of schools, lots of schools.

On the effect of early hardships on shaping later ambitions

I have a sense of it. I can intuit it, but I don't think I can articulate it. I know that I come from a very poor peasant background. My mother was a struggler, my father was a struggler. In this country, we lived in one room, my mother and I until she met her late husband and then we moved to a flat and then a house and so on. My whole life has been a struggle in every way ...

I was enormously lucky in making the connection with New Beacon at the time that I did, and with the Caribbean Artists Movement. It provided a perfect kind of ambience to inspire and stimulate somebody like me at the time ...

I really wasn't ambitious as far as poetry was concerned or even making records was concerned. I had academic ambitions. At first I wanted to become an accountant. Then I wanted to become an economist, because my sixth form tutor thought that I could be another Michael Manley and go to the LSE. And then, later on, you know, I wanted to continue with my sociological studies. All this poetry business and making records is an accident. I never set out to become a professional poet. I never set out to become a recording artist, you know, these things just happened.

On record company contracts

In the contract I signed with Virgin Records, the record company had everything and I had nothing. My royalties was something like 9% of 90% of the retail selling price, less 15% of packaging, less 20% of this and 10% for that and they took 50% of my publishing, 50% for life. I think all that's changed a bit now. Most people, when you start, you know, and you sign a recording contract with a record company, there are two things. You get your royalties as the artist performing the thing and, if you're the composer, you're supposed to get what they call 'mechanical royalties'. Now, what they try to do, they try to tie in the two and say. 'Well, if you don't give us 50% of your publishing we can't do this deal'. And I mean you're dying to go on vinyl, and you're dying to make your first record so you just go along with it and probably think it's a normal thing to do anyway.

On the labels attached to his poetry

Well, in Jamaica, I think so called dub poetry has taken firmer roots than it has in this country. I think in this country what we've got is a lot of what they call 'performance poetry', which is good, bad and indifferent. I mean, when I began to write, let's face it, when I began to write verse, I didn't know nothing about poetry. I don't claim to know an awful lot about it now. But at least I read it. I would read a lot of different kinds of people. I used to experiment. My poetry would imitate whoever I was reading at a particular time. I remember imitating the poetry of Brathwaite, who was a big influence and dabbling with some of the surrealist poets at the time. But a lot of these performance poets, they don't read. You can't get them to read a book. They don't think it's about reading. They think that if they talk, once it's about 'black', the theme is about black people and black oppression and it's hip, you know, that's it ...

I don't call myself a dub poet, you know. I've never called myself that. Other people have called me that. I've always called what I write 'reggae poetry'. I published two poems in *Savacou*. I think they came out in 1977 and they're published as two reggae poems by Linton Kwesi Johnson. I'm not responsible for this dub poetry because I never called myself that.

On performing his work with and without music

Well you know I wear two different hats, and I separate the two completely. If I'm reciting poetry, I'm reciting poetry to a poetry audience, people who have come to hear the word. When I'm playing with a band I'm conscious of myself as a reggae performer and I have to meet the criteria of people who pay their money to come to be entertained by reggae music so it's a different thing entirely, and they both have their rewards.

Of course, I think performing to 10,000 people in a big park or auditorium with musicians could never be as rewarding as performing to 50 people in a room like this. It's a different thing completely. One is very impersonal and the other is very intimate. And, yes, I do get a bit more of a buzz. I do get a buzz out of doing intimate poetry readings. But, you know, you also do get a buzz out of 5,000 people screaming for more after you've just come off stage with a band ...

I did my *LKJ Acappella* CD which was a way of reminding people that I had begun with the word to give people an opportunity to hear the words without the distraction of the music. And sometimes when I'm performing with a band, I do make a point of doing at least one or two numbers without the musicians to give the audience an idea of what it would sound like without the music

On performing in Brazil

Well, it was extraordinary. It was an extraordinary experience. It was like being in Africa. You had a strong sense of this Yoruba/Nigerian culture and the people were so friendly and hospitable. We were a bit disappointed with the gig because we had some problems with equipment and all kinds of other things, but I was astounded at the extent to which the black people in Brazil have preserved their African heritage almost intact. We have lost so much in the Caribbean. The other thing that struck me as well was the level of poverty amongst the black people and the amount of children on the streets, the street children.

Response to John La Rose's invitation to end with a poem

I've chosen to recite this particular poem and I don't know why because I haven't got it here with me and it's recent so I hope I don't make too much of a mess of it. It's for a poet sister friend of mine, called May Ayim who some of you might have met through the Book Fair. She was born of mixed parents in Hamburg in Germany. Her father was a Ghanaian medical student, her mother was a German woman. She was raised by foster parents. She had a very unhappy childhood. Somehow she managed to survive, to come through, gave herself an education, became involved with the black movement in Berlin and started an Afro-German woman's movement in Berlin. Last Spring she had a nervous breakdown and subsequently discovered that she had multiple sclerosis and went to a high-rise building and threw herself down from the thirteenth floor and she died. There was a memorial service for her in August, on my birthday, which I attended, and her father came back for her, and took the body back to Ghana to bury it. So this is for May. It's called 'Reggae Fi May Ayim'.

Linton Kwesi Johnson

REGGAE FI MAY AYIM

it weard ow life wid det kyan canspyah
fi shattah di awts most fragile diziah
ow histri an byagrafi kyan plat gense yu
an dem 'angst' an dem 'anomie' gang up pon yu

afro-german warrior woman
from hamburg via bremen
den finally
berlin

it woz in di dazzlin atmosfare
a di black radical bookfair
dat mi site yu
sweet sistah
brite-eyed like hope,
like a young antelope
who couda cope

wid di daily deflowahin
a di spirit wid di evryday erowshan a di soul

two passin clouds you and I
inna di dezert a di sky
exchingin vaypah

but in di commerc a di awt
woz it fair trade in regret
in love an lauftah?

mi nevah know
mi coudn tell
mi shouda site seh

Linton Kwesi Johnson

tru all di learnin
di teachin
rizistin
an assistin
di lovin
di givin
organizin
an difyin

dat di kaizah a darkness
did kyapcha yu awt
dat di lass time mi si yu
would be di lass time mi si yu
dat you woz free
fallin screamin
terteen stanzahs doun
yu final poem in blood pan di groun
dat soh sudden dat soh soon
you wouda fly out
pon a wan way tickit to ghana
gaan ketch up wid you paas
mongst yu ancestaz

wi give tanks
fi di life
yu share wid wi
wi give tanks
fi di lite
yu shine pon wi
wi give tanks
fi di love
yu showah pon wi
wi give tanks
fi yu memahri

(c) Linton Kwesi Johnson, 17 September 1996.

Linton Kwesi Johnson

Linton Kwesi Johnson was born on 24 August 1952 in Chapelton, a small town in the rural parish of Clarendon, Jamaica. He came to London in 1963, went to Tulse Hill secondary school and later studied Sociology at Goldsmiths' College, University of London. Whilst still at school he joined the Black Panthers, helped to organise a poetry workshop within the movement and developed his work with Rasta Love, a group of poets and drummers. In 1977 he was awarded a C. Day Lewis Fellowship, becoming the writer-in-residence for the London Borough of Lambeth for that year. He went on to work as the Library Resources and Education Officer at the Keskidee Centre, the first home of black theatre and art.

Johnson's poems first appeared in the journal *Race Today*. In 1974 Race Today published his first collection of poetry, *Voices of the Living and the Dead*. *Dread Beat An' Blood*, his second collection, was published in 1975 by Bogle-L'Ouverture and was also the title of his first LP, released by Virgin in 1978. That year also saw the release of the film *Dread Beat An' Blood*, a documentary on Johnson's work. In 1980 Race Today published his third book, *Inglan Is A Bitch* and there were four more albums on the Island label: *Forces of Victory* (1979), *Bass Culture* (1980), *LKJ in Dub* (1981) and *Making History* (1983). LKJ, Johnson's own record label, was launched in 1981 with two singles by the Jamaican poet Michael Smith, *Mi Cyaan Believe It* and *Roots*. During the 1980s he became immersed in journalism, working closely with the Brixton-based Race Today collective. His 10-part radio series on Jamaican popular music, *From Mento to Lovers Rock*, went out on BBC Radio 1 in 1982 and was repeated in 1983. From 1985-88 he was a reporter on Channel 4's *The Bandung File*. He also toured regularly with the Dennis Bovell Dub Band and produced albums by the writer Jean Binta Breeze and by jazz trumpeter Shake Keane. Recorded at the Queen Elizabeth Hall in London, the album *LKJ Live in Concert with the Dub Band* was released independently in 1985. This was followed by *Tings An' Times* in 1991, also the title of his Selected Poems co-published by Bloodaxe Books and LKJ Music Publishers the same year. In 1992 Linton Kwesi Johnson and Dennis Bovell collaborated to produce *LKJ in Dub: Volume Two*. In 1996 the album *LKJ Presents* was released, a compilation of various artists including Linton Kwesi Johnson. His most recent album is *More Time* (1998). He has also released *LKJ A Cappella Live*, a collection of 14 poems including some unpublished works. Linton Kwesi Johnson has been made an Associate Fellow of Warwick University (1985), an Honorary Fellow of Wolverhampton Polytechnic (1987) and received an award at the XIII Premo Internazionale Ultimo Novecento from the city of Pisa for his contribution to poetry and popular music (1990). He has toured the world from Japan to the new South Africa, from Europe to Brazil and his work has been translated into Italian and German: unsurprisingly, he is known and revered as the world's first reggae poet.

Quotes about Linton Kwesi Johnson

'... the newest and most original poetic form to have emerged in the English language in the last quarter century' Fred D'Aguiar, poet and novelist

'... his poetry is meant to recoup lost structures, identities, pure "rhythm and roots", poetry integrating audience and performer in one collective voice' Cyril Dabydeen, World Literature Today

78

Linton Kwesi Johnson

'One of Britain's most influential and original voices' The Arts Council of England

'... one of the world's foremost black poets ... an innovator and educator' Portland Press Herald , USA, 1990

' The Black Londoners of the 1970s are no longer lonely in the old way, and Johnson is the first West Indian writer to document their new life styles and capture in verse rhythms the despairing apocalyptic mood, its menace and its mounting delusions' Professor Kenneth Ramchand, Trinidad and Tobago Review 1977

'Brilliant Jamaican poet - the alternative poet-laureate' Time Out, 1996

Books
Voices of the Living and the Dead (London: Race Today, 1974)
Dread Beat An' Blood (London: Bogle-L'Ouverture, 1975)
Inglan Is A Bitch (London: Race Today, 1980)
Tings An' Times (Newcastle & London: Bloodaxe Books and LKJ Music, 1991)

Discography
Dread Beat An Blood (Virgin, 1978)
Forces of Victory (Island, 1979)
Bass Culture (Island, 1980)
LKJ in Dub (Island, 1981)
Making History (Island, 1983)
LKJ Live in Concert with the Dub Band (LKJ Records, 1985)
Tings An' Times (LKJ Records, 1991)
LKJ in Dub: Volume Two (LKJ Records, 1992)
LKJ Presents (LKJ Records, 1996)
LKJ A Cappella Live (LKJ Records, 1996)
More Time (LKJ Records, 1998)

Courtenay Griffiths

photo: Deo Persaud

Courtenay Griffiths
with Ian Macdonald in the chair (14.4.97)

John La Rose introduced the session

John La Rose: I've known both the chairman and Courtenay over a long period but I want to start by saying it has not been easy to be a black lawyer either as solicitor or barrister in Britain. I came here in 1961 so it's 35 years since I've been living in this country. When I came here there were essentially no black solicitors or almost no black solicitors and though I knew any number of students from the Caribbean and from Africa who were doing law either in universities or in the inns of court, the problem was that at the end of their studies it was difficult, if they didn't have the money to return home, to settle in their professions. It was impossible to get a brief. This was the situation in 1961. Fortunately I had a relationship with Ian Macdonald which goes back to the period of the struggles of tenants when he was the leader of the tenant struggles in London and in Islington. I used to take my children to demonstrations about the tenant struggles that we had here, especially the family called ...

Ian Macdonald: The de Lusignans?

John La Rose: The de Lusignans.

Ian Macdonald: The rubbish people.

John La Rose: The rubbish people. That's right. He had brought to my attention the fact that there was this tenant who had been accused of prostitution and she had gone to court and pleaded 'Not Guilty' but had been convicted and he thought we should do something about it. At this time, in the 1960s, I went to the meetings of the West Indian Standing Conference which had come out of the Notting Hill Riots in 1958. I went and I spoke every month there at their request about the situation in the Caribbean. At one meeting I devoted my talk to the case of the tenants of the de Lusignans, who had been wrongly convicted. I shall go into that case with you, if you wish, later on. But what we decided then to do at that meeting of the West Indian Standing Conference was to set up a committee as to how best to tackle it. This committee had Len Woodley, who is now a QC and acting judge and head of chambers - Len Woodley who surprisingly, because the age difference between us is about five years maybe, I had also taught at St Mary's College in Trinidad - and Neville Maxwell who was then Chairman of the West Indian Standing Conference, and Chris Le Maitre who I knew from Trinidad and who had either finished or was about to finish doing his LLB examinations. And that was a committee set up with the support of the West Indian Standing Conference.

We came to the conclusion that there were so many qualified barristers that we knew, who were doing all kinds of menial jobs at the time because they couldn't get work as barristers prior to returning to the Caribbean or Africa where they came from, that a West Indian legal panel would make their services available to all those numbers of people who were being framed as we said by the police, and who were not prepared to plead guilty because they would say frequently to us during those campaigns that, 'I am not pleading guilty because I am not guilty'. And we would challenge the courts and challenge the police and challenge the lawyers about not pleading guilty.

So the West Indian Legal Panel which we formed brought all these cases in a place in Notting Hill and there were the lawyers who were qualified and giving advice and so on and sometimes they would suggest the kind of solicitor they should go to so as to get proper representation and so on and that's what happened. So this West Indian Legal Panel was purely voluntary and it was the first legal aid centre ever established in this country and it went on for many years. I was involved with it and it is important that this history be recorded. It has been recorded but not enough. We need a longer and better study on what they did and how they did it. For example, one of the people whom I knew and who was involved with this panel was Maurice Bishop. He was then a student in the Holborn School of Law and Commerce as it used to be called in those days. That's when I knew him because Chris Le Maitre said, 'You must meet this man. I think he is going to be important to the Caribbean in the future'. He was absolutely right and because of that I met with Maurice Bishop at the Holborn School of Law and Commerce.

It is now not as difficult as it was then but the kind of commitment which we have seen from the past from people like Ian and people like Courtenay has made this road much less difficult than it was when I came here when we were fighting all these cases all over the country in the 1960s and 1970s and 1980s up to the New Cross Massacre Black People's Day of Action. I think I've said enough but this gives some idea of what the George Padmore Institute is attempting to do where we present people who have been involved in these battles, like Ian has been, like Courtenay has been over these years.

Ian doesn't need much recommendation in a meeting like this because a number of you here might know Ian. But Ian has been a Senior Counsel for years and he has been a QC some years now and he is Head of Chambers at Two Garden Court, Inner Temple, and there are one or two people who I can see here who are aware of that situation. But there was a time when it used to be said in London, if you are black and you have a case, you must have a black lawyer and we stood out against that position. We said first it was important to have a competent lawyer. Second it was important to have a committed lawyer and if both were possible with a black lawyer fine. We knew Ian, and we knew Courtenay, and we knew people like that and those were our recommendations in all the cases we fought around the country. Not only that but we were able to challenge that kind of conception of what had to be done and how it had to be done and that enabled us to organise cases in a way that nobody else had organised cases in the country before and win most of those cases.

I mean there were people who said if Ian Macdonald and Darcus Howe got involved on the case the police can't win. That used to be the case because we were able to organise ourselves in a way that we were able to keep the courts an arena of struggle for the people who were involved in these cases at the time.

Ian is head of Chambers at Two Garden Court with Owen Davies. As you can see I've known Ian since the 1960s. We've been friends and comrades since that time and we always said and I always said to people who raised this issue of the kind of representation that people should have, there was one lawyer I knew and I could put my head on a block for that lawyer, that was Ian Macdonald. We kept saying that and people began to see that what we were saying was absolute truth and eventually when the famous New Cross Massacre came, three of them helped. Rock Tansey, Ian and Mike Mansfield appeared at that inquest at the GLC.

So Ian is chair of this meeting. He is a great expert on immigration law. Lots of people who have immigration problems that I've known, I've sent them to Ian and he's been a great help to them and he is one of the leading criminal lawyers in the country.

Courtenay, I hope you've been reading his biography because I really felt he was the kind of person we wanted at this stage of the *Life Experience With Britain* to present to an audience for serious examination. Courtenay I welcome you here this evening.

Ian Macdonald: Okay John. When I first came to the bar in 1963, it's a long time ago, there weren't many black barristers. If they were there and they did some practice, they were really only doing it part time. One of the people that I used to co-defend with quite a lot and met in the courts a lot was Learie Constantine. Now he was very much a part-time person and I can't remember whether it was before he became the High Commissioner for Trinidad or afterwards. Then there were obviously lots of the people who were students who intended to go back home. Richard Small was a person who decided to go back home and has made a very distinguished career as many of you know in Jamaica. Chris Le Maitre was another person who went home and Maurice Bishop was someone who as we all know went home and I used to have long discussions with Maurice Bishop about whether you could be a revolutionary lawyer or not. I think I came to the conclusion that you couldn't and he came to the conclusion that you could and certainly went on to prove it.

Then there were people like Darcus Howe who read for the bar but never actually practised and who went into other things. Then came perhaps a more controversial figure Rudy Narayan, who made possible I believe the passage for people like Courtenay, he made the way forward for a lot of people. But he was liable to say anything in court. He didn't have any fear. The trouble was that sometimes the things he said really didn't help his case or his client and it's got to be said that Rudy has faded out of the picture. But I think we do at a meeting like this have to acknowledge the debt which a lot of younger black lawyers coming forward owed to him because he certainly made the courts places that black lawyers need not be so afraid of when they appeared.

What was then the next stage was in fact people like Courtenay who first did his pupillage, second six, in our chambers. I think we are the left-leaning set of chambers referred to in his biography and he is being very kind. Of course in a sense the kind of solidity and well-based practice that someone like Courtenay has, has also been I think a beacon of light to an even younger generation of black lawyers who are coming forward and who look to people like Courtenay. He's going to have to buy a hat that's about two sizes bigger by the time we've finished this meeting. Let's make no bones about it, Courtenay is one of the leading lawyers of his generation defending clients. He is in demand for clients who are part of Liverpool networks and Manchester networks. I know he says he's a specialist in Yardie defences, but he also gets a very, very big clientele from within the white criminal fraternity who ask for Courtenay. I've co-defended with Courtenay and I know how brilliant he is in court and it is a pity that his brilliance hasn't yet been rewarded with silk but I'm sure that we will see that if not next year then at least the year after but more probably next year. And so it's with pleasure that I introduce my friend, colleague in chambers and occasional co-defender in the courts, Courtenay Griffiths.

Courtenay Griffiths: Thank you Ian. I certainly do hope that I get silk next year, Ian, because I might end up wearing it as much as you. But I had good cause last year to start thinking about the route by which I came to be in the position I'm in now because it's almost exactly a year since my father died, aged 86, in Yonkers in New York where he was resident with my mother and had been for some ten years. We all decided that there was no way that we were going to allow his bones to be laid to rest in New York, to put it more bluntly, in a white man's country. We wanted him back in Jamaica. We put him to rest in the red dirt of Dovecote Cemetery in Jamaica.

In the process of preparing myself to give an address at the funeral in celebration of his life, I had cause to think how is it that coming from where we did, growing up at an address 66¾ Chisholm Avenue - remember in Jamaica in some parts they don't have a, b and c, you have 66 ¼, 66 ½ and 66 ¾. We grew up at 66 ¾ Chisholm Avenue which is off the Walter Park Road which is part of West Kingston. My elder brothers all went to Jones Town Primary and Trench Town School and I've got seven of them. I'm the second youngest and one sister. I remember even then in the 1950s them having to run the gauntlet of knives and so on from school to make it back to Chisholm Avenue. And you see our roots are very deeply rooted in the Jamaican working class in that sense. My father was a carpenter and a cabinet maker and so on many occasions he had to leave my mother with this large family to go abroad and work. Thus it was that during the Second World War he was working on the rebuilding of the Panama Canal and again thereafter went fruit picking in the United States, because that was the way of life during that period because of mass unemployment and under-employment in the Caribbean.

So it was that when I was ten weeks old in 1955 my father left Jamaica leaving my mother with all of us to look after, and I never saw him to recognise him until I arrived off the boat train from Calais at Charing Cross some five years later in 1959, having just completed a three week sea crossing from Jamaica, when we went around the various islands picking up people and ended up in Genoa in Italy. And they put us in a sealed train all the way across Italy and France to Calais and then on a boat, the ferry across to Dover and then up to Charing Cross. A train full of black people coming here to do the shit jobs.

I remember when we arrived in Coventry. The first large black family in Coventry and we arrived in October. No winter clothes whatsoever and there's Daddy and Mummy taking these eight kids down to Coventry shopping centre, because that's where my father had decided to settle because there were a lot of opportunities in the building trade there because it had been badly devastated during the war. So we're walking through the precinct in Coventry and all these white people would be stopping, 'Can we touch them?' 'Can we touch their hair?' And so we had to be running this gauntlet on a daily basis. But in time we settled in Coventry and I was fortunate in the sense that being one of the younger members of the family, I came here of an age where I could take advantage of the educational system and so it was that I was lucky enough to win a scholarship to go to an independent boys school in Coventry.

Now I'm relating some of this because, as I've said, it's the route by which I come to be where I am now. My view is that my effectiveness as an advocate, and without blowing my own trumpet, I am a very effective advocate in court, has much to do with that grounding and much to do with my experiences as a young black person growing up in Coventry and thereafter moving to London and it also had much to with the guidance given me by people like Gus John who knew me when I was 16, 17. Gus, I don't know if you recall the time when you and I were driving from Coventry up to Manchester. Remember that red Cortina you used to have? Remember that? How we went and stayed up in your house up in Manchester then. We're talking about people like Gus giving me that guidance.

But also school was, I think, a major reason why I find myself where I am now because the kind of school I went to is the kind of school where you're taught, not that you're going to be a worker on a production line, you're taught that you're going to be one of the power brokers in this society. You're taught not to have fear, in certain environments, at a school like that. I see that difference even between myself and some black colleagues at the bar today. That in certain situations they lack the confidence that comes from that kind of educational background. It is a fact that I benefited from my schooling in that way.

Of course there was the disadvantage of being the only child of African origin in the school for the time I spent there from age 11 until 18½ nearly 19 when I left. For example, when I was in first year, there was a group of boys in the third year who were giving me a seriously hard time. And it wasn't the done thing, as I mentioned in the biography, to complain to the teacher because you were not supposed to be a squealer or a grass. But they didn't reckon with the fact, you see, they didn't know that I had all these older brothers. So one day we waylaid them. We waited for them outside school and gave them the most serious kicking. Thereafter I never had a problem in school at all. I became the firm favourite with teachers and fellow pupils. And as I say in the biography, it taught me a lesson. When one is dealing with racists and racism of that type, one has to be up-front and if needs be one has to be prepared to go to the step of adopting violence to put an end to it and that's one lesson I learnt from that experience.

But at the same time it's very easy for a black child growing up in that kind of environment to become seduced by it and lose contact with their roots. Again I see many black people at the bar who have become seduced by the fact that they went to public school and Oxbridge. They have extreme difficulty in relating to their own kind. Now there was never a risk that that would happen to me coming from my family. There is no way I could go home speaky spoaky, because my brothers would have bashed my head in. There is no way they would have allowed me to come in there popping style at them, as they would say, because it was just not a possibility. That was important for me in the sense that I was able to retain that side of my character and experience as a black person. This allied to the schooling, to my mind, made a formidable combination. Even today in court that ability to cross the boundary between those two lines is, to my mind, one of the unique abilities that I have and which I can deploy in the court room.

And not only was it my family's influence that gave me that edge. It was also work that I was involved in, work which Gus, for example, knows about. Ian speaks of Chris Le Maitre. I remember when Chris was working in Notting Hill in a project over there, meeting him at various conferences. At that stage I stayed on after my A-levels and did Oxbridge. And I actually got a place at Worcester College to do history but I was dead set on doing law. I wanted to become a barrister. The reason why I wanted to become a barrister was that to my father

Courtenay Griffiths

I knew having one of his sons become a barrister would be a major big deal. Remember where he's coming from. A barrister was on a level he couldn't even imagine where my father was coming from. Up in Saint Elizabeth in Jamaica where till now dem say 'foot know path' - you know what that means - at night it's so dark you can't see, so your feet have to know the paths and your feet lead you home. That's where I'm coming from - bush! And to him the idea that he has a son now who's a barrister was an aspiration he wouldn't have believed possible back then. And so I decided I was dead set on doing the law but I stayed on, did Oxbridge, didn't get the place to do law that I desired. But after that because then you took the Oxbridge exam in November I took the period off until the following September to basically idle around.

During that time, and again Gus was helpful in this, we managed to con Coventry City Council and the Commission for Racial Equality out of some funds and using those funds we opened up ourselves a youth club in the centre of Coventry, Holyhead Road Youth Centre. Now out of that youth centre came the Specials and the Selector and the Two Tone label. In fact one of my greatest disappointments is the fact that when they started off in the youth club, because I was the only one who could read sheet music, because my parents had been sending me to piano lessons since I was about five, I used to play keyboards with them, and as soon as I left and went to university they hit the big time and I missed out. I missed out. But they came out of that experience. We were dealing with a time when everybody was dread, a time when the one night club in the centre of Coventry, the Locarno Ball Room, you'd have a situation where you'd go down there and they'd say, 'Sorry mate, you can't come in you haven't got a tie on'. So you'd go home and come back next week with a tie, 'Sorry mate, you can't come in. You're not allowed in with jeans on', or the next week it might be, 'You can't come in with a hat on'. So we could never get in these places right.

So organising the youth club was one way of creating our own space and out of that came a sound system and I used to be a toaster on the sound system. We used to play at blues and my father got seriously worried about me around this time because he thought,

'Here's my son, good A-level grades, university place and from Friday evening he go out the house and I don't see him till Sunday morning', because we'd play out with the sound in the Midlands right, in Leicester, Birmingham and so on. So you'd play all through the night from like 10 o'clock till 6 o'clock in the morning and that would be Friday night and Saturday night. And it's funny, you know the youngster Heskey, who plays up front for Leicester City football club, his old man I know well because he used to run a sound system in Leicester and in fact me and him had a fight over the sound system when we had sound war over there at this club that they used to have in Leicester. So I know him well.

But that experience, I feel, was invaluable because it gave me an insight into the mentality and the background of the kind of people that I now end up defending for the most part. It gave me a knowledge of where they're coming from and an ability to articulate their experience which I feel very few lawyers have. And happily for me I was able to continue that relationship with that community when I came down to London. Ian hadn't started earning big bucks yet so we couldn't tap him. So to finance my way through pupillage I started working part-time in a youth club down in Brixton, Dick Shepherd. Now I had some experience down at Dick Shepherd, one of which John knows about, because the Race Today Collective used to organise a football tournament.

So I took my boys, my team from Dick Shepherd down to the tournament. A fight broke out and I remember, John you don't remember this, Leila and I forget the other sister's name from the Race Today Collective, who were doing the organising. When my boys were saying, 'Now we're banned from this tournament', and they were saying 'Courtenay you've got to act on it!' So I went up and talked to them and I remember Leila saying, 'Don't you come here with your barrister bit!' But these were some of the roughest characters you can believe. Nowadays when I go down to Brixton Market shopping, when I see them, I dodge. Because they're going to come up to me with some hard luck story, 'Courtenay, I just got hauled up last week and ...', and I'll be there for half an hour trying to sort out his defence and I ain't got time for that. What about me, I want buy me banana and go home. I took them up to another tournament in Coventry, a five-a-side team, playing away, one of them gets tackled hard, next minute he pulls a ratchet out of his sock and chops this guy. SPG (Special Patrol Group) called. I've got to load them in the coach and hop it down the M1 motorway back to London. We take them to Den Haag in Holland to play some teams over there. Same thing. We're miles away, separated by the English channel and these boys are picking, it's not as though we could jump on a coach and run, and these boys are picking fights out there as well. Those are the kinds of characters that were there.

But again as I say, it was an invaluable part of my education, dealing with that category of citizen because it made you realise that at one level there but for certain lucky breaks went I. It made me realise that minus the suit, minus the qualification, I'm a member of that class popularly defined as being mugger, as being riot prone. I'm a part of that category and that recognition never left me. As I say it has proved a very useful and central core part of the way in which I go about the job now.

Now turning to the job itself. Having qualified, I went off and worked for the GLC as legal assistant to Paul Boateng on the Police Committee Support Unit for a while. Perhaps the most useful thing I learnt from that is never trust the Labour Party. But, I mean, when you think about the boy Blair and that smile you know, you just wonder what is happening to organised politics nowadays but that's an aside and let me not get diverted by that. The most important experience and lesson I learnt from that was that I would never get involved in organised party politics. It's just not for me. It's full of too much hypocrisy. It's full of too much lies and falsehoods and I don't feel that if one is committed to a certain politics you can prostitute them in the way that so many party politicians do.

After I'd finished there, I went off to the States and worked for a while teaching as a visiting professor at City College in New York which is in the middle of Harlem. Now that was a very useful experience for me because it made me realise that the experiences that I've had as a young black person growing up in Coventry, further developed when I moved down to London, but that those experiences were shared by black people all around the globe. And that whereas in Harlem, for example, the accent might be different and the numbers greater, the characters you were seeing were characters who had been part of my life and my experience for a while. So you could recognise them immediately.

In any event after that very instructive experience I came back to the United Kingdom and happily for me my practice took off. I think in part that my practice took off precisely because I was able to relate in the way I've suggested. But the next turning point and a major turning point in terms of my attitude to the job, came with my involvement in the Blakelock murder trial. I was junior to Mike Mansfield and we were representing one of the three juveniles charged with the killing. Barbara Mills, now head of the Crown Prosecution Service was lead council QC for Silcott. Roy Amlot who was prosecuting, was sitting on the end of the bench there. Barbara Mills and her junior, then me, then Mike Mansfield. So I had good cause to watch Mrs Mills at work.

The important lesson that I learnt from that experience, watching that one-time prosecutor defend a black man in such an emotionally and politically charged trial, was the fact that we can't entrust our future, we can't entrust our lives to persons in court who are not committed, who don't appreciate the politics of the situation and hence know how to operate and to defend properly in a case like that. Now Mrs Mills sat down and her game plan was, because the sole evidence against Silcott was only these two small portions in his interview, 'I'm going to play the nice tactical prosecutor bit, keep my head down, don't really say a great deal, then say to the jury at the end of the day, "Ladies and Gentleman, can you convict this man on this?"' Of course they're going to convict a black man on that in a trial like that. Of course they're going to do it. What did she expect? It required a much more up-front defence. The Crown had to be taken on from word go. This she was not prepared to do. The only person in the trial prepared to do it was Mansfield and he was ridiculed by the other counsel for doing it. 'Why are you challenging them Mike when this is a riot?' 'Everybody knows that it is a riot'. Riot it may be but whose riot was it? That was a valid issue to be aired in the trial.

And from that experience I said to myself, 'I'm going to try and push myself as far as I can go in this profession because if possible and another Blakelock type situation emerges, I want to be in there. I want to be in there able to input my experience, my tactical awareness of the situation into that legal environment'. It has made me driven.

My wife Angela complains that she never sees me. I work extremely hard. On many occasions I work until two or three in the morning and I'm up at 6.30 again perhaps to get a train to go to Manchester. And I probably won't get back until past nine o'clock the next day and I do that on a regular basis. To work on a Saturday and Sunday is not abnormal. It's very hard work to do this job properly. You've got to put the time in and you've got to be disciplined. And Ian mentioned Rudy Narayan. Rudy Narayan is one of the most brilliant criminal defence advocates the bar in this country has seen this century. But his failing was a lack of discipline and furthermore a refusal to prepare and gird himself to the needs of the job in the way that I do. Rudy wouldn't do that and yet a man of such ability, had that been allied with a capacity for hard work, he would have been phenomenal because he was a phenomenal advocate, Rudy. And as Ian says he paved the way for my generation. Yes, I'm now looking at perhaps getting silk and I want it. I want it because I know I can use it effectively. It's as far as I want to go in this job and if the Lord Chancellor is fool enough to give it to me, he'll only realise his mistake afterwards because he'll realise that the person he thought he was giving it to is a completely different animal altogether. Given that I've got no ambitions beyond that I can say what I like.

Ian Macdonald: Don't tell the Lord Chancellor that.

Courtenay Griffiths: So that's my attitude to the job now and as I say a lot of the work I'm doing now, as Ian has pointed out, is serious crime. We're talking about crime, serious drug importation, armed robberies and the like and defending both white working class and black defendants. At one level, one of the striking aspects of the job is seeing the similarity in the experience of those two groups. They might be divided by colour but, interestingly, in terms of their attitude to life one of the most striking things is the way in which white working class youth have become infected with certain aspects of black youth culture and black people's attitude to life. Now think about it. All this was a major problem with black young people in the 1970s, it's only now becoming a major problem, or in recent times, for white youth. Under-employment and unemployment has long been a part of our culture. We've learnt how to cope with it. They are now realising that many of the strategies we developed to cope with that situation are useful strategies and they are adopting it. One of the curious features of that group is the fact that black youth culture has extended into so many lives. It's global. Black young people are some of the most creative people on this planet. When you think of what they've achieved in cultural terms. You can't pass a billboard without seeing Michael Jordan or some other personality, or this youngster, Tiger Woods who is going to be a billionaire. And if you contrast that with the economic deprivation of the mass of black youth, yet they have that creativity.

I've always said that one of the reasons, for example, on this same vein, why the government decided to deregulate radio in the 1980s is because black youth had got hold of the technology and set up pirate radio stations. They had no choice and in many ways they've been at the cutting edge of many of the cultural innovations taking place globally. Being able to work with that group and being able to see at first hand that influence is very rewarding for me. But it does have its down-side.

I've mentioned defending Yardies. I finished a trial at the Old Bailey just before Christmas where my client had entered the United Kingdom on a false passport, at the end of May. By the beginning of June he'd been implicated in one murder and seven attempted murders spread around the country from Birmingham to Hackney to Notting Hill to Peckham. In Notting Hill a 19 year old kid had been paralysed when he was shot. They'd had a running gun battle through Peckham High Street at about 9 o'clock one Friday night. The 171 bus had to stop to let them go past. It was like the Wild West. In a couple of months.

Now it does prick your conscience doing cases like that. You wonder on occasions, and I'm not judging the client, that's not for me to do and I'll adopt the normal lawyer's cop-out and say that's the jury's job. But it does, as a committed black person, as a political animal, it does worry you on occasions that you're using your abilities as a mercenary, as a hired gun to put back out on the street people who might well through their actions be preying on your community. How do you deal with that situation mentally? How do you deal with that? Now I haven't got a complete answer to that and I see it as my job to continue defending people in court irrespective of what they're charged with although I do draw certain limits. But it is a question and it may be a useful kicking-off point for our debate. Thank you very much Ladies and Gentlemen.

Responses to questions and comments from the audience

Femi Fatoba: As a man of conscience, you used that word, and as a lawyer how do you decide which cases to take? Do you refuse cases? If you do how do you decide which ones because you just mentioned people who might be preying on our communities.

Courtenay Griffiths: Well for the most part the decision as to which case I take lies with the clerks and with my availability. That's always a major problem - when there is space enough in the diary to do it. But equally there are certain kinds of cases which I never do. For example, I've never prosecuted and I've never acted for racists although on occasions people have called up the clerks and asked if I'm available - members of the National Front and the BNP to defend them. And you can understand the thinking behind it. That if I go into court with a black lawyer, how can I be a racist. In the same way that many female advocates end up doing purely sex cases at the Old Bailey because many rapists feel if I go into court with a female lawyer, how can I be a rapist. So for that reason I draw the line at those kind of cases because I realise that to take them on would leave myself open to exploitation. That's the bottom line. But beyond that I really don't draw any kind of moral line. I don't. Because at the end of the day ours is a mercenary profession.

Returning to the comment Ian made earlier about the debate he'd had with Maurice Bishop about whether it was possible to have a revolutionary lawyer, I think in a sense it's a contradiction in terms because to be a lawyer makes you at one level, whether you like it or not, part of the establishment. To be a lawyer also means that you operate according to certain rules which are given and within those rules I have to operate. My job is to use those rules to the best of my ability to my client's advantage and I don't really pause apart from reflective moments like this to consider those kind of moral issues. In all honesty I don't.

Ian Macdonald: Courtenay, can I just take you up on that because there is a sense in which you do because you hold yourself out as being available more often than not in certain areas than in others. I mean we aren't a commercial set of chambers. We are not representing the Sheikh of Abu Dhabi suing Chase Manhattan Bank or something like that. So there is an element of choice about where if you like you set up your taxi rank. You can set up your taxi rank outside the Savoy Hotel or you can set up your taxi rank outside Lunar House. I've chosen to set mine up outside Lunar House. You've chosen to set yours up outside Brixton Station say. That's important. There is an important choice being made about your availability.

Ray Hendricks: I classify myself as a community worker. My experience is similar to yours but I came from Guyana from a different family background and different social background ... I feel that what needs to be done now is a programmed response where we're actually putting people into the black communities for people to actually address systematically the issues facing those communities. It can't be just one person. Now I wonder if in terms of the level which you're at, you've spoken about some people who are there perhaps where things have gone right for them all the way along but do you get the sense that as a whole black lawyers have a consciousness of the role that they have to play?

Courtenay Griffiths:I think there are a number of black lawyers around with that consciousness and I think in fact that the vast majority do have that consciousness in varying degrees and it's very encouraging that there are so many young black people coming into the profession. In fact perhaps the most important and worrying aspect, in a sense of this influx, is the gender imbalance in the black people coming through. As in other areas where black people live, the States, Jamaica, the Caribbean, and here, finding that the vast majority, a disproportionate number of those coming through and being successful are black women. As a rule young black men aren't doing as well and that's the worrying aspect. But in terms of consciousness to return to your question, there are lots of black people at the bar with that consciousness. I don't think we've done enough as a group to organise the skills that we have and make them more readily available to our communities. I don't think for example that the Society of Black Lawyers has been a particularly effective tool in channelling those kinds of legal skills down to our communities. I don't think it has been. There are a number of reasons for that which I needn't go into but it's something that I think we as black lawyers have to address.

Gus John: Last October, November, I gave a keynote address to the Society of Black Lawyers' Northern Chapter in Manchester and what I found fascinating about the discussion around the point that I was making was that many of the black lawyers there were expressing a kind of trepidation about adopting an up-front position. Particularly within legal firms in Manchester, Sheffield and so on, both within their chambers, within their practices and indeed in court. The impression I got was that the more they felt empowered by the general politics within the chambers, the more confident they were in court for fairly obvious reasons. What I thought was particularly disturbing was that the Society of Black Lawyers doesn't seemed to have forged for itself a role in relation to supporting and empowering such lawyers. You were in the very fortunate position, you collectively, in London, in chambers such as Ian's or Mike Mansfield's and so on. But as Ian can tell you the situation for many black lawyers in those nether regions is pretty dire. I have now some practical cases in Manchester and many of them gravitate towards me and other colleagues there for some sort of community based support, but I'm just wondering what role the Society of Black Lawyers might play in relation to such individuals, many of them isolated and intimidated. Particularly as I say women lawyers in chambers with some very reactionary, if not racist, white men. That I think is a particular concoction which mediates against the kind of thing Ray Hendricks was just talking about.

Courtenay Griffiths: Well I understand perfectly, Gus, the point you've made because it is a profession in which experience and age count for a lot in terms of confidence. If you're a young black person joining some of the sets of chambers out in the provinces, at one level they're very conscious of the fact that they need to tow the line if they wish to progress in any way. Tow the line not only in chambers and their relationships with their colleagues but to tow the line in court because you know this is a profession in which a running list is maintained on you by grey men and women in suits in rooms up in the Lord Chancellor's Department. So many of us are conscious of that and it does have a debilitating effect in terms of their performance in court. Now to what extent the Society of Black Lawyers can address that problem is difficult to know apart from providing a wider network of support of people to whom you can talk and people with whom you can socialise. It must be said that when we have a conference of the Society of Black Lawyers one of the most enjoyable and useful functions are the social aspects of it. There is the fact that someone who is isolated in chambers in Preston say or Bolton can come into a situation where everybody there is black and they're all fellow lawyers. But beyond that it is difficult to see how in a profession that is so individualistic as ours, as competitive as ours, we can provide much greater support than on that level. It is very difficult to see how that can happen apart from, for example, making yourself a resource so that people can call you up. Many young barristers call me up and say, 'Courtenay I'm in court tomorrow, I've got this problem. How should I go about it?'. The phone is always going in that kind of way. Beyond that it's very difficult to see what kind of support we can give.

Ian Macdonald: I agree.

Aggrey Burke:I lived in Saint Elizabeth and I was born there and you could see yourself as a Chisholm Road or a Saint Elizabeth man. I'm putting it in that context because I have a feeling that whether you're a Saint Elizabeth man or a Chisholm Road man, it's a political issue and that one must find a way which is a political way to modify the environment and influence others on issues which are relevant to us. I was very interested in that early experience you described of the independent school. There were lots of things you described and the snippets were very, very fascinating like the fact of the big brothers defending your right to be a citizen in the school and the big brothers saying to independent school boys, watch my brother or watch yourself. Eventually they had to watch themselves and it freed you. I think that is a very powerful political statement of organised rebellion, you can say, or organised protection. I think this is a problem we have in this society. It's wildly dangerous in Kingston in the area you're proud of, the most dangerous part of the world actually, it really is that part. Saint Elizabeth is nice and safe at the moment. I think that here we have a situation that you then went on at the end to talk about how ... I say I feel I'm a plumber and you say you're a carpenter and that's fine but in England plumbers and carpenters and all of us in those settings are forced to have a political view at the end of the day. I just wondered if you have a sense of what that political view should be?

Courtenay Griffiths: Political view? I've always been a political animal in the sense of appreciating that unless changes affect the mass of people then it is not real change at all. Looking at the current political climate, for example, it is of great concern that all the political parties seem to be pandering to the wishes and desires of the middle class. The working class as an interest group has in effect almost been totally disenfranchised and that has been the case for black people, and young black people in particular, for a long time. How you address that problem, how you empower those people to feel a part of this society I must say, although I have a political position on it and I want that change to come about, it is very difficult to see any theory of life or any project on the go at present which is either providing any meaningful answers or might even provide such meaningful answers. It's very difficult to see such projects afoot now because of the level of splintering and the level of fragmentation which has taken place. When you think of some of the vibrant black groups that were operating in communities in the 1970s. What was the brother's name at the hostel for black kids in Islington here? Brother Herman. Then there was the George Jackson House in Manchester. There were a number of such projects going and this was at a time when we weren't dependent on local authorities for funding, for money. We were doing it off our own backs in many ways and yet now none of that is going on. The experience I had in New York in a sense prepared me for that process of fragmentation because over there, to my eyes, it's even worse at that level. To be quite honest, although I have a political view on it in the sense that I appreciate that it requires the political will to change that situation, I can't say that I have any thought-out program as to how that is going to be brought about.

Brian Alleyne: It seems to me that the notion of black lawyers is a very problematic one in the way that perhaps the notion about black trade unionists might not be. You've made it very clear that you're working within the strictures of your given profession even though you did say for example that you wouldn't take a brief or take a case from racists. Although I cannot imagine that neither would Ian Macdonald either. I'm thinking also about Ian Macdonald's comment that the chambers wouldn't for example take a case of Abu Dhabi versus City Bank. So where is the space for a distinctively black politics as opposed to a progressive politics? I mean it's good that a black person can become a lawyer in Britain and overcome a number obstacles but how would you respond to somebody who says, well okay tell me what's special about being a black as opposed to a progressive lawyer?

Courtenay Griffiths: There is a level at which there is a large measure of truth and common sense in your comment and it reminds me of something I heard. Lincoln Crawford, who many of you might know, has been elected as first black chair of the Bar's Race Relations Committee. They had a meeting last week to which I was invited. At that meeting there was a representative from the Council of Legal Education which is the body charged with training new barristers and he was talking about the difficulties faced by people in getting pupillages even after they've completed the course. What was very interesting about what he said was this, that at that level it's more an issue of class rather than race in the sense that he's found black students on the course from the independent schools from the Oxbridge background who never have a problem at all, whereas white working class kids along with black people from that background have the most difficulties. I start with that point because, yes, there is a level at which being a progressive lawyer is in a sense more relevant than being a black lawyer. Nonetheless I do think that being a black lawyer has it's own special content and I do think that there is something particular about our experience which benefits the law here. I think that our experience through slavery, through the Civil Rights Movement in the 1960s gives us a particular distinction when it comes to the law, human rights and issues such as that. I do think we have that special input to make and I do feel that we as black people have a particular voice which should be heard in the court room, independent of issues of class. I think that the two must go hand in hand and that you must be conscious of both at the same time in order to make a meaningful contribution.

Member of audience: Please don't get this wrong Courtenay. I see and I feel that there is great sincerity in everything you've said, and integrity. But earlier on you were saying how you felt the politicians were hypocrites and I must also agree with you there. But isn't there an element of hypocrisy on your part if you're defending a guy and getting him off the hook when you know he's done something wrong and he might do it again and against your own community for that matter?

Courtenay Griffiths: That's certainly one way of looking at it and certainly as I've mentioned earlier it does prick your conscience where you're defending in certain cases. Now it would be very easy for me to give you the stock barrister's answer which is that it's not for me to decide guilt or innocence - that's the jury's job. I'm there doing my job and if the consequence of that is that the Crown can't prove their case well that's not my fault. That's the stock barrister's answer. It's down to the jury, it's not me. But I do agree with you that there is a level at which operating in that arena of course you have ideas about where the rights and wrongs of a particular prosecution might lie, of course you do. As I said earlier it's something I still haven't resolved and if that difficulty is branded as hypocrisy then yes you may well have a point. There may be a level at which we are hypocrites in the way we approach the job but nonetheless I do think that it is important that the law is kept under constant focus by defence lawyers because experiences show that without such constant vigilance the kinds of miscarriages of justice which have tarnished the English criminal justice system over the last 20 years or so will occur. The only way of ensuring that those things don't happen is to be in there fighting irrespective of the character or nature of your defendant.

Member of audience:I'm a teacher in North London. I met Courtenay a long time ago in the canteen of the LSE and as a working teacher one thing that frightens me and I find quite alarming is that the number of black kids coming through the system and making progress in terms of careers is still very poor. I find it very difficult to motivate them beyond hanging out in the shopping precinct. They are not being encouraged to actually aim high. I remember my careers advice was restricted to becoming a typist and that was the end of that. I think a lot of our kids now do need that extra push. The girls can be persuaded to study. It is not a part of the boys' culture and it is really quite alarming that they do not see it as part of their culture to study. My experience shows that a large number of them spend all their time being excluded and the numbers of excluded are ridiculously high for black boys. In a meeting such as this where you have got role models of various occupations, I'm sure if I walk into my school tomorrow and say, 'Did you know or do you realise', they would not believe me. There are lots of conferences set up, careers conventions, if you like, where students are invited and given opportunities like this to actually speak to and hear from people. I wonder if there is a possibility of similar things being set up to actually encourage not just black kids but young people in general to say there is life beyond the shopping precinct and beyond the dole queue.

Courtenay Griffiths: That's a very important point actually because one of the most worrying aspects of our community's development right now is the extent to which young black males in particular are under-achieving. It makes you pause and wonder how it is that they are creative on certain levels, a creativity bordering on genius at certain levels, whether it be athletics, whether it be entertainment and so on, but yet in other spheres, particularly in education and on the economic level, they are not displaying, or not being allowed to display, to be more accurate, the same creativity. I think it is a reflection of the racism within this society and in the different ways in which is affects black people in gender terms. Yes, it would be encouraging for black youngsters to have more role models of that type but I still think that there are much bigger hurdles that we're going to have to cross in order to solve this particular problem. I don't know if merely having on display these role models is going to be enough. Changes need to take place in the school system for example. So the schools aren't seen merely as warehouses for black kids to keep them off the streets from nine until four and the mentality that goes with that warehousing. Those kinds of things also have to be addressed apart from just putting role models on show.

Member of audience:I'm a solicitor. I want to ask you why you don't want to become a judge?

Courtenay Griffiths: For this simple reason. It's boring. No seriously it's boring. It's not that I'm against sitting as a judge. In fact a couple of years ago I applied to sit as an assistant recorder. Going back to the same problem of young black kids and role models, I would like to sit as a part-time judge at a court like Inner London and I think it would be very useful for somebody like me to be seen filling that role at somewhere like Inner London in the sense that it's one of the courts around London which has a high number of black defendants. I think that would be very important and I would do it. But it really comes down to a personal thing that I know, from speaking to many judges, that it's a very boring and isolated life and I'm not so sure, particularly now. Maybe when I get to Ian's age I might be more interested. But personally...

Member of audience:I was wondering if there is a political objection?

Courtenay Griffiths: No there isn't a political objection at all. There isn't a political objection at all and in fact I've been trying to encourage as many people as I can to sit. A member of our chambers, for example, will be sitting which I think is a very good thing. When you go to a court like the Old Bailey, for example, 18 courts and the central criminal court, and if you were to walk around those courts on any particular day I bet you more than 20% of them are engaged in trying black defenders on very serious charges because that's all they do at the Old Bailey, murder and rape. It would be nice to have a black judge in there. It would be nice for someone to have the kind of consciousness to be able to bend where possible the rules to get blacks on a jury. It would be nice to have that kind of influence. It's just that for personal reasons I'm not ready for that.

Ruel White: What I was sticking my hand up for was to talk about the presentation of the story, in the sense that you arrive at that problem at the end, you might defend a black person who is guilty and then get him off and they come back into the community and commit a grave offence. But the way the whole thing is constructed, as you said first off, you describe your brothers going up to the school to beat someone up, you describe the football matches and the fights and then you come up with the dilemma at the end. But the thing is that most black people who end up in court, in my opinion, are not in that situation and everybody's got the right to defence. And the overwhelming majority of black people won't end up in court so I just have a problem with the story, the way you give the story and come up with the dilemma at the end of it, basically going through a series of violent acts then you would at the end have to ask that question. But if you were to propose that people don't get involved in serious, violent acts then that wouldn't arise.

Like Brecht, you talk about the law and revolutionary lawyers but you know what Brecht uses to talk about perspective. He goes to the law and talks about the guy who gets knocked off his bicycle and people see it and the police turn up and ask people if they know what actually happened. Two people give two different stories and the most believable story is the one that convinces people so that if you make things into basically a story so that at the end of the day I felt that most people that go to court are innocent, most black people don't go to court and if they go to court then they deserve to be defended and that's the end of it. It's not a matter of violence or any thing of the sort.

Courtenay Griffiths: So are you saying there are no black criminals in the community you would like to see behind bars?

Ruel White: There are black criminals I would like to see behind bars. There are white criminals I would like to see behind bars but I think that everybody has the right to the most effective means of defence available and that's not a particular dilemma for the black community. If you construct a situation where you put black people in the situation where they're going up to the school to defend you violently or they're doing some other violent act then that is the ultimate question that

105

you must come to at the end. But if you don't believe that black people commit so much violent acts and all the rest of it then that question does not arise at the end. Just give him a good defence. I don't think you're a hypocrite. I think when you stay out of party politics what you don't like about politics is the politics, because politics is about hypocrisy. But on the way the presentation was given I thought you had no alternative but to come up with that question at the end.

Member of audience: I'm just going to ask if you would advise students to study law. I feel that a lot of black students especially in law are disproportionately failing. They're not getting the right grades in their first degree, having to re-sit and facing a lot of obstacles. Would you advise someone to study?

Courtenay Griffiths: Of course. I think the more of us who come in and the more of us beating on the door, the more likely it is to fall down. When I'm asked that question I always remember a comment made by an ex-member of our football team who is now a black cab driver. He got his knowledge about ten years ago and at the time when he got his knowledge Dave was one of the first black cab drivers around London. He said to me after he got his knowledge he was speaking to some of the drivers of black cabs who were saying to him, 'Hey Dave don't tell your mates about this down in Brixton', and he said he turned around and he said, 'I'm going to tell a million of them!' That's my attitude. I want a million of us to enter this profession because it's the only way we're going to beat the door down. And despite the problems and despite the obstacles there you've just got to show the commitment and you've just got to show the resolve within yourself, 'Yes, I'm going to do this.' This is the route I've charted for myself. 'I'm going to do this.'

Member of audience: When I was at school they asked me, 'Why don't you become a secretary, why don't you become a nurse?'. But I didn't listen to them and I went on and sat my A-levels and went to university. I went on and did what I had to do but it's very frustrating that you've got so far and yet it's really difficult to get training contracts and it's not that I don't think I've got the capability or I'm not competent. I know I can do it and its frustrating.

Courtenay Griffiths: Well I know how frustrating it is because if you know the number of black graduates I know who have done the course and can't get the training contract and are just idling away doing jobs that they don't want to in order just to make ends meet. I know that is a major, major problem, particularly in the solicitors' side of the profession.

Member of audience: And bear in mind that it costs a lot of money. My parents couldn't afford it and I had to get a loan. It's frustrating that the Law Society has taken so much money from students knowing that there are not enough jobs out there and I think it's wrong. It's really wrong. I mean the medical profession is taking a certain amount of students because at the end of the day they know they've got that amount of jobs out there. The Law Society take 5,000 or 6,000 a year, not just in my institution but all over the country, and there aren't the jobs out there.

Courtenay Griffiths: And there is a further aspect to it as well because on the barristers' side of the profession they've widened the numbers coming in because it's not only the Council for Legal Education which will be offering the Bar vocational course but a number of institutions around the country will be so the numbers graduating from the Bar vocational course is going to quadruple. Now where do you think all those barristers are going to go. There aren't places in chambers to do pupillages and tenancies. What are they going to do? It is frustrating I know but you've got to have the determination within your self to say, 'This is the route I'm going to go and I am going to go.'

Member of audience: Out of interest what is the proportion of black people entering into law as against whites?

Courtenay Griffiths: The last time I saw figures I think at the Bar it was something like 20% and in the solicitors' profession it was something like 6% but don't quote me on that because I think those figures I got years ago when I was working at the GLC but I haven't seen a recent breakdown, not at all.

Azim Hajee:I wanted to explore the point that was made earlier about the parameters of working as a black lawyer and the parameters of working as a black trade unionist. I'm a black trade unionist. At the moment I represent people working in the Lord Chancellor's office. There are not many black workers there but I remember about 10 to 15 years ago, at that time we were very strident about the need to break down existing structures, and we had a campaign for law centres to be more representative of the communities they worked in. We argued for the sorts of cases the law said you shouldn't take up. We represented people accused of racial attacks and so on. Fine but the other one is about the dilemma of collective battles and individual battles. There is the whole experience that John talked about of campaigns using the cutting edge of lawyers, serious, competent and committed lawyers and there are loads of examples of that. Yet some of the things that you've said don't draw out the lessons of that. Presumably there is a fair amount of experience there but that doesn't seem to have happened as effectively more recently and the experience of black lawyers in that experience certainly hasn't come out very clearly. Something has to be said about that experience of the greater number of black lawyers.

Courtenay Griffiths: I agree with you that we haven't seen the kind of defence campaign geared defences in recent years in the same way as we did during the Bradford 12 and so on. In fact even a trial like the Blakelock murder trial didn't have the same kind of support as other trials did. That's partly because I think the kind of issues and the kinds of occasions which generated trials of that type to my experience haven't been occurring as regularly in recent times. For example, five or ten years ago, there'd be at least two trials a year in which myself and other colleagues would be involved in, a violent disorder type situation involving a fight between racists and black kids or something like that, but I haven't seen many of those kinds of trials coming up in recent times. They've been more particular individual criminal offences. I also think that the infrastructure that had been built in the 1970s, which made those kind of defences possible, has in a sense withered on the vine. There isn't that infrastructure anymore which could, for example, in the case of the Bradford 12 mobilise support in London and other parts of the country for people to go up to Leeds. I'm not so sure that is there. So in terms of the collective versus the individual that's one aspect of it and also another aspect of it is with experience the type of work that I do has changed. It's changed considerably. For the most part the kind of defendants I am representing now are not the kind of defendants who would endear themselves to the kind of people who might become involved in a defence campaign. In fact perhaps quite the opposite. So it is a reflection of the type of work I'm doing now that I personally have not become involved in those kinds of cases so there's that too.

Now dealing with your first point, I remember speaking at a conference, it was the Law Centre Federation Conference. It was up in Leeds a few years ago and yes I do recall that in my younger days I was a bit of a firebrand, in the same way that my good friend Mac here will recall the days when he was a bit of a firebrand in court. But I guess it's a function of age that you mellow and you come to see that there are different ways to skinning a cat.

Ian Macdonald: It's the judges that mellow.

Courtenay Griffiths: And also with the experience that I've gained and with the fact that my face is now well known around certain courts, you don't have to be fighting the same kinds of aggressive battles with judges as perhaps I had to five or ten years ago because I do have a very effective tongue and if they were to make the wrong comment I won't be slow in coming forward. So as a result they tend nowadays to leave me alone to get on with the job. As I say I've mellowed, come to maturity. I've got grey hairs to show for it now.

Courtenay Griffiths

Yvonne Brown: This young lady in the front - it is disheartening when there are young people who are bright and keen and they become disheartened. But I think a lot of it's to do with careers advice. I know one particular lady who had been put off from doing law and I said, 'Well this is a growing area. It doesn't matter which side you're on, whether you're for Greenpeace or for the big companies, you're going to get yourself involved, acquire other skills, not just the pure law skills.' I think that perhaps the careers advisers could tell people that it's not just the pure law that you need to go for and that maybe the majority of black lawyers work in welfare type areas but there are many that are not and I think you need to argue for picking up those skills and going forward and that you have to be very creative as well.

The opportunities are not just going to come. I'm sure that for myself they came because of many of the other things that I did. And they did come, but they came out of industrious efforts and not just expecting it to come by the formal route. For those who went through independent schools like Courtenay and many of the others, it will come automatically. But they won't come for the majority of working-class black people. They just won't. Sometimes they will but I think you have to look in other areas as well. I just wanted to make that comment.

Gus John: In relation to politics and the role of a black lawyer, it seems to me that the context of the dispensation of justice within the society will always be surrounded by and informed by racism. It seems to me that the practices of certain police officers and certain police stations around the country become over time more notorious than others. Then we're in danger of getting into a situation where that whole experience of group oppression, which young people particularly face and where there needs to be constant vigilance and political intervention, resistance against that, becomes diffuse because black communities themselves internalise this notion that they're either drug pushers, or Yardies or criminals and therefore it isn't worth mobilising around what is happening.

It seems to me that politically it is important for the state, for the justice system to understand that black communities are concerned

Courtenay Griffiths

about the circumstances by which people become criminalised and the whole route that the criminal justice system takes to them. And one of the important things about the campaigns was precisely that - sending a clear message to magistrates and judges and the rest of them that that was no private act between them and this particular individual, who some policeman determined or defined in a particular way but that it had a lot to do with the very roots of people's oppression in communities, especially black young people. In 1981 when I was chair of the Moss Side Defence Committee following the uprisings there, we dealt with something like 100 cases. Yes, some of those young people were guilty of busting up shops and looting but the fact of the matter was that the police and the courts were doing something quite specific. They were actually trying to send out the message to the population at large, aided by Thatcher and Whitelaw and the rest of them, that they were in control. So they trampled over everybody's rights and old women going to church and prayer meetings and stuff were pounced upon by the police and we had to intervene in all of that as well.

So it's basically how we form and generate a counter culture about the operation of the legal apparatus, the police and those people, in relation to our communities and particularly those who are most vulnerable within them. Still now in Moss Side there are young people being planted by the police largely because there's a general drugs and gun culture there and as Courtenay was saying there are very few defence committees amongst those young people and many of them are finding their way into jail because there are lots of lawyers making deals with the police and the crown court. It leaves an enormous sense of oppression and injustice within those communities and people know it. So it really is how that then gets expression on a wider, more collective basis within communities rather than people saying well drugs are killing our children in Moss Side. We should not be involved in ensuring that we are custodians of what the police do within those communities and in relation to those young people. In that context black lawyers are important and it is in a sense a political statement to be a black lawyer in this country in the way that John was suggesting.

111

John La Rose: All I want to say is we fought all these campaigns from the 1960s right until the 1980s. A lot of campaigns, a lot of successes against the police in courts and so on because of the political organisation which we brought and the methodology of fighting those cases. Not only the methodology that we brought. For example, if you had a case it was important that the parent or the person knew that it was their case and not the lawyers' case and whatever happened, if they wished to be able to defend themselves properly in court, they had to be well prepared, and solicitors didn't have the time for that. If solicitors spent the time preparing a case as well as we took the time to prepare it, it would mean that they would not be successful economically. So we took on a lot. For example, in the Newton Rose case which Ian brought to my attention, I spent one whole week with Newton Rose's father going through all aspects of what had happened in the Newton Rose case, after which we knew that we could make a defence for Newton Rose. Eventually in a matter of months he was out of jail and he was a person who had been committed to Wormwood Scrubs. He was there for life. He was found guilty of murder. But the campaign and the organisation around it took him out of jail. He could not have possibly committed that murder. But nevertheless he had been convicted in court in the Old Bailey for having done it.

Okay, the point I'm making here is that that methodology was taken up by a lot of organisations around Britain, not only around London, around Britain. In some cases very opportunistically, because people wished to be able to make their politics of getting members for the SWP, for the Labour Party, the Communist Party, for whatever organisation to which they belonged. But we always said it was a case for the person who was accused, for his or her friends and family to organise and we would be supportive in organising their case and we would then involve a barrister, a solicitor who would be prepared for the case. That's how we did it. Sometimes the solicitors and barristers came and met the clients and so on. But we said whatever happened at the end it is not the lawyer who is going to jail, it is the accused who is going to jail and therefore it is a political show that you're fighting in the arena of the gods. Now it is as clear as that in terms of the ideology of that kind of organisation. Some cases have been pursued. Some cases have not been pursued. Nevertheless, it was generally accepted that in that way you could win your case and we won lots of cases. As I said the police stopped winning unfair cases because they couldn't win unfair cases. They were losing them of course. But I see they are bringing some of them in again nowadays. So it depended on that, to be able to defend that kind of situation in the past.

But I must say something else because it really does effect what I have described. Everybody involved was voluntary and committed. But then the legal aid centres and that kind of thing came along and a lot of people saw it as a job. It wasn't any longer a community political commitment, it was simply a job working in a legal aid centre. You worked for whatever time that you worked and there were very few of the people, I see two of them here today, who were politically committed and fought cases in a way that we had been fighting cases prior to that.

Section 11 which is what the government used as a settler for blacks and revolts was a way of pacifying that. The government sought after all those riots of that period, Brixton, everywhere, to create a black middle class rapidly as they created it in the Caribbean after 1937. I have lived through both experiences and I knew what it meant. It meant that a number of people were being pulled out of that kind of political commitment and struggle compared with those who had been in there earlier. But I am for a black middle class. I am for a white middle class because you need those in societies. But the question is that you have to make a political struggle to get to that stage where that means something in terms of the social transformation of the society. I mean industrialisation produces middle classes. That's what it does and therefore one should expect that. Okay, some of the problems that I know about from my own experience over that long period and also which I heard both Ian, to some extent, and mostly Courtenay and others here speaking about. I am aware of the difficulties.

Deo Persaud said some people asked him, 'What is the George Padmore Institute about?' He said, 'The George Padmore Institute is about preparation for the 21st century.' You have to go through those phases in preparation and then people take their stand as to where they want to go. Like this young lady here and this lady here, they take their stand as to where they want to go. They chose their road and they live by that kind of conviction and having done that we see the changes. I mean there are massive changes in this society. There is no doubt about that. I can go into that more with you. We can talk about it here at the George Padmore Institute in the future. But the point is that people have to know and understand what it means in terms of the kind of commitments they take.

We were not concerned whether a lawyer was black or white. We said a black defendant does not have to have a black lawyer. We also said the first thing is competence because there were so many incompetent lawyers in the courts in those days. I mean it made me feel ashamed to see how some of them were in the courts. Because of the lack of cases they would take cases and you would see the papers were not there in their brief. They were not properly briefed in court. We saw all of that happening in court at that particular stage. We said the first thing was competence and secondly commitment. What he said is absolutely true. I knew the case of Courtenay. I knew the case of Ian. The case is a heavy struggle in the court and he has to go home and prepare for the next day until two or three o'clock in the morning. I know that. That's a serious, competent lawyer. You cannot be a serious, competent lawyer except you do that. I know that. There were a lot of them around and it was those we sought out in terms of the cases we fought. I knew many unserious and incompetent black and white lawyers and that is an issue which we face. I mean some of the problems which we talk about are telling lawyers how to defend people.

If we organise the way we did politically it really meant that we had a greater chance of succeeding in the courts with the defendants whom we worked with and it meant that the courts were an arena of political truth. It was said, I know from my experience in the Caribbean, a political case is not a case where a politico is accused or charged. That is not a political case. A political case is a case where people are organised politically to defend themselves in the courts as an arena of struggle for their rights so that is what we kept on saying and explaining and why we said it.

I really want to thank Ian particularly for coming here today and I know he's way out in Manchester and he came here. And I forgot to mention the fact that Ian is also a trustee, an important trustee of the George Padmore Institute. So I want to thank him very much for making it possible to chair this session as one of the distinguished lawyers in the country and one of the great experts on immigration law and also European immigration law. So you should talk to Ian privately if you have certain ideas on this question because we've got to make changes in the legal system.

I mean in the colonial system it was even worse than what we've got here now. I experienced that. When people talk about racist police and oppressive police I knew that in Trinidad and they were black. They weren't white. They were black and we were fighting them. These are police called commandos and they were coming like in West Kingston and I got arrested.

The only time I got arrested in my life was there. The police were making a sweep and I was in the street with my comrades and the police were making a sweep. Some guys dressed up in the dirtiest clothes you could find, they were policeman making this sweep. The guys in the area knew this is police and started scattering. I as a black middle class person with rights, when the police came to me and not all the others and said, 'Move!' I said, 'For what?' The police didn't answer me for what. He brought the car and the arresting officer right there and they pushed me in a car and arrested me and took me to the nearest police station. My comrades fortunately ran behind the police car to the police station. And although I was charged with obstruction at that particular moment because there was a pack of people outside saying, 'Release the man, release the man, yes!' About 50 or 60 people saying, 'Release the man outside.'

There was someone called Jim Barrette, who was a great one as an oral historian who knew about the 1930s and the 1940s, and he said, 'Listen John when you go to court, you're not going to believe the story you're going to hear about what happened'. I said, 'How you mean man, they can't do that!' So he said, 'Listen boy you better learn what goin' happen'. The police case was that I had come out of the shop and I was drunk and they had to arrest me because I was creating an obstruction. I have never been drunk in my life. He said, 'You ever heard of cite me and relate me?' I said, 'What is cite me and relate me?' I hadn't run that experience therefore I didn't know. So he explained and said, 'You better learn about cite me and relate me'. Anyway I went to court and I was given a suspended sentence. I had to pay my lawyer five guineas which was a lot of money in those days and I got a suspended sentence for three months. My only case I've ever had which is really quite lucky because they tried to arrest me on the Newton Rose campaign, outside Hackney police station. All the comrades came around and they drew me out of police hands. They couldn't take me inside the station and I could remain there with a mass behind me and confront the police on the campaign on the Newton Rose case that Ian had brought to our attention.

Now that means that you have had certain kind of changes but this is an interim period and it's preparation for what remains of the 20th century and preparation for the 21st century.

Ian Macdonald: Thank you John and I would also like to thank Courtenay for coming and I think for demonstrating very, very clearly that a lot of the day-to-day stuff that lawyers do in court is not the big stuff but that you are honing your technique, you are practising your law, and what you have to be ready for is when the important cases do come along you haven't gotten yourself into a position where all you can do is a deal. You haven't gotten yourself into a position where you don't really give a damn, where you don't prepare any more, where you don't stay up until two in the morning or even later. And Courtenay has demonstrated very well, particularly when he says, 'You watch it when I do get silk, the Lord Chancellor will regret it'. It's that kind of preparation that we all have to do to keep ourselves in readiness with what may be quite routine cases, for whatever kind of cases we may be doing tomorrow. And it's just the same as the people who want to become lawyers who have to prepare yourselves and study. I think those of us who are practising, I think a lot of the time we are preparing ourselves for the important case because it's not every time in your career that you're going to have important cases like the New Cross Massacre Action Committee or some of the cases Courtenay has cited in his Curriculum Vitae that he's submitted. But the awful thing would be, and I think there is a serious risk that this can happen, is that a lot of people get into the profession and they then get so carried away by making money, by getting the big house and mortgage and all the rest of it, that they forget where they've come from. They forget that and I think that is something that Courtenay has demonstrated to us tonight. He hasn't forgotten where he has come from. He hasn't lost that commitment and what he's doing in the meantime is that he's honing his talents. He's building his experience and there'll be a lot more of us who can go into the courts, John, than in the days that you were talking about when there were about two or three and that's what we at Two Garden Court are committed to doing.

Courtenay Griffiths was born in Jamaica in 1955, the eighth child of a family of nine. His father emigrated to England when he was just ten weeks old. Courtenay followed at the age of five. His father had settled in Coventry primarily because of the opportunities available in the building trade in that city so devastated by bombing during the Second World War. They were the first black 'family' to arrive in Coventry. He recalls that when his father took them all into the town centre to purchase winter clothes the traffic stopped and people approached asking if they could touch their hair and skin.

He attended an independent boys school and was the only student of African descent during the seven years he spent there. He recalls that the initial years were a real test, when he was constantly bullied and subjected to racial taunts. It was not the done thing to complain about such behaviour, but this treatment eventually stopped when he enlisted the help of his brothers and discovered that racists only continue in their cowardly ways until confronted violently. He did well at school both academically and in sport.

In 1975/76, between school and going to the London School of Economics, Courtenay experienced what he describes as *"one of the most valuable experiences of my life. I lived with my own kind. I learnt the difference between the sheltered world of my schooling and my position in the world as a young black man. I worked as an unpaid developer of a youth club in Coventry, out of which came The Specials and The Selector, the Two Tone record label. This was the period when homelessness was a major problem for young black men. We were also just starting to attract the systematic attention of the police. There were few entertainment facilities open to us in the city so we had to create our own. This was also the period of skinheads and I recall many violent clashes between us and them around the city centre and in the area around Coventry City football ground, Highfield Road, which was close to where we lived.*

"This was the period when we as young black men discovered Rastafari. Out went the skiffle and the Tonic suits to be replaced by Red Green and Gold. I had a head full of dreads

117

Courtenay Griffiths

at this time. I was also seriously into sound systems. I used to deejay on a sound we formed called 'Jah Baddis'. I also organised a football team which for a while played in the local leagues under the same name.

"This was a rich and formative period for me. My political education began at this time fuelled by black literature sent to me from New York by one of my elder brothers who had migrated there in the early 1970s and who had become involved with the Black Panthers. This was the time when I appeared on the front page of the Morning Star speaking at a conference organised by the Gulbenkian Foundation and held in central London. I was a regular conference goer at this time, many being organised by the Commission for Racial Equality. Indeed it was at such a conference that I met Angela my wife."

Courtenay went to the London School of Economics in 1976, during which time his interest in politics continued. He had a group of friends in Brixton, two of whom ran a youth centre in Brixton called Dick Shepherd. They encouraged him to become involved and of course the money came in useful. It was an extension of the work he had done in Coventry. *"One of my abiding interests has been football and I was instrumental in organising various football teams at the centre. I have often thought when watching overpaid premier league players that I have worked with much more talented individuals. The problem with our teams was one of discipline. Fights were always breaking out. I recall taking a five-a-side team to a tournament in Coventry when a member of the Dick Shepherd team pulled a ratchet from his sock during the game and cut an opposing player. We took them to Holland to play in another tournament and the same thing happened. You had to have 'bottle' to deal with these guys. When you're on the door and a man comes in with a machete intending to do grievous bodily harm to another you cannot call the police you have to deal with it yourself. So it was that on one occasion we held a 'Sound Clash' at the centre featuring all the major South London Sound Systems. Some men from 'The Line' saw this as an opportunity to enrich themselves and robbed some of the takings. Panic set in and it needed baseball bats and a great deal of 'front' to restore order. The South London Press made this front page news reporting that an ILEA run youth centre had been taken over by gangsters who had for several hours run amok on the premises. Nothing could have been further from the truth."* Courtenay continued working at the centre until he had completed his Pupillage in 1981.

During his Pupillage he discovered that even in a 'Left-Leaning' set of chambers solicitors were not over-anxious to brief a black person. In 1981 he had an opportunity to work as Legal Assistant to the Greater London Council's Police Committee Support Unit, where he was able to combine his legal knowledge with real political activity. He stayed at the GLC until 1984. His job involved drafting model legislation, in particular for a Police Authority for London; writing on policing and legal issues as diverse as the retention of trial by jury, critiques of Central Government legislation (e.g. The Police and Criminal Evidence Act 1994, The Public Order Act 1986.), the criminalisation of black youth, and police crimes; and organising public campaigns against, inter alia, The Police and Criminal Evidence Act 1994. This involved every aspect of developing public debates from designing campaign literature to recording a campaign record, to speaking at public meetings, to organising marches and concerts.

He comments that although this work at the GLC was very fulfilling it also caused him to develop a marked aversion to party politics and the hypocrisy of politicians.

From 1985-1986 he was a Revson Fellow on The Urban Legal Studies Programme at the City College, New York, based in the middle of Harlem. He found this another

Courtenay Griffiths

important learning experience. *"For me to spend a substantial period of time in a setting in which for once I was in the majority was an eye opener. I used to spend hours walking the streets of Harlem just watching and taking in the smells and the sounds and the myriad faces. My experience in New York did serve to make me more driven. I realised that the skills I had acquired now needed to be properly tested in the arena of the courtroom."*

In 1986 he returned to 2 Garden Court Chambers to re-commence work as a barrister. His practice is crime-based. Amongst the cases in which he has appeared are 'The PC Blakelock' murder trial arising out of the Broadwater Farm riot, following the death of Cynthia Jarrett in October 1985; the trial of the man said to have made the bombs planted in Brighton which almost killed Mrs Thatcher; the last Crown Court trial of Frank Critchlow and The Mangrove community; the Risley Remand Centre riot; the Dartmoor Prison riot; and the Colchester 'Poll Tax' riot. In the past couple of years he has made a speciality of defending 'Yardie' gangsters. These latter experiences have caused him to ponder the role of the criminal defence advocate: *"I would not be honest if I did not accept that on occasion I have successfully defended individuals who have gone on to commit further grave crimes, many within their own communities. How does the committed individual square these unique demands of the profession with his conscience?"*

An increasing aspect of his work involves suing the police. One of his clients received the highest award of damages ever made by a jury against the police: £305,000.

Courtenay has varied interests outside the Bar. He has lectured at universities and Home Office conferences. He retains a keen political interest, although not as a member of any political party. He has been involved with a broad range of community groups, including the black theatre group Talawa, and has been active in community protests around police brutality and racial harassment. He is a keen follower of sport generally and football in particular.

For the past few years he has deliberately withdrawn from any kind of political activity as he feels his two youngest sons require his attention. As he says "I have seen too much of a certain style of life to take my responsibilities as a black father of black sons lightly." Courtenay Griffiths was appointed a QC in 1998.

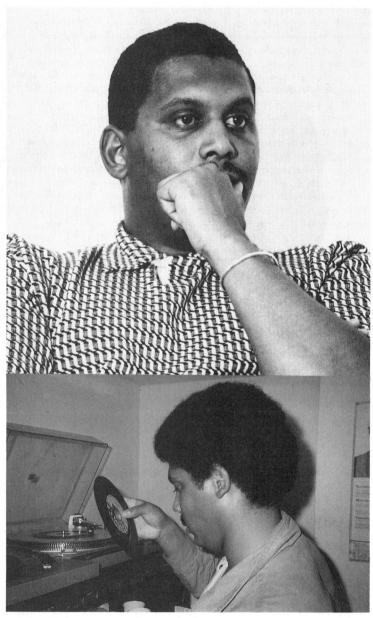

Michael La Rose (inset at the sound system controls in the 1980s)

photos: Deo Persaud & inset Roxy Harris

Michael La Rose
with Roxy Harris in the chair (12.5.97)

Roxy Harris: Good evening everybody, we have a very interesting and exciting session tonight which I am looking forward to a lot. Michael is going to be talking about the rise of the sound system in popular culture and social life in Britain and really he is one of the few people in the country who could do such a talk, in not only being a participant, but also, analysing and thinking about it for the whole of the last 25 years, I should say. For some of the people who are younger here, I first met Michael probably around 1974/75. At that time he was a youth and, in fact, I toyed with the idea of bringing a picture to show you, but I decided not to embarass him. In the picture I had in mind he had big hair like that and big trousers like this and big platform kind of shoes. So that's how long I have known Michael, but in particular with the sound system. I have also known him as a very important person not only in political activities, which we shared over all of that time, but also particularly with music. And Michael is going to give a talk about his entry and participation in the sound system, but also he is going to try to analyse it a bit not only just say what he did but how he sees it, and one of the things he is going to talk about which I have always admired, is that all throughout that period Michael's sound system always played every kind of music at a time when lots of people said they are only going to play reggae, or they only going to play soca or they are only going to play one style, he always had the vision to play all styles. And now most people who run the music promotion business play all styles. So I am going to hand you over to Michael and I hope you will give him a hand and encourage him to talk.

Michael La Rose: What I'll be talking about today is a period in the history of black people in Britain which was very important, very important for what is happening today, very important for what people are doing today. First of all, I want to tell you what period I am talking about. I am talking about from the late 1960s, beginning of the 1970s till the end of the 1980s. That is the kind of period I am talking about. I need twenty years.

First let me tell you about my coming to Britain. I came to Britain as a little six year old from Venezuela, a South American country, with the Caribbean just coming off the tip of it. And there we had colour TV. We had skyscrapers, we had big cities. So when I came to England, I did not come as a 'country bookie' as someone who didn't know anything. I came and I saw England as a very grey green, a very dull place, a lot of soot in the air, people wearing grey suits and brown suits and everybody wore the same kind of clothes. The houses were all the same colour, they were all green and dark green for some reason. And the houses all looked the same, there were no skyscrapers there were just little houses so I thought this was a country of little people as there were just these little houses everywhere. That was my impression of England from the train.

My first real experience of England, I used to live on Nelson Road in Hornsey just up the road here, and I went to what I know now as a sweet shop. I didn't know what it was at the beginning but in England we used to have little threepenny pieces, a coin with lots and lots of sides, they don't make them any more, and I went to the shop and I can't remember what I was buying, and I said how much was it and the shop keeper told me the price and I showed him this three penny piece because I didn't know what the money was either, I just gave it to him and they said 'Thank you little wog'. I said, 'Uh, that's OK'. I went home and I told my Mum: 'I went to the shop and the man said to me "thank you little wog"'. She said, 'What!'. And she marched me back to the shop and made a big fuss in the shop and cursed the man and everything. That set the standard for our life in Britain. You had to respond and react to that racism, and I think nothing much has changed in that sense. It set the standard for all blacks in Britain at that time in that we responded every time to that racism, either physically or in words. We just did not take it. And that was, as if it set the standard for my whole generation growing up, young people growing up at that time. We would mash the place up, burn it down if we found that kind of racism against us.

Michael La Rose

Today, I am going to say things as they were, rather than paint a nice picture of it. I am going to say how things really were. I remember in school another incident. I told my teacher I wanted to do eight O Levels. He said, 'O Levels, to do what?' I said, 'Well to do A Levels and go to university.' He said, 'No, no, no, you're aiming much too high. You should try to get on a course and be a mechanic.' I said, 'Why should I be a mechanic? Going to university is no big thing.' My cousins in Trinidad were lawyers and doctors and they went to university and it was not such a big thing. O Levels is not such a big thing. But for young blacks in Britain, they wanted to stop you from going to university, to take your O Levels or whatever. They wanted to block your aspirations, keep you in place.

This was a constant battle the question of being black in Britain, you had to defend it or go under and an important part of our identity of feeling strong, of feeling of worth, of feeling that we could take on all our enemies and all the things we had to face, was the music and sound systems. We had to listen to our music only in special places and they were like secret places because these were shops that were in back alleys sometimes, not on the high streets, and that's where we would hear the records. We would hang out in the record shops for hours. Some people would stay there from the time the shop opened until it closed. That's what they did. And we used to listen to records in people's houses especially when their parents were out and we could turn the music up loud. There was only one programme that played black music at that time and it played black music on a Sunday, that was Steve Barnard's 'Reggae Time' on Radio London. We have a GLR (Greater London Radio) person here tonight, that is the long tradition that they have been in. We went to clubs like Phoebe's in Stoke Newington, Bluesville in Wood Green, Pastor Morris's Youth Club on West Green Road, the Methodist Hall up in Archway which is still there, Noreik in Tottenham, it got knocked down completely, and Cobweb in Hornsey.

I'll tell you a little story about Pastor Morris's club. It was a youth club but in there was a resident sound system. Pastor Morris was the kind of guy who wanted to influence these youths through the sound system and he actually paid for the sound system for the bigger 'badder' boys. Their sound was called Scrap Iron and they used to play in the youth club. We used to have fights in there, stabbing fights and knife fights. All kinds of things used to go on in there over stupidness. But when the police came, and they came often, we would all unite against the police and my main image of that Pastor Morris Youth Club on Stanley Road, in Tottenham was of one night when police tried to get in through the front door and all the youths, ran into the back and grabbed empty milk bottles and threw them over the roof. As you know, it was a church, with a very very high roof and the youths would throw the milk bottles over the high roof at the police at the entrance on the other side of the youth club. That was the day-to-day running at that time. That was the day-to-day battles we had with the police at that time, over where we could play our music, where we could be, where we could congregate. Because as black youths congregate anywhere, there was a big problem.

We started our sound. Like a lot of young people at that time, we used to go to what they called blues, that's a party where they sold drinks. A sound system would be playing and all the youths would come in and go through all night. You would pay an entrance fee at the door. The sound system is a business as well as a means of cultural identity. It is a business with promoters and all kinds of businessmen involved. And in our area in North London there were sound systems established before us. The generation before, that is our parents' generation, and a set of people, some youths about four years older than we were, they also developed sound systems. And in our time in this part of London would be Fat Man, Sir Dees, Sir Biggs, Metro Downbeat and Chicken. These were the sounds in this area.

But coming back to what we faced as young people at that time, we saw ourselves as waging a fierce war against racism and where was the war fought? First of all, it was on the streets with the police. When I was 12 years old, I was walking down Stroud Green Road here, there used to be a shoe shop here, and I was walking with my Dad to buy some shoes. Suddenly two police vans came from different directions. One grabbed me, one grabbed another guy further down the road and another guy was chased up the road somewhere. Why was I arrested? I was 12 years old, yes? I was arrested because there had been a robbery in the area and, the police description was that three black guys had done it. So any three black guys who were on the street got arrested. Needless to say my Dad kicked up a big fuss and I got out of the police van but it was a common thing to be arrested, from 12 years old onward. This was common, everybody was at risk. Some people were luckier than others. When I used to walk up Oxford Street, I would be stopped four times by police, searched on the street and asked what I was doing and where I was going. Four times in one day in Oxford Street. When I got a car, I got stopped three times on my own street, Uplands Road, three times on the same street on the same day. That was the daily routine of our battle with the police.

In the schools there was the instinctive rebellion, our instinctive rebellion against what we thought was training for 'shit' work. That is what we thought of cleaning the streets, working on the buses, or working in hospitals. We knew our parents had to do it, but we did not have to do it. We went to school with all the other white boys and girls and we felt that we had the same rights as they had in Britain and we were not going to be channelled into those jobs. There was a lot of racism in what was being taught in schools and we stood up against it. Ours was a battle for dignity and identity. We had to battle to wear our Afros, as Roxy was telling you. At that time you weren't allowed to wear Afros in school or little badges saying black power and other slogans or little pendants with black fists on them. But we forced the school authorities to allow that and we wore our Afros and we wore our pendants and badges and so on.

In the courts, the magistrates believed everything the police said and a lot of young blacks were up in the courts. A lot of them were stitched up, a lot of them got a record, a lot of them are just coming out of jail now. There was a friend of mine with whom we used to play football in a little garage at the bottom of Uplands Road, in Hornsey, North London, that's where all the youths used to gather. Occasionally every month there would be a police raid on that garage, not because there was anything wrong going on, but because we were congregating in that garage. And they singled out that friend called Ivan, and when they raided and everybody scattered, they would chase just this one guy to the ground and they would beat him. They would take him in the van, beat him in the van, take him to the police station, beat him there, not arrest him, and then send him home, just this one guy. In our social events and our dances, wherever we gathered, there was the question of police interference or people complaining. Any congregation of blacks was seen as aggressive. We had to have our parties and blues in condemned houses because that's all that was available. You couldn't hire a hall, you couldn't hire a hotel, that is how it was in those times. No one would give you the booking.

And then there was the question of the racist media. We didn't exist on the television. We were always described as West Indians or coloureds even though a lot of us were born in England. And any time there was any kind of serious crime, it was always a black face that was put up on the television screen and there was absolutely no black music on Radio One or 'Top Of The Pops'.

There was at this time also a lot of political activity. There were the remnants of the black power youth movement, and a kind of black consciousness movement here in Britain with organisations of black youths slightly older than we were, about four years older than we were and they were in organisations like the Black Unity and Freedom Party, the Black Liberation Front, the Black Panther Party, and they all had their newsletters and their newspapers and we read them all. We were also encouraged by those newspapers to read certain books written by revolutionary and progressive authors, like, Huey Newton, Malcolm X, Walter Rodney, Marcus Garvey, Amilcar Cabral. Another important factor was the question of Rastafarianism which was very very strong. It was rebellious, anti-establishment, and against materialism and a "Babylon mind" as they said. It had pride, consciousness and a lot of contradictions. It was more a way of life than a religion, but it affected us very much and we listened very carefully to what was said and a lot of people became Rastafarians, at that time, at least a lot of my friends did. And also on the international scene there was a lot of active resistance with people in Africa taking up arms against the colonial authorities especially the Portuguese colonies. Angola, Guinea Bissau, and Mozambique were all fighting wars for independence. These were all factors that affected us very greatly at that time.

Now what I want to do at this point is just play a couple of tunes that give you an indication of feeling of the music at that time. This is especially important for the younger ones here. The first track is 'The Israelites' by Desmond Dekker which was the first tune I ever heard on the radio. I think it was No 1 in the British charts. And then there was a tune called 'Blood and Fire' talking about rebellion and burning down, and an Al Green tune made into reggae. There was always a reggae version. That's one of the geniuses of reggae, you can always make a version, a reggaefied version or a Caribbean version of anything you wanted to hear. And finally you will hear one of the most influential toasters at that time, what you call MCs now, a guy called Big Youth who had gold teeth and locks and was the epitome of all that we wanted to be at that time.

Music Plays.

I hope that brings back memories for some people and I hope it educates others.

What was sound system culture? First of all, you made your own boxes (speaker enclosures) and amplifiers and the best sound systems were those who had people in them who were carpenters and electrical engineers. They were the best sound systems. The actual sound was very important. The tops, I'll just say how it is and how I know it was and you can ask me later on what it means. The tops (treble) had to be clear, that is, the voice (mid range) part of it had to be very clear, the chip had to be very sharp and the bass line had to 'lick your chest', it had to knock you over. We used to use one deck and a toaster to fill the gaps. The toaster is what we call now an MC and our heroes at that time were toasters called I Roy, U Roy and Big Youth. The currency was the records. I told you about those record shops where we could get those records. They were imported from Jamaica and we called them pre-releases. That is records available before they were released in Britian. But we shortened that word to 'pre' They were called 'pres'. They were very precious and not only did you not want another person to have it, because of the competition between you, what you did was you tore the labels off so that nobody else could get it. If someone looked at your deck and looked at the record, they would not know what the record was. I've got a lot of records at home where I don't know who the artist is.

How could we afford these records? They were very expensive, they were imported records. Well, how could we afford the material for the boxes? How could we afford the equipment? This was expensive heavy duty equipment. How was it possible? I have been thinking about this very recently. Remember we were youths, most of us were either at school, or unemployed, very few had work, but those who did work, got HP, and we also put our money together collectively. We also stole the equipment.

There is a film called *Babylon*. It is a film about a sound system. It is the only film I know about a sound system in Britain. It's by Franco Rosso. And there is a scene, and we all laughed about it because that is what really happened to us, where they were stealing a speaker from a train station, you know the PA system, that's what happened to us, we did that. We took the whole thing, we unscrewed a bracket off the wall, and ran away with the speaker. Anyway you could get the equipment that's what happened. So if you get a chance, see that film *Babylon* see that scene because that's realistic, that's what really happened. It happened to us and it must have happened to other people.

People used to gamble to get the money. They used to gamble on the horses; people used to stay in the betting shop all day trying to make some money. Other sounds would make their money through selling weed or ganja, that's marijuana. I don't even know what it's called now. I only know the old name. Some were full time criminals and did armed robberies and that's how they got their money to buy their equipment. And some people were ex-gunmen from Jamaica who were holeing up in London. There was a kind of civil war going on in Jamaica at that time between the PNP and the JLP, and after these political gunmen killed too many people in Jamaica, it was too hot for them. They used to come to London and they continued to get paid. They used to buy expensive cars and they started record labels and they started sound systems. That's how you paid for it. There were all different ways of paying for a sound system.

As I said to you, the record shops were very important and in this area, there were two record shops run by two Jewish women, one was in Stamford Hill, and one was in Finsbury Park. Right, right here and they sold these imported records, these 'pres'. But sometimes, even they used to keep some back to make sure that there was a little market so that there would be exclusive records and you would whisper in their ears to say, 'I don't want anybody else to have this record when you've sold me it'. So there was all that kind of thing going on. There was on this street, on Stroud Green Road, a record shop called Junior's and this was a black run record shop, and Junior had the label called Ashanti, or Abeng. You remember them? And he later on became one of the organisers of Sunsplash in Jamaica. There is another guy down in Turnpike Lane and we called that record shop Derrick's, this was another black run record shop. But it was funny that this guy was a black Conservative, about the only black Conservative that I knew at the time, and he used it to influence black people and the youths. There used to be a hall on Tottenham Lane called Conservative Hall, the Conservative Party's hall, and we used to have dances in there because he used to sublet the hall to all these local sound systems as a way of winning over these black votes. But, needless to say, he never won at the elections, so it was a waste of time. Then there was Fat Man's record shop. He had a sound system and a record shop in Tottenham. The other places we had to go were record stalls at Ridley Road Market, Brixton Market and Shepherd's Bush Market.

People went into sound systems first to make money, to do better than the sounds that were there already, to entertain, and for fame. It may sound a bit strange because it wasn't on TV or any radio station anywhere, but it was a local thing and that's what people ran the sound system for. Right now I want to play three very influential LPs at the time that all of us bought. A lot of youths bought these albums and sat down for hours listening to them because they were that influential. They were *Natty Dread* by Bob Marley, it was his third album, but it was the first album that the black community responded to. That was in 1974. The next tune is 'Slavery Days' by Burning

Spear, from an album called *Marcus Garvey*, in 1975. And the third tune is called 'I Need a Roof' by the Mighty Diamonds off the *Right Time* LP in 1976. Now those three albums were the most influential albums for our generation, and as you can hear they are 'message music', that is, committed music, music that comes over with a message.

Music plays

We used to check out other sound systems. We used to go and look and see how they set up their speakers, if they had eight basses on this side, and if they had two trebles up that side, how they put it in the room, what kind of amplifiers they used, try and see what kind of records they were playing, try and look at the names. Our heads used to go like that. So that's why when people come up to you as you play records, there is a bit of aggression still because you are going back to the old days when there was that kind of competition.

I want to give you some of the names of these sound systems, especially the ones that were formed a generation before us, because without them we could not have happened. They were the establishment of it. They were: Coxsone, Fat Man, Sir Dees, Sir Biggs, Neville King, Chicken, Duke Vin, and Count Suckle.

My generation of youths were the big population of youths here in England, so there was a lot of us. A group of youths, just slightly older than we were by about three or four years, was very influential on us. They were big men to us youths. They ran sounds like Sofrano B, Metro Downbeat, Java, Sufferer and Shaka, at that time it was called Jah Shaka. From our generation in this part of North London, there were sounds like El Rico, Orpheus, El Paso, Heavy Weight, Unity, and Front Line. Every area was known for its sound. So if you said Wood Green, you will say, 'Oh I know, this sound or that sound is up there'. You knew the area by the sound. The reputation of the sound, gave a reputation for the area. Every sound system's posse was known in the area and it was their claim to fame. That's the fame I was talking to you about. There were a lot of youth sounds especially in areas like Battersea, and in our part of North London, Tottenham, Wood Green

130

and Hornsey. It was a nationwide community, up and down Britain. The questions of culture and identity, were very important to us, and you could not call yourself a sound system if you didn't have the equipment to play. If you hired equipment you were, in those days, thought of as being soft. You were nothing. Only if you had your own equipment were you something. There was an oral history and tradition in the sound system culture.

For instance, I told you there was this older age group, there was a sound called Sufferer and all of us knew this story, it doesn't matter in which part of London you were, you knew this story. Sufferer played at a place called Burtons in Cricklewood and the police raided it and if you know the Burtons in Cricklewood, it's got a narrow staircase that goes up to the dancehall area and the police had a real battle to fight people up and down the staircase to get in. Eventually, they called enough police to get up the stairs and when they got up the stairs they confiscated Sufferer's equipment, his amps, his speakers, and it was like blasphemy. And part of what we talked about was, were we willing to fight the police and go to jail for our equipment? And the answer was yes. That's how serious it was. I must tell you who were in Sufferer. There was a guy in Sufferer called Black Beard, that's what he was known as, Black Beard, or Professor Black Beard. His name comes up again in the history of British reggae. His real name was Dennis Bovell, a very influential person in black music in Britain. But just remember, Sufferer, Black Beard and the confiscating of the sound. Maybe that led him to get into music properly. But that's one of the stories about the oral history of the sound system.

The other thing was about northern sounds. People in London feared northern sounds because we felt that they had more time on their hands, more unemployment up there. So they could build bigger and better systems. They used to go overboard. I mean seriously. I mean a whole wall of speakers. I always remember a sound from Birmingham, because Birmingham had a reputation for having sounds with seriously big equipment. And what was interesting about this sound was its name. It's name was Quaker City. It was only years after that I understood what this meant, because names were very

131

important in sounds. Everybody thought very hard about the names for their sounds. So Quaker City, what did it mean? Quakers were some of those people who dressed in funny clothes and were on porridge boxes, and why should a sound system call themselves after that? It was later on in my upbringing I found out that Birmingham is known as a Quaker city. So that they were the first sound that I can remember that called themselves after their area, their locality, some place in Britain. They were anchoring themselves in Britain.

There were a lot of black youths at that time who were not even willing to say they were born in Britain. Everybody said, 'I was born in Jamaica', even though they were Trinidadian, Grenadian, St Lucian. Everybody was born in Jamaica because to be a Jamaican was to be hard, and if you were hard you could be in the sound system. But that was the start of being grounded here in Britain, to say that I am British, I'm black and I am staying here.

Part of the sound system culture was what we called 'Box Boys'. I don't know if people understand this term. If you wanted to be around the sound system and go where they played, but you could not afford to pay to get in, you helped them lift the speakers, and that was the hierarchy of things, that's how you entered into a sound system. You started off as box boys, then you became a toaster maybe, then a selector and maybe you ran the sound afterwards. But how you joined up in a sound system was starting off as a box boy. And a lot of people I know have nearly broken their backs trying to get in a dance free and being box boys for people like Shaka who had some seriously big speakers. That's one aspect of it.

The second thing was violence, because the sound system, as I told you before, was very competitive. People used to pull guns and pull knives on each other. Each sound had its own supporters. Sometimes you 'turned up' on each other. That is, you would play as loud as your amps would go on maximum volume and he would turn up as well. You agreed in the beginning that you would play two tunes each, and let the crowd decide who is best, by cheering or whatever else. But these arrangements always broke down and you would turn your music up and he would turn his music up and you would turn up on each other and there would just be this noise, and usually the only way to stop the noise was to fight or people would cut wires or pull guns or whatever else. That was all part of it. It was called a sound clash.

Now into this arena we came as People's War Sound System. First of all, I'll just tell you about the name because I told you about Quaker City before. When we were growing up in in this politicised era, there were these people in Mozambique fighting the war of independence against the Portuguese and they had a Support Committee in London and they had a poster with a man looking very serious with a gun and it said 'Victory to People's War'. We were talking about forming a sound system in 1975, all friends together, about eight of us, because we needed more cash within what we were doing to produce a sound system, and we said, 'Yes, that's the one we want, People's War. That's why we are called People's War, but everybody else chose their names for different reasons. Sounds' names are very important.

One of the decisions we made at that time sounds very strange now. As Roxy was saying just now, we decided that we would play all types of black music, that is, we would play reggae, we would play soul, and we would play calypso at that time, and another type of music called high life from West Africa. Now it doesn't sound like a big decision, but there was a lot of competition between the sound systems and a lot of false nationalism and threats. At that time there was an unwritten rule that a sound system could only play reggae. That was the rule but we were not going to follow that. We had to physically fight to keep that policy, wherever we played out and whenever we played in sound clashes as well. They used to cut our wires. In those times your speaker had to have strong mesh on it so people could not punch your speaker, or, you know, push a screw driver through it. But when that happened we had to do it back otherwise you were going to be trampled over. So we had to physically fight back to keep that music policy. It sounds strange now, but that's what had to be done. It was about knives and guns and screwdrivers and fighting. But it had to be done, scuffling and carrying on.

The sound system was a social organisation of young blacks because there are very few things that could organise them at that time. The sound system disciplined black youths' lives. It made you get your equipment, sort your money, sort out where you were going to store the sound. I think that is one of the biggest headaches of a sound system. We were lucky we had my mother's house and there are still speakers in some of those rooms today. It is important because if you don't have a place to put the speakers, what are you going to do, because they would get stolen, or something else would happen to them. So what in effect would often happen is that you have speakers in somebody's house, another one in a cousin's house, and one in an uncle's house over there and when you are playing out you had to get all the equipment together put it in a van, go up the road and play in a party, and at four or five o'clock in the morning, come back, try and knock the door quietly, to get in with all the stuff, trampling and knocking down things and scraping the walls and all kinds of stupidness. So, as you can imagine, it is not a popular thing having a sound system in a house. Every Saturday, every Sunday, every Friday, maybe, this is happening at four o'clock or five o'clock in the morning. So that an older person who has property is very important for a sound to operate. We were very lucky. We had our mother where we could put our stuff in and we could come in at four o'clock or five o'clock in the morning. Other sound systems had a more stable situation as some people had whole basements, bigger than this, where they could store equipment.

You had to test the equipment because it used to break down all the time. You had to test it before you played out to make sure it did not break down while you were playing out. You wanted to avoid this at all costs. The embarrassment and loss of face made sweat used to come out of your forehead and the music is gone. Nobody knows what to do and you pretend you are fiddling around with it and the crowd are getting mad. So it is very important to have an engineer who knows what to do when the thing breaks down or to have reliable equipment that you know is not going to break down. So you have to make specialised equipment rather than ordinary domestic stereo systems. You have to hunt for these special engineers, or have an engineer within your organisation. So that to make a sound system, it is not an easy thing, especially if you have a lot of people looking at you and waiting for you to fall on your face, a lot of your opposition people whom you are playing against, or some guy at school who has a sound system and feels he can do better than you. So that's what unified and organised these young people into sound systems posses.

And part of this was to organise yourself to make money, to hang together, to be together, talk nonsense all night, to organise against other groups, plan against other groups. These were organised cells of the black community. Sound systems and their posses were organised frontline troops of the black community, black youths who would unite against the police, the schools, the social security, and the racist enemies like the National Front, and the BNP or some shop that was giving black people a hard time. We used to organise ourselves to deal with all of these people in the sound system organisation. That was the organisation.

Examples of the intervention of these small organised cells of the black community go through the whole history of black people in Britain and I just want to make some sound system examples. Count Suckle, of the sound of the same name, organised people during the Notting Hill Riots in 1958, when blacks were being attacked by white racists in the Notting Hill area. It was the sound system people that mobilised and organised people to fight the police in 1976 at the Notting Hill Carnival when the police tried to flood the area with blue and intimidate us from participating in Carnival. The same goes for the Brixton riots. And if you can remember these were the first kind of victories then of black youth against the enemy, the enemy at that time was the police. But there was a little period before then when there were initial skirmishes. That was the 1970s. The National Front was marching in New Cross in South London and there were sound system guys who attacked one of the National Front marches for the first time. Finally, in the 1981 Black People's Day of Action for the New Cross Massacre, there was mobilisation up and down the country, through the sound systems, through the MCs of the sound systems telling people to come to that march up and down the country. It was the most powerful demonstration of black people in the history of Britain so far with 20,000 people marching and chanting through London from New Cross to Hyde Park. What I am describing now is a period of black struggle in Britain and with black youth as the people on the streets, a period of organising and winning for the first time in Britain. The shock troops, the people out there on the streets doing the fighting were organised around the sound systems, that's how they organised. But that was never enough to win some of the victories that we were winning at that time. We also had organised black struggle and I and other people here tonight were part of that in the Black Youth Movement, the Black Parents Movement, and an organization called the Alliance. We organized the New Cross Massacre Black People's Day of Action, 20,000 people, eight hours on the streets in London. Black political organisation built the resistance against the banning of Carnival and the police take over in 1976. The numerous small routings of the police in areas up and down the country, in youth clubs here, in Leeds, in Leicester, in Birmingham, all up and down the country and winning cases in courts of police fit-ups and police malpractice and police aggression. The sound systems of that era, ready to take on the powers that be politically and physically, helped to shape a new black identity in Britain.

I told you about this guy, Dennis Bovell, Black Beard, he did one of the first interesting things in local music. In England, there was this talk that black people in Britain can't make reggae. It was only yard people who could make reggae. So this guy, Dennis Bovell, under his name Black Beard, made some dub albums. Dub is just drum and bass. And what he did was send them to Jamaica and pressed them and imported them back into Britain as pre-releases. His records sold a lot. And then there were bands coming through. Again Dennis Bovell, was a founder of a band called Matumbi in this time. And the first kind of black youth band of my generation was a band called Aswad. They were from Ladbroke Grove, youths from Ladbroke Grove. The drummer, Drummie Zeb, was taught by a steelband guy I know. And in Bob Marley's concert at the Rainbow here in Finsbury Park in 1977, on the supporting bill, to open the concert, was a reggae band from Birmingham, which we had never heard of before, called Steel Pulse.

So things were happening in reggae and shortly after this, this same guy, Dennis Bovell, introduced a new type of music that was black and British and we called it Lovers' Rock and we wore slacks and sovereigns. Do you know what slacks and sovereigns are? Slacks were trousers and sovereigns were rings made from gold sovereign coins. So rings on your fingers, with crocodile shoes and silk shirts was the style for this music. Very expensive, very slick. Things were beginning to change. And there was also a young music producer called Paul Robinson. He and his brothers formed a very good band called One Blood. He later became the singer we know today as Barry Boom. I'll get to what he produced later on.

So right now I want to play this new British reggae which is coming through. It will start off with Junior Murvin which is not British reggae but it was a record called 'Police and Thieves' which is about the atmosphere at that time; then there is Aswad singing their first single 'Back To Africa' which made everybody think, 'Who is this band? It must be a new Jamaican band'. We did not believe it was from Britain; and thirdly, is their song 'Three Babylon' about the riots in Notting Hill Carnival in 1976.

Music plays

There was an explosion of reggae labels and black British reggae artists. In Jamaica Britain was recognized as the new reggae market. There were new voices and styles emerging. Towards the end of the 1970s, new voices arose recording the previous struggles rooted in sound system culture and tradition. For me, the most authentic and creative voice in the toast tradition called himself a poet. The form was called dub poetry, and the poet was Linton Kwesi Johnson. In his work he recalls the violence, the dread, the force of the music which was important to us; in the identifying of the enemies, the analysing of ways forward he was unapologetic. Yes, we did burn down the place. Yes, some people smoked ganja, fought with knives and robbed and mugged. Yes we revolted against oppressors and rejoiced in our own culture. If you listen to *Forces of Victory*, *Inglan is a Bitch*, and *Bass Culture*, you will have that history recorded right there. Again it is Dennis Bovell who pops up in this time because it is he who produces the music to go with the poetry. Right now, I am going to play some of that and the first tune is 'It Dread Inna Inglan' by Linton Kwesi Johnson, from the *Dread, Beat and Blood* album, 1978, and it traces a campaign to get George Lindo out of jail in Bradford and we have someone from Bradford at the back there so he would probably have heard of this George Lindo campaign. It was a national campaign that a lot of us in this room were involved in. The second tune is 'Want Fi Go Rave', and it is from the *Forces of Victory* album, 1979, and that for me captures the spirit of the young people at that time. They would do a lot of bad things, but they were very clear on what they were up against in terms of what was oppressing them, and what they wanted was to be in a sound system party, a rave. And finally, 'Street 66' from the *Bass Culture* album, which is the only song that I can think of that talks about the feelings within a sound system dance, when a sound system is playing and the bass 'licks your chest'.

Music Plays.

Well at this point I would like to take any questions on what I have said and I am going to finish off with a kind of analysis of where that experience took us but if anyone would like to ask anything to clarify what I have just said there.

John La Rose: I want to make a comment. You referred to the police invasion in Burtons and I just want to add to the story. Because eventually when the police invaded there, as all those people who were there were getting out of the building, there were police on both sides of the stairs beating them as they passed, and it became a very famous affray case and Rudy Narayan appeared in that case. We did not fight that case. Rudy Narayan fought that case and eventually they won it. It was the last major defeat the police suffered in affray cases. We had fought affray cases as you will remember with the Wood

Green 22. You were involved in that. You had brought it to our attention because they were being harassed by the police and the black girls with the Alliance fought the case and we won. But those were the times of affray cases, and affray is very simply defined in law as something that somebody is saying that they were afraid by the event occurring. They did not have to prove it. All they had to say was that they were afraid and the police would bring a witness to the court and say this woman said she was afraid even though there was absolutely no reason why she should have been afraid. Affray cases were one of the techniques of dealing with the youths of that particular period. Sus was another way of dealing with these youths. You mentioned that you had been stopped four times. Sus was Suspicion of Committing an Arrestable Offence. You didn't have to commit an offence, you just had to be suspected of committing an offence, and a lot of youths were criminalised on that basis and we campaigned against it. I'll just mention those two, especially the Burton case, that you referred to because of Black Beard or Dennis Bovell, because Dennis Bovell is really a genius and we shall have him on in the future, looking at the band.

Member of audience: I would add to that. It was the first time I saw policemen break down and cry like hell in the dock, when Rudy Narayan fought that case. That was the prime of his time really. So that's interesting.

Member of audience: I just wanted to say I know a bit more about parental involvement, as you already mentioned scraping the walls with speakers and it reminded me about what parents were doing in the early days.

Michael La Rose: There were two ways where parents were involved. First there is one way where you lost a place to put your speakers because parents would say, 'Nah, I am not having those boxes in my house again', and that was it, you had to find another place. So that you always had to be looking for another place to put the speakers. That was one thing. The second thing was that most of the people who took the money at the door or who looked after the bar, because sound system is about making money it is a commercial activity as well, were the older generation. Some really bad men, some guys would take up the whole of the door area. There were some wild youths around. So you would have bad people to be on the door. They would be from that generation. They would also run the bar and would have some really exploitative prices. The drinks at that time were Special Brew, Red Stripe and Babycham, and they would sell them for about three and four times the original price, so that's also part of the blues culture. That's what really happened in blues.

Member of audience:I want to find out, Michael, a bit about what role women, your contemporaries played. Was it only the affair of young men? Were women involved in the sound system culture? And how?

Michael La Rose: There are two aspects of it. One was that essentially the sound system started as groupings of boys or young men, but as it developed more into a business situation it was about how to win over the young women as well. When we took the decision to play all types of music, we said we were not just going to be a sound clash sound, that is when you defeat your other opponent. We want to be entertainers, we want to entertain the crowd and the crowd would be predominantly men and women. But when it turned into a sound clash, it would be predominantly men, because only men would stick around for this big fight that was going to happen. So that basically there were two strands to it, going different ways. The entertainer line came on top to the point where a lot of the promoters, or the people who got together to put on dances were women. A lot of the people who put on blues, the older people whom I was telling you about, were women who knew how to mobilise people. Most of them used the proceeds to pay for their mortgages.

Member of audience: What about the Hibiscus Club, Michael, was it in the brand of entertainment?

140

Michael La Rose

Michael La Rose: The Hibiscus was very important in that it was a club where mainly Eastern Caribbean people went. People from Grenada, Trinidad, Dominica and St Lucia, who had a much more open view about the music, so we played calypso, soul and reggae, and a bit of high life at that time. It was a club where the DJ there, got sick, and it was how we entered into the sound system business. When he got sick, we played because we were regulars at the club. It was my brother Keith and my friend David Barnwell who hung around together and bought a lot of records who were confident that we could be DJs at the Hibiscus. The regular DJ used to play in a club called Q Club in Paddington at the time, Count Suckle's club. He used to play at Q Club and he was a very good DJ, excellent. He knew all types of music very well and that influenced us very much. The other person that influenced us was Fat Man, because, although he was in the traditional sound system way, he had a very broad musical repertoire in what he was trying to do as well. And those two things, the Hibiscus Club and Fat Man, were our main influences when we were coming through.

Member of audience: You mentioned about getting the records and one of the things about getting the records, did you ever get just one copy?

Michael La Rose: As I told you, we would whisper in the woman's ear and tell her, 'Don't sell this record to anybody else you know'. What people used to do in the end was either to send to Jamaica for the records or go to Jamaica themselves and make the contacts to get the pres and dub plates before they were released in England.

Member of audience: Certain DJ's I heard on the radio they would say, 'This is the only copy of this tune, yes? This is the only copy of this tune until it is released.'

Michael La Rose: Yes people used to do that and they used to be called acetates, this was the actual test copy before you go into production, and they would bring this back to London or sell it in

London. These were called dub plates. If you were to be able to get hold of that tune and then play it and then the other sound couldn't play anything else that was in any way similar or play another version of that same tune you would be hailed as the victor. Your sound would win the clash.. The idea was that you would play a tune and if the other sound couldn't play another version of the same tune, they were defeated. So the idea of getting this one exclusive record was the purpose of the dub plate.

Member of audience: What, if anything, were the reactions of the white working class youth or the white youths of the community? There was no mention of conflicts.

Michael La Rose: Yes, I'm going to get to that in a moment, but I would just say that the first interactions of white youth with black music that I remember was when the first skinheads came out. Skinheads at that time wore Ben Sherman shirts and braces, jeans and boots and fought each other at football matches ...

Member of audience: Bovver boots!

Michael La Rose: ... Bovver boots, yes, and fought at football matches and they were looking for some hard music. They lived a violent life style and they wanted some hard music and they got into ska just when it was changing into reggae and there is a tune, 'Skinhead Moon Stomp'. You heard that tune? The skinheads were into all those kinds of ska-reggaeish tunes just when it was changing over into reggae. The white youths bought the music. In the film *Reggae* there is a concert, if you see the crowd it is all white youths, skinheads.

Member of audience: Is that the same skinheads that used to beat up black people?

Michael La Rose

Michael La Rose: Later, they joined the BNP and the NF and all those fascist groups, but at that time, no, they were just disaffected white youths looking for fights.

Member of audience: Did you have any problems like violence because of this to get you into serious trouble?

Michael La Rose: Not serious trouble or else I would not be here now. Yes, we got into a lot of trouble, basically defending. We were not attacking anybody at that time. We were saying that we can play any music we want, and even if they cut our wires, or threaten us with knives and so on, we would stand up to them. I think we had a few scuffles, nothing too serious. Nothing to get anybody in jail.

Okay, if you can hold your questions to the end, I will just carry on with more analysis.

What was the impact of these organised units of black youths which were organised around the sound system? First of all for British society in general, they helped to expose the racism of the police force and were the only force on the ground who could defeat them, who could militarily defeat the Metropolitan Police, or the police in Yorkshire, or the police in Manchester, or the police in Carnival.

With the help of black parents they raised the question of working class education in Britain. The question of the type of education that ordinary people had in Britain and with organisations like the BPM, BYM and the Alliance, in conjunction with that movement, allowed that to happen.

They raised the issue of language within British society. British society is very class ridden and the question of language is very political. And we raised the question of language so that a lot of white youths today say 'wicked', 'babylon' or 'raas' these are now common words, we just take it for granted, but this is the kind of influence we have on society.

It changed the musical knowledge of the white British youths. I told you about the skinheads in the 1960s, there is also the Two Tone musical movement in the Midlands, which had a ska revival. Bands like Buster Blood Vessel, The Specials, UB 40. There was also

143

Madness in London. This was a whole set of white youths looking back into the history of black music. Reggae and soul were in the British charts. And on Radio One records like *Everything I Own*, Ken Boothe, *The Israelites*, Desmond Dekker, Althea and Donna's *Uptown Top Ranking* all got airplay. From the sound system came people who went into trying to redress the question of black music in the media and formed themselves into pirate stations. The first wave was a wave of white youths playing soul and the second wave was blacks playing reggae and so on but then the authorities clamped down on them and then another wave of black pirate stations came back up and right now it is only a weekend thing because the legal black stations are now telling the authorities where the pirate stations are.

There were also blacks in the mainstream media, mainly Radio London with Alex Pascall every night with Black Londoners and then another black presenter called Miss P on Radio One and then GLR (Greater London Radio) later. So things were happening. White DJs and artists were being influenced. Bands like UB40, Police, Paul McCartney, and Wings. A lot of white DJs on the Radio, we used to call them the white mafia, because they used to keep black music, especially the soul, at that time for themselves and would not allow any black DJs to come in. DJs like Tony Blackburn, Robbie Vincent, David Rodigan, Tommy Vance, who did a TV programme on reggae, Charlie Gillett, Steve Walsh, a load of these DJs on the radio, white DJs, who were trying to fill the gap in the media for this black music, but weren't allowing blacks into the media to do it for themselves.

There were also white reggae and white soul record companies like Island, Greensleeves, Dub Vendor and later on a lot of house and rave sound systems like Ministry of Sound. Soul sound systems developed in the same tradition of the sound systems except that they played pure soul. Out of that came Rapatak, Soul to Soul and Rampage. Soul to Soul then became a recording artist collective, but they came out of an earlier sound called El Rico which operated in this area of North London. There was a lot of pressure on the specialist record shops, the same record shops I told you about that we used to go to, and who were providing a service to young blacks by providing this music. But in the later period now they were under pressure because HMV, Our Price, Virgin and other record shops stocked up black music, soul, reggae, world music, African and Caribbean music for a new white audience. A market had been developed. They wouldn't have done it otherwise. So that initial kernel of the sound systems has developed a new set of white DJs playing to a new white audience and market in Britain. The social habits of white youth changed due to this influence. When I used to go out to clubs, you would go out at 12 pm by bus, and when the clubs closed at 4 am, there used to be an army of black youths walking through streets from the West End of London to their homes. They didn't have cars and there were no night buses. You walked from the West End and you walked from Stoke Newington all through the night, like ghosts, just these people walking. And, as we used to go out, the white guys I used to know in school used to be coming in. They had just finished in the pubs and they were going to bed and we were going out. Today, that is completely different. The rave, house and acid scenes see thousands of white youths going out at 2 o'clock in the morning and coming in at 8 o'clock in the morning. That is the reality in Britain today.

And in reggae a new black sound came out from some South London sound systems. The new sound was called fast style. It was a way of toasting very, very fast. But this new style told a story, and it was about what was going on in Britain. It was nothing about going somewhere else, or back to Africa, or going back-a-yard or anything like that. It was about what was happening here and it was originated by a guy called Peter King, on a sound system Saxon International. Later on the leader of that sound called Muscle Head, got involved in the rave scene providing his sound system for the music as his sound system was so big that he could provide his sound system for big venues, with thousands of people in it. Saxon International dominated the sound system world with this fast style sound. Nobody else could do it. It was a black British invention, and they took the sound to different parts of England and to New York, to Jamaica, to Miami. And sounds in England started to go international themselves, doing tours of Europe and Jamaica, sounds like Saxon themselves, Nasty Love and Asher World Movement.

Right now I want to play the fast type of music. The first record is the first white label we heard of this new fast style, it was by a guy called Papa Levi in 1983, and is called 'Mi God, Mi King'. Attached to that Saxon Sound were not only toasters, but singers, because in sound systems we had toasters, MCs, as well as singers. And one of their singers came with a new type of singing influenced by this same guy called Barry Boom, and his name was Maxi Priest, and the song we are going to play here is called 'In the Spring Time'. And lastly, there is another one of these fast style stories and is called 'Complain Neighbour', about people complaining about sound systems, a normal thing in Britain. The battle was about sound systems making noise and whether it should be allowed. This guy is called Tippa Irie and it came out in 1985.

Music plays.

The final part now is about the effect of sound systems in Britain. The sound system and the young people around it have been at the cutting edge of the changes in the political and social life in Britain. I told you about the all night parties and the raves of white youths. The rapping, toasting, MC styles are present in the music of mainstream music, Peter Andre, or the Spice Girls. Outdoor festivals are looked forward to in Britain like Carnival, like summer festivals in Hackney, and shows all over the place. New types of music have been developing. Black music has been splintered into a thousand different forms and I like a term I heard on a TV programme the other day called MOBO ('Music of Black Origin'). It may not be even performed by blacks, but it is the music of black origin, stuff like rave, house, techno, drum and bass, jungle, acid, ragga and ragga soca. It influenced the clothes and fashions in Britain and even today there is a kind of revival back to those times, where Jah Shaka sound system plays, in Archway and Holloway to large audiences of rasta whites.

Sound systems were the resistance against the cultural domination of the commercial stations. Sound system posses staff many pirate radio stations like RJR, Groove, Station FM, CFM, Ragga FM and SLR. They had both a commercial and cultural agenda. Now black functions are held at various venues from hotels to the Hammersmith Palais to the Cafe Royal. Legal black commercial radio stations have been formed. There have also been the white stations influenced by blacks like Kiss FM or proper black stations like WNK and Choice FM. There are TV programmes on a Saturday for young people with a black format or styles calling themselves with black names. Present day sounds like Rampage play r&b, hip hop, ragga, jungle, Miami bass and soca, not just one type of music.

The establishing and the survival of the black commercial record industry comes out of the sound system experience. People like Blacker Dread in Brixton, Hawkeye record shop in Harlesden, Body Music in Tottenham and Deptford, Regal Music in Clapton, Classique in Wembley, are still the major reggae and black music distributors and record sellers. Mr Palmer and Jet Star have been the black music selling pioneers and leaders for years. You cannot write the history of black music in Britain without writing about the sound systems and about Mr Palmer and Jet Star. If you buy a CD now you will get the reggae version, the soul version, the house version.

This has all come out of the sound system culture. That's all I have to say for the time being.

Michael La Rose was born in Trinidad. He was taken to Venezuela when he was two years old and later migrated to England from there in 1963 at the age of six. He attended state schools in north London where he was reasonably successful both academically and in sport. As a teenager he represented Haringey and Middlesex in athletics and football. At that time he was keen to become a professional footballer and for a period played in one of the nursery teams for Arsenal. Laurie Cunningham and Glen Roeder also played in that team. In 1978 he formed his own successful amateur team, Uniques FC. In its heyday, in the early 1980s, it won or was runner up in many local competitions. Uniques are still in existence and are currently playing in the local Sunday leagues. Michael is now the manager and is no longer a player in the team.

Michael La Rose's other great interest was music. He began to DJ with his brother Keith in the West Indian-run Hibiscus Club in Stoke Newington. His experience expanded when the club gave them their own weekend spot as DJs in the Hibiscus. Later, in 1975, he formed his own Sound System with his brother and other friends, and they called it Peoples War Sound System. This was one of the first proper sound systems to play from a moving truck in 1978 at the Notting Hill Carnival innovating with an electric generator on the lorry to make this possible. Michael La Rose has been active in the Carnival movement in London

Michael La Rose

since 1973. He became Vice-Chairman of the first organisation of Carnival bands, the Carnival Development Committee (CDC). In 1983 he formed his own masquerade band, The Peoples War Carnival Band, with friends and supporters. He is both its designer and the bandleader. In 1989 he became the first chairperson of the Association for a Peoples Carnival (APC), an organisation which arose out of the protest movement against the over policing of the 1989 Carnival. The Association's aim is to inform and educate people in Britain and throughout Europe about the history and culture of Carnival and to acknowledge the Notting Hill Carnival as the biggest and perhaps the most significant festival of popular culture in Britain.. The APC has produced regular newsletters since its foundation. Michael edited a booklet *Mas In Nottinghill: documents in the struggle for a representative and democratic Carnival 1989/90*, which was published in 1990. For many years he has also been giving lectures and talks on the history and culture of the London and Trinidad Carnivals. Michael was a founding member of the Black Youth Movement in 1976. The BYM together with the Black Parents Movement fought many successful campaigns through the 1970s and 1980s both against police arbitrariness and oppressive conduct and for a better education for black children in British society. The BYM, BPM and Race Today collective formed the Alliance, which spearheaded the New Cross Massacre Action Campaign and organised the crucial Black Peoples Day of Action on March 2, 1981.

Michael has also been involved with the supplementary school movement over many years. He was a founding pupil of the George Padmore Community School formed by his father, John La Rose, in his own house in 1969. A basic objective of the Black Supplementary Schools, as they were then called, was the teaching of Pan African history and culture. The purpose was to give black students confidence in their own origins and histories while studying English, Maths, History and Sciences. Among the important books used at that time were *Marcus Garvey 1887-1940* by Adolph Edwards and *Groundings With My Brothers* by Walter Rodney. Michael's own children later attended the George Padmore Community School, and he has also been one of its voluntary teachers. Having completed an HND in Applied Biology at the South Bank Polytechnic, he then worked as a lorry driver for a couple of years. Michael later joined New Beacon Books in 1983 as the Sales Director and Books Distribution Manager. He is still one of New Beacon's directors. He worked with New Beacon for nearly ten years and during that time was one of the principal organisers of the International Book Fair of Radical Black and Third World Books, which began in 1982 and was held annually until the 10th Book Fair and Book Fair Festival in 1991. There were two further Book Fairs, held biennially, the 11th in 1993 and the 12th in 1995. In 1992 he returned to university study and became a mature student at Middlesex University. There he successfully completed an honours degree in Applied Environmental Science, and is currently an Inspector with the Health and Safety Executive.

Alex Pascall

with John La Rose in the chair (16.6.97)

John La Rose: Today we have with us Alex Pascall. I have known Alex Pascall long before he became famous with the BBC Black Londoners Programme. He has always lived around here like I have. He lived around here and became quite well known with the Alex Pascall Singers. That is something in Alex Pascall's history that is virtually unknown these days. I had heard about the Alex Pascall Singers and I located him and one of his friends who was part of that - Allister Bain, I see here. Allister Bain, the dancer and actor. So that was the Alex Pascall Singers and then subsequently there was all the excitement about dancers and drummers and all those things with which Alex was associated. Finally he became very well known in this country because of the BBC Black Londoners Programme and we became very closely associated in that period because of the number of interviews we were doing about various things on the police and education. These were being reported in the Black Londoners Programme which was a nightly programme. And there was something which Alex always said, 'Those behind closed doors', meaning those in jail. He always ended the programme by remembering 'those behind closed doors' because there were a lot of people in jail who should not have been there. There were a lot of people who were framed and in jail who ought not be there because of police brutality as well as police arbitrariness and we were campaigning during that period about all those things. But more important was the period which related to the New Cross Massacre Campaign. I was the Chairman of The New Cross Massacre Action Committee - and I also became the Secretary-Treasurer of the New Cross Fire Committee and Alex was its Chairman. So we both had responsibility for the money which we collected which we passed on to the parents and their families for all the funerals, and there were a lot of funerals, as well as for the injuries which the families sustained as a result of that fire at New Cross on 18th January 1981. And we raised, it seems almost impossible to believe at this moment, £27,000

149

Alex Pascall

photo: Roxy Harris

for the parents without any of the grants that people tended to rely upon. It was all that people contributed including what students in the streets collected because of their concern over other students who had died in the New Cross Fire in 1981. And on the Black People's Day of Action, which is the important event of that particular period, there were 20,000 people on the street for eight hours which was the beginning of the kind of situation we saw where the creation of the black middle classes emerged after 1981. So I want to welcome Alex here and welcome you all and I give the floor to Alex Pascall.

Alex Pascall: Thank you. Thank you John. Before going into the topic, John, let me pay you this tribute and the spirits that are around this house. When you speak of Padmore I must speak of Sam Morris because Sam Morris was one of the early broadcasters and he worked with Padmore. I owe this good brother on my side every respect because throughout the years and up to this moment he is one man that I can always walk down, ring the bell and philosophise with, John La Rose. And your building here, I hope the few words of a contribution that I'm to make now, will add so much to it. It's nice to see faces, faces of yesterday that are still here today. Pearl, well the sweetest thing is to see Allister in the back but then that is the man who gave it all to me. The whole beginning came from Allister Bain.

I walked out of the Grenada Boys Secondary School in the year 1957 and I went straight into the Bee Wee Ballet Dance Group. I wanted to be a dancer but I was put on drums. He says, 'You can't dance Alex'. I had a knock knee and with Allister I turned the knock knee into having a joke. I think the strength of me there was I had just finished research at the Grenada Boys Secondary School prompted by an American who was at the school, Mr Talaska. And he said, 'What do you want to go on to do?' And I said, 'I want to study the culture as I see it from here'. And we went to what was then called the poor house, the crazy house and the colony hospital. I must say that the people who were in there were saner than the people who put them in there. They were not mad at all. That's one of the problems of this very place Britain and the colonial period.

Alex Pascall

Let me talk a little bit about the background of where I am from so that when pundits write the history about me and Black Londoners in the future, not as they have always been saying, it's other people helping Alex to create the pandemonium. Whatever I did, I did it my way. Because at the time, John, when you started your shop, when people like us came here and I remember the first person I met in this country was Barry Holness. Allister took us there and there were these other people, Salkey and the others. All I knew about the BBC was the voice that I heard from home. The voice of truth it was supposed to be. You couldn't tell your father or your mother what the BBC said was rubbish and most times it was rubbish. That's a fact. It was propaganda to make us think the way they wanted us to think. What was beautiful about the school that I went to is that we had those teachers who were very British and other teachers who nursed what T. Albert Marryshow, the father of federation, had said, 'The West Indies must be West Indian'. Proud I was to grow up on an island with a man like that and others, like Butler, who went to Trinidad and my great philosopher in calypso, the Mighty Sparrow. Never leave that out. He's here now. I haven't seen him but that doesn't matter.

At school I was trained as an elocutionist. I was trained and understood Shakespeare. You see you had studied *The Merchant of Venice* and you saw what happened to Shylock and you understood later *Julius Caesar* and the art of Mark Antony how he did his thing and the soothsayers that went ahead. If you don't read between those lines, you couldn't come to Britain to face a media. These were great groundings. And the drums in the village and the shango. People, that tamboo bamboo around. I grew up in the tamboo bamboo period, yes? I grew up with the old people whose philosophies I nursed. I really cherished them. And therefore the extension of a family beyond what is a blood family gives me that real backing to say, 'Don't be frightened when you have to face the issues'. With two drums in my hand and a grip, not a suitcase, I left the Caribbean to join Allister here to do a documentary film that never happened. But by the time we got here on August 19th 1959, we, Allister and I and others, were on television with Shirley Bassey, Chelsea at Nine. I learned then that colour meant a lot. They showed my hands. They showed our feet.

You saw some of our faces. That was very interesting. And in recent years when I tried to recover the film from the archive, they can't find it. That's not surprising. A lot of things cannot be found. Those things made me make one decision. You said you want to study modern communication and you want to go to Africa to study rhythm, do it! I joined the London Transport against my wishes. Allister hated to see us in uniform on the London Transport. It's true. My wife to be hated the uniform. It stereotyped us. I always speak about the test. I don't want to labour it because I want to get right into the topic but this hinges on the topic. I remember the arithmetic. If you had a box of matches and you lit two how much would be left. I thought that was insulting. I remember the test I had, the physical test, with a man taking that rod lifting up my private parts and looking at them attentively. I thought that was handsome of him but I put that aside. It was degrading. Those things told me while on the transport study the social fabric of the British people. I began studying trade unionism as a study on London Transport. My depot was High Barnet and I went up and down the Northern Line from 1959 November until August 1964. From sweeping the platform, cleaning the toilets to the guard motorman. I went to school to study voice with an opera teacher in Camden Passage. She wanted me to be Paul Robeson but there was just one Paul Robeson. Nobody could be another Paul Robeson. I wanted to make money. Therefore after taking six lessons I decided, 'Let me do my voice training on the trains'. So as the motorman turned and I pushed the button, mmmm, that's where I did my voice training. And I can teach people to this very day how to train voices without going for those heavy lessons that don't do anything. It is there likewise I got to know the bowler-hatted creatures and I was able to pick you up as whether you just come or you living around. I could sus you out.

I then started a 21 piece choir, a 10 piece band and I went into one of the two night clubs in Britain - the Paint Box, 27 Foley St. That is a whole history in itself. I could only say in Britain, that and other things I saw reminded me of when 'man turned beast' overnight. There were lords there, jockeys and otherwise. Jockeys yes and that's where I realised that life in England is quite different to the history that I read, the colonial history. There was one thing we all knew, that we had to make it in Britain. And going back home and crying was not in the book. I came for five years, 1959, you understand and I'm still around. There were pioneers long before us and we began to pick them up. Pearl, it's great that you're sitting here this evening, because while we're sitting here, we would all remember the Mighty Sparrow in the Seymour Hall in 1962, the beginning of something that was different. The fabric of a carnival that had already started in other town halls, that Black Londoners later on had to see. When I hear people today talk about the history, Mrs Laslett you did us very well, but Claudia Jones is who did it, and let it not be otherwise written or documented. Let the rest who came around her, many of us, pay tribute as the years go by. Let's put history right.

How did I get into radio? Oh my goodness. I served as a dirty comedian for one year previously, meaning a stand up comic in working men's clubs. I hated it but I had to work for money. I got nine pounds at the weekend for doing two pieces. If I had worked for the whole week on music I would get seven pounds. It was better money so I did it for a while. We knew all of the hierarchies. In those days, as far as people were concerned, we all sang calypsos, we all could limbo. I'm giving you this as a background so that when people say we had to be trained to get into the BBC, apart from technology, there was very little that could have been taught to many of us.

Of course there was the World Service. When I was offered the programme, and I will go into a little bit before that, I went to my brother here John, I called Andrew Salkey. Salkey annoyed me a little bit. I must be honest because Salkey said to me, 'Boy, I'll meet you to talk – Alex, what you going into the BBC for?' He was just coming out. I didn't realise what Salkey was saying. But you see what might have been his experience might not have been mine. We didn't meet so that he could brief me about the BBC Bush House where we sent Christmas messages back home, the privileged ones. Come on let's face it, it was not for the masses. As a matter of fact looking back to Bush House as part of the embryo, we didn't hear it here. We heard it back home – the World Service. History later on showed me that people like Una Marson and many other people, Louise Bennett,

Pearl, your husband Edric, Learie Constantine and many others. And Pansy Jeffreys, who is not here, but I wish to pay tribute to her, contributed to the development of black media here.

Since the year 1962 they were talking, because of the BBC's Charter, that there should be programmes for minorities and I'm afraid to say, apart from the two people, Pansy and Learie, it appears that others didn't want it because, they might have been right, they said we spoke English and we were British, so we didn't need a special programme. I was sitting home and my phone rang 'Alex, Sam here'. Brother Sam, he's in the back. 'We down at the CRC'. The CRC was in Bedford Square. You had the CRC and the Race Relations Board. 'We down here at a meeting'. Lots of people. I wouldn't go into the names today. 'There's a lot of argument about who should front this programme and I tell them I know a man and if you don't front it I break up the meeting'. That's brother Sam. That's how he was. That's how he is. Sam you're certainly there. I know that. He's in the back. And Sam it is who introduced me to the programme. Barry Clayton who was then a resting producer from Yorkshire Television lived in Highbury. James Cummings, David Shackman from Hammersmith CRC, Ray Cruikshank and a few others. Lots of names. CRC people, police. Police, yes, police. They were all wanting this programme because race problems were developing. There was nothing in the papers but rhetoric thrown at us and we had no response. *West Indian World* was there, yes? Lots of papers and magazines, *Tropic* and others were there but they couldn't answer to what the British press was putting over. Enoch Powell was at his top. He was doing it. And I went in. We discussed from July right down to November and the name of the programme was interesting in the discussion. I suggested we should call it Links and somebody say, 'Alex get those chains off your head now man'. My reason was we had not been linked as a Caribbean people until we jumped on board the ships to come to Britain, or those of us who were privileged to meet during the inauguration of the Federation of the West Indies. So we sailed and we were here. Then David Shackman, after much argument, said, 'Why don't you all call it Black Londoners then?' He was a white man.

We sat and we finally agreed. They wanted the signature tune to be 'Island in the Sun' - Island in the Sun - we were in Britain man. I loved Belafonte. He did a lot for us but the times were changing. The 1960s had brought some newness that we had to address from America to here. Say it loud, I'm black and I'm proud! And we needed something to make us really get together. If we said Africa, the Africans and the West Indians would fight. If we said Jamaica well the rest would fight. We saw it through the Federation in 1962. This was the land where we had got to and we needed to hold something together. Money, forget about that. The CRC gave us £200. Barry had £100. I had £100.

The BBC gave us Access – that meant airtime. They argued that people like me could not be trained because I was not British. It didn't do me bad really. I went to the City Lit just to defend the fact. They forgot that I had voice training. I used to hold microphones and dealt with the whole thing before. They didn't bother. They did not even train their own staff. They put me in the education room. Whether to be educated or for me to educate them that's the question. I was given a chair. The men I met there, and I put praise to Keith Yeomans, Barry Clayton, we made a policy that this programme would represent the people. It was a six month programme, a magazine style programme. Nobody knew what it was supposed to have in it. We went to Brixton to see Gloria Cameron, who then had a group, and we met a number of people to ask them what they would want because Brixton was always the capital for black people here. And the people said to me, 'Alex, you damn well know what we want, why the hell don't you go back and make the damn programme. It's typical all you men'. I said, 'Well, look, I haven't even started yet and you're all giving us this'. And they said, 'Yes, as soon as we attack all you men, you all ready to back out!'. That made me decide, 'Don't back out'.

Contents, the signature tune? The BBC put £60 down and it was recorded first at the Aelioan Hall with Gloria Cameron's group. That was pretty tough. It was badly recorded and I decided that cannot represent us. So my wife, Joyce, and I took £90 out of our hard-earned money and with friends, Helen Fleming and others, we re-recorded the song. And that was to be something that spoke. I decided that

Alex Pascall

calypso had to be it. We had already a reggae programme – Reggae Time. Radio London was supposed to represent minorities. From 1972 onwards, Steve Barnard's reggae programme was there and Steve daren't play a calypso. They'd kill him. That's not hedging the words. If he played a calypso on Reggae Time he would be knifed by the time he walked out the station. It was vicious times. I sat down with my wife at home and we looked at a format. Although it would start once a week with a repeat, with a phone in, even the phone in was repeated, and I can go back to the first caller - not tonight, that will be for the book to come. Boysie Grant he was, a musician. Oh and it was wonderful, 'I am the first caller man!' Oh man it was touching. The equipment at the BBC was so dilapidated. In Hanover Square where we started, not Marylebone High Street, they were propping it up really. I had more producers that evening but Arif Ali came with the *West Indian World*. And Arif gave us a proud front page as a beginning. It was wonderful. It was written by Iolette Thomas. I remember that and we decided that the doors will be open for people to walk in. That was a problem. I remember walking in the first time into Hanover Square and when I saw Steve Barnard on the step my heart was leaping. This guy was somebody that I cared about as a listener, because I remember presenting shows and when the last minute to go if somebody's leaflet wasn't mentioned their show died. I was at the Roundhouse at the time when I was Mc-ing a show and you couldn't find the man who was running it because it wasn't mentioned. That's the power Reggae Time had. Everywhere you walked around you hear Reggae Time. And I thought it over very carefully. I was proud to meet Steve.

The first tape recorder we were given to go and interview a young man that had come by a plane and didn't want to get off. It was in Hammersmith and I didn't realise that the tape recorder had a flat battery. It was hell to borrow the tape recorder from John Murray the deputy manager. You had to sign paper and all sort of thing to get it. I was never trained to handle a tape recorder. At those times they would even ask me what questions and everything else. They meant well. They did. No, no, some of them meant well. Not everybody. Because when we write history we really got to try and balance some situations. And the young man just turned to us and he said, 'Why don't you try the battery it might be weak'. He knew more about a tape recorder than I knew about it myself. That was really something. We went back.

We then went to interview Hugh Fraser MP, and also Alex Lyon who was a minister. I used to call him Minister for Dandruff. He was hard to interview. I mean that. No holds barred. Going up the lift to interview Hugh Fraser we tested the tape recorder - flat again. So it was a real joke boy when we got up there for us to do the interview. We can't go back because it's once a month and the thing is tomorrow. So there I am. I'm talking and he talking, and Barry's looking at me as if to say, 'I hope this damn man don't ask us to play back to hear anything'. And he didn't but one of his guys, I think the press officer, realised that we had a flat tape recorder so he said, 'Sir Hugh, I don't think I was quite pleased with that question. Would you like to run it back for us again'. We went back and we were in trouble and that is when I realised that the BBC had something called quality control. You could send the tape across there. Those were days.

Sybil Phoenix, at that time she began fostering, she was on the first programme. I could name everybody but it's not the time to do that. The evening to start that programme, Oh Lord, they were propping me up from all corners. They had me 26 times doing something as a leader for the programme. I was faking. Let me be very honest with you here. I had to do a lot of acting during that period. I had a headphone put on my head and the producer down there talking to me while I'm on air. And I always knew one thing, you could hold me down, but wait man once you put me live you can't stop me boy! So I used to move the piece from this side and that side. So when they thought that I was not listening they would say odd things and I would just say, 'I hear you'. It was not always nice. I remember one of them saying, 'You will make a very good broadcaster one day', in this sort of demeaning and patronising air. It didn't matter to me. Sam said after a time when they would not put money, 'Alex why don't you drop the damn thing?' I said, 'Sam, that is what they want. I ain't dropping it'. My experience was after five months I got a cheque for £50. That's what it was. I have the receipt. They can't doubt it. We were not allowed to play more than one record for needle time of three minutes. That was the policy for the programme. So I had to lie and even say 'Belafonte is record and all the other things are cultural material.' Friends came in and did things gratis whether they were professional or not. Everybody wanted this programme to succeed. Prior to me there was Louis Marriott working with Radio London, the Jamaican guy who became Mr Manley's press officer. He caught his backside. I learnt about it afterwards. Louis started something called 'New Londoners' with Asians and other people. And I only got to know that because when I had the group, the Alex Pascall Singers, that's where we got our first little broadcast. Carl Binger, one of the singers knew Louis Marriott so we got a little piece on. It was not easy. After the broadcast got going, during those days, they would ask me, when they were short of programme material, 'Could you tell an Anansi story to fit in five minutes?'. And I used to go on air and do a live, created Anansi story watching the needle ticking down. That was the training I had. That was the training. No matter how I asked for training they wouldn't give it. I was then asked to go and see my High Commissioner, Oswald Gibbs. Ossie said, 'Well boy, the country poor and ting, we don't have money', and so on. So that's why I went to the City Lit, for a course in voice training and breathing techniques, to defend myself against the accusation that I wasn't trained. During that period there were lots of people in the upper strata of the black community, our community. Pontificators who were attacking Alex like hell, boy. 'He cannot talk!'. 'We must get him off'. 'The programme ain't good'. There are articles written in *West Indian World* by Mike Phillips and others about it and I will come back to that a little bit later. I'm painting the picture to remind people that they gave us only air time and I took the rest aided by two committees. One was the Black Londoners Committee which the BBC wanted to advise but had no power. The other one came during the 1981 period, the Black Londoners Action Committee, which took action. We'll come into that later because that is very important.

The programme was always placed close to Question Time in the House so the edited version of Question Time came sometime before or after the programme. We were always the last to come before night fell. Every politician liked to hear themselves so they all tuned in for Question Time and in so tuning in they were well tuned to the vibes of Black Londoners. The signature tune, (Alex sings) 'Ba da ba dap, ba da ba dap, Black London, ba da ba ba, ba da ba bab, Black London, brother, brother, let's get together, get with it and stay on the beat with Black London. Feeling high or feeling low, tell it to us on radio, London London' and so on. So I can voice me little pieces, 'Good Evening and welcome to Black London. Hello Miss Wet Pants'. Yes, there was a lady called that. There were reasons. 'Hello North, hello South, hello Brixton. This is the BBC, the Brixton Broadcasting Co-operation'. I made those jokes. There was this gentleman, the deputy manager of the station. I would say things like, bien aca bien aca (come here), well, talking Creole and other languages and after the programme he'd say to me, 'Alex, I just love to hear you on air. Why don't you explain some of the things that your people and yourself exchange?'. I said, 'Okay John hold it now. Are you trying to tell me you worried that I'm passing messages? Forget about that'. So I used to go back on air and say to people, 'All you people when you call the programme talk English because I think they're getting worried that I'm passing messages'. I was always a frank speaker. If I upset anybody you all mustn't take it that way because I'm a frank speaking person. That's what I am like. I remember when Rhodesia was to become Zimbabwe, I started calling it Zimbabwe and he said, 'Alex, I'd like to see you for a moment'. I said, 'Yes, John, three bags full'. 'Well, I don't think you should be saying Zimbabwe until they have actually gained their independence'. I said, 'Alright three bags full'. And I lay off again. And I go back and I say, 'Well from this evening I will not be saying Zimbabwe anymore'. They knew at that time I'm lying.

They used to write scripts for me and I had to pretend I couldn't read because the script was written in language that I don't want to speak. I am an oral person. Strategically trained to say what I want. And when you work in the medium of the calypso it is very immediate, you know what I mean. You see a thing. You feel a thing. So you do your thing. And it went on. The people. I had four people,

Alex Pascall

Pat Bell, Pat Philo, Gerlyn Bean and Mia Morris. And many others who started the programme, all free. No money. Nothing for fares.

It is true to say that the BBC proper and its governors might have wanted to give us something, but the then manager of Radio London during my first three months period had stated when he was approached about the programme, 'Do you think they have enough to actually merit a one and a half hour programme?' These were the words of the manager, Peter Redhouse. He can't deny this. It is written down. The next manager within three months who took over in Hanover Square was Alan Holden. That man is who saved and kept Black Londoners alive until 1980. I don't care what people say about Alan. I speak to him and remain his friend up to this day. For those who do not know, you've got to paint the picture. You've got to understand how to manoeuvre. He was one person who said to musicians, who argued all the time, they couldn't get air time. He said, 'Gentleman ...' He used to give me money to buy drinks and invite them in. I sat him there. 'You all could talk till the cows come home, there is only one way you will win. Form an organisation together. Come back to me as a power. Talk to me and then I will talk to the authorities'. They never did it. So those who want to grumble today that we did not get together to attack the BBC in order to have our music represented, many, many of the people who were making music at that time have to blame themselves for it. They did not stand up. I only remember two people, Dennis Harris and Eddy Grant come in to save Reggae Time when they were kicking off Steve Barnard.

Then they made me the producer at that time. So that any fire that was coming in the station would land on me. I understood that, but I was proud they would call me a producer for once. I argued always about my status. I used to be called the guy who gathered the material. All sorts of names. They never knew where I got my stuff from. That was one of the things. And I would walk in with nothing in my hand, take two records and I could make a programme. Because we had a format and a name called 'Speak Out on Friday Evening', and that was powerful. There was no topic we did not touch, honest to God. We created. The programme went from 1974 to 1976, one and a half hours with a repeat. In 1976 it became one hour and we had it once a week. From 1976 to 1978. May 8th 1978 was when it went daily.

Prior to it going daily, I was given a sum of money to go to the Caribbean to create new links. Mark this because the BBC said afterwards that it had no money to bring in things from overseas. They were broadcasting to overseas but you see Louise Bennett's poem is very interesting, 'Colonisation in Reverse', they didn't like it. This was the time, not to colonise, but to educate England about those of us who came and our nostalgia about where we came from, Carnival and Christmas and so on. I was to go to six Caribbean countries. I landed in Jamaica having last seen my two suitcases in Miami airport. I landed in Jamaica with a little bag on my side and my tape recorder. They stole everything in Miami but because of the link through Allister, the Bee Wee Ballet, Ivy Baxter, Louise Bennett and so on, when I hit Jamaica I rang these people and told them my dilemma. In no time I had more clothes and everything else. Everybody says leave the hotel come stay with us. I was beginning to gather a type of momentum. Everybody realise we needed something. Christmas greetings began to come from here to there. Not the sophisticated ones, 'Hello mummy, hello daddy'. No, 'Wha' happ'n boy'. You understand we begin to break down the language because in the early times you had to be able to speak properly. John will remember that. Otherwise you can't go on the BBC World Service at all. You had to be a student. You hear that. You had to be intellectual my dear good brothers. Yes, you had to be. So it was changing times. I remember when we did the first programme and sent it. They said a new day had dawned and I was listening. So I was caught up between who put me inside the BBC and who am I supposed to be representing or was I responsible to, the BBC or to the community? See it's easy to answer that. This little thing here says contributions are open to and indeed welcomed from all black people in and around greater London and in some cases outside London and white people who feel they have a contribution to make.

The initial episode magazine type series to be run on Radio London. The programme is aimed at London's community with a view to dispelling through information some of the fears and misconceptions held by whites and blacks. At that period we were called coloured. Black Londoners has revolutionised a change from calling people coloured to black. There were lots of black people who I met who were against the name Black Londoners because it's a whole history. Go back from home, we were once slaves, we were then niggers, we were coons and I could name them until we came up to what is stupidly called now ethnic minorities and all this rubbish. You know the history is there and we are helping each other to sort of carry them through. I hate it. That's whose problem it is. Good luck to them. I'm a black man. I'm an African man. I was born in the Caribbean with deep African roots and that I will go with until that last day. Go back to the Caribbean man, everybody happened to see me. I got up in the morning in time to record the cocks crowing, the donkey braying. I went to Antigua where they were having battles on the air over the missiles. Do you remember that John? Right across Jamaica.

John La Rose: Yes, yes, Jamaica, Barbados …

Alex Pascall: I had picked up the vibes. Eugenia Charles was at that time in opposition. She could not even get an interview on her own radio station. When I came back to London I had to tell people this is a voice of a woman you are going to hear. She's got a very mannish voice. It's true. So I'd be gone, politicians used to come through this country, Prime Minister or otherwise nobody heard them, nobody saw them. High Commissioners were here, pompous lot, most of them were. They gave me hell. The number of them who wrote the BBC to get rid of me. Some of them are dead now, unfortunately, because, no I didn't do it. Not like Gairy. Gairy always used to say his enemies are in the graveyard. I'm not like that, no, no, no. That's history. It's no sense me sitting here and not tell you the facts. I used to be shown the letters written by them but never given a copy. It's true. It was rather hurtful. In 1978 as I came back to bring the programme daily, my wife and I created the format. Monday would be this. Tuesday would be that. Visitors to London would come on that day and so on.

Alex Pascall

Music policy. I agreed not to play American music because Americans were getting enough coverage black or otherwise. I said let me play preferably calypso and deep African-rooted music. Here and there I played a reggae because Steve Barnard was already there putting out the reggae so why should I go into conflict? I remember that record 'Sugar Boom Boom' pretty well because it was the first record that broke the deadlock between the people of the south and the people of the north. It was the first time Reggae Time played a calypso. Steve Barnard before wouldn't play it. He couldn't play it because they will have him. We had this island north south divide that was frightening. How could you give me a programme for one and a half hours to meet what is called Britain's black community? Look at the volume of people that you're giving me to deal with. I had to make sure that I put a little snip of everything. The French Creole went on. People used to sit their children and family down in an evening, 'You have to listen to Black Londoners!' I meet people and young children that grew up, 'I grow up with you, you know boy'. I'd say, 'That's nice to know'. 'My father used to make damn sure that I don't move away from the radio.' That was good. That's all we had.

We had nothing else and we were able to know what was happening in and out of this country, more than what we do know at this present time, although it was called a ghetto programme. Easy we'll come back on that. A ghetto programme. You see anything we blacks are in charge of it has to be given a type of degrading name to make us feel degraded. Apart from Hanover Square with the one chair I had, when we went to 35 Marylebone High Street, I was put in the basement. That was a big fight. I fought them like hell to get out of the basement. Even the riots took me in the basement and it was after the riots that they realised, 'Things are happening boy, move him upstairs'. It was interesting.

I have to talk about the coup. I wouldn't call the name of the person. It will be reflected in the book. But people know who he is. I left two people to run the programme in my absence. One was Mike Phillips, and the other one was Hilton Fyle, for this reason, that the African should begin to come in because everybody thought it should be a

Caribbean programme. They forgot I was talking as a black programme. The Chinese came in because they had nowhere to go. All disenfranchised minorities came in to me to get on the air and the door was open for them to get on the air. I changed the policy of the doorman. The same doorman who blocked me when I was taking the tape of the Alex Pascall Singers. He doesn't know that up to today. He's the same guy who became my best friend and everybody who was asked to sign he said, 'No man, it's Alex, go in man'. It just tells you as Mandela said, 'As long as there are human beings in charge I knew I stood a chance to come out'. I knew we could get through. I came back to start the programme on Monday. I'd come back from the Caribbean and to my utmost surprise there was a host of letters that Keith Yeomans had gathered. He called me in a corner, 'Alex have you seen this campaign of letters against you?' Signed by names. I wouldn't bother to go into the names but I can call names without fear because it's documented. To get rid of me. I was boring. And there were other people who climbed very high in the BBC later on who were part of it likewise. Very hurtful those type of things. Because there we were I was given something with no money, no training, and then I got the most hell from a certain strata of the community while the other people on the ground were fighting like hell to maintain it.

There were some Dominican women, I tell you what, praise to them. If the BBC had interfered with me they'd have taken over the station overnight. It's true. I had to tame them. The women gave me a type of support that I could never understand. Well now I do. It was not about sex. It was like if they had an understanding as to what struggle was all about and we mustn't forget that. In my room all the people who came into work, they were all women. As soon as I got a couple of men they started giving trouble. Jockeying for positions. Well we had a meeting downstairs. And Sebastian Godwin, who many people know as Kuba Assegai, when he saw the letters and he knew who had orchestrated them he went crazy.

The programme began and it was my duty to bring in as many people – 'drop in' as the signature tune says. Ratings, there was a book written and the rating of the programme showed that 59% of

Radio London's listening audience listened to Black Londoners. 56% of blacks listened to it. If there was one thing that you had it was an immediate telephone line to me. Everybody knew it. My home on average was taking 27 calls a day through the history of the programme and I had to return the calls. The phone bill, I paid the bill. It was not until 1978 I began getting about £25, I think £27.50 to do each programme. That's what. A part from the CRE's and a part from the BBC. The youth problem, the police problem, the Notting Hill Carnival. In 1975 there was a group that got together to get rid of it. By then Darcus, Selwyn were all in Trinidad and if it were not for the stand of that programme and the people understanding, Notting Hill Carnival with the press would have been wiped out. There was nothing to save it. Black Londoners educated the people of Britain. Black, white and indifferent. That's a term I developed during that because I found there were black people who were indifferent and there were white people who were indifferent. So I created those terminologies to talk to people.

I remember the fights we had to put up for Black Londoners. The carnival riots, that was something else. In 1976, when the sun came out, Greg Edwards with Capital Radio came with that big bus, man, and I with my one microphone there they wiped me off the street. I didn't go away. I still stayed there. Within that period I'd done something for Radio 4 called 'Black and Blue' – blacks versus the police. After I'd done that documentary I went sick for about three weeks. I was so depressed with what I had experienced because it was the 'Sus' period. The Linton Kwesi Johnson record that he speaks about 'Mother' ('Sonny's Lettah'). The problems on the streets was hilarious but everybody had an in.

I was told when I went to the BBC that there were three people I should not interview – Darcus Howe, Althea Lecointe, Farrukh Dhondy. Isn't it funny? Isn't it funny? Today they are the big people. When I brought Darcus in and I had him on the air, you see I had a principle, never to introduce you. I would always pretend I don't know your name because I felt you could talk for yourself. Like Pearl, I would say, 'And I have in front of me a lady with a lovely red hat, and Madam is the lipstick kiss proof'. I would go into all the funny

Alex Pascall

thing as a laugh. 'What's your name? Why don't you tell people your name?' And they'd say, 'But Alex, my name is Pearl Connor', and so on. It was a smart way of not telling them always who I was going to interview. Nothing was by chance because they were watching me. It's only later on I got to know after the riots of 1981 when there were four phones downstairs all ringing from around the country telling me where would go up next. The newsmen were upstairs looking for the news. I had the news. They thought I was part of setting up the riots. You see people on the outside, some people who even created the programme, they attacked me at times saying Alex you turned it into music, you did this, you did that. They don't know. So I forgive them. Because the time has come, John, believe me, if it wasn't for John, I ain't coming out to talk about this now because every time I go into it it hurts. I know I have to write it otherwise history will go wrong. It has to be done and I'm skimming the top. What lies below is yet to come.

The time went by and Juliet Alexander joined me. I was not allowed to have a say in who was coming to work with me. Management ruled me out until Alan Holden said, 'This nonsense cannot go on!' It was a man in the newsroom, and here we go with history, who told me when I noticed many people were going off to trips and I felt I should be sent on one of them. He said, 'Alex, if you will get me a black bit of pussy that's it then you can always get a trip elsewhere'. There are lots more things too they did. Ann-Marie Grey should tell you about the picture of the monkey they put on her desk. I don't want to go into these things because its too deep to tell you without analysing the facts around it. But the same Ann-Marie Grey was extremely reluctant to give over a whole Black Londoners programme to Louise Bennett.

I had some damn good times inside. Good Friday man! I remember Good Friday, the first time we put gospel music on the air. Oh, it was a beauty. A woman told my wife while she was lying in hospital once, 'You mean that man is your husband? Lord have mercy. The day I heard his gospel on the air, I felt like stripping. I didn't know what to do'. It affected her. I remember taking the white producers to Lewisham, the Pentecostal Church and it was like, if it was opening, when the vibes start man, they couldn't take it. There's a thrilling

167

story about three tapes. I missed the second one the day of the broadcast, the evening before the broadcast I rang up the Pastor and said, well I'm in trouble and he said, 'Just tell me how the first one ends and the third one begins and come back with a tape recorder'. Later on I found the tape and I matched them. They were dead on. That's a lovely story. To tell you that pastors know their business. Boy, know their business, how to handle it.

News. Black Print. Mrs Robinson, a lady, a Dominican lady is who started to collect the papers to say we must have a newsprint section. The community deciding. Syd Burke came in with me for a certain time. Somebody came over to buy me off to put me on LBC in a way of stalling Radio London and then it was either me handing them Syd Burke or Mike Phillips and I preferred to hand them Syd Burke that's how he got the job. Honestly. There were lots of other people. Search, people looking for each other. You might have lived in nearby streets. Veronica Lovindeer was there and she did her thing. They put a little bit of money afterwards and we had Monday as the youth programme training young people. I have a letter here that shows the BBC did not want to train us at all. They offered to train me way down and you should hear the pomposity of the training, what they offered. That again came from Mr Murray. I love that guy. He stated that really and truly I did not need anything else. And he felt that I needed to learn how to take orders. That's the training they wanted. 'Don't try to destroy his style but he must learn how to take orders'. I was quietly asked at a meeting whether I used to go to bed with any one of the girls that worked with me. Maybe it was a policy inside the BBC but I never carried it out. You understand. I didn't.

Don't let it be all that bleak because when guys like Sparrow came in 1977, what a thrilling year to remember. Oh, Lord. Roots! Taxi drivers pulling up on the road and call in. What a time to remember. Muhammad Ali going through. The blues singers coming through. Alex Haley coming through. Everybody's linked to Black Londoners. Switzerland. That's where they got the news from. All the West Indians there used to tune in. I was asked, I asked to go to the Black Festival, FESTAC, in Africa 1977. Leslie Scafe from the CRE granted £168 through the committee we had and he told Keith to make sure that I came back and reported properly. Leslie Scafe did that. £168! The fares were more than that. My money I took from my pocket.

Pearl, when I met us all in the dust, it is my money and a little tape recorder, that I later lost, that documented all the things in the village. When I came back here I was reported to the BBC about doctoring a tape that I had brought back by a gentleman they had sent down to Nigeria and they beat his backside and put him back on the plane. I think he was a rugby player. You know who we talking about. I'm still being careful although I have proof, you know John, but this is history brother. It was so nice when you meet a fellow coming from the Caribbean. Mighty Sparrow gave a thrilling thing here to Clive Lloyd. Man Ezeike recorded 'Who's sorry now? Who's sorry now? Da, da, da, da, You had your way'. That's when Greig had made that statement that he would make the West Indies grovel. What a time. I used to go there on the sidelines and record sideline commentary. Nice that. So while the ball comes up and he bowls you hear a fellow, 'what the blasted ...' So you had two types of commentaries. It was wonderful. I enjoyed those things really.

Let me move on to the 1981 period because, John, that is dynamite. We were at home. Arif, myself, all of us in the media, or emerging media, despite watching each other, we had a friendship going. Something happened we would buzz, buzz, buzz, buzz and it was a network. Where is it now? Those with Choice FM Radio would say, 'Alex you're too old and too controversial so we can't have you on our station.' I don't care a shit about it. That's good. Let them run. Money time has come. I'll come to that. We got to Sybil Phoenix's house and the lady lifted her head and I did the original interview and within seconds the cops were there. I had the interview already. They couldn't change nothing. If it was not for that interview there would be maybe hundreds of young blacks in prison to this day. What was it like? Thirteen dead, nothing said in the march I was. Everything of that period is recorded. Gathering the money, the prisoners from Wormwood Scrubs, I met them afterwards, who raised hundreds of pounds inside of the Scrubs and sent it to us. 'To you and those behind closed doors, Good night'. For one or two days, if I forgot to say that

I would get letters coming through from the prisons. But did I totally mean prisoners? Not totally. All of us live behind closed doors. Lonely. We were in this country. We have nobody. You from there. I don't know where you were. It was a linking thing to remind people that we were there. The authorities looked at me as dangerous for making those turns.

John, now and then I play some of those pieces of tapes and they frighten me. There's one piece that frightens me. I remember when the horses cornered us at Cavendish Square and they were arresting a little boy and the chorus began like that 'Let him go!' My tape recorder was running here, and one that I always wear under my belt. I told my wife and children if anything is wrong just ask anybody if they found the little one on my side. My family was well tuned into everything I was doing. This chorus, 'Let him go! Let him go! Let him ...' I call it orchestration of fury. Then I really saw, I was so close and I can't run away and I say well if I have to die this way I like to go this way. It wasn't the days like now when you see distant black people on programmes that tell you they are now Black Brits. No, I was a servant of the people. They could know where to wait for me in front of my yard. And they knew I never drove. They knew where to find me. From 1981 the tempo change within the BBC. Alan Holden had gone and a new manager came in. Derrick Amoore the greatest man for divide and rule but a loveable person for defending his staff. Some influential people of Caribbean background opposed my treatment of the death of Dr Eric Williams. He was a lover of the classics. Himself and C.L.R. intellectuals. They might not have seen eye to eye but they were men of deep thought. I rang Trinidad through contacts here to bring C.L.R. James up on the line and I did a different style of obituary not downing Doctor Williams at all and behind it I laid a piece of steel band music classic. Although the BBC logged no calls, these influential people said there were lots of calls from Trinidadians and other West Indians who said I disrespected the Prime Minister.

Looking back we could question whether, without the power of institutions like Black Londoners, the BBC would have felt the need to appoint a black governor like Jocelyn Barrow. The times went on and then there was a real discovery of a private leaked paper to me, they going to kill Black Londoners. And this is the first time in a conference in Birmingham I saw the BBC fly three people up. I had Vince Herbert and Juliet Alexander and I sat them in the audience to just drop the paper. Those were the turmoils that were going on at Bush House and everywhere there. But what was nice about it, black people were loving each other. We were together. The functions were everywhere and there was positiveness in the air. Seeking to get places, asking. 'Oh don't talk about the rallys, MPs. The number of MPs later during the Labour Party period that supported this programme. Maybe I can't dislike Labour because I've got the most help from them. I can't tell you no matter what I tried with Mr Powell to invite him, he would not come. His letter. My letter to him. He copied it to the BBC stating, 'Britain has no such thing as a black community', etc., etc. Enoch. The way they sacked people that they brought in and the campaigns we had to run going to big conferences. Vidya Anand who became the chairman of the Black Londoners Action Committee. Very interesting the things we did to save the programme. Alfonso Charles, lord, the most dedicated human being I've ever met to stand up for the programme. Tony Banks stood in front of the BBC campaigning. Mr Denis Healey stood in front of the BBC campaigning. Bernie Grant was a great supporter. Give Bernie that, always whatever came up, and people rallied that way.

John, there are so many other things within this. I brought a couple of things that I want to quote from because if I don't read a couple of these letters where they said the station stunk after a programme and let me explain why I brought food and drinks into the room. In a deprived country, so called the third world, poor people when they come to you to do favours they always bring a gift. They take anything they could catch, you know Pearl, a bottle of rum. A lot of the record people came with money and sometimes to save myself from them I said what about a drink. Maybe I was stupid somebody told me the other day. No, no, no, my conscience is clear. I couldn't collect. No it was not like that. So instead I said to everybody coming, bring some food. Then I thought how do I get the restaurants to be publicised?

So restaurants used to send food. Fellows bring a bottle of drink. So no matter what time you come to the station ... and that how the newsroom begin to change. The sweet smell and the nice taste. Sweet food kill cow. Them come and they begin to change. You had to use strategies. I avoided. I remember once when asking to go into somebody's house to monitor the noise in Wandsworth. They going to pay me £60. On Friday when they came back to decide I say to them, well I've been on the road and I price every coffin and I can't find one for £60. They were mad with me, John, they were really mad with me.

I remember another occasion where a producer from the newsroom came down and he said, 'Alex we're dressing up such and such a person to go down in Brixton to do a programme on mugging.' And he said, 'Could you help us find three muggers'. I said, 'You've got one right here. There you are'. And I'd walk out the road and the first black person I meet, 'That's the second mugger'. It wasn't difficult. Embarrassing times. Oh, Lord, yes. You see, you had to give and take. I would do a piece of news and give it to them in order to diversify the whole programme's format within the station. They wouldn't take it. So I handed it to Radio 4. Radio 4 put it out and they copied it and put it on their programme. Such is the power. Mark you the BBC proper starved local radio. So the confusion that was going on in local radio you have to realise that it was not totally those inside but what the main Beeb was doing with the funding.

The greatest evening in history, Bob Marley meets the Mighty Sparrow, the north–south divide will end with two major stars coming on air and I have Paul Keens-Douglas in the middle because I'm building him up to balance because Jamaica alone used to get things on the air, southern Caribbean nothing in the line of poetry. Let me create a balance. Ooh, I went into problems with that too. Boy, what an electrifying evening it was. The next morning where did I find the tape? In the recycling bin. Oh Lord, I could have kicked, I mean if you touched me in that morning I was going to blow up the place. I managed to save it. Any cab driver pick up a black man going to the BBC they drop him to me. Ha, ha, ha, a big mistake. Once Sam King came to the BBC and was automatically directed to me and became

Alex Pascall

very impatient. He said I was keeping him waiting. So I interviewed him but later I was accused of stealing interviewees. A similar thing happened with major stars. Marvin Gaye, 1½ hours live. Teddy Pendergrass going to Radio One. I want to show you that it is not only the white structure of the BBC that was the problem. We were part of the problem ourselves and therefore we created something to allow them to orchestrate the killing of it from 1984.

John, when I think of Grenada's revolution, let me come back, let me bridge that a little bit here. As a Grenadian what was it like to sit in a station hearing false propaganda? Listening to people talking openly around me and I had no power except the telephone book to phone up Grenada, man. Even when the bomb fired I was on the phone. I knew Maurice Bishop, I could just phone people direct and talk to them. The prime ministers became nobody, I would just phone them, through the Caribbean because the high commissioners wouldn't give me the news and then the high commissioners would attack the BBC for, 'This boy, Pascall'. That's what they called me, 'This boy Pascall'. I'll never forget it. If they're supposed to represent us and they treated me like that, radio has power. 'Alex', says one, deceased, 'You should not allow people who speak badly to come on the air'. My answer was, 'Run your high commission, I will run my programme'. In the Caribbean you can't say that to a prime minister or a minister. You're joking! You're out of your job the next day. That's one thing I was able to do here.

When you tune in in the evening during the riots, the riots was on, and when Grenada came they didn't pay for me to go to Grenada. The West Indian Standing Conference collected some money. Another man whose name I would not name gave me a free ticket. I landed in Barbados and I got an American plane that dropped us off on the tarmac and by my stupidness, not finding out, not wanting to go by my relatives to put them in trouble. Which house did myself and Henderson Dalrymple rent? The only house that was free was where Gadafy's people were staying. But we didn't know. I was in trouble. But I knew every Grenadian. My nephew had a bullet through his brain. I had to be fighting to get him out. Through all the police and everybody else to talk but they didn't want to talk to me. Sir Paul

Scoon would never talk to me. Tough things you can't forget. A gun being put behind your back. Not paid. I wasn't paid to go to Grenada. My nephew was in prison. A gun put behind my back and ordered out of the prison yard because I said I was taking a photograph, and all of the whites who were there taking photographs. I was the little spider so they took advantage. Don't talk about jamming the airwaves when I tried to report here. They wanted to kill me. I left Grenada two days before I was due to leave and there were two women who took me from house to house every night to make sure that I remained alive. I was fleeced by one of my ex-school pals and security followed me to Barbados.

You see when I hear what others say about Pascall and what they don't know about behind what went on, it hurts. Then its blocking the progress we should be making because we have as a people made immense progress since the Windrush. You see this street along here. John La Rose have a book shop. Look at bluggas (a type of banana) selling down the road, plantain selling down the road. When that reach England that's to tell you that we have entrenched ourselves and the economy is buzzing because if it wasn't for corner shops and the rest of us where would it be? And our children's children that we nurture, look at them at this moment. So don't forget that we have made strides. I resent the fact that many people, and there are many who pass through Black Londoners, when they doing up their CV's now they don't say that they work with Black Londoners because they know that they wouldn't get a job if you worked with Pascall. They say they worked with the BBC and that includes nearly all of them. They got to change. And the word Black Brit. Black what? Black Brit. I remember Marc Wadsworth introducing himself to me as a maverick and a Black Brit. There is no such thing like that. Dr David Pitt always said, 'I'm Dr Pitt and if I'm walking down the road when they're cutting people's backside, will they stop and say, "Hi Dr Pitt, we going to cut your backside"?'

When the Brixton riots came and I went to the police and I said, 'I'm Alex Pascall from the BBC I'm going down there', that time they can't send no white person down there. Oh that time I could work all through the night. I could get every taxi I want. Those were the days when they sent you out. He said, 'Son I appreciate what you say, but you see my men down there they are frightened. I can't tell them in their fright to look after you? No we are all on our own tonight'. When I went down Railton Road that's where I saw the human hand strip galvanised metal out. Those were terrible times. I heard people curse Rene Webb. I could never forget that. And he stood up in tears and said, 'Oh, God, I'm just one of we. Just one of we man'. There was a house there and there was a guy who knew because he was behind closed doors. When he saw me with the tape recorder, Juliet was holding on to me in deep fright. She didn't know what to do and she said, 'Pas, don't go in the house'. I had my tape recorder, one running there and he's taking me in and the words that were coming out would make the whole of Europe pregnant if I repeated them to you. And he said, 'Unu man know who that is? Unu man, say goin raas'. Oh boy, oh boy and I'm going in. When I reach it he said, 'This is the man, said "once you and those behind closed doors", Pascall it you boy, well you raas come go and tell Margaret Thatcher'. I said, 'Man I can't do that'. 'Well nah come back in Brixton ...' Ooooh, and I say to them, 'I can't put that on the air'. 'Well don't come back.'

That time the Radio London manager was sitting down there and nobody could come down to Brixton. He said to me 'Alex, did you get anything?' I say, 'yeah'. He said, 'Can I hear it?' and I said, 'yeah'. And I edited it and I hid it and I said to the studio attendant, 'Not until I tell you to put on that', because I had made up my mind to take the sack. I didn't understand. They never trained me you see. It was death you facing and I said, 'To those of you who are sitting nice and cosy and wants to know what the news is like at Brixton and I put my hand up and the bad words flowed man for five minutes. And the manager ran in jumping up in the air and he said, 'Yes, you've done it, you've done it. The other bastards couldn't get it' and stopped.

Then I realised that during war time you could report anything. I didn't realise until the Iraq war that a lot of people who interviewed me afterwards was real big security people in this country. Watching me and looking at me. You know what I mean, serious scenes. No reason why they wanted to oust me. When 1984 came I was tipped off, 'Alex your time has come. Let's go for a drink'. Why I believed that man because he had already leaked something to me before, which was true. So I trusted him. It's true. He wanted to really prove that he was a brother. And he said, 'Don't work late in the night anymore. They will set up a woman one of these nights and she will be shouting rape just at the time the commissioner is coming in. Nothing will save you.' It had come to the point to back out – 1984.

Luckily the Commonwealth Institute Caribbean Focus was coming in. So for half the money I was working for I took a job to present Caribbean Focus around the country. Not many people knew why I left the BBC. I created SOCA Lift Off and I took over many of the things that the so-called black programme was doing then. Hal Austin will admit to you that he was asked to strip every piece of material from the room. They wanted to clean it up. He would admit that to you. The map on the wall that I educated everybody and myself about the Caribbean and Africa, the maps taken down. Luckily I had photographs of everything before I left. I wasn't stupid. All the tapes that I had left was in the dustbin, was in a big skip at the back. Such was what it was.

SOCA Lift Off – S.O.C.A. – Sounds Of the Caribbean and Africa. When they gave it to me, they didn't think of that. They thought they had given it to me to play music so I would just shut up and play music. That was not the scene. I'm saying that to tell you how much effort had to be put in to make something. Link up to America, link up to this, link up to that. The fight for the liberation of South Africa, the fight for the liberation of Rhodesia, the changes, the political changes within the Caribbean. Everything came through. To raise money for the floods, the hurricane and all of that that happened down there. Rotarians helped to do that. Don't condemn every English person. Don't condemn everybody within the BBC. It's an establishment. It is an interesting one. I remember one little postcard and that meant a lot that said, 'Alex don't believe all of us are against you.' That's the only postcard I got in my lonely times. It was really relieving and I always smile with that man when I see him. Very, very interesting. Stanley Charles played a very important role in the programme. I don't want to go more into that. Very important. Yes.

Alex Pascall

When 1988 came the writing was on the wall. I gave an interview. I was told that the station was closing down. It had to close because I had blackened it. The format had changed. I had made it open that there was money, if they were going to sell Radio London, to buy it. There were people who were talking money in my ears. People inside the Beeb that was telling me what to do. Radio 5 was at our reach to have but some of our people didn't understand. They wanted community radio. Black Londoners was the real format. It gave birth to what was supposed to be community radio which has today become incremental radio. There was no way. All our things that we had taught, the economy that we brought through this programme, the education that we had brought through, Britain had it now. It was time to close it down, says one, 'Because the material you're putting over now is for you old fellows. The young people want their own programme'. On my telephone I found a message, it says, 'Don't come back'. It ended on the telephone.

But to show you that there was love within the programme I have a very interesting card. You see this? I'm going to read it for you. To tell you how you may not even know who's writing to you and you possibly could be misinterpreted by what they write to you. It reads, 'Alex, my sweet, sweet lover in dreams. You were fantastic. I can still feel you with me close, smile. Your love is like a blanket. It covers me from head to toe and keeps me warm. Don't keep me waiting too long darling, for you are divine. SOCA music drives me crazy and that sexy feeling. I had put my feelings to sleep until you came and gently you woke it up. But your beautiful dream has done something out of this world. Alex, I love you. You are more than words can say.' Lipstick all over. Now why I read this card at the end is to say to you that Black Londoners brought love to this country. Black Londoners is the thing that has, you see those on air now, Moira Stuart, she used to come to it. Most of the people, they question what I meant by training, access to me and the inner sides of the BBC is training. Sit and watch, make your mistakes as I did, that's training. To speak all the time like this my dear without people understanding you is not training. You understand. Communication is what I believed in. And I hope that this will remain what we have built all of us, the black, the

177

white and the indifferent, what we have built through Black Londoners must go on for posterity. Nothing is permanent. That's the beauty about it. You see the Tory Party went. The Labour Party come back. Nothing's going to stay. Margaret never thought she would have to and she went. Therefore I am hopeful that within our lifetime, John, some type of material, some type of programming will return again and I want to thank you for inviting me.

John La Rose: We will open this session for questions and comments. I'm very sure many of you here who lived through this period might want to say certain things, might want to comment about some of the things that were said by Alex. I want to just refer to one thing and that was the New Cross Massacre Campaign. I was out to lunch that day and I came back home at about 6.00 pm which was the time of the meetings of the Black Parents Movement on that particular Sunday. All of us were getting together on that particular Sunday for the meeting of the Black Parents Movement. I hadn't been hearing the radio. So when I got back Irma said, 'Did you hear about what's going on?' I said, 'What?' She said, 'People got killed in New Cross'. I said, 'No, I've been out all day and I don't know what this story's about'. She said, 'Well yes, I heard this story about midnight or sometime early in the morning and it appears that it was some black people that got killed'. She worked that out. So we all became interested and just after that it was the 6.00 pm news so we said, 'The meeting shall not start we'll go upstairs and listen to the news'. So we went and we listened to the news and we saw this happening in New Cross and we decided when we came back down, we would intervene in this process immediately.

So the Alliance of the Black Parents Movement, the Black Youth Movement and the Race Today Collective members who were present at the Black Parents meeting decided that we would go down there immediately. This had happened during the morning. Before I went down, I rang Alex. Not very far away. And I said to Alex, 'What news do you have on this situation?' He told me what he had and that he planned to go and see Sybil Phoenix that evening. So I said, 'Okay we'll pass and pick you up', and we went in Roxy's car, Roxy Harris's car. We decided that the delegation would be myself, Roxy and Darcus. The three of us went down to Sybil Phoenix's house. I rang Sybil who I knew very well and said, 'We're coming', and she said, 'Fine'. When we picked up Alex and we went in Roxy's small Morris Minor down to Sybil Phoenix's house and there was Mrs Ruddock on her bed in that place.

That day was really quite terrible for everybody. Really terrible. As we got in I asked Sybil what was happening. She said the police were coming to see Mrs Ruddock. I said, 'The police?' She said, 'Yes'. So I said, 'Okay', and then before that happened we would like to see Mrs Ruddock and Alex and I went in to see Mrs Ruddock and Alex asked if she would do an interview, and she said, 'Yes'. He interviewed her. These were climactic moments. We made decisions at that time. They had reverberations for a long time afterwards. She said, 'Yes', and Alex interviewed her. He has that tape. I've got that tape. We've got that tape. As to what she said. That tape was broadcast the next night on Alex's programme and we had an interview with Darcus and myself and the police. They had already decided this was not a racial attack and we were questioning what they were saying in that programme because already they had come to that conclusion. They said they had 50 people on the case. Now what was interesting about that was that at that very moment her brother came in. Her brother came in and we were there still talking to Sybil and the other people who were there and we went back in to see Mrs Ruddock with her brother. Her brother was very worried about what had happened. We turned to Mrs Ruddock and asked if she needed any help. The brother intervened and said, now this is how history is made, the brother intervened and said, 'She really needs help you know but she doesn't know how to ask for it'. That's what the brother said. We said, 'Well we'll form a committee to raise money'. Right there and then we took a decision and we formed this committee and there's one person on that committee who never functioned on the committee, that was Rudy Narayan because he had been there earlier in the day. The committee was to have been Ken Williams, Darcus, myself, Alex and Rudy, five people. But Rudy never functioned. So there were four of us who functioned. Right there I became Secretary Treasurer, Alex

179

became the Chair of the New Cross Fire Fund and right there from that moment onwards the Black Londoners came into trouble with the BBC.

Alex Pascall: Oh God yes, heavy, heavy.

John La Rose: Because it was a live programme. I as the chairman of the New Cross Massacre Action Committee went to every funeral and reported back to the BBC. It was a live programme reporting on what was happening during the campaign. That meant that the BBC had made a terrible mistake which they will not repeat. A live programme to be broadcast without being edited before it went on air. That continued up till the programme went off the air.

Alex Pascall: Yes I had editorial control. They had editorial control but I had control.

John La Rose: That's right, Alex had control. You talked a lot about what was happening and that is such a critical point in the history of blacks in Britain. What Black Londoners represented at that particular moment has to be part of that major history, of the transformation of British society, through the activities of blacks during that period and prior to that period. There's much more to be said but you'll ask questions and we'll give answers, you'll give comments. Aggrey is here. Aggrey Burke, he's a psychiatrist. I knew for the first time how important he was when he was involved with the priests in the area. They became involved with the parents. They gave a lot of comfort and succour and they went to the funerals. They went to the families and visited. Then there were some social workers. One from this area called Barbara Fletchman-Smith. She became involved with the others who were down there, particularly Sybil and one or two others. Sybil Phoenix I mean. When I say Sybil I mean Sybil Phoenix. I asked Aggrey to be involved with them. He went and took control of something that had never happened in this country until that moment. So we have really made a lot of histories here. I mentioned when Courtenay spoke, Courtenay Griffiths spoke, that we were the first legal aid centre by having the West Indian Legal Panel with Maurice Bishop and these others before then there were no legal aid centres. This is the first time in recent times that you've had social workers and psychiatrists monitoring the situation and intervening in the situation. Aggrey's written about it. He's spoken about it. He's Vice Chairman of the Trust and he is also a leading psychiatrist in this country. All that is of major importance.

Alex Pascall:I think there would have been so much more distortion about Caribbean-African affairs if we didn't have the programme to respond to things. I mean upstairs on the news we gave out one thing and downstairs I would counter that and there was a conflict. I remember the row I had with the Managing Director of the BBC when I refused to talk to anybody lesser than him. They took away my contract for two years and they couldn't sack me. Letters were coming in from the door every morning. Rudy did a great thing for me. I must pay him a little tribute here. He was the lawyer who taught me how to answer questions by questions. When you're in hell, play the game. He really taught me a lot. But I mean this trouble was unending. Have we got better John, that is the point, where are we heading from a positive point of view now? That's what we got to look at as we sum up history.

John La Rose: Okay, questions, comments, anybody else?

Member of audience:I was impressed by the end which seemed to be a hopeful note that what you have done and what has been achieved will not be gone back over and eroded. Which is the question I want to ask. Do you think the road that you've taken will be removed and probably we will have no road behind us eventually?

Alex Pascall: We remain silent and if we don't take, like John has and others, don't wait on publishers because John don't even have the money to help you publish the stories. We have to be individuals to begin to take things and put it in print, put it on that, put it on the other. I know what I'm saying because today it is what we have that is helping the educational problem that we spotted so early in this country. The Carnival despite the games they are playing with it, it is what is changing attitudes. The attitude is no more what it was. It is more serious now. Don't worry about the CRE. Forget about that. Don't worry about whether you're getting grants. You are not getting it anymore. Black people who have a few pounds and they have the knowledge how to do things, please do it and that is the only way that we will not lose out. It is the right time, no I'll speak about 50 years as a point, between now and the year 2000 for those of us who came John it is the last bolt. If you don't put it down now and put something that will represent us after that, forget it.

Member of audience:I appreciate in fact being here tonight because it's brought back a lot of memories to me, very, very important memories. But one thing that I think is very important is the way that Black Londoners was set up, the actual structure of the programme, the structure. It was so important, so deeply rooted that my understanding of what happened with the introduction of GLR, even though you were not there, what you have put in place in terms of Black Londoners, they couldn't just shut down the programme. They replaced you with some questionable characters. I don't want to make any comment about Hal Austin, okay, but I can. I remember being involved in a programme where the African community were called together to talk, to review the year and in reviewing the year of our community the police were invited as part of the review. Well, I stopped them from speaking, basically that's what it boiled down to. I stopped them from speaking. Hal Austin actually threatened to have me arrested. I said that's a pig there, let him arrest me. But I was actually threatened to be arrested because I was disrupting a programme that was supposed to be our programme. If not for the structure of the programme I wouldn't have been allowed into the place. But I could not have been prevented from going into the place because of what you did, what you set up and left there and that is what I think is the most important thing. It was a revolutionary statement that you made by doing that programme that couldn't be removed. It couldn't be wiped out. It couldn't be erased except by

Alex Pascall

destroying the whole station. They had to remove a station to kill a programme and that is what I think was the whole result of that.

Alex Pascall: In 1984 when I gave up the daily thing and then they get stars to come in and do a presentation. Tell you one of the things that happened. When I go into the station the young people there they wouldn't talk to me. They had briefed them not to talk to me.

Member of audience: No one wants to take away the contribution that Black Londoners has made as a programme. My perception of it is that it is the start of a great movement, a movement that started even before the programme. For instance, I don't think you would take the responsibility of saying that Black Londoners was responsible for the riots. That was something that was built, that was coming up a long time before. A lot of people were saying that. A lot of people were saying that unless we have people articulating the concerns of the black community, right. So what I'm saying is that Black Londoners to some extent minimised tension because we had a voice.

Alex Pascall: It gave an opening to people's feelings.

Member of audience:I have a view that the so-called riots of the 1980s, I have a view that the riots had their origin in the New Cross Massacre and the riots brought some fantastic changes. After the riots you suddenly found a lot of money being put into the black community and a lot of groups. A lot of people who were not getting jobs started getting jobs. I was looking and said, 'Boy look at that!' The same happens everywhere. The people who fight on the street don't benefit and it is the people who fought on the street who never benefit financially from this thing. I just think now is a fantastic time to be alive. You see when you get old you understand things so much better. I'm happy. I'm really happy and I think the younger generation will come and they will do their thing because others will come and do their thing. I have tapes that I have recorded from Black Londoners. There was a group which was in trouble the other day and

I had to lend them a tape from the Black Londoners broadcasts in the 1980s so they could do their thing. So thank you for that.

Member of audience: This is my first time here and I have a limited knowledge of the Black Londoners programme but you were discussing earlier about the black media and that's something I'm particularly interested in. Whilst I was at university I tried to set up a black media society and there were two main criticisms against this idea. The first one was that, these are from, I was studying history, so these are serious academics, one of the criticisms was that to set up some sort of black media society, that black issues themselves are nostalgic. I tried to explain that its important because we have an oral tradition and that nostalgia may play an important part in portraying black issues. The second criticism, I think they were trying to say, that it was ephemeral and that black issues are not important and have no place in society and that when we do discuss these issues I suppose that they're portrayed in a negative light so that negates the positive contribution that we want to make. How do we get around that?

Alex Pascall: They should get rid of Jewish programmes. They should get rid of Asian programmes. They should get rid of Scottish programmes. They should get rid of all these programmes. They should get rid of Welsh programmes and all the things that are now going back to be meaningful to individual people. We are the only people that they always attack. We are the people that do not understand why the attack is coming because we got something to say. We got a lot of history. You know Horace James used to make a joke about our brain worth half a crown and others don't and it was a funny joke because he meant it wasn't used and we have so much to come out with. How do we approach it? We ourselves need, like this evening, a proper school, discussion and these within ourselves, to be able to analyse it. Since I left the Beeb they have never allowed me to address one of the classes. All the universities that are teaching here, I don't get one of them to even talk about the history and there is a reason, John, because if you want to talk the truth it is dangerous so don't worry about it. It's not to say you can't talk or you don't know what the whole thing is about. The only time they call me is things to do on race. I do not do things on race anymore. Because as far as I'm concerned my race is to be equal to anybody else. That is the race that I'm after. Colour is not race. Economics and politics is what we are dealing with. The BBC collects so many millions of licence fees. If it gives us, as I once said, 'Give me one third of what you collect of ours. Give me a licence and I will do the rest'. Why is it I haven't got it? They've said about ghettos before like that programme. Community radio what they're charging people for now, isn't it an offshoot? It's no more ghetto is it? They make money out of it and the blacks will take them over. Let me say this, those who make black programmes don't own them. The majority of shares belong to somebody else. Come on what we are dealing with here is economics and politics. If you allow me freedom to talk to each other, to educate each other, that's dangerous.

Pearl Connor:I was going to say my brother's words. I was trying to follow him but I missed out. He's very happy. We are not happy. A lot of us are not happy. We feel we have gone backwards. Backwards 50 years watching it and it's a backward trip. They watch us and they push us back. Right now the academics, all the people I've known in my own lifetime, like you who are breaking frontiers, they stop you there. They block you off. We can't be laughing you know. We can be happy individually in ourselves but the problem of of our people in the world is very dire. The question of blackness, negritude, none of it is solved. It is going on right now and people have imprisoned us in some kind of framework that they want us to occupy and which we have to break out of. I'm sure you know it. I mean, why don't they let you talk and you speak and you speak the truth? You have the knowledge of the reality of something you have experienced. They can't change that so you must be silenced. You must not talk. Those of us, anybody who is articulate here who has experienced anything about life in Britain knows that the situation is back, back, back. We fight for everything we get and we can't laugh. The laughing time may be to come, the Millennium they're talking about, some of us may be laughing then but I don't think now. I think really we have to face the situation as a reality.

Member of audience: Alex, it is interesting that you said how there was the big radio station blasting you out of the way.

Alex Pascall: Yes Capital Radio

Member of audience: Now I have noticed over the years at Carnival, I've been documenting it. I've noticed when I go there. The big sound systems on the way to the station. They're playing techno, they're playing jungle and they're playing this and they're playing that and people can't move ... and the last thing is hopefully with the Millennium this will change and with all the big radio stations not playing calypso and the soca. All they are doing is playing techno and jamming up the place. Where are we going to go with this?

Alex Pascall: Well I was once told in answer to this statement, 'Alex the type of charismatic person you are,' this is almost word for word, 'suppose you and Bernie Grant and Jesse Jackson decided to address the black community at Notting Hill Carnival, that could be trouble'. That's what the manager told me, the deceased manager, Derrick Amoore. I remember when it got further. I wouldn't use the four letter words. He said, 'I'll wait. We'll wait for what you're doing to the Corporation. We'll be there on time and the same papers that are helping you now, they will turn against you. We will make sure.' They did that. There is a danger there. But the creation of *The Voice* newspaper is because of the power of the Black Londoners and my signature signing for the money for which I never got anything. That's another piece of history. It's a serious bit of history.

Why I led into that Carnival is because when I met you all doing Carnival here, when I met Claudia and all of you all around, I was a little guy learning. You know, interested with my drums and just listening to everything that was going on. But I was intrigued especially by your husband because he was a proud man. When he spoke no dog bark. That is a fact. The Carnival that you ask about.

Let us answer this from a Black Londoners' point of view. It's no more there that we can run from camp to camp with a radio car which was what we did. That I can write letters and attack the BBC for not putting it on air. I have all that documentation. It's no more there where I was asked by the former MP of Kensington and Chelsea, Sir Brandon Rhys-Williams, sent by Mr Hurd to ask if I could help move it from Notting Hill, watch it, it's going to Brixton. By the time it's the year 2000, watch it, it's on the move. Because all the streets are being narrowed now and all those who are jumping up they can't see and I watch all the big conferences and people who are talking and they don't know a damn thing about it. There's a vigilance if you want to save Notting Hill. You have to save it now.

There was a Conservative MP Sir Brandon Rhys-Williams, unfortunately he's dead now, who was a shrewd man. He said to me, 'The Home Secretary has asked, because we are going to a meeting, whether you will help us to move the Carnival from Notting Hill, the Royal Borough, to Brixton.' Victor Crichlow and everybody knows that. I told people. I safeguarded myself.

There were African countries that were prepared to put in money because they saw the value of the Carnival. I see something now called the spirit, catch the spirit, you mean catch the ghost? The spirit has gone. Claudia Jones would turn in her grave like hell to see what has gone on. What we talking about? Okay time has moved on. They no more talking about calypso and steel band and these things you know. It is on my dying bed I wouldn't accept this name Lilt Notting Hill Carnival. No way. Can't you see what is going on in the area? It's all about money and money. Look at the stalls. We were charging £25. They bring in £300. The spirit of Carnival was rum and revelry. People. That's gone. They take over all the licensing and everything else and everybody frightened to confront them. It's simple you know. If I wrote the book from behind the Carnival with what I went through and what I know and what all the newspapers cuttings it would cure it. But how do I do that because I would collaborate with many other people. Then what would my life be? I must openly say that, because life is very strange John.

John La Rose: Well Brandon Rhys-Williams had said, I want to remind you, that they also decided that if they couldn't do that they would close down the Carnival.

Alex Pascall: That's true. There was a little green paper that was around. They still want it out of their royal borough.

Member of audience: There's a new MP now in Kensington and Chelsea.

John La Rose: Alan Clark

Member of audience: That's right. What do you think his views will be about that? Because he's worse than Fishburn.

Alex Pascall: The view is set already. It equals money. Let's go with it. London will become Europe's biggest fête city. It will be called Carnival but it will not be the Carnival that we created. No it would not have that. In my book I stated that we'd be all jumping up and paying to go you know. Ray Cruikshank going to feel the guys should put up something, that they should put poles in the road and charge people to go in. Oh, what a lot of nonsense.

John La Rose: Last question.

Aggrey Burke: Alex I'm sorry I missed the first part of your discourse on life but I wondered about the collective hammering and the collective, I think in Grenada they call them lashes, the bruises that we are left with. Because your bruise must be awful ... But there is this real problem that if you continue knocking and knocking and knocking and traumatising you end up in a certain other state ... I just wondered on your reflections on the link between your trip, the women moving you and your returning. In a way it's a struggle with death too. The climactic element of it is one that is eternally fearful and terrorising. So there you were with your fear but the terror was always outside. Always. I'm wondering on your reflections on that.

188

Alex Pascall

Alex Pascall:I told a friend that the nearest I got to death was when the phone rang one morning and I dropped on the floor like a lead and my wife was downstairs and she ran upstairs to take over the phone from me and she was going to call the doctor and I said, 'Don't bother I know what's wrong'. From that day I changed completely because I realised what was stress and the rest of it. The pain that you're talking about, I have a very clear conscience and if our consciences are clear we can go on. I know people today, black and white, whose consciences are worrying them. They meet me at times, 'What happ'n Alex boy, you look good yes'. So, as if to say, 'I thought you'd be dead already'. And I always laugh my head out. What is interesting, they forget this, that behind the doors when you have passed in a position in a country like this, they will always come back to you, the authorities to ask about you or you or you and what we have to be careful is that we don't put pains on other people. Sometimes when I'm attacked by people who don't know the background I just roll my arms and I say, 'I understand, I understand'. Because there are lots of people, I think, those of us in professions, who have attacked us in various ways and later on when they got the gist of what things were they are sorry for it. Not everybody could say sorry. We wouldn't expect it. The psychological pains that you have to handle with many of our people.

I'm going through schools now and I'm watching what has happened to many, many of our parenting people and the little ones and the greatest worry for me is this and I will finish here, when I meet a black person as a teacher, educator or otherwise, especially in a white city, they always worried about how to watch me or how to take me. The little child of mixed race is in a dilemma, serious dilemma and I have to discreetly discuss this with teachers and others now pretty often. And I have begun to work out ways to make approaches and how to help teachers and others who are not interested in the problem because it's confronting them.

You see what should have been happening since we came to this country, in hindsight I can talk about that now, is that we should have been made to educate the host community about life, what was called multi-cultural life as they put it. We had it all already. We knew it all already. But now that the authorities are here and there admitting that they have made serious mistakes, the dilemma on our hands in Britain now is so big that I don't have an answer really as to where we are heading. I just say that each of us has got, as individuals, to do as much as we can do. A youngster called me up today and said she's looking to see whether there were black mini-cab drivers when the mini-cabs just came out and I had to go back deep in history to look and I remember who might have been called mini-cab drivers touting for the little money and so on and I was able to give her a background history and to tell her about two taxi drivers she can talk to of the early ilk. We are very important people with our ages now and our experience and we should use it strategically. They need it. I've been down to Europe and I can see it. Britain, although it has a great name for race relations, is still backward. Yet we are ahead of Europe that is outside there. Think about that.

"**Alex Pascall,** cultural 'guru' for Caribbean people in Britain who has spent 35 years as a communicator par excellence. teaching, performing and promoting Caribbean music and history ... Sir Shridath (Sonny) Ramphal, former Commonwealth Secretary-General, March 1996

This tribute to Alex Pascall was paid at a civic reception by Islington Council in his honour on the day he received his OBE 'for services to community relations' from Her Majesty the Queen in March, 1996. Alex has been a voice for the Caribbean community ever since he was invited to join the BBC in 1974 to present the first daily Black radio programme in British history. Behind that voice there is much more to his work in community development. He was born in Grenada, the eldest son in a family of ten. His formative years were highly influenced by the very African cultural atmosphere around him in his deeply agricultural fishing village. All the people were like a family, whether related or not. Music played a prominent role, as did the cultural rituals and storytelling of the African retentions. "My mother made us tell stories and sing to each other."

His first research into his cultural heritage and retentions was in 1957, when he made up his mind that African Caribbean culture was his destiny. He was highly influenced by his English and drama teacher, D. Baptiste, and by the words of T.A. Marryshow, the Grenadian 'Father of the Federation', who declared: "the West Indies must be West Indian". It was at this time that Harry Belafonte created such a buzz with his film *Island in the Sun. The Bee Wee Ballet Dancers,* who performed the limbo in the film, recruited Alex shortly afterwards as they represented Grenada in the *Inauguration of the Federation of the West Indies* in 1958, The following year Alex followed their leader, Allister Bain, to Britain. Until 1964, Alex worked with London Transport, while founding *The Magnets,* his first ten piece band, and various others. His first singing group, *The Alex Pascall Singers,* Africans and Caribbeans performing songs directly related to their cultures, lasted until

Alex Pascall

1971. Also, working as a stand-up comedian gave Alex many insights into the British society of the day.

His work in developing the programme, *Black Londoners,* from 1974 on BBC Radio London undoubtedly established a black presence in the British media which opened doors to many who are familiar figures in the media today. His studio itself was an open microcosm of the community at large, and thus Alex was able to facilitate little-known minority voices to be heard, influencing change in the entire British radio network. During this period, with his specialist knowledge of African and Caribbean cultures, Alex became an advisor to the BBC on Caribbean affairs. Originally planned as a test series of six programmes, *Black Londoners* had become a daily programme by 1978 and continued under Alex's guidance until the abandonment of BBC Radio London in 1988. Meanwhile, Alex honed his skills as a communicator, co-ordinator and researcher. As an extension to his radio work he chaired the Notting Hill Carnival Arts Committee for five years; this was a natural development of his commitment to grass-roots activity as since his school-days he had come to realise that a people's voice is expressed through its artistic and cultural heritage. Alex was selected to serve as National Co-ordinator of Caribbean Focus '86 for the Commonwealth Institute and the Caricom Governments of the West Indies in 1986. Involving 55 committees across Britain, one of the highlights was the Caribbean Express '86, the only known cultural exhibition train in British history, running educational workshops and travelling to 18 cities in 21 days. What was happening at this time in Caribbean Focus and Notting Hill attracted Europeans in other countries to emulate Caribbean cultural developments in Britain. The Foundation for European Carnival Cities came into existence in 1985, with Alex as a founder member and Vice-President responsible for the arts. Yet another culture train was commissioned, this time to bring British and European carnivalists to the Viareggio Carnival in Northern Italy. Alex was subsequently responsible for linking European carnival cities and the Caribbean in 1981 taking a delegation of 90 European carnival dignataries to the Islands.

Alex first took his stories and cultural work into schools in 1968. Still advancing this pioneering work today, Alex is at the forefront of bringing Carnival arts education, Caribbean folklore and oral history to people of all ages in schools, universities, libraries and community events nation-wide, giving performance lectures and running workshops, training and Carnival residencies.

Alex now has at his finger-tips a significant collection of his own writings, poems, raps, songs and music which he has developed in response to the need he daily encounters to make Carnival arts accessible to all. In addition, the many years of his research and documentation have yielded a vast historical archive on the Black presence in Britain. The documentary programmnes Alex researched and presented for Radios 2 and 3 in recent years include *A Different Rhythm,* reflecting the impact of the Black presence on British music and musicians from the 15th century, *Caribbean Folk Music,* researching its origins in various countries and, forming part of the 1995 VE Day celebrations, and a reminiscence programme, *World War Calypso,* which was shortlisted for the CRE 1995 Media Race Awards.

Colin Prescod

photo: Deo Persaud

Colin Prescod
with John La Rose in the chair (7.7.97)

John La Rose: I heard of Colin before I met Colin, very much like the way I met Lennox Pierre in Trinidad, I heard of him from his brothers before I met him. I heard of Colin from his cousin Edward Phillips.

Edward Phillips was here, he was hoping to get into university here and he was applying for admission to university and he told me of his cousin Colin and Pearl, Colin's mother, and eventually when he couldn't get into university here I told him, 'Why are you wasting your time with British universities, you could go to a French university, apply to the Sorbonne'. He applied, and was admitted to the Sorbonne. He did philosophy at the Sorbonne and of course it started the process and eventually he became a professor of philosophy. So I knew of Colin, and then I met Colin. Over the years with Ricky Cambridge and the *Black Liberator*, at the Polytechnic of North London, and as a matter of fact I gave a talk there at his invitation. Then he became the Chair of the Institute of Race Relations after me. So Colin you're welcomed here and we look forward to hearing your talk.

Colin Prescod: Thank you John and I hope that the George Padmore Institute continues to build slowly. I'm not quite sure how I deserve this, the kind of stature that is implied in the way in which John has announced me. My life is just ordinary. I came here to talk about my life as a primary document, as a photograph which in the moment it is taken is just a snapshot but further down the road it's looked at by people in conjunction with other photographs and suddenly it's an important piece of the jigsaw that helps us to understand how history turns.

Routes

I want to start by reading a poem. It is called 'I Poet' and it's by Jean Binta Breeze who is at the height of her power and who was in London recently. It is an old poem but I am reading it because somehow it resonates with the position, which I have in talking to you all here. I am talking to people who, as John has just been saying, know more things about me than I know and more things about the kind of things that I'm going to talk about than I know and so it is a peculiar position that I'm in. First the poem:

I Poet
ah was readin
readin all de time
fram book
fram play
fram t.v.
fram life
in odder words
fram yuh all
befo ah was writin
ah was readin
yu all
neva did know who yuh all was but
ah was full a love
ah give it here
ah give it dere
neva see no harm
in a likkle share of
de warmes ting ah have
sista, bredda,
older, younger
neva matta
 jus love
like evrybody was preachin
ah was readin
ah was lovin
befo ah was writin

Colin Prescod

ah read all yuh poems
ah read all yuh plays
ah read all tea leaf, palm
anyting wid a good story,
even if it didn't always have
a happy endin
an everyting ah read, ah sey
but how come I know dis story aready? or
I do dat yesterday,
I see dat last night
I live troo dat
so I stap readin fi a while
stap lovin fi a while
jus befo I start writin
I stap evryting
just fi a moment
an I sey maybe, (I humble)
I sey, maybe
it was you readin me all de time
so doah I was well hurt inside
wen yuh all did sey
I wasn't no poet
I never mind
cause I sey
I was poet all de time
so I start write
an I tankful
to madda and fadda
dat ah did read and love firs
fah I know
when I writin
I poem
is you
all you

Colin Prescod

This poem by Jean Binta Breeze, helps to situate me in what I'm doing here. When John La Rose invites me to speak here as part of the Life Experience with Britain, I have to avoid the vanity of thinking that my life is so important that everybody thinks I have done something.

I think perhaps I can make a contribution by giving you my kind of line on the things, the themes and times that have made me, or at least some of the things, and times that have made me, such as my professional practice and my political practice which I think it might be useful to talk to you about. It may stir some people into talking about some other things that relate to my things and times and indeed to present a better analysis on some of the things that I would like to reflect upon.

And so, to the start of my narrative. I am going to do this a little bit anecdotally of course. I thought I'd start by telling you how, as a boy, I came to be routinely first or top of the class when I was in primary school in Tobago just before I came here. Between the ages of 9 and 13 I remember that every Friday, every end of term, every end of the year test, I had to be first in my class or I got licks. I had a cousin called Leonard Prescod who is today a 'Big Boy' as they say in Trinidad and Tobago and who has done very well for himself. He lived in the same household as me in Tobago, and we both had to be first, and if I came out of school at the end of a test and I was second and he was first, or I was first and he was third we both got licks. I had to be first in class. That's how it was.

I tell that story in a way to talk of the heavy discipline in my life, but also to get to who was giving me the licks, who was beating me. I was beaten by my uncle, one of my uncles. My note to myself here, says my failed uncle. I say my failed uncle because he was someone who was born into a situation and who had a lot of potential. He was born into the Prescod family in Tobago. He inherited a lot of land from my grandfather and my great grandfather, somehow that's another story to be investigated and my experience of growing up was of seeing this land being squandered.

He was failed, and I guess now it would take a political economist to understand why. He was failed because he was somebody trying to make a living as a farmer, trying to sell copra, trying to sell cocoa beans from the plantations they had and getting less and less satisfactory deals, and finding it more and more difficult to find good markets and soon it began to dawn on him and his other brother, that a quicker way to make money from this land was to sell it piece by piece, and so they began to sell it off. I describe my uncle in a very particular way and in a very guarded way as my failed uncle. My failed uncle was the person who was beating me and my cousin Leonard - whipping us to succeed.

I was born in Port-of-Spain in Trinidad in Belmont and I lived there for the first nine years of my life. I came to live in Tobago, with my Tobago family at the point at which my mother came to England in 1955. She came here on a singing scholarship. My mother was someone who entered a singing competition and who did very well. She entered the competition, won in the island of Tobago and then went on to Trinidad and won in her class there. She had a marvellous soprano voice and so impressed someone there, whose name I remember to this very day. His name was Dr. Northcote, a Welshman. He was the main adjudicator and I don't know whether it was already arranged that the winners would have top class scholarships arranged for them to go abroad. He made it sound like it was because he was so impressed by this untrained voice, with its natural beauty, that he was going to go back to England and that he was going to arrange for a scholarship for this woman. That was what he told them and sure enough the scholarship turned up. So my mother comes in 1955 to England to the Guildhall School of Music to be trained to sing opera.

At this point I was moved from Belmont in Trinidad to live with my maternal grandmother and my uncle in Tobago, that was how I came to be in Tobago, coming top of the class, getting licks if I failed to do so from my uncle. That was a part of my root that set me on the path of my trajectory, but I had other roots, deeper more hidden roots, but still nourishing.

My father's story is one, which began in Grenada. He came with his mother from Grenada to Trinidad. As I was later to understand, she came to look for better employment and better prospects. He came as a boy of 12 with his mother to Trinidad and had to walk away from the house which his mother made in Trinidad, when he was just a boy of 12, with his little georgie bundle as he said, because the man, who his mother had decided to live with, was a man who was cruel to him, so he had to leave.

The story he tells me, when I eventually sit with him in 1976, because I didn't sit with him before that, is of how he was adopted by some English people who gave him a job and encouraged him to develop a trade. And so he became a master carpenter. So that by the time I was a little boy in Belmont in Port-of-Spain, I knew my father, Hubert Branche, as a foreman of works, working for the government, working as a master carpenter. So that's the story of my father from Grenada.

There is my grandmother's story that I know much less well and which began in Panama. My grandmother came with her mother from Panama to Trinidad and Tobago. She is a dougla woman, my grandmother, and married into these big landholding Prescods in Tobago. I know too little of my grandmother's story, and my great-grandmother's.

Then there are my ancestral roots, which are also part of my hidden roots, and I don't refer to these roots flippantly, which began in West Africa probably, because they were still being registered throughout my young life in Trinidad and Tobago, in obeah and shango ceremonies which happened in my yard. I remember the drums, I remember the fire, I remember the spitting of liquids from the mouth, I remember people catching the spirit, I remember the amazing magic and movements. So this is not a vague notion of ancestral roots, it was absolutely there in Tobago.

My cultural underpinning as a national of Trinidad and Tobago was a really interesting complex weave of heritage and inventiveness from Africa, from Asia, India in particular, and from European influences. This is the backdrop of the little boy who was to become involved with the things that John has asked me to come here to talk about. All this, in time, and in the complexity of things, I would come to piece together analytically. Indeed, I believe that I'm still piecing these things together, along with all the people from the Caribbean.

You may well ask, as I did, why the hell my uncle was imposing such a heavy discipline on me when I was a little boy. What was the point of this heavy licks and discipline. I reason now that his peasant and personal failure was to be recovered in a way by the educated professional success of the next generation of Prescods. That is what he was making sure of. He was saying, 'You lot have to do what I didn't do'. I reason now that there must have been a general buzz about the opening up of the professions to black working class families at that time in the Caribbean.

We were at the time in the transition from colonialism to neo-colonialism and so the space was opening up to natives to take up professional positions which they didn't have before. So, there must have been lots of families I imagine who had peasant, working class roots who at this period were imposing heavy discipline on their children to make them do better and take the education, because there really were going to be openings, for people to take new professional positions in the society which was emerging.

First Footing

There is another start to my narrative, how I came to be in England. I am here in Europe, and I am paraphrasing a phrase that Sivanandan, I think, probably invented in order to make an argument. I am here in Europe, because Europe was in the Caribbean. Sivanandan's brilliant aside was, 'We are here because you were there'. Which is supposed to be the answer that someone gave to a social scientist who was doing research among black people in the 1950s, who had asked a little man from Pakistan or somewhere, 'Why are you here?'. The man said, 'Somehow I think I'm here, because you were there'. I'm here in Europe because Europe was in the Caribbean.

My life is marked by journeys, maybe all our lives are. Maybe this awareness of the fact that my life is marked by journeys put me ahead of others whom I eventually came to teach and whose lives are also embarked on journeys. These are complex interweaving journeys I'm talking about. I'm one of a number of people coming firstly from the periphery to the centre of an imperialised capitalist world system. I was also one of a group of people coming from colonised status to rebel citizen status. I was involved on a journey from peasant condition to proletarian condition. I was involved on a journey from historical object to historical subject. To answer the question of how did I come to be here, I think I was caught up in history, like all the other people who were making the same kinds of journeys as I was, that is how I came to be here.

I believe that it is this particular rich, lived history of race and class and culture contradictions which would have set me up with what C. Wright Mills, an American sociologist, called a 'sociological imagination'. And, more than that, I believe it gave me a predisposition to sociological activism rather than being an academic sociologist. The rest of my story is really only about making sense of life given this predisposition.

And so to my black British experience. In 1958 I made my trip to Liverpool by boat. I arrived in this awful, ugly, dirty place and was happy to be getting on a train which was bound for Euston. Upon my arrival in London, my first nights and days were like they were magical.

I spent my first nights and days literally in theatres, namely the Royal Court Theatre and on film sets at Pinewood Studios. I am coming from the seaside in small island Tobago, and this was, in this glamorous city, my first experience. And this was happening because my mother was an actress, a singer and actress, and, she at that time was appearing in a play called *Flesh To A Tiger* by a man called Barry Reckord, and nearly all the talented black performers in Britain were in this production it seemed to me. So my first night was backstage at the Royal Court and then next day, I was on a film set, literally sitting in crowd scenes at Pinewood Studios. But my mother's circle which I entered did not consist of thespians merely concerned with theatricality although there were some who were only concerned with theatricality. This is where I think, in my mother's circle, I got my anti-racist and anti-imperialist instructions. My first roost in London was at No.1 Bassett Road, in Ladbroke Grove, North Kensington.

Here lived Amy Ashwood Garvey. Here visited Claudia Jones. These were amongst my mother's closest friends. Amy Ashwood Garvey is not merely the second wife of Marcus Garvey, I mean the other wife of Marcus Garvey. I now know that she was present at the 1945 5th Pan African Congress in Manchester, saying very important things about, what was later to be known as feminism, as well as colonialism and anti-imperialist struggles. She was a well known Pan-Africanist. Claudia Jones, as everybody now knows, is generally regarded as a famous person. I didn't know it then, but my mother must have known, that Claudia Jones was somebody who had become very famous or infamous out of the United States of America. Persecuted in McCarthyite America, she came here. She was the person who was the founder of the *West Indian Gazette*. She was the person making some of the first hard politics in this country against racist attacks, on the streets as well as in institutions. These were amongst my mother's closest friends.

There was also, I have to say, a sense of tension in my mother's circle in 1958-59, among the writers, and the actors and directors who came to rehearse and to visit my mother's basement flat, where we'd moved to, in Cambridge Gardens. The summer of 1958 was to throw up the Notting Hill riots, need I say more about that.

Many of the people present here must know what happened at the Notting Hill riots. I as a boy came innocently into Ladbroke Grove to join my mother and these people, and within weeks of my being there, the attacks by young and old whites stirred by Colin Jordan, Mosley and other fascists on black people, who were newly settling, had begun. And it took me some years of research and work, along with people like Cecil Gutzmore, to eventually track down the fact, that the image we have is of black people under siege, and running and being done in by all these attackers. But the attacks business only stopped because black people organised and fought back and fought off the people who were attacking them. The police then came in at the point where the blacks were going on the offensive and at that point slowed it down. But I came into that.

In the immediate wake of the riots I became a founder pupil of the first major comprehensive school in London, Holland Park School. 2,500 students and literally a handful of black kids amongst them. There were a number of Teddy Boys around and I did have to fight on a number of occasions, with my mates, to defend my right to be there, in the playground, to be a part of the school at that point. On the streets also, one had to face confrontations. It doesn't hang heavy with me, because it seems to me that we did away with that quite easily at the time.

At Holland Park I was encouraged. There was inspired encouragement from my teachers, who pushed me to excel in all sorts of ways and I believe that I repaid them, by what I guess, they saw as all round impressive achievements. I did well academically. I did well dramatically and in choral terms. I did well, I did well, I did well. I became Head Boy of the school and so that's another part of the launch pad of my life in Britain, this massive new school. I have to say that the academics that I did well at, probably relied on the rigour of my colonial education, because I couldn't remember working very hard for the first two or three years, although I was always first in class. No uncle giving me licks, but I was always coming first in class. I came into an education system that was very highly streamed, if you can imagine this contradiction. So that if you came top of the class of 3B.1, in the following year you went into class 4A.2. I was always top of the class so that by the 5th year I was in 5A1, but I was not aware of the fact that I was a keen student. It was just the drilling which had been drummed into me from the colonial education system.

And so to the 1960s. You realise I'm handling it simply chronologically. In the 1960s I grew up. I finished school and I left in 1964. I should say that at Holland Park School, I met my wife Nina, who was herself a colonial girl from Australia/Singapore. We remain married to this day. At the end of school I headed off to universities - 1964-1967 the University of Hull, 1968 the University of Essex. I recall that at Hull amongst my university mates were Tony Martin and Ansel Wong who came from Trinidad to study. I had a good easy time there. I was supposed to be studying economics. Even if at that time I had not been introduced to marxist analysis, I was suspicious of marginal economics and didn't take much notice of it to be honest. So I began to divert myself into sociology and social history and those areas, because I didn't like, and wasn't convinced about, what was happening on the economics side.

Colin Prescod

At Hull I was particularly influenced by my tutor John Saville, who turned out to be a very important British socialist historian. He directly identified what I was going to do, because I didn't know what I was going to do. He asked whether I would like to do some research, to go somewhere like Essex to do some work. And I remember him writing to Peter Townsend, who was then a senior Professor at Essex. I went to Essex to read sociology. I enrolled on a Masters intending to go on and do PhD work. I stopped short of doing PhD work because at that time, as you can imagine, I was ambivalent about sticking to academia when stuff was happening on the streets, which required much more immediate activity. And people were suspicious of people who were taking those academic routes. I actually diverted myself from doing the PhD study in order to avoid going off into academia and rising away from the mass. Funny thing, but never mind I was a boy.

Black Power

In the 1960s we witnessed the arrival of Black Power. It came from the United States of America. Stokely Carmichael and others from their organisation SNCC (Student Nonviolent Coordinating Committee) toured the UK and came to my university. My mother and her friends agitated about anti-racism in Britain, about anti-colonialism abroad, about apartheid abroad. I used to be in halls and on stages with my mother and her friends getting things organised in anti-apartheid organisations. I remember readings and being given scripts to read by the people who were making those organisations happen at that time. My mother and her friends lobbied and marched about all these matters.

I remember another famous occasion a march coinciding with the Martin Luther King march in Washington, which Claudia Jones must have been an organiser of. And my mother was there at the front of that march singing, 'We shall overcome' through a loud-hailer. I'm not pretending to name names, the people who are here will know and correct me about any of these matters. But these are part of my roots, the things that rooted me in Britain as I was beginning to grow up. I remember too, just as an aside, a young man by the name of Obi

Egbuna, who was then an activist playwright in this period, as a young man amongst all the other people, who came to my mother's house moving in that circle. Obi Egbuna eventually became one of the first people to be imprisoned by the state here, for racist activities would you believe, for standing up against racism. He was railroaded through the courts for racist activities in public.

The reason I remember this was that many years later in 1981, when I was in Washington, in the United States of America, to give a lecture at Howard University, I was being driven along by someone and out of the window I saw this man, and thought, 'Isn't that Obi Egbuna?' So I wound down the window and shouted, 'Obi', and the person stopped and saw me. And I got out of the car, and I said to him, 'Obi Egbuna, I'm very pleased to meet you, you won't know who I am, but you will know my mother, who is Pearl Prescod. He said, 'What', and he stopped the traffic in the street and he put his bag down, and he was able to reach into his bag and pull out several texts. He was teaching at Howard University - a writer in residence and teacher. He pulled out a text and opened it and on a page was an essay 'Pearl', and he said, 'Look, look, what do you mean, do I remember, look, look'. It was a wonderful essay, a very generous essay, remembering, not to mention romanticising, my mother's situation. He wrote, 'Pearl owned a house in Cambridge Gardens, (in fact we lived in a basement, renting like everybody), and her hospitality was so wonderful, she looked after us all'. And what he was saying was, that without this woman, he would not have been set on his way in life and all the rest of it. He wrote a play called *Wreath for Udomo*. It was with this play, that my mother went to West Africa to FESTAC. So that is how I remember Obi Egbuna, not just as a person. The point is that this man was yet another person, a serious activist, nurturing my very young life, and setting me on this track.

The 1960s saw the beginning of my building my own political practice in support, in the margin so to speak, of the rise of radical British black power organisation and struggle, and the connected Pan Africanism. I say very tentatively that I was a small supporter on the fringe of this. I have to say that I recall at this time, there was this very race conscious politics amongst black people and one that was possibly suspicious of me with my openly white wife. I say this not as a big deal, but I felt it at the time. It was real. I can understand why it was. I'm not making a fuss about it now and I didn't make a fuss about it then. It is interesting for me to remember that it was like that. So, I didn't push myself into the politics at the time. I was there, and this was something which affected how I entered the politics at the time. My mother died in the mid-1960s. 1966 to be exact. Claudia Jones died in the early 1960s. I grew up.

The late 1960s was an extraordinary period of organised as well as spontaneous rebellion. In the world I mean, as well as in our society. There was the black civil rights struggle over there, influencing here. There was anti-war struggle, Vietnam in a big way, the bomb over here. There were hippies dropping out and people turning against notions of the family and their middle class roots. There were students uprisings happening everywhere. There was trade union militancy in Great Britain. There was the closing down of the British colonial era. There was the closing of the immigration door against British citizens in Britain.

In Britain this was the period in which I think we forged Black as a political colour. This is the period in which the people from the Asian sub-continent, from the Caribbean, from Africa as well as with Europeans, were joined in common struggle against racism. It is the period in which this notion of Black that we talk about was constructed. It is old fashioned to talk about Black today, you don't use Black in that way any more, we have awkward phrases like Black and Asian, and things like that, but this was the time that Black was forged.

If the 1960s might be characterised as the period of 'power to the people', the 1970s was to be the period in which the slogan became 'we are our own liberators'. In the 1970s black struggle in Britain shifted from 'resistance to rebellion', to quote a Sivanandan essay title. For me the 1969-70 straddle was marked by the Mangrove trial, now a legend. The first time I saw Cecil Gutzmore and the first time I saw Rhoden Gordon as a very boldly dressed African leading demonstrations on the streets, fighting the police outside court houses and so on. It is the period in which I became aware of Darcus Howe, who was a member of the Mangrove Nine group. It was also the period in which I became aware of the woman Althea Lecointe who is arguably the most powerful and thorough of all the people from that Mangrove Nine period, and of all the people who had leading positions in black organisations at that time.

I remember Althea very much impressing me in this period. But the spirit of the Mangrove Nine, and the court victory that occurred was, it seems to me, the culmination of all of the 1960s political mood that I have been talking about, which my mother, Claudia Jones and various other people had started building. And in Ladbroke Grove, with its history of struggle, from fighting the fascists in 1958, to fighting police harassment around the Mangrove Nine, I realise now that I was living in a hothouse of black politics in Britain.

The 1970s were dominated by the emergence of black political responses to the predicament of young black people, I think, and this was at the centre of my young political activism - the struggle for the first born and first schooled here generation. Parents began challenging schools, when it was realised that the schools were failing and labelling children of Caribbean descent as educationally sub-normal in an alarmingly concerted fashion. Joined with this assault on black people was a police offensive, using the now notorious 'sus' laws. The police were engaged in harassing black kids, particularly black males on the streets and in their recreational spaces, in their clubs, in their community centres, in their parties. To cap it all these young blacks were already discovering how the employment market had built-in discrimination, so they were not getting jobs.

The early 1970s were marked, then, by a number of black organisations and campaigns which were engaged entirely in what was called 'struggling for justice' for what became 'the youth'. By the mid-1970s, the youth were beginning to fight back on their own behalf. The point to remember is that many of us were constantly outside court houses trying to picket and defend people who had been railroaded into the courts, especially young kids on conspiracy charges. There were the Islington 8, the Willesden 12, the Bradford 12, the Sheffield 3 and so on and so on. It was this youth constantly under attack, who at the Notting Hill Carnival, in London, in 1976

Colin Prescod

and 1977 who rioted when they saw there the enemy, if you like, the people who were constantly harassing them and attacking them in the dark corners, and the grey spaces in the society, lined up to police what the state had said was a 'threat to law and order' situation on the streets of our society. The youths faced and fought the enemy on the streets. They were beginning to fight back against the attacks they had been getting. Yes we were constantly on the streets demonstrating in the 1970s.

Busy Being Black

At a recent reunion of late 1960s old Holland Park pupils, someone white in the gathering remembered describing me in the 1970s, and they remembered it gleefully, they said somebody's father had said, 'Oh, that Colin Prescod, he is just busy with being black'. Imagine that. The immigration door had been squeezed shut by the state after a series of hasty and racist legislative moves, and special police and custom agents were humiliating Asians and Caribbeans alike at airports and raiding their homes and workplaces. The youths were under attack by the police and they were picked on when they attempted to resist injustice. They were being railroaded into borstals and prisons. The schools were recklessly failing black Caribbean descent kids in alarming numbers. The job market was offering no work, or what people began to call 'shit work' for the majority of working class black young people coming out of school. So, of course, I was busy being black. Black was the colour of my political response to the injustice, the waste, the humiliation and the brutality that characterised racism against the people I knew and cared about and shared a community with.

The 1970s was when I joined, first the *Black Liberator* and then *Race and Class* journal at the Institute of Race Relations. I will say a little about the *Black Liberator*, which was founded by Ricky Cambridge with some other people. I have never actually tracked down how many people supported Ricky as he founded it. By the time I joined it in 1974, Cecil Gutzmore was already a member of the collective along with Ricky Cambridge and we were Marxist-Leninists and we published a Marxist-Leninist journal.

What we were really, were people who were actively involved in the politics of defending the black community, holding a class line - attacking racism and attacking imperialism. And publishing a journal was a good way to get our voices out and to communicate our analysis of the situation to people. It was a stylish publication, a very good looking publication and probably very expensive to publish. My input to this was down to Ricky Cambridge and others who advised him. It was a constant problem to be able to afford to publish this journal. We sold the journal outside the London underground stations, for the most part, in Clapham, in Brixton, in Ladbroke Grove, in Shepherds Bush mainly to black people.

But this *Black Liberator* journal that we produced used words and analysis that was so high that at one point we had to have a glossary in the journal. And eventually we stopped publishing. And I think that part of what stopped us being able to go beyond the late 1970s, was that in a sense, even with a glossary in it, some of the people to whom we were selling it would have needed glossaries to understand our glossary.

In spite of and in addition to all that the *Black Liberator* collective should be remembered as a group of people who made things happen in many parts of the country. Our real intention was to be part of the politics of organisation and campaigning. We had a journal which was a means of reporting on those things, and indeed of making interventions in all those spaces.

Come the mid-1970s, I was introduced to the Institute of Race Relations, by one of my students, Tony Bunyan, and was invited to start contributing to the journal which was called *Race* and which became *Race and Class*. I was part of the hard argument for changing its title at the Institute of Race Relations, and I remain a member of the working editorial committee of *Race and Class*. And further to this, as John said earlier on, I am now Chair of the Institute of Race Relations.

Insurgent Sociologist
In 1978, I made my first black documentary film which was called *Blacks Britannica*. I made it with a couple who came from the United

Colin Prescod

States of America. The man was called David Koff, a white, Californian Jew and a terrific anti-Zionist, and the last film he made was called *Occupied Palestine* and was about Israel. David hasn't worked since, making films. The conspiracies have been so heavy, that he has not worked since. Before this he had made some fine films on Kenya and the anti-colonial struggles and so on. His wife is a woman called Musindo Mwinyipembe. They came to Britain. They spoke to me, I'd been doing some things with television people up to that point.

They asked me whether I'd be interested to help them make a film and I said, 'On condition that you make a film around the political practice that I'm obsessed with'. We had access to talking to a series of very important people - among them Ron Phillips, Gus John, John La Rose, Darcus Howe, Ian Macdonald and Sivanandan. *Blacks Britannica* is a very important documentary film, yet it is a film that has never been shown on British television to this day, and was made with money from the USA. It was bought by Channel 4 in the early 1980s when it came out of court litigation, and it has never been seen on TV in Britain. I think it remains one of the finest documentaries of our struggle here to this day, showing us how we activated, how we made politics in that period of the late 1970s.

Meanwhile, I'd started to work as an academic sociologist in 1969, at what was first the North Western Polytechnic which soon became the Polytechnic of North London. There is a little tale I want to tell about this actually because I had, by the way, applied for a position in 1968 at UWI in Jamaica. I had begun to come out of my MA and was still thinking of continuing to do research, but in another place. I applied for a job at UWI, and was interviewed by three British professors, white professors, one of them David Glass, and I had the impression that I did very well at the interview. But then nothing happened, and nothing happened for weeks and weeks and months until eventually I thought, 'I'm not going to get anything from the University of the West Indies'. So I applied for a job at North Western Polytechnic. Three years later, to the month, I had a telegram from the University of the West Indies. It was really mysterious. It was at a point when I was just about to set off for West Africa in 1971. The telegram had an urgent thing attached to it, stating, 'Job offer, UWI,

209

Mona Campus, please reply'. Do you know I had not even reapplied for a position at UWI.

The point of my telling you the tale of my applying and not hearing from the UWI is, for those of you who do history, that at the UWI in the period 1968-1969, Walter Rodney had been 'grounding with the brothers', and had upset the authorities and the state and so on, and things must have gotten into such a constriction that they didn't move on anything. So that even if my name had gone forward as somebody who had been recommended to have a job, nothing at all happened. But, here was my link with Walter over there at that point.

So I got my first job at the Polytechnic where I stayed for two decades. To do a very quick thing on my life as a teacher, I thought I'd do three anecdotes. When I first joined the polytechnic I met the senior lecturer there, a man called Brian Herraud. We sat down to talk about my teaching timetable and he said, 'Of course you'll teach race relations won't you?'. 'No', I said and I never did teach race relations. I was constantly involved in anti-racist activity and it got into my teaching, but in 20 years I never did teach a course called race relations.

The second thing I want to tell is about a student a few years ago when I was still teaching. One of my students came to me and said, 'I met somebody who used to be here at the polytechnic a few years ago and they said to me, 'is Colin Prescod still there, Colin Prescod of the RADA school of sociology?' RADA is the Royal Academy of Dramatic Arts and I guess this was a reference to the way in which I performed as I taught my students and I guess a reference to my roots.

The third tale I want to tell, an anecdote out of my teaching time, which sticks with me is that I remember on one occasion, I'd just finished giving a class, and coming out of one of my lectures. We'd gone into a tutorial or a seminar situation, and one of my students, I believe it was an African student, it was a black student, said to me, effectively, 'Wonderful stuff, great terrific, but if we write what you teach us in the exams will we be marked down?' It's funny that while it is touching it is also disturbing. In my early teaching career I didn't want to teach race relations I wanted to teach sociological theory. I'd come out of one of the best schools in sociology, at Essex University.

Colin Prescod

I was absolutely shit hot and I taught theory and I enjoyed it a lot. I also taught myself a great deal, in order to present a course eventually in political economy which I called 'Underdevelopment and the World System'.

I was allowed to do this under a man called Harold Wolpe. He died recently. He was a white South African, a lawyer who had a practice in South Africa and who fled South Africa because he was under pressure for the work he had been doing. He made himself into a sociologist and he came to be the senior lecturer heading up the sociology department, at the Polytechnic of North London which was making the transition from running a degree that was under London University, to running its own degrees. The CNAA had of course been invented to allow polytechnics to start constructing and administering their own degrees, and to free themselves from the universities.

The person who was in charge of getting us, my bunch of staff, together, and we were a bunch of reds to be quite honest, everybody was radical at that time, was Harold Wolpe. He got us to put this degree together and we were putting it together in the face of Baroness, then plain Caroline, Cox and a man called Mr Terence Miller who had done wonderful service to the end of empire in Rhodesia, as it was then called. This man was brought in to be head of the Polytechnic of North London and he in turn brought in this woman, who is now Baroness Cox in the House of Lords, who was a lay nun, and a real right winger. She was brought in to the Department of Sociology and promoted very fast to Head of Department. All of which underlines the fact that we had some real reds in that department and they saw us as being dangerous.

When we finally piece all of this together, do the research, we will then find out how the conspiracies occurred. But it was remarkable that we got Mr Miller at the Polytechnic of North London, as the person who came to be Head of the Polytechnic, and it was remarkable that we had Caroline Cox in our department, who was promoted very fast, to become senior, to frustrate the efforts of Harold Wolpe and the staff, who were trying to construct a critical degree and to teach students critically. Our students were hot, our students were outrageous, our students were challenging everything. These were good times. And they came for us, and the pressure was hard. Harold Wolpe literally began to have heart attacks, because of the pressure of what he was doing in that situation.

From where I was coming from, my professional practice was always a subverting practice. I was constantly adapting the marxism that I taught myself, that I was developing with my comrades at the *Black Liberator*, to help to improve my teaching on the courses which I constructed. I was kind of crazy in that I decided that I would prefer to publish in the form of documentary film than in essays and texts. This was a very personal decision that I made. Maybe I was actually cowed by the notion of writing learned texts, but my decision was to publish in the form of documentary film, a very radical kind of practice at that time - certainly not designed to help me to get on professionally.

In 1982, I made my solo directoral debut with four films for Channel 4, and they were made with a company which was named Race and Class Ltd. The Institute of Race Relations who had formed this non-profit making company to make the films which went under the title *Struggles for Black Community*, and they are films which can still be seen today. They are films which attempted to describe the development of black communities in Cardiff in Wales, in Southall, in Ladbroke Grove and in Leicester. They document the particular and different kinds of strands of black community which all these places had. Cecil Gutzmore, who is sitting here today, was actually a researcher for a large part of this work.

The 1980s saw the shut down of my course 'Underdevelopment and the World System'. This is a course which was allowed to spread over two years of a three year degree course. For two years students did this course, which talked about the third world, and the imperial world systems, and their interrelations. It was the first course of its kind in the country, and at one time the Sociological Association, one of the professional associations, did a survey of all the courses that attempted to handle the third world, and determined that the course, which I had done with Harold Wolpe and all the other folks, was the best thing that existed. These are professional accolades, that nobody sees, but I was pleased about it. It meant that the advice which I'd had from my comrades, on the work I had done, was good advice.

The Change of Life

But, in the 1980s we saw the slow shutdown of the course. Courses became smaller, they began to semesterize things. What I joined teaching for, ceased to be what teaching was about anymore. They said we had to be promotional, we had to chase the market, we had to do things which would allow students to get jobs in institutions and so on, and I hated it. I became somebody who was constantly arguing with my staff, who would say, 'But we have to go this way'. After a while, I guess, I thought to myself, 'Anybody would tell you Colin that if you don't like it you can leave'. So I became interested in leaving teaching and I was seduced into joining the BBC to do television production.

Something else was happening at that time. In the 1980s we saw the defeat of the Left and the falling away of my old allies and fellow travellers. Therefore what we were seeing in the late 1980s was the victory of Thatcherism and imperialism and 'equal opportunitism' which was influencing and affecting even black sections of our population.

The 1980s saw the culminating explosions of black British anti-establishment rebellion, with summer 1981 as its peak. This was something which carried on into the mid-1980s, which saw the arrival, announced in 1979, of Thatcherite ideology infiltrating international politics and national culture for the rest of this century. You may want to debate as to whether and to what degree, the new Labour victory on May 1 1997 has changed things.

I've argued that these two big 1980s interventions contributed decisively to the end of vigorous, radical political campaigning and organizing for rights and against injustice, and for radical political and economic change which had marked the new black British presence since the 1950s.

Thatcherism undermined all our political rights and implanted individualist and opportunist ideologies in the culture. I think, and I've always wanted to suggest, that the marvellous and amazing black

213

Colin Prescod

youth rebellion, which occurred in the 1970s and 1980s, at the same time embarrassed the then existing black organisations which had neither the organisational nor the strategic ability to seize the time, or take the power this black rebellion was pushing to demand. I don't know, and I haven't seen where we have tried to think about this thing. But I have a feeling, because I was present at it, that exactly at that moment of terrific, bold courageous success, we also failed.

There were kids who had come from a tradition of being educated to stand up for their rights, to challenge, to imagine transforming the society, to imagine making history in different kinds of ways, and who in addition had their own immediate frustrations on the street, with police harassment and all the rest of it. And out of all of that, that marvellous explosion of the 1980s came out onto the streets. What I'm saying though is that at the same time we have to register that this uprising embarrassed all our existing black political organisations because we were not up to it, to taking it to the next stage. There are all kinds of reasons why this may have been so. In the 1990s, we have all experienced hard challenges to and for our activism, particularly those of us who remember that history of courageous and militant organised and aggressive resistance. None of the old front line issues have disappeared. Yet we do not have anything like the same political mobilisation. I have myself moved to media struggles as a new front line of exposing and combating the old and new racisms. As an old sociologist I think there is much to be debated and clarified around the shift from black political to black cultural focus at the centre of the black community in Britain. The popular practice of young black people now uses black power as a way to make money and to make social statements within a cultural emphasis.

Among academics some have invented celebratory cultural analysis as a replacement for what used to be sociology, and this doubles as a device for evading the difficult tasks of forging political organisation, and taking on radical political mobilisation. Maybe that is something which we can all participate in discussing here. Thank you very much.

John LaRose: Thank you Colin.

Colin Prescod

Responses to questions and comments from the audience

Linton Kwesi Johnson:I just wanted to say that I do remember the *Black Liberator* very well. it was one of the first publications that would publish any of my verse. It was way back in 1975/76 that one of my poems was published in the journal. Subsequently, the *Black Liberator* also published a paper which I wrote. I remember also that I found it quite unintelligible.

Colin Prescod: So, you see, I didn't speak a lie Linton. I think inside of the collective, I'm not exaggerating, but we could have come to blows over the issue of the writing style of the journal. I believe to this day Ricky Cambridge doesn't talk to me because maybe I spoke too harshly about exactly this. I came to feel that the language we were using, we couldn't justify it. People were buying this magazine, they loved it, they loved the fact that we stood there on the streets, holding a space. But it seems to me that most people were taking it home, but they would not have been able to read too much of it, and our challenge was to do something about it.

Member of audience: The struggles of black people in this country are being severed from what is happening to white people in this country. What we talk about here is 'our people' 'our home'. As a sociologist have you seen us doing anything with reference to our sociological equals in this society or is our struggle always perceived as a black struggle. I suspect that we will always struggle futilely, unless we recognise the links between us and certain other people who are in this society.

Colin Prescod:I can answer that very quickly. First, when I talk about the period which nurtured me, Claudia Jones, Amy Ashwood Garvey, my mother, Nadia Cattouse, in the 1960s. In that movement at that time, these people did not act on their own. Their allies were white people. The CARD movement for example, was something which included white people working alongside black people. My mother and people who were performers in plays and television and so on, would have reached absolutely no place without working with 'white liberals'. People who were interested in creating space, producing plays on TV. It's possible to look back on television at that period and think that the content of programmes was more progressive, than most things that we have had since. Claudia Jones was someone who worked in a broad politics, not simply race politics.

I may look as though I'm talking about black struggle, but the black sections of the working class were leaders in a lot of the political movement in this society. When we challenged schools, we were challenging something that a lot of other people agreed with. When we challenged the police it was the same. Many years later, just to give you a quick example, during the miners strike, I remember them coming down to the Frontline in Ladbroke Grove. Cecil Gutzmore was still working down there at the time, as an activist and a community worker. The coal miners' campaigners were the first to observe that black working class people were very generous contributors to their funds. They said 'we were up there in the country parts looking at you black folks confronting the police and some of us used to be saying, "well they must be doing something wrong, and that is why the police are going for them", and so on. We've lived to come to realise that what you were saying is something that we all have to follow behind'. The politics we made was a race and class politics.

The point to remember is, that when black workers began to organise on their own behalf in this society, they had to fight not only the boss but also the white workers, so it is easy to say we had to use other people, but first we had to do a damn good job on changing the people with whom we were going to be working, into seeing us differently, and getting to understand the authority of our leadership in some of these areas. This is my experience, whether I talk of the school-yard in Holland Park School, or of movements in defence of workers' rights, so that is my response to what you are saying. You're right, that we can't fight the battle to change the world staying inside some ghetto. That is correct, but I don't believe that we ever have.

Pearl Connor: Colin take up this point. Those of us who are thinking of the world at large and of general humanity, it's a great idea, but you have to start on the ground we're standing on. We have to get our own situation anchored and our own ideas solid before we can emerge into the world and make friends with the world. And of course, as you know South Africa is a good example of what is happening with its inter-racial mix. Among the people who liberated black South Africans there were white South Africans. The black South Africans didn't have that kind of power. They didn't have the machinery, they didn't have connections with the outside world, and certainly a lot of Jewish people in the state of Israel, had a lot to do with it. So, I don't think we should be blinkered at all about our own interest in other people. I think we have to get our own security right, our own homes, our own situations must be established and we must be sure about that. It doesn't mean that we should be blinded, but we do need to work on ourselves, otherwise we can be watered down so easily and influenced so easily. We're in the western world, and the media is against us, back, front and side, and its very hard to move the opposition. But, as I said before we do need to integrate.

Colin Prescod: This is where the *Black Liberator* was important, because we came to realise that there was a need, most of all, for us to come to understand our own situation properly. We can't move out unless we are sure of the ground we are moving from. When you look at the situation of black working class people it is massively under-analysed, Caribbeans are massively under-analysed. We're still trying to piece together the whole of our stories, all the bits and pieces which have happened, but it is an effort. I'm not sure how to answer your question, since it is not about turning away from the rest of the world, but about the necessity to understand our own predicament, which is a predicament in the wider world.

Member of audience:I think what has happened with us is that there is not a lot of solidarity between working class whites. Any struggle that I've been involved in, I think there has been more support from white women but not from working class white men. That I find difficult to understand, in that they can't see that a lot of our struggles are theirs. What I'm saying is that when we have a struggle we create a division between us and working class whites. The white woman identifies with the struggle more than a white working class male.

Colin Prescod: My quick glib way, would be to refer to an old marxist way of making argument. When I taught my students and I tried to tell them what class struggle referred to inside marxist analysis, I remember saying that for Marx class struggle referred to not only struggle against the enemy class, but within the class which you belong to, and these are struggles for clarification, struggles for getting rid of negatives, things which obstruct. It is very clear to me that the black working class, and indeed the Asians who came to this country, have had to wage struggles against class oppressors and within the working class. I think I referred to it earlier on. Cecil Gutzmore did some work, many years ago, on Fords, where he talked very clearly and dissected the way in which black workers, even to get their rights in that part of industry, had to struggle with the unions that were supposed to be supporting black workers. It was so in the textile factories in the Midlands. People went through the same kinds of stuff. So, we had to start fighting our own battles. It is to our political credit that people were changed by our participation politics here. I think we have had more and more people, middle class whites as well as working class, joining black struggles. My insistence, from my own experience is that the black working class struggles of which I was part were leading political definers at the time in which we were making these struggles. Everybody else had to come to understand them. When nobody else was providing that clarity, we were.

Aggrey Burke: I have a sense that the sociology of struggle and the politics of struggle is part of how you ended up in the media. What I want to ask is that here we have a very serious period of struggle. The talk about the *Black Liberator* is fantastic, because here is the language of 'Doctor politics', it is part of a structured struggle, which actually allows those at the doctor level to continue the struggle. Baroness Cox, becomes part of the conspiracy as part of the structure.

Colin Prescod

So repeated patterns throughout all of the struggles including America, in the Caribbean and here means that one has to deal with the conspiracies. How does one deal with them. Do you feel damaged by the struggle?

Colin Prescod: No. I say that straightforwardly. Because you ask the question very intelligently. There came a point in my life about 1993 when I said to myself. I am going to refuse to become yet another miserable, resentful black male, educated professional, because you are right, professional humiliations are regular occurrences. I'm certainly looking around at all sorts of people - the Gus Johns, the Morgan Dalphinis's - these are people who come to a certain point, a point where they could achieve a kind of authority in the society, in defining things and, just at this juncture, something cuts away from under them and removes them. Now, you can talk about conspiracy and so on, but I refuse to become another bitter black man. And I say this especially in relation to Peter Blackman who was a giant of a man, a giant. Poet, all sorts of writer, activist, strong man who came here as a young man to study to be a priest, and in the middle of his struggle he discovered how nasty institutionalised racism was, even the most Christian part of this stuff, and moved out and changed himself to be a heavy marxist. At the time I met Peter Blackman, he was writing for the *Liberator*. He was a man who was really very suspicious of everybody who came to him, including black young people who were saying they were militant. And it was off the back of what had happened, of the humiliations of his life. And he was so suspicious and so on that there were people who wanted to be helped, but whom he would not have helped because this man had become so cagey. And it is something worthy of study, to understand the degree to which this thing is happening. Only by piecing it together will we be able to say whether it's a conspiracy or not, or just another part of the working of institutionalised racism in this society.

But it is true that I could become such a person. Because when I sent in my notes to John, the short biography he received, I decided that there should be some reference to the fact that when I was appointed Head of the BBC African-Caribbean Unit in 1991, the

Voice newspaper just at that time published a big spread on the 50 most influential black professionals in the land, and I was one of them. And I was put into the category not because of the practice I was doing all of these years, but because the BBC had given me an accolade and had made me one of them. Within a year of me having that position I was removed. Well I wasn't removed, but I was dissuaded from being there. They shut the unit under me, and they shut it because I was active in terms of the roots I was coming from, and I was insisting in pushing programmes in a certain way. I was insisting that it had to be opened up in terms of handling the African content in a respectful way. The whole of it. The best they could do was to cover South Africa. I believed that they believed that white people were going to be influenced by it. They thought that every time Nelson Mandela farted we were going to be influenced by it. But the rest of the continent was not being handled. I fought huge battles with Alan Yentob and the rest of the BBC to have that happen.

I remember that within two months of my getting that position and making the push that I was making that suddenly reorganisation had to happen with Pebble Mill. They decided that they were going to merge the African-Caribbean Unit and they had to have a new structure and so on, to deal with multiculturalism, because they could no longer justify why there was just an Asian and an African-Caribbean unit. 'What about all the other minority voices', they said, 'We must have something which reflects them'. I said, 'I smell a rat, I don't like this idea'. I argued at every point that I could. I wrote long essays to everybody high up in the BBC and so on. But they carried on, and they shut down my unit and they merged it, and they told me that because I had a staff contract when I started at the BBC because I resigned from my previous job, they told me that I was not redundant, but my position as editor of the unit was redundant. I told them not to treat me and the constituencies which I represent in such a way in such a fashion. I waved as many fingers as I could and walked off and thought I was going to be fiercely independent as a producer.

What happened to me after that was that for two years I didn't work at all, and I was reduced to 'signing on' for about a year of my life.

Colin Prescod

From being highly paid, one of the 50 most influential persons, to that kind of situation. I am now recovering my feet so, I can see that you are being perceptive in how you asked that question. And there is something which is very sad about that, because it seems to me that a lot of our older black people, who had wonderfully educated starts are being undermined in a racist society, and literally going mad because of the influence of this regular practice within our society.

Cecil Gutzmore:I'm looking at the kitemarks of the different varieties of struggle. Some of us were more interested in looking at race and being black, some of us looking at effects, and Ricky, who was influential on the journal, had the habit of doing his learning in public. So, what Ricky was doing, particularly in the glossary and some of the other pieces in there was doing his leninist-marxist learning in the pages of the *Black Liberator*, and that is why all of that over-theorised stuff looks like that. But, remember that it wasn't all over-theorised.

John La Rose: You're right, Cecil, I know Ricky quite well. When I came here Ricky was a member of the Communist Party. I was forming an organisation directed at liberation in the Caribbean, including armed struggle for liberation and I wooed Ricky and his close friend called Miles, into that organisation, and Ricky was then an unformed marxist, let's put it that way. Now what happened in the period of the *Black Liberator* was that that unformed marxism was still there in the *Black Liberator*, and that was my argument with him about his jounal. There was a question of, 'What is it that you're trying to do with a journal like this?'. Therefore that was why *Race Today* was so important, because it was a different kind of proposal and a different kind of understanding of how you write a journal. First, it deals with the activism of the people, in that it reported on what we were doing. That was what it did. It reported and analysed what we were doing, that was what gave it enormous power of airing with relation to the changes occurring in British society.

Colin Prescod

Cecil Gutzmore: The *Black Liberator* was always and declared itself to be a theoretical journal of black liberation. *Race Today* didn't say it was theoretical. It was a popular journal of black struggle. The *Liberator* didn't describe a whole heap of events and social struggles. We did have a very important article in it on Notting Hill and the Mangrove and so on, at quite an important point. So the difference between us and *Race Today*, was that. The other strength which *Race Today* had was that it pulled down very directly on Jamesian politics, and the Jamesian theory was what lay behind it, gave it much more of an immediacy than the non-Jamesian one, which those of us had on the *Black Liberator*.

Member of the audience: What do you think about the cultural politics surrounding certain black icons and how do you differentiate between figures like Muhammad Ali, and other iconic black figures who have taken up reactionary positions?

Colin Prescod: I don't have any need to answer that. I'm not going to fall for that one, because I prefer to think before I express opinions. I was opening it because I think its an area which we ought to examine. What I will say is there is a question, and my question is that people seem to be pleased, especially with regard to young black people, they're in their rap, in their music and so on, their cultural space. I'm not sure that that compensates for the hard political organisations we used to have, or how much all of this contributes to new movements. I'm not saying that I can make a judgement, because it hasn't been studied yet. I'm saying that the first place I saw that rather crudely stated, is in Paul Gilroy's book, when he wanted to say that people like Smiley Culture were emerging as the new political leaders of our time. It seems to me that that signalled that we don't need to look to any political movements or figures anymore. The youths are going to do it themselves. It is true, that a lot of popular culture is full of references to icons and so on. If I were back in sociology, I would say something about it. And, were I to get the space to make intelligent programmes, its one of the things that I would want to use different people to provide analysis. I hear your observation, and your observation is making clear that we have to suspect that within popular culture, cultural politics and icons, here is some easy answer of the way forward.

Cecil Gutzmore: What we need to do is to make politics against the reactionary trends, and make politics with the progressive trends.

John La Rose: I would like to add something to that. We've discussed this issue any number of times at forums in the International Book Fair of Radical Black and Third World Books, in any number of ways, and in private discussions, with Bernice Johnson Reagon, Paul Gilroy and others. These are planned discussions. Now, in the case of Nigeria there is a Yoruba theatre, the most popular thing in the culture of Nigeria. Yet, it was argued among the Nigerians, and by ourselves, that because it was popular it wasn't progressive. We need to keep that clearly in mind, that because it was popular it was not progressive, and we need to look at what clearly it is that the Yoruba popular theatre was dealing with and how it dealt with it. Now Biodun Jeyifo has done a lot of study of that at the University of Ife, as well as others such as Soyinka, Omotoso and others so the discussion went on for a considerable period, but that is question of popular culture versus progressive culture. I would like to say some more about that but I'm chair.

Pearl Connor: I want to talk to Colin about the media. You're talking about magazines and printed word and so on. But when you got into the media we knew that something amazing was happening. We thought, 'Right, we have our man there'. We knew that something very nasty was happening inside when you disappeared. We thought a bit of magic happened there. A few of us were trying to get you there, but we thought that you were too radical, and you wouldn't be able to get your foot in, but when you got in we knew we had a major, thinking man right in there. We knew that the old thing was working, the power was there. Not, power of your mother, but the real thing.

Colin Prescod

Colin Prescod: In truth it's worth responding just a little to that. When I got that position it is true that I was flooded with people. Not people saying, 'Give me a job', but people saying, 'Here are ideas. Thank goodness you're there, can this work?' I guess the people at the BBC must have panicked because people were constantly coming to me. There were sessions in the rooms in the department, I began to set up conferences, and I began to throw in ideas that were challenging to the people who were my line managers at BBC at White City, and I had lots of them, lots. Lots of fights went on, and eventually the shut down. So, yes you're right. I was very upset, which is why I left when they did the business, rather than stay there keeping a job and so on. Because it seems to me to be insulting to everything that I represented and of the people who wanted me to work.

John La Rose: OK. May I thank you all, and may I thank Colin in particular.

In the early nineties *The Voice* newspaper featured **Colin Prescod** as one of the most influential black professionals in Britain. This grandiose accolade was accorded on the basis of his appointment as Editor and Head of the BBC's African/Caribbean Programmes Unit (TV), then located at Pebble Mill in Birmingham. Within a year of his appointment, he was on his way out the door. Under the guise of Birtian reorganisation of the BBC, new line-management at the Corporation's Midlands Region headquarters were determined to shut down the ACPU. Colin put strong arguments against the plan to do away with distinctive Asian and African/Caribbean units and the plan to set up instead a Multi-Cultural Programmes (MCP) unit. His bosses went ahead with their plan and the results were disastrous. Asian programmes flourished under the Asian head of the new MCP unit, but none of the promised new programming for the full spectrum of ethnic minority voices ever emerged and the MCP unit's meagre non-Asian output was particularly insulting to African and Caribbean audiences. At the end of 1995 the BBC quietly disbanded the MCP unit, dismissed its head and set a course to return to the status quo ante. But by then Colin Prescod was long gone and neither he nor African/Caribbean audiences could expect any form of explanation as atonement. Today he continues to work in television - now as a freelance producer.

Colin Prescod was born in Belmont, Port of Spain, Trinidad and Tobago in 1944, where he attended, briefly, Tranquility Boys, Trinidad, and Bishop's High School, Tobago, in quick succession, at the very start of his secondary education. He has been resident in England since 1958, when he came to join his mother, Pearl Prescod, the well known singer, actress and community activist. In London he attended the brand new, massive and pioneering Holland Park Comprehensive School, from 1958 to 1964, where he enjoyed academic and extra-curricular success - becoming head-boy amongst 2500 pupils, university entrant, overall London Schools' 100 yards sprint champion at 16 and 17 years.

Colin Prescod

His formal education was completed at Hull University where he gained the B.Sc. Econ. Hons, 1967, and at Essex University where he obtained his MA Sociology in 1968. He is married to Nina and they have two sons, Adam 29 and Leon 25.

Before joining the BBC, he held one continuous salaried position, from 1969 to 1989, at the Polytechnic of North London, now the University of North London, finally holding the post of Senior Lecturer in Sociology. Here he taught and researched in Sociology, Political Economy and Caribbean Studies for undergraduate and postgraduate degree courses, with breaks for a sabbatical research year in Trinidad and Tobago in 1976, and a Fulbright Visiting Professorship in the Afro-American Studies Department at Syracuse University, USA in 1981. He retains an active interest in academia, lecturing periodically and serving as external examiner to the B.A. Humanities degree, race and culture modules, at the University of Middlesex in London.

Throughout his career, Colin Prescod has mixed and matched the worlds of political activism, popular culture and academia - not a fashionable thing before the 1990s. In the early to mid-1970s he was a member of *The Black Liberator* collective, along with Cecil Gutzmore, Gerlin Bean, Meg Howarth, Neville Fearon and A.X. Cambridge founder-editor of the journal. During the second half of the 70s he became more and more involved with film and television - researching, writing and presenting for the Open University as well as for emerging black film makers like Henry Martin, Menelik Shabazz and Imruh Bakari. By 1978 he was ready to link up with David Koff and Musindo Mwinyipembe to co-produce the landmark documentary *Blacks Britannica* for US television. Four years later he made his directing debut with *Struggles for Black Community* - four documentaries broadcast by Channel Four Television in 1983. During his time at the BBC he commissioned a range of programming including the talk show series *Hear Say* (1991); a BBC2 current affairs series, *Black on Europe* (1991), dealing with African and Caribbean communities across the continent; *Homeboys in Hollywood*, on African-American cinema; and *Out of Darkness* (1992), a six-part series on contemporary African political affairs. He was also Senior Production Consultant on *Will To Win*, the acclaimed six-part series on black sporting achievement, broadcast by the BBC in 1993.

In the late 1970s Colin's 'foco' became the Institute of Race Relations. Ever since that time he has worked closely with his political mentor A. Sivanandan, Director of the IRR and Editor of the journal *Race and Class* - lecturing, organising, campaigning and sometimes writing on and for anti-racism as well as Black and Third World liberation. Currently he is Chairman of the IRR's Council, the previous Chairman being John La Rose and he is a member of the *Race and Class* Editorial Working Collective. Since 1993, Colin has also been Chair of the board of The DRUM, a major Black (British/ African/ Caribbean/ Asian) Arts intervention located in Birmingham and due to open its centre in 1998.

225

Biographical Notes

Abbensetts, Michael Guyanese born playwright and TV scriptwriter. Has had a successful career in Britain since the early 1970s writing for the theatre and TV, including the sitcom *Empire Road* (1978-9) which was one of the first TV series to provide an ensemble of black actors and actresses with opportunities.

Abdallah, Mogniss A journalist and activist of Egyptian/Danish parentage. Coordinator of Agence IM'media in France. Very active in campaigns against racist attacks and murders.

Abrams, Oscar Born in Guyana. Political and cultural activist in Britain. Director of the Keskidee Centre in North London in the 1970s and 1980s. Died 1996.

Adams, Grantley Leader of organised labour in Barbados during the 1940s and early 1950s. Founder of the Barbados Labour Party. First and only Prime Minister of the West Indies Federation from 1958-62. First Prime Minister of Barbados. Knighted.

Adams, Robert (c1900-65) Guyanese born actor. Britain's leading black actor in the 1930s appearing in films with Paul Robeson. A founder member of the League of Coloured Peoples in 1931. Founded the Negro Arts Theatre in 1944, one of the first attempts to create a black theatre company in Britain.

Alexander, Juliet Of Guyanese descent. Worked as a journalist on the *Hackney Gazette* in London. Joined *Black Londoners* as a radio presenter. Also worked as a TV presenter on the BBC's Ebony *Programme.*

Alexander, W.J. Trinidad born teacher who became a lawyer. Member of the first PNM (Peoples National Movement) government in Trinidad in 1956.

Ali, Arif Guyanese born editor and publisher. Founder of Hansib Publications and *Caribbean Times* which he edited for many years.

Ali, Jamal Guyanese poet, playwright and actor prominent in the 1960s and 1970s in London where he was involved with the Dark and Light Theatre in Brixton.

Ali, Tariq Born in Pakistan. Political and cultural activist in Britain. Writer and journalist.

Alleyne, Brian Born in Trinidad in 1965. Anthropologist. Writing a thesis on John La Rose and the network around New Beacon Books in North London.

Alleyne, Keith Born 1918. Barrister. Crown Attorney of St Lucia in 1946 and of St Vincent in 1952. Attorney General of the Windward Islands in 1955.

Anand, Vidya Indian born historian. Involved in Caribbean journalism.

Andy, Bob b. 1944 in Jamaica as Keith Anderson. Well respected reggae artist. Best known by the general public for his major hit record of the civil rights and black power era, *Young, Gifted and Black*, recorded with Marcia Griffiths.

Ardiles. Osvaldo Argentinian footballer who was a world cup winner in 1978 and thereafter played for Tottenham Hotspur for many years, later managing the club.

Armatrading, Joan b. 1950 St Kitts. Moved to Britain aged 6. Brought up in Birmingham. One of the first black female singer songwriters to come to prominence in Britain. Appeared in the musical Hair in 1970. First album *Whatever's For Us* (1972). Still writing and recording.

Austin, Dean Professional footballer who began playing for Tottenham Hotspur in 1992.

Austin, Hal Barbadian born. Well known black journalist in Britain.

Biographical Notes

Ayim, May (1960-96) Born in Hamburg of Ghanaian-German descent. Poet and writer. Author of the poetry collection *Blues in Black and White* and co-editor of *Showing Our Own Colours: Afro-German women speak out.*

Azikiwe, Dr Nnamdi (1904-1996) A leader of the Nigerian independence movement. First president of Nigeria 1963-66.

Babb, Ena Trinidad singer. Came to London in the 1950s. Stage name was Ena Cabayo.

Baden-Semper, Nina Trinidad born actress and singer, who achieved prominence in the British television comedy series *Love Thy Neighbour* between 1972 and 1975.

Bain, Allister b. Grenada 1932. Came to Britain in 1958. Actor. Student of Caribbean folk dance. Founder of Grenada's first professional dance troupe, the Bee Wee Ballet. Partly responsible for dance sequences in the film *Island in the Sun.*

Banks, Gordon b. 1937. One of England's finest ever goalkeepers. He was a member of England's 1966 World Cup winning team. Later played for Stoke City from 1967 onwards. Had his career cut short when he lost an eye in a car accident.

Baptiste, Thomas b. Guyana. Came to London in 1950. Theatre, TV and film actor as well as an opera singer. Early member of Joan Littlewood's famous Theatre Workshop Company. First black actor to have a part in the British TV soap *Coronation Street* in 1963, acted in the film the *Ipcress File* alongside Michael Caine. Campaigned, in the 1960s, for black actors in the actors' union Equity.

Baptiste, Selwyn Trinidad born. A principal organiser of the Notting Hill Carnival for many years. At one stage was director of the Carnival Development Committee.

Barnard, Steve b. St Lucia. Once a DJ at the Q Club. Started *Reggae Time*, the first reggae radio programme in Britain, on BBC Radio London in 1972.

Barnes, John b. Jamaica 1963. Highly successful England international footballer who won many honours playing for Liverpool. Has also played for Watford and Newcastle.

Barrette, Jim (1903-1993) Trinidadian working class activist and labour leader. Founding member of the Negro Welfare Cultural and Social Association and the Workers Freedom Movement.

Barrow, Jocelyn Trinidadian born educationist. Came to England in 1959. Has served with many national and local organisations including as a governor of the BBC. Made a Dame of the British Empire in 1992.

Batson, Brendon b. 1953 in Grenada. Played for Arsenal (1971-73). Has made his mark as a senior official of the Professional Footballers' Association.

Baxter, Ivy Dance tutor and dancer. Leading person in the field of dance in Jamaica.

Bean, Gerlyn Jamaican. Activist in the Black Power Movement.

Beaton, Norman (1934-94) Born in Guyana. Leading black actor in Britain. Worked on the stage, including at the National Theatre, and on TV. Became well known through such sitcoms as *Empire Road* and *Desmonds.* He worked closely with black playwrights.

Bell, Pat Voluntary helper on Black Londoners radio programme. Member of Islington Community Relations Council in London.

Benjamin, Floella Trinidad born actress, writer and TV personality, particularly known for her appearances on children's TV programmes in Britain.

Bennett, Louise Well known Jamaican poet, writer, performer and broadcaster. Known particularly for her pioneering writing and performance in Jamaican creole.

Bentley, Earlene African American singer and actress mainly resident in London.

Berry, James Jamaican born poet and writer. Came to Britain in the 1940s. Author of many books for adults and children.

Biographical Notes

Best, Clyde Pioneering black professional footballer. Played for West Ham from 1969 to 1975 and also played for Bermuda.

Best, George b. 1946. Football legend born in Northern Ireland. Found fame playing for Manchester United. and was a prominent member of the 1968 European Cup Winning team. The first footballer to be treated like a pop star.

Big Youth Manley Augustus Buchanan b. Jamaica 1955. Pioneer of putting the reggae DJ style onto record using the toasting style which was particularly popular in the 1970s.

Bishop, Maurice Grenadian barrister and politician. Leader of the New Jewel Movement and the Grenada revolution in 1979. Prime Minister from 1979 to 1983, when he was brutally murdered.

Blackman, Peter From Barbados where he was part of the literary movement. Came to Britain in the 1940s, originally intending to train for the Church. Became involved in Communist Party politics. Poet, writer, historian, political analyst.

Blackwell, Chris b. 1937, England. Gained worldwide fame first through his company Island Records founded in 1962, and later by internationalising reggae music through the recording, marketing and promoting of the work of Bob Marley.

Boateng, Paul Born in Ghana. Came to Britain in 1966 after fall of Nkrumah. Barrister. Labour MP since1987. Appointed Junior Minister of Health in 1997.

Bonhof, Rainer German international footballer and coach.

Boom, Barry Reggae musician Paul Robinson used this name for his recording career following early success with family band *One Blood* and writing and producing reggae star Maxi Priest's first album.

Boulaye, Patti Nigerian born actress and singer. Appeared in the *Black Mikado* in the 1960s and played in Carmen Jones at the Old Vic Theatre in London in the 1990s.

Bovell, Dennis b. 1953 Barbados. Pioneering British based reggae musician. Often credited with establishing and definiing the British Lovers' Rock style of reggae. Prominent in leading the Dennis Bovell Band which supplies the musical accompaniment to the work of Linton Kwesi Johnson.

Brathwaite, Kamau Born in Barbados. Distinguished Caribbean poet, literary critic and historian. Worked at the University of the West Indies in Jamaica in the 1970s-1980s. Currently a Professor at the City University in New York. Co-founder of the Caribbean Artists Movement in 1966.

Breeze, Jean 'Binta' Jamaica's first and leading female dub poet. Works in Jamaica and Britain. Her collections include *Riddim Ravins, Springcleaning* and *On the Edge of the Island.*

Brooks, Gwendolyn b. 1917. First black American woman to receive the Pulitzer Prize for poetry.

Bruno, Frank b. London 1961 of Caribbean migrant parents from Jamaica and Dominica. Well known world heavyweight boxing champion.

Bullins, Ed African American playwright. Active in Britain in the 1960s when his play *The Electronic Nigger* was performed at London's first lunchtime theatre venue, the Ambience in Queensway, run by Trinidadian Junior Telfer. He returned to the USA and became part of the Lafayette Theatre movement with Leroi Jones (Amiri Baraka).

Burke, Aggrey Born in Jamaica in 1943. Senior lecturer and honorary consultant in psychiatry at St George's Hospital, London. A leading expert on the subject of racism and mental health.

Biographical Notes

Burke, Syd Jamaican born photographer. Later presenter of the programme *Rice and Peas* on London's LBC coommercial radio station.

Burnham, Forbes (1923-1985). Co-founder with Cheddi Jagan of the Peoples Progressive Party in 1950 and then in 1955 he founded and became the leader of the People's National Party. Prime Minister of Guyana from 1964 to his death.

Burning Spear b. 1948 as Winston Rodney in Jamaica. Reggae artist notable for his dedication, from the early 1970s onwards, to the singing of 'conscious lyrics', principally concerning Marcus Garvey and rastafarianism.

Busby, Margaret Born in Ghana of African-Caribbean parents. She is a publisher, editor, writer, poet and painter. Co-founder of the publishing house Allison & Busby in 1966. Compiled the major anthology *Daughters of Africa* (1992).

Butler, Tubal Uriah 'Buzz' (1891-1977) Born in Grenada. Trinidadian trade union leader and politician. Historic figure in the struggle for independence in the Caribbean.

Bynoe, Hilda Grenadian. Medical doctor. Became the first black person and the first woman to be Governor General of Grenada.

Cabral, Amilcar (1924-73) Born in Guinea Bissau. Revolutionary thinker and activist. Founder and leader of the African Party for the Independence of Guinea and the Cape Verde Islands (PAIGC). Assassinated by a party dissident.

Cambridge, A.X. (Ricky) Jamaican born writer. Political activist in Britain from the 1960s. Founder and editor of the *Black Liberator*, marxist-leninist journal of the 1970s.

Cameron, Earl Bermuda born actor. Came to Britain in 1939. Joined the navy. Became well known film actor after the war. Appeared in Ealing studios films.

Cameron, Gloria Jamaican who became well known in Britain in the 1970s for her folk group which recorded Jamaican folk songs and presented Jamiacan folk dances.

Carberry, Dossy Jamaican poet. Later became a leading civil servant in the Caribbean.

Carmichael, Stokely Born in Trinidad in 1941 and moved to New York at the age of 11. One of the key black power movement leaders in the 1960s. Died 1998.

Carter, John Born in Guyana in 1919. Barrister. Representative to the United Nations 1962-66, ambassador to the USA 1966-70. High Commissioner to London in 1970.

Cattouse, Nadia Born in Belize. Folk singer and actress. Appeared on radio, television and the stage in Britain since the 1950s. Served in the British army in World War II.

Césaire, Aimé Born 1913 Martinique. Writer and politician. Part of the négritude movement. Author of the key work *Retour Au Pays Natal* (*Return to my Native Land*).

Charles, Clive born Bow, London 1951. One of pioneering black football players in Britain. Played for West Ham 1972-73. Involved with US team in 1998 World Cup.

Charles, John born Canning Town, London 1944. Footballer and elder brother of Clive. England youth international. Played for West Ham 1963-69. One of the first black London players to break through to professional success.

Charles, Alfonso Dominican. Worked for the Post Office for many years in London. Founder of the Dominica National Oversea Association.

Charles, Eugenia b. 1919. Barrister. Became Prime Minister of Dominica in 1980. First female Prime Minister in the Caribbean.

Chelsea at Nine A Granada TV programme on which Shirley Bassey made one of her earlier television appearances.

Cipriani, Arthur Born into the white Trinidadian planter class. Became President of the Trinidad Workingmen's Association in 1922 after championing the cause of black

Biographical Notes

Caribbean soldiers in Egypt during World War I. Later became leader of the Trinidad Labour Party and a member of the Legislative Council.

Clarke, Sebastian (Amon Saba Saakana) Born in Trinidad. Came to Britain in 1965. Poet, writer and publisher. Founder of Caribbean Cultural International and Karnak House.

Clough, Brian b. 1935. Middlesbrough, Sunderland and England footballer. One of the best goalscorers in top level English league football. Later became one of the most successful ever English club football managers, especially with Nottingham Forest with whom he twice won the European Cup (1979 and 1980).

Coker, Ade born Lagos, Nigeria 1955. Footballer. Played for West Ham 1970-1973. Ended career in the North American League with the Boston Minutemen.

Connor, Edric (1913-68) Trinidad born actor, writer, filmmaker, singer and film star. He was the first black actor to appear with the Royal Shakespeare Company in Stratford in Tony Richardson's production of *Pericles* in 1958. Together with his wife, Pearl, he organised, in the 1950s, an agency to represent black and Asian actors and later, in 1960, they founded The Negro Theatre Workshop.

Connor, Geraldine Born in Britain; daughter of Edric and Pearl Connor. Musical director, composer, choral conductor and singer. Works between Britain and Trinidad. Senior lecturer in Popular Music Studies at the University College Bretton Hall.

Connor, Peter Born in Britain; son of Edric and Pearl Connor. Musician.

Constantine, Learie (1901-1971) Famous Trinidadian and West Indies cricketer. Played in the Lancashire league in the 1930s and 1940s. First Trinidad High Commissioner to Britain after independence. Knighted and later made a life peer.

Conteh, John Brought up in the Kirkby area of Liverpool. Sierra Leonean father. Became World Light Heavyweight boxing champion in 1974. Appeared as an actor in the London West End play *Blood Brothers*.

Coppell, Steve b. 1955. Manchester United and England footballer. Career cut short by knee injury. Chairman of the Professional Footballers' Association 1982-1984. Later went into football management.

Count Suckle Jamaican who was a DJ from the bluebeat period onwards. Started the Q Club in the Paddington area of West London. Leading advocate for the building of black business in Britain.

Cousins, Frank Jamaican actor and director. Started the Dark and Light Theatre in Brixton in the 1970s.

Cox, Stretch Trinidadian 'King of Limbo' dancing. Came to Britain in the 1950s.

Crawford, Lincoln Barrister. Member of the Black Lawyers Association. Secretary to the Scarman Commission into the Brixton riots in 1981.

Crichlow, Victor Treasurer of the Carnival Arts Committee which replaaced the Carnival Development Committee as organiser of the Notting Hill Carnival.

Croker, Ted Played professional football briefly for Charlton (1950), but became well known in football as Secretary of the Football Association. Died in 1992.

Cummings, James Originally from Trinidad. Member of Croydon Community Relations Council in London.

Cunningham, Laurie One of the early black footballers to play for England and commonly regarded as one of the most brilliantly talented players of his generation. Played for Leyton Orient, West Bromwich Albion, Manchester United, Leicester and

Biographical Notes

Wimbledon and also played in Spain after a sensational £1 million transfer to Real Madrid. Killed in a car crash in 1989 aged 33.

Cyrus, Tony Guyanese born singer, actor, guitarist and composer. Resident in Britain.

Dalphinis, Morgan Born in St Lucia. Leading researcher on creole and African languages and an education specialist. Author of *Caribbean and African Languages*.

Dalrymple, Henderson Barbadian born journalist. Has written for *The Caribbean Times* and many other British-based papers. Author of book 50 Great Westindian Test Cricketers (1983), and of the publication *Bob Marley:Music, Myth and the Rastas* (1976).

Dawn, Marpessa African American actress who starred in Black Orpheus in the 1960s.

Dekker, Desmond b. 1942 in Jamaica, as Desmond Dacres. Recording artist. Became internationally famous in the 1960s for his tongue in cheek stage presentation of the Jamaican rude boy street style and his projection of the ska and rock steady musical styles which were the precursors of reggae. Particularly known for his three enduring major hit records *007 (Shanty Town), Israelites*, and *It Mek*.

Denselow, Robin British journalist. Known for his writing on music for *The Guardian* newspaper and his current affairs journalism for BBC television.

Di Stefano, Alfredo b. 1926, Argentina. Legendary international footballer. Famous in the 1950s /1960s as the striker of the brilliant Spanish team of that period, Real Madrid.

Du Bois, W.E.B. (1868-1963) Major US figure in the struggle for the rights of black people. Writer and intellectual. First African-American to win Harvard doctorate. One of the founders of National Association for the Advancement of Coloured People. Author of *The Souls of Black Folk*. Died in Ghana.

Edwards, Greg Grenadian brought up in the USA. Leading radio presenter of soul music in Britain in the1970s.

Edwards, Herman (1925-1998) Born in Antigua. Founded the Harambee organisation which worked with black youth in Britain in the 1970s and 1980s. Popularly known as Brother Herman.

Egbuna, Obi Nigerian born playwright and teacher. Based in Britain in the 1960s when he was involved in the Black Power movement and founded the Universal Coloured People's Association. Later moved to the USA.

Evans, Roy Played football for Liverpool 1969 to 1973. Liverpool manager 1994-98.

Ezeike, Man Jamaican born entertainer. Once hosted a BBC local radio programme in Bedford in the south of England. Later presented a mainly reggae music programme on BBC Radio One.

Fanon, Frantz (1925-1961) Martinique born psychiatrist. Supporter of Algerian liberation movement and major anti-colonial theorist. Author of *Black Skins, White Masks*, and *The Wretched of the Earth*.

Farley, Rawle Guyanese born academic who lived in Britain in the 1950s.

Fat Man Leader of one of the pioneering sound systems based in the Tottenham area of north London. Opened a record shop and helped to found the pirate radio station RJR.

Ferlinghetti, Lawrence American poet. Born 1919 in New York. Prominent member of the beat poets movement in the 1960s. Bookshop owner, publisher, writer and critic.

Fleming, Helen From Grenada. Trained as a nurse. Also an actor, dancer and songwriter.

Forbes, Leonie Jamaican born actress. Appeared in several significant productions in the 1960s.

Biographical Notes

Francis, Pepe Of Grenadian/Trinidadian background. A leading carnivalist in Britain. Manager of the Ebony Steelband.

Garvey, Amy Ashwood (1897-1968) Born in Jamaica. First wife of Marcus Garvey. Political activist in her own right, working in the Caribbean, USA and Britain. Attended the 1945 Pan African Congress held in Manchester and chaired some of the sessions.

Garvey, Marcus (1887-1940) National Hero of Jamaica. Active in the Caribbean and USA. Founded the Universal Negro Improvement Association in 1914 which asserted the principle of negro and African equality and due respect for the African past. His black pride and self help ideas have become influential again over the past 30 years.

Gilroy, Paul Born of Guyanese/British parentage. Professor of Sociology at Goldsmiths College in London. Has also been visiting professor in the USA. Author of a number of books including *There Ain't No Black in the Union Jack.*

Ginsberg, Allen American poet. Prominent member of the beat poets in the 1960s. Died in the mid-1990s.

Gordon, Rhoden Grenadian born community worker and political activist based in the Notting Hill area of London. Founded the Black People's Information Centre. Defendant in the Mangrove Nine Trial in 1971.

Goveia, Elsa (1925-1980) Born Guyana. Appointed Professor of West Indian History at the University of the West Indies in Jamaica 1961. First female professor there.

Grant, Boysie Trinidadian drummer and vocalist.

Grant, Cy Guyanese born actor, singer, musician and writer. Joined the RAF in 1941. Became well known with his regular appearances on the BBC's *Tonight* programme launched in 1957. Set up the Drum Arts Centre in London in the 1970s.

Grant, Bernie born in Guyana. Activist on behalf of black people in Britain as a trade union official, local councillor, and since 1992, as a Labour Party MP.

Grey, Ann-Marie Born in Jamaica, brought up in Britain. Freelance broadcast journalist. Worked on Black Londoners and for the BBC World Service. Later co-hosted Radio London's Rush Hour morning programme.

Gullit, Ruud b.1962 in Holland. Father from Surinam. Highly successful Dutch international footballer. Played in Italy (Milan, Sampdoria) and Britain (Chelsea). Successful manager of Chelsea. Became manager of Newcastle United in 1998.

Gutzmore, Cecil Jamaican born political activist and academic. Prominent in radical black community politics in West London 1960s to 1980s. Now mainly resident in Jamaica.

Hajee, Azim Kenyan born. Trade union official. One of the founders of the Black Workers' Group in Camden in London during the 1980s.

Hansberry, Lorraine (1930-65) Celebrated African American playwright and activist artist. Author of *A Raisin in the Sun,* which opened to critical and popular acclaim in 1958 and brought black audiences to professional Broadway theatre.

Harris, Dennis Jamaican. Owner of record company called DIP Records in Lewisham, London. One of the early organisers of coach parties to the seaside. Committed supporter of Jamaican music.

Harris, George Grenadian born TV and theatre actor. Spent early life in Sweden and trained there as an operatic singer. Came to Britain in the 1960s to appear in the West End in the musical *Jesus Christ Superstar* and has worked mainly in Britain ever since.

Biographical Notes

Hassan, Leila Born in Britain in 1948 of Zanzibar/British parentage. Active in Black British politics during the 1970s and 1980s. A member of the Race Today Collective from 1974 until its closure in 1990.

Heighway, Steve Played football for Liverpool from 1970 to 1980 and also played many times for the Republic of Ireland. Newsworthy during his career as one of the very few professionals in English fooball to have a university degree.

Henriques, Pauline Born in Jamaica in 1914. Actress. In 1946 she and Connie Smith became the first black actresses to appear on British TV acting in *All God's Chillun Got Wings*. In the 1950s she switched to social work and became the first black woman Justice of the Peace in 1966.

Herbert, Vince Once worked on BBC black local radio in Manchester in the north of England. Later worked as a presenter on the Black Londoners radio programme.

Hill, Errol Trinidadian actor, playwright, director and lecturer in drama studies. Author of the pioneering study *The Trinidad Carnival: mandate for a national theatre* first published in 1952.

Hill, Janet British librarian. Head of Lambeth Libraries in Brixton, London, during the 1970s and 1980s.

Hoddle, Glen England international footballer who played for Tottenham Hotspur between 1975 and 1987. Manager of the England team in the 1998 World Cup.

Holder, Boscoe Well known Trinidadian dancer and artist. Formed a well known dance troupe in Trinidad having spent some time in England.

Holder, Ramjohn Guyanese born actor and singer. Has become a household name with his portrayal of the character Porkpie in the TV sitcom *Desmonds.*

Holness, Barry London-based Jamaican whose home was a meeting place for many intellectuals.

Hooley, Joan Jamaican born theatre and TV actress and scriptwriter who came to Britain in the 1950s. Appeared in many episodes of the early British TV hospital soap opera *Emergency Ward Ten* and in 1998 in the BBC TV soap opera *Eastenders*, and wrote scripts for the popular TV black sitcom *Desmonds.*

Howe, Darcus Born in Trinidad in 1943. Active in radical black politics from the 1960s to the 1980s. Member of the Black Panther Movement and then the Race Today Collective and the Alliance of the RTC with the Black Parents Movement and Black Youth Movement. Moved into media journalism in the mid 1980s.

Howe, Don Played football for West Bromwich Albion, Arsenal and England between 1952 and 1966. Subsequently highly successful as a coach with Arsenal and England.

Hudson, Alan Played football with Chelsea, Stoke and Arsenal from 1968 to 1985.

Hughes, Langston (1902-1967) Well known African American poet and writer. Active in the Harlem Renaissance movement of the 1930s.

Hughes, Emlyn Successful Liverpool and England footballer and TV personality.

Huntley, Jessica Born in Guyana in 1927, and active in radical politics there before coming to Britain. Co-founder of Bogle-L'Ouverture Publications in 1969 and the Walter Rodney Bookshop. Along with John La Rose, and her husband Eric, a pioneer of black book publishing in Britain.

I Roy b. Jamaica 1949 as Roy Reid. One of the pioneering storytelling reggae DJ's of the 1970s.

Ikoli, Tunde Of Nigerian/British parentage. TV scriptwriter and playwright. His classic work *Scrape off the Black* was first produced in 1981.

Biographical Notes

Irie, Tippa b. 1965 in London as Anthony Henry. Made his name with the Saxon sound system in South London in developing the 'fast chatting' reggae MC style. Had a smash hit in the UK pop charts in the 1980s with *Hello Darling.*

Jack, Stanley Trinidadian dancer. Performed often in Britain with his dance group.

James, Alby Black British theatre and TV director. Artistic director of the Temba Theatre Company from 1983-1991.

James, CLR (1904-89) Trinidadian born writer, lecturer and influential independent marxist intellectual. Author of *The Black Jacobins, Beyond A Boundary, Minty Alley,* and many other titles on history, politics and culture.

James, Horace Born in Trinidad. Became a well known theatre and TV actor and writer in Britain. A key organiser of early Caribbean folk concerts at the Commonwealth Institute in London.

Jeffers, Audrey Trinidadian. Well known for her social work in Trinidad in the 1930s where she organised The Breakfast Shed to offer meals for the children of the poor.

Jeffreys, Pansy Born in Guyana. Came to Britain in the 1950s as a nurse. Pioneer in developing care for black old people and established the Pepperpot Club in West London for this purpose.

Jet Star The major distribution company for reggae music in Britain. Run by the Jamaican Palmer brothers who were pioneers in releasing reggae music in Britain on their Parma label.

Jeyifo, Biodun Born 1946. Nigerian academic and political activist. Lectures in drama and the sociology of literature. Currently working in the USA where he also edits *Talaka Freedom Courier* a journal opposed to the military regime in Nigeria.

John, Errol (1924-88) Trinidadian born actor and playwright. Won the Observer drama competition in 1957 with his classic play *Moon on a Rainbow Shawl.*

John, Frank Trinidadian poet who was active in the Caribbean Artists Movement in London in the 1960s. Later moved to the United States.

John, Gus Born Grenada in 1945. Came to Britain in the 1960s and has worked as a youth worker, researcher, lecturer, educational consultant, film producer and was until recently Director of Education and Leisure for the London Borough of Hackney. Consistently active in struggles for racial and social justice.

Jones, Claudia (1915-64) Born in Trinidad. Active in left wing politics in the USA and after expulsion from there came to Britain in the 1950s. Founded the pioneering *West India Gazette* in 1958 and was a founding organiser of the Notting Hill Carnival.

Jonson, Bari Jamaican born as Barrington Johnson. Prominent theatre and TV actor in Britain in the 1960s. Also well known for his TV work in Jamaica.

Joseph, Barbara Trinidad born architect. Became a leading figure in the Carnival movement in London in the 1970s as part of the CDC (Carnival Development Committee).

Joseph, Elroy Jamaican born dancer. Came to Britain in the 1950s. Member of the Ballet Nègres dance group. Later developed his original jazz dance techniques in Liverpool. Died in the mid-1990s.

Kani, John South African actor. Caused a sensation in Britain with his performances at the Royal Court Theatre in the 1970s in *Sizwe Bansi Is Dead* and *The Island.*

Keegan, Kevin b.1951. England fooballer who was best known for his time playing in the highly successful Liverpool team of the 1970s. Later had a successful playing career in Germany and entered football management in England.

Biographical Notes

Keens-Douglas, Paul born in Trinidad and spent childhood in Grenada. Popular oral poet and storyteller.

Kelshall, Jack Trinidadian solicitor. Worked for independence and closely with the Oilfields Workers Trade Union and other workers' organisations.

Kelsick, Cecil Born 1920 in Dominica. Barrister. Attorney General of the Leeward Isles in 1953 and of the Windward Isles in 1954. Solicitor General in Trinidad & Tobago 1957-66.

Kempes, Mario Argentinian international footballer who became famous as a goalscorer with Argentina's 1978 World Cup winning team.

Khama, Seretse Born 1921. One-time heir to the Ngwato chiefship, nationalist leader and became first President of Botswana in 1966.

King, Martin Luther (1929-68) Leading African American civil rights leader.

King, Peter Well respected in British reggae circles as the originator of the fast chat style of reggae DJing and as an inspiration from within the south London Saxon sound system for the better known Smiley Culture and Maxi Priest.

Kirby, Alexander Journalist and BBC religious correspondent. Became the first editor of *Race Today* in the early 1970s in its initial period as an independent campaigning organisation linked to the then Institute of Race Relations.

Kizerman, Rudi Born in Barbados as W.R. Brathwaite. In 1968 wrote *Stand Up In The World* , a pioneering novel about black power in Britain in the 1960s.

Kumalo, Alton South African born actor and theatre director. Founded the Temba Theatre company in the early 1970s.

La Rose, John Born in Trinidad in 1927. Influential political and cultural figure, who has been active in both Trinidad and Britain, where he settled in the early 1960s. Co-founder of the Caribbean Artists Movement in 1966. Co-founder of New Beacon Books and Chairman of the George Padmore Institute.

Laine, Cleo Born 1927 of Jamaican/British parentage. Actress and jazz singer. Wife of jazz musician Johnny Dankworth with whom she often performs in concert.

Laird, Colin British born architect who settled in Trinidad in the 1940s and has designed many major buildings.

Lamming, George Born 1927 in Barbados. Well known writer and essayist. Lived and worked in London in the 1950s and 1960s. Presently moves between the Caribbean and USA. His best known work is the novel *In The Castle Of My Skin*.

Laslett, Rhaune Of Central European extraction. Ran North Kensington community organisation in the 1960s. Ran an annual children's parade in the area. Controversial because of the claim that she, rather than a Caribbean person like Claudia Jones, initiated the Notting Hill Carnival.

Lawrence, Stephen (1974-1993) Young black student, born of Jamaican parents in London, who was killed in a racist attack in South London. His parents have waged a long and principled campaign ever since to bring his killers to justice.

Le Maitre, Chris Trinidad born lawyer and journalist. Political activist with the Caribbean Labour Congress. Came to Britain in the 1950s. Later became a leading community relations officer. Founder member of the West Indian Legal Panel established in London in the 1960s.

Lebel, Jean Jacques Poet who took part in the May 1968 French student uprisings.

Biographical Notes

Lecointe-Jones, Althea Trinidadian. Leader of the Black Panther Movement in Britain in the late 1960s and early 1970s. Studied chemistry and then medicine. Has practiced in both Trinidad and Britain.

Levi, Philip (Papa) born as Philip Williams. Another of the key figures in the pioneering Saxon sound system from south London. In 1984, with *Mi God Mi King* became the first UK reggae DJ to top the Jamaican charts.

Lewis, Lennox b. London 1965 of Caribbean parentage. Grew up in Ontario, Canada. In 1992 became the first British born boxer to be World Heavyweight champion.

Lindo, George Jamaican born factory worker living in Bradford who was wrongfully imprisoned for armed robbery in the 1970s. There was a successful campaign to clear his name and he received record damages in compensation.

Lloyd, Errol Jamaican born artist, sculptor, writer and children's book illustrator who has lived in London since the 1960s.

Lloyd, Clive born 1944 in Guyana. Captain of the West Indies cricket team 1974-1985 in some of its most successful ever years. Also captained Lancashire.

Loate, Walter South African singer. Came to Britain in 1961 with the musical *King Kong*. In 1964 joined the famous South African singing group The Manhattan Brothers.

Luthuli, Chief Albert (1898-1967). Nobel-prize-winning South African nationalist leader. President of the African National Congress (ANC) 1952-67.

Macdonald, Ian Born in Scotland. Leading barrister and a specialist in the field of immigration law. Defended in the Mangrove Nine Trial and many other major black cases. Headed the Macdonald Inquiry into racism and racial violence in Manchester schools. Was appointed a Queens Council in the 1990s.

Manley, Michael (1924-1998) Jamaican barrister, politician, trade union leader and writer. Son of Norman Manley. Prime Minister of Jamaica 1972-1980 and again from 1989.

Manley, Norman (1893-1969) Jamaican barrister, politician and trade union leader. Founder of the Peoples National Party in 1938. Chief Minister in Jamaica in 1955 and Premier of Jamaica from 1957-62.

Mansfield, Mike Leading British barrister. One of the representatives of the New Cross parents at the inquest into the deaths of their children in 1981. Subsequently known for his legal work in exposing official wrongdoing in high profile miscarriage of justice cases. Prominent lawyer in the Stephen Lawrence Campaign.

Mapandero, John Zimbabwean enthusiast for the visual arts, particularly African painting and sculpture. Set up the Drum Arts Centre in London with Cy Grant in the 1970s. Returned to Zimbabwe where he continued to be active in the arts.

Marais, Genevieve South African born teacher and author who was a close friend of Kwame Nkrumah.

Marley, Bob (1945-81) Outstanding Jamaican reggae artist. Key figure in the global popularisation of reggae and rastafarianism after his album *Natty Dread* (1975).

Marriott, Louis Jamaican. One of the earliest black broadcasters in the BBC Radio London newsroom.

Marryshow, T.A. (1885-1958) Grenadian politician and journalist. Elected to the Legislative Council in 1925. Campaigned for constitutional change. Advocate of Caribbean unity and opponent of repression in the colonies.

Biographical Notes

Marson, Una (1905-1965) Jamaican. Pioneering poet, BBC broadcaster, playwright and social reformer. Came to London in the 1930s and then worked in the USA in the 1950s and in Israel in the early 1960s.

Martin, Tony Trinidad born writer, publisher and academic. Founded the Majority Press publishing house in the USA. Producer of a number of books on Marcus Garvey.

Matthews, Stanley b. 1915. World famous Blackpool and England footballer. Played at the top level in England until he was 50. Played for Stoke City from 1930-47 and from 1961-65. Knighted in 1965.

Matura, Mustapha Trinidad born playwright and TV screen writer who came to Britain in 1961. His plays include *As Time Goes By* and *Play Mas* and he has also been a scriptwriter for a number of TV sitcoms.

Maxwell, Marina Trinidadian writer, playwright and teacher also known for her work in Jamaican popular theatre.

Maxwell, Neville Born in Barbados. Lawyer and legal tutor at Holborn College of Law and Commerce in London in the 1960s. Co-founder of the West Indian Legal Panel.

Mboya, Tom (1930-69) Kenyan labour organiser, nationalist leader and minister in the Kenyatta-led KANU government from 1963 to his assassination in 1969.

McBurnie, Beryl b. 1915. Leading Trinidadian dancer, choreographer and anthroplogist. Founder of the Little Carib Theatre. One of the pioneers of Caribbean dance and researcher into dance and folk traditions.

McDermott, Galt American composer who wrote the famous musical *Hair*.

McLean, Raymond Trinidadian dancer and dance teacher who originally trained with Beryl McBurnie.

McNish, Althea Trinidad born leading artist and textile designer who has lived in London since the 1950s. Works as an artist, designer and in art education.

Mighty Diamonds Famous Jamaican reggae close harmony vocal trio. Particuiarly well known in the 1970s and 1980s. Still performing in the 1990s.

Mighty Sparrow Born 1935 in Grenada as Slinger Francisco. Legendary Trinidadian calypsonian. Master of many calypso styles. Producer of dozens of albums and numerous classic songs including *Jean and Dinah*. Awarded honorary doctorate by the Univesity of the West Indies in 1987.

Mills, Barbara British lawyer. First woman to head the Crown Prosecution Service.

Minshall, Wilson Artist and father of the well known Carnival designer Peter Minshall. Became head of the Trinidad Tourist Board.

Mittelholzer, Edgar (1909-65) Pioneering Guyanese born novelist. Well known for his *Kaywana Trilogy*.

Morris, "Mia" Of Grenadian parentage. Voluntary worker for Black Londoners radio programme assisting with activities such as publicity leafletting.

Morris, Barney Trinidadian dancer and choreographer. Known for her work with the Little Carib Theatre. Died in the 1980s.

Morris, Pastor Jamaican born church minister based in Tottenham, north London, in the 1960s and 1970s. Ran a club for black youths. Tried and failed to run a carnival in Finsbury Park, north London, intended to undermine the Notting Hill Carnival.

Morris, Sam Uriah b. Grenada. d. 1976 in London. Secretary to Nkrumah in George Padmore's time. BBC World Service broadcaster. Produced an early series of Black Studies programmes on BBC Radio London.

Biographical Notes

Munroe, Carmen Born in Guyana in 1932. One of Britain's most successful black actresses. Has worked widely in theatre and TV. Became particularly well known for her part as Desmond's wife in the TV sitcom of that name.

Mutabaruka b. Jamaica as Allan Hope. Leading Jamaican dub poet.

Naidoo, Bobby Actor from Kenya. Joined the Negro Theatre Workshop in 1960s in London. Died in 1966.

Naipaul, V.S. Well known Trinidad born novelist, short story writer, essayist and travel writer. Author of *A House For Mr Biswas*, *Miguel Street* and many other works.

Narayan, Rudy (1938-98) Guyanese born barrister. Worked closely with legal advice centres in London. Became prominent in fighting some of the main black cases in the 1970s and 1980s.

Newton, Huey (1941-89) African American black power activist. Founder member of the Black Panther Party

Nkomo, Joshua Born 1917 in Rhodesia. Labour organiser and nationalist leader. Founder of the Zimbabwe African Peoples Union together with Ndabaningi Sithole in 1961. Defeated by Robert Mugabe in the post liberation elections in Zimbabwe.

Nkosi, Lewis South African writer, academic and literary critic.

Nkrumah, Kwame (1909-72) His fight for independence established the pattern for all British colonies making him the most important leader in British sub-Saharan Africa. Prime Minister of independent Ghana in 1957 and President from 1960-1966. After his overthrow from power in 1966 he settled in Guinea.

Ntshona, Winston South African actor. Performed with John Kani in *The Island* and *Sizwe Bansi Is Dead* which ran successfully at the Royal Court Theatre in the 1970s.

Nunez, George Trinidadian. Brother of Pearl Connor-Mogotsi. Flew with the RAF during World War II. Was killed in action in 1943.

Nyerere, Julius Born 1922. Leader of the independent movement in colonial Tanganyika. First Prime Minister (1961-2) and first President of the present Tanzania (1962 to 1985).The first African post-independence head of state to retire voluntarily.

O'Connor, Quintin Trinidadian trade union and political organiser, active from the 1930s to 1950s. General Secretary of the Federated Workers Trade Union, Secretary of the Trade Union Council and Treasurer of the West Indian Independence Party.

Omotoso, Kole Born in Nigeria in 1943. Arabic scholar, novelist, playwright, literary critic, writer and academic. Currently Professor of English at the University of the Western Cape in South Africa.

Onuora, Oku Born in 1952 in Jamaica. Leading Jamaican dub and performance poet, who began writing seriously around 1971 when he was in prison.

Ove, Horace Trinidadian born film maker. Pioneered black films in Britain with the production of *Reggae* in 1970 and *Pressure* in 1974, the first full length black feature film. He has also made a large number of films for TV.

Padmore, Dorothy (Dorothy Pizer) The wife of George Padmore and a political activist in her own right.

Padmore, George (1902-59) Born in Trinidad. One of the major figures of the 20th century, demonstrating an independent intellectual and organisational position in the anti-colonial and international socialist movements of the 1930s and 1940s.

Palmer, Mr Jamaican pioneer of reggae music selling and distribution in Britain.

Pele b. 1940. in Brazil as Edson Arantes do Nascimento. Generally regarded as the greatest ever footballer. Played for Brazil over 100 times scoring several goals in the

Biographical Notes

1958 World Cup Finals when he was only 17 including a hat-trick in the semi-final. Won the World Cup three times with Brazil in 1958, 1962 and 1970. Later became Minister of Sport in Brazil.

Phillips, Edward Tobagonian academic. Taught philosophy in Nigeria in the 1970s.

Phillips, Ron Guyanese community and political activist based in the Manchester area of England from the 1960s until his return to Guyana in the 1980s. Died USA 1998.

Phillips, Mike Brought up in London. Guyanese parentage. Writer, journalist and academic. Co-author, with his brother Trevor, of *Windrush:the irresistible rise of multi-racial Britain* (1998). Author of a number of well received crime thrillers.

Philo, Pat Voluntary helper with the Black Londoners radio programme.

Phoenix, Sybil Guyanese born social and community worker in south London. Founder of the Moonshot Youth Club. Became a Methodist mininster.

Pierre, Lennox (1919-93) Trinidadian lawyer, trade unionist, musician, poet and writer. Worked closely with the steelband movement, the trade union movement and in the independent radical politics of Trindad.

Pitt, Dr David (1913-1994) Born in Grenada. Medical doctor. President of the West Indian National Party in Trinidad. Practised as a doctor in Britain from 1946. Active in Labour Party politics. Failed to become an MP but was made a life peer in the 1970s.

Poitier, Sidney Of Bahamian parentage. Leading African American theatre actor and Oscar winning film star. Well known for acting in dramas of racial conflict such as *In The Heat Of The Night, Guess Who's Coming To Dinner* and *To Sir With Love.*

Prescod, Pearl Tobagonian actress, singer, cabaret artist, playwright. National theatre player in Arthur Miller's *The Crucible* in the early 1960s. Friend and comrade of the political activist Claudia Jones. Died 1966.

Priest, Maxi b. London 1962 of Jamaican parentage. Successful international reggae singer. Initially came to prominence as a member of the pioneering south London Saxon sound system. Distinguished from his peers as a 'singing' rather than 'fast chat' DJ.

Puckering, Evrol Trinidadian dancer and choreographer. Came to Britain in the 1960s.

Puskas, Ferenc b. 1927. Legendary Hungarian footballer. A member of the 1950s Hungarian team credited with revolutionising football's playing style, and which beat England 6-3 at Wembley in 1953 and 7-1 in Hungary in 1954. Later had a successful career with Spanish team Real Madrid.

Rajendra, Cecil Malaysian lawyer and poet. Lived in London in the 1970s when he organised a third world cultural forum called Black Voices in the basement of the Troubadour Coffee House.

Reagon, Bernice Johnson African American anthropologist and folklorist, civil rights social activist and a cultural performer. Founding member of the famous black women's accapella group, *Sweet Honey in the Rock.*

Reckord, Barry Jamaican theatre and TV playwright. His plays include *In The Beautiful Caribbean* produced on British TV in 1972, and *Skyvers* one of the early plays to address the black British experience.

Reckord, Lloyd b. Jamaica. Came to Britain in the 1950s. Theatre and TV actor and directed BBC TV documentaries. Returned to Jamaica in 1968 to play a leading role in the development of theatre, including theatre for schools.

Richardson, Tony British theatre and film producer. Particularly prominent in the 1960s.

Biographical Notes

Robeson, Paul (1898-1976) World famous African American singer and actor. Supported the fight against racism and backed working class and independence movements around the world.

Rodney, Walter (1942-80) Guyanese born historian and intellectual. Author of the influential works *Groundings With My Brothers* and *How Europe Underdeveloped Africa*. Assassinated in Guyana.

Rodriquez, Rico b. Jamaica 1934 as Emmanuel Rodriguez. First settled in Britain in 1961. Well respected trombonist in reggae and jazz circles.

Rose, Steven British academic. Professor of Biology at the Open University. Specialist in brain research. Strong opponent of racism in science.

Rose, Newton black British youth from North London. Jamaican parentage. Unjustly jailed for muder at the end of 1981. Freed after 3 months by vigorous campaign led by the Alliance (Black Parents Movement, Black Youth Movement, Race Today Collective).

Rosso, Franco British film director and leading film editor of Italian parentage. Worked with John La Rose on the *Mangrove Nine* film. Produced a film *Dread, Beat and Blood* on Linton Kwesi Johnson for TV in 1976. Has also worked with Horace Ove.

Rotten, Johnny b. John Lydon in Camden, London in the 1950s into an Irish family. Became famous as a pioneer of punk music with his band the Sex Pistols.

Ruddock, Amza Originally from Jamaica. Her house at 439 New Cross Road, Deptford was burnt down in a racist attack on January 18th 1981 which killed 13 young black people including two of her children and led to the New Cross Massacre Campaign.

Rugg, Akua Nigerian born teacher, writer and critic. Works at Lambeth College in London. Author of *Brickbats and Bouquets* (1984), a collection of her reviews of black theatre and film in Britain. Former member of the Race Today Collective.

Salkey, Andrew (1928-95) Jamaican born novelist, children's story writer, anthologist, essayist, broadcaster and academic. Lived in London from the 1950s to the 1970s. Co-founder of the Caribbean Artists Movement in 1966. Taught in Amherst, USA, for the last 20 years of his life.

Samuel, Anselm From Trinidad. Longtime community activist in Britain.

Sanchez, Sonia born 1934, Birmingham, Alabama. African American poet and writer.

Sangster, Donald Burke Jamaican politician. Leader of the Jamaica Labour Party. Became Prime Minister in 1967 after Bustamante retired but died suddenly soon afterwards.

Saville, John British academic. Co-editor of the annual *Socialist Register*, the influential New Left anthology started in the 1960s.

Scafe, Leslie Jamaican. One time officer of the Commission for Racial Equality in Britain. Later returned to Jamaica.

Sekka, Johnny Born in Senegal. Well known TV and film actor particularly during the 1960s. Later successful in the USA.

Selassie, Haile (1892-1975). Regent ruler of Ethiopia 1916-30 and Emperor from 1930-74. In exile from 1936-41. Placed under house arrest in 1974 after a military takeover. Died under mysterious circumstances.

Selvon, Sam (1923-94) Trinidad born novelist, short story writer and lecturer. Lived in London 1950 to 1978. Author of *The Lonely Londoners*, a pioneering novel in its depiction of the life of West Indian immigrants and its use of Caribbean creole.

240

Biographical Notes

Shaka, Jah b. Jamaica. Came to Britain aged eight. Veteran sound system operator. Has remained true to rasta inspired roots reggae and dub from the 1970s to date.

Shearer, Alan b. 1970. England international footballer. Striker with club sides Blackburn and Newcastle.

Shilton, Peter England goalkeeper with a distinguished record which lasted from the 1960s to the 1990s.

Simpson, Christian BBC producer. Assisted the Negro Theatre Workshop. Died in mid-1960s.

Simpson, Lois Sister of Pearl Connor-Mogotsi. Met and married her husband Jack from Blackburn, Lancashire, when he was posted to Trinidad during World War II with the Fleet Air Arm.

Sivanandan, A. Sri Lankan born director of the Institute of Race Relations in London since the early 1970s. Editor of the journal *Race & Class*.

Skinner-Carter, Corinne Trinidadian born theatre and TV actress. Starred in the TV series *Empire Road*.

Small, Richard Distinguished Jamaican barrister. Supporter and co-founder of the Jamaican Council for Human Rights.

Smith, Michael (1954-1983) Leading Jamaican performance and dub poet who took Europe by storm after his electrifying appearance at the 1st International Book Fair of Radical Black and Third World Books in 1982. Stoned to death in Jamaica.

Smith, Tommy Footballer who was a member of the outstandingly successful Liverpool teams of the 1960s and 1970s.

Souness, Graeme Scottish international footballer whose career ran from 1970 to 1983. Best known for his career with Liverpool.

Soyinka, Wole Nigerian poet, playwright, novelist, essayist and academic. Winner of the 1986 Nobel Prize for Literature. Currently living in exile and campaigning for a return to democracy in Nigeria.

Stanley, Macdonald Trinidadian trade unionist and community worker. Active in Britain in the 1950s and 1960s. One of the founders of the West Indian Standing Conference after the Notting Hill riots in 1958.

Stepney, Alex b. 1944. Manchester United goalkeeper who played once for England. Member of Manchester United's 1968 European Cup Winning team.

Stewart, Bob American academic, poet and critic. Studied in Jamaica. Also writer on religion and slavery.

Talbot, Brian England international footballer who played for clubs such as Arsenal, Stoke and West Bromwich Albion between 1973 and 1990.

Tansey, Rock British barrister. One of the representatives of the New Cross parents at the inquest into the deaths of their children in 1981.

Taylor, Gordon Played football for Bolton and other teams between 1962 and 1979. Well known as Chairman of the Professional Footballers' Association.

Thomas, Iolette Guyanese journalist.

Thomas, Michael b. 1967 in South London. Black, England international footballer. Famous for scoring a brilliant last minute goal which won the League Championship for Arsenal in 1989. Has also played for Liverpool.

Toshack, John From Wales. Played football between 1965 and 1983 for Liverpool and other clubs. Has subsequently pursued a career in international football management.

Tropic One of the earlier black magazines in Britain.

Biographical Notes

U Roy, b. Jamaica 1942, as Ewart Beckford. Reggae artist. Started as a sound system DJ. Pioneered the toasting DJ style, in which improvised lyrics are chanted over reggae dub plates (reggae songs with the singing vocals removed).

Verity, Jeremy Jamaican broadcaster. Worked at BBC World Service during the 1950s and 1960s as editor of the Caribbean Service; he later became head of the Jamaica Broadcasting Company.

Villa, Ricardo Argentinian international footballer who was a World Cup winner in 1978. Enjoyed a highly successful spell with Tottenham Hotspur 1978-1982.

Walcott, Derek St Lucian born poet, playwright and academic. Winner of the 1992 Nobel Prize for Literature.

Walke, Olive Trinidadian folk song and dance expert. Founder of the choral group *La Petite Musicale.*

Walker, Rudolph Trinidad born theatre, TV and radio actor. Appeared in the TV series *Love Thy Neighbour, Black Silk* and *The Thin Blue Line.*

Walker, Wilf b. 1945. In the 1980s became one of the first independent black concert promoters in Britain. Founder member of the Arts Council of Great Britain African Caribbean sub-committee.

Webb, Rene A founder of the West Indian Ex-Servicemen's Association in Britain. Became director of the Melting Pot Foundation a welfare organisation for black people.

White, Ruel Montserrat born novelist, short story writer and teacher. Author of one of the first black British novels *Heroes Through The Day* (1990).

Wilkinson, Howard Former professional footballer who has been a successful coach and manager with Sheffield Wednesday and Leeds United.

Williams, Eric (1911-1981) Founder and political leader of the Peoples National Movement in Trinidad and Tobago. First Chief Minister in 1956 and then first Prime Minister of independent Trinidad from 1962 until his death. Outstanding historian and author of *Capitalism and Slavery.*

Williams, Nigel b.1948. British writer of TV and stage plays and novels.

Wilson, T-Bone Guyanese born actor, playwright and poet. One of his plays was produced at the Keskidee Centre in the 1970s.

Wong, Ansel Trinidadian born community worker and educationist. Active in London since the black power movement of the 1960s. Became deputy director of Morley Adult Education College in London in the 1990s.

Woodley, Len Trinidadian born barrister. Founder member of the pioneering West Indian Legal Panel. Appointed a judge in Britain in the 1990s.

Wright, Ian Born in South London to Jamaican migrant parents in 1963. Has had a highly successful career in British football as one of the most prolific goalscorers of his generation with Crystal Palace and Arsenal before moving to West Ham in 1998. Achieved modern legend status in North London during his career with Arsenal where he broke the club's all-time goalscoring record in 1997.

X, Malcolm (1925-65) Leading African American black nationalist leader of the 1960s. His ideas have remained influential throughout the decades since his assassination.

Yashin, Lev b. 1929, Moscow, d. 1990. Famous Russian international goalkeeper of the 1950s and 1960s.

Yeomans, Keith Executive producer of Black Londoners and formerly Head of Educational Programmes for BBC Radio London.

INDEX

SOCIAL PROTECTION
AFTER THE CRISIS
Regulation without enforcement

Steve Tombs

First published in Great Britain in 2016 by

Policy Press
University of Bristol
1-9 Old Park Hill
Bristol
BS2 8BB
UK
t: +44 (0)117 954 5940
pp-info@bristol.ac.uk
www.policypress.co.uk

North America office:
Policy Press
c/o The University of Chicago Press
1427 East 60th Street
Chicago, IL 60637, USA
t: +1 773 702 7700
f: +1 773 702 9756
sales@press.uchicago.edu
www.press.uchicago.edu

© Policy Press 2016

British Library Cataloguing in Publication Data
A catalogue record for this book is available from the British Library

Library of Congress Cataloging-in-Publication Data
A catalog record for this book has been requested

ISBN 978 1 44731 375 5 hardcover

Cover design by Soapbox Design
Front cover images: iStockphoto
Printed and bound in Great Britain by by CPI Group (UK) Ltd, Croydon, CR0 4YY
Policy Press uses environmentally responsible print partners

Contents

List of tables and figures

Tables

Figures

About the author

Steve Tombs is Professor of Criminology at the Open University, UK. He has a long-standing interest in the incidence, nature and regulation of corporate crime and harm. His publications include *The corporate criminal* (Routledge, 2015), *Regulatory surrender: Death, injury and the non-enforcement of law* (Institute of Employment Rights, 2010), *A crisis of enforcement: The decriminalisation of death and injury at work* (Centre for Crime and Justice Studies, 2008) and *Safety crimes* (Willan, 2007) (all co-authored with Dave Whyte); *Corporate crime* (Longman, 1999) with Gary Slapper, and *Toxic capitalism* (Ashgate, 1998, Canadian Scholars' Press, 1999) with Frank Pearce. He co-edited *State, power, crime* (Sage, 2009), *Beyond criminology?* (Pluto Press, 2004), *Criminal obsessions* (Crime and Society Foundation, 2005, 2008), *Unmasking the crimes of the powerful: Scrutinising states and corporations* (Peter Lang, 2003) and *Risk, management and society* (Kluwer-Nijhoff, 2000). He works closely with the Hazards movement in the UK, and is a trustee and board member of Inquest.

Acknowledgements

This book is a new venture for me – my first attempt at a sole-authored monograph. I have, however, been publishing for over 30 years with a diverse group of co-authors and co-editors. Having joint names on any piece of writing is an honest acknowledgement of the fact that none of us autonomously produces nor can claim sole ownership of our ideas, nor how we translate them into words. This book owes something to all of those with whom I have been lucky to work over the years.

Within and beyond those co-authors, however, are people who deserve special mention. These include colleagues, comrades and dear friends; and I am privileged to be able to say that each of these terms could apply to many of the individuals whose names I list here. As I have had a strict rule during my career of publishing 'by alphabet' only, so I want to acknowledge the contributions to my life and to my work of the following, by the same convention:

Anne Alvesalo-Kuusi, Grietje Baars, Andrea Beckmann, Cad and folk at the Institute for Employment Rights, Gregg Barak, Steven Bittle, Jon Burnett, Bree Carlton, Kit Carson, John Clarke, Roy Coleman, Deb Coles and all those who worked at the CCA , Linda Cooke, Deb Drake, Vicky Canning, Vickie Cooper, the European Group for the Study of Deviance and Social Control, Ross Fergusson, Samantha Fletcher, Richard Garside and all at the Centre for Crime and Justice Studies, Pete Gill, Harry Glasbeek, Penny Green, Lynn Hancock, Paddy Hillyard, Hilda, John, Rory, and all associated with the Hazards movement, Ritchie Hunter, Phil James, Janet Jamieson, Dave Jones, Ron Kramer, Kris Lasslett, Linzi, Dawn and Paul and others all of the other inspirational campaigners of Families Against Corporate Killers, Jo Mack, Ray Michalowski, Gerry Mooney, Simon Pemberton, Paddy Rawlinson, Susanne Soederberg, Laureen Snider, Andre Spicer, Colin Sumner, Colin Toogood and the Bhopal Medical Appeal, Louise Westmarland and Joe Yates.

Frank Pearce, Joe Sim and David Whyte are among my closest friends. It's a privilege to be able to write that sentence. It's been a pleasure and inspiration to have worked alongside them over many years; as teachers, researchers, and as people, I am genuinely in awe of each of them.

My thanks go to all at Policy Press who have worked on and borne with this project – notably, Laura Greaves, Victoria Pittman, Rebecca Tomlinson and Laura Vickers. And to Anne Grundy, and more generally the Leverhulme Trust, for the financial (and other) support which made this possible, via a research fellowship, RF–2011–173.

I dedicate this book to my brother Dave, along with Christine, Matt and Ryan. They know why.

ONE

Introduction:
some starting points

Capitalist Society faces a dilemma, either an advance to
socialism or a reversion to barbarism. (Rosa Luxemburg,
1916, *The Junius Pamphlet*, in Waters, 1970, 269)

Introduction

In August 1914, the German SPD – the 'great shining jewel of the
Second International' (Waters, 1970, 257) – voted in favour of funding
Germany's participation in the great imperialist war of 1914–18. For
Rosa Luxemburg, and other revolutionary socialists, it marked the
end of parliamentary social democracy. For her opposition both to the
war itself and to the SPD for supporting the war, Rosa Luxemburg
was imprisoned. From her cell, she wrote the pamphlet, *The Crisis of
German Social Democracy*, widely known as *The Junius Pamphlet*. Probably
mis-quoting Engels, she marked this watershed as one of a descent
into barbarism or a turn to socialism.

One hundred years later, few in the west are writing of socialism, but
many are facing something akin to barbarism. If the almost 40 years
of neoliberalism have undone much of what Alain Supiot labelled the
'social state', on which more below, the flexibility, tenacity and sheer
power bases of this form of political economy, which discursively
counterposes states and markets, with the avowed aim of setting
the latter free of the former, has come out fighting after what some
thought might have been the sucker punch of the financial crises which
unfolded across the globe from late 2007 onwards.

While 'barbarism' has a multiplicity of meanings within Marx's and
Marxist thought (Bellamy-Foster and Foster, 2004), the barbarism of
the current era is regressive – an attempt by a ruling class to restore
any losses sustained through the peculiar hiatus of post-war social
democracy, which one commentator has called the breaking up of
'capitalism's shotgun marriage with democracy' (Streeck, 2014, 64).
In this, the creation of a new hegemonic common sense about the
extent of possibilities and necessities in the world appears to have
been remarkably successful. One generalised response to the current

international recession – and claims of 'sovereign' indebtedness – has seen governments roll out severe austerity measures: widespread social harm measured in rising rates of un- and under-employment, decreases in the social wage, and increasing levels of poverty and inequality have been accompanied by further anti- and de-regulatory pressures in order to 'free' private capital to produce wealth, employment and tax revenues. As I write, from the UK, the government-established Office for Budget Responsibility has characterised the most recent round of cuts as ones which 'would pose a significant challenge' as they reduced 'spending on public services to its lowest since the 1930s' (Reuben, 2014). Use of the term 'barbarism' in this context is hardly hyperbolic.

The key agents of this barbarism are not nakedly imperialist states, or at least they appear not to be: rather, the visible agents of this assault on the remaining vestiges of social democracy and social protection are private corporations, rapaciously devouring what appeared to be public spaces for the provision of goods and services, in the name of liberalisation, privatisation, deregulation and so on. But if we look more closely, we see the hand of the state, perhaps hidden, but at times exposed, centrally involved in the masquerade of creating laissez-faire. Working feverishly to create and recreate the conditions of their apparent powerlessness and increasing irrelevance, states are key agents in the imposition of an age of corporate barbarism.

The starting point of this book is with what appears to be the contemporary 'paradox' of regulation (Haines, 2011): on the one hand, most developed economies, not least the UK, are undergoing class-targeted hardship as a result of crises which many accept had as at least one cause failures of regulation; on the other hand, regulation in most of these economies is, as I demonstrate in this book with reference to the UK, further undermined – it is too expensive for a shrinking state, and represents burdens upon the only path to economic recovery which is private sector economic activity. In short, as I aim to demonstrate, the 'possibility' of corporate *crime* is negated while corporate *harm* is likely to proliferate, through a series of class-initiatives around regulation and enforcement, through which is emerging a new phase of neoliberalism, one in which states and corporations are once more secure – but also, in their new inter-dependencies, potentially more vulnerable.

The state and social protection

There is no doubt that the state has historically been forced to provide some form of social protection – public service, in the form of regulation – across a whole swathe of areas of social life. These forms of social protection had reached their high point in post–1945 social democracies. At their core was law and regulation. The western social protection state had a longer history, having emerged in the nineteenth century 'with the adoption of a new regime of responsibility for industrial accidents' (Supiot, 2013, 99), compensation for 'the human refuse of the industrial project' (Supiot, 2013, 100). Supiot's specific legislative reference point is a law on industrial accidents adopted in Austria-Hungary in 1887. Of course, the first legislation to intervene in the organisation of production had come in Britain, in 1802, in the form of the Health and Morals of Apprentices Act, designed specifically to regulate the working conditions of 'Poor Law' apprentices in the textile industry. Then, from 1831 onwards, a series of Factories Acts were passed – regulating the hours and conditions of young workers and women, extending across industries and workplaces of different sizes, culminating in the consolidation of existing legislation in the Factory Act of 1878. Although largely concerned with limiting the working day, the debates that framed the emergence of this legislation were dominated by concerns about the horrific rate of injuries and deaths by 'overwork' suffered by factory workers, particularly children.

As Marx observed,

> These laws curb capital's drive towards a limitless draining away of labour power by forcibly limiting the working day on the authority of the state, but a state ruled by capitalist and landlord. Apart from the daily more threatening advance of the working-class movement, the limiting of factory labour was dictated by the same necessity as forced the manuring of English fields with guano. The same blind desire for profit that in the one case exhausted the soil had in the other case seized hold of the vital force of the nation at its roots. (Marx, 1867/1976, 348)

Marx documents the efforts of domestic social reformers and the relationships of these efforts to upheavals in continental Europe, widespread employer opposition to the introduction of factory regulation, and clear conflicts among different groups of employers. He also shows that, in the very attempts to impose minimal conditions for workers, the state played a crucial role in forcing the qualitative leaps in the nature of capital investment and concentration of production that were crucial to the development of the factory system – thus effecting the real rather than the formal subsumption of labour. Yet, 'for all that, capital never becomes reconciled to such changes – and this is admitted over and over again by its own representatives – except "under the pressure of a general Act of Parliament"' (Marx, 1867/1976, 610).

The legal protections for workers enshrined in the Factory Acts originated in the need to resolve a contradiction inherent in capitalism, generated by a relentless demand for greater profit which at the same time threatened to exhaust the capacity for sustaining profits in the long term. As Engels noted of the violent system of nineteenth-century production, 'measures had to be taken by the state to curb the manufacturers' utterly ruthless frenzy for exploitation, which was trampling all the requirements of civilised society underfoot' (Engels, 1850). The Factory Acts can be understood as a form of mediation between social protection and rampant profiteering which threatened the viability of the factory system, and, given the social unrest provoked by workers' resistance and growing campaigns by middle-class social reformers, regulatory intervention was necessary to ensure some measure of legitimacy for a very clearly grossly unequal and violent system of production. In short, regulation was necessary, in Carson's (1980a) words, in order to sustain a 'viable class society'.

During the same period in which the Factory Acts were codified, the wider issue of public health in rapidly industrialising towns and cities also emerged in Britain. Chadwick's government-commissioned report into sanitation – *The Sanitary Conditions of the Labouring Population* – was published in 1842. It directly linked living and working conditions with illness and disease. At the same time, as Pearson has argued, the report

> provides an explicit account of the intimate relationship between the various dimensions of public health, housing, morality, criminality, deviance-control, sexuality, and politics. It is through Chadwick's work that we can penetrate the hidden agenda of the origins of the field of deviance. And…this hidden agenda concerns the creation of a stable working population within the rising domination of a factory system of labour. (Pearson, 1975, 166–7)

Chadwick's report was implemented via the Public Health Act of 1848 – which, in true regulatory tradition, was clearly 'a compromise' (Hamlin and Sheard, 1998, 589–60). In 1847, Dr Duncan had been appointed the first Medical Officer of Health, to Liverpool City Council, a city which was 'created in haste for commerce – by men too intent on immediate gain – reared without any very tender regard for flesh or blood' (cited in Ashton, nd, 49–50). Duncan was soon to form part of the first multidisciplinary public health team, alongside

Fresh, the aptly named Sanitary Inspector, and Newlands, the Borough Engineer (Ashton, nd, 51). More generally, it has been acknowledged that the Act itself was to prove 'a powerful catalyst for the development of local government' (Fee and Brown, 2005, 887), an observation of no little irony, as we shall see in this book (see, especially, Chapter Six).

The second half of the nineteenth century also saw the emergence of the first thoroughgoing attempts to install and enforce environmental protection regulation, through the Alkali Act of 1863 (and, subsequently, of 1874, 1881 and 1892). This system – a combination of local authority and centralised agency oversight of environmental law – was to form the basis of a system of regulation that lasted for some two centuries (Pontin, 2007). While the Alkali Act was 'introduced to tackle the legal and financial consequences of pollution from the heavy chemical, or alkali, industry' (Garwood, 2004, 101), it was hardly antithetical to corporate interests. Thus Pontin has described the emergence of law in terms of 'Peers, Pollution and Prosperity' (Pontin, 2007, 194–6).

'Peers' refers to the role of landowners,[1] dominant within the House of Lords, who had seen their land despoiled by emerging alkali and chemicals production – effects which one commentator has claimed were 'devastating...on the value of land and rural produce', (Garwood, 2004, 101) so that support for regulation has been characterised as 'aristocratic self-interest' (Pontin, 2007, 195). The reference to 'pollution' indicates that regulation was also partly a product of concern with pollution of the natural environment per se, a literal concern to conserve, and this was exploited by 'public pressure emanating from some of the world's earliest (if now forgotten) environmental interest groups' (Pontin, 2007, 192). Finally, as noted below, this emerging environmental regulation hardly dented the industry's prosperity – quite the opposite in fact.

Equally important to making the new laws palatable were the ways in which they were enforced. Typically, the new (initially, three-man) Alkali inspectorate 'utilized cooperation, consensus, and conciliation rather than coercion to enforce the law', (Garwood, 2004, 103), and operated on the basis of a clear 'conviction that the Alkali Act was not to be "implemented as a police act"' (Garwood, 2004, 104). Within this enforcement approach, prosecution was rare, 'a distant threat and last resort', (Garwood, 2004, 104) and indeed 'dependent on the perceived moral culpability of offenders...The concept of moral culpability was so powerful that even gross breaches of legal standards could escape prosecution' (Garwood, 2004, 111).[2] And the new law had the advantage of offering order and stability for alkali manufacturers: prior to the Alakli Act, landowners had turned '*en masse*' to use the common law system for compensation for pollution to their land (Garwood, 2004, 101–2), from which the Alkali Act provided a *de facto* protection (Morag-Levine, 2011, 30).

Moreover, central to this enforcement approach was the *advisory* role of the Inspectorate. As, in MacLeod's words, 'peripatetic consultants to industry' (MacLeod, 1965, 93), inspectors quickly became 'the manufacturers' best ally; almost unconsciously, the State was providing a service to industry which would ultimately reverse the relative economic importance of hydrochloric acid waste and alkali product' (MacLeod, 1965, 93). Thus there were several benefits of the new Act(s) for manufacturers. Overall, inspectors and manufacturers negotiated a series of compromises which balanced environmental and economic interests (Garwood, 2004, 113), while favouring protection of the latter over the former (Garwood, 2004, 117), the net result being 'the lowest possible level of regulatory interference with chemical manufacture and profit, while providing for a certain amount of pollution control' (Garwood, 2004, 116).

As well as (potentially) generating a level playing field, 'where, up until then, plants that had condensed their gases were potentially disadvantaged relative to competitors that did not' (Morag-Levine, 2011, 30), regulation offered other benefits to industry. Britain's dominant position in the international chemicals' processing industry meant that manufacturers had room to manoeuvre in terms of internalising any costs that may have been generated by regulation (Pontin, 2007, 196), regulation which at the same time spurred technological innovation – for example, 'new chimney designs, which in turn stimulated further innovations in works design' (Macleod, 1965, 93) – and thus an impetus for greater efficiency and prosperity. In short,

> Industrialist and landed aristocrat classes alike were each major beneficiaries of the mid-to-late Victorian era's unequally distributed economic prosperity. Peers' belief in the scope for robust environmental protection without compromising economic growth could draw support from the existence of vast markets, around a growing empire, creating demand for chemical and other raw materials and goods from Britain's prolific workshop. (Pontin, 2007, 196)

The later decades of the nineteenth century also saw the emergence of a system of food regulation in the UK (French and Phillips, 2000). In perhaps the most celebrated text on this movement for pure food, drugs and drink, Paulus notes how this essentially middle class social movement was 'part of the overall public health movement of the 19th century' (Paulus, 1974, 22). This movement culminated in the 1875 Sale of Food and Drugs Act, enforced through the Local Government Board, 'that was to form the basis of food law in the United Kingdom until 1955' (Paulus, 1974, 1). Although in some way a response to a series of food adulteration scandals, the emergence of this piece of legislation and other regulation was certainly no 'natural' response to any unfolding crisis; rather, state intervention and regulation was an arena of social conflict between 'individuals, interest groups and governmental departments' (Paulus, 1974, 2) pursuing contradictory interests and objectives. Indeed, 'conflict dominated the enactment and the enforcement of the law' (Paulus, 1974, 89) – and in many areas it was 'simply not enforced' (Paulus, 1974, 96). Such were the problems of under-enforcement which typified the 1875 law in practice (French and Phillips, 2000, 47) – alongside low levels of fines and the pro-business attitudes of magistrates (Atkins, 1991) – that these generated concerns about unequal enforcement (French and Phillips, 2000, 45), with some business interests arguing for *greater* enforcement (French and Phillips, 2000, 46).

Within these conflictual processes, some business interests supported certain forms of regulation, engaging in alliances on specific issues with social reformers, not least reflecting the diversity of the food sector, a series of businesses involving farmers and producers, retailers, distributors, both large and small economic concerns, as well as the concerns of domestic companies in the face of foreign imports (French and Phillips, 2000). Accum's (1820) *A Treatise on the Adulterations of Food and Culinary Poisons* had, over 50 years prior to the Act, identified 'unprincipled modern manufacturers', hiding under the guise of respectability, but endangering lives through an 'eager and insatiable thirst for gain' (cited in Wilson, 2009, 29). There is no need to enter into detail here, suffice to make the point that regulation was an arena of conflict, with the shape of regulation which emerged from this an effect of power rather than a benign impulse towards better social or consumer protection, not least because of the obdurate dominance of 'the free trade mentality' (Atkins, 1991, 318).

Crucially with respect to food laws, as we find more generally across the implementation of social protection legislation during this period, it was the shift from its organisation around *mens rea* to a standard of strict liability which secured its institutionalisation (Atkins, 1991). This institutionalisation of strict liability – a process of 'accommodation' and 'expediency' (Paulus, 1974, 102–3) – meant that this and other laws 'became a barrier to criminalisation rather than a facilitator of it'

(Paulus, 1974, 99). Thus what appeared to be legislative benefits for the consumer were 'secondary in the struggle to achieve workable laws' (Paulus, 1974, 103), and the operation of the 1875 law with strict liability 'minimised the risks for *all* parties' (Paulus, 1974, emphasis in original). Thus, 'the legal innovation of strict liability in the mid-nineteenth century created a possibility to protect the public at large from many harms without stigmatising and/or criminalising offenders in the process' (Paulus, 1974, 135).

In summary, this was a key period in the emergence of key pillars of social protection, at least in the context of public health. There are several commonalities in these briefest of overviews of the emergence of regulation that are worth noting since their significances remain. First, as new forms of regulating capital emerged, business offences were separated off as something other than 'crime'. This was partly achieved through the introduction of a different category of culpability, and therefore a secondary class of 'strict liability' offence allowed the crimes of the business-owning class to become conventionalised and understood as something other than 'real' crime (Carson, 1980b). Second, this distinction was achieved through the establishment of a regulatory agency with a very particular attitude towards the regulated, where compromise, negotiation, bargaining were the order of the day, rather than strict enforcement of law – so that formal enforcement, let alone prosecution, was rare. Through these achievements, corporate crime became re-defined into a separate 'regulatory' domain.

Two other characteristics of the regulatory process are worth noting here. First, that in the cases of law and regulation considered here, there was no homogenous business opposition – indeed, as there may have been inter-class struggles over the attempts to develop and reform regulation, so there were intra-class struggles too. Further, and as important, is the fact that in the areas under consideration, the new regulatory regimes proved to be beneficial, albeit in various ways, for capital as a whole, that is, for the development of specific sectors or industries, even as individual business owners and indeed intra-class interests opposed legal reform. Herein are important lessons about how we should understand 'regulation'.

These indications of the emergence of apparently socially protective regimes of regulation are enough to indicate that it is not enough to think of them simply as forms of social protection. For Supiot, the establishment of protective labour law and regulation, social security and social services, was accompanied by a more general challenge to the conception of the state. Instead of being simply charged with the government of men, embodying a power that rules them, the state made itself the servant of their well-being, assuming the face of what in various contexts has been called the Welfare State, État providence, Sozialstaat or République sociale – formulations inscribed within the generic notion of the social state. (Supiot, 2013, 104)

It may be that the idea of social protection is a challenge to the state; but it is also the state's *response* to such a challenge. In some respects, then, and while it points to functions around which some states have, at historically-specific periods, organised and through which they have sought both legitimacy and order-maintenance, the term 'social protection' state is in many respects a wholly ideological term.

However pluralistic, de-centred, increasingly impotent, or, indeed, progressive, social democratic and protective the state appears to be, it is also crucial of course to recognise, at least from a Marxist viewpoint, that the state is always a class state, is always about class power, and is always about violence, at least in the last resort. Always at the centre of state interventions is violence – or, at a minimum, the threat of violence. Therefore, state violence is always implied or connected to the so-called 'soft' forms of power or even social protection. In general, then, as I have argued with colleagues elsewhere (Coleman et al, 2009), to distinguish between force and consent, violent and non-violent means of securing power, then, is to set up a false dualism:

> because this domination has been secured by consent – on the basis of a wide consensus, as the saying goes – that domination not only seems to be universal…and legitimate (not won by coercive force), but its basis in exploitation actually *disappears from view*. Consensus is not the opposite – it is the complementary face of domination. (Hall et al, 1978, 216)

In short, the one principle that the modern state is organised around is its ability to resort to violence. The laws that establish state sovereignty create this as an entity with unrivalled power. Not only are the boundaries of the legitimacy of violence established by law (Green and Ward, 2009), but the power and authority of the state – indeed law itself – is necessarily and intimately bound to violence: 'Lawmaking is powermaking and to that extent, an immediate manifestation of violence' (Benjamin, 1921/1978, 295).

Thus a specific state may at times mitigate or redistribute the level of harms, (Pemberton, 2015) not least those which emanate from corporations – and are borne by workers, consumers, 'the public' and the natural environment – but it is never the solution to the production of those harms. We must avoid a highly ideological reading of the phrase 'social protection' which sees in this the effective triumphing of 'public' interests, represented in and through the state, over those of private capital. But the idea of social protection has potency. On this point, Walklate's (2009) re-versioning of Tilly's (1985) argument that the state is a protection racket whose legitimacy is sustained by its ability to *coerce* order as well as having access to the means of *maintaining* order, is a useful one. Famously, Tilly had noted, in the context of his historical analysis of state formation, that war making and in particular 'state-making' was analogous to a 'protection racket'. 'Which image the word "protection" brings to mind depends mainly on our assessment of the reality and externality of the threat', he wrote. 'Someone who produces both the danger and, at a price, the shield against it is a racketeer' (Tilly, 1985, 171). Walklate thus focuses on the promise of the state to provide 'a public good of protection', and argues that, through constructions of victimhood in particular, this is central to 'the continued maintenance of the (capitalist) hegemonic state'. 'This,' she claims, 'is the state's protection racket!' (Walklate, 2009, 184).

This means, then, that there is no simple understanding of how to view, and what to do, about the state in order to begin to think about the mitigation of corporate crime and harm. We must recognise the 'dualistic' role of the state, as 'simultaneously repressive and protective' (Steve Hall, 2012: 114). In political terms, this means states must be challenged on their own terms of social protection, while also recognising that the state can never be the solution to corporate crime and harm and that it retains essentially repressive, and often more or less violent, inherent characteristics. Demands for more or new forms of regulation may not be transformative (Garside, 2013), but nor are they an irrelevance.

Neoliberalism and *re*-regulation

The central focus of this book is regulation, while a key reference point is 'neoliberalism'. On the relationship between neoliberalism and regulation there is much misunderstanding, much of which is generated by taking claims of neoliberalism on regulation in particular and the role of the state in general at face-value. In this section, I seek to pre-empt some of this misunderstanding, first by some observations on the deployment of 'neoliberalism' here, then through an extended discussion of regulation, deregulation and re-regulation in neoliberal politics.

Since the term 'neoliberalism' is used so widely – and indeed loosely – it seems worth briefly clarifying what is denoted by this term here. Specifically, I refer to a system of political economy which has emerged to dominance across much of the western world, imposed by states from the late 1970s onwards. In other words, the use of the term in this book is distinct from its dominant usage within criminology, which is, following David Brown, 'as governmentality'.

> Assisted perhaps by the standing of its Foucauldian heritage, governmentality has been assimilated into criminological debate, especially in the areas of crime prevention, underpinning established concepts such as 'responsibilisation', 'governance at a distance' and the 'government of populations'; loss spreading and actuarialism; the rise of statistics; and the rise and rise of risk technologies. (Brown, 2011, 130)

The term as used here does encompass the other forms of 'neoliberalism as practice' highlighted by Brown, so that it is at once 'an ideological hegemonic project', 'policy and programme' and as a 'state form' (Brown, 2011, 130).

In this book, neoliberalism is understood via the form of political economy inspired by neo-Chicagoan economics (Pearce and Tombs, 1998), developed through most of the twentieth century (Peck, 2012), and variously translated by different national governments into a diverse range of economic and political management practices. But as I argue here neoliberalism is not merely about the economic and the political: it has significant ideological, cultural and moral elements which in fact prove central to the analysis in the following chapters. In this sense, 'neoliberalism' is deployed to refer to a series of characteristics set out usefully by Colin Hay, upon reading of which it is important to bear in mind both the actual and rhetorical commitments therein:

1. a confidence in the market as an efficient mechanism for the allocation of scarce resources;
2. a belief in the desirability of a global regime of free trade and free capital mobility;

3. a belief in the desirability, all things being equal, of a limited and noninterventionist role for the state and of the state as a facilitator and custodian rather than a substitute for market mechanisms;

4. a rejection of Keynesian demand-management techniques in favour of monetarism, neo-monetarism and supply-side economics;

5. a commitment to the removal of those welfare benefits which might be seen to act as disincentives to market participation (in short, a subordination of the principles of social justice to those of perceived economic imperatives);

6. a defence of labour-market flexibility and the promotion and nurturing of cost competitiveness;

7. a confidence in the use of private finance in public projects and, more generally, in the allocative efficiency of market and quasi-market mechanisms in the provision of public goods. (Hay, 2004, 57–8)

To be clear, there is no attempt to impose a coherence upon neoliberalism, nor a homogeneity of the forms it takes, nor to assert any claim that these above commitments can in fact be translated into practice. The durability and resilience of neoliberal argument and practice is partly an effect of the fact that not just that an ideal-typical neoliberalism has not been achieved but that it is un-achievable. This is more than a recognition of the fact that there are significant varieties of existing neoliberalism (Brenner and Theodore, 2002). Thus, Schmidt and Thatcher highlight five characteristics which have combined to protect the ideological dominance of neoliberalism in general – and, indeed, its commitment to 'reducing regulation' in particular – namely: its diversity and adaptability; the gap between rhetoric and reality, which always creates a space for the promise of 'real' neoliberalism to be fulfilled; the relative absence or weaknesses of alternative ways of seeing the world; the powerful interests which are served by the prevalence of such ideas; and the institutional embeddedness of these ideas over the course almost 40 years, both at national levels and also through supranational institutions such as the European Union (Schmidt and Thatcher, 2013b; see also Cahill, 2014). If neoliberalism is more about dreams than realities (Pearce and Tombs, 1998, 3–33), actually exists in a variety of ways (Jessop, 2013), and is indeed characterised by 'tensions' and 'fault-lines' (Jessop, 2014), not least in relation to the role of the state (Davies, 2014; Peck, 2012), then these are simultaneously points of weakness *and* strength.

In short, and as I shall demonstrate at length in the following chapters, neoliberalism is not equated with any actually existing free market, nor with state withdrawal, nor with a necessary diminution in state power which in a zero-sum sense accrues to national or multinational capital. These are rhetorical claims made within neoliberalism which could not be nor have never been actualised. These are also key to understanding what otherwise might appear to be its 'strange non-death' in the wake of events which unfolded across much of the capitalist world from 2007 onwards (Crouch, 2011).

Prior to that recent financial then economic crisis, that is, in the UK, 30 years on from the first Thatcher government beginning a sustained experiment in neoliberalism, the political – and some might argue academic (see Chapter Four) – consensus was that the era of state management of national economies had clearly passed; so too had the moral collectivism upon which it was founded, replaced by a trenchant ethos of individualism. According to a Randian logic, healthy societies are a product of the competitive self-reliance of men, women and their families. For neoliberal ideologues, the claim is that a shift away from state 'interference' towards greater human spontaneity and creativity represents the triumph of capitalist expansion and efficiency over the inefficiency of both mixed economies and 'totalitarian' regimes committed to centrally planned economies.

For many, neoliberalism was equated with deregulation, so that its effective victory entailed the passing of the reality and the idea of state regulation. On such a reading, the contraction of the state is central to the restoration of neoliberal economics; private capital is granted free rein to operate with little or no interference from the state and its regulatory bodies. However, despite a dominant political and academic consensus surrounding this idea of regulation-as-obstacle, the development of neoliberalism should not be understood simply as a story of deregulation, notwithstanding many of the claims of its advocates, even where this appears most starkly (Booth, 2015; Tombs and Whyte, 2015, 24–5). More generally, the essential role of the state is an inbuilt tension, even contradiction, within neoliberalism, intellectually, economically and politically (Peck, 2012), to the extent that it is a key point of vulnerability for neoliberal ideology and practice. Any simplistic accounts based on a 'state-market' dichotomy – an antagonistic, zero-sum relationship – obscure the fact that neoliberal states work, and must continue to work, intensely to construct 'free' corporations in 'free' markets.[3]

First, simplistic understandings of deregulation are predicated upon a common view of state–corporate relationships characterised as an autonomous (state) agency intervening (or not) against an autonomous (capitalist) organisation. Each then posits a view of the relationship between the state and corporations or 'business' as one of *opposition* and *externality* – that is, the state stands as an institution or ensemble of institutions which is ontologically separate and distinct from civil society. The major distortion which this generates is that regulatory agencies are viewed in one-dimensional terms, itself rooted in the limited understanding of the state characterised by Gramsci as the 'state as policeman' (see Coleman et al, 2009). Gramsci used the term to suggest that we could only ever have a selective, uni-dimensional view of the state if we limited our understanding to the negative, repressive, law-centred role of the state, that is, to 'a State whose functions are limited to the safeguarding of public order and of respect for the laws', and which stands outside of civil society (Gramsci, 1971 [1996], 261). If the state is always and only the negative enforcer, then the relationship between state institutions and corporations is always going to be antagonistic – one facing the other in a battle of opposing wills, one seeking to secure compliance with the law as the other seeks to avoid this, and so on.

Further, this general approach obscures the fact that the state is a *capitalist* state, one that is necessarily if complexly committed to prioritising the practices and values of profit accumulation above 'social' values. The significance of viewing regulation in this context, and thus in the context of relationships between states and capitals, is already clear in Marx's rich discussion of the struggle over the passage of the Factory Acts in Britain from 1832 onwards, in the first volume of *Capital*. Therein, he documents how an *apparently* disciplinary state imposing upon factory owners legal protections *for* workers in the name of social reform was pivotal in the transition to factory production, the shift from the extraction of absolute to relative surplus value, and the real rather than the formal subsumption of labour (Marx, 1867/1976). Thus Marx's analysis of the Factory Acts provides subtle insight into the fragmented and often contradictory way that regulation develops, and of the fissures within as well as between 'state' and 'capital'.

Mahon (1977; 1979), for example, drawing upon the work of Poulantzas, and his most basic insight upon the state – namely that it regulates contradictory class practices to maintain or restore systemic equilibrium – has argued that regulatory agencies should be understood as 'unequal structures of representation' that absorb and dissipate conflicts between opposing interests that are created 'in order to neutralise any threat to hegemony that cannot easily be contained by the normal functioning of the political and administrative apparatuses of the state' (Mahon, 1979, 160). Such agencies, then, are sites where intra- and inter-class struggle, engaged in through a plethora of actors including, but not limited to, representatives of various branches of government, political parties, trade associations, lobbying organisations, various NGOs, trades unions and other more or less organised social movements, is mediated. Moreover, as a site and result of struggle, the nature and level of regulation is never once-and-for-all settled, always more or less precarious.

Thus regulatory agencies emerge as a compromise borne out of social conflict, so that the nature of the regulatory body and its formal mission reflect the balances of forces between *and within* states, capital and populations (Snider, 1991). Regulatory agencies are not, then, simply (actual or potential) 'policemen' – that is, their relation to capital is not merely one of opposition and externality – but in fact play a much more general role in reproducing the social conditions necessary to sustain a capitalist social order. The visible aspects of regulatory agencies – how they persuade corporations to comply with the law, the extent to and ways in which they investigate, enforce, prosecute and so on – are, too, to be seen in the light of this ongoing process. On this basis, one can see what it means to say that corporations exist with some degree of autonomy from states, but also that this autonomy can never be complete, since the state – through regulation – plays a crucial role in reproducing the social conditions necessary for them to survive and thrive. Corporations always exist simultaneously 'inside' and 'outside' of state rules and institutions.

This analysis therefore warns us against adopting an over-simplified idea, inherent within neoliberal and pluralist literature, of the roll-back/roll-out of the state (Coleman et al, 2009). The power of capital depends not upon the rolling back of the state, or diminution of state power, but also on the successful mediation and dissipation of particularly contentious issues, or issues that threaten a stable social order. In this sense we can see very clearly how states intervene in ways that are essential to the long-term interests of capital.

In this context, we should bear in mind a rather important obviousness – namely that the corporation is a creation of the nation-state, and is maintained through an awful lot of state activity. Corporations are institutions that are created for the mobilisation, utilisation and protection of capital within recent socio-historical state formations. As such, they are wholly artificial entities whose very existence is provided for, and maintained, through the state via legal institutions and instruments, which in turn are based upon material and ideological supports. As one recent history of the world's first multinational has succinctly put it, the East India Company was the product of a contractual 'bargain with the state', albeit that this early corporate form 'was on constant life support, repeatedly having to justify its existence to the state' (Robins, 2006, 27). Certainly it is the case that maintaining the conditions of existence of contemporary corporations, even, or perhaps especially, in 'free' markets, requires an enormous amount of state activity. The corporate form and the state are thus inextricably linked to the extent that, in contemporary capitalism, each is a condition of existence of the other (Tombs and Whyte, 2015).

Now, in one sense, states have always existed in a relationship of dependence with capital – for some, this is what makes the capitalist state capitalist. Certainly nation-states have been and remain engaged in a constant 'competitive process of attraction-and-immobilization' (Holloway, 1994, 38) of capital – and, what is as important, one element of this is to provide the most 'favorable conditions for the reproduction of capital within [their] boundaries' (Holloway, 1994, 34–5). More generally, of course, in any capitalist state, private corporations are key sources of providing goods, services, taxation and employment – all of which conditions are necessary, politically, economically and socially, for states. But the forms of such dependence are dynamic and historically specific – constituted in different ways, at different times, with differing intensities and thus having different impacts. As we shall see below, then, these aspects of dependence and inter-dependence have recently been subject to intense re-configuratory pressures as the post-crisis settlement is forged.

Post-1979, as neoliberal ideas became powerful to the point of virtually uncontested dominance, they also helped to produce that which they sought to describe and prescribe, notably in terms of increasing popular dependence upon the private sector. For as new markets were created by states for private capital through privatisation and deregulation, as states formally withdrew from providing a host of goods and services, many people really were made more dependent upon the private sector to provide basic goods and services: increasingly private sector organisations *must* provide goods and services which states have withdrawn from providing – and, having withdrawn from such provision, are less and less able to reassume such a role.

While the period from the mid-1970s to the present witnessed the emergence to international dominance of 'neoliberalism', then this became closely allied to and conflated with 'globalisation', the necessary consequence of the national successes and inherent dynamism of neoliberalism. If, as politicians of all stripes have proclaimed, there was no alternative to the rise of free market capitalism, its internationalisation – 'globalisation' – also increasingly became cast as some form of naturally unfolding reality; a force of nature which gave governments no choice but to embrace policies of deregulation, low taxation and declining expenditures as the price of nation-state integration into this 'global economy'; and in so doing they increasingly relinquished control over domestic policy agendas (Leys, 2001, 8–37). By adopting such a fatalistic stance, and swallowing so easily the idea that the rise of market forces could not be opposed, governments reinterpreted what had previously been the wishful thinking of large corporate interests as the national interest. Neoliberal fatalism on the part of governments became a self-fulfilling prophecy (Tombs, 2007). Thus, the *idea* of deregulation, itself claimed as economically determined by the seemingly naturally unfolding of neoliberalism-as-globalisation, strengthened during this period (Bourdieu and Wacquant, 2001).

In the UK, this period also saw the Labour Party, in political opposition, 'modernise' itself, so that, through the 1990s and in office from 1997 onwards, this dominant understanding of globalisation had been 'internalised by New Labour' (Hay and Watson, 1998, 815). This was confirmed by the first Blair administration's pledge to 'accept globalization and work with it' (cited in Holden, 1999, 531). It was New Labour's fatalistic self-resignation to neoliberalism which partly helps to explain why Blair's governments refused to undo – and in fact consolidated – privatisation initiatives.

This was a logical destination of what had been a long journey. For New Labour had entered office having remodelled itself with a point to prove – that it was not the party of the 1970s; those who championed the modernising project explained the party's 20 years in opposition by reference to a disastrous relationship with trades unions which unravelled during the so-called Winter of Discontent. We should recall that, seeking to prove its fiscal 'responsibility', the party in opposition had pledged itself to stick to the Conservatives' targets on inflation and public spending for the first three years of government administration (Wood, 2010, 12). Significantly, virtually the first act of the newly elected government in 1997, even before the strains of 'Things can only get better...' had faded, was to hand over monetary policy, and in particular the setting of interest rates, to a non-elected Monetary Policy Committee, symbolically and formally relinquishing a key lever over the British economy.

When Blair launched New Labour's manifesto for business in the run-up to the 2001 election before 100 corporate leaders in London, he committed Labour to developing, in its second term, a 'deeper and intensified relationship' with business (Blair, 2001, cited in Osler, 2002, 212). Commenting upon Blair's pledges, Osler notes that, 'Policies on offer that day included deregulation' (Osler, 2002,12). Thus, as

Farnsworth notes, under New Labour the voice of business grew ever stronger:

> So successful was this strategy that the outgoing president of the CBI, Clive Thompson, explained to the Financial Times that the working relationship between the CBI and the Labour government was, in 2000, 'probably closer than at any time in the last 25 years' and certainly closer than under the Thatcher or Major governments. (Farnsworth, 2006a, 89; see also Lambie, 2013)

It was no coincidence, then, that the second Labour government embarked upon a concerted material and ideological assault on regulation (see Chapter Five). Moreover, the Labour government did, of course, institute a series of major 'reforms' to the public sector – much of the welfare state (Farnsworth, 2006b) and, indeed, the voluntary sector (Eikenberry and Kluver, 2004), were subject to marketisation, not least with the rhetorical justification that, familiarly, there was 'no alternative'. These stopped short of further full-scale privatisation (Parker, 2004), but were generally couched in terms of greater 'choice' and 'efficiency', as the interweaving of state and private capital continued at pace (Farnsworth, 2006a; Farnsworth and Holden, 2006). Materially, they tended to take the form of a complex set of arrangements, generally by way of opaque contractual relationships, with the common aim of attracting private capital into areas of state or public activity previously untouched by privatisation or contracting-out. These relationships take various forms, such as, states' (local, regional, national) effective role as joint partners with the private and third sectors in various forms of economic activity, as out-sourcers and contractors of economic activity, and as key purchasers of corporate goods and services. They generally proceed through contracts, new regulatory regimes, regulatory reform, or a combination of each. In short, within neoliberal UK, the state has entered into a plethora of formal, intimate relationships with the corporate sector which have increased popular dependence *on* that sector. 'Marketisation' was 'the cutting-edge of New Labour's neoliberal project' (Stuart Hall, 2012, 18) – of which more in Chapter Two.

One consequence is that it is now virtually impossible to think of any area of any 'publicly' provided good or service in which private capital is not significantly represented (see Boffey, 2012a; 2012b). Moreover, all of these new markets are accompanied by the creation and re-creation of immensely complex[4] regulatory regimes. Thus, over a period of 35 years in the UK, deregulation, privatisation and a variety of new forms of state–capital interdependence has increasingly seen government shift from service provider to the chief architect in the construction, then regulation, of markets. We can also see in the emergence of the 'regulatory state' the resolution to an *apparent* paradox – a government committed to privately owned, 'free' enterprise which has created a complex web of (re)regulation.

Thus if the emergence of neoliberalism in the UK apparently marked a period of state retreat, it is important to recognise the promotion of anti-statism (Coleman et al, 2009) as a hegemonic process. Thus any simplistic dichotomy between an interventionist state on the one hand and a laissez-faire one on the other is ultimately unhelpful when analysing corporate crime, harm and regulation. A key point for us is not that the state *is* anti-statist, but that it represents itself as such (Hall, 1988, 152). Thus we have to differentiate between state retreat as a real outcome of neoliberalism and anti-statism as a hegemonic device (Hall, 1988). In this context, it is clear that the period of the past 35 years or so is not accurately characterised simply as an era of *deregulation*. Rather than acting to control or restrict markets, there emerged in this period regulatory forms that *promoted* market activity. Thus, the 'freeing' of markets in the privatisations of energy, water, telecommunications and, most tortuously, in rail, was accompanied by a mass of regulatory institutions designed to establish and maintain what were effectively new markets (Prosser, 1997). In short, neoliberalism has not sought or achieved 'a shrinking of the state, but a re-imagining and transformation of it' (Davies, 2014, 5):

> Victorian laissez-faire was only one empirical manifestation of the liberal *idea*. Restoring economic freedom would not be achieved simply through withdrawing the state from 'the market', but through active policy interventions, to remould institutions, state agencies and individuals, in ways that were compatible with a market ethos (however defined) and were amenable to economic measurement. The state is therefore a powerful instrument of neoliberalism, though also an object of its constant critique. (Davies, 2014, 5–6)

Hegemony

The above discussion indicates that neoliberalism is, as much as anything, a hegemonic project. Now, perhaps even more so than the phrase 'neoliberalism', the word hegemony is so over-used that it seems to have lost all relationship to its Gramscian origins, so that, even for many academics, it is used synonymously to refer to a dominant set of *ideas*. In this, it is shorn of its material and class-based nature. For Gramsci, there were several key elements to the construction and maintenance of hegemony. Securing hegemony requires the formation of a historic bloc – in and through the state – and members of a historical bloc seek to assert a general common sense which gains dominance in, over and through mainstream social institutions. Such common sense is always 'an ambiguous, contradictory and multiform concept' (Gramsci, 1971 [1996], 423); such fissures provide spaces of leverage for developing counter-hegemonic knowledge. This actual or potential contestation means that hegemony is always secured and maintained through a changing combination of material power and moral and intellectual leadership – Gramsci's well-known combination of coercion and consent – and this in turn requires the constant attempt to fragment counter-hegemonic groupings, whether this means that they are derided, de-legitimated, disrupted, disempowered, surveilled, controlled and so on.

In these struggles, there are roles to be played by intellectuals, including academics. Gramsci (1971 [1996], 3–23) distinguishes between two types of intellectuals: organic and traditional. Organic intellectuals are those intellectuals who emerge to give the dominant hegemonic group 'homogeneity and an awareness of its own function' (Gramsci, 1971 [1996], 5) in the economic, social and political spheres. Traditional intellectuals refer to those intellectuals who, despite the emergence of a new hegemonic order, retain their social position as intellectuals.

For traditional intellectuals, their apparent disconnection from the dominant social group, or from other economic groups – added to the apparent historical continuity that they retain – is proof positive of their political neutrality and ability to produce value-free intellectual work. Denying their role in the class wars of position and manoeuvre, traditional intellectuals are idealised as organically linked to the institutional context within which they work: 'these various categories of traditional intellectuals experience through an "*esprit de corps*" their uninterrupted historical continuity and their special qualification, they thus put themselves forward as autonomous and independent of the dominant social group' (Gramsci, 1971 [1996], 7). Thus, 'the intellectuals think of themselves as "independent", autonomous, endowed with a character of their own, etc' (Gramsci, 1971 [1996], 8).

In the case of universities, the institutional context that ensures historical continuity is the 'academy'. For many university teachers and researchers, the 'academy' – the institutional discipline of academic study – represents a higher loyalty that keeps them above the fray of class struggle. Thus, organic intellectuals may not recognise their role as partisan if it is not immediately tied to an economic group. However, for Gramsci, the idea of political neutrality is based upon a fetishised account of the state and of the sphere of politics:

> since the State is the concrete form of a productive world and since the intellectuals are the social element from which the governing personnel is drawn, the intellectual who is not firmly anchored to a strong economic group will tend to present the State as an absolute; in this way the function of the intellectuals is itself conceived of as absolute and pre-eminent, and their historical existence and dignity are abstractly rationalised. (Gramsci, 1971 [1996], 117)

In this sense, organic intellectuals – acting out their scientific and technical roles, defining truth, setting out the ways in which we are supposed to understand the world and so on – are imagined as possessing an intellectual credibility that rises above the class divisions endemic to capitalist social orders.

The separation of organic and traditional intellectuals is, for Gramsci, a formal one, and in reality, these boundaries are blurred. Indeed, in the context of universities, what academics actually do in many cases is act out simultaneously the roles of organic and traditional intellectuals. University-based researchers may conduct governmental, policy or industry-useful research that can be deployed as part of the hegemonic political project, *and* at the same time may use this research as the basis of their general contribution to the academy, to academic bodies of knowledge and so on. Thus, rather than seeking a crude distinction or dichotomy between categories or types of intellectuals, Gramsci suggests that it is possible to measure the 'organic quality' (Gramsci, 1971 [1996], 12) of groups of intellectuals and their connectedness with the dominant (or, indeed other) economic group(s).

Moreover, as Poulantzas reminds us, the separation between the public and private realm (and indeed state and civil society) is purely a juridical one, a distinction established by law (Poulantzas, 1970, 305). Thus, although some institutions are idealised as private, as part of civil society, they are more accurately viewed as simply part of the state ideological apparatuses. They may only be regarded as 'private' in that they enjoy some measure of relative autonomy from the state. Universities are in this category, and are only distinguished from the formal structures of the state because of a relative autonomy that is largely derived from their assumed status as traditional (as opposed to organic) institutions.

In short, the romantic ideal of the 'ivory tower' has always been a highly fetishised one, a point Gramsci was at pains to stress. For him, the 'concept of free-floating intellectuals, whose roles and functions appeared to have little directly to do with the productive sphere, state policy or political activity, was a myth' (Showstack-Sassoon, 2000, 18). The idea of research conducted within the context of universities as neutral, value free and divorced from the partisan imperatives of economic forces is itself intellectual nonsense, particularly since the period of the emergence of capitalism (Showstack-Sassoon, 2000). Rejecting such preconceptions brings into sharp focus the claims of researchers in academic institutions to neutrality and objectivity. Such claims are no more powerful to the extent that they are in fact vehemently believed by these researchers. Such researchers, whether wittingly or not, create an intellectual, legitimising terminology that explains away the structural inequalities of capitalism and state efforts to retain a mask of neutrality. They may also work for neoliberalism in meeting its demands for 'new breeds of expert – coach, regulator, risk manager, strategist, guru – offering toolkits and advice on how to navigate and act upon a constantly changing and unpredictable environment' (Davies, 2014, 29). Thus, as we see in Chapter Four in particular, much work on regulation is hegemonic: it operates within a terrain upon which neither capitalism nor the corporation are subject to any critical scrutiny; what is at issue are a series of techniques for better mitigating some of the more deleterious effects of the corporation within contemporary capitalism. As we shall see, this work operates within the confines of a liberal pluralism which is not just devoid of any challenge to corporate and state power, but which is actually useful for the maintenance and extension of such power. Here, then, we see a specific instance of Gramsci's general claims that, first, universities play a key role in the mystification of the capitalist social order, and that universities, and academics within them, can do this only by retaining their own mask of neutrality.

On harm and crime

The idea, and at times the practice, of regulation involves the mitigation of some level of harm. In this section, focusing on the UK, I provide some indications of the scale of corporate harms which the regulatory functions of consumer, environmental, and worker protection claim to seek to mitigate. Thus I set out some broad empirical indicators of the scale of corporate food poisoning, corporate killing at work, and corporate air pollution. Such indications stand as a general context for the considerations of this book, but they are not the focus of this book per se. They are set out to make clear that those phenomena which are the subject of regulation – which *is* the focus of this book – are not mere technical violations, by-products of certain economic activities, aberrant accidents or incidents which are relatively isolated. Rather, they are ubiquitous, routine harms, which kill, injure and generate significant levels of ill-health.

It is also important, however, to be clear that producing any such estimates is fraught with difficulty, and certainly data which categorises these as crimes is generally absent or virtually worthless. Since the majority of corporate illegality never gets processed as illegality, subject to a whole range of filters which consistently remove corporate 'offences' from anything approximating 'crime' data (Tombs and Whyte, 2008), we are left with the task of identifying proxies for the scale of corporate offending. This generally entails at least two processes, albeit to different degrees. First, arguing that harms which appear to emanate from the corporate sector might under certain circumstances in fact be violations of law, even in the absence of any process which has formally defined them as such – that is, in Sutherland's terms, that they are punish*able* even if not punish*ed*. The second process is demonstrating that such harms do in fact have *corporate* origins. In the context of both corporate killing and injuring at work, the former process is the greater problem; with corporate food poisoning and corporate air pollution, the latter is the greater issue. Neither of these problems can be overcome definitively. We must inevitably remain in the realms of estimation. And of course in contexts where the message of corporate crime is likely to fall on deaf ears, certainly lost in the unceasing racket about the 'real' crime problem, then that need to estimate always places commentaries on the scale of corporate crime at clear methodological *and political* disadvantages.

These points being made, that is, notwithstanding all of the uncertainties and qualifications regarding much of the evidence presented in this section, my basic point is that *when taken together* it serves to highlight the scale, relative invisibility, and routine production of harms from a variety of corporate activities.

The full scale of food poisoning-related deaths remains unknown, partly because of the poverty of official data, but also because of the complex way in which food infection affects human health. Food poisoning cases are known to have lasting and complex effects on health. For example, it has been estimated that salmonella and campylobacter triple the average person's chances of dying from any other disease or condition within a year (Helms et al, 2003).

What is most commonly referred to as 'food poisoning' is a major source of death and illness in the UK. According to the most recent report from the Chief Scientist, 'Our best estimate suggests that there are around a million cases of foodborne illness in the UK each year, resulting in 20,000 hospital admissions and 500 deaths' (FSA, 2012, 11); clearly a significant 'public health impact', this is estimated to cost the UK about £1.9 billion (FSA, 2012, 7). Even these estimates of food related illness are likely to understate the scale of the problem (FSA, nd; see Tam et al, 2011). While this overall data does not distinguish foodborne from person-to-person infections, the study was able to conclude that in the case of the incidence of campylobacter – which had reached 500,000 cases annually by the year 2008–09 (according to FSA commissioned research, cited in Advisory Committee on the Microbiological Safety of Food, 2012, 18) – 'the majority…was likely to be foodborne' (Advisory Committee on the Microbiological Safety of Food, 2012, 19). Food Standards Agency (FSA) sampling of chickens bought from large UK retail outlets and smaller independent stores and butchers between February 2014 and February 2015 found that 73 per cent of chickens tested positive for the presence of campylobacter (FSA, 2015) – that is, three-quarters contained a pathogen which is the major source of hospitalisation from food poisoning in the UK.

Now, it is certainly the case that campylobacter and many other bacteria carried in foodstuffs can be killed through thorough cooking. But this is rather to miss the point. More relevant is that the prevalence of such bacteria, for example in chicken, is increasing when the conditions under which its spread can be eradicated are well known, and amounting to nothing more than meeting basic standards of hygiene in poultry production and processing. This fact of the increasing prevalence of the bacteria is a consequence of two conscious decisions taken in, for example, the food retail business, both of which are directly linked to the maximisation of profitability: one is the driving down of costs to undercut competitors, not least among the handful of supermarkets which dominate the UK retail food sector – the 'Big Four' (Tesco, Asda, Sainsbury's and Morrison's), even in the face of increasing competition from discount retailers, still account for almost three-quarters of market share between them (BBC, 2014); another is the complex line of sub-contracting which makes effective self-regulation virtually impossible even were it desirable on the part of industry, not least an industry which, while claiming it can self-regulate, flexes its muscle frequently to pre-empt or water down even the mildest forms of statutory regulation (Lawrence et al, 2014; Blythman, 2007).

If we turn now to occupational health and safety harms we find that the scale of these, not least in the UK, is consistent and significant – albeit, as with much corporate harm, obscured. If we begin with deaths from occupational injury, each year the Health and Safety Executive (HSE) releases a statistical bulletin which is press released with a figure for work fatalities – the press release for 2013/14 stated that in that reporting year, 133 workers were fatally injured. But what I have elsewhere called this 'headline' figure is highly misleading. Following the link from the press release takes us to the HSE's *Health and Safety Statistics 2013/14* (HSE, 2014a) which also notes that 'around 13,000 deaths each year from occupational lung disease and cancer are estimated to have been caused by past exposure, primarily to chemicals and dust at work' (HSE, 2014a, 2). But also reportable to HSE are deaths to members of the public which arise out of work activity. HSE's (2014a) Statistical Report does not refer to these at all – although they are generally accessible at a section of their website headed 'Fatal Injury Statistics'. In October 2014, this stated that, for 2013/14, 'There were 70 members of the public fatally injured in accidents connected to work in 2013/14 (excluding railways-related incidents)' – a figure that significantly augments the 133 fatal injuries to workers. Then, in a further, much fuller statistical document, one learns that, 'There were 264 members of the public fatally injured in accidents connected to work in 2013/14. Of these deaths, 194 (73 per cent) related to incidents occurring on railways' (HSE, 2014b, 4). The end result of this trawl through official data takes us from 133 deaths to some 13,400 deaths in 2013/14.

The underestimate does not stop there, however. As HSE now openly acknowledges, there are significant categories of deaths – at sea, associated with air travel, for example – which are occupational but recorded by other regulatory agencies. But by far the biggest omission are the deaths of those who die while driving as a normal part of their work. This omits some 800–1000 occupational deaths *per annum* because such deaths are recorded as road traffic rather than occupational fatalities.

Still, these additions do not capture the full scale of the problem of work-related deaths. For while HSE's data on fatal occupational illness is an estimation, as it acknowledges, it is in fact a gross underestimation. For example, researchers from the European Agency for Safety and Health at Work calculated, in 2009, 21,000 deaths per annum in the UK from work-related fatal diseases, while accepting both that such data 'might still be an underestimation' and that work-related diseases are 'increasing' (Hämäläinen et al, 2009, 127, 132). A UK study has estimated up 40,000 annual deaths in Great Britain caused by work-related cancers alone (O'Neill et al, 2007). And long-term research by the Hazards movement, drawing upon a range of estimates derived from studies (some commissioned by HSE) of occupational and environmental cancers, the percentages of heart-disease deaths which have a work-related cause, as well as percentage estimates of other diseases to which work can be a contributory cause, produces a lower end estimate of up to 50,000 deaths from work-related illness in the UK each year, or more than four times the HSE estimate (Palmer, 2008). This annual total ranks highly in comparison with virtually all other recorded causes of premature death in the UK (Rogers, 2011b).

Finally, we can turn to death and illness caused by air pollution. It is extremely difficult to be precise either about the levels or the sources of such pollution and, specifically in the context of this book, what proportion of air pollution is caused by corporate activity. These points being made, we have enough official indications to begin to approximate the scale of this type of harm.

First, in terms of the scale of harm, there have been a series of UK government estimates in recent years which indicate that the level of death runs into the tens of thousands. For example, the all-Party Environmental Audit Committee concluded in 2010 its report on Air Quality that 'Air pollution probably causes more deaths than passive smoking, traffic accidents or obesity, yet it receives very little attention from government or the media' (Parliamentary News, 2010). It added that evidence indicated that

> air pollution could be contributing to as many as 50,000 deaths per year…Averaged across the whole UK population it is estimated that poor air quality is shortening lives by 7–8 months. In pollution hotspots it could be cutting the most vulnerable people's lives short by as much as nine years. (Parliamentary News, 2010)

A subsequent, 2011, report by the same committee claimed that 'Dangerous levels of particulate matter (PM2.5 or PM10) and chemicals (such as NO_2) in the air are contributing to tens of thousands of early deaths every year in UK cities', estimating that '30,000 deaths in the UK were linked to air pollution in 2008 – with 4,000 in London alone' (Parliamentary News, 2011). Finally, in 2010, discussing upper and lower limits on the relationship between air pollution and deaths, as well as the degree of contribution of such pollution to these deaths, the Committee on the Medical Effects of Air Pollutants[5] concluded that,

> it is more reasonable to consider that air pollution may have made some contribution to the earlier deaths of up to 200,000 people in 2008, with an average loss of life of about two years per death affected, though that actual amount would vary between individuals. However, this assumption remains speculative. (Committee on the Medical Effects of Air Pollutants, 2010, para 21)

The effects of such pollution are not evenly distributed. Research findings have also indicated that 'poor air quality is hitting the poorest hardest' (House of Commons Environmental Audit Committee, 2011, para 10). In general, 'elevated levels of pollution are concentrated among socially deprived neighbourhoods' (House of Commons Environmental Audit Committee, 2011). Correlations with greater exposure have been found with lower incomes, low employment, low educational attainment, ethnicity and lower house prices (House of Commons Environmental Audit Committee, 2011).

On *sources* of pollution, the House of Commons Environmental Audit Committee (2010) stated that, 'industry and road transport are the main sources of air pollution, though domestic combustion and agriculture are also to blame' (House of Commons Environmental Audit Committee, 2010, para 2). Moreover, according to government figures, 96 per cent of sulphur dioxide is commercially produced (Department of the Environment, Food and Rural Affairs; 2001). Meanwhile, it has been estimated that 72 per cent of PM10 – the standard air pollution particle measure – is a result of commercial activity (Greater Manchester Air Quality Steering Group, 2002), as are most of the carbon monoxide, ozone, nitrogen oxide, 1,3-butadeine and lead pollution (all cited in Whyte, 2004, 135). Lorry traffic (House of Commons Environmental Audit Committee, 2011, para 8), buses (House of Commons Environmental Audit Committee, 2011, para 16), as well as aircraft engine emissions, airport operations and road transport to and from airports – all commercial or directly linked to commercial activity – are specifically cited as key sources of pollutants by the cross-party Environmental Audit Committee (House of Commons Environmental Audit Committee, 2011, paras 8, 16, 22).

Taking these three sets of data together, it is clear that corporate activities generate significant deleterious costs. Many forms of corporate activities produce physical harms – deaths, injuries, ill-health – arising out of dangerous workplaces, polluted environments, unsafe goods and services and so on. Meanwhile, governments, taxpayers, consumers, workers, and other companies incur economic costs. Indeed, even if we confine ourselves to economic costs, the best available evidence indicates that these far outweigh those associated with 'conventional' or 'street' offending. At the same time, we also know that the majority of corporate harms, even if they are punish*able*, are rarely so punished (Tombs and Whyte, 2015). Further, these routine yet widespread harms are produced under conditions in which states are intimately implicated, in a variety of ways. Most obviously, states bear some culpability here for their formal legalisation of much of this harm, their failures to develop adequate law and regulation which might mitigate these, their failures to enforce adequately such laws as do exist, and/or their failures to impose effective sanctions where violations of law are proven. Already, then, we can see how any recognition of corporate harm, let alone crime, cannot proceed adequately without understanding the role of the state as bystander, facilitator and even conspirator.

It is with the role of the state that this book is concerned, notably through its regulatory efforts in respect of corporate activity. In some ways, what I attempt to chart in the following chapters is a process of state withdrawal from such regulation; in a more important sense, as I try to make clear, this apparent withdrawal is only possible on the basis of intense, feverish, sustained state activity, hence the claims above that the processes at work are best understood via re-regulation. The empirical focus of the book is with three areas of social protection – environmental protection, food safety and occupational health and safety. These are not the only forms of social protection, of course, but they are key forms of this apparent state function.

Overview of the book

The geographical focus of the book is the UK. Notwithstanding many of the hyperbolic claims regarding 'globalisation', above, this is an unsatisfactorily restricted, yet necessarily limited, focus – regulatory policy, as virtually anything else within a specific nation-state, has a multitude of influences and context beyond borders, and in the case of regulation this is perhaps particularly so. There are significant, missing dimensions here in terms of the EU, OECD, World Bank, US hegemony and the spectres of emerging economies in other parts of the world, as well as a host of other supranational institutions, think tanks and, of course, multinational capital itself. Somewhat differently, but as significant, is another omission – what is offered in the following pages is a top-down account of the trajectories of regulation and enforcement, from which the crucial accounts of resistance, reform, struggle and contestation are absent, except to recognise their necessary presence; the latter stories also need to be told, in all of their rich, multi-faceted and at times inspirational dimensions.

In fact, even the focus on the UK is one that is only partly maintained. That is, where data is used this refers to England and Wales – which has a somewhat distinct local regulatory system to that in either Scotland or Northern Ireland. Food Safety enforcement in the UK operates almost entirely at the local authority level, and is overseen by the national body, the Food Standards Agency. Local functions are divided between Environmental Health and Trading Standards Officers. Environmental Health Officers (EHOs) oversee food safety and food hygiene, enforcing law across all forms of retail food business organisations (restaurant, shops and so on), as well as food processing and food manufacturing outlets. Occupational health and safety regulation is divided between a national regulator, the HSE, and EHOs at a local level; the division is based on the main activity of any premises. EHOs are the main regulators in retail, wholesale distribution, warehousing, hotel and catering premises, offices and the consumer/leisure industries. Health and safety EHOs liaise with HSE in their work. Pollution control is also divided between a national regulator, the Environment Agency, and local pollution control EHOs. At a local level, pollution control covers various forms of non-business activities, notably littering and fly-tipping, and a significant part of the work of pollution control EHOs is with noise, both domestic and commercial. The vast majority of the work of pollution control EHOs that concerns business is with regulation of 'Part B' installations – examples of which include glassworks and foundries, rendering plant and maggot breeders, petrol stations, sawmills and paint manufacturers.

The historical time period most at issue here is that between 2003 and 2013. This is more than a ten-year convenience, although it is partly that. As I shall argue, 2003 was at the cusp of a ratcheting up in re-regulatory efforts in the UK, while this ten-year period also encompasses the financial crisis which rampaged across much of the globe from late 2007 onwards, as well as its economic, political and ideological aftermaths. It also, in the UK, covers three governments, including all three main political parties, two more latterly, since 2010, in coalition. In this way, the analyses herein underscore that the re-regulatory trajectory and agenda is largely a matter of political consensus.

In this introductory chapter, I have attempted to both provide schematic historical, political and social contexts for what is to come, while also laying out some of the social-scientific concepts which are central throughout the argument developed here. The following two chapters will provide further politico-economic context for the specific considerations of the regulation and enforcement of social protection legislation in the UK. The starting point for Chapter Two is the fact that, for almost 40 years now, varieties of neoliberalism have systematically become the dominant form of political economy across much of the developed world. And central to neoliberal political economy are several tenets that bear directly upon the issue of the actual or potential regulation of private capital – not least among which are the ideas that markets are best when 'freer', that state and public sector activity are relatively inefficient, and that states' attempts to regulate private economic activity should be kept to a minimum. These claims have political, economic and indeed, as this chapter will demonstrate, *moral* dimensions. It is with the attempts to construct, and the nature of, the new material and moral realities of neoliberalism, that this chapter is concerned. These transformations in economic, political and social life elevated private capital to newly dominant status, while providing the context within which 'regulation', cast as antithetical to free enterprise and entrepreneurialism, could be so thoroughly undermined.

It is in this context that Chapter Three considers some of the fallout from the financial then economic crises which erupted across much of the world from 2007 onwards. Again, specific attention is paid to the UK experience. This chapter dissects the ways in which these crises have been framed politically, and especially in terms of the significances of these re-framings for dominant understandings of necessary and feasible regulation after the crisis. Thus the chapter examines the ways in which the aetiology of and thus the route from the financial and economic crisis has been reframed in various ways. Crucially, none of these discursive re-framings creates a political conjuncture within which the level of regulation is seen as a central cause of the crisis; and indeed each of them, it is argued, erects a new reality of sovereign debt in the face of which the state must withdraw further from the provision of goods and services, while at the same time there is the need for further 'freedoms' for private capital – and thus 'less' regulation of private capital – since it is increasingly the only game in town for recovery from the 'age of austerity'. Through the ways in which the crisis has been framed, not least through a series of moral critiques, private capital has not only recovered from the crisis to a position of 'business-as-usual', but it appears strengthened in fact.

Chapter Four shifts registers, although what remains at issue are key aspects of the hegemonic definitions of regulation – and the extent to which these have survived, or not, the events of 2007/08. Here it is argued that, from the 1970s onwards, a substantial body of academic work, across criminology and socio-legal studies, has emerged around regulation in general and enforcement in particular. This represents a quite remarkable consensus to the extent that I argue it represents both an orthodoxy and a pro-hegemonic resource. Dominant across these literatures, are a series of empirical, theoretical and normative claims, which view regulatory activities as the outcome and/or attempt to forge a consensus across a plurality of competing claims on the part of potentially – but not fundamentally – antagonistic parties ('business', 'workers', other 'interests'), all of whom, ultimately, are viewed as having a mutual interest in an efficient business sector. Further, within the latter, the idea of the socially responsible corporation performs a series of key functions, and I shall address this literature critically also. While this work is apparently heterogeneous, a critical examination reveals a series of essentially similar commitments within it – organised around, at base, a liberal pluralism to which 'balance' is already integral.

The following two chapters, Five and Six, have a largely empirical focus. First, in Chapter Five, 'Re-regulation in action', I trace some of the mechanisms through which the Labour governments, then, from 2010, the coalition government, sought to embed a new regulatory agenda under the auspices of 'Better Regulation'. This term, utilising many of the key elements of the regulatory orthodoxy, some quite consciously so, operated as a rubric for what amounted to a feverish programme of re-regulation, with four central elements: a long-term rhetorical assault on regulation as burdensome, red tape and so on; a plethora of institutions designed to oversee regulation and regulatory reform; a series of legal reforms – delivering both deregulation and re-regulation; and a perpetual series of reviews of regulatory agencies and regulation per se. As I shall demonstrate, Better Regulation is no mere state withdrawal nor deregulation – rather, it equates with re-regulation, thoroughgoing attempts to reconfigure the relationships between state and private capital under the guise of setting the latter free.

Then, in Chapter Six, I turn to consider regulatory practices: that is, through reference to enforcement trends from 2003 to 2013 in three areas of social protection, spanning national and local regulation: namely, environmental protection, health and safety at work and food safety. The start of this period allows any discernible quantitative effects of the rolling out of the de/re-regulatory 'Better Regulation' agenda (which proceeded nationally then locally) to be captured, and then, at the end of the period, any further effects of the financial crisis, recession, and so-called 'age of austerity' on these statutory regulatory functions can start to be observed. For a series of social scientific data, these are, taken together, remarkable: for all the internal differences, nuances and so on, they all point, unequivocally, in the same direction: that is, towards declining levels of enforcement, of all kinds, declines which in fact undermine the claims for various forms of 'better' regulation within which they are justified and which in some senses provide justifications for them.

Chapter Seven returns to 'bigger' questions of state and economy. Having begun the book with some general, conceptual and contextual considerations, then shifted to issues of governmental-level policies, not least regulatory 'policy', I drilled down further to examine some of the micro-level effects of these, via national, then local, enforcement trends and practices. In the concluding chapter, I address issues which are both more theoretical then, ultimately, questions which are more speculative. What, after all, is regulation? How resilient is the regulatory settlement being embedded in the UK? What role is there for enforcement in this, and what should our attitude to the inevitable 'failures' of regulation and enforcement be? And, finally, how can we respond to these developments which, in sum, have exposed the fragility and contingent nature of the state's 'commitment' to social protection, to the extent that in many respects, whatever it was, it is being abandoned before our eyes? In that context, I address some of the vulnerabilities of the new state-corporate settlement, and how counter-hegemonic forces might act upon these.

TWO

The new material and moral saliences of private capital

We want a society that celebrates and values its business heroes as much it does its pop stars and footballers. So we must remove the barriers to enterprise in this country, reward risk-taking, and encourage innovation and creativity. (Mandelson, 2 November 1998, cited in Elliott and Atkinson, 2007, 47)[6]

Introduction

The nature, level and outcomes of regulation – as well as dominant ideas regarding what constitutes desirable and feasible levels of regulation – are always a product and thus an effect of economic, political and social power. A key, if often under-explored, dimension of the power and resources to which corporations have access is their level of 'moral capital' – the ways in and the extent to which private corporate activity is valorised through a range of representations, claims and assumptions. This chapter examines the shifting moral capital of capital prior to and then, in Chapter Three, in the wake of, the financial and economic crisis. These chapters address an apparent paradox of the 'post' crisis period: namely, that while corporate morality was and remains exposed following the events of 2007, there are also ways in the post-bailout period in which the moral capital of capital has in fact been augmented. The rationale for these two chapters is that understanding this paradox requires an understanding of the social construction of corporate morality under conditions of neoliberalism. Moreover, the fact of the paradox is crucial in thinking about the key issue addressed in this book, namely the prospects for and limits of the more 'effective' regulation of capital in the current era.

I begin in this chapter by tracing some of the elements of the social construction of corporate morality *before* the crisis – that is, the emergence and consolidation of the moral capital of private capital under neoliberalism. In the following chapter, I pay particular attention to some of the 'post crisis' dynamics in the UK, most notably the various ways in which the crisis was framed – and the *moral* aspects and consequences of such framings. These forms of framing – in their own way small, competing morality plays – lay claim both to understanding the crisis, and, concomitantly, to offer lessons or prescriptions as to how, to what extent or even whether any recurrence could be prevented or mitigated. As we shall see, notably absent from the prescriptions that might emerge from such morality tales is any turn to more interventionist and effective forms of regulation: the state, remarkably present as the crisis unfolded, is notably absent from post-crisis discourse, at least as part of any serious 'solution'. These processes can only be understood via the longer term reconstruction of the moral capital of capital, and it is to this process that the chapter now turns.

A new *moral* salience of private capital

If we are to understand post-crisis discourses in relation to the *morality* of corporate activity, then we need to have some sense of moral discourses that circulated in relation to corporate activity *prior to* the crisis – the extent to which the former are able to emerge, be sustained, and gain credence is at least in part dependent upon the extent to which they cohered with aspects of the latter (Froud et al, 2012). In this section, then, we focus on what I have elsewhere referred to as the emergence and consolidation of the 'moral capital of capital' (Tombs, 2001) under conditions of emergent and then dominant neoliberalism.

The changes summarised in Chapter One – the emergence of neoliberalism – amounted to an increase in the structural power of capital (Gill and Law, 1993, 104). But an often overlooked aspect to this augmented power is an increase in private capital's social importance. Indeed, it is possible here to discern a *moral* aspect to the new status of private capital – an elevation which both encourages, and then in turn feeds off, a sustained attack on state, public and regulatory activity; an attack cast in terms of the freeing of enterprise and the valorisation of risk. As Snider has demonstrated (2003), the use of a phraseology of 'burdens on business' and 'red tape' to refer to laws designed to regulate economic activity has become common currency, the unquestioned implication being that such burdens and red-tape should be reduced as far as possible – since they no longer express any public good. The renewed moral status of private capital – to emphasise, not to particular businesses (a task which would be difficult given the evidence of amorality, immorality or criminality on the part of individual business organisations) but to business, or rather 'capital', as a whole – is partly a function of it not being the 'other', that is, wasteful, inefficient, and intrusive public sector bodies. Indeed, it is not just that the latter are inefficient – it is that through their very existence they thwart individual and institutional innovation and competitiveness.

A confluence of economic, political and moral arguments had been developed in the work of the 'law and economics' school. According to this body of ideas, state intervention in the economy poses tremendous dangers to the working of market rationality. For although state activities are usually justified as being necessary to correct allocative problems due to *market failure*, in fact, they primarily function to redistribute resources in a socially inefficient way. For example, we can earn what we are worth and what we are worth, in turn, depends upon how much we have invested in resources including ourselves. The poor are poor because they have decided not to invest wisely and the well-off are well-off because they have invested wisely. Therefore even the existence of unequal distributions of wealth in market economies shows how these economies make it possible for interests to be mutually harmonious. Universal welfare provision, then, is counterproductive. It discourages labour market participation and artificially inflates the wages bill for all areas of economic activity. It would also be quite unnecessary if people were to take responsibility for their actions. These and other related state activities generate inflation, increase uncertainty and discourage productive investment.

One way to deal with market failure is to use regulatory agencies. But in the case of both economic and social regulation, consumers end up paying higher prices than is necessary for the benefit of small groups of highly motivated and well organised actors, be these inefficient firms, full-time regulators and pork barrel politicians, or 'politically motivated' moral entrepreneurs such as environmentalists or some opportunistic politicians. Many of the latter moral entrepreneurs can be motivated by a dangerously irrational ideal, a risk free society. It is irrational because it is unachievable and because it presents risks in an entirely negative light as opposed to recognising that progress requires a willingness to take risks, such as providing entrepreneurs at the leading edge of technology with venture capital. It is dangerous because it obscures the opportunity costs and transaction costs of regulation – excessive regulation leads to the inefficient use of resources and inhibits constructive innovations. Furthermore, since overall the wealthier a society, the healthier its members, then anything that inhibits wealth creation is socially regressive and thus to be restricted as far as possible. Regulation, then, is best achieved by a combination of property rights, market forces and private litigation.

As the law and economics movement shifted from economic, political and moral prescription to informing public policy, the dominant representation and form of the state also shifted drastically – from a (Keynesian) protector of the public good, or a (pluralist) representative of the general interests of capital, to a set of institutions either representing its own special interests or captured by external moral entrepreneurs in order to promote, through regulation, interests detrimental to both economic and political freedom.

If these discourses became powerful, indeed dominant, then they also helped to produce that which they sought to describe and prescribe, notably in terms of increasing popular dependence upon the private sector. At the same time, the moral capital of capital becomes augmented – along the lines of Lukes's third dimension or face of power (Lukes, 1974), its elevated moral status means that certain issues simply do not get raised within political or popular consciousness. The most obvious non-issue is any resumption of ownership of certain areas of economic activity by the state or some other public entity.

Central to the argument that I seek to develop here, then, is that neoliberalism is more than an economic or political project. It is also a project with a moral core (Amable, 2011) – albeit one beset by what are at best tensions, at worst contradictions (see Shorthose, 2011). Indeed, any economic order is both predicated upon and seeks to further specific moralities (Thompson, 1971), so that 'all economies are also moral economies' (Clarke and Newman, 2012, 314; Sayer, 2007). More specifically, or as one particular aspect of this moral element, is that, with the emergence to dominance of neoliberalism, one can discern a *moral* aspect to the new status of private capital: private economic activity was elevated to the status of an intrinsically worthy end in itself (Frank, 2001), as opposed to a *means* to some other end. Consequently, the 'moral capital' attached to business activity has increased dramatically over the past 40 years. Private enterprise, entrepreneurship, risk-taking, the pursuit of wealth and the 'market' have all become valorised not just as the most effective means to certain ends – profits, wages, or various socially necessary and (perhaps) socially useful goods and services – but *as ends in themselves*. Just as paid work came to be invested with moral meaning throughout the industrial epoch, private individuals and institutions that control work and business activity have increasingly come to be seen as positive moral agents within our own society.

As a general context, we can understand this valorisation of private economic activity in terms of two well-documented processes which characterise late twentieth-century capitalism, albeit occurring to different extents across different nation-states, namely marketisation and financialisation of economy, society and culture, processes which indeed also demonstrate the mutually reinforcing effects of the ideological and the material. Together, these are central to the dominance of a neoliberal rationality through which all aspects of social life are cast in terms of economic relations, and through which individuals are increasingly interpolated as entrepreneurial subjects in ever-more aspects of their lives, responsible for themselves and free from the protective state (Giroux, 2008, 172; W Brown, 2005, 41–5).

Marketisation and financialisation

Whitfield (2006) has characterised marketisation as 'the process by which market forces are imposed in public services', and identifies five elements to this general process: 'the commodification of services and infrastructure; the commodification of labour such as the reorganisation of work and jobs to maximise productivity and assist transfer to another employer; restructuring the state for competition and market mechanisms; restructuring democratic accountability and user involvement; embedding business interests and promoting liberalisation internationally' (Whitfield, 2006, 4).

As Whitfield's typology makes clear, however, these processes are not just material changes to the organisation of sectors, but also generate cultural changes. The extension of market activities, logics and mentalities beyond but also within a shrinking public sphere means that, as is well documented, what remains formally social provision in a range of areas including health, welfare, education, criminal justice, even national defence and war have all been sites of an ever-increasing, indeed seemingly relentless exposure to, and reliance upon, private economic actors. In other words, with marketisation comes a new cultural political economy as well as new politico-economic modes of organisation (Wiegratz, 2013).

These processes – a long march through the institutions, to recall a former phraseology – are so advanced that some have referred to 'the capacity of market logics to subsume, rather than just subordinate, "non-economic" domains of social life', so that a quality of markets is their 'unboundedness' (Clarke, 2010a, 376). This marketisation is, then, more than institutional – it is, in a very Gramscian sense, a market populism and imagery which achieves a 'partial colonisation of common sense' (Clarke, 2010a, 378–81).

The pervasive and powerful combination of material and ideological advances is also in evidence in the context of financialisation. In essence, this term refers to 'the increasing importance of financial markets, institutions and motives in the world economy' (Epstein, 2005, 3). These are international, if not global, trends (Epstein, 2005). Moreover, the sheer scale of financial markets, and the largest complex institutions which dominate them, is almost impossible to comprehend. Dowell-Jones has recently provided some stark indicators of this scale:

> World Gross Domestic Product (GDP) is roughly US$70 trillion. The value of shares trading on world exchanges is not much lower than this, at US$63 trillion, before you take into account any other type of financial market. Amounts outstanding on the global bond markets hit a record of US$100 trillion in 2012, up from US$40 trillion ten years earlier. The combined face value of derivatives contracts in existence is a staggering US$700 trillion, ten times world GDP. According to data from the International Swaps and Derivatives Association, most of these contracts are concentrated among a small handful of financial institutions. In 2010 (latest figures available), the 14 largest global derivatives dealers – the G14 Group – accounted for $354.6 trillion of derivatives exposures, roughly five times current world GDP, and the five largest US dealers had $172.3 trillion of contracts – a value equivalent to two and a half times world GDP concentrated in just five financial institutions. (Dowell-Jones, 2013, 430–1)

The significance of the financial sector also assumes different proportions in different national economies. If we consider the UK economy in particular, some have argued that finance capital has long held a peculiar dominance therein (Ingham, 1984; Hutton, 1995).[7] However, here this dominance has been extended, particularly since the 1986 'Big Bang', central to the Thatcherite reconstruction of the City, followed by a long period characterised by light touch regulation during which New Labour generated with and for the City 'a new set of instruments, actors and policies that can be identified in terms of economic patriotism' (Morgan, 2012, 376).

According to the trade association for UK-based financial and related professional services industry, TheCityUK, 'The sector's trade surplus is larger than the combined surplus of all other net exporting industries in the UK. Financial services accounts for around a third of all foreign direct investment into the UK. This is more than any other sector' (TheCityUK, 2013, 5). Moreover, in 2012 financial and related services contributed 12.6 per cent of the UK's GDP (TheCityUK, 2014, 14) – higher than other major economies (with the US share being 8.4 per cent, Japan 5.8 per cent, France 5.1 per cent and Germany 4.3 per cent, respectively) (McKenzie, 2011, 1; see also TheCityUK, 2013; UK Trade and Investment, 2012). This share in the UK had increased during the previous decade, from 5.3 per cent in 2001; the share of manufacturing, by contrast, fell from 16.4 per cent to 11.1 per cent between 2001 and 2009 (McKenzie, 2011, 1).[8] Indeed, for some, finance has not just grown vis-à-vis other sectors of the economy, it has become independent of them, changing the nature of contemporary economic activity per se; thus Urry has claimed that finance less and less functions for, for example, industry, and in effect *becomes* the economy (Urry, 2014, 72). Relatedly, Streeck (2014, 52) refers to the shift from 'the old regime of M–C–M[1] to a new one of M–M[1]': in other words, money creates money in the absence of commodity production, truly a definition of 'casino capitalism' (Strange, 1997; see Sayer, 2015, 179–236).

Thus, on some interpretations, the rise of finance capital and decline of manufacturing in the UK are causally linked. For one thing, financial speculation and profit-generation is increasingly independent of investment in the real economy; for example, in the property bubble between 1996–2007 which preceded and helped to generate the financial crisis, 'bank lending to productive business declined sharply from 30 per cent towards 10 per cent mainly because bank lending to other financial firms and property developers ballooned in the bubble' (CRESC, 2009, 65). In general, City institutions have an external orientation which partly explains the lack of investment in the UK's manufacturing base (Lambie, 2013). In other words, the UK economy is peculiarly dependent on financial services, a dependence which increased dramatically over the past decade[9] and which Wilks has characterised as 'a cornerstone of the New Corporate State' (2013, 107). Now, this growth is explicable due to a host of factors, but it is partly understood on the basis of capital being drawn to the sector by the promise of extremely high, relative rewards. Thus,

> Between 1920 and 1970, the return on UK banks' equity averaged below 10 per cent per annum, with low volatility of around 2 per cent per year. This was roughly in line with risks and returns in the non-financial economy. The 1970s signalled a sea-change. Since then returns on UK banks' equity have averaged over 20 per cent. Immediately prior to the crisis, returns were close to 30 per cent. The natural

bedfellow to higher return is higher risk. (Alessandri and Haldane, 2009, 3–4)

Thus there are very real motivations for the process of financialisation to accelerate, and there is no necessary reason why recent events in the financial services sector can provide any 'break' upon these. Chima and Langley define financialisation in terms of three processes: a 'finance-led growth regime'; politically enabled, increasing opportunities for financial speculation 'that liberalise and deregulate markets and individualise welfare provision'; and patterns in household saving, occupational pension provision and the revolution in so-called 'financial services' since the 1980s.[9] Growing numbers of the population hold a stake, however meagre, in the 'mass investment culture' (Chima and Langley, 2012, 412–13). But the significance of financialisation is pervasive. The material realities of the dominance, spread and 'success' of finance are likely to lead to the logic of finance 'getting wired into a growing number of economic sectors' (Sassen, 2013, 27). It has international dimensions and effects not least through distorting the flow of capital (Tabb, 2012), has (detrimental) effects upon corporate cultures and forms of corporate governance (Ireland, 2009), and may lead to the generalised financialisation of culture, especially in the UK and US, the developed capitalist states where neoliberal programmes have been pushed furthest. Thus Johnson, former Chief Economist at the International Monetary Fund, with reference to the US, captures this cultural pervasiveness beautifully:

> As more and more of the rich made their money in finance, the cult of finance seeped into the culture at large. Works like Barbarians at the Gate, Wall Street, and Bonfire of the Vanities – all intended as cautionary tales – served only to increase Wall Street's mystique. Michael Lewis noted in Portfolio last year that when he wrote Liar's Poker, an insider's account of the financial industry, in 1989, he had hoped the book might provoke outrage at Wall Street's hubris and excess. Instead, he found himself 'knee-deep in letters from students at Ohio State who wanted to know if I had any other secrets to share…They'd read my book as a how-to manual.' Even Wall Street's criminals, like Michael Milken and Ivan Boesky, became larger than life. In a society that celebrates the idea of making money, it was easy to infer that the interests of the financial sector were the same as the interests of the country – and that the winners in the

financial sector knew better what was good for America than did the career civil servants in Washington. Faith in free financial markets grew into conventional wisdom – trumpeted on the editorial pages of The Wall Street Journal and on the floor of Congress. (cited in Simms and Greenham, 2010, 59)[10]

This interpenetration of corporate, financial and market logics into civil, economic and political spheres is significant – not least, as argued in the next section, in its role in creating and maintaining (while also being effects of) an elevated moral status for private capital (Hansen, 2014).

Most fundamentally, then, we have lived through a period in which a new common sense has circulated: business interests – which are by definition sectional (class) interests arising out of activity conducted for clear motives – are increasingly represented as 'general' or 'national' interests. We are increasingly persuaded that what happens to individual businesses and business in general matter to us, albeit that this process is highly contradictory. Further, business activity is increasingly represented as *a good end in itself*, as opposed to what it actually is – namely a *means* to some other end, whether this is profits, wages, or various socially necessary and (perhaps) socially useful goods and services.

One index of these developments is that as citizens we have increasingly been, and remain, constantly encouraged to believe that the 'success' or 'failure' of business activity matters to us. Witness, for example, the massive growth in business and financial reporting across a range of media in the past quarter of a century, the routine reporting across various mass media of stock exchange movements from Hong Kong to New York, the build up to and dissection of the financial statements of individual companies, and the entrance of some individual business-people into the cult of celebrity – witness Branson, Gates, Sugar, Trump and so on (see Snider, 2000) or even as the key architects of progressive social change (Dienst, 2011, 95–119). Thus there is a very general, 'background', yet new, reality, namely that 'perceptions about the economy and prevailing business climate occupy central importance within everyday political debates' (Doyle, 2006, 434). What is important, however, is that this is not to say that this level of reporting aids popular understanding of financial and economic matters (Doyle, 2006), nor that these perceptions regarding the corporate world are at all accurate.

Yet the increasing salience of private capital is no 'mere' ideology or appearance (Geras, 1972; Fisher, 2009). In many very real senses, the business world affects a much greater number of us than was the case 40 years ago. There is a material basis for the elevated status of private capital – one which makes 'freedom' for capital not just difficult to resist but, as we shall see, increasingly so in the dominant version of the 'post-crisis' settlement. Analogously, as Cameron and Palan note of globalisation discourses, these are reproduced through 'countless, small, incidental performances on a daily basis', thus contributing to their overall 'normalcy' or 'plausibility' (Cameron and Palan, 2004, 160). Thus as public provision of goods and services has been scaled back in many industrialised nations, the private sector certainly does impinge more readily upon our lives as citizens – whether this be in the provision of education, healthcare, transportation, telecommunications, basic utilities and so on. Moreover, while claims of a 'popular capitalism' are much more illusory than real, there are now up to 10 million shareholders in the UK – albeit that 'the vast majority hold only a few shares, and many of those will have come from privatisations, de-mutualisations or from former employments', while these 'shares are rarely traded' (UKSA, 2005).[11] The proportion of privately owned homes increased from about just over a half in 1979 to over two-thirds in 1990 (Graham, 1997, 121) – hence popular concern with interest rates – while the number of individuals owning shares rose from one in twelve in 1981 to one in four in 1990 – hence some passing stake in the stock market (Graham, 1997, 121).[12] More significantly in terms of the latter, as social insurance has diminished, people have increasingly come to have stakes in either private pensions or in savings schemes linked directly to company and stock exchange performance; many of us have had or do have monies invested in pensions, in PEPs, TESSAs, AVCs, ISAs, in endowment policies and so on. One consequence of this development is the fact that if many people have been encouraged to believe that business activity matters more to them, then this is because it does: certainly many people have some personal stake in financial services, while more generally such developments have created the reality or the belief of having a stake in the effective functioning of the central institutions of the corporate world and of finance capitalism in particular, and indeed *of capitalism in general*. Thus,

> The penetration of finance into the everyday life of households has not only created a range of dependencies on financial services, but also changed the outlook, mentality and even morality of daily life. Financial calculation evaluates

everything in pennies and pounds, transforming the most basic goods – above all, housing – into 'investments'. Its logic has affected even the young, who have traditionally been idealistic and scornful of pecuniary calculation. Fertile ground has been created for neoliberal ideology to preach the putative merits of the market. (Lapavitsas, 2014a)

This in turn furthers the claim, as noted above, that business interests are synonymous with 'general' or 'national' interests.

Thus, private capital increasingly dominates in the provision of both essential and peripheral services, creating a new class of dependent consumers – not citizens (Hansen, 2014, 627) – often in oligopolistic markets where there is in fact little 'choice' to be exercised. Indeed, both practical and psychological dependencies upon private capital have come to be an intractable part of contemporary life. Such changes raise the status – the moral and cultural capital – of private business and of the men and women who control, manage and work successfully within them.[13] At the same time, crucially, these shifts also serve to undermine the legitimacy of those charged with *controlling* corporate activity. Inevitably, state regulators increasingly operate upon a terrain in which their cultural capital and leverage has been significantly reduced. As these new realities interact, what is deemed acceptable in and on behalf of the corporate world shifts, which in turn shifts cultural definitions of illegality towards support for greater freedoms for corporate activities from the anti-entrepreneurial instincts of states and their regulators. These are points to which I now turn.

Celebrating private capital

These processes can be further explored via a closer look at one specific aspect of this increasing moral salience of private capital, namely the emergence of the business-person-as-entrepreneur as both role model and celebrity. This is a telling feature of neoliberalism – and one that, it could be argued, assumed ever greater prominence under the years of New Labour.

What is important here is that what constitutes entrepreneurship – and who constitutes an entrepreneur – is a site of discursive struggle, and crucial within this contestation are the moral valorisations which underpin the application of the label (Jones and Spicer, 2009). Thus, it is more than plausible to argue that, for example, those working in the illegal economy, or in what Ruggiero (2000) has called the 'urban bazaar', might in fact much more resemble the entrepreneur than those concrete individuals to whom this label actually gets successfully applied. While the latter often simply use their various resources, not least financial, crudely to exploit dominance in oligopolistic or oligopsonistic markets, it's the former who display what we might recognise as entrepreneurial *qualities*, though they will never acquire the *status* of entrepreneurs. That is, for those in the urban bazaars, working and surviving, let alone prospering, requires the flexibility to move between licit and illicit worlds to take whatever opportunities present themselves so that reward at least *appears* therein to accrue to talent and versatility (Ruggiero, 2000, 28–43).

Such figures, however, are not cut out to be the heroes of neoliberalism – this is clear, even if it is not always clear who or what the entrepreneur is. As many commentators have noted, the figure of the entrepreneur is a common one, often invoked,[14] albeit an 'imaginary', so that 'The entrepreneur becomes a floating signifier imbued with a wide range of meanings' (Perren and Dannreuther, 2013, 611), its deployment being central to establishing neoliberalism as it helps to create interpellated subjects whose fates are immediately in their own hands (Hall and Winlow, 2012). But its very utility is in both its elusiveness *and* in the fact that it is not a category freely offered to all potentially entrepreneurial subjects. This differential labelling is one used in common political, economic and social discourse, but it is also underpinned by those in business and management 'education' who invoke this totem. There, the poverty of scholarship in this area is notable:

> talk about entrepreneurship is, more often than not, a shiny veneer behind which there is much that is troubling… almost all of the intellectual efforts – both by academics and by practitioners of entrepreneurship – have rested on shabby grounds, unthought premises, weak argumentation and scant evidence. (Jones and Spicer, 2009, 3)

Consistent with one of the themes of this text – that is, the relationship between academic work and its political uses – Jones and Spicer have argued that the poverty of intellectual work around the entrepreneur is functional, and indeed that '[e]ntrepreneurship has become a mantra that has worked, paradoxically, by repetition of the same. Business gurus repeat the same platitudes about the virtues of enterprise', platitudes then 'echoed by politicians seeking economic cures' (Jones and Spicer, 2009, 2). This very process of repetition has been crucially facilitated by the growth in business reporting alluded to above – although, as one study of newspaper reporting has concluded, it is often difficult here to distinguish whether 'what is being offered is financial news in the guise of entertainment or vice versa' (Doyle, 2006, 448). Far from being restricted to the economic and business spheres, however, the hegemonic status of the entrepreneur has also come to permeate the world of popular culture. Taking on the identity of celebrity, 'successful' entrepreneurs have entered popular consciousness, not least through fronting or participating in entertainment shows such as *The Apprentice* or *Dragon's Den*.

A key figure in the emergence of the entrepreneur as celebrity – and, indeed, of a cool or 'hippie' capitalism – at least in the UK, was Richard Branson; and, indeed, in his career are paradigmatically evident some of the key contradictions within such nomenclature. Describing the 'slipping' of his 'halo' at the end of the 1990s, Bower recalls how the Virgin business empire was exposed in this period as generally loss-making, while his only 'two profitable companies – airline and trains – relied on government franchisees for protection from competition, while all his businesses exposed to normal market competition were debt-ridden' (Bower, 2001, 298). As Bower documents, this exposure marked the cracks in a long career of instrumentalism, not least in his strategic alliances forged with politicians of all political stripes – so long as they were near to or at the heart of government – and journalists. His instrumentalism extended to his relationship with the law: willing to use the law to prevent exposure where necessary, but with a 'relaxed' attitude to taxation, accounting and competition law (Bower, 2001, passim). Such is the power of the image, however, that Branson remains a go-to figure as entrepreneur, for politicians and journalists alike.

While the sheer volume of 24/7 broadcast media is clearly relevant to the absolute level of 'business entertainment format' (Kelly and Boyle, 2010, 229) appearing on screen, there is more at work here. Kelly and Boyle, for example, note that 'it is significant that with regard to its news output the BBC did not have a business editor until 2001', while over the two decades preceding this, on both sides of the Atlantic, the representation of business as entertainment had been a mixture of 'crooks, conmen and clowns' (Kelly and Boyle, 2010, 230). In the UK, a watershed moment came in 1990 when former chairman of ICI, Sir John Harvey Jones, starred in *Troubleshooter*, a series in which he went into a variety of failing firms to turn them around. This marked a new form of business programming in which the entrepreneur was either heroic in some form and/or 'contributing to these new types of programmes in other ways, namely as "experts", "mentors" and "judges"' (Boyle and Kelly, 2010, 335). Later examples of the genre broadcast on mainstream channels were *The Apprentice* (BBC2, 2005 onwards), *Dragons' Den, Mary Queen of Shops,* BBC2, 2007), and *Property Ladder* (Channel 4, 2001) – though it is interesting that in the period from *Troubleshooter,* in 1990, through to the mid-2000s, with *The Apprentice,* the tone of the programming had become more confrontational and aggressive, perhaps mirroring changes in business, and wider neoliberal realities.[15]

Of course, none of these examples of broadcasting are simple representations of the heroism of either entrepreneurs in particular nor of private economic activity in general. Indeed, in my view at least, one of the most striking features of *The Apprentice* is the sheer lack of both intellectual ability and social skills on the part of many of the 'contestants' – but in this they are harshly judged by an archetypal entrepreneur and his hired men and women, demonstrating the need *both* to talk the talk (which many of the aspiring apprentices have taken to the point of ridicule) *and* to walk the walk, which separates out the real 'wannabees' from the *real* entrepreneurs – the latter both adjudicated and represented by Sugar, of course, but also Margaret Mountford, Nick Hewer and more latterly Karren Brady, as well as the various business successes who 'grill' each candidate in the interviewing round. Business success requires something special. Meanwhile, *Dragons' Den* is equally mixed in its detail if clear in its overall message. What we see in this show, emphasised by the stacks of money which sit in front of the 'dragons' as they adjudicate harshly, is in fact not entrepreneurialism at work, but its very opposite. The potential for entrepreneurialism, the creativity, determination, inventiveness and hard work, as well as the ability to self-delude, sits with the contestants. By contrast, the 'dragons' use their bullying, overpowering wealth to buy the rights, as venture capitalists, to creativity upon which they are clearly entirely parasitic. Yet in the sole ability to pass judgement through cash they stand as a leitmotif of that to which everyone who enters the 'Den' seemingly aspires.

Thus,

> Through television's system of 'delegated looking'…the viewer is regularly aligned with the viewpoints of Sugar and the 'dragons' and is thus encouraged to draw upon the skills, knowledge and expertise put forward by these entrepreneurs before going on to judge the contestants and participants accordingly. It is also the case that these figures perform a certain 'nasty' role that has become appealing to audiences schooled in reality TV and which is indicative

of the televisual skills they have acquired. However, this does not necessarily make them appear inauthentic, as their ruthlessness is again legitimised by their offscreen achievements within the demanding world of business. (Boyle and Kelly, 2010, 337)

Often, and notably at times of recession, the extreme wealth of these figures was explained by a rags-to-riches narrative (Boyle and Kelly, 2010, 338). Further, such was their expertise that governments increasingly turned to business either to join them in government or to act as special advisers, or, increasingly known as Gurus, on some specific aspect of public policy, from school dinners to housing or high street planning policy (Boyle and Kelly, 2010). Indeed, one commentator has drily noted, 'The rollcall of government experts sometimes reads like the pages of the *Radio Times*' (Rankin, 2013). Indeed, in the specific context of the UK, becoming a celebrity entrepreneur appeared to be a virtual guarantor of being invited to head some or other special government initiative – a recent phenomenon quite separate from the well-known and long established transparent and opaque revolving doors between business and politics which ensures that the latter never stray far from preserving and furthering the interests of the former.[16]

With no hint of irony, rather than some specific expertise being used here for the public good, what often happened was that a flagging business career was revitalised. At the same time, politicians were often left frustrated in their search for stardust, as business men and women soon or eventually left their posts expressing pique at the bureaucratic world of government which had prevented them getting things done – that is, being 'entrepreneurial'. The mythical dichotomy of private good and public bad is thereby reinforced: business people (albeit failing as business people) succeeding as celebrity which results in them being invited into government on the basis of that celebrity rather than their business performance per se; yet their failures to effect changes in government are in turn blamed on anti-entrepreneurial governmental structures and practices. This perhaps reached its zenith when Gordon Brown assumed his role as Prime Minister in 2007 with a stated determination to oversee a 'government of all the Talents', and invited a series of unlikely bedfellows (and they were mostly fellows) into a labyrinthine of advisory – non-elected – posts. One notable such appointment was (Lord) Digby-Jones, former head of the employers' organisation the CBI. On resigning his post as Trade Minister in 2009 Digby-Jones argued that 'top businessmen' – and not 'incompetent politicians' – should run major government departments: 'Health, education, business, transport, defence and security are too important to be left any longer to enthusiastic amateurs and their honest and hard-working but risk-averse civil servants' (cited in Walters, 2009).

The new elevated status of business people was further highlighted, albeit somewhat differently, by the death of Steve Jobs in 2011, when he was hailed as an innovator of style who had changed people's lives and the ways 'we' live our world; with only a hint of hyperbole, one commentator noted that on his death, 'The deification of Steve Jobs is Apple's greatest marketing triumph to date' (Gold, 2011). But if it is a marketing triumph, it is also more than that: for in the glorification of the life-changing and aesthetically path-breaking products of Apple, the company's staggering levels of profit were not just acceptable but validated as *just reward*. In July 2011, it had announced global revenues of $28.57 billion and profits of $7.31 billion, up 90 per cent and 124 per cent respectively, year-on-year (Gold, 2011). Indeed, it is hard to imagine such levels of profit being generated by anything other than a ruthless, profit-maximising, global entity – which is, of course, exactly what Apple was, and remains. Thus the considerable and indisputable evidence of the appalling conditions under which Apple products were being produced by its Chinese supplier became both well-known[17] but relatively ineffectual in undermining the brand of design-led, West Coast capitalism which Jobs claimed to embody.

Finally, not content with being models of 'entrepreneurialism', some business people have sought to represent themselves as figures central to charitable and even humanitarian activities – a process, indeed, through which business-people have become celebrities and celebrities recognised as business-people (Barker, 2013). Thus, for example, while heading a corporation mired in a long-running refusal to pay European Commission-levied fines for anti-competitive practices, to the tune of hundreds of millions of US dollars, popular representations of Bill Gates – an archetype of the new 'cool capitalist' (Boltanski and Chiapello, 2007) – have tended more to focus on his Foundation which, among various 'philanthropic' activities, is currently freeing the under-developed world from malaria. Of course, as Dienst observes in his searing 'Letter to Bono', such initiatives are more part of the problem than any solution. Of Bono in particular then, he must 'surely know that the economic and ideological machinery that creates global rock superstars is inseparable from the vast machinery that creates and maintains global poverty' (2011, 96). Dienst's critique of celebrity fuelled attempts to 'Make Poverty History' through selling coloured wristbands is a timely antidote to the puffed-up philanthropy that is claimed by and for 'responsible' capitalists (see also Fisher, 2009).

Such is the power of Žižek's 'liberal communists' (Žižek, 2009b); their cultural as well as economic domination ensures that they are often perceived as a panacea to economic and social problems, and this domination is more than just hegemonic, as I have said, but inscribed in the neurological systems and desires of many of the children of neoliberalism. This is a prime example of moral capitalism at work: the potential for accumulation is achieved (here, via record sales) while claims to progressive moral, charitable, and even political action is claimed. In this way, and more generally as I have sought to show in this section, through a plethora of synoptic vehicles, celebrity entrepreneurs are represented as *ego ideal* – and in this way, atomism, acquisitiveness, avarice and ruthlessness (see Steve Hall, 2012) are all valorised.

Conclusion

The elevated moral capital of private capital in general, just as the rise of the celebrity entrepreneur in particular, cannot simply be understood as pure 'ideology', but are a product – and also further impetus to – material changes in the organisation of economic and social life: the increasing salience of private capital is not 'mere' ideology or appearance, since in a whole series of ways the fortunes of private capital are much more closely tied to many of our fates than was the case 35 years ago. Indeed, it is the combination of the ideological strength and thoroughgoing material basis for the elevated moral status of private capital which makes 'freedom' for capital not just difficult to resist, but is increasingly so in the 'post crisis' settlement.

The ideological transformations discussed here have involved ascribing a moral status not so much to *particular* businesses – this would be a difficult task given the evidence of amorality, immorality or criminality on the part of individual business organisations – but to 'business', the 'private sector' and 'entrepreneurs' and 'entrepreneurialism' in general. Nor, to be clear, does this moral valorisation mean that business people and business organisations are immune from criticism – quite the opposite, in some ways. Thus as Winlow has recently noted, 'the asocial institution of the corporation' is frequently and perhaps increasingly vilified through, for example, Hollywood blockbusters – but so entrenched are these corporations, so effective has been the creation of a no-alternative discourse, that their constant exposure as villains meets only 'cynical realism and cultural passivity' in the absence of genuine oppositional politics (Winlow, 2013, 30). The superiority of the private over the allegedly wasteful, inefficient, intrusive and freedom-negating public sector is now *obvious*.

At the same time, this distinction between capital in general and specific companies or businessmen and women at specific times allows a further paradox to be ideologically 'resolved'. If, as I have claimed, popular investment (literally and metaphorically) in the private sector is real as well as ideological, then this creates a challenge where corporate *wrongdoing* is exposed. In other words, how can wrongdoing on the part of particular companies be managed politically in an era where minimal regulation is deemed preferable? Where regulation is largely organised off political and popular agendas, as this book documents is increasingly the case, then, as Chapter Four seeks to demonstrate, the answer to this paradox is supplied by the increasingly ubiquitous claims of 'corporate social responsibility' (CSR). That is, the rise of CSR discourse squares the circle of greater risk and less regulation; or, more accurately, both deregulation *and* forms of re-regulation which in themselves create greater risk in the form of opportunity structures for criminal motivations and activity. At the same time, it allows for normal business behaviour to be decried as aberrant or marginal.

THREE

Framing the crisis: moral critique and the renewal of 'business as usual'

> Everywhere the crisis of the private financial system has been transformed into a tale of slovenly and overweening government that perpetuates and is perpetuated by a dependent and demanding population. This is an amazing transformation of the terms in which our circumstance is to be understood. For about 10 days the crisis was interpreted as a consequence of the ineptitude of the highly paid, and then it transmogrified into a grudge against the populace at large, whose lassitude was bearing the society down to ruin. (Robinson, 2012)

Introduction

In September 2008, in contrast to any other social catastrophe – global warming, widespread hunger, poverty and the routine deaths of millions of children, AIDS, TB and malaria epidemics, about which 'there always seemed to be time to reflect, to postpone decisions' (Žižek, 2009a, 80) – one issue presented itself as 'an unconditional imperative which must be met with immediate action': the 'banks', for which read finance capital in particular and the global neoliberal order in general, had to be saved (Žižek, 2009a). In the UK, 'golden parachutes' (Žižek, 2009a, 12) were handed out to the UK banking system: in December 2009 the National Audit Office (NAO) (2009e) produced an 'overview of the government's response to the crisis' which showed that 'the purchases of shares by the public sector together with offers of guarantees, insurance and loans made to banks reached £850 billion, an unprecedented level of support'. The financial commitments made by governments since September 2008 have included purchasing shares in banks to enable re-capitalisation, indemnifying the Bank of England against losses incurred in providing liquidity support, underwriting borrowing by banks to strengthen liquidity, and providing insurance cover for assets. The government 'cash outlay' is said to have peaked 'at £133 billion, equivalent to more than £2,000 for every person in the UK' (House of Lords and House of Commons, 2013, 14).

In the US, the Troubled Asset Relief Program (TARP), developed on the back of the 'Paulson Plan', effectively bailed out the US financial services sector, representing what has been labelled a 'financial coup' (Harvey, 2009; Johnson, 2009). Under TARP, the US Treasury committed up to $700 billion to promote stability in financial markets through the purchase and guarantee of 'troubled assets' (Congressional Budget Office, 2012, 1), and by February 2012, $431 billion of this had been disbursed (Congressional Budget Office, 2012, 2).

These 'financial coup[s]' (Harvey, 2009) marked the beginning of a new 'age of austerity' characterised by sovereign debt, where the already most vulnerable within, and across, societies are targeted as the price worth paying for capitalist recovery. Moreover, these financial packages in both the US and the UK were accompanied by relatively unprecedented levels of state 'intervention' in parts of the corporate sector. Notably, for example, numerous governments, including the UK and UK, provided various forms of assistance to the automobile industry, 'including subsidies to firms and direct involvement in industry restructuring plans', as well as varieties of car scrapping schemes to increase sales (OECD, nd, 2). During this period, many governments allowed the banks to ignore competition law – the supposed bedrock of neoliberal markets; in the UK, for example, a merger between HBOS and Lloyds, two of the country's largest banks, was supported by government.

Despite states rescuing capital from the crisis, however, there has emerged – not least in the UK – a dominant set of *consensual* responses which may provide the basis for the further march of neoliberal ways of organising and seeing the world. It is with some of the ways in which this remarkable outcome could be achieved that this chapter is primarily concerned.

Crisis, whose crisis? Discursive frames and morality plays

Introduction: framing the crisis

In Chapter Four, I address various criminological and socio-legal 'responses' to the crisis. Here I wish to consider the various ways in which the crisis has been politically and popularly *framed* – ways which have allowed, as I shall develop throughout this text, business-more-or-less-as-usual to proceed in its aftermath. Here the focus is upon various discursive initiatives and narratives which were constructed and utilised as, and since, the crisis unfolded. The starting point is with the claim that, 'Narratives are important instruments…because they co-construct and legitimise regimes by framing the way we see the world. Narratives are not author-less discourses, but represent specific, powerful interests' (Hansen, 2014, 636).

Writing from the discipline of cognitive science, Lakoff has contrasted the worldviews of liberals and conservatives in the context of US politics (Lakoff, 2002; Lakoff and Halpin, 2005). Of interest for this text is his discussion of the relationship between common sense and unconscious thought. And central, for Lakoff, to the ways in which unconscious thought informs common sense is through reference to metaphors. Thus metaphorical common sense helps to convey complex claims in ways which we all readily understand, even without having to stop to reflect why we understand it. More than that, within this logical structure of common sense, metaphors are used instead of, and are more powerful than, facts. Of Conservatives (albeit in the US context), in particular, he notes that they have learnt that 'politics is about family and morality, about myth and metaphor and emotional identification. They have, over 25 years, managed to forge conceptual links between morality and public policy…with powerful slogans, repeated over and over again…until the connections have come to seem natural' (Lakoff, 2002, 1).[18]

Such a characterisation of political debate is ideal-typical and over-simplified, as Lakoff himself recognises, and it does not even attempt to engage with the work of neoliberal organic intellectuals in a long-term construction of a new form of reasoning (Peck, 2012). But this argument does help us to understand why and how framings can be so successful in defining a social problem – and, thus, the limited range of credible solutions that can emerge in response to that problem. Indeed, if such social problems or even crises disrupt 'business-as-usual neoliberalism', successful framing of them can ensure that this endures for a 'relatively brief moment' (Peck, 2012, 181), and may in fact give certain aspects and agents of neoliberalism greater impetus (Lakoff and Halpin, 2005).

As early as 2009, Thompson had identified four main ways in which the financial crisis was 'being packaged for public consumption'. One is a 'business as usual' narrative, which identifies the key task as re-securing the stability of the financial system, alongside some blaming of a few 'bad apples'; politicians represent their task as acting decisively in restoring business as usual, while evading responsibility. Second – and partially related – is to invoke problems associated with 'globalisation', which thus require concerted *international* re-regulation. Third is a 'strong critique' of 'greed, profits and growth at any cost'; a fourth is a (predominantly US Republicans/Tea Party) response which calls for the return to '"sound finance" and balanced budgets' and a rejection of state intervention and regulation. For Thompson, each frame entails not just a claim about the causes of the crisis and concomitant resolution(s), but also invokes a specific public mood or animus in whose name it speaks – whether this public mood is, respectively, nervous, sceptical and disaffected, greedy, or resentful and vengeful.

Whether one agrees with Thompson's initial characterisation of post crisis packaging, several things are at least clear from this. First, most obviously but crucially, the crisis contained threats for capital, threats which required responses. This is even more the case if one accepts that the events which began to unfold from 2007 from specific parts of a mortgage industry rapidly spiralled into wider credit, financial then economic crises, which were themselves overlain by a series of related crises in what some have argued represented a conjunctural moment (Garrett, 2012). Second, that the crisis provoked a whole series of discursive responses – some complementary, some competing, some clearly contradictory. Third, that while each was backward looking by way of explanation, each frame at the same time carried with it prescription and potential resolution. Thus, writing in November 2008 as the discursive terrain appeared relatively open for what was in fact to be a brief moment, Žižek observed that, 'It all depends on how it ["the financial meltdown of 2008"] will be symbolised, on what ideological interpretation or story will impose itself and determine the general perception of the crisis. When the normal run of things is traumatically interrupted, the field is open for a "discursive" ideological competition' (Žižek, 2008).

Fourth, many of these framings contain an implicit or explicit moral element – and I would argue that moral responses were necessary, since the specific crisis of the financial services sector itself generated a moral critique which for a very short period of time seemed to have the potential to be overwhelming. Finally, Thompson's outline reminds us that these processes of framing need to relate to, and are at the same time also seeking to shape, some aspects of the public mood – so that they are about securing consent, about addressing, and negotiating with, publics; thus these are processes requiring 'intensive ideological work' (Clarke and Newman, 2012, 300), always fraught with difficulty (Clarke, 2010a, 391; Clarke and Newman, 2010). Indeed struggle for consent itself indicates a long-term *'continuing failure of hegemonic projects to secure a new settlement that stabilises a political-cultural formation'* (Clarke, 2010b, 348, emphasis in original). Attempts to forge such settlements always involve utilising elements of existent and past, albeit still somewhere resonant, discourses – and hence the significance of the argument in the previous chapter regarding the growing moral capital of capital extending beyond a quarter of a century prior to the crisis.

Identifying blameworthy subjects

Having the benefit of greater hindsight than Thompson regarding those discourses which emerged to explain, and prescribe ways out of, the financial crisis allows me to be a little more expansive than his, earlier, characterisation. Here I wish to highlight a series of such responses – some complementary, some competing, some more powerful and some more enduring than others and, crucially, some with more system-threatening potential than others.

First, there emerged a series of morality plays which had their origins in regarding individual bankers as 'villains that brought down the world' (Whittle and Mueller, 2012, 119). Whittle and Mueller's (2012) analysis of the UK Treasury Select Committee hearings of 2009 into the banking crisis and in particular the questioning of four senior bankers therein demonstrates clearly that these were processes of moral condemnation. The conduct and substance of the Select Committee is typical: within these generalised morality plays, senior individual figures at the head of financial services companies – prime examples being Fred Goodwin, Stephen Hester, Andy Hornby and Tom McKillop[19] – were identified and vilified, often over very long periods of time. Moreover, such processes took place on both sides of the Atlantic (Froud et al, 2012, 44–5). Indeed, these were effectively quasi 'degradation ceremonies' (Garfinkel, 1956; Goffman, 1963) – *quasi* because although they were clearly ceremonial, and certainly involved formal denunciation, not least in moral terms of blame and shame, lacking was any formal calling to account even if for some who had been vilified, their lives were changed, though this generally meant a lower profile rather than any significant diminution in their material standard of living (Harris, 2012b). A variation of this ceremonial denunciation of specific, named individuals involved intermittent, less focused, much broader swipes at the guilty men and women of the City or Wall Street. This in turn drew upon distinct, but not entirely unrelated and hence utilisable, discourses of *rogue* traders (Pludwin, 2011, 470–2), itself a common discursive mechanism for separating out harms and crimes perpetuated in the corporate world from the normal functioning of that world.

In any case, what emerges from this generalised framing of specific or a 'class' of individuals is that, if there were 'lessons to be learned', they were about eliminating bad apples, or 'tricksters' (Kelsey, 2014) – and not, therefore, about the necessity of the external restructuring of markets, sectors or fundamental practices within them through re-regulation. Thus, for example, reflecting upon the causes of the global credit crisis and the international recession, Lord Myners, the then Financial Services Secretary in Gordon Brown's Labour government was able to state,

> The failures have not been failures of the market economy. They have been failures of men and women who forgot that market discipline meant that they had to be disciplined in order to get results out of the marketplace. Too many people got complacent and lazy – and the market responded as we should have predicted. (Myners, 2010)

However, it is worth noting that such was the level of this outrage directed at a broad sweep of leading financiers that this discourse was never easily nor wholly contained simply at the level of specific bad apples; as indicated, popular sentiment extended to 'the bankers', bankers' pay and bonuses, sporadically if briefly widening out to both executive pay and, possibly more significantly, to 'crony capitalism' – to which I return, below.

That this was a protracted process of blaming is indicated by the fact that 'banker bashing' entered the popular lexicon. Indeed, some sought to call it to a halt: in January 2011, within days of taking over as CEO of Barclays, Bob Diamond told a parliamentary committee that he thought that 'There was a period of remorse and apology for banks and I think that period needs to be over' (Treanor, 2011). As Werdigier put it, he argued that it was time 'to move on from criticising and to let banks and the private sector create jobs and economic growth' (Werdigier, 2011). For Diamond, the question was 'how do we put some of the blame game behind' (cited in Werdigier, 2011). It has become a common refrain by the industry and its apologists. Fraser Nelson, editor of *The Spectator*, lamented in 2013 that 'It has been almost five years since the crash and still the guilty men are being tracked down and subjected to what seems like a never-ending trial for financial war crimes' (cited in Cohen, 2013), while Anthony Browne, chief executive of the British Bankers' Association and his former hatred of rent-seekers has vanished. 'We need to put banker bashing behind us' (Cohen, 2013).

This was not a view shared by all of course. Interestingly, Mervyn King, who as Governor of the Bank of England was hardly immune from criticism himself in the incubation of the crisis, said before the Treasury Select Committee, in March 2011, in reference to the fall in living standards on the part of 'innocent families', that this was, in fact, the fault of the financial services sector – and that he was 'surprised the real anger hasn't been greater than it has' (cited in Aldrick, 2011).

As intimated, this generalised opprobrium took some dangerous (from the point of view of capital) turns. At a most general level, there was a long-term popular and political outrage at 'executive pay' – an issue that has certainly erupted from time to time in the UK, not least under conditions of neoliberalism in which the UK has experienced widening levels of income and wealth inequalities, trends exacerbated under conditions of post-crisis austerity which the government was attempting to impose under the rubric 'we're all in this together'.[20] Government responses to this both sought to acknowledge, even to claim at times to share, the popular discomfort but to represent such levels of remuneration as unavoidable in a globalised market – Britain Plc had to attract and retain the best people at the head of their largest companies in order to continue to compete effectively in globalised market-places, and thus to facilitate recovery from recession. This latter claim appears to hold considerable sway – perhaps through repetition and a simplistic understanding of labour markets – despite there being absolutely no evidence for it (Bolchover, 2013; Gigliotti, 2013; High Pay Commission, 2011a; 2011b). Were this actually to be the case, then it might be noted that, compared to its European counterparts, the City of London must have some exceptionally talented people: a 2013 report by the European Bankers' Association found that there were 2,400 bankers in the City paid over €1 million in 2011 – a total which was more than three times as many as in the rest of the EU put together (Treanor, 2013b).

A second general way in which blame has been apportioned is via the construction and use of a series of moralistic dichotomies. One which has circulated widely in the UK has been between retail (good) versus investment (bad) forms of banking, a discourse which gained such power that it sits at the heart of the major reform to the sector which has resulted from the crisis, the so-called ring fence to be erected within banks to protect the former from the risks of the latter (see below, on Vickers). This rather conveniently obscures the fact that the three major waves of consumer victimisation that have occurred in the sector in the past three decades – private pensions, then endowment mortgages, then payment protection insurance 'mis-selling' – all occurred within the retail sector (Tombs, 2013).

A further, slightly distinct, moral dichotomy has been that between 'good' and 'bad' borrowers (the latter being the sub-prime borrowers in particular) and predatory as opposed to responsible lenders (Brasset and Vaughan-Williams, 2012, 35). Such divisions have class-based and, in the US, racialised and gendered dimensions – and, while pernicious, these also have resonance as they bear a relationship (albeit distorted) to reality, since saturated markets for mortgages saw less financially able groups exploited as a new, untapped source of super -profit for business (see, for example, on the distribution by ethnicity of sub-prime lending in the US, Sassen, 2013, 31–2; and Dymski et al, 2013).

While there are elements of the bad apple claims here, this applies to wider populations, so that this resort to endless victim-blaming discourses (Weissman and Donahue, 2009, 9) created the basis for a wider encompassing of 'suspect citizens' and their 'culture of debt' (Pludwin, 2011, 472). In some ways this used the suspect lending practices of financial services forms and turned responsibility on its head. As Dymski et al have noted of the post-2007 exposés of sub-prime lending in the US, 'The defining aspect of the crisis was not that subprime loans and other forms of predatory lending disproportionately victimised minorities and women, but that borrowers were myopic, overly greedy, or both' (2013, 125). This also created the basis for a further, useful slippage, one that then allowed moral blame to be attached to many of us, itself related to a slightly wider claim that 'we' were all somehow personally responsible for borrowing too much, enjoying easy credit, living beyond our means and so on (Brasset and Vaughan-Williams, 2012). Thus, in general,

> The relationship between individuals, their houses/homes and their investment and saving habits was suddenly produced as a category of moral analysis in the public sphere. Fear, guilt, shame and anger were mobilised and sovereign responses, typically couched in the humanitarian vocabularies of salvation and helping victims, as we have seen, were not only justified but seen to be necessitated. (Brasset and Vaughan-Williams, 2012, 41)

The emphasis upon bad borrow*ing* as opposed merely to bad borrow*ers* also opened up discursive space for the emergence of the credit card analogy (Broome et al, 2012, 5). This analogy was to prove crucial in the institution of the idea that nation-states had overspent. In 2008, while in opposition, Cameron used the *News of the World*[21] to claim that the Labour government 'has maxed out our nation's credit card – and they want to keep on spending by getting another. We believe we need to get a grip, be responsible and help families now in a way that doesn't cost us our future' (Conservative Home, 2008).[22] Thus, although such an analogy is empirically (Reed, 2012) and conceptually (Pettifor, 2012) ludicrous, it had power since it resonated with the relatively successful balanced household budget analogy deployed over 35 years ago by both Thatcher and Reagan as they ideologically softened up their respective populations for monetarist experiments. Indeed, Konzelmann charts 300 years of key themes within narratives designed to justify austerity – within which 'appeals to ethics and morality' which in turn are 'reinforced by misleading analogies drawn between government budgets and the accounts of…households' have been central (Konzelmann, 2014, 701). As I shall expand upon below, such claims proved pivotal in the very quick shift from the construction of the crisis as one of private, capitalist institutions to one of national debt, especially debt incurred through public sector and welfare spending, and thus a more general, public lassitude (Robinson, 2012). More generally, then, this renewed attention to a diet of good monetary and fiscal governance via belt tightening on behalf of a gorged population helped to make austerity not just palatable but necessary, both economically and indeed morally (Blyth, 2013b, 1–15).

Such discourses also segue into a third group of morally-condemnatory frames, namely those which we can reduce to the claim that everyone and everything was to blame for the crisis (McLean and Nocera, 2011). Thus, 'Who's not to blame? The mortgage brokers were out of control. Regulators were asleep. Home buyers thought that they were entitled to Corian counters and a two-story great room… This was an episode of mass idiocy' (Pludwin, 2011, 472). If there was idiocy, claiming that this was ubiquitous is important: *if* we were all to blame, then no-one or nothing in particular was to blame; and *if* we were all to blame, then it follows that we should all share the pain of 'recovery' – hence, again, the UK government's easy refrain that we are all in this together, albeit a claim always somewhat vulnerable in the context of clear empirical evidence as to the distribution and effects of austerity measures. The ubiquity of blame coupled with the facile credit card analogy are double movements underpinning the representation of private as public debt and ideologically fuelling the legitimation of austerity.

These indications are enough to highlight the prevalence of blaming strategies, albeit this discussion is not exhaustive, for blame also extended at specific times to specific institutions (such as ratings agencies; Sinclair, 2010), or to specific practices engaged in by institutions (such as 'short-selling', limited forms of which were banned in the UK for six months from September 2008) (see BBC, 2009a). But enough has been said to emphasise that what ties these discursive responses together is that such processes of actively naming and producing blameworthy subjects serve

> a political and ideological function by focusing attention on individuals and groups and away from a confrontation with the normative and systemic violence of capitalism itself. In a moment of economic crisis one cannot merely say, 'This is simply the natural force of the market at work,' since such a statement would certainly raise questions as to the soundness of the broader system. The restaging of responsibility to the active 'discovery' of guilty parties helps maintain the integrity of capital and sustain the mythology that the market is rational, objective, and natural, but had been undermined and polluted by a few bad apples. (Pludwin, 2011, 475)

Silencing blame discourses

Pludwin correctly states, in the above quotation, that a response to the effect simply that the crisis was a *natural* effect of 'the market at work' would have called into question the market system itself. However, there were some discursive responses which did in fact invoke forces of nature to 'explain' the crisis. Thus, a fourth discursive response to the crisis transcends the paradigm of blaming – albeit while retaining systemic-insulating effects. This entailed the generalised use of the language of the *tsunami*, a force of nature which in fact made victims of individual bankers just as much as financial institutions, governments and taxpayers (Brasset and Vaughan-Williams, 2012; Broome at el, 2012; Whittle and Mueller, 2012). This invoking of the tsunami was so strong and generalised that it became metaphorical – the financial crisis *was* a tsunami. Thus, giving evidence to a Congressional Committee in 2008, Alan Greenspan, Chairman of the US Federal Reserve until 2006, while acknowledging a long list of 'regulatory mistakes and misjudgements', referred to the crisis as a 'once in a century credit tsunami' (BBC, 2008). As Greenspan spoke, fears were expressed that the tsunami which had started in the US and 'rolled across the UK' would then move on to 'the Continent' (Priest, 2008). Within a year, political leaders of developing countries were telling the G20 that

'All the warning signs suggest that the financial crisis has produced a tsunami heading directly towards some of the most vulnerable parts of the world' (Woods, 2009). Months later, within the Eurozone, the crisis in Greece, formally defined as one of national debt, was generating fears of a 'Lehman-style tsunami' as the crisis was seen to threaten Spain and Portugal (Evans-Prichard, 2010). More latterly, within the UK, the coalition government has sought consistently to represent the UK as a safe haven from the after-shocks of the tsunami affecting Eurozone states – after-shocks now represented as storms, presumably because of their longevity and creating the idea that *some* protection could be offered by nation-states. At the same time, of course, demonstrating that ideological frames need not be consistently drawn upon, the failures of the UK economy to 'recover' were consistently explained, at least partially, by the coalition government via references to external, uncontrollable shocks *upon* the UK economy *as a result of* 'the crisis in the Eurozone'.

This metaphor has several related effects and elements, albeit not necessarily, at least on face value, consistent with each other. First, it renders us all as victims – and this status as victims in the face of uncontrollable external events was one of the moral appeals made by UK bankers to evade responsibility (Whittle and Mueller, 2012, 126–9). Second, it depicts that which has victimised us as somehow both natural but also unnatural – it was a force of nature but also something that could not have been expected nor prevented, and somehow aberrant in the normal workings of the world of finance. Third, it is plausible – since it is entirely consistent with the ways in which markets, market forces, economic outcomes and so on are and have long been represented, as if natural, literally a product of nature, which of course at the same time 'severs the economy from political life' (Pludwin, 2011, 467) and thus any form of human agency – representations which dominant forms of academic economics have been crucial to upholding (Jackson, 2013; see also Blyth, 2013a). Fourth, the analogy with the tsunami also provides the basis for a 'state of exception' since, as is the case following any natural or other, specific 'disasters' (such as 9/11), these justify, in fact necessitate, states instituting emergency measures – albeit ones for which we would all have to pay, both now and in the future, in exchange for some future state-promised if not state-delivered protection (see Broome et al, 2012; Brassett and Vaughan Williams, 2012). Thus, the financial tsunami allows 'the government to justify incredibly large interventions to recapitalise the banks on behalf of such anxious citizens; the trick of course being that it was actually the citizens who were to subsidise the protection of the very banks that created the excessive lending in the first place' (Brassett and Vaughan Williams, 2012, 27).

In general, across nation-states, bailouts, bail-ins, emergency budgets, state nationalisation of banks, have all taken place as executive acts – which in effect have liquidated democracy and exist in a space beyond the rule of law (Agamben, 2005).

A further key feature of the idea of a tsunami is that it carries with it the connotation that what occurred across the international financial services sector could not have been known in advance. That is, it constructs the crisis as one of a lack of knowledge, or ignorance, albeit one that runs counter to 'the common assumption that modern economies are knowledge societies', an ignorance which is at the same time an active silencing, a closing of the possibility of critical debate (see also Mathiesen, 2004). Thus Davies and McGoey examine 'the double value of ignorance: the ways that social silence surrounding unsettling facts enabled profitable activities to endure despite unease about their implications and, second, the way earlier silences are then harnessed and mobilised in order to absolve earlier inaction' (Davies and McGoey, 2012, 66). More than this, 'the ways that the fallibility of expert knowledge are alternately highlighted and downplayed are marshalled as a vital defence mechanism against unwanted governmental intervention' (Davies and McGoey, 2012, 73). This in turn chimes with the consistent narrative in 'official accounts' of the financial crisis which invokes '"complexity" in the nature of the securities transacted and in the structure of the financial industry as a way to convey difficulty to understand or apprehend, and thus to predict financial dynamics and regulate financial institutions' (Datz, 2013, 459).

Of course, it would be erroneous to imply that such processes are secure – they are, in fact, subject to intense struggle, and silencing, pulverisation and the general attempts to insulate institutions from fundamental critique are only more or less successful. We can see the fragility involved in attempts to respond to a crisis of legitimacy through containment and attempts to 'close the universe of discourse' (Shorthose, 2011, 108) by the fact that more system-threatening discourses about the crisis did intermittently and incoherently circulate.

Blaming capitalism?

Thus there have been two specific versions of discursive response which have had greater potential for placing some of the more individualised accounts into a wider context. Thus the individualised moral critiques of personal greed have intermittently extended, or threatened to extend, beyond purely individual levels – from widespread vilification of 'the bankers' though to a general critique of the relationship between pay, bonuses and poor performance, and into wider critical considerations of banking culture and 'crony' capitalism.

One strain here has been to invoke critically a wider, albeIt meso-level, immoral banking *culture*, with echoes of what Will – following others – has called, in the context of the US, a Ponzi culture (Will, 2013), one characterised by the valorisation of 'debt, speculation or gambling, and the belief in rapid "investment" growth' (Will, 2013, 48), 'a product of the symbiotic relationship between government and financial institutions' (Will, 2013, 60). Problematic elements of 'banking culture' revolved around greed, short termism, 'excessive' risk-taking – all, if not specifically individualised, are shorn of their structural and institutional supports, even determinants. This decontextualising was further bolstered, in the UK, by the establishment of the 2013 Parliamentary Commission on Banking Standards, the terms of reference of which were to 'consider and report on: professional standards and culture of the UK banking sector, taking account of regulatory and competition investigations into the LIBOR rate-setting process; lessons to be learned about corporate governance, transparency and conflicts of interest, and their implications for regulation and for government policy; and to make recommendations for legislative and other action' (www.parliament.uk/bankingstandards). What is of interest here is how, from the litany of offences in which the financial services sector has been clearly implicated in recent years – from waves of 'mis-selling' to consumers of pensions, endowment mortgages and payment protection insurance (Tombs, 2013), to money-laundering, inter-bank lending rate manipulation, sanctions busting and tax evasion (Bowers, 2012; Sikka, 2012; Treanor, 2012a; 2012b; 2012c; 2013a) – *one* specific issue, the 'problem' of culture, is addressed through only *one* of these offences, the fixing of the inter-bank lending rate. It is unsurprising, then, that the report of the Commission (House of Lords and House of Commons, 2013) did nothing to address the destructive, systemic features of the sector (Economist, 2013).

In its formal, political treatment in the UK, then, this focus on culture acts as a mechanism through which the crisis is reduced and confined at best to second order phenomena, via which it is also subjected to 'de-democratisation' through 'efforts to refuse social and political dimensions of the financial system, its purposes and its governance' (Clarke and Newman, 2010, 713). If publics are not duped by such efforts, they certainly contribute to an anaesthetising cynicism with public life – hardly any surprise then that at the time of the announcement of the Inquiry, 71 per cent of those polled 'do not think banks have learnt their lesson from the financial crisis' while only a quarter thought the parliamentary inquiry into banking ethics would 'lead to positive change among the UK's lenders' (Guardian, 2012).

A second, but this time *macro*-level, moral critique has surfaced and resurfaced periodically and briefly – one which has actually spoken the word capitalism, albeit in the context of a series of simplistic moral dichotomies, between 'good' and 'bad', 'moral' and 'immoral', and 'crony' and 'responsible' capitalism. Indeed, in invoking 'crony capitalism, we are seeing the resurrection of a term that last circulated widely in the context of an earlier financial crisis, which afflicted Japan and neighbouring Asian states at the end of the 1990s (Sinclair, 2010, 91).

At times in the UK, the term 'crony capitalism' has been subject to high level, political rhetoric. Notably, in the space of a few weeks at the start of 2012, all three main party leaders made major political interventions on this issue (Mason, 2012; Miliband, 2012; politics. co.uk, 2012; Pratley, 2012a; Wintour, 2012). As one might expect, however, the level of political 'debate' was anodyne.

First, Miliband followed up his party conference speech of 2011, where he focused upon 'a system of irresponsible, predatory capitalism based on the short term, rather than productive, responsible behaviour which benefits business and most people in the long term' (Miliband, 2011a). Therein, he mocked the seeming 'passion' of government to 'take on "crony capitalism"', since all this did was to highlight 'an agenda for responsible business that our business leaders already champion' (Miliband, 2012). Then, within days, Clegg called for an end to crony capitalism and encouraged companies to follow the 'profit-sharing' model of the John Lewis department store group (Mason, 2012). Cameron himself urged 'reforms' for greater accountability to shareholders (Pratley, 2012a). Such interventions only paved the way for Cameron to be able to emphasise the role of a socially responsible private capital forging an economic recovery while performing many of the functions with which the state had previously been charged, under a 'Big Society' tent, so that:

> what I want to argue today is that those of us who believe
> in markets, business and enterprise need to come together
> and prove the sceptics wrong...we've got to take on certain
> snobbish attitudes. The snobbery that says business has no
> inherent moral worth like the state does...that it isn't really to
> be trusted...that it should stay out of social concerns and stick
> to making the money that pays the taxes. (politics.co.uk, 2012)

Now, these latter discourses, regarding the 'need' for a renewed moral capitalism, which by definition involve a critique of some form of immoral capitalism, are not insignificant. They raise a system-critique, with echoes in contemporary, albeit marginalised, political claims such as those articulated by Occupy, the Indignados or Attac; and they jimmy open spaces for other generalised outrage at, for example, tax avoidance or food adulteration. In so doing, they create specific political risk, perhaps even crises of legitimacy for states, which are contexts in which albeit limited regulatory reform can be pushed through (Almond, 2013; Bittle, 2012). Thus they are instances where moral critique pushes up to the limits of political safety. That said, and at the very same time, they are in themselves not of great significance (yet?) since they have not, at least in the UK, assumed discursive dominance – this is partly related to the contemporary balance of social forces, partly an effect of generalised political scepticism and demoralisation, and partly because they in fact have nowhere meaningful to go except that place which all state, institutional and organisational power will be deployed to prevent them going. For these discussions about a moral capitalism are perfectly analogous with the claims for corporate social responsibility, discussed in Chapter Four; and, to preview my argument therein, they are futile, void of empirical or conceptual substance, and are better understood less as the basis for any meaningful economic reform, more as a tactic of virtual last resort, a 'Maginot' line in defence of capitalism (Glasbeek, 1988). The only place to which they can go is a place where they *cannot* go – that is, a more or less adequately conceived 'post'-capitalism.

Whose crisis? From private to public debt

In 2008, even as the government was in the middle of bailing out the financial services sector, Prime Minister Gordon Brown was keen to adopt the tone not of regulation nor criminalisation, but of moral re-energisation. In doing so, he was able, crucially, to draw upon the moral capital of private capital which had been developed and strengthened over the previous decades. This latter 'common sense' – and all that it implied for the gamut of potentially available regulatory strategies – was remarkably un-dented by the financial collapse and international recession (Crouch, 2011). Thus, despite having overseen an unprecedented bailout of the banking system – a massive state subsidy funded by the taxpayer that effectively socialised the consequences of long-term, systematic private greed and possible (albeit never to be uncovered) illegality – the UK's Labour government *underscored* their commitment to the 'free-market system' and 'light-touch regulation', while again declaring their continued faith in business morality and corporate social responsibility: 'Our government is pro-business; I believe in markets [and] entrepreneurship, and there are many areas of the economy that need the spur of more competition. But the events of the past months bear witness, more than anything in my lifetime, to one simple truth: markets need morals' (Brown, 2008).

On one level the claim that 'the markets' – a purely reified, fictitious entity – need morals (not, note, regulation) is just *non*-sense; on the other hand, the fact that such a statement can be made attests to the power of the hitherto constructed *common* sense. This formal political response was soon to form the basis of a consensus, [23] one accepted by all major political parties in the UK as they fought the general election of 2010 (and, indeed, one common to most governments across the capitalist world).[24] Specifically, senior political figures frequently espoused the need for 'improved regulation' of the financial services sector – albeit what this meant was never (and never-to-be) specified. In fact, the 'main parties competed only to represent themselves as the most competent to foster the health of the city' (Froud et al, 2012, 53). Alongside these mantras ran the equally consensual and consistent claim that regulation in general remained over-burdensome and required reduction. The Labour Party, in its 2010 election manifesto, stated that 'banks will face tighter regulation' (1:4), before going on to say of regulation more generally that, 'We will continue to simplify regulation and avoid unnecessary red tape' (Labour Party, 2010, 1:6). Cameron had, in a series of public statements from Autumn 2008 onwards, been 'quick to emphasise that the party still favoured light-touch regulation as far as possible' (Dorey, 2009, 265), and in its main 2010 election manifesto (Conservatives, 2010a), as well as in its pre-election policy paper, *Regulation in the Post-Bureaucratic Age* (Conservatives, 2010b), the Conservative Party sought to document the extent to which Labour had added significantly to the regulatory burdens upon business, claiming that that 'a lot of Britain's regulatory burden is created because we resort to state regulation and red tape when other, lighter touch alternatives would do the job just as well instead' (Conservatives, 2010b, 13). One exception to this was Vince Cable who, as Treasury Spokesman for the Liberal Democrats, talked toughest and in most detail on regulating financial services. By contrast, in his first speech as Business Secretary after the formation of the coalition in May 2013, he in fact promised, 'radical steps…against red tape' (Horton, 2010).

More generally, by this time,[25] the financial crisis had been transformed into a national debt crisis – the logical response thereby being to reduce public expenditure significantly while re-creating the conditions in which private capital could flourish. Thus, in the UK,

> Rather than regard finance as broken, the politicians have chosen to regard government as broken. New Labour set out a blueprint for an assault on the state; the Coalition has merely intensified this assault. The financial sector demanded a fiscal consolidation, and the government has pledged itself to deliver. The ease with which our politicians have attacked civil servants and the social benefits that have been the birthright of UK citizens since the Second World War contrasts markedly with an almost non-existent approach (so far) to financial sector reform. (Simms and Greenham, 2010, 53)

Of course, this reframing of the causes and thus the road from the crisis has occurred at the international level, too, through 'epistemic communities' (Deacon, 2011) which framed national policies.

This reframing has been most violently in evidence in the Eurozone. Thus when Fox Piven notes that 'a kind of coup d'état has been worked through the European Commission, influenced by the banks, putting entire national populations at risk of serious austerity measures and even default' (Fox Piven, 2012, 82), it is crucial to understand that this has only been possible by representing these as crises of sovereign debt rather than further transfers to banks. Not only were national crises problems which governments needed to address domestically, but they were also represented for some states – notably, Cyprus, Greece, Ireland, Italy and Spain – as situations in which national governments needed *to be saved from themselves* by external agencies, whether inter- or non-governmental. The policies of structural adjustment, generally enforced upon developing economies, had been imposed upon highly developed economies at the heart of Europe. And, to be clear, one basis upon which a translation could be achieved was that it was able to draw upon the instilled common sense which had always-already[26] constructed states and the public sector as bad and inefficient, private capital as good and efficient.

Thus, within what was quickly to become known as the 'age of austerity', the price of 'recovery' was to reduce significantly the social wage across the western world. Government debt, re-cast as state over-spending rather than the socialisation of the effects of reckless, capitalist profit-taking, means that unemployment insurance, the deferred wages that are pensions, public services, and the often still minimal protections offered by regulation are luxuries that can now be barely afforded.

Clarke has described these processes in terms of the 'nationalisation' and 'statilisation' of the crisis. The former was achievable through invoking the national interest – 'the conditions of the national economy, the fate of vital national industries, the loss of jobs in national economic sectors', which in itself represented a moment of exposure for neoliberal globalisation, where the state, apparently so shorn of capacity, had become 'the means of salvation' (Clarke, 2010a, 387). Thus the crisis was statilised: 'the state comes to be regarded as a powerful and resourceful political agent for managing the economic and political dynamics of the crisis' (Clarke, 2010a, 387). In these shifts, many of the various framings of the crisis are useful resources. Certainly in their combination, these clearly work to pre-empt new forms of regulation of the financial sector in particular or indeed the corporate world in general.

Perhaps most significant in this remarkable transformation was that which on first appearance is the most banal: namely the variations on the credit card analogy. Yet this had power precisely because it encapsulated both long-term capitalist, as well as financialised neoliberal, common sense: we always-already knew, ingrained from the ideological origins of ascetic capitalism, that frugality was the morally superior lifestyle to accompany industriousness (Weber, 1905/1978); more recently, at the dawn of the era of financialised capitalism, we always-already knew that prudent 'housewives' (so rhetorically beloved and effectively deployed by Thatcher), households and nations should 'balance their budgets'; we always-already knew that under financialised capitalism, credit had been easy to come by as well as that – at least *at the level of individual consumers* – failure to pay our debts necessarily generated punitive monetary (as well as, at times, social welfare and criminal justice) responses; and we always-already knew that – even if many of us had not directly 'enjoyed' it ourselves – the previous decades had been partly defined by the most grotesque[27] forms of conspicuous consumption, so unnatural, so odd, so deformed, bizarre and absurd that this could not continue without some price, ultimately, being paid.

Thus, as Osborne was able to state in 2010,

> Let me tell you what a structural deficit is. It's the borrowing that doesn't go away as the economy grows, and we have £109 billion of it. It's like with a credit card. The longer you leave it, the worse it gets. You pay more interest. You pay interest on the interest. You pay interest on the interest

on the interest…Delay now means pay more later. Everyone knows it's the most basic rule of debt. (Osborne, 2010b)[28]

Further, it needs to be emphasised that this redefinition of private to national debt was also highly manageable since it is hardly a novel achievement. Marx's dialectics of debt and credit – bound in a 'dynamic and unstable antagonism' (Dienst, 2011, 51) – recognised a fundamental characteristic of the capitalist economy, namely that, 'The only part of the so-called national wealth that actually enters into the collective possession of a modern nation is – their national debt' (Marx, *Capital Vol 1*, cited in Dienst, 2011, 29). Just as crises are endemic to capitalism, so, too, is the privatisation of profit and the socialisation of risk and the consequences of the realisation of those risks.

So when introducing his budget to the Commons shortly after the formation of the 2010 coalition government, Chancellor Osborne could quite confidently lay bare the shift from private to public debt, by then already a *fait accompli*, which generated measures of urgent fiat, as denoted by the very fact and naming of the budget as an 'emergency' budget: 'Questions that were asked about the liquidity and solvency of banking systems are now being asked of the liquidity and solvency of some of the governments that stand behind those banks…This Budget is needed to deal with our country's debts…This is the unavoidable Budget' (Osborne, 2010a).

Here, however, it should be emphasised that, in this reframing of the crisis from one of finance capital and capitalist speculation, to a crisis of individual rogues and aberrant rogue practices, but most fundamentally of state over-spending, pro-capitalist cheerleaders in government have not had, nor are they likely in the future to have, it all their own way. Governmental efforts to re-cast a new, post-Welfare capitalist settlement have met no little popular resentment and some resistance. State responses to such resistance have followed similar patterns: a combination of ideological mystification backed by the often heavy hand of power, flexed brutally on the streets of Athens, Madrid, Nicosia, London, New York, Toronto and numerous other cities and towns across the world.

Indeed, some of the state's more forceful responses to resistance lay bare the fact that austerity is political as well as economic – it is, in fact, about power, and thus also about violence, a violence which may be observable, involving batons, tear-gas and rubber bullets, or is structural, involving workfare, geographical displacement and dis-entitlement, thus exacerbating already-existing inequalities with devastating social, cultural, psychological and very material effects

(Galtung, 1969; Galtung and Hoivik, 1971). It is 'an assertion and a consolidation of power, capable of cancelling out custom and social accommodation'. As such, it 'claims the force of necessity', and is able to sweep away the fruits of struggle that might represent some forms of social progress to 'proceed confidently, and moralistically, in the face of common sense and painful experience' (Robinson, 2012). Thus, austerity, mystification, violence and a lack of accountability are intimately connected, so that opposition,

> has been met by a 'hardening' of the state and the characterisations of a new phase of 'authoritarian neoliberalism'. This claim is based, in part, on the further strengthening of executive power and insulation of economic policy from parliamentary accountability that we noted above. But it also arises from the incredible multiplication of legalised restrictions and policing modalities for the disciplining of dissent by the 'austerity state' (Albo and Fanelli, 2014, 21).

Perhaps, too, and not unlike the early responses to 9/11 in which consumers were encouraged to defy the terrorists and support the US economy and Wall Street by continuing to spend (Whyte, 2008), the reductions of interest rates in the UK to 0.5 per cent, the reductions in both stamp duty and then VAT, as well government attempts to get banks to start lending through injections of capital into them, not least via various rounds of quantitative easing, were encouraging much the same popular response. Thus, through encouraging a renewed form of market patriotism (Whyte, 2008, 2013) and via increasingly high levels of public investment in the private sector, the UK government fused the interests of 'nation' with those of private capital in the most brazen of ways. The practices and values of marketisation and financialisation were thus strengthened: 'the manner of the movement between victimhood and survival involved an even stronger pact with the sovereign power of finance and the affirmation of the particular category of liberal financial citizenship' (Brasset and Vaughan Williams, 2012, 39), through 'the (re)production of sovereign power, liberal financial subjects and the very market practices that were implicated in the crisis' (Brasset and Vaughan Williams, 2012, 21). More generally, and also analogously to 9/11, the financial crisis has been re-created as an opportunity for a significant power and wealth grab on the part of capital and political elites.

Conclusion

What emerges from the material and discursive responses to the crisis, then, is a crucial meta-narrative – that the conditions for, and nature of, recovery places governments and populations as even more dependent upon private capital. This in turn immediately and necessarily – *for all our sakes* – reduces the scope for reinvigorated regulatory regimes. And the dominance of such discourses is important – they crucially underpin systems of regulation which, while varying across nation-states and indeed across different areas of social protection, remain predicated upon the assumption that most companies most of the time are essentially law-abiding, not least through having some form of social responsibility – a view still dominant among academic scholars of regulation, as documented in Chapter Four.

The ideological foundations upon which our economy is based have hardly been undermined, then. Rather, if somewhat paradoxically, these may in fact have been strengthened and deepened (Albo and Fanelli, 2014, 14) by the economic crisis: private capital is trumpeted as the only feasible response to economic crisis. *Increasing* 'freedom' for capital has been prescribed as the solution to the problems created in the first place by the excessive freedoms of capital. Thus, while the UK government put together the biggest single rescue package for its banking industry (Alessandri and Haldane, 2009, 23; Simms and Greenham, 2010, 33), it has remained the key bulwark against reforms in global financial regulation (Prieg et al, 2011). Cameron has also claimed that it is in the national interest to defend 'the City' against EU-driven reform of financial services (BBC, 2011a) so that 'safeguarding' UK financial services from the new dynamics of EU regulation must be 'at the very top' of the list of priorities in any EU negotiations (Booth et al, 2011, 4).

Thus it can now more clearly be seen how the morality plays discussed above were both effective and neutralising. They were effective, that is had a social and cultural power with some momentum, because they reflected realities – bankers *had* demonstrated greed, recklessness and at best a moral indifference, economies *had* boomed on consumption based on ever-easy access to credit, access to risky credit *was* disproportionately distributed to ethnic groups and class fractions who were sold lifestyles which could not be supported by low paying, under- or precarious employment, and the popularised myths of the end of boom and bust really *had* meant that, in some senses and for some, the crash did come unexpectedly, as if of no-one's making but also of everyone's making. But these discourses were also effective precisely because individually, and in their combination, they individualised, isolated and pulverised the crisis, thereby neutralising the systematic nature of the financial and broader economic system from the critical, perhaps fatal, popular scrutiny that the events from 2007 onwards merited.

In these ways, a series of 'mystifications' which shuttled 'between a market-centred responsibility and an agentic-centered blame model of responsibility' both served to 'sustain the supposed sanctity of the market' (Pludwin, 2011, 476) and, crucially, the dominant actors within it. However, it should be emphasised that 'these multiple and competing definitions of the crisis are indicative of more than a matter of different points of view: rather, they suggest that the present forms a conjuncture in which different forces, different tendencies and even different crises come together' (Clarke, 2012, 45). Moreover, these are also more than economic and political: 'there are also' persistent and paradoxical crises of morality (and authority, perhaps) which 'seem an integral part of the present' (Clarke, 2012, 48).

None of what has been discussed here was any simple trick nor straightforward process – though trickery, literally the creating of illusions, played its part. There is no sense in which the narratives that were eventually to be more successfully attached to the crisis and its aftermath were *necessarily* to be successful. There was discursive struggle (Whittle and Mueller, 2012) over which narrative would triumph, contests as to 'how' to make sense of events (Breit, 2011; Stanley, 2012) – whether through greedy bankers, consumer responsibility, a gorged nation, a nation of victims of something akin to a force of nature, risky cultures, practices or indeed systems. At least two issues were crucial in determining which narratives succeeded. First, what power and interests could be mobilised *around* which narratives – and, here, the long-term mobilisation and consolidation of interests around the claims of free market economics was crucial (Blyth, 2013a); and, second, to what extent did those narratives *have* power, specifically, which were more authoritative (Stanley, 2012), more plausible, more convincing and cohered with an already existing moral narrative (Whittle and Mueller, 2012). And it is in this latter context that the previously constructed moral capital of capital becomes crucial – or, in quite literal terms, gets cashed in – because the solidity of the moral stock of capitalism as a whole generated over the previous 35 years (not to mention the de-moralised, parasitic and overly bureaucratic state, public sector and welfare system) was to insulate the system as a whole from any effective, thoroughgoing critique, let alone a moral one. Neoliberalism had not just been socially (Cahill, 2011), but also culturally embedded. To paraphrase Massey (2012), then, and to be clear: none of this just happened; it was the product of a great deal of ideological work over many years.

FOUR

Regulation, orthodoxy and hegemony:
crisis, what crisis?

Decent chaps don't check up on decent chaps to see that they're behaving like decent chaps. (Sir Desmond Glazebrook)[29]

Introduction

In one sense, it would be hard to over-estimate the extent to which the financial crises that rolled out across many parts of the globe from the end of 2007 onwards changed political, social and economic landscapes in many of the nations most affected. At the same time, several observations seem incontrovertible, and are assumptions upon which this chapter proceeds: first, that much of what was enmeshed in the aetiology of 'the crisis' involved not just harm but various forms of crime engaged in by major financial institutions across the world; second, that one of the causes of the crisis was not just risk-raking behaviour on the part of these institutions, but the nature and level of regulation at both national state and international levels which either allowed or encouraged such activities – in other words, the crisis represented not just forms of corporate crime and harm, but of state–corporate complicity in these. Third, that the state–corporate relationships which generated these harms and crimes are, to put it mildly, in urgent need of reform – and that this reform is most likely, under current politico-economic arrangements at least, at the point at which state and corporate activities most manifestly meet, that is, in the practice of regulation.

A question thereby raised is this: what can criminology or socio-legal studies tell us about the causes of the crises or ways in which further such crises might be prevented, mitigated, responded to? This is a pertinent question to ask of criminology, since one of the phenomena at issue in the crisis is potential or actual crime, and certainly widespread harm, a concept which has recently found its way into the discipline (QAA, 2014). And it is also a question of direct relevance for socio-legal studies because, in general, this sub-discipline is the place where most academic work on regulation gets done. These two questions provide the framing context within which this chapter proceeds. The focus is specifically upon British academia, albeit it is impossible to demarcate this clearly and neatly.

From the 1970s onwards, a substantial body of academic work, across socio-legal studies has emerged around 'regulation'. Dominant within this literature is a particular strand, with empirical, theoretical and normative dimensions, which views regulatory activities as the outcome and/or attempt to forge a consensus across a plurality of competing claims on the part of potentially – but not fundamentally – antagonistic parties ('business', 'workers', other 'interests'), all of whom, ultimately, are viewed as having a mutual interest in an efficient business sector. This chapter provides an overview of this literature, examines its responses to the financial crisis – in part, the result of a failure of regulation – and argues that this dominance has not been disrupted by the events that unfolded from late 2007 onwards. This latter claim, it will be argued, is a matter not of the accuracy nor the cogency of ideas, but of hegemony and thus of power per se.

An orthodoxy: introducing the main contours of the literature

In a review of socio-legal studies research in Britain conducted in the mid-1970s, a period by which it was said to constitute 'a coherent field of activity', Campbell and Wiles attributed the following general characteristics to this body of scholarship:

> First, the hegemony of law is accepted and furthered, even though some of the particular provisions of the law may be thought to require change. Second, the nature of the legal order is treated as unproblematic, especially in its relationship to the rest of the social world. Equally the general functions of law in society tend to be taken for granted or are assumed to involve the balancing and regulating of different social groups and their interests. Such a perspective assigns high priority to ensuring that the law is informed by liberal and reformist sentiments. Research is unambiguously utilitarian and pragmatic in orientation, and the suggestions for reform which flow from it tend to be limited in scope and of a legalistic nature. (Campbell and Wiles, 1976, 553)

Also from the 1970s onwards, a substantial body of academic work, across criminology and socio-legal studies, but also spanning political science, public and social policy, and management studies-related disciplines, has emerged around regulation in general and enforcement in particular. As I shall argue here, the dominant assumptions within these literatures shared the characteristics which Campbell and Wiles have attributed to socio-legal research.

Almond and Colover (2012) recently characterised work on regulation in terms of a '"deterrence school" of thought' (more widely referred to as a 'command-and-control'[30] approach, below) and a 'regulatory orthodoxy'. The former advocates 'tough penalties and a proactive enforcement strategy' and is inherently punitive, based upon a prescriptive, command-and-control model of regulation. In contrast, what they term the 'regulatory orthodoxy' suggests a more selective use of the threat of prosecution as a 'last resort' (Almond and Colover, 2012, 1010) and in general,

> gives support to approaches that utilise enforcement rarely and prioritise compliance-centred, accommodative, self-regulatory strategies of risk *management* (Ayres and Braithwaite, 1992; Baldwin and Black, 2008; Gunningham and Johnstone, 1999; Hutter 1997…Under this view, adversarial enforcement action only occurs in a limited number of cases when alternative approaches have been tried and failed. (Almond and Colover, 2012, 1000, emphasis in original)

Thus, some 25 years ago, in what was to become a rather acrimonious debate, Frank Pearce and myself drew attention to what we called a compliance or 'Oxford' school on regulation and enforcement. We argued that proponents of a 'compliance' (as opposed to a 'policing') regulatory strategy claim that the nature of corporate illegalities calls for different forms of regulation than is the case for other kinds of law breaking. Thus, businesses and particularly corporations are not, as many would have it, typically 'amoral calculators', but rather 'political citizens' who may indeed sometimes err but more because of 'organisational incompetence' than deliberate wrongdoing. Although some corporations sometimes act as if they are 'amoral calculators', this is neither necessary nor typical; where regulations are violated, this is usually the result of factors other than pure economic calculation. Corporations can and do have a primary commitment to act in a socially responsible fashion, are not essentially criminogenic, and will not cease to commit violations because of attempts at deterrence (Kagan and Scholz, 1984, 67–8; see also Hawkins 1984, 110; Hutter, 1988, 45–7, 80; Richardson et al, 1983, 125–49). To accept a view of the corporation as an amoral calculator entails a corresponding view of the most appropriate regulatory response to such corporations, namely, 'strict enforcement of uniform and highly specific standards, backed by severe penalties', with regulatory officials acting quite literally as 'policemen' (Kagan and Scholz, 1984, 72).

In fact, even as we were engaged in that debate, the academic *and* policy scales had tipped significantly and decisively towards those forms of regulation and its enforcement which we were subjecting to critique. Our own arguments for alternative forms of regulation (the so-called 'command-and-control' approach) had already become generally accepted as unworkable, unrealistic, undesirable.

The current dominance of the regulatory orthodoxy traced back to the 1980s, when, politically, the emergence of neoliberal governments meant widespread aim was taken at a variety of programmes for regulating private economic activity, while academically descriptions of and prescriptions for compliance-oriented enforcement and self-regulatory strategies began to gather momentum. Some three decades later, a new political and academic common sense around the viability of regulatory strategies has been consolidated.

Of interest for us is the way in which this shift was and is often characterised, since it is one shorn of agency, interests, power, conflict, but rather imbued with an inevitability and the emergence of a reasonable, realistic and indeed sophisticated and nuanced common sense. Typically, then, Hutter has claimed that the late 1980s 'witnessed a growing disillusionment with state regulation' (Hutter, 2006, 1), and that in the US and Europe, 'there was a strong deregulatory rhetoric, centring on claims of overregulation, legalism, inflexibility and an alleged absence of attention being paid to the costs of regulation' (Hutter, 2011a, 10; 2011b, 460). As Hutter notes, these 'shifts' were linked to wider changes regarding new public management, the de-centring of the state and a shift from government to governance (Brady, 2007, 5–6). The momentum of such 'shifts' was overwhelming, as Job et al emphasise:

> During the 1980s, a shift began in the public service in the western world from administration to management, with the expectation that results would be achieved in a fast, efficient, and innovative manner…Disillusionment with a command-and-control style of regulation promoted

interest in cooperative compliance, a style of regulation
that relied less on coercion and obedience and more on
education and persuasion. Cooperative compliance was
regarded with scepticism by operatives who frequently
encountered intransigent non-compliance, but it became
popular rhetoric among the advocates of deregulation. (Job
et al, 2007, 88; see also Brady, 2007, 5–6)

Thus by the start of the twenty-first century, what some were claiming[31] had been the 'dominant policy position' of 'CAC' (command-and-control) had been undermined as the widely cited criticisms of it – as 'inefficient, costly, stifling innovation, inviting enforcement difficulties and focusing on "end-of-pipe" solutions' – had 'been widely accepted' (Fairman and Yapp, 2005, 492–3); thus, 'remedying the perceived deficiencies of command and control has become a driver in the regulatory reform initiatives taking place worldwide', not least through the OECD (Fairman and Yapp, 2005, 493; see also Vickers, 2008) and other international pro-capitalist organisations. For some, then, a shift from CAC had been 'necessitated' (Ojo, 2009, 9). It was certainly 'widely accepted by policy-makers' (Vickers, 2008, 216). Thus, 'an earlier, simplified view of regulation…sometimes referred to as "command-and-control", had been superseded by "new governance research" which had "grown up in response to" it' (Carrigan and Coglianese, 2011, 114), so that by the start of this century, victory seemed complete:

> In business regulation circles these days, there is not much
> contesting of the conclusion that consistent punishment of
> business non-compliance would be a bad policy, and that
> persuasion is normally the better way to go when there is
> reason to suspect that cooperation with attempting to secure
> compliance will be forthcoming. (Braithwaite, 2002, 20)

Now, as we note below, there is no doubting the fact that there has been a concerted effort to undermine the validity of arguments for what is here caricatured as the CAC approach to regulation, and that these have been successful. Moreover, in these efforts, there has been an unholy alliance between academics and policy makers, to which we return below.

Crucially, at the same time as were engaged in our 'debate' with Hawkins, at the start of the 1990s, Braithwaite was forging the concept of responsive regulation in an explicit effort to transcend what he and

Ayres viewed as a sterile debate over 'deregulation'. Its origins were in an enduring problem for students of regulation: how to develop effective regulation in the face of inevitable resource constraints on the part of regulatory agencies. This approach had already been made clear in an earlier piece by Braithwaite and Fisse (1987), extensively drawn upon and developed in *Responsive Regulation* (Ayres and Braithwaite, 1992, 101–32). The former piece had considered the prospects for self-regulation as a strategy to control corporate crime on the basis that, 'we know it is politically and fiscally unrealistic to expect that our generation will see the public resources devoted to corporate crime control approach anywhere near those expended on crime in the streets' (Braithwaite and Fisse, 1987, 221). Therein, they went on to argue that 'there are many reasons' why 'corporations spend resources on private policing programs', that is, self-regulation:

> First, the question assumes an overly economically rational view of corporate behavior: corporations are at times moral actors that are concerned to obey the law because to do so is ethically right, even if costly. Second, corporations are in many ways even more concerned about their reputations than are individuals – individuals often subjugate economic rationality to preservation of their good name and self-respect, and so too do corporations. Third, corporations often invest in self-regulation to pre-empt the less palatable alternative of government. Indeed, governments sometimes enter into a tacit social contract with business: unless business makes self-regulation work, public intervention will be the result. There are other reasons as well, but we need not devote time to them. (Braithwaite and Fisse, 1987, 222)

I return to these claims later in this chapter. But it is such claims which were to form the basis of Ayres' and Braithwaite's development – in a text which has gained 'canonical' status (Parker, 2013, 2) – of the idea of responsive regulation. This concept has been applied, developed, tested, affirmed and subjected to critique across Australasia, North America and Western Europe in a diverse range of contexts from 'corrections to school bullying to international peacemaking' (Burford and Adams, 2004, 12; Nielsen and Parker, 2009, 376–7; Wood et al, 2010). Central to responsive regulation is the prescription of a regulatory enforcement strategy which these authors characterise in terms of a regulatory pyramid. Most regulatory activity with most companies involves forms of self-regulation, while the most punitive tactics need only to be resorted to in dealings with a small number of firms – hence the self-regulatory base of the pyramid is far larger than the punitive peak. Thus most companies have 'demonstrably effective self-regulatory systems', so that 'scarce regulatory resources' should be 'concentrated on companies that play fast and loose' (Ayres and Braithwaite, 1992, 129).

A slightly distinct – and increasingly now voluminous – variant within regulation literature has sought to establish a 'risk–regulation' paradigm (see, for example, Black and Baldwin, 2010). Since the publication of *Responsive Regulation*, the use of risk technologies to inform regulatory targeting has become part and parcel of the regulatory landscape, with risk-based forms of regulation now ubiquitous across UK regulatory bodies (Black, 2005; Hutter, 2005; Rothstein et al, 2006). In practical terms, risk-based regulation increasingly forms the basis for regulatory policy across a wide range of regulatory areas in diverse national contexts (Tombs and Whyte, 2006; Tombs and Whyte, 2013b). Thus, 'In a striking wave of regulatory homogenisation, risk-based regulation is becoming widespread across the globe and in areas as diverse as environment, finance, food, and legal services' (Black and Baldwin, 2012, 2).

The 'risk–regulation' couplet has established itself as academically pre-eminent in the past decade. Much of this development has taken place within institutional academic circles – notably, in the UK, such claims regarding regulatory policy and enforcement have coalesced around the ESRC Centre for Analysis of Risk and Regulation (CARR), and have been central to the further renewal of the regulatory orthodoxy. Thus, CARR 'has rapidly established itself as an international reference point'[32] for 'risk regulation studies' – and what is particularly of interest is the very couplet, 'risk–regulation'. For here are the simultaneous ideas that risk is ubiquitous, that regulation always needs to be balanced against risk, and that determining this balance is not necessarily, or even, the task of government or regulatory agencies per se (Hutter and Jones, 2006). Thus, 'risk regulation refers to the governance, accountability and processing of risks, both within organisations as part of their risk management and compliance functions, and also at the level of regulatory and other agencies that constitute 'risk regulation regimes'[33]. Regulation extends beyond, and indeed is 'de-centred' from, the state (Black, 2002) – to various non-state bodies within the economic sphere, not least operating through market-based relationships, and through civil society (Hutter, 2006). 'At a minimum', determining the risk–regulation balance 'entails the use of technical *risk-based tools,* emerging out of economics (cost–benefit approaches) and science (risk assessment techniques)' (Hutter, 2005, 3, emphasis in original).

The affinities between these two independent bodies of work are, in fact, widely recognised in the regulation literature. For example, in a series of papers, Baldwin and Black have argued recently for *really responsive risk-based regulation* (Baldwin and Black, 2007; 2008; Black and Baldwin, 2010), in an explicit attempt to develop the affinities between both sets of literature. Thus, if work within the risk–regulation paradigm is clearly independent of that on responsive regulation, and has developed its own, diverse trajectories, this burgeoning and now voluminous literature shares several assumptions with that around responsive regulation. One is that state capacity has dwindled with respect to private actors and 'the market', while state resources are not and never will be sufficient for the task of overseeing compliance with regulation. A second is that this requires a targeting of regulatory resources at those firms or sectors where risk is greater or the chances of non-compliance are more significant, or both. Third is the assumption that the preferred regulatory option is to leave the management of risks to institutions beyond the state – notably to business organisations and their managements themselves, but also other private actors including trade associations, insurers and investors – so that corporations should be encouraged to act as responsible, self-managing, risk-mitigating organisations. A fourth assumption is that this is not only desirable but also feasible, because anthropomorphised corporations[34] can and do have moral commitments to preventing and mitigating risks – they are not reducible to artificial amoral, calculating entities, legally constructed as purely profit-driven, which in fact will routinely kill, injure, poison, lie, cheat and steal based upon (accurate or erroneous) cost–benefit analyses.

Returning explicitly to Ayres and Braithwaite's (1992) claims for responsive regulation, this means being responsive to both 'industry structure' – since different structures require different types and levels of regulation – and to 'the differing motivations of regulated actors'. Further, regulation 'should respond to industry conduct, to how effectively industry is making private regulation work' (Ayres and Braithwaite, 1992, 4). What characterises this key statement on responsive regulation, and those that have followed in this tradition, is a rejection of a 'strict enforcement' model. This rejection, for Ayres and Braithwaite is how we move beyond the 'deregulation' debate. Thus, time and time again, regulation theorists assert and reassert that 'strict enforcement' is a counterproductive strategy (see, for example, Simpson, 2002; May and Burby, 1998; Nielsen and Parker, 2009).

This insistence is in itself an interesting one since a deterrent enforcement philosophy, transmitted via command-and-control regulation, has *never* featured predominantly in any liberal democratic system of *corporate* regulation. Notwithstanding temporal, geographical and sectoral differences, empirical studies of a range of regulatory bodies across various jurisdictions overwhelmingly point to the facts that non-enforcement of the law is the most frequently found characteristic in regulatory regimes; enforcement activity tends to focus upon the smallest and weakest individuals and organisations, and sanctions following regulatory activity are invariably light (Snider, 1993, 120–24). In this sense, then, reference to 'pathologies of command and control' (Hawkins, 2002, 15) invokes an ideal-typical characterisation of an imagined regulatory system. Thus the idea of deterrence, as it is applied in the field of corporate regulation, serves the function of a myth: to act as some kind of cautionary tale or a sacred narrative which explains exactly why the regulatory system is the way it is and why it has to be so.

In fact, responsive and risk-based regulation are mutually compatible and reinforcing concepts that have achieved intellectual hegemony. In spite of (or perhaps as a consequence of) this hegemony, those who argue for such forms of regulation have largely been spared the hardship of defending their positions. While such positions have been subject to some empirical, but certainly conceptual and theoretical, critique, these arguments have tended either to be ignored or dismissed summarily as simply unrealistic or crude idealism. Indeed, the advocates of responsive regulation have positioned themselves as the representatives of the *only feasible* site for discussing regulation, a terrain which, we are seduced into believing, has transcended the 'deregulation debate', to paraphrase the sub-title of Ayres and Braithwaite's book – that is, 'the intellectual stalemate between those who favour strong state regulation of business and those who advocate deregulation' (Ayres and Braithwaite, 1992, 3).

The argument here is that the emergence to dominance of regulatory orthodoxy-related concepts combined within wider theoretical and normative schemas around regulation and enforcement is to be explained less by empirical, conceptual or theoretical robustness, and much more by political attractiveness and convenience. The broader political economy within which this position is generally articulated has allowed regulation scholars to peddle their claims in an environment which has protected their assumptions from critical scrutiny.

An orthodoxy?

Despite not insignificant differences among the writers and approaches I have referred to here, then, there has emerged a remarkable degree of academic (and policy) consensus, a dominance to such an extent that even at the start of the 1990s Frank Pearce and myself described this as an academic orthodoxy achieving the status of ideological hegemony, while at the same time we argued that this group of academics constituted a school, that is, a 'compliance school', centred around the Oxford Centre for Socio-Legal Studies.[35] Of the idea of a school, we noted that this need not and would probably not be a conscious identification, but members of a school would 'share a set of implicit and explicit theoretical assumptions' and 'similar assessments about what kinds of interventions in the world are possible'. Moreover, and crucially, a school can be identified by 'that which it is not, by that which it sometimes attacks, and as often ignores or evades'. Further, members of a school tend to cite each other's work approvingly, edit and contribute to the same journals and books, exchange unpublished papers and seek constructive criticism from each other when writing, 'not least when they are policing boundaries' (Pearce and Tombs, 1991, 421).

Hawkins baulked at the idea of a 'compliance school' – always used in inverted commas – since for him it was a claim which cobbles together (Hawkins, 1990, 445) authors and research work focusing upon the quite distinct spheres of regulatory policy (strategy) and regulatory enforcement (practice), as well as focusing upon the US and UK, which have quite different regulatory cultures. Yet to the extent that there was an ongoing series of relationships between many of the authors whose work we were subjecting to critique, and a shared set of assumptions regarding regulatory policy *and* practice, albeit with differences in details, the existence of such a school seemed incontrovertible. It is notable, for example, that many of the authors we had subjected to criticism in our 1990 article were acknowledged by Hawkins in his first response to that (Bartripp, Hutter, Lloyd-Bostock, Kagan) (see Hawkins, 1990, 444). More significantly, since that period, there has been a considerable circulation of personnel between two key institutions. We had argued in 1990 that the compliance school might be also be labelled the Oxford School, given that compliance-oriented arguments found their clearest expressions through the work of researchers associated with the Oxford Centre for Socio-legal Studies. A decade later, the key institutional site for logically related regulation discourse was to be found at the Centre for the Analysis of Risk and Regulation at the London School of Economics.

CARR was a significant initiative, established in October 2000 with £2.58 million ESRC funding, with a further £2.86 million in October 2005; it has also generated significant funding from private sector sources, including £4.7 million from Deutsche Bank (February 2000), £2.1 million from PriceWaterhouseCoopers (July 2000) and sums in excess of £200,000 from AON (February 2001) and BP Amoco (January 2000) respectively.[36] Through its very title, it helped firmly establish the risk–regulation couplet.

The circulation of personnel between Oxford and CARR is significant. Bridget Hutter, Senior Research Associate and Professor of Risk Regulation at CARR had previously held a Research Fellowship at the Centre for Socio-Legal Studies, Oxford; Julia Black, CARR Research Associate and Professor in the LSE's Law Department studied there; Sally Lloyd-Bostock, professor in LSE's School of Law since 1997 after working at the university's Centre for Socio-Legal Studies since 1973, is a research associate at CARR; Keith Hawkins has been a visiting professor at CARR for several years.[37]

These academic relationships have also extended across international borders to incorporate like-minded academics across the world, notably in the key centres of regulatory study in Australia and the US. In the former, Braithwaite, Gunningham and Parker have all been CARR visitors, as has Bardach, co-author of the touchstone anti-'punitive' enforcement text, *Going By the Book* (Bardach and Kagan, 1982; 2002). Other key institutional centres of the regulatory orthodoxy include Regnet (the Regulatory Institutions Network,[38] located at the Australian National University, Canberra) and the Penn Program on Regulation. At August 2012, current Regnet staff included Ayling, Braithwaite, Drahos, Grabosky, Gunningham, Haines, Johnstone and until 2013 had included Sherman (who was also listed as an 'Adjunct Professor', from UPenn);[39] Job and Shearing were visitors to Regnet in January 2014[40] and former Regnet staff included Haines, Levi-Faur, Parker and Scott.[41] Meanwhile, Coglianese and Carrigan were both on the staff at the Penn Program on Regulation,[42] which lists, among its academic links, CARR and Regnet.[43] The key academic journal outlet for the orthodoxy is *Regulation and Governance*, founded by John Braithwaite, Cary Coglianese and David Levi-Faur (see Braithwaite et al, 2007); its editorial board as at January 2014 listed many of the figures cited above.[44] Finally, the leading book series to publish monographs and collections of work in this orthodoxy[45] was centred on Oxford: Keith Hawkins was a long-time general editor, with an editorial board containing a majority of Oxford's Centre for Socio-Legal Studies staff, and publishing numerous texts over many years by Ayres, (Robert) Baldwin, Black, Braithwaite, Grabosky, Gunningham, Hawkins, Hutter and Christine Parker.

Though perhaps generally unintentional, through the dominance of literatures which shared essentially similar assumptions and which operated across the same liberal pluralist terrain, and in their (surely less unintentional) failures to acknowledge or engage with alternatives, these academics and institutions played a central role in the long-term process of commonsense construction and manipulation – and thus were well placed also to respond to particular crises to the hegemonic order – in these senses having something of an 'organic quality' (Gramsci, 1971 [1996], 12).

It is clear why academics might baulk at the idea of a school or orthodoxy. Any position appears much more persuasive and indeed rigorous: *if* it appears as one cited for its internal persuasiveness and rigor per se, rather than as one sharing a problematic with other, albeit varying, sets of claims and arguments; *if* it appears to be one of a range of commonsense views rather than as representing a school engaged in a hegemonic project to establish the common sense; and *if* it appears to stand on a terrain of reasonableness shared by a wide range of other authors and researchers, outside of which alternative views always-already appeared unreasonable, lacking rigour (rather being polemical, political and partisan) and *therefore* lacking support. As Davies has observed,

> An orthodoxy may not eliminate rivals, but its influence means they lack intellectual leverage and can be caricatured, recuperated, censored or ignored by its protagonists. Orthodoxies are best understood as the unwarranted assertions and silences of dominant paradigms. Vital questions…are bracketed in favour of 'pragmatic', often normatively inspired questions about how to manage or democratise…society. (Davies, 2011, 3)

If we substitute Davies' focus on governance for the concern here with regulation in the following quotation, we find perfectly parallel, and key, insights on the ways in which the regulation orthodoxy is maintained, its characteristics, and its effects:

> much…research is biased towards studying the positive effects of networking, ignoring manifold negatives.

> Lotia and Hardy (2008, 471) comment: 'A theme that characterises all the work discussed above is the assumption that, when it can be made to work, collaboration is clearly beneficial'. The literature is 'thoroughly functionalist', concerned with finding 'practical solutions to practical problems', underpinned by the normative bias towards networks. (Davies, 2011, 3)

Indeed, it is not surprising that the searing critique of network and governance claims in which Davies engages (2011) for the most part applies to regulation orthodoxy since for many regulation scholars, eschewing the role of the state in so-called CAC regulation, networks and governance, not least through self-regulation and a plethora of private actors, are both the desired and necessary basis for contemporary forms of regulation. It is no coincidence, for example, that the key journal in this area, established in 2007 by Braithwaite and colleagues,[46] should be entitled *Regulation and Governance*, while the new realities of governance – steering not rowing – are ubiquitous across this literature (Braithwaite, 2000).

Further, again in the context of a critique of network and governance claims, but again perfectly appropriate for considering regulation orthodoxy, Davies continues by noting that, 'During the 1990s and 2000s, a positive feedback loop emerged between the theoretical and the political fields, encompassing intellectuals celebrating networks and their political counterparts attempting to cultivate them' (2011, 30). Thus, Bordieu 'defined the "theory-effect" as remaking society in the image of ideas about it' (Davies, 2011, 31). Indeed, and more generally Aune (2001) has traced the ways in which policies based roughly on neoclassical economic theory were diffused from think tanks and specific universities based in the United States to government (see also Tombs and Whyte, 2003).

Politics, hegemony and the regulatory orthodoxy

The ideas being cultivated and diffused were intimately related views of feasible and desirable regulation and its enforcement – located within an essential *a priori* commitment to a liberal, pluralist democracy (Tombs and Whyte, 2010a). More than this, this fundamental commitment makes such views in principle coherent with a neoliberal perspective on regulation, those which primarily advocate the solution to the proliferation of regulation and regulatory over-enforcement via a shift to market-based and third party forms of regulation, beyond the state (Whyte, 2004). Whether intentionally or not, such intellectual, interpersonal and institutional relationships have the net effect of marking out of an academic and political terrain, an area constituting the acceptable range of views (see also Davies, 2011; Tombs and Whyte, 2003). In his critique of liberal interventions in seeming opposition to the contemporary politics of security over liberty, Jackson sets out forensically how, despite this seeming opposition, such liberal critique *ultimately aligns* itself with the dominant ideology and thus the state – so that it is critique in appearance only, and may therefore actually perform a legitimating function. Intriguingly, Jackson advances his argument through a critique of the work of leading liberal public intellectuals who seem to represent an apparently diverse set of views and with internal disagreements, the cumulative effect of which is, through their occupation of the same essential logic, not least commitments to liberal democracy and free market capitalism, and to human rights *within* these, to seek to offer a '"third model" or "middle way" between alternatives' (Jackson, 2011, 170).

The proclaimed option of representing or identifying a middle ground is far from coincidence, for here is the central liberal claim of being able to *balance* opposing concerns. Jackson consistently notes the significance of the balance metaphor in liberalism – a discursive device widely used (Pantazis and Pemberton, 2012, 656–7, 660–2). The shared 'politics of compromise' (Jackson, 2011, 171) thereby generated demarcates the terrain of legitimate and acceptable political critique, position and response, serving to 'marginalise and de-legitimate conflict and deny any potential for truly alternative politics' (Jackson, 2011, 174), not least any which would reject the legitimacy and validity of capitalism.

Here we find perfect analogies with the regulatory orthodoxy. Two intimately related balances are always-already central within this orthodoxy. First, the need to balance the socially productive effects of private corporate activity against the deleterious ones: worker, consumer, community and environmental protection is always to be balanced against the (never contested!) 'right' of private corporations to accumulate, which in turn produces social benefits in the form of employment, goods and services, tax revenues and so on. Second, the desire to regulate must always be balanced against the need to recognise the necessity of, and even to valorise, risk and risk-taking – a claim which ranges from the banal observation that there is no such thing as a risk-free society to the highly ideological claim that risk-taking entrepreneurialism is the motor of contemporary capitalism. Taking these two observations together, the regulatory orthodoxy takes as unquestioned the relative freedom of private capital to accumulate while accepting some – albeit always unspecified and indeed relatively unexplored – levels of socialised harms as a consequence of this. This is the axis around which any 'balance' is to be achieved.

In the UK, the Labour Party's modernisation process was in many ways a re-balancing; and, coming to government in 1997, the first Blair government committed itself precisely to transcending regulation/ deregulation, drawing upon the Third Way discourse popularised by Giddens (1998), a neither-right-nor-left charade which drew intellectual succour from a communitarianism to which Braithwaite was also committed (Tombs, 2002). Such transcendence was based upon a rejection of the idea that regulation is a process that seeks to resolve fundamentally antagonistic social relations in favour of a conception of regulation as aimed at 'win–win' solutions, 'wherein actors are seen as virtuous when they take seriously not only their own concerns but the concerns of others' (Braithwaite, 1997, 356–7).

As we shall see (in Chapter Five), a watershed moment for regulatory strategy occurred in 2004 when the Labour government launched the Hampton Review, which sought no less than to reconstruct the 'regulatory landscape' (Hampton, 2005, 76). Of interest here is the fact that Hampton's conclusions were informed by a concept of responsive and risk-based regulation. Certainly, it was significant in so far as it openly acknowledged the influence of this concept in the development of UK regulatory policy. Noting the merits and the influence of this work, Hampton explicitly acknowledged Ayres' and Braithwaite's arguments that 'regulatory compliance was best secured by persuasion in the first instance, with inspection, enforcement notices and penalties being used for more risky businesses further up the pyramid'. 'This approach', it continued, 'has been adopted by many regulators, and has resulted in the largescale random inspections of the past being replaced by more targeted intervention.' Thus, '[f]rom these developments has come a general acceptance among business and regulators that inspections are an inefficient enforcement mechanism in lower-risk or high-performing businesses, and that risk assessments should inform the work programmes of Inspectorates' (Hampton, 2005, 27).

Now, it is arguable whether Hampton's analysis was *entirely* consistent with the approach adopted by Ayres and Braithwaite. Indeed those authors might legitimately claim that Hampton has exploited their work in order to legitimise a withdrawal from inspection on a scale that they would never have advocated (see Chapter Six). However, what is instructive is the ease with which their work has been used to bolster what is in essence a politically driven neoliberal agenda.

This is a function of there being a logically consistent relationship between the two frameworks, of the assumptions and givens contained therein, of what is ruled in and ruled out of the terrain upon which each set of arguments works and which each marks out. If we add to these characteristics the explicit policy-orientation of the academic orthodoxy, this had made it particularly vulnerable to the process whereby, 'power typically *selects* ideas...while in the long term ideas tend to *conform* to the realities of power' (Simpson, 1998, xxix, emphases in original). Thus the work of the regulatory orthodoxy has inadvertently provided intellectual support for the political consensus of and trajectories around regulation – so that while at times denying any normative or political elements (Hawkins, 1990), the orthodoxy in fact contains both and thus is pro-hegemonic in function.

More specifically, Hampton used a responsive regulation approach to resolve the tension between the withdrawal of scrutiny and the need to secure compliance. He does this by using the following line of argument. First, regulatory resources are limited, and indeed are likely to be limited further; because enforcement strategies are resource intensive, regulatory agencies can no longer be expected to maintain current levels of inspection and enforcement. Second, reduced inspection and enforcement does not necessarily lead to less effective regulation; regulation may indeed become more effective under conditions of reduced resources if a series of compliance levers are used to secure self-regulated compliance. Further, Hampton bases his argument about a further reduction of regulatory activity upon a set of technical claims. Here, his argument turns to what is now loosely referred to as a 'risk-based' approach. This approach relies upon the claim that the most likely offenders can be clearly identified through a series of knowable variables that allow the likelihood of offending to be predicted. In this argument, Hampton severs 'reactive' regulatory activity from 'risk-based' regulation. Thus, while risk-based regulation is often narrowly cast as a method whereby scarce inspection resources are allocated, it has a wider and increasingly significant impact upon regulators. It helps regulators to 'structure choices across a range of different types of intervention activities, including education and advice' (Black, 2010, 186). In other words, the complex and often convoluted logic of risk-based regulation provides a rationale for a shift towards more consensus or compliance-based strategies which appeal to the cooperation and goodwill of business.

The aim of the risk assessment strategy set out in the *Hampton Report* is to withdraw regulatory scrutiny from those who, in the terms used by Hampton, had 'earned' their 'autonomy'. This was essentially rooted in the regulatory pyramid devised previously by Braithwaite and colleagues. Thus, and as we shall see in the following chapters (Five and Six), in strident pro-business climates, governments can extend 'risk-based' regulatory strategies *in the place of* enforcement. And, indeed, risk-based forms of regulation are now ubiquitous across UK regulatory bodies – as noted, the 'risk–regulation' couplet has established itself conceptually in the past decade as a key element of the new common sense regarding the nature and limits of regulation.

It is hardly unsurprising, then, that risk-based regulation is both central to the Better Regulation agenda (Black, 2010, 186, 189, 210; Hutter and Amodu, 2008, para 24) – at both UK and European levels – as well as being as much a 'legitimating device' for regulatory agencies themselves (Black, 2010, 188) as it is a series of techniques for regulatory practice. Moreover, as Julie Black has noted, this 'framing of the regulatory task' 'has the potential to have more than a rhetorical effect: it imports particular conceptions of the problem at hand, and leads to the framing of a solution in a particular way' (Black, 2010, 188).

Central to this framing is that, across a heterogeneous variety of regulation scholars, as we have seen above, there is a generalised rejection of 'deterrence-based' approaches. Thus, for example, scholars who describe or prescribe compliance-oriented (Hawkins, 1984), twin-track (Gunningham and Johnstone, 1999), smart (Gunningham and Grabosky, 1998), problem-solving (Sparrow, 2000), risk-based (Hutter, 2001), private or market-based (Hutter, 2006), and most significantly those who advocate varieties of responsive regulation (Ayres and Braithwaite, 1992) – including really responsive (Baldwin and Black, 2008) or really responsive risk-based regulation (Black and Baldwin, 2010) – all assume that what is generally referred to as 'command-and-control' regulation, where the state prescribes closely what constitutes compliance and then responds punitively on the basis of a deterrence-oriented approach, is unsustainable.

Moreover, also as noted above, a deterrence enforcement philosophy coupled with command-and-control regulation has *never* been anything like reality, but has acted as convenient myth. Indeed, the invoking of this myth as a means of justifying a particular regulatory strategy is by no means confined to academic critiques of regulatory and enforcement styles; indeed, it is a myth that has been a highly convenient one for politicians seeking to impress business. In a key speech to the CBI by Gordon Brown as UK Chancellor of the Exchequer (at a time when he was enthusiastically driving a business-friendly strategy of re-regulation) he told the CBI: 'In the old regulatory model – and for more than one hundred years – the implicit principle from health and safety to the administration of tax and financial services has been, irrespective of known risks or past results, 100 per cent inspection whether it be premises, procedures or practices' (Brown, 2005b).

Brown's contrived revulsion for an era that never actually existed mirrors the same mythical cautionary tale that we find in the mainstream scholarship on regulation. In UK politics then it is the re-imagination of a central straw person within this myth – the figure of the inspector who strictly enforces the law – which pervades and underpins claims regarding over-regulation, and the creation of unnecessary, state-initiated burdens on productive enterprise. The same figure has also been academically invoked as at the centre of 'the problem of regulatory unreasonableness' (Bardach and Kagan, 2002). Yet what is notable in both the political and academic 'common sense' is the lack of attention given to the clearest and most empirical evidence that would render such claims incredible. There is a myth of deterrence at the core of this common sense; a myth that is revealed by the perennial low-level of resources granted to regulatory agencies and the persistently – if, recently, rapidly declining – low levels of regulatory oversight which this permits.

> A consensus developed among mainstream scholars that things never quite work out as they ought when legislation is translated into administration. Rather than focus on what kind of practices were nonetheless achieved, the research depicting regulatory inadequacies became fodder for normative projects decrying public regulation alongside policy to de-regulate (Botero et al, 2004; Besley and Burgess, 2004; Alesina et al, 2005). While scholars may have sought regulatory reform, their work was appropriated to fuel regulatory retreat. (Coslovsky et al, 2010, 14)

Indeed, in setting out ten *Draft International Best Practice Principles for Improving Regulatory Enforcement and Inspections*, the concept of responsive regulation, attributed to the work of Ayres and Braithwaite, was explicitly proposed as one of these principles (OECD, 2013, 5, 14), as an essential element of part of an overall risk-based approach.[47] It is clear, then, that Ayres and Braithwaite's work is viewed, in this highly influential policy document, as the conceptual basis for opening up risk-based practices of targeted intervention.

The dominance of these approaches – all with their variations, but all, to be clear, placed firmly on a similar and essentially liberal pluralist terrain – ensured that there was, by the start of this century, a dominant politico-academic consensus on the nature, rationale and aims of regulation. The remaining issues appeared essentially technical, as academic after academic vied to deliver more effective how-to toolkits for local, national and international regulatory bodies – even as some, it must be emphasised, still bemoaned the fact of over-regulation and over-punitiveness (see, for example, Baldwin, 2004a; 2004b)! In sum, then, as captured by Haines, writing in 2011:

> The regulatory literature contains many strategies for regulators to consider should they want to be more effective. Suggestions for a thoughtful approach to regulation variously point to the value of smart regulation (Gunningham and Grabosky, 1998), meta-regulation (Parker, 2002), responsive regulation (Ayres and Braithwaite, 1992; compare Silbey, 1984), problem-solving regulation (Sparrow, 2000), and most recently, really responsive regulation (Baldwin and Black, 2008). This literature places the regulator within a broad governance framework, where the enforcement of rules within narrow prescriptive frameworks is eschewed in preference for policy mixes, combining instruments, third-party actors, and enforcement regimes that collectively can both 'push' and 'pull' (Gunningham and Grabosky, 1998, 259) regulatees into a reflexive appreciation of the goals the regulator wants to achieve and lead them to act in a diligent manner to bring the goals to fruition. Taken as a whole, this writing is pragmatic and positive; it argues that regulators can both design and enforce regulations in a manner that ensures regulatees pay sufficient attention to risk reduction and take appropriate action. (Haines, 2011, 119)

Regulation has become, thus, 'post-political':

> many contemporary attempts to regulate organisations and their practices can be understood as post-political in the sense that the organisation of these global governance efforts reflects a post-political vision, premised on consensual relationships, and where conflicts of interests and unequal power relations tend to be made invisible and/or irrelevant. We have not suggested, however, that these forms of regulation or governance are not political or that they are disinterested – rather, that their political nature is downplayed or concealed…[O]ur argument is that

the overall conflictual space in these forms of regulation has been narrowed down by the regulatory design, and that the frames are set in ways that limit the options and constrain the legitimate voicing of alternatives. (Garsten and Jacobsson, 2013, 432)

The functions and dysfunctions of corporate social responsibility

The article by Garsten and Jacobsson from which the above quotation is taken is, among other things, a critique of 'soft law' in the form of corporate social responsibility (CSR) initiatives. And this brings us neatly back, full-circle, to the earliest statement of what was to become the regulatory orthodoxy, namely Braithwaite and Fisse's 1987 essay which set out the three reasons why corporations would effectively self-regulate (above), central to which was a rather weak claim in support of the moral or socially responsible tendencies of the private corporation. Indeed, and as discussed above, in Chapter Three, the initial and consensual political response to the financial crisis in the UK was to eschew the need for more regulation through a focus on morality as a lens through which economic actors could be seen as central to any solution rather than the problem.

There has long existed an enormous literature on CSR – although, within that literature, there is little agreement on what it is, how it can be achieved or how it should be measured. As van Oosterhout and Heugens (2008, 198) have recently observed,

> The problem is that it is not clear what CSR is, that we do not understand its causes and consequences, and that the notion is not very helpful in understanding what is desirable or required at the business–society interface. We conclude, therefore, that the notion of CSR is better dispensed with altogether.

These points being made, most fundamentally CSR involves the claim that corporations can or do recognise a social responsibility, consisting of meeting legal and regulatory requirements which pertain to various spheres or aspects of their activities. Thus corporations may seek to respond to more general concerns, values, or pressures in society – that is, to take on commitments over and above those placed upon them by legal duties. More recently, it has become rather modish to invoke the notion of the 'triple bottom line'. Thus CSR 'involves a shift...from profit maximisation for shareholders within the obligations of law to responsibility to a broader range of stakeholders, including communal concerns such as protection of the environment, and accountability on ethical as well as legal obligations'. This is the shift from the "bottom line" to the "triple bottom line" (McBarnet, 2007, 9), consisting of economic, social, and environmental performance.

In general, this literature is notable more for its quantity than quality, and tends to evidence three clear, and inter-related, characteristics: first, much of it takes the form of prescription and normative reasoning; second, much of this is based upon an inadequate theorisation either of the nature of the corporation or of the economic and political contexts within which these operate; and, third, the literature lacks a clear empirical evidence base, usually revolving around case studies in support of what the socially responsible is or might be, alongside an attempt to squeeze 'analyses' of these into typologies. However, such weaknesses do not undermine the actual power or significance of these claims.

Most fundamentally, this literature fails to advance any coherent reasons in support of the claim that corporations can act according to a rationale other than profit maximisation. In general, it is crucial to understand the particular economic, political and legal conditions within which such calculations are made, so that the extent and nature of external pressures upon specific corporations *and* the corporate sector in general must be taken into account. And such latter pressures include what Snider has called the existence and cohesiveness of 'pro-regulatory forces' (Snider, 1991), within which balances of class forces are crucial (Pearce and Tombs, 1997). As Glasbeek has carefully demonstrated, to claim that the pursuit of profitability can be subjugated 'to some extent' is a logical incoherence upon which all corporate social responsibility arguments founder (Glasbeek, 1988, 401, and passim).

Moreover, in some business sectors, a strategy of social responsibility may make more business sense than others – notably those where corporations may wish to protect their reputations, the second support Braithwaite and Fisse (1987, 221–2) give for their willingness to engage in effective self-policing. But we need to be clear that this concern may apply to only a subset of corporations and is even then highly contingent. Thus, those which operate in competitive markets where they deal directly with individual consumers, for example – notably, high street stores – may have 'reputational' concerns to the extent that they seek to gain competitive advantage through CSR claims. More generally, then, CSR may represent a 'corporate social opportunity', to use the title of a widely used management handbook on the subject (Grayson and Hodges, 2004). Such a stance may have value in crude

PR terms, as well as in attempts to reposition external relationships with customers, or a wider public audience (Fryzel, 2011). Indeed, in so far as CSR has become a routine technique for corporations seeking to project their socially beneficial impact, it has also become part and parcel of the synoptic effect of corporate power (Tombs and Whyte, 2015). Further, CSR claims may enable corporations to enter emergent markets. Mooney and Miller, for example, have documented how '[l]obbying, think tanks, elite networking and policy planning groups, corporate social responsibility (CSR) and corporate philanthropy' have all been crucial in the strategic colonisation by private corporations of formerly public sector spheres of activity such as education, health and welfare (Mooney and Miller, 2010, 460), as well the plethora of new market opportunities afforded by the specific vehicle of the PFI (Edwards, 2009a; 2009b; Ruane, 2010; Pollock, 2011).

CSR has also been crucial in corporate efforts to enter or extend activities in markets which seek to build the allegiance of consumers, workers and publics and to create new forms of emotional ties to particular companies and brands (Klein, 2000), not least by embracing social entrepreneurship, community voluntarism (Sklair and Miller, 2010, 486–7) and even, in recent years, by adopting the language and symbolisms of resistance (Fleming and Jones, 2013, 76–8), most notably around environmentalism, so that '[w]ords and terminologies once used by environmental activists suddenly became corporate jargon' (Rowell, 1996, 103). In these senses, CSR opens up *new* techniques of profit-maximisation. In other words, it is not useful to think of CSR *merely* as a propaganda exercise or a smoke screen (Hanlon and Fleming, 2009).

Finally, claims to social responsibility are also, of course, made with much more cynicism on the part of corporations. Thus the calculative orientation which is central to corporate activity informs actions which appear to have quite a different rationale. This may form an integral part of the strategy of a business (Carr, 1985) as it assumes 'the cloak of social responsibility' for actions which 'are in the long-run interest of a corporation' (Friedman, 1970, 124). Again, CSR is not something antithetical to profitability, but is one of the strategic means by which profitability might be secured, protected, extended, maximised. CSR is a strategy for profit maximisation, and thus has a whole series of conditions of existence – and there is an element of contingency about all of these conditions of existence.

Nowhere has CSR's use as a means of enhancing corporate political leadership been brought to bear more effectively as it has in the sphere of legal regulation. If hardly stated explicitly, the principles of voluntarism and self-regulation that sit at the core of CSR strategies are always implicitly aimed at pre-empting, weakening or indeed displacing legal responsibilities – even if the prospect of law *enforcement* against corporations is slim and, in most contexts in the UK at least, getting slimmer, as we shall see in the following two chapters. As Baars (2012) shows, firms' CSR documents and policies can and do serve the function of diverting legal processes or, if these cannot be diverted, of mitigating the impact of enforcement and punishment of legal violations. CSR is a strategy that dilutes or deflects law enforcement thus allowing 'corporations to continue being harmful in a more controlled manner' (Baars, 2012, 298). An adjunct political function, as Shamir argues convincingly, is that CSR has been used as part of a more general political strategy to 'block the use of legal methods' for taming corporations (Shamir, 2004a, 7). Thus, CSR is deployed as a strategy to dilute or ward off legal regulation (Shamir, 2004b), and, contemporaneously, provides arguments for the extension of market-based forms of self-regulation. The irony here is that this is the third of Braithwaite and Fisse's arguments as to why corporations should self-regulate – 'to pre-empt the less palatable alternative of government' (Braithwaite and Fisse, 1987, 222) – and in fact underscores the claim made here that CSR is an act of corporate strategy. Further, it ascribes a rationality and instrumentalism to the corporation which the authors in fact wish to deny. Thus, while denying that corporations can and do necessarily act rationally, the regulatory orthodoxy claims, or assumes, that corporations will act rationally to produce socially responsible outcomes – not just because they are moral entities but because this pre-empts 'stricter' external regulation!

To be clear, then, CSR claims have a double function in relation to the law. They represent a means of protecting, extending and exploiting the *spaces within* the law and they at the same time obscure or mitigate the effects of exploiting spaces *between* laws. The latter has been discussed in detail elsewhere, notably by Michalowski and Kramer (1987), and is often crudely captured by the idea of regime-shopping, a strategy open to multinational corporations, of course, but also to companies operating within states as local growth regimes compete within domestic borders to attract and retain capital. But it is on the first set of process, the spaces within laws, which I focus here briefly.

Spaces *within* law are created actually or potentially in several ways. First, there is the ubiquitous phenomenon that law vis-à-vis corporations, and especially larger ones, is under-enforced, so that under-enforcement is the norm (Snider, 1993). Second, via the anti-regulatory initiatives which discursively and materially undermine the ability of those charged with enforcement in order always-already to tie the hands of the latter and to disempower them, key elements of the Better Regulation strategy which unfolded in the UK, then across the EU and the OECD (Chapter Five). A third space is potentially available in relation to the question of what constitutes compliance. This question is a far from unproblematic one. Much regulatory law sets out general duties or performance standards against which compliance is to be judged by external regulators or inspectorates. What constitutes compliance is thus subjective, ambiguous and, crucially, determined through negotiation and bargaining – so the outcome is always an *effect of power* – and a consequence of this is that corporations may adhere to minimalist interpretations of law yet still cast themselves as law-abiding. More generally, legal ambiguity allows corporations to adhere to the letter, rather than the spirit, of the law, and there are very significant differences between these two forms of 'compliance' (Hargreaves, 1975, 2). Accepting the minimal 'satisfying' of legal requirements as consistent with being 'responsible' in fact allows – even encourages – corporate irresponsibility. In the UK, this is evidenced, recently, in the clearly porous line between tax avoidance and tax evasion (Farnsworth and Fooks, 2015). In any case, all of these techniques have the aim of jimmying open wider, effectively legalised, spaces for corporate freedom.

Thus, it is no coincidence that the emergence of neoliberalism provided an impetus to the proliferation of CSR claims. For example, Frederick, a leading advocate of the CSR movement, speaking from the context of the US, noted that the election of Reagan was a crucial year in the 'story of corporate social responsibility':

> With the 1980 election of Ronald Reagan as US President, business hopes rose that some of the extreme pressures from social critics would be eased. The thicket of new social regulations and their costs had eaten into profits and complicated corporate decision-making. It was a watershed year, signalling a turn away from government and favoring private enterprise…Unwittingly, President Reagan had given a boost to CSR. (Frederick, 2006, 57)

As they gathered momentum, 'free market', anti-regulatory discourses and practices were creating a space to be filled – and CSR was ideally placed to do so. CSR, then, may be viewed partly as a defensive strategy, utilised at times of popular social censure, as 'a Maginot line' (Glasbeek, 1988) designed to defend capitalism; or more aggressively, as a proactive strategy for filling the spaces created by de- and re-regulatory moments.

If the search for means to fill such spaces – both 'between' and 'within' the laws (Tombs and Whyte, 2009) – has led to the re-emergence of claims for corporate social responsibility, then this points less to the substantial merit of the claims for or evidence of this concept, in any of its rather slippery guises; rather, it needs to be understood as the very product of that which it claims to remedy, that is, the regulatory crisis created by the international consolidation of neoliberalism (Snider and Bittle, 2010), while the embracing of such strategies by the various critics of corporate activities is, in 'a post-regulatory' – indeed, 'post-political' (Garsten and Jacobsson, 2013, 433) – context, merely born of desperation (Snider and Bittle, 2010).

States' apparent inabilities or unwillingness to regulate corporate activity create the space which the idea of corporate social responsibility seeks to fill. CSR is used strategically to support 'self-regulation' and to claim that corporations can comply with the law with little or no external oversight. What is perhaps most surprising and indeed depressing is that so much academic energy is devoted to detail the ways in which both CSR and self-regulation could and might work – despite the fact that there is simply no good conceptual nor empirical reasons to support either hope. None.

What bolsters such hopes, what makes them impossible to shed even in the light of no relationship to the reality of corporate practice, is ultimately a commitment to liberalism. Analogous to academic arguments for varieties of self-regulation – whether 'responsive', 'risk-based' or 'really-responsive' and 'really risk-based' – all variations of CSR claims stand squarely within an essentially liberal pluralist terrain. And central to them is the essentially liberal idea of achieving balance between opposing concerns (Jackson, 2011).

Most centrally, one form of balancing is always-already central to both CSR and self-regulation claims, namely the need to balance the socially productive effects of private corporate activity against the deleterious ones: worker, consumer, community and environmental protection is always to be balanced against the never contested 'right' of private corporations to accumulate, which in turn produces social benefits in the form of employment, goods and services, tax revenues and so on. Thus, 'the differential power positions of actors involved are being increasingly overshadowed and invisibilised by appeals to agreement, consensus, and morals. And in this process, some choices and trade-offs are removed from contested space while other ideals and choices are naturalised. Antagonisms are reformulated into win–win terms' (Garsten and Jacobsson, 2013, 433).

What crisis? Academic business as usual

The preceding argument perhaps helps to explain the extent to which the regulatory orthodoxy has – or has not – engaged in self-reflection following the financial then economic crises which unfolded from 2007 onwards. In short, and as I have demonstrated elsewhere,[48] just as the crisis has barely had an impact on criminology in general nor regulation studies in particular in terms of an object of study, the dominant body of work on regulation has hardly been disturbed at all by the failures of the forms of regulation it described, sought to conceptualise, and consciously or unconsciously, implicitly or explicitly, advocated for some 25 years or so.

In one of the few criminological or socio-legal papers even to address the crisis (Tombs, 2015a), Dorn has argued that the crisis exposed the ways in which dominant forms of regulation created common blind spots, and he argues for a 'regulatory diversity' which corresponds to

> a political strategy of democratic steering of regulatory agencies, diluting, if not displacing, the currently dominant notion of financial market regulation as a purely 'technical' discourse. In concrete terms, this implies shifting systemic regulatory oversight responsibilities away from 'independent' agencies, to government bodies and/or departments that are held accountable to their parliaments and electorates. (Dorn, 2010, 23)

Dorn in fact began his article thus: 'Criminology may still be making up its mind whether the emergence of the crisis in global financial markets is a matter for it or for other disciplines' (Dorn, 2010, 23). The benefit of hindsight allows us to respond to Dorn's then equivocal statement – both British criminology and socio-legal studies appear collectively to have made up their minds that the emergence, dynamics and fallout from the crisis is *not* a matter for either as a discipline. And the lack of such interest is not confined to Britain (McGurrin, 2013a; 2013b).

In another of the rare treatments of the economic crisis from a criminological perspective, however, the editors of a Special issue of the US-based *Criminology and Public Policy* were able to conclude in a way which takes us to the heart of the nature of the 'response' to the crisis by criminologists and indeed regulation scholars more specifically – and the problems with such a response:

> There is currently a remarkably optimistic consensus in some academic quarters about how to reduce the harm caused by privileged predators. The heart of it lies in the presumed promise of pluralistic, cooperative approaches, and responsive regulation. These assumptions highlight the need for enhanced prevention, more diverse and more effective internal oversight and self-monitoring, and more efficient and effective external oversight. They have gained use throughout a variety of regulatory realms, many since their earliest, albeit embryonic, formulation nearly three decades ago... They make sense theoretically, and we endorse them. We do so not because they have a record of demonstrable success but principally because sole or excessive reliance on state oversight and threat of criminal prosecution is difficult, costly, and uncertain. Still, we are mindful, as others should be, that the onset of the Great Recession occurred during and despite the tight embrace of self-regulation, pluralistic oversight, and notions of self-regulating markets by policy makers and many academicians. (Grabosky and Shover, 2010, 641–2)

In short, the financial then economic crisis have not disrupted the overwhelming majority of the academic literature on crime or regulation. This is not to say that regulation scholars have not addressed the crisis and its possible fallout, not least for their own work. However, as with Grabosky and Shover, above, they have tended to 'find' not only that their assumptions have not been found wanting, but that it is only themselves who can tweak conventional wisdom on regulation to establish the new, slightly revised, post 2007 orthodoxy. Certainly what is not on their agendas are considerations of anything resembling CAC, more punitive, more state-centred, nor more interventionist forms of regulation.

The optimism here is as staggering as it is unavowedly unfounded. These authors state quite explicitly that an academic consensus persists in its 'assumptions' regarding the 'presumed promise of pluralistic, cooperative approaches, and responsive regulation' – albeit that the policy approaches they suggest have no 'record of demonstrable success'!

Similarly, in the one special issue of any British based journal devoted to issues of regulation and the crisis (Moschella and Tsingou, 2013), its editors point to at least one general conclusion, namely that:

> The crisis and the reactions in its aftermath, marked by political activism and calls for re-regulation, have led a number of commentators to identify a general reorientation in the philosophy that underpins global financial governance. The argument is that the pendulum has moved away from deregulation, self-regulation, and market discipline to a more assertive and interventionist role for the public sector. However, the evidence assembled in this special issue does not provide clear-cut support for these propositions. While it is true that the activity and competence of the technical and expert policy communities analyzed in the case studies that follow was initially discredited, their grip on the regulatory process has not been seriously dented. (Moschella and Tsingou, 2013, 409)

These are clear indications that the crisis has not disrupted the academic nor policy assumptions regarding regulation. Certainly what is not on dominant agendas are considerations of any forms of more state-centred, more interventionist, nor more punitive forms of regulation.

To underpin this insularity and complacency, it is worth turning, briefly, to a special issue of *Risk Regulation*, the in-house organ of the Centre for the Analysis of Risk and Regulation (CARR, 2008). Therein, there is little sense that much has changed for the legitimacy of a particular approach to regulation – it may, in fact, have been rendered more significant and more urgent. Thus, the then current Director asked,

> what does this financial crisis and calls for a new financial architecture mean for the academic study of regulation and risk? Have academics been asleep on the job and are they now required to radically revise their reading lists… regulation as an academic subject was not asleep at the wheel because the study of unintended consequences and inevitable failures featured in research over the last few decades – not just at CARR…Just what caused contemporary events and discussion on continuing regulatory responses will occupy social scientists for years to come, but so far little suggests that the key regulation literature assumptions need revision. (Lodge, 2008, 13)

Similarly, another contribution, by the former Centre Director, urged

> a period of careful and systematic reorganisation. We therefore need to beware knee-jerk reactions. Typically, we can expect a flurry of post crisis activity but it is essential to contemplate proper longer-term solutions, taking time to appreciate what has happened and reflect on the coming inevitable competing explanations and accounts…Now is not the time for a regulation see-saw, moving first to strong, then back to weak…We must learn that the 'scientific' models of risk and business activity need to be underwritten and overseen by an ethos of responsible behaviour. We must learn that organisations need to re-assemble a sustainable trust and confidence structure across national borders and so bring Europe together. And we must learn that whatever we do, any solution has to embrace all the global players. (Hutter and Dodd, 2008, 6)

More generally, the regulation literature proceeds *as if* the events of 2007/08 have not happened, *as if* trust in the responsible corporation remains possible, *as if* the state remains incapable of regulating or intervening in the economy, and *as if* the basic assumptions of the literature hold true, simply in need of more research funding for further research for greater fine-tuning within but never questioning of its liberal pluralist paradigm. Reading quotations from articles such as those cited above, one wonders if it is merely a coincidence that CARR sits within the LSE – the former location of Anthony Giddens of whom, famously, Bourdieu and Wacquant scathingly summarised his services to the powerful as performing the role of their Pangloss (Bourdieu and Wacquant, 2001, 5).

Conclusion

> The characteristic feature of the new regulation is that it has been shaped by the financial institutions themselves, and its purpose has been to ensure the ability of the financial system to grow and extract profits. It has not contributed in the slightest to avoiding financial bubbles nor to imposing the costs of financial crises onto those responsible for them. On the contrary, contemporary regulation has led to society bearing the brunt of financial disasters, while private individuals associated with finance have reaped the

benefits of expansion. Society has little to expect from more regulation of the type we have known for four decades now. (Lapavitsas, 2014b)

The focus of this chapter has been on the emergence, nature, and maintenance-of-dominance of a regulatory orthodoxy. It should not be read as a critical reflection on the state of criminology nor socio-legal studies in general – though I do find both fields of academic endeavour relatively depressing. That said, the intention of this chapter has not been to obscure the considerable body of counter-hegemonic work being produced on a genuinely international scale by scholars, some well-established, many relatively early in their academic careers, on a range of counter-hegemonic projects which have either re-analysed, or extended (or both) some of the traditional empirical, theoretical, methodological and indeed political assumptions and commitments of criminology. There are so many examples that it would be invidious to highlight a few for mention here.

That said, one can read most criminological and socio-legal literature on *regulation* and find virtually no reference whatsoever to the financial crisis, its aetiologies, its political and economic consequences, its aftermath of drip, drip revelations regarding widespread corporate crimes, harms and immoralities, and that where there are such concerns they proceed with little sense that they might entail rethinking regulation.

In sum, the academic literature on regulation is a small industry, a torrent of self-referential banality from which considerations of power, capital, class *and even crime or harm* are notable for their absences. Therein, regulation is viewed largely as a technical issue, a search for mechanisms to empower anthropomorphised, essentially responsible firms to comply with law, in a world of stakeholders and conversations, where those who might suggest resort to criminal law are simplistic, anachronistic embarrassments, a world where power is never concentrated but dispersed, where sources of influence are polycentric, and where the state is certainly de-centred, relatively and increasingly impotent, just one among a range of actors, not least those which inhabit the private sector itself. So regulation might be responsive, better, smart, twin-tracked and risk-based – but it is always so 'realistic' that it is never about controlling pathological, calculating, profit-maximising entities as one element of a broader struggle for social justice.

Thus there is an absence of searching for regulatory solutions beyond tinkering with the forms of regulation which have prevailed. There are very few regulatory scholars who are even considering alternative forms of corporate ownership and controls, programmes for re-appropriation, state controls on exchange and interest rates and of international capital flows, debt audits and corporate and or individual sanctions as interventionist, potentially punitive and infrastructural state responses.

In his reflections on the financial crisis, Moran concludes that there are three lessons that regulation academics 'must urgently take on board'. First, that *'Democracy matters'*, referring to a 30 years' experiment 'designed to insulate regulation from democratic politics' which 'proved to be a disaster'. Second, *'Ideology matters'*, pointing to the fact that this same period had seen a *'naturalisation of markets: an exercise in ideological hegemony that pictured them as subject to quasi-scientific determined laws'*. Third, he recognised that powerful *'Interests matter'*, specifically 'a new Anglo-American plutocracy in the markets', the 'fantastic wealth of the financial sector' and a hegemony within which 'the stories of regulation before the crisis…are of timidity and subordination on the part of public regulators' (Moran, 2010, all emphases in original).

Now, I can agree with all of these observations – but the logic of the regulation orthodoxy seems virtually immune from being affected by them. To take Moran's exigences in turn: for the orthodoxy, *democracy* entails the liberal balancing act so that the right of capital to generate private profits is reduced to one of several social interests; *ideology* is the characteristic of those, such as Bittle, Glasbeek, Pearce, Snider, Whyte, and others who see corporations as inherently destructive and criminogenic; while the *interests* of power and the powerful are virtually entirely absent from the orthodoxy's analyses. In general, as I have argued, responses to the crisis by academics working in and around the orthodoxy have been either absent or complacent, lazy, self-referential and self-serving. The net effect of these, whether conscious or not, and bolstered by the reassertion of the neoliberal idea in the wake of the crisis, has been that the hegemony of the regulatory orthodoxy has been rapidly re-established. Across this orthodoxy, regulation is ever-more reduced to pragmatic tools and techniques ('toolkits') for balancing interests. And this, in turn, is an effect of the fact that liberal-pluralism predominates and continues always-already to de-legitimate alternative approaches to regulation.

Thinking about and beyond regulation – to follow Lapavitsas's challenge at the head of this section – is analogous to Jackson's conclusion to his critique of security intellectuals, thus:

confrontation with the logic of security must involve, if not begin with, confrontation with the intellectuals that provide it with a critical source of legitimacy and render it closed to critique...A truly alternative politics...must refuse to work with the logic of security and eschew all validity of a reformist approach. (Jackson, 2011, 185)

The regulatory orthodoxy is, for critical, counter-hegemonic scholarship, part of the problem not the solution. *Contra* the pro-hegemonic, liberal-pluralist assumptions which define this orthodoxy, regulation must be viewed not as a set of technical ameliorations to a world where private accumulation is always prioritised over social protection – represented through a pluralist balancing act – but as an object of struggle, power and social forces. Despite their protestations, the non-ideological work of the liberal orthodoxy is highly ideological and politicised, and needs to be challenged – following Jackson, this means eschewing narrow reform and daring to engage in radical intellectual work which not only reinstates the possibilities of regulatory options, but recognises that regulation by a capitalist state can only ever deliver a more effectively functioning capitalism – so that the real focus of regulation study must be on the symbiotic relationships between corporate and state forms, an exigence which means transcending the boundaries of criminology and socio-legal studies and embracing a wider political economy of transformation.

FIVE

Re-regulation in action: 'Better Regulation'

The argument is not the old one – more regulation against less regulation. Our focus is on getting regulation right – better regulation…regulation that will improve, not hinder, business competitiveness. (Blair, 1998, 18)

We are sticking to the task. But that doesn't just mean making difficult decisions on public spending. It also means something more profound. It means building a leaner, more efficient state. We need to do more with less. Not just now, but permanently. (Cameron, 2013)

Introduction

As indicated in Chapter One, the Labour government, elected in 1997, set itself on a concerted effort to *prove itself* as the party of business in a way the Conservative Party, as capital's natural representatives, have never had to do. Integral to this effort were two key, underlying convictions which underpinned its repositioning as the party of business.

The first was that Britain's global economic competitiveness hinged upon the creation of a business-friendly environment. Behind this rationale was an apocryphal fear of capital flight; the idea that over-regulation would result in the displacement of firms to more business-friendly foreign locations. On this basis, Blair sought to make Britain 'A great place to do business. Labour is now the party for business, the entrepreneur's champion' (Blair, cited in Osler, 2002, 57). The second was the central conviction that private economic activity is inherently and necessarily better than public sector activity. New Labour bought into a set of neoliberal claims that proposed, on grounds of economy, efficiency and effectiveness, the private sector as the most appropriate provider of goods and services. The logical consequence of this is that private businesses can also deliver *regulatory* outcomes more effectively than government mechanisms.

On entering office, those two rationales framed New Labour's approach to the regulation of business and enabled regulation, as a necessary evil, to be repositioned along neoliberal lines. These rationales were to be rolled out within the over-arching rubric of 'Better Regulation', a concept which can be traced back to the 1990s, but which in the UK and in the EU received particular impetus from the first Blair government.

Blair emphasised the bases for 'Better Regulation' in 1998 in the context of Britain's Presidency of the EU. In a Comment piece for the *Financial Times*, from which the quote at the head of this chapter appears, he set out his views on regulation – neither 'old left nor old right' (Blair, 1998, 18), in a classic articulation of the then-still fashionable 'third way' approach (Dodds, 2006, 526), and in terminology reminiscent of Ayres and Braithwaite's opening up of the discursive space for responsive regulation.[49]

Thus he committed his Presidency of the EU to ensuring that better regulation becomes 'a priority for Europe' (Dodds, 2006). In fact, it was to be Blair's second Presidency of the EU in 2004 which was to prove one of the pivotal moments in advancing Better Regulation through the EU (Wiener, 2006). So much so that, by 2007, one commentator was able to note that, 'Better regulation has become "*one of the most fashionable terms circulating in the corridors in Brussels*"' (Allio, 2007, 82, cited in Smith et al, 2015, emphasis in the original).

The European Commission's vice-President Verheugen was clear on both the nature and the aim of Better Regulation in 'a highly publicised press conference' in 2005. There, he stated that 'Better Regulation at all levels constitutes a central component in the Commission's proposal for revitalising the Lisbon process' (cited in Allio, 2007, 94) – the process which was being 'revitalised' to focus simply on 'growth and jobs', jettisoning its original commitments when launched in 2000 to 'sustainable economic growth, with more and better jobs and greater social cohesion and respect for the environment' (European Commission, 2010, 2). 'The equation is simple', continued Verheugen: 'less red tape = more growth and jobs' (cited in Allio, 2007, 94).

In this chapter, I trace some of the mechanisms through which the Labour governments, then, from 2010, the coalition government, sought to embed a new regulatory agenda under the auspices of 'Better Regulation'. To be clear upfront, this is not the most stimulating read, in the sense that it refers to initiative after initiative, most of which in isolation are hardly of great significance, many of which are essentially similar in substance and tone: but that, in a key sense, is the point. For what is being described here is a concerted programme of re-regulation, with four central mechanisms, albeit that the significance and dominance of any one of these has changed at different points during this time period: a rhetorical assault on regulation as burdensome, red tape and so on; the establishment of a mass of institutions within and around government; various legal reform initiatives which have delivered both de-regulation and re-regulation; and a constant stream of reviews of specific regulatory agencies and of the practice and purpose of regulation in general. In short, and crucially, these forms of mutually compatible activity indicate that it would be mistaken to view Better Regulation as deregulation – what we have witnessed is a concerted effort at re-regulation, attempts to re-configure the relationships between state and private capital. Moreover, the claimed effect here is that capital is being set 'free' – but these processes are more accurately viewed as generating a deeper and more intense inter-dependence between state and capital.

Regulating for 'better regulation': 1997–2010

Institutions and legal reform

An early indication of New Labour's enthusiasm for radical re-regulation came from its first year of office, in 1997, with a series of early, key institutional initiatives. First, the Conservative's flagship Deregulation Unit was consolidated as the 'Better Regulation Unit', with the Better Regulation Task Force (BRTF) established in the Cabinet Office. Then, the government formally launched its Better Regulation agenda, aiming to 'minimise the burden of regulation'. Better regulation entailed three elements: 'simplifying regulation by designing new regulations better and simplifying or removing old ones'; reducing 'the administrative burden on business of regulation, that is, administrative activities businesses would not undertake in the absence of regulation'; and reducing 'the burden on business of inspection and enforcement activity' (NAO, 2008a, 6).

In 1998, the Better Regulation Guide (Cabinet Office, Better Regulation Unit, 1998) introduced Regulatory Impact Assessments (RIAs). In 1999, the Better Regulation Unit became the Regulatory Impact Unit, with a remit to ensure that RIAs were being implemented across government departments. RIAs were the key legal reform of this period: they claim to measure the costs and benefits on business of all proposed policy and legislative reforms. Yet they contain structural biases towards less rather than more regulation in at least two ways. First, since their very rationale is the need to consider 'the impact of any new regulations, before introducing them, to ensure any regulatory burden they add is kept to a minimum' (BRE, 2008), their basis is in *reducing* regulation. Second, their economic form is likely to produce outcomes for less rather than more controls on business activity since the costs of meeting new regulatory requirements on the part of businesses are generally more calculable than are the economic or social benefits of such regulation (Cutler and James, 1996; Campbell, 2014).

RIAs, and the bias against regulation which they embed, proved to be central to a series of institutional structures established at the heart of governmental policy-making during the New Labour administrations. Meanwhile, one of the last acts of Labour's first term of office was the passage into law, in April 2001, of the Regulatory Reform Act. Crucially, this provided for Regulatory Reform Orders (RROs), which enabled a Minister to remove regulation if it represented a burden (defined tortuously by the Act) (see Regulatory Reform Act, 2001, section 1), a move that had been 'warmly welcomed by business organisations' (Lea, 2006).

Subsequently, and again demonstrating a zeal for institutional change through which to embed better regulation across government, the BRTF was succeeded by the Better Regulation Commission (BRC) in 2006. The BRC acted upon the BRTF's five principles: to ensure regulation and enforcement was proportionate, accountable, consistent, transparent and targeted. Its most significant contribution was to place 'assessing and managing risk' at the centre of the government's Better Regulation agenda via two reports, *Risk, Responsibility and Regulation – Whose Risk is it Anyway?* (BRC, 2006) and *Public Risk – the Next Frontier for Better Regulation* (BRC, 2008a), where it was argued that it was unrealistic and undesirable to try to completely eliminate risk. In January 2008, The Prime Minister announced the establishment of the Risk and Regulation Advisory Council (BRC, 2008b). A year later, in 2009, the Regulatory Policy Committee was set up to ensure that proposals for regulation are 'supported by a sound and robust evidence base' in the form of RIAs (Regulatory Policy Committee, 2011, 8).

Moreover, alongside the BRC was established the Better Regulation Executive (BRE). Located within the Cabinet Office, this was 'charged with driving through the government's better regulation agenda'. Additionally, there existed 'a Panel for Regulatory Accountability (PRA), a sub-committee of the Ministerial Committee on Regulation, Bureaucracy and Risk'; chaired by the Prime Minister, it was to consider 'all new regulatory proposals likely to have substantial burdens on business' (UK Parliament, 2006).

Rhetoric

These institutional developments were accompanied by a long-term rhetorical assault on the idea of regulation. This in many respects continued a low level rhetoric that could be traced back at least through to the Thatcher governments which cast regulation as burdensome, red tape, a barrier to enterprise and so on. But it was in the early years of the second New Labour administration that this ideological attack on regulation was ratcheted up – as if by design, across a plethora of political and media sources, precisely to accompany the establishment and the report of the Hampton Review (on which, more below).

This period saw a key series of high profile speeches decrying the anti-entrepreneurial effects of regulation, the dangers of risk averseness for not just economic but also for social and personal development, and the need for a new, 'sensible' debate about the relationship between risk and regulation. These were played out against the backdrop of simultaneous ratcheting up of the anti-regulation thematic across print and broadcast media. Underlying much of this was often to be found a more or less thinly disguised anti-European, or EU, sentiment, the latter being seen as the source of a whole plethora of attempts not just to over-regulate Britain, but even to undermine 'Britishness'. It also cohered with populist railing against so-called 'political correctness' (Heffer, 2004).

It is worth emphasising that, in isolation, any of these rhetorical interventions might appear irrelevant, spurious, or even downright silly (see, for example, Clarkson, 2004). But the issue is not at all any one speech, newspaper article or radio package in isolation – albeit some are significant, given their source; their significance is in their steady stream, seemingly ubiquitous, from senior politicians, civil servants and regulators through to a raft of media outlets, from tabloids to broadsheets, and across TV and radio outlets. From Tony Blair as Prime Minister and Gordon Brown as Chancellor of the Exchequer, across the *Guardian* (notably via Simon Jenkins and Simon Hoggart) to the *Daily Mail* and *Daily Telegraph* (especially through the writings of Simon Heffer), BBC Radio 5's daily evening *Drive* show, and Clarkson's *Topgear*,[50] there was a constant drip, drip of undermining of the *very idea* of regulation – in effect, the sound of a new common sense being constructed, within which regulation was always-already illegitimate, irrelevant, nanny state-ish, counterproductive, burdensome, pernicious, anti-entrepreneurial and even, at the personal level, antithetical to 'normal' human development. As Campbell has put it, high level rhetorical interventions are key in framing that common sense:

> The foundation of any regulatory regime is set at the top. This is where the tone and expectations, guiding rules and procedures, and budgets – the regulatory culture – are established…[G]overnment's laissez-faire attitude to regulation is reflected in its incessant use of the term 'red tape,' which implies that regulations are a burden on business rather than a legal mechanism to protect the public interest. (Campbell, 2014, 24)

Many of the 'regulatory myths' (Almond, 2009, 354–60) propagated during this period tended to focus particularly on health and safety, which became the *bête-noire* of the over-regulation mantra, but had the effect more generally of undermining regulation and regulators. It is no coincidence that two of the most infamous stories can both be dated back to 2004, the year in which Hampton was appointed to undertake his major review of regulation: one, the claim that local councils had begun to ban hanging baskets, the other, that some schools had started to ban the use of conkers in their playgrounds (Almond, 2009, 355–56).

Thus it was that in the period leading up to the establishment of Hampton, and in that surrounding the publication of the *Report*, there was what appears to be a concerted political initiative around risk-aversion and the need for sensible regulation. In his budget speech as Chancellor of the Exchequer on 17 March 2004, Gordon Brown foreshadowed the deliberations of Hampton and the assault on inspection and enforcement by a commitment, 'working with business', to identify 'further regulatory reforms in Britain and in Europe', including the commitment to 'review the burden of inspection and the overlap between enforcement regimes' (HM Treasury, 2004).

A year later, Brown unveiled Hampton's findings in his budget speech, in March 2005, stating that,

> it is also right to lessen the burden of regulation and enhance our flexibility while still ensuring high standards. So instead of a one size fits all approach which can mean that unnecessary inspections are carried out while necessary ones are not carried out, the best practice risk-based regulation now means more inspection only where there is more risk and a light and limited touch where there is less risk. (Brown, 2005a)

Brown also used the pages of the-then Labour-leaning *Financial Times* to continue to urge 'a new, risk-based approach to regulation to break down barriers holding enterprise back' (Brown, 2005a) For Brown, 'a new trust between business and government' was possible, founded on 'the responsible company' and 'government concentrating its energies on dealing not with every trader but with the bad trader. This new risk-based approach has wide application from environmental health to financial services and even taxation' (Brown, 2005a).

Also coinciding with the publication of the *Hampton Report*, Lord Hunt, then Health and Safety Minister, called for a common sense approach to risk management as he formally launched a debate on the causes of risk aversion in health and safety. Speaking at the launch organised by the HSE in the House of Lords he said:

> We must concentrate our efforts on the big issues that cause real harm and suffering and remember that excessive risk aversion does damage too. It hits organisational efficiency, competitiveness, restricts personal freedoms and damages the cause of protecting people from real harm. We know that something is seriously wrong when we read stories of schools asking children to wear goggles to play conkers in the playground...It is my intention to bring about a balanced approach to risk that have at its heart an emphasis on the importance of communicating risk effectively. (HSE, 2005)

HSE Deputy Director General Jonathan Rees said at the same meeting: 'HSE's approach to regulation is very much based on sensible risk management. Risk is ubiquitous. Some degree of risk, whether financial, environmental or in terms of safety, is necessary for progress.'[51]

Two months later, Blair made a crucial intervention in London, presenting essentially two versions of the same speech. What was to prove a key speech in the context of the EU's embracing of Better Regulation, which by then was already said to be 'sweeping' through the EU (Wiener, 2006, 65), was titled 'Risk and the State' (Blair, 2005a), and was reformulated in the afternoon of the same day in a call for a 'Common sense culture not compensation culture' (Blair, 2005b). It is worth focusing on Blair's speech(es) in a little more detail. As Prime Minister, it is notable that he recycles well-worn myths which by that time had attained the status of truths and were being reiterated ubiquitously. Blair framed the 'issue' as something which, 'if it goes wrong, has the capacity to do serious damage to our country'.

It is what I call a sensible debate about risk in public policy making. In my view, we are in danger of having a wholly disproportionate attitude to the risks we should expect to run as a normal part of life. This is putting pressure on policy-making, not just in government but in regulatory bodies, on local government, public services, in Europe and across parts of the private sector – to act to eliminate risk in a way that is out of all proportion to the potential damage. (Blair, 2005b)

While in fact Britain 'compares favourably with its competitors on regulation', Blair illustrates some of the dangers of regulation:

something is seriously awry when teachers feel unable to take children on school trips, for fear of being sued; when the Financial Services Authority that was established to provide clear guidelines and rules for the financial services sector and to protect the consumer against the fraudulent, is seen as hugely inhibiting of efficient business by perfectly respectable companies that have never defrauded anyone; when pensions protection inflates dramatically the cost of selling pensions to middle-income people; where health and safety rules across a range of areas is taken to extremes. (Blair, 2005b)

He then slips between perception and reality, citing a 'compensation culture' as dangerous for the *belief* that one exists despite there being no evidence for its existence (Blair, 2005b), before invoking some infamous regulatory myths:

You may recall the stories of the girl who sued the Girl Guides Association because she burnt her leg on a sausage or the man who was injured when he failed to apply the brake on a toboggan run in an amusement park...

Public bodies, in fear of litigation, act in highly risk-averse and peculiar ways. We have had a local authority removing hanging baskets for fear that they might fall on someone's head, even though no such accident had occurred in the 18 years they had been hanging there. A village in the Cotswolds was required to pull up a seesaw because it was judged a danger under an EU Directive on Playground

Equipment for Outside Use. This was despite the fact that no accidents had occurred on it. (Blair, 2005b)

Having thus rolled together civil law, public bodies, local authorities and the EU as part of the problem, he urges that we cannot then 'regulate to eliminate risk', for 'we pay a price if we react like this', namely, 'We lose out in business to India and China, who are prepared to accept the risks' (Blair, 2005b). Thus 'practical steps' to address this problem, via Better Regulation, were to be forced through UK - and EU-based law and regulators. Taking this forward would ensure 'a proper and proportionate way of assessing risk and the response to it. Government cannot eliminate all risk...A risk-averse business culture is no business culture at all' (Blair, 2005b).

Dodds has summarised such claims, and interventions made on their basis, in terms of the establishment of a new risk tolerance. As he notes, this had been discursively established by the middle of the decade, and found support on both the political right and left (Dodds, 2006). It had also found academic justification in the 'third way' and New labour theorist, Giddens, who promulgated a view of this where state activity was circumscribed, so that individuals, while more aware of risk, were also 'more sceptical of the state's ability to control them' (Dodds, 2006, 538).

The term 'risk averse', and the newly calibrated balance towards risk-tolerance which it required, had by this time become well established as code for over-regulated. More generally, during this period, it is no exaggeration to say that a new language emerged through which to speak of regulation, a language most sharply honed in the context of 'health and safety'. It is at once familiar, and part of a spectrum, one which derides the illegitimate demands of state bureaucracies ('bad') upon private enterprise ('good'), and invokes a plethora of 'conkers bonkers' type tales which now pervade political and popular discussion – such as the nonsense peddled, not least, by former PM Blair. Health and safety has gone mad. We need a more balanced approach. Less regulation, less enforcement. This is all so familiar that it circulates relatively unchallenged – who, after all, can argue for *more* burdens, *more* red tape, *more* bureaucracy, when these are always-already negatives?

The kinds of stories re-cycled by many including no less than the Prime Minister may be 'frivolous' – lacking 'objective seriousness' and with a 'derisive tone' (Almond, 2009, 354). But in isolation and combination they raise the spectre of regulators enforcing in over-zealous ways, focus attention not on any potential offender or offence but on the inappropriateness of regulation, and thus (re)inforce the chasm of good sense between the 'ordinary man' and 'a powerful, impersonal regulatory bureaucracy, thereby establishing the essential "otherness" of regulators' (Almond, 2009, 353–4).

Reviews: the Hampton agenda

Gordon Brown's appointment of the Chairman of Sainsbury's, Philip Hampton, to lead a wholesale review of business regulation in 2004 should have attracted some controversy. Hampton had been British Gas Group's Financial Director at the time one of the Group's subsidiaries, Transco, caused a gas explosion in Larkhall that killed a family of four. Transco was later fined a record £15 million. The judge presiding in the trial noted Transco's 'serious maintenance failure', following significant cuts to the company's maintenance budget. Hampton had also been Finance Director of Lloyds TSB during the period that the Bank was embroiled in a 'stripping' scheme in which it falsified its records to mask transactions from Iranian and Sudanese banking clients in violation of US law. The company was forced to pay fines and forfeiture totalling $350 million in a deferred prosecution settlement with the New York District Attorney's Office (Tombs and Whyte, 2010b).[52]

The Hampton Review was charged with considering 'the scope for reducing administrative burdens on business by promoting more efficient approaches to regulatory inspection and enforcement without reducing regulatory outcomes' (Hampton, 2005). Its remit encompassed 63 major regulatory bodies – including the Environment Agency, the Food Standards Agency, the Health and Safety Executive, and not to forget the Financial Services Authority (Hampton, 2005, 13) – as well as 468 local authorities (Hampton, 2005, 3); in other words, every agency which played a role in the mitigation of and response to corporate crime and harm. There is no little irony that in what was to prove to be a searing critique of existing regulators and their practices, Hampton singled out the Financial Services Authority as 'a model regulator, consolidating functions and using thoroughgoing risk profiling/assessment' (Hampton, 2005, 62), an assessment repeated two years later – the same year as the financial crisis began to unfold – in an NAO review of its work (NAO, 2007).[53]

Hampton's report – *Reducing Administrative Burdens: Effective Inspection and Enforcement*, published in 2005 – called for more focused inspections, greater emphasis on advice and education and, in general, for removing the 'burden' of inspection from most premises. Specifically, Hampton called for the reduction of inspections by up to a third – across all regulatory agencies, this would equate to one million fewer inspections

– and recommended that regulators make much more 'use of advice' to business. The report drew upon risk-based claims as the basis for withdrawing regulatory scrutiny from those who, in the terms used in the *Hampton Report*, had 'earned' their 'autonomy'. The 'consensus' established in and through this review and report (Vickers, 2008, 215) marked the consolidation of the era of Better Regulation, the triumph of the policy shift from enforcement to advice and education, a concentration of formal enforcement resources away from the majority of businesses onto so-called high risk areas, and the consistent efforts to do more with less, bolstered by (somewhat Orwellian) claims that less is more (Vickers, 2008).

As we saw in our review of the regulatory orthodoxy in Chapter Four, this risk-based, targeted model of regulation relies upon a series of assumptions: that most businesses are law-abiding; that they are likely to comply when faced with a combination of persuasion and market incentives; and, therefore, that only the minority of recalcitrant businesses need to be monitored via inspection regimes. Moreover, this risk-based model assumes that businesses are *capable of*, and given the correct information and advice, are *likely to*, comply with the law. It also assumes that regulators can know who the law-abiding businesses are – and, more generally, have sufficient intelligence on which to base their judgements of relative risk. As we shall see in Chapters Six and Seven, this latter claim appears ever more spurious to the extent that regulators have less and less contact with businesses.

Taken together, these claims and assumptions have proven to be materially and discursively crucial. On the basis of these, Hampton prescribed a series of 'Principles of Inspection and Enforcement':

- Regulators, and the regulatory system as a whole, should use comprehensive risk assessment to concentrate resources on the areas that need them most.
- No inspection should take place without a reason.
- Regulators should provide authoritative, accessible advice easily and cheaply.
- All regulations should be written so that they are easily understood, easily implemented, and easily enforced, and all interested parties should be consulted when they are being drafted.
- Businesses should not have to give unnecessary information, nor give the same piece of information twice.
- The few businesses that persistently break regulations should be identified quickly, and face proportionate and meaningful sanctions.

- Regulators should recognise that a key element of their activity will be to allow, or even encourage, economic progress and only to intervene when there is a clear case for protection.
- Regulators should be accountable for the efficiency and effectiveness of their activities, while remaining independent in the decisions they take.
- Regulators should be of the right size and scope, and no new regulator should be created where an existing one can do the work.
- When new policies are being developed, explicit consideration should be given to how they can be enforced using existing systems and data to minimise the administrative burden imposed. (Hampton, 2005, 7)

In isolation and in total, these cement the notions that regulation: is always-already somewhat illegitimate; is at best inefficient and at worst parasitic; must be minimised; and impinges upon the freedoms of law-abiding businesses. Hampton marked the key moment when the practices, and indeed the very idea, of regulation were pushed decisively on the back foot.

Reviews: the problem of local enforcement

Hampton had also explicitly addressed issues of local enforcement – recognising, indeed, that *most* enforcement (in terms of businesses regulated, numbers of regulators and so on) operated at this level. His starting point was with the frequently raised 'problem' at local level – inevitable, perhaps, given the hundreds of local authorities – of inconsistency in enforcement. Immediately, he identified this as a lack of any uniformly utilised risk assessment which, he claimed, produced not merely inconsistency but 'over-inspection at local level' (Hampton, 2005, 5). This inconsistency took many forms and 'generated several difficulties', namely: 'difficulties arising from the lack of effective priority-setting from the centre; difficulties in central and local coordination; cross-boundary problems; inconsistency in local authorities' application of national standards; variations in activity' (Hampton, 2005, para 4.86)

Indeed, regulation itself was identified as *a cause* of business law-breaking:

> the regulatory environment is so complex, but the very complexity of the regulatory environment can cause business owners to give up on regulations and 'just do their

best'. This is particularly true in respect of small businesses, many of whom, through pressure of time, take a conscious decision to avoid finding out about regulation. (Hampton, 2005, 35)

In this context, the Review expressed concern that inspectors might enforce the law rather than advise on compliance, that is, 'prioritise inspection over advice' (Hampton, 2005, 36).

Moreover, while accepting that local authorities had their own priorities, so that variations across authorities were inevitable, the 'inconsistency' this generated created 'unfair burdens upon businesses', and thus needed eradicating via more effective national control and coordination (Hampton, 2005, 4.100–4.106). It was in this context that the 'Rogers Review' was established, turning attention 'to the Trading Standards and Environmental Health professionals in local authorities who, considered together, form the country's largest body of enforcement officers' (Rogers, 2007, 5). The 'key aim' of the Review was to 'help solve' the difficulties with local enforcement which Hampton had identified (Rogers, 2007, 8). To effect this, Rogers sought to identify a series of national enforcement priorities which would inform the work of all local authorities regulators. In so doing, Rogers assembled a mass of evidence attesting to the harm which enforcement failures in each of these areas of social protection generated (Rogers, 2007, 59–63, 97–183). He first identified 61 priority areas, reducing these to 24, before reaching the final six. Of the evidence invoked, 'some was descriptive, some explanatory; many policy areas were supported by good qualitative data but there was limited quantitative data in certain areas. Despite this, identifying those policy areas that met the criteria for national enforcement priority was, for the most part, relatively straightforward' (Rogers, 2007, 57).

The enforcement priorities so determined were as follows:

- air quality, including regulation of pollution from factories and homes;
- alcohol, entertainment and late night refreshment licensing and its enforcement;
- hygiene of businesses selling, distributing and manufacturing food and the safety and fitness of food in the premises;
- improving health in the workplace;
- fair trading (trade description, trade marking, mis-description, doorstep selling).[54]

They were to be significantly disrupted by a quite different set of priorities, determined during the first year of the subsequent, coalition government.

Reform and review: after Hampton

Also in the same month as the *Hampton Report*, March 2005, the Cabinet Office's Better Regulation Task Force published its review of regulation, *Less is More: Reducing Burdens, Improving Outcomes* (BRTF, 2005). This tellingly entitled document proposed a crude mechanism for controlling the regulatory 'burden': a 'one in, one out' approach to regulation, whereby all new regulations were to be accompanied by the withdrawal of existing regulations (BRTF, 2005, 7). It was also in this document that 'The Five Principles of Good Regulation',[55] first outlined by the BRE in 1998, but now to become all pervasive across the UK re-regulatory agenda – were to be established most firmly (BRTF, 2005, Annex B, 51–2).

Many of the recommendations of these reports came together in the Legislative and Regulatory Reform Act, which passed into law in November 2006. The stated aim of the law was to 'enable delivery of swift and efficient regulatory reform to cut red tape' (Cabinet Office, 2006). The Act further facilitated removing or reducing burdens resulting from legislation, with a much clearer, and indeed very broad, definition of 'burden' than the 2001 Act, namely as 'a financial cost, an administrative inconvenience, an obstacle to efficiency, productivity or profitability, or a sanction, criminal or otherwise, which affects the carrying on of any lawful activity' (Legislative and Regulatory Reform Act 2006, S1(3)(a)–(d)). Here, and more generally in this Act, we see a clear codification of the Hampton reforms which had at their heart a very carefully constructed rationale which defines regulation first and foremost in terms of its *economic* burden on business. This represented – in legislation and in policy – a very open statement of a direct relationship between the shift towards self-regulation and a neoliberal profit-maximising agenda.

The explicit economic rationale at the heart of the Hampton reforms reached a new level in the new *Regulators' Compliance Code*, published in December 2007 (BERR, 2007), by the newly formed Department for Business, Enterprise and Regulatory Reform (BERR), the creation of which was one of Gordon Brown's first initiatives when he finally made it to Number 10 in the summer of 2007. This Regulatory Code was introduced to address how 'the few businesses' (Para 8) that break the law should be handled. In general, regulators were advised to facilitate compliance through a positive approach (Para 8), 'to reward those regulated entities that have consistently achieved good levels of compliance' (Para 8.1), and to take account of the difficulties small businesses may have in complying with law (Para 8.1). But most crucially, the new realities of regulation could not have been made clearer when it emphasised that '[r]egulators should recognise that a key element of their activity will be to allow, or even encourage, economic progress and only to intervene when there is a clear case for protection' (Para 3). In this specific requirement, the scope and reach of the burdens on business agenda is foregrounded directly in the day-to-day work of inspectors, further marginalising their enforcement role.

Also, by 2006, the Treasury had already begun to review the extent to which the recommendations of the *Hampton Report* were being implemented (HM Treasury, 2006). In 2007, it established the Local Better Regulation Office (LBRO) to 'ensure that local authority regulatory services, including trading standards, environmental health, and licensing are included within the scope of the Hampton Code of Practice. Like national regulators they will need to have regard to the Code when setting their enforcement policies' (HM Treasury, 2006, 4). What followed was a torrent of oversight activity. A series of 'Hampton Implementation Review Reports' were conducted on the work of 36 national regulators. Phase 1, completed by the NAO by December 2007, covered the five 'most significant in this country. The Environment Agency, Financial Services Authority, Food Standards Agency, Health and Safety Executive and Office of Fair Trading [which] regulate millions of businesses, covering some key areas of economic activity, while protecting the interests of us all' (NAO, 2008f, Foreword; see also NAO, 2008a; 2008b; 2008c; 2008d; 2008e). Phase 2, up to December 2009, assessed the Hampton-compliance of 31 further regulators, while the aim was to begin a second round of reviews of the first five (Phase 1) regulators, although only one was completed prior to the general election of 2010 (BIS, BRE, 2010).

Such was the energy directed at re-regulation by the Labour governments that the last[56] OECD report on member countries,[57] 'Regulatory Management Systems' (OECD Regulatory Policy Committee, 2009), indicate both that the UK was 'a leader in terms of regulatory management' – better or re-regulation – and that it was an early if not the earliest starter on almost every indicator of such (see also OECD, 2010; Jacobzone et al, 2007). Moreover, so well cemented was this new common sense regarding the limits to be set upon regulation in a globalised world that, as has been seen in earlier chapters, it was not even to be undone by the near collapse of the financial services sectors which dominated the last two and a half years of the Labour government.

Re-regulation under the coalition: 2010 onwards

Following its establishment in May 2010, the coalition government moved quickly not just to continue, but to accelerate, acting on the consensus around the burden of regulation in general. Again, the four forms of mutually reinforcing initiatives – a *rhetorical* assault on regulation, the establishment of a plethora of *institutions* within and of government, various *legal reform* initiatives and a constant stream of *reviews* of regulation – were clearly in evidence.

Rhetoric

Just three weeks into the new government, Vince Cable, who in opposition had been a key advocate of more interventionist financial services' regulation, established a Reducing Regulation Committee when installed as Business Secretary; its aim was to put an 'end to the excessive regulation that is stifling business growth'. As Cable put it, 'The deluge of new regulations has been choking off enterprise for too long. We must move away from the view that the only way to solve problems is to regulate' (BIS, 2010).

The rhetoric against regulation was consistent, and often coming from the highest level of government, notably from PM Cameron. A few highlights suffice to make the point of the level of vitriol aimed at regulation and regulators. On 6 August 2011, disorder broke out in Tottenham, North London, following a demonstration at the police shooting of a young black man, Mark Duggan. Within three days riots followed across many London boroughs, towns and cities in the West and East Midlands, as well as in Bristol, Liverpool and Manchester. Three men were killed in Birmingham, another two in London, hundreds of millions of pounds of damage was caused to businesses and homes, shops were looted, police lost control for periods of major urban centres and within a week over 1,000 people had been arrested. In other words, this was a major series of incidents. Nine days after the killing of Mark Duggan which had triggered the first outbreak of disorder in North London, the Prime Minister made his first major, set piece speech to comment upon these events. Quite incredibly, in that speech in Birmingham, on 15 August 2011, Cameron decided to include references to health and safety regulation. He 'announced' that the government would 'review every aspect of our work to mend our broken society', including focusing upon 'the obsession with health and safety that has eroded people's willingness to act according to common sense'. Indeed, what he went on to call 'the human rights and health and safety culture' was a source of 'damage [to] our social fabric' (Conservative Home, 2011). Weeks later, at the Conservative Party conference, he continued the theme, in a fashion that would be funny were it not a signal of virtual hatred for a key element of social protection:

> one of the biggest things holding people back is the shadow of health and safety. I was told recently about a school that wanted to buy a set of highlighter pens. But with the pens came a warning. Not so fast – make sure you comply with the Control of Substances Hazardous to Health Regulations 2002. Including plenty of fresh air and hand and eye protection. Try highlighting in all that. This isn't how a great nation was built. Britannia didn't rule the waves with arm-bands on…At long last common sense is coming back to our country. (BBC, 2011b)

In January 2012, Cameron made a 'New Year's resolution'

> This coalition has a clear new year's resolution: to kill off the health and safety culture for good. I want 2012 to go down in history not just as Olympics year or Diamond Jubilee year, but the year we get a lot of this pointless time-wasting out of the British economy and British life once and for all. (Cited in politics.co.uk, 2012)

It was a resolution to be repeated the following January, when he derided the fact of 'Health and safety rules stopping children getting work experience in companies':

> We need to encourage businesses to offer that work experience, we need to simplify health and safety rules, we need to say to schools, 'every school should have a plan for how you are going to teach children about enterprise and business'. (Cited in Hope, 2013)

More latterly, he has invoked regulatory myths as he previewed a new Deregulation Bill, enacted in 2014 (below). Thus he told the Federation of Small Businesses,

This government has already stopped needless health and safety inspections. And we will scrap over-zealous rules which dictate how to use a ladder at work or what no-smoking signs must look like. We've changed the law so that businesses are no longer automatically liable for an accident that isn't their fault. And the new Deregulation Bill will exempt 1 million self-employed people from health and safety law altogether. (Prime Minister's Office et al, 2014)

Reviews

Weeks into the life of the new government, it launched a review of 900 'quangos' (formally, Non Departmental Public Bodies, NDPBs), which reported in October 2010 that '192 quangos were to be abolished' (www.bbc.co.uk/news/uk-politics-11405840) as the start of its attack on what was now widely referred to as 'the quango state' (Maer, 2011, 1). In 2011, the Cabinet Office produced guidelines for Triennial Reviews of all main national regulators (Cabinet Office, 2011). These stipulated that all 'Non Departmental Public Bodies' should be reviewed 'at least once every three years' (Cabinet Office, 2011, para 4.1), with reviews having two 'principal aims':

> (i) to provide a robust challenge of the continuing need for individual NDPBs – both their functions and their form; and (ii) where it is agreed that a particular body should remain as an NDPB, to review the control and governance arrangements in place to ensure that the public body is complying with recognised principles of good corporate governance. (Cabinet Office, 2011, para 5.1)

That guidance provides a checklist of 'delivery options' to be considered when reviewing the work of any such agency – 'Departments are encouraged to think creatively when reviewing how functions might be delivered' – with the first listed such option being to 'abolish' (Cabinet Office, 2011, Annex A).

By July, the government had also established a 'Your Freedom' website, claimed to be a forum for the public to suggest regulation that they think should be removed or changed. Deputy Prime Minister Clegg claimed, 'For too long new laws have taken away your freedom, interfered in everyday life and made it difficult for businesses to get on' (Prime Minister's Office, 2010).

Also within weeks of its formation, the new government appointed Lord Young to investigate 'concerns over the application and perception of health and safety legislation, together with the rise of a compensation culture over the last decade' (Hope, 2010). The appointment of Lord Young to oversee this 'review' was of no little significance. As a life peer at the heart of Thatcher's government, central to the construction of the idea of the 'enterprise culture' (Morris, 1991), he had overseen two deregulatory White Papers, *Lifting the Burden* (Cmnd 9571), in 1985, and *Building Business – Not Barriers* (Cmnd 9794). His report, *Common Sense, Common Safety*, was published in October 2010, with a series of recommendations aimed 'to free businesses from unnecessary bureaucratic burdens' (Young, 2010, 9). Close reading of Young's report is instructive, since his report was merely the latest in a line of futile government searches for the existence of a 'compensation culture'. Young concluded that 'The problem of the compensation culture prevalent in society today is, however, one of perception rather than reality' (Young, 2010, 19).

Then, in March 2011, the Löfstedt Review was established by the Prime Minister, with a remit to 'look into the scope for reducing the burden of health and safety regulation on business' (DWP, 2011a). Due to its attempt to bring together a broad range of stakeholders (small and large business, trade unions, academics and politicians), it was arguably the most significant attempt to engineer a consensus around a new anti-regulation and enforcement agenda (Almond, 2015).

The government then launched, in June 2011, its 'Red Tape Challenge'. At the launch, Employment Minister Grayling noted, 'This is an opportunity that every beleaguered business leader, incredulous community group or outraged newspaper reader has been waiting for – a chance to directly change the laws underpinning Britain's health and safety culture' (HSE, 2011). In fact, health and safety was only *one* focus of the 'Challenge', which invited visitors to a website to submit their views on cross-cutting, general areas of regulation on a *series* of themes, in turn, within a five week window – the other five areas chosen for what the government termed its 'spotlight' being 'Equalities', 'Employment Related Law', 'Company and Commercial Law', 'Pensions' and 'Environment'. It is notable that both health and safety was foregrounded in Grayling's announcement (see Chapters Six and Seven) and that 'food safety' or a broader reference to 'consumer safety' were absent here, although there was coverage of these in the more detailed themes that proceeded within each 'spotlight', notably within the theme 'hospitality, food and drink'.[58] Responses to the Red Tape Challenge would allegedly feed into government departments making 'proposals to the Reducing Regulation Committee' and seeking 'policy clearance' for removing specific legal coverage.[59]

During the same summer, a '*Transforming Regulatory Enforcement*' consultation was held, to access 'the most pressing concern for millions of businesses: the day to day experience of regulatory enforcement at the front line'. The stated aim, then, was to 'hear, first-hand from businesses, views on where reform of enforcement was needed and where the state's methods of enforcing regulation could be lightened or made to work in more constructive ways with business' (BIS, 2011, 5).

When the Löfstedt review reported, in November 2011, it in essence concluded that the current framework of health and safety regulation was not in need of a fundamental overhaul but did propose a range of recommendations for reform. Among those it identified as 'key' (Löfstedt, 2011, 9) were a series of recommendations for further review, for example of all existing Approved Codes of Practice, of a series of sector-specific regulations, and of regulatory provisions that impose strict liability. Notably, it also recommended 'exempting from health and safety law those self-employed whose work activities pose no potential risk of harm to others' (Löfstedt, 2011, 3); and that 'health and safety inspection and enforcement activity' be directed 'to ensure that it is consistent and targeted towards the most risky workplaces' (Löfstedt, 2011, 5).

Taken together, the report stated that its proposed reforms and reviews would, 'help to ensure that all key elements of the regulatory and legal system are better targeted towards risk and support the proper management of health and safety instead of a focus on trying to cover every possible risk and accumulating paperwork' (Löfstedt, 2011, 7).

The Löfstedt report's focus on 'low-risk' proved to be crucial, however. In fact, the report used the phrase 'low-risk' in four senses: 'low-risk' work activities, 'low-risk' businesses, 'low-risk' sectors and 'low-risk' workplaces. Now, although the report notes the difficulty of defining what constitutes 'low-risk' (Löfstedt, 2011, 36), none of these concepts are actually defined in any useful sense – curious, given that Löfstedt is Professor of Risk Management and Director of one of the UK's foremost university centres of risk management. In fact, such a vague, flexible use of this phrase proved highly useful for a government which went on to use this report as the catalyst for formal removal of enforcement from 'low-risk' sectors (James et al, 2013; and see below). In its formal response to the report, the government accepted all of its recommendations (DWP, 2011b). Löfstedt subsequently raised concerns in public about the withdrawal of inspection legislated for by government on the basis of his report (SHP Online, 2012).

The following year, in December 2012, a 'Focus on Enforcement Review' was unveiled, aimed at allowing business to tell government where enforcement can be improved, reduced or done differently; inspectors across regulatory agencies were to be encouraged to 'have regard for growth' (http://discuss.bis.gov.uk/focusonenforcement/). This is not to be confused with the 'Business Focus on Enforcement', announced by Michael Fallon in March 2014, inviting business 'to help run an initiative that puts driving the reform of regulatory enforcement in the hands of business'. As part of the initiative, bids for government grants were invited to help businesses and trade associations prepare cases 'to challenge problems like duplicated paperwork, inconsistent advice or unhelpful guidance and present the case for change directly to regulators and ministers – who will be required to respond to the evidence industry presents' (BIS, 2014).

Legal reform

The key overall regulatory strategy document for the new coalition government was its *Reducing regulation made simple: Less regulation, better regulation and regulation as a last resort* (HM Government, 2010a). This document was notable for setting out post-implementation reviews (PIR) and 'sunsetting' requirements, both ostensibly designed to reduce regulation.

Post-implementation review (PIR) refers to reviews of regulation which complement the 'ex-ante appraisal contained in the impact assessment' (HM Government, 2010a, para 47). Sunset provisions 'build on' these processes (HM Government, 2010a, para 48). In practice, 'sunsetting' refers to several processes and procedures: one is the use of a 'review clause', that is, 'a statutory duty to carry out a review of the relevant regulation on a specified timescale but does not provide for automatic expiry'; a sunset clause per se 'provides for automatic expiry after a specified period'; (HM Government, 2011, 7). Where any review recommends that regulations be maintained, this recommendation must be passed to the Reducing Regulation Committee for approval; meanwhile, sunsetting is 'mandatory for new regulation introduced by Whitehall departments, where there is a net burden (or cost) on business or civil society organisations' (HM Government, 2011, 3). Further, all Departments are required to conduct thematic reviews of regulations – 'to undertake reviews of their existing "stock" of regulation to identify opportunities to remove or revise regulations' (HM Government, 2010a, para 52), such as those of health and safety regulation.

In addition to these processes and procedures, the document also sets out the need for 'streamlining' systems of enforcement (HM Government, 2010a, para 3.4), including 'developing co-regulatory approaches' (HM Government, 2010a, paras 63–5), since 'More needs to be done to ensure that, where businesses have a good track record of compliance, this is taken into account by regulators, who will then reduce the inspection burden for them' (HM Government, 2010a, para 64). These co-regulatory approaches are explicitly defined as giving 'appropriate recognition to a business's own efforts to comply with regulation' (HM Government, 2010a, 63).

One initiative, by the Department for Business, Innovation and Skills (BIS), was to introduce the 'one in, one out' policy, in September 2010, first trailed under the previous government, as noted above. This required any government department introducing one new regulation that imposed a direct net cost on business to remove or modify another regulation at equivalent cost (BIS, 2010). This itself was superseded by 'one in, two out': from January 2013, every new regulation that imposes a new financial burden on firms must be offset by reductions in 'red tape' that will save double those costs (BIS, 2012a).

On 1 April 2011, the government had introduced a three-year freeze on new UK regulation for businesses with fewer than ten employees, including start-up businesses. What was originally known as the 'micro-business moratorium' was extended in June 2013 to 'small businesses', those with up to 50 employees (BIS, 2012b; 2013b).

Changes in inspection regimes also gathered pace under the coalition. In March 2011, health and safety inspections were reduced drastically in an act of fiat by employment minister Chris Grayling. Claiming that Britain's 'health and safety culture' was 'stifling business and holding back economic growth' (DWP, 2011a), he announced that proactive inspections by HSE were to be severely limited, 'by one third, around 11,000 inspections per year' (DWP, 2011d, 9), while at local level these would be ended completely, amounting to a reduction of 65,000 inspections per annum (DWP, 2011d, 10). Each soon became policy (HSE and Local Government Group, 2011; HSE and Local Authorities Enforcement Liaison Committee, 2013). These were workplaces in the sectors deemed to be 'low risk' – that is, all local authority regulated sectors and, for HSE, the following: agriculture, air, bricks, cement products, ceramics, clothing, computer products, concrete products, courier services, docks, electrical engineering, electricity generation, electronic products, emergency services, fabricated metal products, footwear, glass and glazing, health care, laundries, leather, light engineering, mineral industries, optical products, other food and drink, other manufacturing industries, paper and board, plastics, postal services, printing, prisons, quarries, road haulage, rubber, social care, textiles, and the transport sector (O'Neill, 2011).

Furthermore, in October 2011, Deputy Prime Minister Clegg unveiled a policy on enforcement to small business leaders, stating that 'bodies responsible for inspection…need to understand that their job is to make your life easier, not harder. So there will be a major shake-up of business inspection – going through the regulators, asking 'Are they still necessary?'; 'Should they still exist?' (Winnett, 2011). Then a further government report, published in November 2011, proposed to review all regulators, seeking: 'to make sure each one is making the fullest possible use of the range of alternatives to conventional enforcement models, working with business and others and reducing state activity wherever possible. We will expect to see a significant reduction in state-led enforcement activity' (BIS, 2011, 6). It urged a 'transparent and light-touch risk-based system' (BIS, 2011, 7–8).

The torrent of legal reform did not end there; 5 April 2013 was announced as 'Freedom Day' for Business, with a package of deregulatory reforms introduced by Michael Fallon claiming that these would set 'business free from the restrictions that hold back enterprise [and] is a compulsory step on the road to growth. We've listened to firms and taken prompt action where regulation presents barriers – but there is a huge amount still to do' (BIS, 2013a). Later that month, the Enterprise and Regulatory Reform Bill passed through Parliament, and within a year, in February 2014, a further Deregulation Bill extended exemptions from regulatory law and its enforcement. The final legal reform to be made during this period was perhaps the most significant. A further (2014) revision to the *Regulators' Compliance Code* embedded and extended the exigence in the 2007 version (above), namely that '[r]egulators should recognise that a key element of their activity will be to allow, or even encourage, economic progress and only to intervene when there is a clear case for protection'. The 2014 version was based on the so-called growth duty: that is, '*Point 1*' of the new Code emphasised that, 'Regulators should carry out their activities in a way that supports those they regulate to comply and grow' (BRDO, 2014b, 3).

Institutions

With this renewed urgency to reducing regulation, a more complex institutional configuration was developed inside government. Installed into each department was a 'Better Regulation Minister' – 'challenging policy-makers to meet the government's reducing regulation commitments' (HM Government, 2010a, para 14) – supported by Board Level Champions (BLCs), senior officials 'who champion the new approach within their departments' (HM Government, 2010a). The latter, in turn, are 'supported by a network of working level contacts in Better Regulation Units (BRUs) within departments who... support their policy colleagues in making the changes needed' (HM Government, 2010a, para 15).

Sitting 'above' these was a Better Regulation Strategy Group (BRSG), 'representing business (both employers and employees), consumers and government' and which 'acts as an advisory group to government right across the regulation agenda' (HM Government, 2010a, para 18). Further, the Reducing Regulation Committee was given 'an enhanced role in the new government's plans to introduce a new approach to regulation' (HM Government, 2010b). As a Cabinet sub-Committee, it would 'take strategic oversight of the delivery of the government's regulatory framework'. Its 'broad terms of reference' included 'scrutinising, challenging and approving all new regulatory proposals as well as proposals for transposing EU obligations' (HM Government, 2010a, para 30). This strengthened remit was to be overseen by Business Secretary Cable (Regulatory Policy Committee, 2011, 7).

In January 2012, an Independent Regulatory Challenge Panel was also established. This would investigate complaints regarding advice given by HSE or local authority inspectors which applicants consider to be incorrect or going beyond what is required to control the risk adequately.[60]

Reviews: the problem of local enforcement re-visited

As discussed earlier, the Rogers Review had, in the wake of Hampton, turned to local authorities to 'help solve' the problem of enforcement at that level (Rogers, 2007, 8). Rogers identified five enforcement priorities, around air quality and pollution, alcohol and licensing, food hygiene and safety, workplace health and fair trading – based upon a review of a considerable amount of evidence attesting to the harm which failures in regulation around each generated.

Four years later, during the first year of the subsequent, coalition government, this work was jettisoned, on the basis of adherence to a quite different methodology and set of rationales. In 2011, the last Act of the LBRO was to publish its Priority Regulatory Outcomes Final Report (LBRO, 2011). This noted that Rogers had established his priority enforcement areas through working with an expert user group of local authorities, professional bodies, national regulators and central government departments (LBRO, 2011, 6). The LBRO reported that it had, in contrast, having worked with the Institute of Local Government Studies, University of Birmingham, and seven local authorities, concluded that, 'the priorities did not take sufficient account of the importance of local priorities and the need for regulatory services to effectively demonstrate how they were contributing to locally important outcomes' (LBRO, 2011, 6).

In 'refreshing' the national enforcement priorities, LBRO in fact abandoned them. Thus, a new set of 'priority regulatory outcomes were determined', as follows:

- support economic growth, especially in small businesses, by ensuring a fair, responsible and competitive trading environment;
- protect the environment for future generations including tackling the threats and impacts of climate change;
- improve quality of life and wellbeing by ensuring clean and safe neighbourhoods;
- help people to live healthier lives by preventing ill health and harm and promoting public health;
- ensure a safe, healthy and sustainable food chain for the benefits of consumers and the rural economy. (LBRO, 2011, 7)

It further argued that, 'The regulatory system as a whole, and local regulators individually, should tailor their approaches to support businesses into compliance in a way that meets their needs' (LBRO, 2011, 11). This, and the first stated priority above, both accord with the first duty to be enshrined in the later (2014) *Regulators' Compliance Code*, the so-called Growth Duty (BRDO, 2014b).

Also crucial to note here is that the term 'enforcement' had been entirely removed from these regulatory priorities, quite explicitly so:

> Given the pressure on public finances, it is even more important to look for evidence of what works – which activities will deliver maximum impact and progress towards improved outcomes.
>
> The shift away from the terminology of national *enforcement* priorities towards priority regulatory outcomes serves to reflect the breadth of activity local authority regulatory services and partner organisations carry out to support business compliance and prosperity and to

protect citizens, workers and the environment. Delivering outcomes depends on the careful allocation of resources across a range of regulatory activities. (LBRO, 2011, 22, emphasis in original)

Thus, following Hampton, the efficient use of resources should be based on 'risk, taking into consideration differing customer needs and use of alternative approaches to regulation' (LBRO, 2011, 22) and thus targeted (LBRO, 2011, 22–3). With this document, the LBRO was dissolved, to be replaced by the Better Regulation Delivery Office (BRDO) as the key coordinating body for local regulatory services, on 1 April 2012. This would enhance working relationships between businesses and regulators and thus 'strengthen the overall package of regulatory reform by bringing these two elements together within government' (Local Government Lawyer, 2012). BRDO describes its aims as

working towards a regulatory environment in which businesses have the confidence to invest and grow and citizens and communities are properly protected. We do this by operating Primary Authority [on which more later, Chapter Six] to ensure consistent regulation, improving the professionalism of front-line regulators, and giving businesses a say in their regulation.[61]

But to be clear, what this LBRO document also did, as indicated in the final quotation from it, above, was to remove enforcement from the lexicon of local authority regulatory priorities. This, alongside the statutory removal from enforcement for swathes of businesses by type and sector, indicated elsewhere in this chapter, are clear indices of the institutionalisation of a new form of regulation: *regulation without enforcement*.

Conclusion

This chapter has traced some the key mechanisms through which both Labour and coalition governments up to 2014 have sought to embed a new regulatory agenda under the auspices of 'Better Regulation'. There have been four different mechanisms deployed consistently throughout this period, across three governments, as has been noted: a rhetorical initiative, the creation of re-regulatory institutions, various legal reforms and incessant reviews of regulation in general. This has been a period of intensive re-regulation.

These initiatives have had an impact, variously, upon the idea of regulation, as well as the policies and practices of regulation. I would argue that key to understanding the effects of these is in their synergistic rather than isolated effects. In short, and crucially, these forms of mutually compatible activity indicate that it would be mistaken to view better regulation as a form of mere state withdrawal or simple deregulation – what we have witnessed is a concerted effort at re-regulation, attempts to re-configure the relationships between state and private capital. Moreover, the claimed effect here is that capital is being set 'free', even if the effect is actually to generate further inter-dependence between state and capital.

Several concluding observations follow.

First, it is noteworthy that the trajectory, if not priority attached to, these initiatives traverses not just several governments but, crucially, the period leading up to, during, and then subsequent to the financial crisis. This remarkable consistency of anti-regulation can only be understood within several broader contexts: in terms of the longer term assault on the idea and practices of regulation, associated with the emergence of neoliberalism in its specific UK variants (Chapter Two); on the basis of the ways in which the crisis was framed, and specifically how this framing excluded the regulatory antecedents of the crisis but instead cast it as over-extension by bloated, inefficient and meddlesome states bureaucracies, so that 'recovery' was at the same time framed as setting free an entrepreneurial, growth-giving private sector (Chapter Three); and, in terms of a logical compatibility between a political and an academic consensus regarding feasible and desirable forms of regulation – and, concomitantly, the necessary limits upon these – forms of consensus and compatibilities which, for all their differences, are located upon pro-market, liberal-pluralist terrains (Chapter Four).

Second, the nature of the effects of these various initiatives within and across forms of regulation clearly varies. Some have significant ideological effects, the most obvious instances here being the rhetorical onslaught against the idea of regulation, encapsulated in the stream of anti-regulatory rhetoric that characterises political and popular references to the issue. Also with important ideological effects are various reviews of regulation, as well as the plethora of institutions designed to control or check regulation; both are dependent upon, but also feed further, the common sense that there is too much regulation, that it is counterproductive, to be resisted and so on. Equally both of these types of initiative have more or fewer real, practical effects –

because reviews and institutions lead to changes in the volume and nature of regulation, albeit often not to the degree that may be claimed for them. Finally, legal reforms have predominantly material effects, that is, they alter the regulatory landscape, in terms of what regulators can do, where they can do it, and how they can do it. All of these changes, I would add, alter the balances of power between the regulated and the regulators, undermining capacities of and/or creating crises of confidence among the latter, and thus emboldening the former.

This latter point links into a third observation to be drawn here. Once regulation has been has been so thoroughly defined as a problem, indeed over a long period, so consensually and broadly, then it is difficult to disrupt the amplification processes that are generated and fuelled by this new common sense. If regulation is always-already problematic, then there would seem to be no logical limits on the extent to which this problem must be addressed. The legal reforms from a 'one-in, one-out' to 'one-in, two-out', the extension of businesses covered by the 'micro-business moratorium' on new regulation, and the 2007, then 2014 revisions to the Regulators' Compliance Code, noted above, each illustrate and encapsulate this logic.

Fourth, while the detail presented in this chapter has been selective only, it should be clear even on the basis of the coverage herein that while regulation *in general* has been subjected to various forms of reform and assault, one specific form of regulation in particular, namely that associated with occupational health and safety protection, has been by far the most vigorously targeted. This is clear, for example, in the rhetorical attacks on regulation. While these are often aimed at regulation in general, as we have seen above, the illustrations provided there also faithfully reflect the fact that, where specific forms of regulation are highlighted for verbal opprobrium, these are, latterly at least, almost exclusively and most vehemently reserved for health and safety law and its enforcement. We find this particular focus on health and safety regulation reflected in governmental reviews – both Young and Löfstedt, for example, were established within a year of the coalition government being formed; and HSE also has been subjected to *two* triennial reviews of its functions and fitness for purpose. Further, legal reforms have proceeded most thoroughly in this area – so that, for example, the formal institutionalisation of low-risk has seen proactive inspections across the vast majority of workplaces formally prohibited. In other words, and consistent with the analyses in the following two chapters, health and safety regulation has been a specific target within generalised initiatives upon the idea and practices of regulation.

It remains, finally, to be noted, albeit not discussed in this chapter, that regulation has been subject to reform via central government (and local authority) spending priorities, decisions and allocations. There is a tendency of course to view reductions in expenditure, certainly since 2008, as responses to a fiscal crisis of the state (notwithstanding the mystified origins of that crisis – see Chapter Three). While reductions in government expenditure in general have some bases in economic and fiscal policy, they are clearly at the same time, if not *more* usefully viewed as, political initiatives (Gamble, 2015). Thus as Prosser has noted, citing the Treasury Select Committee on the Chancellor's first (June 2010) budget statement, George Osborne had 'been explicit that his aim is not only to reduce debt, but to rebalance the economy away from the public and toward the private sector' (cited in Prosser, 2011, 597). Thus, the 2010 Spending Review was explicitly presented as part of 'a radical programme of public service reform', thereby 'incorporating goals other than economic management' (Prosser, 2011, 598) – it was the basis of what was to become the mantra of the Conservatives during the coalition years, namely of the need to 'shrink the state' and, in particular, to systemically reform the welfare state (Taylor-Gooby, 2012). Here, the politics of Better Regulation, and the institutionalisation of a new form of *regulation without enforcement*, dovetailed perfectly with the economics of government policy, a suggestion that will be developed in the following chapter.

SIX

Regulatory inaction?
Regulation without enforcement

'Increasingly we're told that our main job is to facilitate business, industry and so on.' (Environmental Health Officer, interview, Merseyside)

Introduction

The focus of this chapter is on the trajectories of state enforcement of regulatory law in the context of three areas of social protection, spanning national and local regulatory bodies in the UK: food safety, namely the quality and hygiene standards associated with food bought for consumption in the home or otherwise; health and safety at work, the protection of the health, safety and welfare of employees and members of the public from harms associated with work related activities; and pollution control, part of a general environmental protection function, that is, protection of land, air and waterways.

The central claim of the chapter is that various forms of quantitative and qualitative evidence[62] relating to these enforcement activities provide clear and consistent indications that the economic, political and ideological attacks on the *idea* of regulation have combined to produce regulatory regimes that are based, variously, upon declining levels of enforcement. In this context, it is important to note that the trends set out in this chapter have attracted virtually no critical political nor social comment. Furthermore, even at the end of the period under examination, 2014, it remains the case that political and social references to regulation and enforcement continue to be couched in the same terms, as burdensome, antithetical to economic efficiency and thus prosperity, and so on. That said, the vehemence of these ideological and associated material assaults on regulation and enforcement varies, and plays out distinctly, across regulatory functions and specific regulators, an issue addressed in this and the concluding chapter.

National and local regulators

By way of summary introduction, it should be emphasised that regulation across the three areas of concern here is something of a patchwork of national and local responsibilities. Food Safety enforcement in the UK operates almost entirely at the local authority level, but is overseen by the national body, the Food Standards Agency (FSA). Local functions are divided between EHOs and Trading Standards Officers. Food safety EHOs oversee food safety and food hygiene, enforcing law across all forms of retail food business organisations (restaurant, shops and so on), as well as food processing and food manufacturing outlets. Occupational health and safety regulation is divided between a national regulator, the HSE, and health and safety EHOs at a local level; the division of labour is based on the main activity of any premises. Pollution control is also divided between a national regulator, the Environment Agency (EA), and pollution control EHOs. At a local level, pollution control covers various forms of non-business activity, notably littering and fly-tipping, and a significant part of the work of pollution control EHOs is with noise, both domestic and commercial; the focus here is on the pollution control efforts aimed at businesses. I now turn to provide a little more detail on these regulators and their functions, activities and so on.

Food safety and hygiene

The FSA was established by the Food Standards Act 1999. With the exception of its Meat Hygiene Service, the FSA does not undertake inspection and enforcement.[63] Thus, local authorities carry out most of the UK's food standards and safety inspections, with the Agency monitoring them and running an audit programme. The risk assessment programme for food safety and standards 'is set out in considerable detail in the Food Safety code of practice, which derives from European legislation' (Hampton, 2005, 110). However, in the earlier years of the FSA's existence, concerns were consistently expressed about the robustness of this monitoring function (see, for example, FSA, 2006; 2009) which resulted in a 'Changes to Local Authority Enforcement Arrangements' Project (FSA, 2009) and, from 2008/09, a new reporting system as regards local authority enforcement activities, including, for the first time, a calculation of FTE enforcement officers (see Table 6.1).

In England and Wales,[64] enforcement of food safety and hygiene lies with food safety EHOs, with food standards (that is, information and labelling requirements) overseen by Trading Standards Officers – except in London where EHOs combine both roles. (Hutter, 2011a, 64–70).

Table 6.1: Full time equivalent (FTE) professional local authority staff engaged in UK food law enforcement

	31/3/2009[a]	31/3/2010	31/3/2011	31/3/2012	31/3/2014
Food hygiene	1,957	n/a	n/a	1,869	1,821
Food standards	904	n/a	n/a	840	624
Total	2,861	2,889	2,774	2,709	2,449

Note: [a] This was the first year where this data was returned and collated, and 'no comparison or trends can as yet be identified from the data. However, anecdotal evidence from local authorities indicates that their regulatory resources are being reduced, and this trend is set to continue' (Food Standards Agency, 2010, 14).

The functions under consideration here are food safety and hygiene: food safety requires that 'food should be fit for consumption, have no adverse health effects, be of substance/quality demanded by consumer' (Hutter, 2011a, 64); food hygiene covers 'activities of preparation, processing, manufacturing, packaging, storage, distribution, handling and offering for sale/supplying foodstuffs' (Hutter, 2011a, 64).

In 2012/13, food safety EHOs enforced law in 608,143 businesses.[65]

Occupational health and safety

The HSE regulates work-related health and safety in Great Britain in partnership with local authorities in accordance with the Health and Safety at Work Act 1974, through which a variety of existing inspectorates were amalgamated into HSE.

In general, HSE is responsible for enforcing health and safety at workplaces including: factories, farms, building sites, nuclear installations, mines, schools and colleges, fairgrounds, gas, electricity and water systems, hospitals and nursing homes, central and local government premises, offshore installations. Local authorities' health and safety EHOs are responsible for health and safety enforcement in offices, shops, hotels, restaurants, leisure premises, nurseries and playgroups, pubs and clubs, museums (privately owned), places of worship, sheltered accommodation and care homes.[66]

In 2004/05, government funding for HSE was £209 million (HSC, 2005, 74); total funding received by HSE from DWP for the financial year 2013–14 was £154 million (HSE, 2014c, 91). HSE reported in 2014 that it had experienced 'a 40 per cent real term reduction in resources from 2011/12 to 2014/15' (HSE, 2014c, 60). Indications of both the absolute numbers of health and safety inspectors at national and local levels, as well as trends in these across a ten-year period, are provided in Tables 6.2 and 6.3.

Table 6.2: Total HSE (including HSL and ONR[a]) staff in post by full-time equivalents (FTE) and occupational group

	1/4/2004	1/4/2007	1/4/2010[b]	1/4/2013 (31/3/2013)	1/4/2014
Frontline staff (of which are frontline inspectors)[c]	1,551 (1,483)	1,405 (1,312)	1,464 (1,342)	1,322 (1,241)	1,059 (981)
Inspectors working in functions other than frontline	122	128	153	126	70
Other professional or specialist staff	1,359	1,350	1,425	1,268	1,111
Other staff (of which are apprentices)	987	699 (4)	660 (118)	459	381 (3)
Total staff[d]	4,019	3,582	3,702	3,183[e]	2,621

Notes: [a] HSL is HSE's Health and Safety Laboratory; the ONR (Office for Nuclear Regulation) was established on 1 April 2011 to create a single nuclear regulator.

[b] Pesticides Safety Directorate (PSD) transferred from Defra to HSE on 01/04/2008.

[c] Frontline staff comprises operational and other health and safety inspectors fulfilling frontline roles, and visiting officers who support inspectors in the delivery of key health and safety messages.

[d] Total staff = the sum of all rows excluding the figures in brackets.

[e] Includes eight 'contingent labour' FTEs, is defined as temporary staff not on HSE's payroll which may include agency workers, specialist contractors, interim managers and so on.

Sources: Health and Safety Executive and Commission annual reports, various.

Table 6.3: Local authority health and safety inspectors

	1/4/2004	1/4/2007	1/4/2010	1/4/2014
FTEs holding appointments under S19 of HSW Act.	1,140	1,100	1,050	800

Sources: Health and Safety Executive and LACORS, nd, 2006, 2008; HSE and Local Government Regulation, 2010; Tsavalos, 2014.

In 2012/13, the HSE enforced law in 870,000 businesses. In the same year, health and safety EHOs enforced law in 1,670,000 businesses.[67]

Pollution control

The Environment Agency was established in 1996 under the Environment Act (1995), and is the regulatory agency mandated 'to protect or enhance the environment, taken as a whole, as to make the contribution towards attaining the objective of achieving sustainable development' (NAO, 2008a, 33). It regulates and enforces across a wide range of areas, and those areas which directly affect business include waste, pollution and emissions to air, land and water. It also oversees a range of permits and licensing schemes.[68] On its establishment, it took on the responsibilities of a diverse range of existing regulators, including HM Inspectorate of Pollution, the National Rivers Authority and waste regulation (www.legislation.gov.uk/ukpga/1995/25/section/2).

The various ways in which EA grant-in-aid, income from non-governmental sources, gross and net expenditures are calculated makes year-on-year comparisons across a ten-year period virtually impossible to determine. However, the following provides a summary of staffing, net and gross expenditures for the last six financial years.

To provide some context to the sums in Table 6.4, total EA *income* in 2005/06 was £1,027 million – a figure which had virtually doubled from 1996/97 (£564 million) (House of Commons Environment, Food and Rural Affairs Committee, 2006a, 5). In fact, the 2005/06 expenditure represented a high point – following year-on-year increases since 2000/01, the following years were marked by year-on-year *decreases* (House of Commons Environment, Food and Rural Affairs Committee, 2006b, 157 of 309). The EA's Annual Report for 2013/14 noted that expenditure on flood and coastal erosion accounted for over half of spending in 2012/13 and 2013/14 (57 per cent and 53 per cent respectively). Funding allocated to 'environment and business' declined from £571 million to £500 million over the same years (representing 47 per cent and 43 per cent of spend respectively) (Environment Agency, 2014, 28). This decline in overall funding, alongside the fact that the flood defence budget is ring-fenced, means that staffing levels beyond these functions are in disproportionate decline (Marshall, 2013),[69] even if this is not reflected in total staff numbers, as can be seen in Table 6.5.

Table 6.4: Summary of EA expenditure (£m) 2009–14[a]

	2008/09	2009/10	2010/11	2011/12	2012/13	2013/14
Staff costs	489	419	403	365	395	373
Gross expenditure	1,280	1,231	993	1,167	1,207	1,164[b]
Net expenditure[c]	876	813	577	750	772	736

Notes: [a] Edited from Table 1: Five-year summary of our income and expenditure, 2013–14, Environment Agency, 2014, 27 and Environment Agency, 2013, 22.

[b] Includes an extra £270 million of funding that the government has allocated for flood and coastal erosion risk management in response to the winter floods.

[c] Gross expenditure minus income.

Table 6.5: Environment Agency FTEs (all employees), 2003–13

	31/3/2004	31/3/2007	31/3/2010	31/3/2013
FTEs (all employees)	11,336	12,252	12,359	11,765

Source: Freedom of Information (FoI) Request, Environment Agency, Response NRSEP53, 2/10/2013.

In 2012/13, the Environment Agency enforced law in 108,885 businesses.[70]

The Environment Agency has no formal relationship with EHOs, with the two sets of regulators having clearly delineated responsibilities for enforcement. That said, Defra guidance notes that, 'It is general good practice for local authorities and the Environment Agency to co-operate over the regulation of IPPC and LAPPC installations' (Defra, 2012b, para 22.1), not least through a Memorandum of Understanding between the Environment Agency and the Local Government Association (Defra, 2012b).

Premises regulated by local authorities are known as Part A2 activities and Part B activities. There are about 80 different types of such premises, including glassworks and foundries, rendering plant and maggot breeders, petrol stations and concrete crushers, sawmills and paint manufacturers, and dry cleaners (Defra, 2012b, 2). Pollution control EHO's regulatory roles encompass 'the initial authorisation or "*permitting*" of processes; the inspection of operational installations; and the prosecution of operators in those cases where processes fail to comply with regulations' (Hartley McMaster Ltd, 2012, 1, emphasis in original). Part A1 installations – 'larger, more complex and more hazardous' – are regulated by the Environment Agency (Hartley McMaster Ltd, 2012).

In 2003/04, there had been 16,932 'Part B' processes and 48 'Part A2' installations registered with local authorities across England and Wales (Hartley McMaster Ltd, 2005, 10, 12). By 2012/13, pollution control EHOs enforced law across a combined total of 18,291 premises (Defra, 2014a).

'Better' regulation in action?

By way of a contextual recap, I argued in Chapter Five that the attempts to secure the increasing dominance of Better Regulation proceeded through four mutually reinforcing processes, namely: a long-term rhetorical assault on regulation; the establishment of a series of re-regulatory institutions within and of government; various legal reforms; and a constant stream of reviews of regulators and regulation.

In combination, I argued that these initiatives sought to cement the assumptions and aims of Better Regulation, which in short are that: most businesses comply with most regulations most of the time; enforcement resources should be targeted at the non-compliers, and for the most part involve advice not sanctions; and less regulation and less enforcement are the keys to a growth economy. Thus, via political and, latterly, economic pressures, both national and local regulators are increasingly under pressure to do more with less (OECD, 2014, 4). The net effect is the institutionalisation of regulation without enforcement as an emerging political initiative.

In this section, I present some overview, quantitative data which provides some indication of how the idea of Better Regulation has affected three key protective fields in the sphere of social regulation. The data refers for the most part[71] only to two indicators of enforcement activity inspections (or 'visits' as some regulators record these) and prosecutions (and/or cautions where prosecutions are either not used or are used negligibly). Aside from reasons of space, these two indicators highlight the level of, and trends in, regulatory activity at the two ends of an enforcement continuum. On the one hand, data capturing the numbers of inspections/visits made by enforcement officers is indicative of the most basic, routine activity of inspectors and thus indicates the extent to which an inspectorial presence, as even potential enforcers of law, is more or less real. Moreover, in the context of the variants within the regulatory orthodoxy, this basic activity is crucial: it is this which can determine, on the basis of intelligence, whether for the most part specific businesses can be left to self-regulate, and where business owners can gain advice or education as regards compliance; it is also the pre-condition for any form of relationship being established between the regulator and the regulated. In short, the inspectorial presence is the *sine qua non* of a regulatory strategy. But at the same time, it is the *bête-noire* of anti-regulation, and the fundamental target of Better Regulation, since '[i]nspections often create unnecessary burdens both for the state and those inspected' (OECD, 2014, 4).

Quite differently, prosecution is the 'last resort' of all social regulators, at least in Britain (and probably more generally) (Snider, 1993). All of the regulators considered here have recourse to a range of other enforcement techniques – variously, verbal and written warning, letters, notices of varying kinds of severity – which fall short of prosecution and which are used more frequently. Two points are relevant here. First, in the absence of any significant turn towards punitiveness on the part of an enforcement authority, then it is likely that, to the extent that inspectorial activity in the most basic form of visits or inspections is in decline, then it is likely that all forms of enforcement activity which follow from this are also likely to decline. Second, prosecution has a special *symbolic* significance within the regulator's enforcement toolkit. It is that which indicates social and moral censure, expresses a normative commitment to 'do something' about companies which violate the law egregiously, and indeed which might become an even more pressing need – to retain moral legitimacy for regulation – in contexts where regulation and enforcement are generally being undermined (Almond, 2013, 32, 77, 159, and passim).

The following tables and figures present data on food safety, health and safety, and pollution control respectively; no commentary is offered. This is not to claim that the data speaks for itself, but it is to claim that there is a remarkable consistency across this data – a claim developed in the summary commentary which follows the presentation of the data on pages 145-53.

Food safety

Table 6.6: UK foodstuff statistics: UK inspections

	2003	2004/05	2005/06[a]	2006/07	2007/08[b]	2008/09	2009/10	2010/11	2011/12	2012/13
Food hygiene	307,526	291,657	450,792	276,380	196,410	287,428	288,048	290,934	277,403	269,962
Food standards total	121,961	115,835	167,090	100,005	71,244	90,961	89,977	94,516	99,294	79,725

Notes: [a] There is a clear spike in activity in inspectorial activity in 2005/06, especially in food hygiene inspections. While it is not possible definitively to explain, a plausible explanation for this spike is the impact of the outbreak of E.coli which began in South Wales in September 2005 (and was declared over on 20 December). The outbreak resulted in 157 cases, 118 of which were confirmed, and 109 were of a unique strain of E.coli 0157. A five-year old boy, Mason Jones, died following the outbreak. The source of the contamination was found to be cooked meats sold by John Tudor & Son, who supplied the school attended by Mason Jones. Unsurprisingly, the outbreak attracted UK-wide publicity. A public inquiry under Professor Pennington was established, while William Tudor pleaded guilty to seven food hygiene offences and was sentenced to 12 months' imprisonment. Ironically, Pennington's report went on to say that the 'light touch' enforcement in relation to John Tudor & Son had been 'wrong' (para 45), and concluded that 'Regulatory and enforcement bodies should keep the choice of "light touch" enforcement for individual food businesses under constant review' (Pennington, 2009: recommendations 7, 17 and 328).
[b] For 2007/08, the data collected was for the nine months from 1 April 2007 to 31 December 2007 only – this was to allow for local authorities to implement the new Local Authority Enforcement Monitoring System (LAEMS).

Sources: Food Standards Agency Freedom of Information Request FOI 1573/1033/2014, 11 June 2014; Food Standards Agency Freedom of Information Request FOI 1131, 20 February 2012; Food Standards Agency Freedom of Information Request FOI 874, 15 May 2010; Food Standards Agency FSA 12/11/06 Open Board – 13 November 2012; CIPFA, 2003, 2004, 2005, 2006, 2007, 2008, 2009, 2010, 2011, 2012a; Rhodes, 2012

Figure 6.1: UK foodstuff statistics: UK inspections

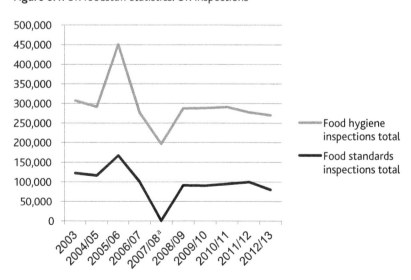

Table 6.7: Prosecutions (no. of establishments)

	2003	2004/05	2005/06	2006/07	2007/08ᵃ	2008/09	2009/10	2010/11	2011/12	2012/13
Prosecutions	552	570	538	443	368	388	467	495	413	398

Note: ᵃ For 2007/08, the data collected was for the nine months from 1 April 2007 to 31 December 2007 only. This was to allow for local authorities to implement the new Local Authority Enforcement Monitoring System (LAEMS).

Sources: Food Standards Agency Freedom of Information Request FOI 1573/1033/2014, 11 June 2014; Food Standards Agency Freedom of Information Request FOI 1131, 20 February 2012; Food Standards Agency Freedom of Information Request FOI 874, 15 May 2010; Food Standards Agency FSA 12/11/06 Open Board – 13 November 2012; CIPFA, 2003, 2004, 2005, 2006, 2007, 2008, 2009, 2010, 2011, 2012; Rhodes, 2012.

Figure 6.2: Prosecutions (no. of establishments)

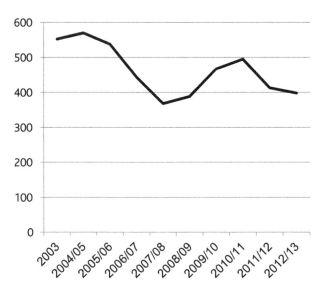

Health and safety

Health and Safety Executive

Table 6.8: Field Operations Directorate inspections

	2003/04	2004/05	2005/06	2006/07	2007/08	2008/09	2009/10	2010/11	2011/12	2012/13
Inspections	58,796	45,823	31,263	30,043	21,793	23,004	27,104	29,293	26,217	27,849

Sources: Freedom of Information Request Reference No: 2010020046, 12 April 2010; Freedom of Information Request, HSE Response, 2014060117, 2 July 2014; Temple, 2014; Sharman, 2013; Health and Safety Executive, 2012a, 2012b, 2014.

Figure 6.3: Field Operations Directorate inspections

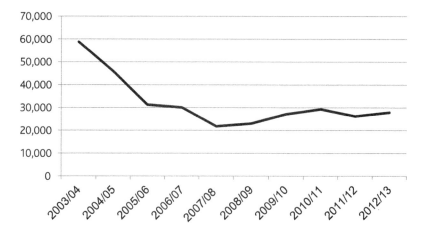

Table 6.9: Prosecutions: offences

	2003/04	2004/05	2005/06	2006/07	2007/08	2008/09	2009/10	2010/11	2011/12	2012/13[a]
Number of offences prosecuted	1,618	1,241	1,047	1,041	1,006	1,034	885	912	991	973
Number of convictions	1,243	957	831	846	849	841	730	771	781	849

Note: [a] Provisional data.

Sources: Freedom of Information Request Reference No: 2010020046, 12 April 2010; Freedom of Information Request, HSE Response, 2014060117, 2 July 2014; Temple, 2014; Sharman, 2013; Health and Safety Executive, 2012a, 2012b, 2014.

Figure 6.4: Prosecutions: offences

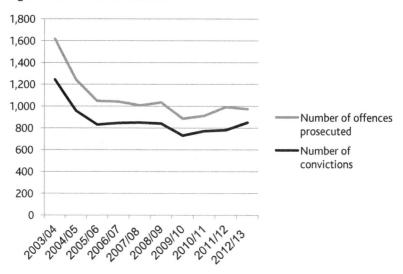

148

Health and safety enforcement (local authorities)

Table 6.10: No. of visits by local authorities

	2003/04	2004/05	2005/06	2006/07	2007/08	2008/09	2009/10	2010/11	2011/12	2012/13
Preventative	147,000	140,000	120,000	120,000	129,000	129,000	118,000	106,000	70,700	14,400
Total	242,000	234,000	215,000	209,000	224,000	209,000	196,000	194,200	151,000	106,200

Sources: Freedom of Information Request Reference No: 2010020046, 12 April 2010; Freedom of Information Request, HSE Response, 2014060117, 2 July 2014; Temple, 2014; Sharman, 2013; Health and Safety Executive, 2012a, 2012b, 2014.

Figure 6.5: No. of visits by local authorities

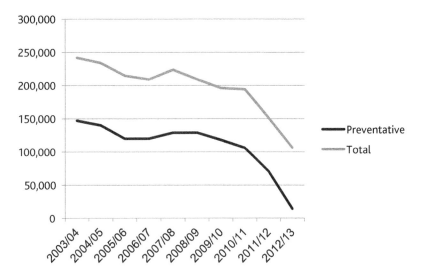

Table 6.11: Prosecutions and convictions by local authorities

	2003/04	2004/05	2005/06	2006/07	2007/08	2008/09	2009/10	2010/11	2011/12	2012/13[a]
Informations laid (known ooutcome)	410	332	257	340	354	329	287	294	199	244
Number of convictions	354	281	247	314	334	309	254	270	187	220

Note: [a] Provisional data.

Sources: Freedom of Information Request Reference No: 2010020046, 12 April 2010; Freedom of Information Request, HSE Response, 2014060117, 2 July 2014; Temple, 2014; Sharman, 2013; Health and Safety Executive, 2012a, 2012b, 2014.

Figure 6.6: Prosecutions and convictions by local authorities

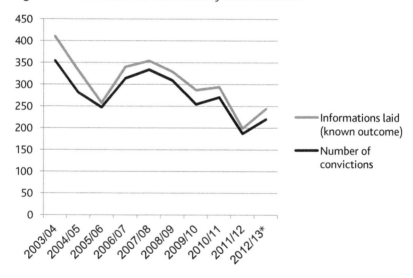

Pollution control

Table 6.12: Environment Agency inspections

	1999/00	2000/01	2001/02	2002/03	2003/04	2004/05	2005/06	2006/07	2007/08	2008/09
Total inspections	220,747	214,057	181,219	176,309	194,495	198,666	157,366	128,659	119,897	106,803

Source: Data obtained by David Whyte from Environment Agency Planning and Performance Team by Freedom of Information Request, 5 November 2009.

Figure 6.7: Environment Agency inspections

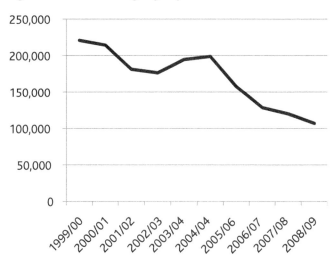

Table 6.13: Environment Agency cautions and successful prosecutions against businesses, 2003–12

	2003	2004	2005	2006	2007	2008	2009	2010	2011	2012
Cautions	184	188	230	228	220	169	176	11	164	106
Successful prosecutions	269	301	324	339	346	297	257	217	208	125

Source: FoI request, Environment Agency, response NRSEP53, 2/10/2013

Figure 6.8: Environment Agency cautions and successful prosecutions against businesses, 2003–12

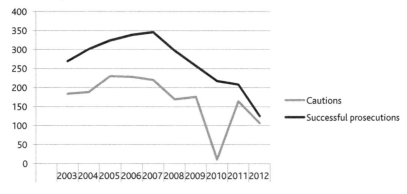

Table 6.14: Local authority pollution control enforcement. EHO enforcement activities, Part B installations

	2003/04	2004/05	2005/06	2006/07	2007/08	2008/09	2009/10	2010/11	2011/12	2012/13
Inspection visits	24,861	22,164	21,683	22,520	23,954	22,696	18,590	15,174	15,318	12,939
Total notices served[a]	1,899	1,619	1,919	2,038	2,088	2,419	4,225	2,369	2,067	1,337

Note: [a] Notices rather than prosecutions are used, since the latter are so few as to render data almost meaningless; for example, during 2012/13, Pollution Control EHOs took three successful prosecutions; in 2003, they took six (Department for Environment, Food and Rural Affairs, 2014, 11, 13)

Sources: Department for Environment, Food and Rural Affairs, 2014; Hartley McMaster Ltd, 2003, 2004, 2005, 2006, 2007, 2008, 2009, 2010, 2011, 2012.

Figures 6.9a and 6.9b: Local authority pollution control enforcement. EHO enforcement activities, Part B installations

6.9a: EHO inspection visits (Part B)

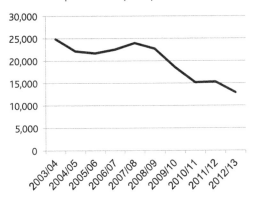

6.9b: EHO total notices served (Part B)

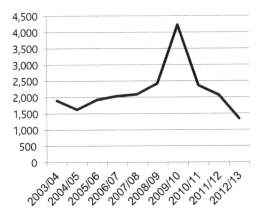

Commentary

In short, between 2003/04 and 2012/13,[72] Tables 6.6 to 6.14 and Figures 6.1 to 6.9 indicate the following.

Local EHOs enforcing food safety and hygiene law undertook:

- 12 per cent[73] fewer food hygiene inspections;
- 34 per cent fewer food standards inspections;
- 28 per cent fewer prosecutions.

HSE inspectors, the national health and safety regulator, undertook:

- 53 per cent fewer inspections (on the part of Field Operations Directorate, the body within HSE which undertakes by far the vast majority of inspections);
- 40 per cent fewer prosecutions of offences, resulting in 32 per cent fewer convictions.

Local EHOs enforcing health and safety law undertook:

- 90 per cent fewer preventative inspections;
- 56 per cent fewer total inspections;
- 40 per cent fewer prosecutions, resulting in 38 per cent fewer successful convictions.

Environment Agency officers engaged in national pollution control undertook:

- 52 per cent fewer inspections (between 1999/2000 and 2008/09);
- 54 per cent fewer successful prosecutions, while issuing 42 per cent fewer cautions (both 2003–2102).

Local EHOs enforcing local pollution control law undertook

- 48 per cent fewer Part B inspection visits;
- 30 per cent fewer Part B notices[74]

Taken in isolation, perhaps no one individual data set on any specific aspect of enforcement activity data relating to any one regulator over a ten-year period is particularly surprising. What *is* remarkable, certainly for a set of social scientific data, is that *each set of data reveals precisely the same trends*: that is, notwithstanding variations across regulators, the form of law being enforced, and indeed within regulators and specific forms of enforcement activity by year, *each set of data unequivocally indicates a long-term downwards trend in every form of enforcement activity*.

There are some further observations which might be made on this data.

First, while the trends in relative declines are striking, indeed uniformly so, this should not be allowed to obscure the fact that for the most part the data also indicates some *absolutely* low levels enforcement activity. This is certainly the case in health and safety regulation where, for example, by 2012/13, if we combine HSE and health and safety EHO data, there were just over 130,000 inspection visits – albeit, between them, these regulators enforce law across more than 2.5 million workplaces. Food safety EHOs, in contrast, visited more than half of their premises for which they are responsible in 2012/13, a combined total of almost 350,000 visits to just over 600,000 establishments. At local levels, pollution control EHOs, enforcing law in 18,291 premises, undertook 12,939 visits.

Second, this data indicates that for all of these regulators, prosecutions are the formal enforcement action of last resort. For example, if we combine HSE and health and safety EHO prosecutions for 2012/13, we find there were 1,169 successful prosecutions completed in 2012/13 across these two sets of regulators (with a combined regulated population of over 2.5 million businesses). For food safety EHOs, almost 350,000 visits led to just 398 prosecutions. In terms of pollution control, the over 100,000 businesses (at 31 March 2013) regulated by the Environment Agency generated 125 prosecutions and 106 cautions (in 2012). Pollution control EHOs took so few prosecutions that it was not worth attempting to plot trends over the period – during 2012/13, pollution control EHOs took three successful prosecutions; in 2003, they took six (Defra, 2014a, 11, 13). Their 12,939 visits to premises in 2012/13 generated 1,337 notices.

Thus, taking the above two observations together, two points are worth emphasising. First, even if there are significant differences across the regulators in terms of the absolute level of inspectorial presence, it is clear that formal enforcement is rare indeed; and, second, this is striking when set against what we know about the levels of deaths, injuries and illnesses associated, variously, with poor levels of environmental, food and occupational health and safety, as indicated in Chapter One.

Third, even a cursory glance at the data reveals differences between the various regulators, not just in terms of their levels of activity, but also in terms of the severity of the downward trends in activity of all kinds across the five sets of regulators and three functions. Certainly in the context of the latter, what we find is that it is health and safety enforcement which has declined most significantly during this period, while food safety and hygiene enforcement has declined least significantly. Somewhere between these two extremes sits pollution control, both locally and nationally, notwithstanding the relative paucity of data here. This does seem to bear out the finding in the previous chapter – that health and safety has often been the most specific target of, as well as perhaps a battering ram into wider, anti-deregulation practice and discourses. This relative weighting of the undermining of regulatory and enforcement functions is also borne out in the next part of the chapter, which presents some qualitative data based upon interviews with local enforcement officers.

Regulation and enforcement at local authority level

Elsewhere, largely on the basis of considerations of documentation, Board minutes, memoranda and so on internal to the three national regulators under consideration here, I have documented (Tombs and Whyte, 2012; 2013a; 2013b) how, at this level, Better Regulation has been translated through policy and practice. Others have also examined Better Regulation at the level of national regulation in general (Dodds, 2006; Vickers, 2008), as well as at international levels (Smith et al, 2015). This section of the chapter focuses specifically upon regulatory enforcement law in food safety, occupational health and safety and pollution control at local level, which has, in academic social scientific terms, passed almost entirely below the radar. The data here draws upon a case study of regulation and enforcement in the local authorities which make up Merseyside (below). Locally, these three functions are enforced through EHOs, usually located in 'Regulatory Services' departments of local authorities. This section of the chapter will present some qualitative data from interviews with EHOs in four[75] of the five authorities of Merseyside.

First, some brief observations on Merseyside as a region. Merseyside is a populous conurbation, and is also one of the poorest, if not *the* poorest, in England (Table 6.15). The Index of Multiple Deprivation is a ranking of all English local authorities, where 1 is the most and 326 the least deprived local authority, based upon government's measurement of 38 indicators across seven domains of deprivation, namely income, employment, health and disability, education skills and training, barriers to housing and other services, crime and living environment. Liverpool is, on the government's Index of Multiple Deprivation, the 'poorest' local authority in England, Knowsley the

Table 6.15: Basic data by Merseyside local authority

	Population 2013[a]	Businesses 2012[b]	IMD Rankings 2010 (2007)[c]
Knowsley	146,086	2,735	5 (5)
Liverpool	470,780	11,955	1 (1)
St. Helens	176,221	7,510	51 (47)
Sefton	273,207	4,180	92 (83)
Wirral	320,295	8,355	60 (60)
Merseyside	1,386,589	34,735	(n=326)

Notes: [a] http://liverpool.gov.uk/council/key-statistics-and-data/data/economy/
[b] Office for National Statistics (ONS, 2013). Active businesses are defined as businesses that had either turnover or employment at any time during the reference period
[c] Department for Communities and Local Government (DCLG). The Index of Multiple Deprivation is a ranking of all English local authorities, where 1 = the most deprived local authority and 326 the least deprived, based upon the government's measurements of 38 indicators across seven domains of deprivation, namely Income, Employment, Health and Disability, Education Skills and Training, Barriers to Housing and Other Services, Crime and Living Environment. Liverpool is, on the government's Index of Multiple Deprivation, the 'poorest' local authority in England, Knowsley the fifth poorest; three of Merseyside's five local authorities are in the poorest decile of local authorities in the country.

fifth poorest; three of Merseyside's five local authorities are in the poorest decile of local authorities in the country. Moreover, all of the five local authorities of Merseyside have higher than the national average of unemployed, and benefit claimants; of those employed, all of the five local authorities have higher than the national ratio of part-time to full-time jobs (Liverpool City Council, 2014, Tables 2–5b). All have a higher percentage of public sector jobs and a lower than national average of jobs in the private sector (Liverpool City Council, 2014, Tables 2–4a and 2–4b). In general, these observations all indicate a far great reliance of the local population upon the local state for a range of welfare, social and public services, as well as employment opportunities, so that changes in any of these have a disproportionate impact upon local people, as residents, consumers and workers (Centre for Local Economic Strategies, 2014a).

The most recent count of active businesses in Merseyside records 34,735 of these (in 2012; see Table 6.15); in the four authorities from which my interview data is drawn, there are about 27,000 such businesses. Across these four authorities there were, at April 2013, 27.75 full-time equivalent (FTE) food safety EHOs, 13.5 FTE EHOs whose primary responsibility was pollution control, and 8.4 FTE health and safety EHOs. This is indicated in Table 6.16, along with a count of interviews conducted in each authority.

Table 6.16: Environmental Health Office staff (FTEs) 2 April 2013

Local authority	Food safety	OH&S	Pollution control	Total (FTEs)	Interviews conducted[a]
C	1.6	1.4	1.2	4.2	4
D	12	2	2	16	5
E	5	3	4	12	3
F	9.15	2	6.3	17.45	13

Note: [a] A total of 35 interviews were conducted between 16/08/13 and 06/10/14. In addition to those included in this table, the wider project from which this chapter comes also consisted of interviews with Regulatory Services managers from two other North West local authorities, senior civil servants within the government's Better Regulation Delivery Office, individuals in the Chamber of Commerce and Federation of Small Business, the Chartered Institute of Environmental Health, UNISON as the relevant trade union, one Council Cabinet's Member for Environment and Sustainability and a programme leader for an MSc in Public Health.

Sources: Freedom of Information Request F2014-12-864; Freedom of Information Request 357573 Response; FOI – Sefton Environmental Health Officer Numbers, 19 January 2015; FOI 856837 – Steve Tombs – Environmental Health Staffing.

The focus on Merseyside – or, rather, four of its five local authorities – is a focus upon four metropolitan boroughs which have real peculiarities. The data presented below may not, then, be generaliseable across all metropolitan authorities, let alone all local authorities in general. There is no claim here regarding representativeness; but at the same time, there is no need to accept that the use of a case study need 'be diminished by a belief that the findings may be idiosyncratic' (Bryman, 1988, 88). Indeed, Flyvbjerg has argued that it is possible to 'generalize on the basis of a single case, and the case study may be central to scientific development via generalisation as supplement or alternative to other methods'. Further, he claims, 'formal generalisation is overvalued as a source of scientific development, whereas "the force of example" is underestimated' (Flyvbjerg, 2006, 228). I am clear, then, that what is presented here may reflect peculiarities but not mere idiosyncrasies. And the qualitative insights offered add to the quantitative data set out above – specifically, to enhance an understanding of how the politics and more latterly the economics of Better Regulation might affect local authority enforcement efforts.

In what follows, three general themes[76] explored in the course of the interviews are addressed. First, I set out some of the more general views, perceptions and understanding of 'Better Regulation' at local levels; second, I focus on some of the perceived effects of the political imperatives towards Better Regulation when combined with the unfolding economic exigencies of austerity; third, I address views upon the likely futures of regulation and enforcement at this level, and do so partly via consideration of a flagship Better Regulation initiative, namely the Primary Authority scheme.

General views on the origins and nature of Better Regulation

Several different kinds of views about Better Regulation in general were expressed by respondents. A minority view, expressed solely among (a minority of) managers of EHO departments and teams, was that the Better Regulation agenda was positive; one, for example, talked about constant efforts to 'push this agenda forward' (C1).[77] For another, it chimed with his view of the EHO function: 'it's about effecting change in business, positively', 'what it says in the book doesn't always work, you've got to help business grow' (F5). And one enforcement officer said, it was 'the future' of the role, which he characterised as, 'I'm your advisor, you pay the business rates, we provide the service' – 'trying to get away from the image of EHOs as scary men in white coats', the latter being 'a stigma' (F6).

The dominant views of Better Regulation, however, were to see this in negative, or cynical, terms, or both. One respondent saw Better Regulation as an impediment to enforcement – 'It seems that everything is being put in our way, they're making it as difficult as possible for local authorities to protect public health' (D4) – while another translated Better Regulation into being increasingly 'controlled' and feeling 'under the hammer' (F11). For some, it was an anti-enforcement agenda in the name of business: 'the message is that for the sake of UK Plc, the message is don't enforce against business' (E1). A sizeable minority of respondents were simply cynical, and cited the Better Regulation agenda as emanating from, and suiting the interests of, large corporations and free market economics: 'a few large businesses setting the agenda and whispering in his ear, they "dominated" Hampton' (E3).

Another was highly critical about 'the burdens on business agenda': 'if we're there for an hour once every five years, how can that be a burden?'; this respondent added that she thought that it was 'the likes of Tesco's, Sainsbury's and the big boys, they're whispering into government's ear about burdens' (F11). For another, 'The coalition has tried to roll back regulation under the guise of red tape, bureaucracy' and 'regulation has been rolled back anyway in terms of funding' (D2).

Finally, there were those who were somewhat dismissive of Better Regulation, claiming in various ways that it was largely irrelevant since it required local regulators to do that which they had been doing anyway: 'we've always risk-rated our premises…so operating on the basis of risk targeting is nothing new for local authorities'; (C1) 'it's what we were doing anyway'; (E1) 'I think we've been doing this before Better Regulation came in…we'd expect our officers to be following these principles without them being written down'; (E2) and, 'we all want to encourage business' (F2).

These latter observations also chimed with characterisations of enforcement styles gleaned through the interviews. In general, the practice of enforcement reported to me was one ostensibly advocated within Better Regulation discourses. Thus, for one EHO, enforcement was characterised as being about 'advice and education' in the expectation that 'compliance was a long-term outcome' (F4), while similarly: 'The key part of our role is to communicate with businesses' (F5); 'enforcement is about building relationships…slow, long-term work, education, education, education' (F7).

It was noted by many respondents that not all EHOs shared this view, and that there was a minority who sought to use the law and were enforcement-oriented. So EHOs were classified in a series of ways to characterise this difference. There were references to 'soldiers, the anti-Better Regulation people', 'they are just concerned with their regulatory function' (F5). It was expected that this 'deadwood in the Department' would be 'cleared out' through staffing cuts (F10). Thus, these 'resisters' were those who 'have been here for 20, 25 years, they are stuck in an insular, traditional, local government model' (F1). Others drew dichotomies between the 'young, academically bright' and the 'old bastards' or 'old buggers' (F2), 'the advisers versus the enforcers' (F10).

These points being made, many respondents were not naïve about what they could achieve. One EHO who described his role in terms of 'negotiation' nevertheless noted that, 'most businesses do not comply with most law, but for the most part this isn't malevolence, probably much more ignorance. This applies to the big, reputable companies who you would expect either to know or comply with the law' (F2). And, similarly, from others: 'lots of big food and pub chains, they're on the edge of compliance, they do what they think they can get away with' (E1); 'We should be able to trust petrol stations run by big companies like BP to comply effectively, and to focus on others, the independents, the smaller outfits, but we can't' (F8).

In other words, and in general, there seems to be some sympathy towards the principles of Better Regulation, while also some sense of problems with some of its central assumptions. In the context of this overall general assessment, two further issues raised through the interviews are worth exploring. First, it was variously noted how attempts to continue to roll out Better Regulation within conditions of austerity have combined to make the formal principles of Better Regulation less feasible, even contradictory. Second, through the qualitative data generated it appears that the effects of austerity may actually have revealed the essential rather than apparent nature – or at least likely trajectory of – 'Better Regulation', that is, creating conditions where businesses are relatively free of local *enforcement*, where regulation and compliance are increasingly defined by businesses themselves, and where businesses are able to call on local authority resources in order to support accumulation. It is these two observations upon which I wish to focus for the rest of this chapter.

The economics of austerity and the politics of Better Regulation

During the latter half of the period under examination here, it is clear that the politics of Better Regulation became substantially overlain – in fact, over-determined – by the 'economics'[78] of austerity. To gain some sense of how these two processes were mutually reinforcing in their effects upon local regulatory services, both in general and on Merseyside, I want to take a brief detour to consider some trends in local authority funding before returning directly to some of the qualitative findings from interviews.

There are a whole series of streams which make up local government funding. Roughly, about three-quarters comes from a series of central government grants, about one-quarter from council tax (Crawford and Phillips, 2012, 127). Of interest is that, analysing funding for local authority services across the last Labour administrations, 1997–2010, local government funding increased from 2001/02 through to 2009/10, albeit less rapidly towards the end of that decade (Crawford and Phillips, 2012, 138–40). Lupton et al find that, 'All groups of authorities experienced an increase in funding over the period, and funding became more redistributive towards poor authorities. For unitary authorities, most of this increase came between 2001/2 and 2005/6. The top two quintile groups (most deprived) became relatively better funded compared with the bottom three groups' (Lupton et al, 2013, 5).

Thus, funding for local authority services was progressive under at least the first two Labour governments for all unitary authorities – as well as for the poorest among these (Lupton et al, 2013, 5).

From 2009/2010, local government funding from central government came under pressure and, if not immediately apparent from the mix of streams by which local government is funded, 'grants from central government (excluding those specifically for education)[79] were cut by 13.3 per cent in real terms between 2009–10 and 2011–12' (Crawford and Phillips, 2012, 131).

According to the Office for Budget Responsibility (OBR) in 2014, 60 per cent of planned government cuts had still to be effected – so will take effect in the next parliament. In its words, the 'implied squeeze on local authority spending is simply severe' (cited in Centre for Local Economic Strategies, 2014a, 3) Indeed, of all the cuts to government departments between 2010 and 2016, the Department for Communities and Local Government (DCLG) is affected most of all. During that period, its funding is 'being cut by over a half. DCLG's cuts across both communities and local government represent nearly two-fifths of all real terms departmental cuts, highlighting the disproportionate share that local authorities across the country have to bear' (Centre for Local Economic Strategies, 2014a, 3–4; see also IFS, 2015). Bearing in mind core areas of service delivery,[80] other local services at local authority level, including regulatory services, will fall *on average* by 46 per cent between 2015 and 2020 (Centre for Local Economic Strategies, 2014a, 4). The 'on average' calculation masks two factors: first, that within the non-protected services, cuts will be differentially distributed; second, that the cuts will have a disproportionate impact upon poorest local authorities (Centre for Local Economic Strategies, 2014b).

Drilling down to cuts by service, Crawford and Phillips calculate that 'planning and development' face by far the greatest cuts, largely due to 'significant cuts in spending on economic and community development programmes'. The next largest reduction is in 'regulation and safety' (Crawford and Phillips, 2012, 135). It is little wonder that many local authorities, even very early in the life of the coalition government, had been or were planning to use their reserves to meet increasing funding shortfalls (Illman, 2011a; 2011b). Moreover, the effects of these shortfalls are likely to lead disproportionately to cuts in those areas where functions are not statutory and where funding is not ring-fenced (Local Government Association, 2013a, 25–6). Budgets for regulatory services are not ring-fenced (Hampton, 2005, 102).

Now, to be clear, if local authority regulatory services are significant in terms the national regulatory effort, 'each regulatory service department is a small part of the local authority it sits within. In 2005/06, the overall spend on local authority regulatory services was only 0.7 per cent of total Council spending' (Rogers, 2007, 24). But even in 2007, when funding was still rising, the Rogers Review noted that, 'over two-thirds, 67 per cent of authorities find it difficult to fulfil their enforcement responsibilities due to the lack of allocated resources within their council' (Rogers, 2007, 24). The same review had also cited a LACORS study which showed that 'very few Local Area Agreements, a key strategic document for local authorities, explicitly refer to regulatory services' (Rogers, 2007, para 2.14).

It is difficult to drill down further beyond 'regulatory services' in general in order to determine precisely what these trends in funding have meant for environmental health and trading standards services. Wall (2011) reports research by the LBRO which documented cuts in Environmental Health services in England and Wales of 8 per cent between 2010 and 2011 – above average in the context of local authority cuts. Graham Russell, LBRO chief executive, said, 'If we want to continue to have a regulatory system that we can be proud of, then we must adapt to the changing reality of the economy and public expectations. We must embrace change, embrace the challenge, and innovate our way to doing more with less' (cited in Wall, 2011). A further source which allows some approximation of this is a recent document which seeks to provides an indicative picture of local authority regulatory services budgets for the financial year 2011–12 compared with 2010/11 (Trading Standards Institute et al, 2012). The analysis is based upon the first year's experience of the effects of the Spending Review 2010, an examination of how budget reductions affected these functions and an attempt to project these through the four years covered by the review. This analysis confirms that, in general, regulatory services will face greater reductions than most other areas of local authority activity.

A second source is through a brief survey of some of the specialist/trade media.[81] Therein, reports of redundancies, non-replacement and the end of recruitment across authorities in environmental health are now constants within the specialist press; see, for example: reports on Gateshead, Bradford, Swindon, Sheffield City Council, Bolton Council, Neath Port Talbot County Borough Council, City of York Council and Middlesbrough Council (Wall, 2011; Wall, 2012b; Williams, 2012a; 2012b; 2012c; 2012d), or a later report to the effect that Crawley Borough Council had, in 2011/12, reduced its environmental health team by a third, losing six of a 17-person team. A council spokesperson noted, 'The changes required by central government on our approach to health and safety' meant 'that it was an appropriate time to review the service', adding that a review of functions allowed the Council to 'refocus on the key public health and environmental services needed by Crawley' (cited in Williams, 2012b).

Concluding on the general state of public finances, it is worth noting the remarkable observation of the (usually sober) Chartered Institute of Public Finance and Accountancy (CIPFA). It stated, in 2012, and prior to the announcement of further public sector budget reductions in April 2013:

> To date the overall performance of public bodies in planning and executing cuts has been positive, helped by the fact that public opposition has, on the whole, been relatively muted. Whether this continues to be the case remains one of the critical variables in the equation. There is no room for complacency because the scale of reductions planned is unprecedented in modern times…While total public spending has increased in real terms more or less consistently over the past four decades, a completely different trajectory is planned post 2010. But public disquiet and the risk of dissent are bound to increase as public bodies are forced to consider cuts to ever more sensitive services which have direct implications for the quality of people's lives and their life chances. (CIPFA, 2012b, 7)

Analyses of the distribution and impacts of these cuts indicate overwhelmingly that they have the heaviest impact upon poorer local authorities as well as those with greater reliance on public sector employment (Centre for Local Economic Strategies, 2014b; Hastings et al, 2013) – in other words, the 'cuts' in general are likely to have an impact as much if not more upon the local authorities of Merseyside than in any other part of England or the UK. For example, DCLG data released in 2014, based on the amount per household that councils are losing between 2010–11 and 2015–16, indicated that

> Councils covering the 10 most deprived areas of England – measured according to the index of multiple deprivation – are losing £782 on average per household, while authorities covering the richest areas are losing just £48 on average. Hart district council in Hampshire, the least deprived local authority, is losing £28 per household, while in Liverpool District B, the most deprived area, the figure is £807. (Sparrow, 2014)

In these contexts, then, the contents of the open letter sent by leaders of three northern City Councils to Chancellor Osborne late in 2012 are hardly surprising.[82] Therein, they warned that budget cutbacks were leading inexorably to, 'Rising crime, increasing community tension and more problems on our streets', which would 'contribute to the break-up of civil society if we do not turn back'. Speaking not simply of the absolute levels of budget reductions but also of the regressive effects of these in terms of under-resourcing northern towns and cities at the expense of already richer south-eastern areas, these three council leaders went on to warn that, 'The unfairness of the government's cuts is in danger of creating a deeply divided nation. We urge them to stop what they are doing now and listen to our warnings before the forces of social unrest start to smoulder' (cited in Helm, 2012).

In the course of the interviews, I was able to gain a clearer sense of what some of this data means in practice,[83] not least in poor local authorities where there is greater demand on local authority spending. Indeed, 'the cuts' were by far the strongest theme across all respondents within all local authorities. As concrete indicators of the general reductions of funding, the following are helpful in understanding the local effects of such national data. In one local authority, from 2011 to 2013, 35 per cent of environmental health resource was cut; in 2014/15, environmental health expenditure needed to be cut by another 20 per cent; as one respondent noted, 'all of these savings have to come from staffing costs. Resources, staffing, is very problematic' (D1). In another authority, one respondent noted something indicated to me more generally – that food inspectors would try to 'keep an eye out for health and safety issues' in the businesses they visited, 'we use food officers to pick these up' (D2). In another authority, I was told that the level of allocated resource to health and safety had declined by 75 per cent between 2011 and 2014 (E2). In general, in that same authority, it was reported by the Head of Regulatory Services that, 'We've lost 30 per cent of resource in last three years, a further 20/25 per cent in next two years, yet even, at present, we can't meet our statutory duties' (E1).

Through a series of requests made under the Freedom of Information Act 2000, I sought to verify these indicators of staffing declines through accessing data of staffing levels by function across the four local authorities in which I was able to conduct interviews. Table 6.17 presents the results of those requests.

Incomplete as this data is, it nevertheless demonstrates clearly that: staffing levels across each of the functions across all of the four local authorities have diminished; where data exists, these reductions appear most marked since 2010; and the relative distribution of staff FTEs reflects the greatest number being devoted to food safety and hygiene,

Table 6.17: Environmental Health Officers (FTEs), 2004–13

Environmental Health Officers (FTEs), by principal responsibility	1/4/2004	1/4/2007	1/4/2010	1/4/2013
Local Authority C				
Food	N/A	2.45	1.85	1.6
Health and Safety	N/A	1.45	1.65	1.4
Pollution Control	N/A	2.7	2.7	1.2
Total staff	N/A	6.6	6.2	4.2
Local Authority D				
Food	14	14	14	12
Health and Safety	4	4	4	2
Pollution Control	5	5	5	2
Total staff	23	23	23	16
Local Authority E				
Food	N/A	N/A	5.5	5
Health and Safety	N/A	N/A	3	3
Pollution Control	N/A	N/A	6	4
Total staff	N/A	N/A	14.5	12
Local Authority F				
Food	11*	10	8.95	9.15
Health and Safety	5*	5	5	2
Pollution Control	8*	7	7	6.3
Total staff	24*	22	20.95	13.45

Note:*No records available; manual reckoning

Sources: Freedom of Information Request F2014-12-864; Freedom of Information Request 357573 Response; FOI – Sefton Environmental Health Officer Numbers, 19 January 2015; FOI 856837 – Steve Tombs – Environmental Health Staffing.

the fewest to health and safety. Finally, it is worth noting the absolutely low numbers of staff resource at issue here, in any authority in any year, but notably by the final year for which data is provided, that is, 2013. The data on staffing levels presented in Tables 6.17 and 6.18 certainly coheres with what were remarkably similar phrases used to describe the state of regulatory and inspectorial resources in the course of the interviews: 'to be honest we're now doing statutory stuff only' (F9); 'there's nothing left to cut now' (C1); 'there is no padding left, we're below the statutory minimum...there are no areas of discretion left' (E1); 'there's nothing else to be cut' (D3). Three respondents spelt out the implications of such reductions in staff resources in remarkably similar terms:

> Where we are now, we're at the point where worker safety is being jeopardised. (F2)

> It's going to come to the point where it is going to affect the residents, the local population, in many ways we are at that point now, where public health and protection is being eroded. (D4)

> We're at the point where there is no flesh left, this is starting to get dangerous, a danger to public health. (F7)

Other themes emerged, which clearly cohered with the findings of the enforcement data, collated for each function over the ten-year period, above. Thus it is hardly surprising that the interviewees raised the issues of a long-term decline in inspection, a long-term decline in the use of formal enforcement tools, and a decreasing use of prosecution. On the latter, another clear message from the data was of increasing obstacles to the ability to prosecute. The latter included: a lack of staff time; fear of losing cases; lack of support from legal services departments to prosecute; and an increased political risk ('flak') in prosecuting. Moreover, these types of responses are indicative of a political context for regulatory enforcement where the idea of regulation is under attack, and are a useful illustration of how discourses and policies at national level can translate into barriers to enforcement at local levels.

Table 6.18: Four local authorities combined

Environmental Health Officers (FTEs), by principal responsibility	1/4/2004	1/4/2007	1/4/2010	1/4/2013
Food	N/A	N/A	30.3	27.75
Health and Safety	N/A	N/A	13.65	8.4
Pollution Control	N/A	N/A	20.7	13.5
Total Staff	N/A	N/A	64.65	49.65

One of the clearest messages to emerge from interviewing EHOs and their managers was that the different regulatory functions have been differentially affected by the political and economic pressures upon them. In this context, a virtually unanimous reference was the contrast between 'food' and 'health and safety' functions – with the environmental protection function barely referred to. Food safety was seen as a priority – for the EHOs and for the public – and in interviews this priority was often explicitly contrasted with the health and safety functions of EHOs. Thus when asked about the relative vitality of the three functions, the robustness of food enforcement was generally raised – this is indicated by the quantitative data, above, that is, when compared with environmental protection and health and safety functions. In this context, the significance of public perceptions was made clear to me. Thus, for example, one respondent noted that, food inspections are 'the ones that people bother about', these inspections 'are up there in the eyes of the public'. Also of note is that specific food 'scares' – the horsemeat scandal and stories of e-coli were mentioned – were said to have been 'helpful' in that they maintained the profile/importance of food safety. In fact, for this respondent, public expectations around food safety and food hygiene were actually increasing. This, she contrasted with health and safety, which 'has been rubbished in the eyes of the public' (F9). The same respondent claimed that, food – as opposed to environmental protection or health and safety – 'was an area where there is less conflict with the regulated' (F9), a point to which I return in the concluding chapter.

This relative prioritisation of food over health and safety was reiterated variously: 'health and safety is going down' (the respondent also noting that former health and safety EHOs were being transferred to food safety work) (F5); 'food is the main priority…that's what the public think and that's what the public want' (F6); 'health and safety is the poor relation to food' (F2); 'the poor relation is health and safety, probably always has been', and thus 'attracts fewer resources' (E2). In short, 'Food is not vilified like health and safety.' Local authorities' food safety functions 'connect with the public in a way that the health and safety doesn't'. (F5)

Following from that last point, one of the variables also mentioned here was the different types of relationships between national and local regulators in the context of food as compared with health and safety – and the potential significance of these. Frequently mentioned was the highly prescriptive role of the FSA in terms of the work of food safety EHOs, and the levels of inspection required of various categories of establishment by risk-rating within this overall prescription. This helped to ensure that in the context of declining resource for local authority enforcement overall, 'health and safety enforcement will necessarily go'; 'FSA prescriptions means that food has retained some resources over health and safety' (D4). Others referred to the fact that, at local authority level, the FSA was 'a key presence and influence here', noting that 'it's very clear, with its codes and so on, very prescriptive' (E2). For other respondents, this level of prescription had generated tensions in the past, but there was a general claim, certainly since the 'horsemeat stuff', that 'they had really improved communications with local authorities' (F2).

In many ways, the comments on HSE–health and safety EHO relationships seemed a mirror image of those regarding FSA–food safety EHO relationships. One respondent was typically critical of HSE's current relationship with EHOs – albeit understanding of the reasons for this. During her time she described a shift from having barely no relationship with HSE to a period when she/they felt very supported by this relationship to more recently when this had 'completely dried up'. Although she accepted why this was the case – in her words, because HSE had been 'hollowed out and is under constant pressure' – she remained critical of the fact that they were now 'so defensive, we have virtually no contact', 'they've just stopped, just pulled back'. (F11). Another EHO also discussed a previously 'supportive relationship' with HSE, but noted that this had changed 'in recent years', so that 'HSE have withdrawn, they don't want to know now'. (F2) As a third observed, 'HSE is now completely in the background' (E2).

To return to the issue of resources in general, it should also be noted that, if all of the local authorities to which I gained access had experienced loss of staff, as indicated above, this did not just mean a loss of *overall* resource, but the loss of a *particular* kind of resource, that is, expertise and experience. Most notably, redundancies did not only mean that staff were not replaced, but meant a loss of specialist expertise alongside pressures for regulators to become generalists (A3). As one respondent put it, 'the last two years have been a nightmare', the authority had lost staff and expertise – 'it's the experienced staff who have gone, so we have lost numbers and expertise' (C1). In fact, the shift from regulators being specialists to generalists was one consistent theme across the interviews, referred to by numerous respondents and in every authority: 'People have had to become generalists', and 'most of them are just thankful they've still got a job' (C1).

Moreover, the loss of staff combined with a shift from a specialist to generalist inspection focus had made re-training necessary. However, another clear theme to emerge from the interviews was of declining opportunities for training – at the time when most needed. As one Regulatory Services manager put it to me, 'We have a training budget, but it is now business hardened' (E1) – by which he meant that there was 'little access' to training, 'except to free online courses'. An EHO translated this into the effects on an individual: 'I used to go on 6 to 10 courses a year, now perhaps one or two, I'm supposed to do 10 hours of CPD [continuing professional development] a year but am struggling to manage that' (F10).

There is one further observation regarding the *education* of EHOs, that is those training to become inspectors and who might, eventually, find jobs in the profession. Changes in education appeared both to have extended the influence of the private sector and to have reflected and/or hastened the general shift away from the EHO function as an inspectorial one.

EHOs attain professional status through a degree course accredited by the Chartered Institute of Environmental Health (CIEH) and taught at various HEIs. In 2011, the curriculum was overhauled, partly, in the words of one interviewee, a programme leader of one such course at a North West University, to reflect 'the shift in the profession from not being seen as inspection focused' (HE1). In the words of another respondent, a student EHO, 'CIEH is increasingly making the content of degrees more private-sector friendly' (F5). This process had already begun as a result of local authorities' inability to offer paid placements for students, while students require placements in order to complete the main assessment on their degree course. Several respondents told me that local authority funded students simply no longer exist – the one student EHO I interviewed was working in the authority part-time, unpaid. More commonly, since students still have to undertake a placement, they now take these where they can be paid, or at least receive expenses, that is, in the private sector – Asda, Sainsbury's, Tesco's were all mentioned as significant sites for such placements in the food sector. Obviously, and as was said to me, this also means that the values and perspectives of the private sector, the regulated, are prioritised for the student EHO over those of the regulator. In such subtle ways are the mind-sets and thus practices of a profession shifted.

The Primary Authority scheme – and the future of local regulatory services?

A further, and key, way in which the private sector has become embedded in local authority regulation is via the Primary Authority (PA) scheme, which in fact represents a paradigmatic example of how the politics and economics of Better Regulation have combined to produce a fundamental shift in the practice and principles of regulation and enforcement. The PA scheme was introduced by the Labour government in 2009, but given considerable impetus by the coalition government from 2010, notably following the establishment of the BRDO in 2012, for which oversight of the scheme was a key priority. According to the BRDO, the scheme allows businesses to be involved in their own regulation. It enables them to form a statutory partnership with one local authority, which then provides robust and reliable advice for other councils to take into account when carrying out inspections or addressing non-compliance. The general aim is to ensure that local regulation is consistent at a national level, but sufficiently flexible to address local circumstances. The business can decide what level of support it requires, and the resourcing of partnerships is a matter for the parties concerned. A primary authority can recover its costs. (BRDO, 2014a, 2)

By April 2014, over 1,500 businesses had established PA relationships across 120 local authorities (BRDO, 2014a, 2).

The PA is a classic Better Regulation initiative – and, at local level, the *key* formal initiative. It allows a company – and, since April 2014, franchises and businesses in trade associations – operating across more than one local authority area to enter an agreement with a specific local authority to regulate *all* of its sites, nationally, even in the absence of being able to visit those outside their specific jurisdiction. Thus, for example, a supermarket like Tesco's may have stores in every one of the local authorities in England and Wales. Under the PA scheme, it can reach an agreement with *one* local authority to regulate its systems across *all* of its stores in *every* local authority for complying with a relevant body of law – occupational health and safety or food hygiene. To regulate its systems, the company makes a payment to the local authority, agreed through contract. The benefit for the company, of course, is the absence of oversight in the vast majority of its outlets. These can be visited in other areas, but any enforcement action needs to be undertaken through the local authority which is the PA. Should a local authority wish to prosecute a company in a PA agreement, for example, it can only do so with the permission of the local authority which is party to that agreement. Then, under the scheme, any consideration of a potential prosecution must entail prior notice being given to the company; the company can then request that the matter be referred to the BRDO for determination (Williams, 2013).

Thus civil servants at the BRDO – created by the coalition government in 2012 to drive through the Better Regulation agenda across local government from its location in the Ministry of Business, Information and Skills – stated[84] that the PA scheme is 'a big success', citing the numbers of businesses who have entered agreements with local authorities, and 'what businesses say about it, the savings it has generated', as well as the fact that 'every major business has been snapped up' (BRDO, 2014b).

It's clear, however, that the scheme was proving highly problematic for local regulators, even as they sought to enter into PA agreements in order to generate income – 'this is why we are really pushing the PA scheme' (C1). Another referred to ongoing negotiations with a company, stating that although she'd 'always been opposed to the scheme', it 'would generate about £18K in the first year when systems and so on are being set up, this is peanuts for a multinational but half a job for us' (A4). So although one regulatory services manager noted that the scheme 'did not really work', he and his local authority were constantly pursuing them (D1).

As one respondent put it, while 'in theory it could work well, in practice it protects large companies from local authority enforcement' (D3). Others noted similar problems with the scheme, for example: 'under PA they [companies] only have to demonstrate the existence of systems' (D2); local authorities have a 'disincentive to take enforcement action because PA schemes are a source of income' (D2); PA schemes 'protect companies from inspection and enforcement' (D5); they operate 'in my experience at the level of a tick-box rather than real co-operation or taking responsibility' (F7); PA schemes 'work on paper only, there are hundreds of businesses in the scheme and I can't see how these can all be genuine' (E2).

In general, then, as one enforcement officer noted, 'Primary Authority has had a real impact on what we can and cannot do'; the claim was made at length that businesses 'pick and choose' which local authorities with which to enter into PA agreements, insisting that 'they wouldn't pick an authority like Liverpool', they will pick the 'no-one-knows-anything authority', that is, a local authority with no experience of the industry/business (D4). Moreover, in the processes of negotiation to draw up the contract which represent the PA agreement, local authorities are at a distinct disadvantage – there is an 'asymmetry of expertise' (Social Enterprise UK, 2012) between local authority negotiators and private companies in such contractual negotiations, as well, of course, as a structural power accruing to private companies operating across numerous authorities to drive down the terms of contract with any one local authority.

The Primary Authority scheme represents a fundamental shift in the nature of local regulation and enforcement. It is a classic vehicle of Better Regulation, since it reduces inspection, exacerbates the power imbalance between regulators and regulated, builds in checks against regulation and enforcement, and operates on a marketised, contract-based system. Discussion of the PA scheme was, then, inevitably used as a way of discussing the future trajectories of local regulatory services. And, when respondents were asked where they thought their service might be in five to ten years, responses were a variation on a theme, encapsulated pithily by the response, 'I don't know if I'll be here in one year let alone five years' (C1). Those who expanded upon this rather dispirited response indicated that the function would become marketised or privatised or likely some hybrid of the two – reflecting more general prognoses of how local authorities would respond to the pressures of funding cuts (Hastings et al, 2013).

Such indications are hardly pure speculation. The wholesale outsourcing of regulatory functions has been realised in two local authorities. In October 2012, North Tyneside Council announced the transfer of 800 employees to Balfour Beatty[85] and Capita Symonds (BBC, 2012). Then, in a much bigger contract, in August 2013, the London Borough of Barnet saw off a legal challenge to a contract to hand over its services to two wings of Capita,[86] under what has become known as the 'One Barnet' model. Business services – estates, finance, payroll, human resources, IT, procurement, revenues and benefits administration, and customer and support services – have been outsourced to Capita in a ten-year contract worth £350 million. A range of other services – including regulatory services – were contracted to its subsidiary Capita Symonds, in a £130 million contract, also for ten years (Smulian, 2013; Spear, 2013). However, these wholesale shifts from public to private provision are the mere visible tip of a significant iceberg: recent research by the New Economics Foundation for the TUC calculated that, 'Environmental and regulatory services is the sector with the second biggest proportion of expenditure paid to external contractors, at 44 per cent' (Trades Union Congress and the New Economics Foundation, 2015, 59). The arrangements under which this outsourcing proceeds are complex and opaque, confounding accountability and often even transparency (under clauses of 'commercial confidentiality'), and include diverse arrangements such as the use of strategic service partnerships (SSPs), joint venture companies (JVCs), shared services, and collaborative outsourcing (Trades Union Congress and the New Economics Foundation, 2015).

It was no surprise, then, when one of the respondents noted that, in contexts where all possible savings had been made, notably in terms of in-house staff, that there would likely be more merging of functions and more outsourcing – claiming that 'the Capitas of this world' would take over functions and make savings by 'driving down pay and conditions', so that there would be left 'a rump of people working for a council who commission services' (D2). Several respondents noted that the most likely scenario was to become a commissioning authority. Indeed, this was also a view held by the one elected member[87] whom I interviewed as part of this research, a Labour Councillor and former NEC member of the Communications Workers Union. In his words, given resource constraints and the fact that 'it's the Council's duty to set a legal budget', 'nothing is off the table', so that what he called 'the Barnet privatisation…might be something we'd consider in the future' (Co1). Another interviewee raised these two developments critically, arguing that 'enforcement should be kept in house', and explicitly raising 'the problems' of 'a private company enforcing against private companies' – this was, in her words, 'a conflict of interest' (F11).

As I argued in the previous chapter, once regulation is successfully cast as a problem, to be reduced, a drain on state resources, private entrepreneurship and economic growth, and once that view is furthered through regulatory, legal and institutional reform, then the momentum against regulation becomes virtually unstoppable – if *less* state regulation and enforcement is *always* to be preferred, then *how little is little enough?* This issue emerged in interviews with two staff at the BRDO, referred to in what follows as BRDO1 and BRDO2.[88] For each of these, they were clear that Better Regulation was established to 'restore trust' on the part of business with regulators, a relationship which one described as having been 'broken'. Of interest was the view, even after some 15 years of Better Regulation initiatives, that regulators failed to understand that 'regulation and economic development and prosperity go hand in hand' (BRDO2), rather viewing the former 'as a matter of enforcement' – and claiming that this was especially problematic at the de-centralised level of local regulation (BRDO1). Thus, for each of these interviewees, the Better Regulation message had not been effectively delivered at local level: 'Most [EHOs] didn't know and many still won't where their local Economic Development programme sits within the authority.' Thus the task was still to get regulators 'to see themselves in a different light in relation to business, to reposition themselves in terms of businesses' (BRDO1). This 'requires a commercial mindedness that most local authority regulators simply do not have' – albeit there was optimism that newer recruits were more likely to be imbued with this attitude, and thus to embrace Better Regulation (BRDO1). This was reflected by one of my respondents, a Regulatory Services manager who had enthusiastically embraced Better Regulation: 'We need to be more business friendly and get our customer focus right' he stated, later adding, 'I am in the business of collaborative regulation…there must be growth, and that is the context in which we must support business to comply with the law' (F1).

Better Regulation: regulation without enforcement

It seems hard to avoid the conclusion that Better Regulation is not really about 'better' regulation but, put most simply, systematically more business-friendly systems of law and law enforcement, the latter amounting in fact to declining levels of enforcement on all key indicators. This observation, reached, in earlier chapters, conceptually, is thoroughly under-scored by the qualitative and quantitative data reported above. What is more, these observations, taken together, reveal a fundamental contradiction in the central claim made for Better Regulation – and which also sits at the heart of the regulatory orthodoxy.

Given the way that the orthodoxy positions optimum regulatory strategies – a focus upon prevention, the relationships it aims to foster with duty holders to encourage compliance, its commitment to information and intelligence gathering – then no matter how far such strategies move towards risk-based, targeted enforcement, inspections remain central to the potential efficacy claimed for such strategies. At the same time, risk-based targeting is promoted as a mechanism, and provides a rationalisation, for increasing withdrawal from formal inspections. So it seems reasonable to argue that, in the absence of either robust historic intelligence or the ability to maintain existing levels of intelligence regarding compliance as a function of a dwindling proactive inspectorial resource across the agencies discussed here, it is difficult to see how a risk based model and any coherent programme of targeted inspections/interventions could be sustained; yet the whole thrust of the shift towards targeted inspection is precisely to reduce the numbers of overall inspections.

This contradiction regarding the role of inspection in a risk-based regime was raised, both tangentially and very directly, in a series of National Audit Office Reviews of the implementation of the Hampton agenda across each of the national regulators considered here, in 2008 (NAO, 2008a; 2008b; 2008c; 2008d),[89] that is, more or less precisely at the mid-point of the period at issue in this text and, arguably, before the economic effects of austerity were overlain onto the political drive towards Better Regulation. In its overarching report, the NAO stated, as its first conclusion, that 'Regulators accept the need for risk-based regulation and, in most instances have established mechanisms to assess risk and direct resources accordingly' (NAO, 2008a, 2). However, it continued:

> Some businesses interviewed for the reviews nevertheless believed the regulatory attention they received was not sufficiently related to their actual performance. These businesses felt that the regulatory effort was targeted at dealing with the inherent risk of a business activity and ignored firms' own capabilities for managing the risk and history of compliance. (NAO, 2008a, 2)

This then produced one of series of 'common challenges' highlighted in the report, namely the need to improve the use of intelligence (NAO, 2008a, 4). Central to this challenge was that the lack of inspectorial presence within businesses meant a lack of intelligence about those businesses – the intelligence upon which risk-ratings are, partially at least, to be based. At the same time, the NAO continued to raise the problem of *over* enforcement and *over* inspection. Thus it criticised the Environment Agency for the fact that 'absolute levels of inspection' remained high compared to other regulators', and that, 'while many EA staff feel strongly that there is a link between inspection frequency and securing environmental outcomes, the EA did not supply us with any evidence of this' (NAO, 2008b, 7). Similarly, on the FSA, the NAO, while noting that its risk-based approach to regulation had become 'embedded' (NAO, 2008c, 5), at the same time subjected it to various criticisms, including for extending its mandate beyond 'protecting' the interests of consumers (NAO, 2008c, 7), as well as for not making sufficient use of advice and guidance' (NAO, 2008c, 8). In general, a 'more nuanced approach' was required, by the FSA 'to its relationship with the industry and its contribution to economic progress' (NAO, 2008c, 33). Thus the then Code of Practice which set out a risk-rating determining (as we have seen, a *relatively* high) frequency of inspection was 'unnecessarily prescriptive and directive' and the Report looked forward to FSA reviewing this 'enforcement strategy, with a view to affording local authorities greater flexibility' (NAO, 2008c, 25). Turning to HSE, the NAO (2008d, 5) rated HSE 'highly' in terms of its working within the 'Hampton principles', endorsing the fact that it 'works well with business, including recognising the need to minimise burdens on business' (NAO, 2008c). With no hint of irony, however, this assessment of HSE's enforcement activities revealed the fundamental contradiction at the heart of a targeting strategy. The report's central criticism of HSE practice – the first of five 'Issues to be addressed' (NAO, 2008c, 7–8) – was the fact that HSE needed to make 'better use of intelligence' 'in order to improve its targeting of business' (NAO, 2008c, 7). Targeting was being undermined in particular by the focus on high risk issues, rather than duty-holders' 'past performance and other factors', which it stated were inadequately taken into account (NAO, 2008d, 21). And this deficit was attributed to the relative lack of inspections: 'Due to the relatively small number of inspections undertaken by the HSE, it may frequently be the case that the HSE has little or no information on past performance of an individual firm' (NAO, 2008d, 23).

While such observations reveal the fundamental contradiction within Better Regulation, government in general, and the NAO in particular, has continued since 2008 to be critical of the degree to which these agencies have embraced risk-based targeting, while at the same time each of these national regulators has committed to becoming even more risk-attuned and to the desirability or inevitability of conducting fewer inspections. Indeed, each of the three national regulators has reasserted the desire to be more risk-oriented *even in the past year*.[90] Thus, the Environment Agency stated its determination to focus pollution control efforts 'in the highest risk sectors' – this immediately following the observation that, 'In the last year, there has been an unexpected increase in the number of serious and significant pollution incidents, in particular from regulated but non-permitted sites. We are currently investigating why this increase has happened' (Environment Agency, 2014, 14). The FSA has launched a new regulatory strategy for 2015–20, including the 'principle' that 'Our future regulatory approach should be truly risk based and assessed in terms of impacts. This means that our greatest efforts should be focussed on the areas and issues that pose greatest risk to consumers' (Ainsworth, 2015, Annex A, para 3.5). Meanwhile, HSE's Annual Report for 2013/14 claimed as its first and third key initiative that it had continued to ensure that 'proactive inspections are targeted on areas of highest risk', and that the new Local Authority Enforcement Code, published in May 2013, would require 'LAs to follow HSE's own practice of targeting proactive inspection at high-risk activities in specified sectors, or where there is intelligence of a business failing to manage its risks properly' (HSE, 2014c,4). These points being made, of these three bodies, the FSA continued to proclaim that it would 'act as a powerful and well informed champion for consumers' (Ainsworth, 2015, 1). This 'championing' of the regulated, however rhetorical, sets the FSA somewhat apart from the other regulators discussed here – and is interesting in the light of the NAO's 2008 review of the Agency's Hampton-compliance, in which it stated,

> The FSA has a clear statutory role to *'protect public health from the risks which may arise from the consumption of food and otherwise to protect the interests of consumers in relation to food'*. The review team felt that the FSA has taken this further and in some circumstances presents itself more as 'championing' the consumer interest as distinct from 'protecting' those interests. In order to implement its duty, the Agency has a clear role in influencing industry. However, this pro-consumer stance, we believe, can complicate the Agency's engagement with and understanding of business. (NAO, 2008c, 7, emphasis in original)

What, in any case, the preceding indicates is that claims around both inspection in particular – and indeed enforcement in general – can be little more than rationalisations within the framework of Better Regulation; indeed, rationalisations which cannot withstand either logical or empirical scrutiny. As we have seen, through our brief analyses of inspection trends across three areas of socially protective law enforcement, there is an external, economic and political pincer-like attack on inspection per se. And this simply cannot be reconciled via the language or practice of targeting: the levels and accuracy of intelligence upon which targeted enforcement is based depends – *inter alia*, of course – upon an inspectorial presence within workplaces rather than just a reliance on company-generated data and information; in the absence of inspection, or significant numbers of audits, the latter data needs to be taken increasingly on trust – hence the centrality of notions of the responsible corporation in a desperate attempt to square the circle of non-intervention.

Thus, the necessary corollary of the (in)ability to target (declining) resources effectively is the assumption that most corporations for the most part can and do comply with existing bodies of law. And here we again meet the logical affinity between neoliberal, risk-based, targeted forms of Better Regulation and the regulatory orthodoxy. And this affinity of course is a key reason why the dominant body of regulation scholarship has a *political* appeal to contemporary policy makers (Tombs and Whyte, 2013a), and one of the qualities that makes it pro-hegemonic. Crucial here is that this scholarship can be invoked by governments to justify the withdrawal of enforcement resources, not simply to justify 'no cost' compliance outcomes but in fact to support claims that overall levels of compliance can be *improved* at the same time as inspection and enforcement is diminished. Thus, paradigmatically, Ayres and Braithwaite grounded their concept of responsive regulation in the need to focus upon limited regulatory resources – and the pyramid enforcement schema which they develop is central to this task, focusing such resources on those among the regulated who present the greatest risk through recalcitrance. Such conceptual schemas, then, provide perfect cover for the contemporary rhetoric used to justify the allocation of ever decreasing levels of regulatory resources. More generally, this approach by the orthodoxy is something of a sleight of hand: what we find in this scholarship is a starting-point which recognises that corporate regulators have never been granted anything comparable to the resources that various branches of police forces or other mainstream criminal justice agencies have; this is then followed by analyses which seemingly accept this as a contemporary reality, *while forgetting* its historical fact. This is a subtle but rather significant shift that creates a major distortion in regulatory studies.

Moreover, whatever the level of actual regulatory resource, the various regulatory prescriptions set out by academics across the orthodoxy ascribe some role for 'credible' enforcement: that is, non-compliance must at some point carry the threat of a more punitive approach by regulators (Ayres and Braithwaite, 1992). Indeed, the greater the heights of punitiveness to which an agency can escalate, the greater its capacity to push regulation down to the cooperative base of the pyramid (Ayres and Braithwaite, 1992, 40). Recent trends in levels of inspection – as we have seen – make detection ever less likely, and with that any potential for escalation diminishes.

Conclusion

This chapter has examined enforcement trajectories, spanning national and local regulatory bodies in the UK, in three areas of social protection, namely: food safety, health and safety at work, and pollution control.

Most centrally, this chapter has documented the systematic creation of regulatory regimes where there is now little or no enforcement. In this context, it is important to note that the trends set out in this chapter have attracted virtually no critical political nor social comment – so that even at the end of the period under examination, 2014, it remains the case that political and social references to regulation and enforcement continue to be couched in the same terms which have undermined these.

Better Regulation has continued, and will continue, apace. It is a long-term political initiative, effectively designed to break the link between regulation on the one hand and inspection or external oversight on the other. To paraphrase Fooks's prescient analysis of financial regulation of the City of London in the 1990s (Fooks, 1999), what we are witnessing is a shift from the regulation *of* business to regulation *for* business. As one analysis of the effects of spending cuts on local authorities has concluded, these will lead to a 'repositioning' of authorities in relation to 'individual well-being and quality of life as well as economic leadership' (Hastings et al, 2013, 3), with

> A renewed emphasis on developing and managing economic growth as a means both to generate income and to develop the economic competitiveness of the local authority and its region in the longer term. (Hastings et al, 2013, 4)

There is good reason to suggest, on the evidence of this and the previous chapter, how regulatory functions will likely be increasingly re-cast as part of *growth* initiatives – that is, as part of a permissive and facilitative regulatory regime (Bernat and Whyte, 2014). Certainly this chapter has provided some qualitative indicators as to the nature of the increasing penetration of business interests and assumptions into local and national constructions of appropriate forms of regulation, itself facilitated by and further fuelling a plethora of political, economic and ideological initiatives, and generating shifts towards marketised forms of regulation. More latterly, the imposition of austerity from the Treasury to other government departments and from Whitehall to local authorities, appear central to re-regulation and to the retreat from enforcement. But the argument here is that austerity policies have been of a particular kind and trajectory precisely because they were put into effect in policy, practical and discursive spaces created by 'better regulation' over many preceding years.

At the same time, 'austerity' has been one of the ways in which some of the stated rationales of Better Regulation have been exposed as contradictory, or mystificatory, or both. *Better Regulation, like neoliberalism, is resilient precisely because it is not a coherent whole, but is essentially fractured and contradictory, flexible within the parameters of the need to support the maximisation of capitalist accumulation.* Thus, like neoliberalism, the contradictions within Better Regulation make it also potentially fragile. In the final chapter, I turn to consider how the insatiable tendencies towards re-regulating state–corporate relationships, through regulation and enforcement in particular, are likely to play out, become accelerated, or be challenged and reversed.

SEVEN

After regulation?

> It was never a question of regulation or no regulation, of
> state control or laissez-faire; there were, rather, the questions
> of what kind of regulation and by whom... The stability and
> future of the economy is grounded, in the last analysis, on
> the power of the state to act to preserve it. Such support
> does not end crises, nor does it eliminate antagonisms in the
> very nature of the economy, but it does assure the ability
> of the existing social order to overcome, or survive, the
> consequences of its own deficiencies. (Kolko, 1963, 4, 302)

Introduction

Gabriel Kolko's magisterial political history of the Progressive Era
in the US re-interprets this as an 'era of conservatism'. This period,
at the turn of the nineteenth century, up to approximately 1920, is
widely referred to as an age of social reform most notably marked by
significant and unprecedented state interventions in the economy, and
thus departures from laissez-faire orthodoxy, via varieties of regulation.
The key mis-interpretation of what this wave of regulation represented
for US capital and capitalist development is based in misunderstandings
of regulation per se – that it automatically benefits the general welfare,
is antithetical to the interests of capitals, capitalists and capitalism,
reflects the state as some neutral arbiter among competing interests,
mistakes government intervention as representing the furtherance of
popular, democratic control over elite interests and, equates regulation
with government activity, and 'deregulation' as the withdrawal of such.

Thus, for Kolko, the years spanning the Presidencies of Roosevelt,
Taft and Wilson are best understood via what he calls 'political
capitalism' – the utilisation of political mechanisms to secure the
dominance of economic interests. Its basis was a political consensus
among business and political leaders about the social good, and a shared
set of social values, 'ultimately, class values' (Kolko, 1963, 284), allowed
the development of a 'functional unity of major political and business
leaders' (Kolko, 1963). Its key vehicle was regulation.

Kolko's thesis is introduced not because it is wholly unproblematic, nor because his objects of analysis equate precisely with those of this book – far from it. But where he was prescient was in setting out a view of regulation which problematises this as inevitably antithetical to capital, and indeed for specific businesses. One of the key themes of this book has been to advance precisely this point, not least in the context of an argument which maintains that UK governments and state institutions have worked feverishly and relentlessly to further the emergence of forms of regulation which are increasingly shorn of effective enforcement capacities. Moreover, in the last two chapters we have seen how these forms of re-regulation have been increasingly re-cast as part of an overall central and local government *growth function*. This argument coheres precisely with the shaping of a new form of 'political capitalism'.

In this final, concluding chapter, I wish to return to the macro-level considerations with which I began, before I drilled down into, and then emerged from, meso-level concerns with governmental regulatory 'policy' and then its more micro-level effects on local enforcement officers and their enforcement practices. Here, my focus is upon bigger questions of state and economy, precisely to muddy this, and other, simplistic binaries, as well as to engage in some more speculative thinking about how the emerging order, a newly shaped 'political capitalism', might play out in terms of the resiliencies and vulnerabilities of neoliberalism after the crisis.

On neoliberal resilience

Much of this book has considered various processes which preceded and then followed the financial crisis of 2007 and beyond. At this point, it is worth reiterating, and expanding upon, some of the *non*-effects of the financial crisis.

First, what we have *not* seen in the UK as fallout from the crisis is any generalised moral panic about any of the core activities of finance capital in particular, let alone capital in general. One of the possibilities raised by moral critique of actions and inactions, alongside very public folk-devilling, is the possibility that a more generalised moral panic may gain momentum. And, while these have been 'conventionally associated with the interpretations of youthful action imposed by powerful state or media forces' (Woodiwiss and Hobbs, 2009, 106), the creation and use of such panics is not restricted to young people and conventional criminality – witness the moral panics around 'organised crime' and terrorism in both the US and Britain, for example. That said, what one tends to find in the context of *corporate* crime and harm is that, while many of the elements for a moral panic appear to exist, the scale and extent of outrage is managed more effectively by political elites, albeit as a consequence of a great deal of work. As Levi has noted, one element of this is precisely the mobilisation of folk devils of the kind that we have indicated above, in Chapter Three: 'in order for officially preferred risk-management strategies to maintain their legitimacy for dealing with the majority of corporate infractions, a number of business people and activities must also be selected for the more populist folk-devilling assuagement of public outrage' (Levi, 2009, 50).

Thus, as we have seen, rogue individuals, specific bankers, some of their aberrant practices, and an amorphous phenomenon known as 'banking culture' have been the objects of opprobrium – but not finance capital, capital, nor capitalism per se. Even where moral outrage has found specific targets, they have ended 'not with a bang but with a whimper' (Levi, 2009, 51). Why this should be the case is clear if we return to Cohen's original formulation of 'moral panics' (Cohen, 2011). There we find that what is less likely in the context of elite deviance – where the activities of the relatively powerful are at stake – is that there will be a successful process of deviancy amplification (Wilkins, 1964), with those who have engaged in primary deviation able to resist, to refuse to accept, that such actions in fact make them deviants (Cohen, 2011, 9). They may be able to ignore or rationalise the label or only 'pretend to comply' (Cohen, 2011, 6), responses made all the more possible in the absence of effective social control measures, even at the level of reform, given that deviance 'emerges and is stabilised as an artefact of social control' (Cohen, 2011, 6). Thus if it is the case that 'it is more likely that if the deviant group is vulnerable, and its actions highly visible, it will be forced to take on its identities from structurally and ideologically more powerful groups' (Cohen, 2011, 12), then the converse holds: where, on the one hand, the deviant group is in fact relatively powerful and relatively invisible – the latter being a support and an effect of the former (Tombs and Whyte, 2003) – and, on the other hand, those seeking to apply the label of deviance are the less powerful and more vulnerable, then deviancy amplification is less likely. Of course, as we shall see below, these processes are not iron laws, they are not immutable. Not all 'bankers' have been immune from prosecution, nor all specific acts insulated from moral panic-type discourses. But the individuals to whom the label is applied and sticks tend to be middle- or lower-level managements; meanwhile, the issues which have generated the greatest moral censure – bonuses, high rates of pay, and specific practices such as 'short-selling' – are those which are hardly central to the viability of a sector which trades trillions of dollars per day.

Consistent with this framework, Levi, and others, account for this process of moral un-panics according to a series of logics. One is that the potential for generalised moral panics is 'defused by the willingness of police, politicians and regulators to treat them as issues for compensation (restorative justice) rather than for punishment (retributive justice) and by the diffusion of culpability in organisational settings' (Levi, 2009, 63). This is furthered by dominant conceptions of 'real' crime (Slapper and Tombs, 1999, 85–109), so that even where folk-devils, moral outrage and panic emerge, there often remains a chasm between what are recognised as immoral and illegal practices and real '*crimes* with the requisite "mental element"' (Levi, 2009, 50). This is signalled by the words we use in relation to corporate crimes: accidents, leaks, mis-selling, scandals, spills and so on. Moreover, states often pre-empt the development of panics via the staging of enquiries, commissions and public hearings – a phenomenon which happened, as we saw in Chapter Three, and to which we return briefly below, on both sides of the Atlantic in the wake of the crisis.

What tends to emerge from these non-criminalising processes are at best largely symbolic pieces of law (Bittle and Snider, 2011; Bittle, 2012; Almond, 2013), so that governments help to reproduce moral un-panics (Bittle and Snider, 2011, 375). Again, the status of private capital and the 'magic of the market' (Clarke, 2010a) are key ideological bulwarks against more thoroughgoing legislative and criminal justice responses.

The net effect of this process of un-panic is that what might have begun to approach a crisis '*of* capitalism' remained at best a crisis '*in* capitalism' (Resnick and Wolff, cited in Bittle and Snider, 2011, 385). This is not to say there has been *no* state response to the crisis; much of this book has detailed a range of such responses, albeit that in the UK these have been to accelerate a longer-term process of regulatory reconstruction, one which has sought to protect and strengthen private capital. Certainly, then, if the nature and level of regulation of finance capital had been a key factor in generating the crisis, one would not notice this from state responses to it. Of course, the 'free market' did not look quite so 'free' when governments rescued banks and other financial institutions. That it was only governments which *could* respond to the crisis – under the guise of creating 'the conditions for a new expansion' – is not in itself at all remarkable (Gamble, 2009, 97). What *is* remarkable, however, is that in so doing, the idea of the necessity and desirability of regulatory retreat has persisted across mainstream political spectrums. As noted above (Chapter Three), in the UK, for example, all three major political parties which fought the general election in 2010 were committed to *reducing* regulation: regulation in general was inherently burdensome and only to be an option of last resort, a minimalist necessary evil; and, in any case, regulation entailed costs for both the state and for business, costs that had to be restricted in the new 'age of austerity'. Thus regulatory costs had to be minimised on the one hand as part of the overall attempt to tackle the new fiscal crisis of the state, and on the other hand to reduce the costs for the private sector, which was seen as the only vehicle for economic recovery. Absent from this political discourse was any sustained, critical consideration of the forms of state regulation which had fuelled unsustainable levels of profit maximisation on the part of financial services operating in the shadow-economy of derivatives and securities, a toxic process which created the very crisis to which more of the same poison was to prove the necessary cure.

Thus, in the UK, certainly, there has been no thoroughgoing attempt to confront or undermine the power of the financial services sector. In fact, the only concrete proposal with an element of ostensible 'social protection' was a rather belated proposal for a flimsy fence between retail and investment banking – not to be erected until 2019 (well beyond the life of the government that introduced it). Nor has there been any inclination to alter radically those parts of it that are now effectively under state ownership; nor any thoroughgoing inquiry into the potential illegalities involved in the near collapse of this sector. There have, of course, been some very public, showpiece political responses.

Notably, in November 2008, the House of Commons Treasury Committee announced a 'Banking Crisis Inquiry' (House of Commons Treasury Committee, 2008). This held 17 oral evidence sessions and produced four reports between April and July of the following year, on: the impact of the failure of the Icelandic banks (House of Commons Treasury Committee, 2009a); dealing with the failure of the UK banks (House of Commons Treasury Committee, 2009b); reforming corporate governance and pay in the City (House of Commons Treasury Committee, 2009c); and on regulation and supervision (House of Commons Treasury Committee, 2009d). Alongside these were a series of related reviews of practices within the financial services industry as well as regulation of it. Notable among these were, first, the Turner Review (March 2009), which even the Third Report of the Banking Crisis Inquiry criticised for the fact that it 'downplays the role that remuneration played in causing the banking crisis', so that it questioned whether the Financial Services Authority 'has attached sufficient priority to tackling remuneration in the City' (House of Commons Treasury Committee, 2009c, 16). Then, in November 2009, the Walker Report on corporate governance in UK financial services appeared, albeit to widespread criticism (see, for example, Allen, 2009; Finch, 2009; Jenkins, 2009). Its most widely heralded recommendations were those regarding the need for such financial services' firms to report on the number of people earning more than £1 million (but not to name them) – even though Walker himself claimed that this was 'the least important' part of the review (Treanor and Finch, 2009). Its specific proposals on bonuses led to a new FSA code on remuneration via bonuses, much watered down, and derided as 'cosmetic' – within months 'BAB' became a common shorthand for 'bonuses are back' in the City (Sinfield, 2011, 68).[91] Finally, and perhaps of greatest longer-term import, was the final report of the 'Vickers Commission', published in September 2011 (the Independent Commission on Banking, 2011). Even at its establishment, Vickers had been criticised for its limited terms of reference which centred almost entirely around the prevention of future financial crises rather than 'the wider place of banking in the economy' (Trades Union Congress, 2012). Among various proposals contained in the Report, that which attracted most attention was a proposed ring-fence between investment and retail banking – to be in place by 2019, a date later revised by Chancellor George Osborne, who stated that these would be in place by 2015 (in exchange for some softening of the proposed raised capital requirements on banks) (Peston, 2011). The report was described by one commentator as 'modest' and '[u]ltimately…a failure' (Kettle, 2011). On the subsequent White Paper on the proposals, Vickers himself responded by saying that the government 'should go further', and urged that it 'resist pressure to weaken their effectiveness' (Treanor, 2012c). It was hard to disagree then, even before the 'lobbying victory by the big banks' (Pratley, 2012b), that Vickers' proposals are likely to have significant effects on the sector: even Andrew Tyrie the Conservative Chairman of the Treasury Select Committee, said of the proposed UK ring-fencing that it is 'so weak as to be virtually useless' (Armistead, 2013).

This brief discussion does not, of course, exhaust the range of formal responses by government to the crisis. But what we do know, for all the inquiries, hearings, commissions and reports, whatever their import or consequences prove to be, is this: there have been no significant prosecutions developed by the Serious Fraud Office or the Financial Services Authority. More specifically, we do not know, nor are we likely to know, to what extent criminal activity was implicated in the events leading up to the crisis,[92] nor the forms and extent of criminal activity which those companies in receipt of financial assistance continued to engage in even while receiving that assistance. Nor do we *really* know the financial costs of the long-term bailout of the sector. Further, it is also not unreasonable to ask what has happened to the bailouts (and indeed to the 'cash' injections provided by various rounds of quantitative easing in the UK, the US and, latterly, the EU), which on the face of it appear largely to have been hoarded by banks to prop up reserves and balance sheets – and thus profits for shareholders (Konzelmann, 2014) – rather than engaging in the stimuli which most post-crisis economies desperately needed and which central banks at least claimed was their intention. On one estimate, virtually all of the £200 million created by the Bank of England in the first round of Quantitative Easing was used by banks to restore profitability, while lending actually declined (Murphy, 2010).

While different states are characterised by their own specificities, the lack of effective legislative response to the crisis is hardly confined to the UK. In the US, for example, brief periods of optimism for advocates of regulation engendered, first, by the wake-up calls that might have been Enron, WorldCom and Tyco, followed by the introduction of the Sarbanes–Oxley Act (SOX), then, later in the decade, with the election of Obama to the US Presidency, proved short lived and ultimately of little import in responding to corporate crime and harm. SOX proved to be relatively ineffectual, at best seeking to address the symptomatic issues of corporate governance rather than underlying structural issues of neoliberal capitalism which systematically produce crime and harm (Soederberg, 2008). Meanwhile, the approach of the Obama administration to corporate wrongdoing, not least in the wake of the economic crisis, is most pithily encapsulated in the *Who* line: 'Meet the new boss. Same as the old boss' – perhaps unsurprising given his choice of key economic advisors (Peck, 2012, 231–69). Thus the crisis has prompted little or no credible legislative response:

> None of the key guilty parties have been sent to prison; rather, Wall Street almost immediately called for returning to 'business as usual', has aggressively contested relatively modest new regulatory initiatives, and has altogether done well for itself while much of the balance of the economy and the American people continue to suffer. (Friedrichs, 2011)

Barak had identified, by the spring of 2012, three criminal cases – all against those 'pretty far down the financial food chain' (Barak, 2012, 102), so that 'no senior executives from any of the major financial institutions had been criminally charged, prosecuted, or imprisoned' (Barak, 2012, 95) – as well as 12 civil cases arising out of investigations connected to the US financial crisis (Barak, 2012, 91–113; see also Petras, 2012). Meanwhile, in Canada, if the first decade of the twenty-first century 'witnessed renewed interest in the regulation of corporate crimes' (Bittle and Snider, 2011, 373), the two key pieces of legislation which the Canadian state was forced to enact – Bill C-45, ostensibly designed to address safety crimes, and C-13, aimed at tackling markets fraud – were almost immediately to 'fall into a state of virtual disuse' (Bittle and Snider, 2011, 374). Thus, as one commentator has noted, even where it reached political agendas, 'financial reform has stalled in all major jurisdictions' (Bryan et al, 2012, 310). This consistency in state inaction is even more remarkable in the light of the relentless litany of crimes in which financial institutions have been embroiled *since* 2007 – internationally, these include the fixing of LIBOR and FOREX, sanctions-busting, money laundering, cartelisation and insider trading, while the apparently clean retail arms of these companies have been engaged in an uninterrupted series of waves of mis-selling in the UK since the 1980s (Tombs, 2015b).

Little wonder that various commentators highlighted how quickly 'business as usual' was restored – Blyth, discussing the lack of any politico-economic paradigm shift, wryly claims that 'we were all Keynesians for about 12 months' (Blyth, 2013a, 205–6).

Across some four decades of neoliberalism, a new way of ordering and thinking about 'states' and 'markets' has become dominant. Within this, a new view of regulation – and, concomitantly, enforcement – has also assumed dominance, politically, popularly and academically. The cataclysmic events set in train by the unravelling of criminogenic financial institutions from 2007 onwards created a moment where this hegemony might have been threatened. In fact, such was the material and moral strength of capital within this mode of political economy that the narratives available to explain the crisis, and to severely limit solutions to it, have rendered neoliberal ordering and views of the world stronger (Mirowski, 2014). As much of this book has sought to demonstrate, so too were the ideas and practices of regulation which contributed to the crisis also strengthened. One of the consequences of this seemingly paradoxical set of processes has been that the state's historically assumed role of social protection – forced upon it through a variety of struggles and compromises over 150 years – has been significantly diminished. This role incorporates welfare and benefits systems, housing provision, health services and security in old age, as well as consumer, environmental and worker protection, changes to which have attracted political, popular and academic scrutiny. The forms of social protection central to this text have been significantly undermined below virtually any critical radar.

There can be no greater testimony to the power of the re-regulatory agenda that had been set over the previous 35 years: 'The persistence of this rhetoric of market efficiency is indeed remarkable. The perseverance of both the faith in free markets and the use of that key dichotomy – free versus constrained, private versus government controlled – is simply astonishing' (Harcourt, 2010, 87).

Thus 'the market' – and private capital as the dominant force within this – has not simply retained but has re-energised the promise of possibility and inherent expansiveness. For, 'markets can always be perfected even if a particular example may not have functioned perfectly' so that they always have the potential to create 'more wealth, more goods, more results, more possibilities' – albeit at some *future*, usually unspecified, point (Clarke, 2010a, 377).

As noted in Chapter One, for some commentators, such claims are part of the resilience of neoliberalism itself. It will be recalled that Schmidt and Thatcher highlight five characteristics which combine to shore up the ideological dominance of neoliberalism in general – and, indeed, its commitment to 'reducing regulation' in particular – namely: its diversity and adaptability; the gap between rhetoric and reality, which always creates a space for the promise of 'real' neoliberalism to be fulfilled; the relative absence or weaknesses of alternative ways of seeing the world; the powerful interests which are served by the prevalence of such ideas; and the institutional embeddedness of these ideas over the course of almost 40 years, both at national levels and also through supranational institutions such as the European Union (Schmidt and Thatcher, 2013a; 2013b). That said, none of these elements of neoliberal resilience, if taken in isolation, looks entirely secure. Within and across these, then, there are potential points of dislocation, 'cracks', through which neoliberalism is rendered vulnerable. Thus in the growing chasm between the future but never quite attained and indeed unattainable (Peck, 2012, 7) promise, and the current, ongoing, very real experiences of most people in most nation-states, state and corporate power remains vulnerable. If cynicism, mistrust and resignation *for now* act as bulwarks against popularised discontent, these are hardly robust, long-term defences for power. For all the discursive depth to, and power of the idea (and ideas) of neoliberalism, it remains fundamentally cursed, in Peck's terms, in a way which the crisis has again – but most spectacularly and dangerously – exposed: namely, it can live neither with, nor without, the state (Peck, 2012, 65).

The central argument developed in the previous chapters has been that under conditions of advanced neoliberalism, the UK state in particular (though clearly not uniquely) has been involved in a long-term, if latterly feverish, process of re-regulation, involving ceaseless initiatives on a range of mutually reinforcing political, institutional, legal and discursive fronts. A related argument is that given the internal logic of Better Regulation, perhaps no better captured by the 'less is more' leitmotif, *there is no logical end point* of this drive towards regulation without enforcement. Once regulation and enforcement are defined as 'too much', it is impossible to perceive when there will be 'little enough' of either or both.[93] Better Regulation might thus mark the beginning of the end of the state's commitment to, and ability to deliver, social protection.

The objects of this regulatory activity, private businesses, have not formed a key consideration of this text (save in passing, for example in Chapters Two and Four).[94] To be clear: one of the key effects of the processes documented in this text is that the activities of private corporations have been effectively legalised or decriminalised, while the terrain upon which private corporations can legitimately act is being redrawn also. Witness the developments in Barnet and North Tyneside (Chapter Six), and other manifestations of commercialisation in the work of national regulatory agencies and local authorities, as but specific instances of the wider opening up of new markets in what were formerly publicly provided goods and services.

In this context, it is worthwhile bearing in mind some obviousnesses – if not obvious to all (see Chapter Four). Certainly corporations are not beneficent institutions. Their *sole* purpose, their raison d'être, is not any social good, but is simply the accumulation, indeed maximisation, of profit. Nor is it the case that their economic and social benefits make deleterious, even destructive 'side-effects', a 'price worth paying': in fact, harm and crime is not marginal but central to corporate activity and profiteering, generated through corporate personhood, the techniques and mindsets of 'externalities' (below), the corporation's dehumanising structure of irresponsibility, and its necessarily amoral, calculative rationality (Pearce, 1993; Tombs and Whyte, 2015). Yet some still claim that, even if corporations appear to act illegally and irresponsibly, corporate activity might be refashioned along socially responsible lines, and that, in the minority of instances where autonomous corporate social responsibility fails, the state can and will enforce the law, in order to bring recalcitrant corporations into compliance. It is further claimed that, even if such law enforcement efforts are often relatively inadequate, the potential for them effectively to balance economic progress with social welfare is always within our grasp. Neither set of claims is sustainable in either empirical or theoretical terms.

Chapter One provided some fleeting indications of the extent to which the corporate drive for profits kills, maims and causes illness, as a matter of course.[95] In turn, this book has sought to indicate the dynamic ways in which corporations (and thus, the corporate power to act and to commit harm) are in so many ways dependent upon their relationships with states, a dependence mediated crucially through law, not least through the apparent freedoms and legalities for which states create and maintain spaces. In short, this means that the corporation's ability to cause harm and crime with relative impunity is also underpinned by state and law – including, crucially, the nature and level of regulation and enforcement. The corporation and the state, as was argued in Chapter Five, stand in an inter-dependent relationship – while the specific nature of this increasingly symbiotic inter-dependence is a shifting one. It is partly in this context that I have argued throughout this text that the processes described herein cannot adequately be captured by the term deregulation, but that they need to be viewed as re-regulation. This is a long-term and ongoing reconstruction of the relationships between states and the private sector, within which markets and the rules that licence activity within them have been consistently constructed and reconstructed. There is no zero-sum relationship between the rise of the corporation and the decline of the nation state, nor is the relationship between states and corporations simply or necessarily antagonistic. Rather, the state–corporate relationship is revealed as essentially *symbiotic*: the power of the corporation rests upon the power of states, and *vice-versa*.

If it is *increasingly* helpful to think in terms of *state–corporate relationships and inter-dependencies* as the sites and mechanisms through which harms and crimes are produced, an alternative, pluralist view of the relationship between states and corporations remains embedded across academic literatures. From this pluralist perspective, this relationship is seen as one of external opposition: that is, the state stands as an institution or ensemble of institutions which is ontologically separate and distinct from civil society. From this perspective, governments generally do things to protect the public interest (they 'regulate') to protect us all from the harms and illegalities. Indeed, as we have seen, for many, states do not have to do very much law enforcement work at all, since corporations are actually or at least potentially good citizens. But I have sought to indicate how this view of state–corporate relations as one of externality is useful neither as a practical nor theoretical guide to understanding regulation and enforcement, nor, indeed, corporate crime and harm.

One of the central themes of this book is that we need to abandon, once and for all, the tendency to view 'states' and 'corporations' as a kind of crude oppositional duality, a view which arises from a narrow understanding of what Gramsci calls the 'state as policeman' (Coleman et al, 2009). As noted in Chapter One, by this he means that what is normally understood in a formal sense as the 'state' – the 'safeguarding of public order and of respect for the laws' – subordinates our understanding of the centrality of 'private forces' in the historical development of states. For Gramsci, the 'state as policeman' approach is a 'limiting hypothesis' (1971 [1996], 261). Gramsci counterposed the 'state as policeman' with the 'ethical' or 'interventionist' state and argued that, '[T]he concept of the interventionist state is of economic origin, and is connected on one hand with tendencies supporting protection and economic nationalism and on the other…the protection of the working classes from the excesses of capitalism' (1971 [1996], 262). It is in this role of the state that we see the crucial part that regulation as social protection has played in state practice and state and corporate legitimacy. It is within this frame that one can perceive both the resilience and the vulnerability of neoliberalism and in particular the unfolding post-2008 settlement.

What is regulation?

The question, 'What is regulation?', is one which is at times asked across the regulatory literature, to be answered in textbook style in terms of a series of techniques, organisational mandates, bodies of law to be invoked and so on. Here I propose a somewhat different answer, albeit one prefaced by raising a prior question, one which is rarely addressed in literature on regulation: *why regulate?*

Most fundamentally, regulation exists because in its absence, as historical record demonstrates (and see also Chapter One), the result is the widescale production of death, injury and illness, destruction and despoliation, not to mention systematic cheating, lying and stealing.[96] Now to me this is a very straightforward observation – yet it is one that is 'forgotten', albeit in an organised (Giroux, 2014) and motivated[97] way. Such motivated forgetting often requires a great deal of energy – a key element of hegemony construction and maintenance.

Davis, for example, has documented how the potential criminalisation of corporate violence is *continually* negotiated and elided by state, regulatory bodies and business 'in ways that preserve and enhance the legitimacy of corporate capital' (Davis, 2000, 303). Moreover, in forgetting why corporations are regulated there is always-already a greater legitimacy added to claims regarding the ethical, law-abiding, or moral inclinations of those who manage, own or control corporations, claims central to the regulatory orthodoxy. To borrow a phrase from the historian Linebaugh, this is a prime example of the '*violence* of forgetting' (Linebaugh, 2001).

The term 'violence' is perfectly apt here. We would do well to remember that the 'social murder' documented by Chadwick and Engels (Chernomas and Hudson, 2007) is neither a matter of mere historical record, nor was it mitigated by enlightened capitalism:

> The people subject to these horrific conditions did not sit passively by and accept their fate. The next hundred years or so constituted a running battle to create institutions – either using the state, which passed protective legislation, or outside the state, by creating things like unions – to alleviate the more debilitating conditions of capitalism. (Chernomas and Hudson, 2007, 4)

Quite so. *Remembering* some of the historical origins of regulation also requires us to ask questions regarding the nature and function of regulation. As indicated above (Chapter Four), such questions tend to be elided by the obsessive search for the regulatory mix and the toolkit which will provide the necessary regulatory balance, so fetishised by the regulatory orthodoxy in all its variants. And really inquiring into the origins of regulation should remind us that the state is a key part of the story. In fact, not simply any old state – but a capitalist state. So let us remind ourselves that *the state in a capitalist society is a capitalist state* – an obviousness, but one worth bearing in mind, not least given the failures of much social science, let alone criminology, actually to refer to capitalism (Winlow, 2013), class (Lynch, 2015) or, indeed, the state (Coleman et al, 2009). Thus, as argued in Chapter One, what has been termed the 'social state' emerged through conflict, struggle and compromise, but ultimately the regulation and enforcement which followed from it was not antithetical to capitalist interests. How could it be otherwise in a capitalist state? In fact, in creating the reality or appearance of greater equality of competition among private companies, in securing the longer-term sustainability of capitalism per se, and indeed in forcing technological and work organisation improvements which have the effect of facilitating the production of surplus value, the form and levels of social protection that emerged represented something other than a defeat for capital. Quite the opposite, as Kolko would have it. More specifically, what appears as social protection is just that – but, as a regulatory compromise at a certain historical moment, regulation as social protection also ultimately benefits capital.

None of these observations are at all undermined by the increasingly prevalent *idea* about regulation, promulgated through the emergence of neoliberalism from the mid-1970s onwards, that states and markets are somehow antithetical, and that regulation per se is burdensome upon business. Yet as we saw in Chapter Two, neoliberalism consists of institutions, practices and ideas, not necessarily complementary, but certainly each important for its emergence to dominance. Thus it was argued there that neoliberalism is more than set of politico-economic arrangements – it is a hegemonic project and, as Chapters Two and Three argued, it is a hegemony which makes moral claims, claims which have allowed capital in general and the dominant idea of regulation not just to survive but to flourish in the aftermath of the financial crisis at the end of the last decade. It was further demonstrated in Chapter Four that, as a hegemonic project with a key educative and mystificatory elements, the work of intellectuals, not least those who discuss and write about regulation, has been important in its durability.

It is worth turning, then, to a body of research produced by critical and neo-Marxist scholars which emphasises the importance of *conflict* in the formation, and in the implementation, of regulatory regimes. This literature notes that regulatory controls have often been established only after long and bitter struggles by organised groups of workers and other social movements (Kramer, 1989; Snider, 1991; Tucker, 1990). At the same time, historically, businesses and their representatives have fought bitterly in opposition to regulation when it is not in their clear, immediate and particular interest. They obfuscate, lie, cheat and make threats to disinvest, often fighting fierce public relations campaigns and behind the scenes political manoeuvres to avoid or to influence regulatory reform (Monbiot, 2000; Tombs and Whyte, 1998; Woolfson et al, 1996; Palast, 2003). Critical scholars and neo-Marxist commentators therefore argue that conflicts between pro- and anti-regulatory forces from outside the state – and, I would add, at times, from inside the state also – are crucial to understanding the origins of regulation, and its subsequent level of enforcement (for example, Carson, 1979; Davis, 2000, 14–18; Harris and Milkis, 1989; Navarro,

1983; Pearce and Tombs, 1998), even if such conflicts around the definition and enforcement of the law are not always visible (Grigg-Spall and Ireland, 1992; Lukes, 1974).

In this context, Snider's (1991) analysis of the emergence and level of regulation is useful, and revolved around two central sets of claims. She argued, first, that regulation must be understood dialectically, via a dynamic complexity of 'specific mechanisms' which affect 'the balance of power between the regulated firm and the regulatory agency' (Snider, 1991, 210). Second, these relationships need to be set in the context of a similarly dynamic set of relations between the state and capital, and between the state 'and the broad electorate, as represented by relevant pressure groups' (Snider, 1991). Through this at once simple yet sensitive schema, Snider analyses four areas of regulation, including 'occupational health and safety laws' and 'crimes against the environment'.

On occupational health and safety, she notes that crucial considerations are that: occupational health and safety is not viewed as necessary for capitalist survival; enforcement in this context may be antithetical to capitalist interests (in terms of a direct attack on profitability) (see Szasz, 1984); states are most likely only to make symbolic efforts to regulate; but that pro-regulatory forces are potentially strong since they are most likely to originate in organised labour, while the imagery of victimisation is powerful in this context. To this it might be added that the key problem for employers here is that of fatal injuries – since these are immediate, visible, perhaps attract wider public sympathy, and are easily associated with a specific employer and, perhaps, working conditions or practices. This is in contrast to ill-health, which often has such long incubation periods and causal chains so that any particular company evades virtually all responsibility for these – albeit that the costs of compensation for a *limited* sub-set of such illnesses may have ultimately to be borne by the state itself.

In the context of environmental protection, measures to improve this may also detrimentally affect profits in the sense that production processes may be altered or, indeed, externalities pushed back onto the firm and onto its balance sheet. On the former, of course, it might be added that controlling the use of raw materials and waste produced, for example, may make some production processes more efficient, so that costs may be reduced. On the latter, the issue of externalities, this demonstrates again how regulation and enforcement can often highlight the costs of production and the distribution of the surplus. 'Externalities' are costs in the form of dealing with the inherent effects of many forms of 'productive' activity: greenhouse gases causing climate change, routine air pollutants causing health effects, leachate to soil and water, and the 'lower level' environmental effects of production such as noise, smell and litter. Standard cost-accounting mechanisms absent these externalities from corporate balance sheets and shifts the costs of these to 'society', thereby privatising profit and socialising costs, so that regulation always involves the proportions of the costs of production which are privatised or socialised.

More generally, attempts to protect the natural environmental are antithetical to capitalist philosophy, which is to view everyone and everything as a potential resource, a factor of production, to be exploited. By contrast, conducive to more rather than less regulation is the fact that, in this sphere, there are now significant social movements with an environmental focus – although it might be added that these have tended to be co-opted into reformist responses to capitalist production rather than being anti-productivist per se. It should also be noted that such movements can at times draw upon very widespread public support – but so widespread that it may be weak in its diffuseness, lacking the organisational base of a longstanding movement such as trades unions, and the rights that such forms of organisation have won, not least at the point of production itself. To this it might be added that the consequences of illegal or indeed harmful pollution are also often not immediately apparent – and indeed environmental damage may occur, as with occupational ill-health, across periods that transcend the historically specific set of institutions which constitute any given state ensemble.

The analytical logic set out by Snider can be further extended and developed in the context of food safety and hygiene. Here, in the processing and sale of foodstuffs, there may be *some* coincidence of interest between capital and consumers. Food poisoning is diffuse and may not always be attributable to a specific source – but often it can be, particularly in the event of any widespread outbreak. Clearly all things being equal, retailers and processors would prefer not to endanger customers – albeit, of course that all things are often not equal, and there is significant room for manoeuvre for illegality and harm-production both through supply chains and at points of sale. In some senses, as in the case of retail outlets at least, the sale and use of food is an archetypal capitalist exchange – a product is bought on the basis of what it claims to be, for immediate use, and then replaced through further purchases and so on. Thus there is some pressure both for the state to oversee some degree of probity in this context, while there is also a sense in which retailers seek to create and retain customer loyalty – from the largest retailers to small sandwich shops. If consumers are individualistic, diverse and not organised collectively, their purchasing power and the varying degrees of choice that they have (depending on the specific form of purchase being made) combine, in this context, to generate some reputational[98] demands on businesses. Thus, on balance, there may be good reasons why food safety and hygiene remains an area where there is at least some generalised acceptance of some degree of regulation via enforcement as part of a market through which there can be generated some relatively equal conditions of competition. Indeed, in this context it is worth noting that for small retailers, not well versed in either food safety and hygiene law per se, let alone with what constitutes compliance, the presence of enforcement officers provides a key business service which supports profitability (see, for example, Fairman and Yapp, 2004). Such an observation marks out food law enforcement as very distinct from occupational safety and health, clearly, and less strongly but certainly so, from environmental protection. Further, it complements the quantitative and qualitative data presented in the previous chapter, Chapter Six, which highlighted some differences in the decline of enforcement across these three functions. Therein, it was found both nationally and locally that food law enforcement had been the area least undermined by the period of re-regulation and anti-enforcement. The distinctiveness of this area of regulation and enforcement should not, of course, be exaggerated, nor should the power of the general analytical framework I have set out be obscured.

Thus, we saw in Chapter One how the food sector is one which causes significant levels of harm. Meanwhile, although we found, in Chapter Six, that rates of inspection were relatively high and that these had not diminished to the extent that they had in other enforcement areas under examination, we also noted that 'food' prosecutions were relatively and absolutely very low. Thus while 130,000 inspections by national and local health and safety regulators produced 1,169 prosecutions completed in 2012/13, in the same year food safety EHOs made almost 350,000 visits to premises which generated under 400 prosecutions. The food sector is one area where we have widespread data on generalised violation of law. As reported in Chapter One, for example, some three-quarters of chickens sold in 2014/15 tested positive for the presence of campylobacter, a major source of hospitalisation from food poisoning in the UK. Perhaps if offending is so widespread, then, and notwithstanding the fact that campylobacter is easily prevented, there is relatively little widespread demand for changes in enforcement on the part of most businesses – such widespread sale of contaminated food in fact denotes an equality in the conditions of competition among retailers in this sector?

If we shift back to the wider framework for understanding regulation, a dialectical view, we see how regulation and enforcement are likely to take different forms in different sectors of the economy in relation to different bodies of law. Moreover, according to this perspective, regulation and regulatory agencies are typically formed by states in order to pre-empt, absorb and dissipate struggles between conflicting social groups – inter- *and* intra-class conflict, extending to wider social movements (Snider, 1991). They do this by claiming to represent the interests of pro-regulatory groups at the same time as protecting the general interests of society. This does not mean that regulatory agencies are neutral or balanced in the way that they deal with corporate crime; rather they are 'unequal structures of representation' (Mahon, 1979, 154). Regulatory bodies tend to subordinate the interests of non-hegemonic groups to the interests of business, but since their purpose is a stabilising one for capitalist social orders, they may subordinate the immediate interests of particular businesses to the long-term interests of capital as a whole. In turn, the likelihood that they may regulate in order to placate or dissipate movements of opposition makes regulatory agencies vulnerable to pressure (Shapiro, 1984; Snider, 1991). From this perspective, the shape of regulatory regimes and strategies of enforcement also depend upon a range of external factors that shape the confidence and the capacity of sub-dominant groups to engage in struggle (Tombs, 1996).

This perspective also implies that regulation is not solely or *perhaps even principally* about 'controlling' corporate harms. Herein, regulation in capitalist societies appears as much about social order maintenance as it is about control efforts per se. Regulation maintains the steady rate and function of the machinery of industry and commerce (Whyte, 2004; 2015). As such, its purpose is to seek a stable and uninterrupted system of production, distribution and consumption. The consequence of looking at regulation from this perspective is to recognise that the regulation of corporate activity by government may seek to ameliorate the harms of corporations, but that this is by no means its primary purpose. It is by pursuing its *primary* purpose – to maintain the optimal conditions for the production and realisation of surplus value – that regulation produces and reproduces corporate harm; relatedly, and in a variety of ways, it prevents such harms being identified, processed or formally recognised as *crimes*, or, if they are recognised as crimes, to engender responses which effectively decriminalises them while generally leaving management autonomy within corporations wholly unscathed. In other words, regulation through the state in a capitalist society must always – even if only 'in the last instance' – reproduce the conditions for effective profit maximisation, 'maximisation' being contingent upon a series of factors and phenomena, not least the balances of social forces.

In short, regulation is a complex and often contradictory process of mediation, one that struggles to negotiate a path between competing social forces and their interests and aims; it is a process which always seeks to translate class conflict into the language and practice of liberal-democracy. Enforcement, or any other regulatory activity, has precisely this purpose: a means of translating fundamental social conflict into something that can be managed by the state, whether directly or at some distance. There can be no illusions about this, no reification of one form of regulatory activity as some kind of panacea with which to tame or sanitise business. But this does not mean that different regulatory strategies and different levels of and trends in enforcement practices do not have very different material and symbolic significances: regulation is not only shaped by, but *also plays a role in shaping*, the balance of social forces. There is always something to struggle for through regulatory agencies, no matter how captured or neutered they appear to be by a particular interest or set of interests.

One object of struggle must be around enforcement of existing law. In Chapters Five and Six, I examined the feverish and relentless ways in which dominant ideas of regulation were reconstructed away from enforcement, and how these efforts were translated into policy and practice. This period encompassed the unfolding of the Hampton Agenda which instituted in policy and practice what was euphemistically termed 'Better Regulation' – and while a long-term political initiative, the trajectory towards its implementation has been drastically underwritten by the austerity economics of the post-2008 era. Thus, a key element and effect of 'Better Regulation' as a re-regulatory project has been to re-position regulation as a phenomenon and idea which can be sustained, indeed can be improved, via *less* – or indeed *in the absence of* – enforcement. Moreover, built into the idea of 'Better Regulation', for all its internal contradictions, is a self-impelling logic – once less enforcement is assumed to be better, then there can only be too much enforcement if regulation is to be better.

To challenge this formal and practical shift from enforcement must be part of the counter-hegemonic struggle in which pro-regulatory forces engage. To point to under- or non-enforcement of law is a common political tactic of such groups. But this is not simply an instrumental opportunism. Seeking to defend and extend enforcement levels and strategies is crucial for a variety of reasons, not least from the point of view of those whom enforcement ostensibly claims to protect – the lack of, or declines in, enforcement undermines the ability and confidence workers, local communities and consumers to demand that the law is complied with by businesses and enforced by regulators, that is, to demand their protection on the terms on which it has been offered by the state.

Further, I would argue, not least on the basis of the time spent with many of my interviewees in local authorities to generate the data drawn upon earlier (Chapter Six), and indeed with many regulators across many years, that to expose *non-enforcement* does not equate to an attack upon, but in fact should seek to embolden and support, enforcement *officers*. The latter do not set regulatory policy, codes of practice, budgets, enforcement priorities and the like. As this text has demonstrated, these, along with the long-term rhetorical assaults on the functions that enforcement officers perform in the name of public protection, and the attacks on them as parasitic bureaucrats, serve precisely to undermine their material, social-psychological and emotional abilities to perform their roles as enforcers of law against non-compliant businesses. In fact, what is often most impressive about those who enforce the law on the ground is their commitment to public service when many could be earning far more and enjoying greater status within corporations, as hygienists, safety officers, environmental protection advisers, risk managers and so on. In other words, a key counter-hegemonic strategy must be to support those within the state who remain committed to public protection – the state is never a monolithic, homogenous entity, but is always an ensemble of institutions and actors within which there are fissures, different priorities, goals, commitments and so on. So the struggle for enforcement is also a struggle for those who might enforce.

None of this equates to any romanticised notion that law enforced by regulators can significantly empower counter-hegemonic interests. However, as part of the regulatory process, workers' demands for improvements in their working conditions, consumers' rights for food fit to eat, or communities' demands for cleaner air are also demands upon the regulator to enforce the laws that both ostensibly exist to protect them, even while knowing that such protection can never be achieved through law. Just as demands upon managements for improvements in standards of food safety, or demands on government for working hours restrictions, constitute a process of regulation, so do demands upon regulators to enforce the law constitute part of the process of regulation. Where businesses are successful in minimising enforcement, then this is also part of the regulatory process and contest.

These points being made, enforcement cannot be advocated and supported for enforcement's sake. A recent case study of a chipboard plant in Merseyside demonstrates this point well enough (Tombs and Whyte, 2014). Over 14 years of its operation, the factory, owned by Sonae, was the site of numerous fires, explosions, leaks of toxic substances to air and waterways, a litany of major injuries to workers and three deaths. During that period, it attracted considerable regulatory attention from the local authority pollution control EHOs, the fire service, the HSE and Environment Agency. It also amassed a virtually unique record of enforcement actions against it, including numerous prosecutions. Yet the company was able to absorb this level of regulatory scrutiny – scrutiny at considerable cost to a very poor borough, since enforcement costs are also externalities for the corporation – given what was in fact a level of generalised tolerance and pitiful levels of fines following prosecutions related to the most egregious violations of law. So what looked like tough enforcement needs to be placed in the context of the level of offending, the outcomes of enforcement actions, and the wider costs externalised to state and community. More productive might have been simply for local government (Knowsley Council) and/or the UK government to have withdrawn various operating licences. This, however, carried too great a political risk, given the welcome (and financial subsidy) offered locally and nationally to a plant which would employ 200 people in one of the most deprived wards in England, and which was to be a flagship for growth and regeneration in the borough (Tombs and Whyte, 2014). Thus, what appears to be, and in many respects is, relatively tough enforcement action should be understood within a generalised regulatory tolerance – resulting in enforcement which was ineffective and costly for the local state and population.

Thus, law enforcement can have both instrumental and symbolic effects, but may not necessarily be the only nor best option in specific instances. But it must at all times exist as a credible option – the very basis on which the orthodoxy can argue that, as the ever-present-in-the-background 'big stick', it need not be used. To argue for the reality of enforcement is not, I would emphasise, to advocate that each and every violation be detected and prosecuted, nor does it represent a crude defence of enforcement per se, charges often levelled against 'punitiveness' in defence of varieties of the orthodoxy (see, for example, Hawkins, 1990; 1991; Braithwaite, 2010). In fact, such charges are generally couched within highly simplified dichotomies: self-regulation *versus* strict enforcement, consensus *versus* conflict or, for Almond and Colover (2012), an orthodoxy *versus* deterrence theory. Such binary approaches to regulation can lead nowhere, because, at least on the basis of the view developed here, they do not understand regulation.

On neoliberal vulnerability

Earlier in this chapter, and indeed throughout this book, I have pointed to what Peck has labelled the fundamental 'curse' of neoliberalism, namely, that it can live neither with, nor without, the state. As Peck puts it, 'For all its creativity, neoliberal discourse has never provided an elemental answer to this question' (Peck, 2012, 65). And nor can it.

It is in this last, irresolvable, tension, inherent within neoliberalism, that its vulnerability is most apparent. The inter-dependence between state and private capital is dynamic, always in flux, far from secure, constructed on the bases of shifting historical, legal and political foundations. The bank bailouts – and the increasingly obvious imbrication of states and corporations in the still-unfolding post-crisis settlement – certainly remain a moment of exposure for states and corporations and the tales each weaves of their antagonistic, independent relationships, tales so skilfully and feverishly spun over decades as part of the wider construction of a neoliberal reason (Peck, 2012). The reassembling of the international capitalist economy has seen widespread state rhetoric regarding the essential role of private capital in 'recovery', calls for a reduced state, and a handing-over of 'public' functions to 'private actors' as a consequence of a claimed fiscal crisis. But this game is far from over.

The essential role of the state in responding to the crisis of private capital raises to the surface the inherent contradictions within neoliberalism, intellectually, economically and politically, to the extent that it is a key point of vulnerability for neoliberal ideology and practice. As Chapter Three indicated, states re-packaged private debt into national debt, reframed private corporate recklessness into public profligacy and lassitude, and recast the corporation from a potential problem to the only hope of economic recovery. Thus, on the back of a fairy tale construction of a fiscal crisis of the state, governments, not least the UK government, now claim to further 'free' markets, opening up ever greater terrain for private capital to take on ever more formerly public functions. These are overseen by national and local states, however, albeit through a complex myriad of contractual and inter-organisational relationships – so that if scratched, the surface appearance of private delivery reveals only too clearly the essential imbrication of corporate and state structures. This creates risks for state and capital. In particular, these new and emerging inter-dependencies risk undermining the 'moral capital of capital' which was so integral to its very process of colonisation of 'public' spheres of activity. Moreover, the claims that could once be generated and circulate effectively regarding the efficiency of private sector delivery of goods and services when key elements of the latter were in the hands of inefficient, bureaucratic, sclerotic states are no longer so easily made nor available, given that virtually no elements of what was public provision can now legitimately be defined as such, such is the penetration of private economic activity (Meek, 2015).

Thus, as Chapter Two, demonstrated, over some 40 years, the superiority of the private over the wasteful, inefficient, and freedom-negating public sector was constructed as common sense, as obvious. So enduring was this new hegemonic settlement that, as Chapter Three argued, the aftermath of the crisis saw private capital further elevated, so that increasing 'freedom' for private capital was widely prescribed as the only solution to the economic crisis – not least via consensus of mainstream political parties. However, precisely because these were part of ongoing hegemonic constructions, they required, as I indicated at the close of Chapter Three, a great deal of ideological work over many years, work which must be ongoing, so that hegemony did not and does not preclude persistent and paradoxical crises as an 'integral part of the present' (Clarke, 2012, 48).

There are, thus, a series of vulnerabilities integral to the still-unfolding post-2008 settlement between inter-dependent state and capital, not least around regulation and enforcement, which allow strategic exploitation as part of a counter-hegemonic challenge.

First, the mystification of private efficiency risks being increasingly exposed as corporations are seen to fail to deliver goods and services in new markets. From the delivery of 'fitness for work' social security programmes by ATOS to Capita's contract to regulate the private sector in the name of worker and environmental health in the Borough of Barnet; from G4S's role in providing security at the 2012 London Olympics to Serco's consistent inabilities to provide suitable GP services, the private corporation, as always through state activity and state support, becomes more vulnerable. Its claims to be more efficient are consistently undermined as evidence mounts that it *cannot* deliver – and indeed, cannot deliver to the extent that previous publically owned services did, even without having a misty eyed view of them. Somewhat differently, there may be some areas of social provision in which private companies find that they simply cannot make a profit, or that the risks of entering are too great. In 2012, Hinchingbrooke Hospital in Huntingdon became the first privately run NHS 'franchise' hospital, by Circle; in March 2015, following a highly critical Care Quality Commission report, the company announced its decision to hand it back to the NHS. The evidence against the private sector's efficiency will mount. *Such observations demonstrate that new markets created through re-regulation necessarily result in no more, and often ostensibly less, efficient delivery of goods and services.*

Second, if inefficient and benefiting from economies of scale coupled with market power – rather than any competitive superiority – the extending reach of these corporations increases the opportunity structures for and likely incidence of harm and crime, and so renders them, again, vulnerable. Thus following the death of Jimmy Mubenga on his deportation from the UK, the decision by the CPS to prosecute three low level employees of G4S, one of the state's go-to private security firms, but not the company itself, was clearly 'perverse, not just in a moral but in a strictly legal sense' (Webber, 2012). A renewed focus on A4E, central to the government's Work Programme (Harris, 2012b),[99] followed criticism of poor performance – and ended up exposing fraud, resulting in the resignation of the Company's Chair Emma Harrison, who one day before had also resigned as Cameron's 'families champion' (Peacock, 2013). In July 2004, the *Daily Telegraph* ran the headline, 'Serco profits from crime', detailing how the marketisation of criminal justice delivery was the basis for the expansion of it and other private security firms (Simpkins, 2004); the headline took on a rather less welcome hue almost ten years later when Serco and G4S were fined for charging the Ministry of Justice for tagging offenders who were either in prison or dead. These types of incidents are frequent, usually involving the same well-known big 'four contractors' (NAO, 2013, 46), and they will proliferate.

In this context, it is of interest that recently the Howard League for Penal Reform audited the performance of the four main private companies involved in the delivery of criminal justice in the UK, an attempt to begin 'a process to collate individual failings to show systemic issues in the privatisation of justice' (Howard League for Penal Reform, 2014, 5). Reviewing the performance of G4S, Serco, Sodexo and GeoAmey on the basis of publicly available data, much from national news sources, the report documents over 160 'examples of failure' on the part of these companies between 2011 and 2014, many of which appear to be at least punishable, if not in fact punished, violations of bodies of law (Howard League for Penal Reform, 2014, 9–62). *Such consistent and mounting evidence increasingly calls into question not simply the probity, but may combine to signify the recidivism, of key private players within specific market sectors.*

Third, even if the 'willingness' on the part of state institutions to 'control' corporations exists, the ability effectively to respond to these crimes and harms is limited. Having relinquished functions to private capital, states become more dependent upon them. Thus, for example, the obvious and perhaps most effective response of the government to the fraudulent way in which G4S secured the contract to provide security at the London Olympics (based upon expertise and staffing it simply did not have) or the inflated numbers of tagged offenders for which Serco billed the Ministry of Justice, might have been legal action, but it should at least have led to governments refusing to contract the same companies for other services, a form of *post hoc* contract compliance. But this is less and less possible as state institutions relinquish ever more service delivery to a sector which is, and appears, more evidently concentrated in small number of private hands. Thus, for example, while still embroiled in a scandal over tagging fraud, under investigation by the Serious Fraud Office, and 'effectively barred' from bidding for new government contracts, G4S again began to secure such contracts (Osborne, 2014); and with four companies dominating this sector of the market, such a *volte-face* was inevitable. Thus, while such cases of illegality and incompetence abound, enforcement – not least in the form of contract compliance or the sanction of barring specific companies from bidding for contracts – appears an obvious governmental response, but one which it is less and less able to adopt.

Thus ATOS, Capita, G4S and Serco have oligopolistic control of some sectors in which they operate, certainly in the UK, for example: 'there are some public services that are only provided by a few large providers. For instance, there are three providers of private prisons (Serco, G4S, Sodexo), two providers of child custody (Serco and G4S), and two providers for medical assessments (Atos and now Capita)' (NAO, 2013, 26). In general, there in fact exists an increasing inter-dependence between states and private capital, from which each is less and less able to break away. *More specifically, the very existence and obviousness of such corporate oligopolies undermines central claims of neoliberalism, and also indicates clearly and consistently the limitations of state claims to be able to regulate such markets, corporations or even contracts.*

Fourth, it is not just that, for some services, states are increasingly dependent upon companies such as ATOS, Capita, G4S and Serco – the latter, too, are largely reliant upon local and national-state contracts for a significant proportion of their income. This will remain the case unless markets in, for example, the delivery of criminal justice, are subject to formal, wholesale privatisation and a mass of new corporate entrants to the sector – neither of which seems, for the foreseeable future, likely, to say the least. A recent survey of these four companies by the NAO calculated that, at 2012/2013, the combined value of public-service contracts involving these four companies was some £4 billion (NAO, 2013, 20–1). Moreover, using data provided in the same NAO report, the share of public sector contracts as a proportion of UK revenue for the companies was significant: for ATOS, 50 per cent, Capita, 34 per cent, G4S, 37 per cent, and for Serco public-service contacts made up 66 per cent of income in 2012/13 (NAO, 2013, 60–4). This is such a level of state-dependency that it might best be summed up by the term 'corporate welfare' – and is of course antithetical to claims of efficiency, competitiveness and so on.

The phrase 'corporate welfare' is a potentially very useful resource in counter-hegemonic discourse. It is, in fact, a relatively recent entrant to the political lexicon, and is defined by Farnsworth, following Glasberg and Skidmore, as encompassing a vast range of 'efforts made by the state to directly or indirectly subsidise, support, or rescue corporations, or otherwise socialise the cost and risk of investment and production of private profits and capital accumulation of corporations' (Farnsworth, 2012, 6). In a forensic analysis of this multi-faceted phenomenon, Farnsworth documents how hidden forms of corporate welfare have risen substantially since the 1980s (Farnsworth, 2012, 75–101) – that is, co-terminous with the emergence to dominance of neoliberalism, but which he discusses at an international level, via the concept of 'globalisation' (see Chapter One, above). At the same time he observes that the net effect of the 2008 bailouts and austerity politics which followed has been a 'major redistribution of welfare effort towards corporations and away from individuals' (Farnsworth, 2012, 197 and 180–97, passim). His call for a proper debate about corporate (alongside social) welfare is a reasonable one – but one which corporations and the state are likely to resist. For here, of course, lies a further, key source of vulnerability for each set of parties in their inter-dependent relationships. The state, via corporate welfare, 'keeps some companies on life-support' (Farnsworth, 2013, 51), which reverses the claims made for autonomous, efficient, competitive and entrepreneurial private capital which have been so crucial to 'freeing' it from state 'interference'. *To expose corporate welfare is to expose these central claims, while at the same time opening up a potentially much wider, and socially and politically volatile, contestation over who or what is a benefit scrounger, parasitic on the state, kept alive only by handouts from general taxation.*

Fifth, a further key dimension to the new and increasing inter-dependence of states and corporations is the undermining of a central plank of 'laissez-faire' discourse – that is, the separations between market and state, economy and politics, private and public. All of these dichotomies are highly ideological, and neither bears much relationship to the reality each claims to signify, nor in fact ever could. But they have been highly significant, crucial in fact, to the claims for the superiority of private capital being left to operate in relatively unfettered markets free from state 'interference', and indeed assuming ever greater state functions, from the 'public sector', in the name of efficiency. As the lines which separate the phenomena denoted within each of these couplets become increasingly blurred, what then remains of the claims of neoliberalism? They can still be advanced, of course, but here the disjuncture between the 'imaginary' and the 'real' social order, in the phrase Frank Pearce (1976) used to describe the emerging US economy almost four decades ago, becomes ever greater. This risks not simply exposure, but poses very specific challenges.

This has been alluded to elsewhere. Crouch has argued that one effect of the elevated status of corporations under neoliberalism, coupled with the overwhelming mantra to the effect that states are inefficient, has placed a greater onus on corporations to provide moral and political leadership. Thus, increasingly, the

> argument that the job of business is just business, and nothing to do with morality or politics, falls to the ground; leading firms are of their own accord, and sometimes virtually officially, taking on moral and political roles. The very ideology that proclaimed the autonomy and superiority of economic motivations has produced complications for those same motivations. (Crouch, 2012, 369)

More generally, as we saw in Chapter Four, one of the planks of the regulatory orthodoxy is that corporations can and do act morally – and thus should be left relatively free of command-and-control regulation. This is intimately related, as I argued, to wider claims for corporate social responsibility (CSR). But while bestowing upon corporations the abilities and willingness to comply with and indeed exceed minimal legal requirements in the absence of external oversight, CSR also allows, and in some versions requires, corporations to present themselves as corporate citizens who engage positively in politics and in social development, indeed who can do both better than government and politicians – as we saw in Chapter Three. CSR thus allows corporations to defend and extend the autonomy of their decision making, and affords them a plausible position from which to challenge, for example, the encumbrance of socially protective laws and their enforcement; but it exposes them as both fully political and not merely economic actors. *Thus, the long sought-for and crucial separation between politics and economics, state and market, breaks down, an achievement in itself, but which may also lead to demands being made upon corporations and states which neither is capable of meeting.*

Transcending regulatory reform?

In short, we may be witnessing a period of increasing corporate vulnerability, which is simultaneously an increasing exposure for the state, the institutions of which paved the way for, maintain, and pronounce the superiority of, the 'private sector'. In the context of the specific focus of this book, that is, on regulation, enforcement and social protection, the vulnerabilities raised for the state – as well as those which are raised by implication for the corporate sector, above – are three-fold, and mutually reinforcing.

First, the state's ability to regulate and enforce is so diminished that any popular confidence in regulation as the antidote to capitalist excess looks likely to be ever diminished also. Second, notwithstanding its knee-jerk instincts, notwithstanding its ideologues, notwithstanding much of the regulatory orthodoxy, capitalism *needs* regulation and law enforcement – not least for the very reasons these were first introduced over 150 years ago. Just as the corporation cannot live without the state, so neither can the state nor the corporation live without regulation: 'capital' wants less and less regulation but at the same time needs regulation – and this in turn entails some minimal level of enforcement. But both regulation and enforcement in the UK are currently less and less credible. This is one of the senses in which 'victorious capitalism' may be its own worst enemy (Streeck, 2014, 50).

Third, and significantly, the five dimensions of vulnerability indicated above raise the spectre of increasing and mutually-reinforcing crises of legitimacy for the state – and this is particularly the case given that one of the legitimating supports of the state has, for 150 years, been based upon its ability to provide some forms of social protection. At this point, it is worth recalling Radice's searing critique of 'the Left', who castigated it for 'ignoring Gramsci's conceptualisation of the hegemony of capital', so that it 'has seriously neglected the relentless ideological campaign waged by the right to shape the public's "common sense" about the economic role of the state'. The effect, he argued, is that 'most of our fellow citizens now think that the state is not competent to deliver measurable economic goals, but only to "enable" the private initiatives of entrepreneurs' (Radice, 2013). Translating Radice's words in the context of this book, I would argue that a key task in the defence and furtherance of social protection is a consistent counter-attack on the moral capital of capital and its promulgation and defence by the state.

Environmental, consumer and occupational health and safety protections are only a very small part of social protection of course; but there is no doubt that the processes outlined in this book should be viewed as part of 'a much broader trend that removes previously hard won legal entitlements from working populations to ensure the wellbeing and continuity of capitalism itself' (Winlow and Hall, 2013, 8). If the state is incrementally abandoning its commitment – and indeed its *ability* – to provide social protection, this will not be an easy series of tasks to accomplish.

To be clear. The state can never be the solution to corporate power, crime and harm – it is part of the problem. This does not mean that one can adopt a simple understanding of how to view, and what to do, about the state in order to begin to think about the mitigation of corporate crime and harm. Neocleous (2003, 86) criticises those who argue that the inability of the state to pursue corporate criminalisation is the result of a lack of political will, while also noting that such political will will not be found 'in the current structures through which mainstream politics is organised' (Neocleous, 2003). The task of resisting the corporation is, indeed, one that requires social forces which can challenge 'the state and the individualising tendencies of bourgeois law, as well as capital itself' (Neocleous, 2003, 86–7). As we have seen through, for example, reference to the work of Snider earlier in this chapter, and also through the discussion of the emergence of the social protection state in Chapter One, states do not autonomously regulate nor enforce – pro-regulatory forces are always required to push efforts to limit the freedom of manoeuvre for capital onto the state's agenda. And on this point, it has to be recognised that in the UK at least, to which the explicit focus of this book is restricted, there appears to be a dearth of anti-hegemonic forces which might genuinely be viewed as pro-regulatory to take on such task. Notably, the historical bearers of 'pro-regulation', trades unions, have been weakened, co-opted, or both. Yet even some trade union organisations, as well as environmental groups, and a plethora of more local or regional, grassroots campaigning organisations, retain a commitment at least to defending what existing levels of enforcement remain, and to seek to extend some forms of protective regulation. Moreover, in this context I would add that academics need to recognise that their work has pro- or counter-hegemonic effects – despite their liberal fantasises or best intentions, academic output is never neutral, let alone value free (Tombs and Whyte, 2003).

At the same time, such social forces need specific points of resistance or pressure on which to work and, *contra* Neocleous, these cannot start with challenging the whole structure of the corporate form – nor indeed some abstraction called 'the state'. On the latter, it is crucial to maintain a dualism as regards the state, without descending into dualism in terms of political strategy – that is, of what is to be *done* about the state. Steve Hall, recently, comes close to this conflation, when he writes, 'where the right imagine monstrous criminals, the liberal left imagine monstrous publics and panoptic-punitive states' (Hall, 2012, 113) – even if, as he quite rightly goes on to note, the problem in the case of corporations ('the banks', for example) is that 'we have far too little control' (Hall, 2012, 113). His left–right schism is not helpful, but his critique of some left positions in failing to recognise the 'dualistic' role of the state, as 'simultaneously repressive and protective' (Hall, 2012, 114), is crucial:

> Despite the noises this left-liberal project made for radical transformation, it continued to rely for its political application and funding on the regulatory and redistributive ability of the underlying social-democratic framework that managed the capitalist economy. In other words it remained dependent on a significantly imbalanced compromise with the state–capitalist partnership it criticised and sought to transform. (Hall, 2012, 115)

Indeed, in this respect he echoes Kolko, who chides the left for a blind faith in regulation per se, more specifically because, historically, it held,

> a naïve, axiomatic view that government economic regulation, per se, was desirable, and also because many ignored crucial business support for such measures by focusing on the less important opposition that existed. The fetish of government regulation of the economy as a positive social good was one that sidetracked a substantial portion of European socialism as well, and was not unique to the American experience. Such axiomatic and simplistic assumptions of what federal regulation would bring did not take into account problems of democratic control and participation, and in effect assumed that the power of

> government was neutral and socially beneficent. (Kolko,
> 1963, 286)

Neither of these important insights, however, means abandoning struggles around regulation and enforcement; rather, each, for me, raises the political reality that states must be challenged on their own terms of social protection, but also that this can at the same time be pursued while recognising that the state can never be the solution to corporate crime and harm and that it retains essentially repressive, and, indeed, violent, inherent characteristics.

As well as challenging the capitalist state, we must also challenge the corporation; and that partly entails thinking *beyond* the corporation. The corporation is an amoral, essentially destructive entity which causes unquantifiable physical, social and economic harm, and cannot effectively be held to account through criminal, administrative, company or regulatory law. As I have emphasised, this is not to say law can achieve nothing, but progressive reform will not be achieved solely via regulation nor enforcement per se. That said, what appear to be quite piecemeal demands can be of significance, with quite radical potential. For example, the campaigning work of two quite different groups – Uncut and the Tax Justice Network, the former very much focused on direct action,[100] the latter a 'think tank' style organisation[101] consisting of academic researchers and activists – has combined to put a very simple, limited and persuasive demand on the political agenda: that high-earning individuals and corporations should pay their taxes. This has been a part of opening up a debate about what a just taxation system might look like which is on national and indeed international political agendas. In other words, this is a very limited demand for enforcement of existing law which has enormous potential in terms of social and economic justice.

Quite differently, in the realm of criminal law, we can still identify reforms which have the potential to be transformative – that is, which maintain the potential for more radical reform, rather than ultimately bolstering the power of capital through a limited instrumentalism, a mere symbolism, or indeed both. Key contemporary examples of legal reforms which might radically undermine the legal protections which corporations currently enjoy are those which seek to pierce the corporate veil – that ideological and material, legal construction through which the corporate form exists as if independent of those who own and control it, guaranteeing a compartmentalisation of legal (and moral) liability. For many years, as its form was being debated through the political process, it seemed that the Corporate Manslaughter and

Corporate Homicide Act (2007) might embody this radical aim, albeit that, eventually, this proved not to be the case (Tombs and Whyte, 2015). That said, proposals continue to circulate in the context of legal liability for workplace killings that precisely establish a clear legal relationship between such deaths, the corporate form, and the senior officers and shareholders of that corporation. These are potentially radical, and are on various political agendas (Tombs and Whyte, 2015, 173–5).

There are further, logically related demands, to be pursued through other bodies of law. We should maintain the demand for radical reform of company law, so that a diverse range of stakeholders are increasingly empowered, not through weak reforms to corporate governance but through building collective organisation with rights inside companies – for example, firms with legally-protected, effective trade union safety reps and safety committees have half as many recorded injuries as those where these countervailing sources of power do not exist (James and Walters, 2002; Reilly et al, 1995). Consumers and local communities should be similarly empowered. Even reforms to rights of and protections for whistleblowers, however limited and individualising such forms of challenge may be, can have some minor progressive effect here (Pemberton et al, 2012). Empowering any or all of these organisations and functions would place some limits on management autonomy within the firm itself, an imposition of some degree of control which can function and develop beyond or at the margins of states and state acceptability.

There are, however, wider challenges to be faced than legal reform. We should be continually demanding that a range of services should be (re-)nationalised and taken out of the for-profit sector, as the latter demonstrates its inability to deliver these according to its own promise, and as the state consistently demonstrates its inabilities to hold consistent corporate failure to account. Thus we must also challenge corporate claims of efficiency, of freedom, of choice, of autonomy from (and superiority over) government, claims which are disproven for all of us on a daily basis, perhaps so obvious that we almost become anaesthetised to the supporting rhetorics of corporate power?

This is a heterogeneous set of demands, from the reformist to the utopian. But there is no necessary contradiction here: the idea that there is a mutual exclusivity between 'reform' and 'revolution' or 'practical' and 'utopian' is not the concrete experience of many counter-hegemonic organisations. And there is a lesson here for academics, since neither utopianism nor radical imagination can emanate from an atomised realm of 'mere' thought. As Haiven has put it, imagination is not a thing that we, as individuals, 'have'. It's a shared landscape or a commons of possibility that we share as communities. The imagination doesn't exist purely in the individual mind; it also exists between people as a result of their attempts to work out how to live and work together. The imagination can, therefore, be extremely dangerous…The radical imagination is a matter of acting otherwise, together. (Haiven, 2014, 218)

A key task here is to reject the idea that being idealistic can never be pragmatic or useful in winning concessions or influencing policy. In the context of regulation and enforcement, this means challenging the orthodoxy which claims a monopoly over pragmatism, albeit one increasingly narrowly defined within the economic and political logics of the moment, and one which is reduced to a re-balancing act, at best. Thus our demands and our actions must be achievable yet at the same time unashamedly utopian. And, following Jacoby, these should be utopian in an 'iconoclastic' rather than 'blueprint' sense (Jacoby, 2005). Thus, while this is a book inspired by and imbued with politics – not least since regulation and enforcement are essentially political processes – it is no political manifesto. Further, not least if we are to avoid political immobilisation, we should, as one commentator has recently put it, 'learn to think about capitalism coming to an end without assuming responsibility for answering the question of what one proposes to put in its place' (Streeck, 2014, 46). But this is also to argue for a 'radical imagination', which requires not just a future; it also has a present and a past (Haiven, 2014). This radical imagination transcends liberalism, balance, the acceptance more or less that things cannot change so much, and indeed a terrain of hope and possibility that narrows and narrows to the extent that it becomes a perverse ground from which to measure, analyse, argue:

the current conjuncture's dominant liberal culture has redefined idealism and pragmatism to realign the usual opposition between them. Now, those who adopt the 'pragmatic' position of slightly modifying the existing system's socioeconomic framework are redefined as the idealists. Conversely, in this current period of economic crisis and rapidly approaching environmental change to believe that the current order can continue indefinitely should be defined as idealistic – even insanely so – but, instead, it is defined as pragmatic as we seek individual solutions tailored to the systems 'problems' as they crop up. To adopt such a position means turning away from a reality judged too traumatic to be faced head-on, and falling victim to the belief that any attempt to change it will only succeed in making things worse. (Winlow and Hall, 2013, 167)

Thinking about what social protection might actually mean, and how it can be achieved, requires an iconoclastic utopianism 'essential to any effort to escape the spell of the quotidian. That effort is the *sine qua non* of any serious thinking about the future – the prerequisite of any thinking' (Jacoby, 2005, Preface). Utopian thinking is not the opposite of seeking reform. Reforms not only co-exist with, but are often sustained by, utopian thinking. Indeed, reforms without a utopian spirit are likely to lapse into reform*ism*, not just with relatively few positive effects, but indeed are likely to be counterproductive, bolstering the corporation as it seems to have been somewhat tamed. If we cannot even imagine a world without the corporation, the state and regulation, then we will never inhabit a world without them – and the devastation that the corporate form wreaks on human life, with state and regulatory support, the state-corporate barbarism that has been the spectre pervading this book, will become an increasing fact of life.

Notes

1. Notably, those owning estates in the north-west and north-east of England (Pontin, 2007, 194), where early chemical production was concentrated.

2. What Miller has called the inspectorate's 'traditional reluctance to prosecute' persisted – 'between 1929 and 1966, for example, only 2 prosecutions are recorded' (Miller, 1997, 309).

3. Albeit there are quite distinct views of how such activity proceeds (see, for example, Polanyi, 1971/1944; Sayer, 1995; Vogel, 1996).

4. And, many might add, highly inefficient – though this somewhat raises the question of the task of different regulatory regimes (see Haines, 2011, 31–61).

5. COMEAP 'provides independent advice to government departments and agencies on how air pollution impacts on health' (www.gov.uk/government/ groups/committee-on-the-medical-effects-of-air-pollutants-comeap).

6. On this basis, both Mandelson and Blair could, during the New Labour years, infamously state that they were 'seriously relaxed' about rising income and wealth inequalities – with the caveat added by both that, 'as long as they pay their taxes' which is, as Dorling notes, 'a view of taxation rather like charity' (Dorling, 2010, 406).

7. This dominance is structural in nature and has historical origins. However, it has other dimensions, some much cruder and instrumental. A September 2011 analysis by the Bureau of Investigative Journalism has calculated that 'hedge funds, financiers and private equity firms contributed more than a quarter of all donations to the Conservative party in the past year' – that is, 27 per cent, or £3.3 million, of the £12.18 million donated to the party. Moreover, 'the proportion of donations to the Conservatives from the entire financial services sector has now reached 51.4 per cent'. Both figures (and percentages) had increased on the previous year, prior to the Conservatives being in government (Mathiasen, 2011).

8. By 2010, manufacturing as a percentage of GDP had fallen below 10 per cent, to 9.6 per cent (*Guardian*, 2013).

9. It is worth noting that financial services accounted for just 3.8 per cent of *employment* in 2010.

10. A very similar point is made by Giroux who, discussing the onslaught of neoliberal rationality, notes how the central figure of the 1987 film Wall Street, Gordon Gekko, while 'meant to be shocking and provocative' for his 'embrace of greed as the most fundamental human value' appeared in fact 'not only a source of inspiration…but *central* to a set of neoliberal commitments that are now utterly normalised' (Giroux, 2008, 165, emphasis in original; see also Hansen, 2014).

[11] Meek has noted that, 'Privatisation failed to turn Britain into a nation of small shareholders. Before Thatcher came to power, almost 40 per cent of the shares in British companies were held by individuals. By 1981, it was less than 30 per cent. By the time she died in 2013, it had slumped to under 12 per cent' (Meek, 2014).

[12] To note this empirical trend is not, of course, to accept the claims of 'popular capitalism' espoused by Thatcherites and which such data was supposed to evidence – in many respects, the Thatcher years saw share-holding become more concentrated (see Coakley and Harris, 1992, 49–53).

[13] Which in turn of course, creates new opportunities for the ruthless psychological motivations of the entrepreneurial 'undertakers' to cross the border into criminality: to put this in familiar criminological terms, new, intensified and ubiquitous forms of motivations and techniques of neutralisation simultaneously become socially produced and available.

[14] Dannreuther notes the massive rise in references to 'entrepreneur' in UK Parliament from the 1980s onwards, before which the word was virtually unused in formal political discourse (Dannreuther, 2013, 5).

[15] An obituary of Harvey-Jones noted that, 'In 2006 he criticised *The Apprentice* star Sir Alan Sugar, branding him a power-exploiting bully. In an attack on business reality TV shows he dismissed the trend towards aggressive management styles, insisting the ethos behind his shows was always one of constructive guidance' (Mail Online, 2008).

[16] So clearly demonstrated over 40 years ago by Miliband in *The State in Capitalist Society* (1973, see especially chapter 3), notwithstanding the well-worn critique of his over-instrumentalist view of the state, a critique which tends to overlook the enduring insights of the book (Coleman et al, 2009).

[17] See, for example, the mass of documentation collated by *China Labour Watch*, (http://chinalaborwatch.org), or *Corporate Watch* (www.corpwatch.org/).

[18] Lakoff argues that US conservative morality is captured by an ideal-typical 'strict father' model (2002, 65–107) which, if hardly unproblematic, does broadly characterise the political uses of commonsense morality tales which have dominated as a crisis of private sector institutions became socialised and then 'necessitated' a series of economic and social policy 'responses'.

[19] The appearance of bankers before the Select Committee prompted a stream of vitriolic press headlines (BBC, 2009b), most infamously in the *Sun* which ran the front-page headline 'Scumbag millionaires' alongside images of Sir Tom McKillop, former Chairman, and Sir Fred Goodwin, former Chief Executive of RBS Group. (Hawkes and Pascoe-Watson, 2009; see Stanley, 2012).

[20] There is now a mass of evidence attesting to the facts that: the UK, among other industrialised nations, is experiencing rising levels of income and wealth inequality; that, internationally, these trends towards widening inequalities are associated with nation-states where neoliberalism has been embraced most

thoroughly; and that these levels of widening inequalities are associated with a wide-ranging cluster of economic, physical and social harms (see, notably, Dorling, 2014; Lansley, 2012; Lansley and Mack, 2015; Pemberton, 2015; Sayer, 2015; Therborn, 2013; Wilkinson and Pickett, 2009).

[21] In 2009, the *News of the World* had a *readership* of just under eight million people (Rogers, 2011a).

[22] Moreover, in such claims, the Conservatives were pushing at an ideological open-door in that they have over decades cast Labour governments as beset by over-taxing and over-spending.

[23] Just as there had been an all-party consensus on the virtues of 'light touch regulation' in the years prior to the crisis (Straw, 2011; Furness, 2012), although this was of course denied and caused fleeting embarrassment for many senior political figures in the later years of the decade.

[24] This is not to make any claim about contexts beyond the UK (see White, 2013).

[25] Indeed, for quite some time (see Radice, 2011).

[26] That is, in the Althusserian sense, wherein individuals are interpellated as subjects, recruiting or transforming them into an 'imaginary relationship' to 'real conditions of existence' (Althusser, 1971, 162).

[27] Quite literally so: 'comically or repulsively ugly or distorted' and 'incongruous or inappropriate to a shocking degree' (www.oxforddictionaries.com/definition/english/grotesque).

[28] While dissenting from the specifics of its use, Miliband as leader of the Labour Party had also endorsed the analogy: 'Yes, the government's argument that if you have a credit card bill you need to pay it off as quickly as possible sounded attractive. And yes, any family, faced with a debt, needs to be very careful with its budget and make some savings. But everyone knows you can't pay off a credit card bill if you lose your job, or see your income fall' (Miliband, 2011b).

[29] The fictional Glazebrook is the Chairman of a bank who meets with permanent Secretary Sir Humphrey Appleby in a bid to cover up bank fraud in the episode 'A Conflict of Interest' of *Yes, Prime Minister*, Series 2, Episode 4, December 1987. (Thanks to Joe Sim for pointing out this quote and indeed episode.)

[30] Even more pejoratively, often abbreviated to 'CAC'!

[31] Erroneously, as I note below.

[32] www.lse.ac.uk/collections/CARR/aboutUs/Default.htm

[33] www.lse.ac.uk/collections/CARR/aboutUs/Default.htm

[34] While responsive regulation rightly draws attention to the need to understand the motivations and contexts of actors and sets of actors within firms, I note the tendency to anthropomorphise the corporation.

[35] Established with funding from the then Social Sciences Research Council in 1972 as a dedicated, interdisciplinary research unit (Harris, 1983, 319).

[36] Freedom of Information Request, London School of Economics and Political Science, February 2012

[37] CARR (www.lse.ac.uk/accounting/CARR/visitors/visitors2002.aspx)

[38] RegNet 'is an internationally acclaimed interdisciplinary program that serves as the central node for a network of centres, projects, institutions, practitioners and academics involved in exploring and understanding critical domains of regulation' (see http://regnet.anu.edu.au/).

[39] http://regnet.anu.edu.au/people/academic-staff

[40] http://regnet.anu.edu.au/people/visitors

[41] http://regnet.anu.edu.au/people/former-staff

[42] www.law.upenn.edu/institutes/regulation/people.html

[43] www.law.upenn.edu/institutes/regulation/links.html

[44] See http://onlinelibrary.wiley.com/journal/10.1111/(ISSN)1748-5991/homepage/EditorialBoard.html

[45] http://ukcatalogue.oup.com/category/academic/series/law/osls.do

[46] The founding editors stated that 'The mission of *Regulation and Governance* is to open regulatory studies to the turn toward governance' (Braithwaite et al, 2007, 4). At the time of writing (December 2014), the Editorial Board of the journal contains many of the key 'compliance school' figures (see http://onlinelibrary.wiley.com/journal/10.1111/(ISSN)1748-5991/homepage/EditorialBoard.html).

[47] These were to become 11 principles in the subsequently published statement, although responsive regulation remained (OECD, 2014).

[48] A content analysis of six British-based journals from January 2009 to the end of 2013 (Tombs, 2015a) found that out of a total of 922 articles, just 13 pieces deal at all centrally with the economic crisis; that is, just over 1 per cent (1.4 per cent) treated the crisis as a thematic issue, seeking to understand either its aetiology or legal and regulatory responses to this (see Alessandrini, 2011; Baker, 2013; Bholat et al, 2012; Block, 2013; Braithwaite, 2009; Dorn, 2010; Frerichs, 2013; Helleiner and Thistlethwaite, 2013; Moschella and Tsingou, 2013; Rixen, 2013; Verbruggen, 2013; Xenakis and Cheliotis, 2013; Young, 2013).

[49] Ayres and Braithwaite defined their task as seeking 'creative options to bridge the abyss between deregulatory and pro-regulatory rhetoric' (Ayres and Braithwaite, 1992, 15). This recognised that, during the 1980s, 'whatever country one examines, the mixed and somewhat Pyrrhic victories conservatives have won on the question of deregulation can give cause for gloom on the right' (Ayres and Braithwaite, 1992, 12), while rejecting the claims of 'the gloom-mongers of the Left' who would 'see capital as structurally impregnable' (Ayres and Braithwaite, 1992, 12).

[50] Certainly since its 2002 relaunch.

51 Cited in *OSHWORLD, News.* July 2005 (www.sheilapantry.com/oshworld/ news/2005/200507.html)

52 Hampton was subsequently knighted for his services to business in 2007 – although in his budget speech, in March 2005, Gordon Brown had already referred to him as 'Sir' Philip Hampton (www.independent.co.uk/news/ business/analysis-and-features/the-interview-man-on-a-mission-has-quangos- quaking-6150293.html). A year later, in 2008, Hampton was appointed as chairman of UK Financial Investments Limited, the firm set up to manage the UK government's shareholding in banks following the bailouts.

53 'The FSA is highly regarded within the financial services industry in the UK and internationally and its risk-based approach is increasingly seen as a model to follow by other regulators' (NAO, 2007, 5).

54 An additional sixth, time-limited enforcement priority of 'Animal and public health, animal movements and identification' was identified.

55 To reiterate, these were: proportionality, accountability, consistency, transparency and targeting.

56 And, at the time of writing, still the most recent.

57 OECD member countries are Australia, Austria, Belgium, Canada, the Czech Republic, Denmark, Finland, France, Germany, Greece, Hungary, Iceland, Ireland, Italy, Japan, Korea, Luxembourg, Mexico, the Netherlands, New Zealand, Norway, Poland, Portugal, the Slovak Republic, Spain, Sweden, Switzerland, Turkey, the United Kingdom and the United States.

58 See www.redtapechallenge.cabinetoffice.gov.uk/all-themes/

59 The 2013 Budget speech announced a second phase of the Red Tape Challenge.

60 www.hse.gov.uk/contact/challenge-panel.htm

61 www.gov.uk/government/organisations/better-regulation-delivery-office/ about

62 The chapter draws upon a larger research project which, among other things, attempts a longitudinal, quantitative mapping of local authority regulatory services, from 2003 to 2013. It also aims to set this alongside data for national regulators working in cognate areas for the same time period – so, for example, HSE data would be considered alongside data for local authority EHOs with health and safety functions. These apparently straightforward ambitions were difficult and in some specific contexts impossible to realise, due to a host of problems in accessing and using relevant data. These included: incompatibilities in data across time; differences in the quality of data held by different regulators; inconsistencies within different data sets held by the same regulator; and the problem of discerning trends when absolute numbers are so low – for example, in prosecutions by local authorities' pollution control officers; and, finally, the fact that much local authority data is held by a private body, the Chartered Institute of Public Finance and Accountancy (CIPFA), a professional

accountancy body specialising in public services and which, while a registered charity, requires a subscription to access such data. Finally, the data used in this chapter relates to England and Wales.

[63] The Meat Hygiene Service inspects abattoirs, slaughterhouses and meat cutting plants – though this service is not part of the research upon which this chapter nor this book is based.

[64] There are 373 local authorities in England and Wales.

[65] Freedom of Information Request, Food Standards Agency Response, 1573/1033/2014, 11 June 2014.

[66] www.hse.gov.uk/contact/authority.htm

[67] Freedom of Information Request, HSE Response, 2014060117, 2 July 2014.

[68] www.environment-agency.gov.uk/business/default.aspx

[69] Thus, one report in October 2013 anticipated a decline in overall Agency staff up to October 2014 from 11,400 to 9,700 (Marshall, 2013).

[70] Freedom of Information Request, Environment Agency, Response NRJUN30, 25 July 2014. In the years covered by the data and considerations here, the EA regulated in England and Wales. From April 2013, Natural Resources Wales assumed responsibility for regulation in Wales (Environment Agency, 2012, 7).

[71] Except where data is either unavailable, or where it is so absolutely low as to make attempts to indicate trends meaningless.

[72] Or, most recent set of ten-year data available.

[73] All percentages in this summary are rounded to the nearest whole figure, whether upwards or downwards.

[74] Notices rather than prosecutions are used, since the latter are so few as to render data almost meaningless.

[75] Four, because I was unable to gain access to one of these authorities.

[76] There were others, not considered here, since they are of less relevance for the focus of this book.

[77] Respondents were assigned a letter, according to the local authority in which they worked, and a number, by order of interview; no other significance should be attached to this notation, which is used purely to guarantee anonymity.

[78] Austerity is very much a political choice, as argued in previous chapters, albeit a political choice which is implemented partly through economic means. This 'choice' is not one accessible to all states of course – UK governments have made this policy choice, while others have had this forced upon them by supra-national and not even remotely democratic institutions, such as the EU's Troika or the IMF (see Blyth, 2013b).

[79] Education is one area over which local authorities have no or relatively little discretion in terms of expenditure (Keeling, 2013a).

[80] As Duffy (2013) notes, local government's primary function is to provide social care to children and adults.

81 And see also qualitative indicators in UNISON, 2012a.

82 Nick Forbes, Leader, Newcastle City Council, Julie Dore, Leader, Sheffield City Council and Joe Anderson, Mayor of Liverpool (see Forbes et al, 2012).

83 See also UNISON, 2012a.

84 Two interviews were conducted at the BRDO, in May 2014.

85 In 2013, central and local government contracts to Balfour Beatty were worth over £371 million (the 2012 figure was almost £600 million) (Rutter and Gil, 2014).

86 In 2013, central and local government contracts to Capita were worth over £800 million (the 2012 figure was over £650 million) (Rutter and Gil, 2014).

87 A councillor in one of the authorities to which I had access, and who had been widely described as a 'local champion' of regulatory services; he was the Council Cabinet's Member for Environment and Sustainability.

88 On the BRDO, see Chapter Five.

89 And numerous others, see, for example, NAO, 2009a; 2009b; 2009c; 2009d.

90 That is, 2013/14.

91 While Britain long acted alone at EU level to seek to resist a cap on bankers' bonuses (Kanter, 2013).

92 Certainly, most criminologists on either side of the Atlantic have barely bothered to give the crisis a second glance (Tombs, 2015a), albeit that there have been some exceptions; for discussions of such work, as well as its relative absence (see Barak, 2013; Burdis and Tombs, 2012; Deflem, 2011; McGurrin, 2013a; Pontell and Black, 2012; and Pontell and Geis, 2014).

93 The struggle over regulation and enforcement is ongoing as I write and will be as you read. At present, May 2015, the siren calls of 'over-regulation' support those who wish to renegotiate the terms of membership of, or leave, the European Union, as a Conservative government prepares for further re-regulatory initiatives at home, while purporting re-regulatory initiatives within the EU (notably, REFIT) (see http://ec.europa.eu/smart-regulation/refit/index_en.htm, and the High Level Group on Administrative Burdens, http://ec.europa.eu/smart-regulation/refit/admin_burden/high_level_group_en.htm) and beyond (notably, the Transatlantic Trade and Investment Partnership, http://ec.europa.eu/trade/policy/in-focus/ttip/index_en.htm).

94 But see, for example, Bakan, 2004; Glasbeek, 2002; Pearce, 1993; Tombs and Whyte, 2015.

95 Documented clearly through the vast literature on corporate crime.

96 That these terms may jar when applied to corporate activity is in itself instructive, because the language applied to the deleterious effects of corporate activity is largely one that is quite distinct from that applied to harmful and illegal acts on the part of individual men and women, particularly those from marginalised, lower class groups.

97 A term first used in this context in conversation with me by Joe Sim.

⁹⁸ On this *specific* point, there is some limited agreement with one of the central claims of the regulatory orthodoxy. However, the claim that concerns for reputation are a significant driver of compliance is far too generalised in the orthodoxy. It is based upon the assumptions that: consumers have choices to exercise – while most markets are in fact oligopolistic (Tombs and Whyte, 2015); consumers can link harm or detriment to a specific company, which is often not the case; and that it is possible to generalise a classic customer–retailer version of capitalistic business, which in fact obscures complex supply chains and the fact that most trade is between companies themselves and between companies and local and/or national governments, contexts where 'consumer sovereignty' is rather distorted.

⁹⁹ A 'payment-for-results welfare-to-work programme' rolled out by government in the summer of 2011; 'central to the coalition government's ambitious programme of welfare reform', it is 'delivered by a range of private, public and voluntary sector organisations' (DWP, 2012, 2).

¹⁰⁰ UK Uncut describes itself as 'a grassroots movement taking action to highlight alternatives to austerity. We use acts of creative civil disobedience to show our opposition to the government's cuts to our public services' (www.ukuncut. org.uk/); a central plank of this opposition has been to highlight tax evasion and avoidance.

¹⁰¹ TJN describes itself as 'a fast, flexible, expert-led, activist think tank' (www. taxjustice.net/about/who-we-are/goals/).

References

Accum, F, 1820, *A treatise on the adulterations of food and culinary poison: Exhibiting the fraudulent sophistications of bread, beer, wine, spiritous liquors, tea, coffee, cream, confectionery, vinegar, mustard, pepper, cheese, olive oil, pickles, and other articles employed in domestic economy, and methods of detecting them*, London: Longman, Hurst, Ress, Orme and Brown

Advisory Committee on the Microbiological Safety of Food, 2012, *Annual report 2011*, Food Standards Agency (FSA), www.food.gov.uk/multimedia/pdfs/committee/acmsf-report–2011.pdf

Agamben, G, 2005, *State of exception*, Chicago, IL: Chicago University Press

Ainsworth, R, 2015, Developing the future regulatory strategy, FSA 15/01/04, Food Standards Agency (FSA) board meeting, 28 January, London: FSA

Albo, G, Fanelli, C, 2014, *Austerity against democracy: An authoritarian phase of neoliberalism?,* Toronto: Socialist Project

Aldrick, P, 2011, Anger at the banks is justified, Mervyn King says, *Telegraph*, 1 March, www.telegraph.co.uk/finance/economics/8355475/Anger-at-the-banks-is-justified-Mervyn-King-says.html

Alesina, A, Ardagna, S, Nicoletti, G, Schiantarell, F, 2005, Regulation and investment, *Journal of the European Economic Association*, 3, 4, 791–825.

Alessandri, P, Haldane, A, 2009, *Banking on the state, Bank of England*, www.bankofengland.co.uk/publications/Documents/speeches/2009/speech409.pdf

Alessandrini, D, 2011, Regulating financial derivatives? Risks, contested values, and uncertain futures, *Social and Legal Studies* 20, 4, 441–62

Allen, K, 2009, Campaigners blast Walker report on banks, *Guardian*, 26 November

Allio, L, 2007, Better regulation and impact assessment in the European Commission, in C Kirkpatrick, D Parker (eds) *Regulatory impact assessment: Towards better regulation?*, pp 72–105, Cheltenham: Edward Elgar Publishing

Almond, P, 2009, The dangers of hanging baskets: 'Regulatory myths' and media representations of health and safety regulation, *Journal of Law and Society* 36, 3, 352–75

Almond, P, 2013, *Corporate manslaughter and regulatory reform*, Basingstoke: Palgrave Macmillan

Almond, P, 2015, Revolution blues: The reconstruction of Health and Safety as a 'common-sense' form of regulation, *Journal of Law and Society*, 42, 2, June, 202–29

Almond, P, Colover, S, 2012, The criminalization of work–related death, *British Journal of Criminology* 52, 5, 997–1016

Althusser, L, 1971, *Lenin and philosophy*, London: New Left Books

Alvesalo, A, Tombs, S, 2001, The emergence of a 'war' on economic crime: The case of Finland, *Business and Politics* 3, 3, 239–67

Amable, B, 2011, Morals and politics in the ideology of neo-liberalism, *Socio-Economic Review* 9, 1, 3–30

Armistead, L, 2013, Andrew Tyrie: Bank reform legislation 'so weak as to be virtually useless', *Telegraph*, 8 July, www.telegraph.co.uk/finance/newsbysector/banksandfinance/10167457/Andrew-Tyrie-bank-reform-legislation-so-weak-as-to-be-virtually-useless.html

Ashton, J (nd) *The history of public health in Liverpool: Upwards and onwards, pendulum or helix?*, www.evolve360.co.uk/Data/10/Docs/workhouse/Poor_Ashton.pdf

Atkins, P, 1991, Sophistication detected: Or, the adulteration of the milk supply, 1850–1914, *Social History* 16, 3, 317–39

Aune, J, 2001, *Selling the free market: The rhetoric of economic correctness*, New York: Guilford Press

Ayres, I, Braithwaite, J, 1992, *Responsive regulation: Transcending the deregulation debate*, Oxford: Oxford University Press

Baars, G, 2012, *Law(yers) Congealing capitalism: On the (im)possibility of restraining business in conflict through international criminal law*, Thesis submitted for the degree of PhD (Laws), London: UCL, http://discovery.ucl.ac.uk/1348306/1/1348306.pdf

Bakan, J, 2004, *The corporation: The pathological pursuit of profit and power*, Toronto: Viking Canada

Baker, A, 2013, The gradual transformation? The incremental dynamics of macroprudential regulation, *Regulation and Governance* 7, 4, 417–34

Baldwin, R, 2004a, The new punitive regulation, *Modern Law Review* 67, 3, 351–83

Baldwin, R, 2004b, *Better regulation: Is it better for business?*, London: Federation of Small Businesses

Baldwin, R, Black, J, 2007, Really responsive regulation, *LSE Law, Society and Economy Working papers* 15/2007, London: London School of Economics and Political Science

Baldwin, R, Black, J, 2008, Really responsive regulation, *The Modern Law Review* 71, 1, 59–94

Barak, G, 2012, *Theft of a nation: Wall Street looting and federal regulatory colluding*, Lanham, MD: Rowman and Littlefield

Barak, G, 2013, The flickering desires for white-collar crime studies in the post-financial crisis: Will they ever shine brightly?, *Western Criminology Review* 13, 3, 61–71

Bardach, E, Kagan, RA, 1982, *Going by the book: The problem of regulatory unreasonableness*, Philadelphia, PA: Temple University Press

Bardach, E, Kagan, R, 2002, *Going by the book: The problem of regulatory unreasonableness*, Piscataway, NJ: Transaction

Barker, M, 2013, Celebrity philanthropy: In the service of corporate propaganda, in R Fisher (ed) *Managing democracy, managing dissent: Capitalism, democracy and the organisation of consent*, pp 96–110, London: Corporate Watch

BBC, 2008, Financial crisis 'like a tsunami', *BBC News Online*, 23 October, http://news.bbc.co.uk/1/hi/7687101.stm

BBC, 2009a, UK ban on short-selling expires, *BBC News Online*, 16 January, http://news.bbc.co.uk/1/hi/business/7832486.stm

BBC, 2009b, Papers angry at 'scumbag' bankers, *BBC News Online*, 11 February, http://news.bbc.co.uk/1/hi/uk/7882805.stm

BBC, 2011a, David Cameron: EU 'constant attacks' on City of London, *BBC News Online*, 28 October, www.bbc.co.uk/news/uk-politics-15487674

BBC, 2011b, *Full text: David Cameron's Conservative conference speech*, www.bbc.co.uk/news/uk-politics-15189614

BBC, 2012, *Union condemns North Tyneside worker outsourcing*, 2 October, www.bbc.co.uk/news/uk-england-tyne-19797229

BBC, 2014, Aldi, Lidl and Waitrose supermarkets increase market share, *Business News* 8 April, www.bbc.co.uk/news/business-26936146

Bellamy-Foster, J, Clark, B, 2004, Empire of barbarism, *Monthly Review* 56, 7, http://monthlyreview.org/2004/12/01/empire-of-barbarism

Benjamin, W, 1921/1978, Critique of violence, in P Demtz (ed) *Reflections: Essays, aphorisms, autobiographical writings* (translated by Edmund Jephcott), New York: Schocken Books

Bernat, I, Whyte, D, 2014, The prestige oil spill: A state-corporate regime of permission, Paper presented at *Resisting the demonisation of 'the Other': State, nationalism and social control in a time of crisis. The 42nd annual conference of the European group for the study of deviance and social control*, 3–6 September, Liverpool

BERR (Department for Business, Enterprise and Regulatory Reform), 2007, *Regulators' compliance code: Statutory code of practice for regulators*, London: BERR

Besley, T, Burgess, R, 2004, Can labor regulation hinder economic performance? Evidence from India, *Quarterly Journal of Economics*, 119, 1, 91–134

Bholat, D, Dunn, A, Gray, J, 2012, Share and share alike? Hedge funds, human rights, and owning enterprise in Britain, *Journal of Law and Society* 39, 185–212

BIS (Department for Business, Innovation and Skills), 2010, *New rules to hand over powers to individuals and companies by cutting red tape and bureaucracy*, 5 August, www.gov.uk/government/news/new-rules-to-hand-over-powers-to-individuals-and-companies-by-cutting-red-tape-and-bureaucracy

BIS (Department for Business, Innovation and Skills), 2011, *Transforming regulatory enforcement: Government response to the consultation on transforming regulatory enforcement*, London: BIS

BIS (Department for Business, Innovation and Skills), 2012a, 'One-in, two-out': Government to go further and faster to reduce burdens on business and help Britain compete in the global race, 19 November, http://news.bis.gov.uk/Press-Releases/-One-in-two-out-Government-to-go-further-and-faster-to-reduce-burdens-on-business-and-help-Britain-compete-in-the-global-race-6838c.aspx

BIS (Department for Business, Innovation and Skills), 2012b, Reducing the impact of regulation on business, Gov.UK, 12 December, https://www.gov.uk/government/policies/reducing-the-impact-of-regulation-on-business/supporting-pages/reducing-regulation-for-small-businesses

BIS (Department for Business, Innovation and Skills), 2013a, 'Freedom day' for business as cuts to red tape come into force, Press release, 5 April, www.gov.uk/government/news/freedom-day-for-business-as-cuts-to-red-tape-come-into-force

BIS (Department for Business, Innovation and Skills), 2013b, Fallon: Red tape freeze extended to more small businesses, Gov.UK, 6 June, https://www.gov.uk/government/news/fallon-red-tape-freeze-extended-to-more-small-businesses

BIS (Department for Business, Innovation and Skills), 2014, Business invited to help reform enforcement of regulation, Press release, 10 March, www.gov.uk/government/news/business-invited-to-help-reform-enforcement-of-regulation

BIS (Department for Business, Innovation and Skills), BRE (Better Regulation Executive), 2010, The Environment Agency: A review of progress since its Hampton implementation review, London: BRE

Bittle, S, 2012, Still dying for a living: Corporate criminal liability after the Westray mining disaster, Vancouver: UBC Press

Bittle, S, Snider, L, 2011, 'Moral panics' deflected: The failed legislative response to Canada's safety crimes and markets fraud legislation, Crime, Law and Social Change 56, 373–87

Black, J, 2002, Critical reflections on regulation, Centre for Analysis of Risk and Regulation (CARR) discussion paper 4, London: CARR, London School of Economics and Political Science

Black, J, 2005, The emergence of risk based regulation and the New Public Management in the UK, Public Law, Autumn, 512–49

Black, J, 2010, Risk-based regulation: Choices, practices and lessons being learnt, in G Bounds, N Malyshev (eds) Risk and regulation policy: Improving the governance of risk, pp185–236, Paris: OECD

Black, J, Baldwin, R, 2010, Really responsive risk-based regulation, Law and Policy 32, 2, 181–213

Black, J, Baldwin, R, 2012, When risk-based regulation aims low: Approaches and challenges, Regulation and Governance 6, 2–22

Blair, T, 1998, Tough on red tape, Financial Times, 9 March, 18

Blair, T, 2005a, *Speech on risk and the State*, University College London, 26 May, www.astrid-online.it/Qualit--de/Studi--ric/Archivio-21/Blair_Risk_State_Speech_26May05.pdf

Blair, T, 2005b, Full text: Tony Blair's speech on compensation culture, *Guardian*, 26 May, www.theguardian.com/politics/2005/may/26/speeches.media

Block, F, 2013, Relational work and the law: Recapturing the legal realist critique of market fundamentalism', *Journal of Law and Society*, Special Issue: Towards an Economic Sociology of Law, 40, 27–48

Blyth, M, 2013a, Paradigms and paradox: The politics of economic ideas in two moments of crisis, *Governance: An International Journal of Policy, Administration, and Institutions* 26, 2, April, 197–215

Blyth, M, 2013b, *Austerity: The history of a dangerous idea*, Oxford: Oxford University Press

Blythman, J, 2007, *Shopped: The shocking power of Britain's supermarkets*, London: Harper Perennial

Boffey, D, 2012a, Public services, big earners: A sector-by-sector analysis, *Observer*, 26 February

Boffey, D, 2012b, Who is making the money as private firms move in on the public sector?, *Observer*, 26 February

Bolchover, D, 2013, *The myth of global high pay talent market*, London: High Pay Centre, http://highpaycentre.org/files/CEO_mobility_final.pdf

Boltanski, L, Chiapello, E, 2007, *The new spirit of capitalism*, London: Verso

Booth, P, 2015, Thatcher: The myth of deregulation, *IEA Discussion Paper No. 60*, London: Institute of Economic Affairs

Booth, S, Howarth, C, Persson, M, Scarpetta, V, 2011, *Continental shift: Safeguarding the UK's financial trade in a changing Europe*, London: Open Europe, www.openeurope.org.uk/Content/Documents/PDFs/continentalshift.pdf

Botero, JC, Djankov, S, La Porta, R, Lopez-De-Silanes, F, Shleifer, A, 2004, The regulation of labor, *Quarterly Journal of Economics*, 119, 4, 1339–82

Bourdieu, P, Wacquant, L, 2001, NewLiberalSpeak: Notes on the new planetary vulgate, *Radical Philosophy* 105, January/February, 2–5

Bower, T, 2001, *Branson*, London: Fourth Estate

Bowers, S, 2012, HSBC Jersey accounts investigated by UK tax authorities, *Guardian*, 9 November, www.guardian.co.uk/business/2012/nov/09/hsbc-jersey-accounts-uk-tax-hmrc

Box, S, 1983, *Power, crime and mystification*, London: Tavistock

Boyle, R, Kelly, L, 2010, The celebrity entrepreneur on television: Profile, politics and power, *Celebrity Studies* 1, 3, 334–50

Brady, J, 2007, Taking advice: The relationship of advice to the risk of non-compliance, *2nd Annual Cambridge Conference on Regulation, Inspection and Improvement. The end of zero risk regulation: Risk toleration in regulatory practice Centre for Business Research*, 12 September, Cambridge: University of Cambridge

Braithwaite, J, 1997, On speaking softly and carrying big sticks: Neglected dimensions of a Republican separation of powers, *University of Toronto Law Journal* 47, 305–61

Braithwaite, J, 2000, The new regulatory state and the transformation of criminology, in D Garland, R Sparks (eds) *Criminology and social theory*, pp 47–70, Oxford: Oxford University Press

Braithwaite, J, 2002, Rewards and regulation, *Journal of Law and Society* 29, 1, 12–26

Braithwaite, J, 2009, Restorative justice for banks through negative licensing, *British Journal of Criminology* 49, 439–50

Braithwaite, J, 2010, Foreword, in A Quirk, T Seddon, G Smith (eds) *Regulation and criminal justice innovations in policy and research*, pp xiii–xviii, Cambridge: Cambridge University Press

Braithwaite, J, Fisse, B, 1987, Self-regulation and the control of corporate crime, in CD Shearing, PC Stenning (eds) *Private policing*, pp 221–46, London: Sage

Braithwaite, J, Coglianese, C, Levi-Faur, D, 2007, Can regulation and governance make a difference?, *Regulation and Governance* 1, 1–7

Brassett, J, Vaughan-Williams, N, 2012, Crisis is governance: Subprime, the traumatic event, and bare life, *Global Society* 26, 1, 19–42

BRC (Better Regulation Commission), 2006, *Risk, responsibility, regulation: Whose risk Is It anyway?*, London: Better Regulation Commission

BRC (Better Regulation Commission), 2008a, *Public risk: The next frontier for better regulation*, London: Better Regulation Commission, http://webarchive. nationalarchives.gov.uk/20100407162704/http:/archive.cabinetoffice.gov.uk/ brc/upload/assets/www.brc.gov.uk/public_risk_report_070108.pdf

BRC (Better Regulation Commission), 2008b, *Passing the baton*, http://webarchive. nationalarchives.gov.uk/20100407162704/http://archive.cabinetoffice.gov.uk/ brc/upload/assets/www.brc.gov.uk/passing_the_baton_070108.pdf

BRDO (Better Regulation Delivery Office), 2014a, *Primary authority extension: Nurturing partnerships for growth*, Birmingham: Better Regulation Delivery Office

BRDO (Better Regulation Delivery Office), 2014b, *Regulators' code*, Birmingham: Better Regulation Delivery Office

BRE (Better Regulation Executive), 2008, *Scrutinising new regulations*, at http://webarchive.nationalarchives.gov.uk/+/www.berr.gov.uk/bre/policy/ scrutinising-new-regulations/page44076.html

Breit, E, 2011, *On the discursive construction of corruption: A critical analysis of media texts*, Helsinki: Hanken School of Economics

Brenner, N, Theodore, N, 2002, Cities and the geographies of 'actually existing neoliberalism', *Antipode* 34, 49–379

Broome, A, Clegg, L, Rethel, L, 2012, Global governance and the politics of crisis, *Global Society* 26, 1, 3–17

Brown, D, 2011, Neoliberalism as a criminological subject, *Australian and New Zealand Journal of Criminology* 44, 1, 129–42

Brown, G, 2005a, Full text: The chancellor's budget speech, *Guardian Online*, 16 March, www.theguardian.com/politics/2005/mar/16/economy.uk

Brown, G, 2005b, *Speech to CBI Annual Conference*, 28 November 2005, www.ft.com/cms/s/2/9073a120-600d-11da-a3a6-0000779e2340.html#axzz2EpjhRxuG

Brown, G, 2008, America has embraced the values of progress, *Observer*, 9 November, www.guardian.co.uk/commentisfree/2008/nov/09/barack-obama-gordon-brown

Brown, W, 2005, Edgework, *Critical essays on knowledge and politics*, Princeton, NJ: Princeton University Press

BRTF (Better Regulation Task Force), 2005, *Regulation – less is more: Reducing burdens, improving outcomes*, London: Cabinet Office

Bryan, D, Martin, R, Montgomerie, J, Williams, K, 2012, An important failure: Knowledge limits and the financial crisis, *Economy and Society* 41, 3, 299–315

Bryman, A, 1988, *Quantity and quality in social research*, London: Unwin Hyman

Burdis, K, Tombs, S, 2012, After the crisis: New directions in theorising corporate and white-collar crime?, in S Hall, S Winlow (eds) *New directions in criminological theory*, pp 276–91, Cullompton: Willan

Burford, G, Adams, P, 2004, Restorative justice, responsive regulation and social work, *Journal of Sociology and Social Welfare* 31, 1, 7–26

Cabinet Office, 2006, New Bill to enable delivery of swift and efficient regulatory reform to cut red tape, Jim Murphy, *Cabinet Office news release 12 January*, London: Cabinet Office Press Office

Cabinet Office, 2011, *Guidance on reviews of non-departmental public bodies*, London: Cabinet Office, www.civilservice.gov.uk/wp-content/uploads/2011/09/triennial-reviews-guidance–2011_tcm6-38900.pdf

Cabinet Office, Better Regulation Unit, 1998, *The better regulation guide*, London: Cabinet Office

Cahill, D, 2011, Beyond neoliberalism? Crisis and the prospects for progressive alternatives, *New Political Science* 33, 4, 479–92

Cahill, D, 2014, *The end of laissez-faire? On the durability of embedded neoliberalism,* Cheltenham: Edward Elgar

Cameron, A, Palan, R, 2004, *The imagined economies of globalisation*, London: Sage

Cameron, D, 2013, Lord Mayor's Banquet 2013: Prime Minister's speech, 11 November, www.gov.uk/government/speeches/lord-mayors-banquet–2013-prime-ministers-speech

Campbell, B, 2014, *Willful blindness? Regulatory failures behind the Lac-Mégantic disaster*, Ottawa: Canadian Centre for Policy Alternatives

Campbell, C, Wiles, P, 1976, The study of law in society in Britain, *Law and Society Review* 10, 4, 547–78

CARR (Centre for Analysis of Risk and Regulation), 2008, *Financial crisis special*, London: CARR, London School of Economics and Political Science

Carr, A, 1985, Is business bluffing ethical?, in J desJardins, J McCall (eds) *Contemporary issues in business ethics*, pp 3–10, Belmont, CA: Wadsworth

Carrigan, C, Coglianese C, 2011, The politics of regulation: From new institutionalism to new governance, *Annual Review of Political Science* 14, 107–29, http://arjournals.annualreviews.org/eprint/pPY7G2avfgZ8ufSUx9pT/full/10.1146/annurev.polisci.032408.171344

Carson, WG, 1979, The conventionalization of early factory crime, *International Journal of the Sociology of Law* 7, 1, 37–60

Carson, WG, 1980a, Early factory inspectors and the viable class society: A rejoinder, *International Journal of the Sociology of Law* 8, 2, 187–91

Carson, WG, 1980b, The institutionalisation of ambiguity: Early British Factory Acts, in G Geis, E Stotland (eds) *White-collar crime: Theory and research*, pp 142–73, London: Sage

Centre for Local Economic Strategies, 2014a, *Austerity uncovered*, London: TUC

Centre for Local Economic Strategies, 2014b, *Summary of austerity in the North West and a case study of Blackpool Council*, London: TUC

Chernomas, R, Hudson, I, 2007, *Social murder and other shortcomings of Conservative economics*, Winnipeg: Arbeiter Ring Publishing

Chima, O, Langley, P, 2012, Putting Humpty Dumpty back together again: Financialisation and the management of the subprime mortgage crisis, *Global Society* 26, 4, 409–27

CIPFA (Chartered Institute of Public Finance and Accountancy), 2003, *Regulatory Services Statistics 2002–2003*, London: CIPFA, www.cipfa.org.uk

CIPFA, 2004, *Regulatory Services Statistics 2003–2004*, London: CIPFA, www.cipfa.org.uk

CIPFA, 2005, *Regulatory Services Statistics 2004–2005*, London: CIPFA, www.cipfa.org.uk

CIPFA, 2006, *Regulatory Services Statistics 2005–2006*, London: CIPFA, www.cipfa.org.uk

CIPFA, 2007, *Regulatory Services Statistics 2006–2007*, London: CIPFA, www.cipfa.org.uk

CIPFA, 2008, *Regulatory Services Statistics 2007–2008*, London: CIPFA, www.cipfa.org.uk

CIPFA, 2009, *Regulatory Services Statistics 2008–2009*, London: CIPFA, www.cipfa.org.uk

CIPFA, 2010, *Regulatory Services Statistics 2009–2010*, London: CIPFA, www.cipfa.org.uk

CIPFA, 2011, *Regulatory Services Statistics 2010–2011*, London: CIPFA, www.cipfa.org.uk

CIPFA, 2012a, *Regulatory Services Statistics 2011–2012*, London: CIPFA, www.cipfa.org.uk

CIPFA, 2012b, *The long downturn*, London: CIPFA, www.cipfa.org.uk

Clarke, J, 2010a, After neo-liberalism?, *Cultural Studies*, 24, 3, 375–94

Clarke, J, 2010b, Of crises and conjunctures: The problem of the present, *Journal of Communication Inquiry* 34, 4, 337–54

Clarke, J, 2012, What crisis is this?, in J Rutherford, S Davison (eds) *The neoliberal crisis*, pp 44–54, London: Soundings/Lawrence Wishart

Clarke, J, Newman, J, 2010, Summoning spectres: Crises and their construction, *Journal of Education Policy* 25, 6, 709–15

Clarke, J, Newman, J, 2012, The alchemy of austerity, *Critical Social Policy* 32, 3, 299–319

Clarkson, J, 2004, Health and safety and the death of television, *Sunday Times*, 11 April, www.thesundaytimes.co.uk/sto/news/Features/Focus/article217694.ece

Coakley, J, Harris, L, 1992, Financial globalisation and deregulation, in J Michie (ed) *The Economic Legacy, 1979–1992*, pp 37–59, London: Academic Press

Cohen, N, 2013, Bankers carry on unabashed, unscathed and unashamed, *Observer*, 7 April, www.guardian.co.uk/commentisfree/2013/apr/07/brtish-bankers-unpunished-unashamed

Cohen, S, 2011, *Folk devils and moral panics*, London: Routledge

Coleman, R, Sim, J, Tombs, S, Whyte, D, 2009, Introduction: State, power, crime, in R Coleman, J Sim, S Tombs, D Whyte, D (eds) *State, power, crime*, pp 1–19, London: Sage

Committee on the Medical Effects of Air Pollutants, 2010, *The mortality effects of long-term exposure to particulate air pollution in the United Kingdom*, http://webarchive.nationalarchives.gov.uk/20140714084352/www.hpa.org.uk/webc/HPAwebFile/HPAweb_C/1317137012567

Congressional Budget Office, 2012, *Report on the troubled asset relief program: March 2012*, www.cbo.gov/sites/default/files/03-28-2012TARP.pdf

Conservative Home, 2008, Labour has maxed out Britain's credit card, says Cameron, 9 November, http://conservativehome.blogs.com/torydiary/2008/11/labour-has-maxe.html

Conservative Home, 2011, Cameron post-riots speech in full, http://conservativehome.blogs.com/thetorydiary/2011/08/cameron-post-riots-speech-in-full.html

Conservatives, 2010a, *Invitation to join the government of Britain: The Conservative Party manifesto 2010*, London: The Conservative Party

Conservatives, 2010b, *Regulation in the Post-Bureaucratic Age*, www.conservatives.com/~/media/Files/Policy%20Documents/BetterRegulation.ashx?dl=true

Coslovsky, S, Pires, R, Silbey, S, 2010, The pragmatic politics of regulatory enforcement, *Jerusalem Papers in Regulation and Governance Working Paper* 29, Jerusalem: The Hebrew University

Crawford, R, Phillips, D, 2012, Local government spending: Where is the axe falling?, in C Emmerson, P Johnson, H Miller (eds) *Institute for Fiscal Studies (IFS) Green Budget 2012*, pp 124–41, London: IFS

CRESC (Centre for Research on Socio-Cultural Change), 2009, *An alternative report on UK banking reform*, Manchester: ESRC Centre for Research on Socio Cultural Change, The University of Manchester, www.cresc.ac.uk/sites/default/files/Alternative%20report%20on%20banking%20V2.pdf

Crouch, C, 2011, *The strange non-death of neoliberalism*, Cambridge: Polity

Crouch, C, 2012, Sustainability, neoliberalism and the moral quality of capitalism, *Business and Professional Ethics Journal* 31, 2, 363–74

Cutler, T, James, P, 1996, Does safety pay? A critical account of the Health and Safety Executive document: 'The costs of accidents', *Work, Employment and Society* 10, 4, 755–65

Dannreuther, C, 2013, *The enduring myth of the entrepreneur, ideology after the Crash*, 27 November, Leeds: University of Leeds

Datz, G, 2013, The narrative of complexity in the crisis of finance: Epistemological challenge and macroprudential policy response, *New Political Economy* 18, 4, 459–79

Davies, J, 2011, *Challenging governance theory: From networks to hegemony*, Bristol: The Policy Press

Davies, W, 2014, *The limits of neo-liberalism: Authority, sovereignty and the logic of competition*, Los Angeles, CA: Sage

Davies, W, McGoey, L, 2012, Rationalities of ignorance: On financial crisis and the ambivalence of neo-liberal epistemology, *Economy and Society* 41, 1, 64–83

Davis, C, 2000, *Corporate violence, regulatory agencies and the management and deflection of censure*, unpublished doctoral thesis, University of Southampton

Davis, C, 2004, *Making companies safe: What works*, London: Centre for Corporate Accountability

DCLG (Department for Communities and Local Government), 2013a, *Local authority revenue expenditure and financing: 2013–14 Budget, England. Local government finance statistical release*, 31 July, London: DCLG

DCLG (Department for Communities and Local Government), 2013b, *Increasing the number of available homes*, 20 August, www.gov.uk/government/policies/increasing-the-number-of-available-homes/supporting-pages/new-homes-bonus

Deacon, B, 2011, Global social policy responses to the economic crisis, in K Farnsworth, Z Irving (eds) *Social policy in challenging times: Economic crisis and welfare systems*, pp 81–100, Bristol: Policy Press

Deflem, M (ed), 2011, *Economic crisis and crime: Series in sociology of crime, law, and deviance*, Bingley: JAI Press/Emerald Publishing Group

Defra (Department for Environment, Food and Rural Affairs), 2001, *e-digest statistics about: Air quality: sulphur dioxide (SO2)*, http://webarchive nationalarchives.gov.uk/20130123162956/http:/www.defra.gov.uk/environment/statistics/airqual/download/pdf/aqtb08.pdf

Defra (Department for Environment, Food and Rural Affairs), 2012a, Discussion paper: Triennial review of the Environment Agency and Natural England, London: Defra

Defra (Department for Environment, Food and Rural Affairs), 2012b, *Environmental permitting: General guidance manual on policy and procedures for A2 and B installations. Local authority integrated pollution prevention and control (LA-IPPC) and local authority pollution prevention and control (LAPPC)*, revised April 2012, London: Defra

Defra (Department for Environment, Food and Rural Affairs), 2014a, *Defra official statistics release: Local pollution control statistics in England and Wales, 2003 to 2013*, London: Department for Environment, Food and Rural Affairs, www.gov.uk/government/uploads/system/uploads/attachment_data/file/323347/Management_summary_cleanv2.pdf

Defra (Department for Environment, Food and Rural Affairs), 2014b, *Statistical release, 25 June 2014*, London: Defra

Dienst, R, 2011, *The bonds of debt: Borrowing against the common good*, London: Verso

Dodds, A, 2006, The core executive's approach to regulation: From 'better regulation' to 'risk-tolerant deregulation', *Social Policy and Administration* 40, 5, 526–42

Dorey, P, 2009, 'Sharing the proceeds of growth': Conservative economic policy under David Cameron, *Political Quarterly* 80, 2, April–June, 259–69

Dorling, D, 2010, New Labour and inequality: Thatcherism continued?, *Local Economy* 25, 5–6 (August–September), 397–413

Dorling, D, 2014, *Inequality and the 1%*, London: Verso

Dorn, N, 2010, The Governance of Securities: Ponzi finance, regulatory convergence, credit crunch, *British Journal of Criminology*, 50, 23–45.

Dowell-Jones, M, 2013, Financial Institutions and human rights, *Human Rights Law Review* 13, 3, 423–68

Doyle, G, 2006, Financial news journalism: A post-Enron analysis of approaches towards economic and financial news production in the UK, *Journalism* 7, 4, 433–52

Duffy, S, 2013, *A fair society? How the cuts target disabled people*, Sheffield: The Centre for Welfare Reform, www.centreforwelfarereform.org/library/type/pdfs/a-fair-society1.html

DWP (Department for Work and Pensions), 2011a, Reforming Britain's health and safety regime to put common sense back, Press release, 21 March, www.gov.uk/government/news/reforming-britain-s-health-and-safety-regime-to-put-common-sense-back

DWP, 2011b, *The government response to the Löfstedt report*, November, www.kcl.ac.uk/sspp/departments/geography/people/academic/lofstedt/review/lofstedtUKgovresponse.pdf

DWP, 2011c, Reforming Britain's health and safety regime to put common sense back, Press release, www.gov.uk/government/news/reforming-britain-s-health-and-safety-regime-to-put-common-sense-back

DWP, 2011d, *Good health and safety, good for everyone: The next steps in the government's plans for reform of the health and safety system in Britain*, www.gov.uk/government/uploads/system/uploads/attachment_data/file/66745/good-health-and-safety.pdf

DWP, 2012, *The Work Programme*, www.gov.uk/government/uploads/system/uploads/attachment_data/file/49884/the-work-programme.pdf

Dymski, G, Hernandez, J, Mohanty, L, 2013, Race, gender, power, and the US subprime mortgage and foreclosure crisis: A meso analysis, *Feminist Economics* 19, 3, 124–51

Economist, 2013, *Reforming Britain's banks*, June 22, www.economist.com/news/britain/21579834-parliamentary-commission-attempts-nothing-less-fundamental-change-bankings

Edwards C, 2009a, *Private gain, public loss: The PFI and the Norfolk and Norwich University Hospital*, www.uea.ac.uk/polopoly_fs/1.116274!Private%20Gain%20and%20Public%20Loss%20-%20June%202009.pdf

Edwards, C, 2009b, *House of Lords Select Committee: Private Finance Projects and off-balance sheet debt. Supplementary memorandum by Dr Chris Edwards*, www.publications.parliament.uk/pa/ld200910/ldselect/ldeconaf/63/09111007.htm

Eikenberry, A, Kluver, J, 2004, The marketisation of the nonprofit sector: Civil society at risk?, *Public Administration Review* 64, 2, 132–40

Elliott, L, Atkinson, D, 2007, *Fantasy island: Waking up to the incredible economic, political and social illusions of the blair legacy*, London: Constable

Engels, F, 1850, The English Ten Hours' Bill, *Neue Rheinische Zeitung Politisch-Ökonomische Revue*, no. 4, English translation, https://marxists.anu.edu.au/archive/marx/works/1850/03/10hours.htm

Environment Agency, 2012, *Environment Agency annual report and accounts 2011 to 2012*, HC 360, London: The Stationery Office

Environment Agency, 2013, *Environment Agency annual report and accounts, 2012–2013*, London: The Stationery Office.

Environment Agency, 2014, *Annual report and accounts for the financial year 2013 to 2014*, HC 357, London: Her Majesty's Stationery Office

Epstein, G, 2005, Introduction: Financialization and the world economy, in G Epstein (ed) *Financialization and the world economy*, pp 1–13, Cheltenham: Edward Elgar

European Commission, 2010, *Lisbon Strategy evaluation document*, Brussels: European Commission, http://ec.europa.eu/archives/growthandjobs_2009/pdf/lisbon_strategy_evaluation_en.pdf

Evans-Pritchard, A, 2010, Fears of 'Lehman-style' tsunami as crisis hits Spain and Portugal, *Telegraph*, 4 February, www.telegraph.co.uk/finance/financialcrisis/7159456/Fears-of-Lehman-style-tsunami-as-crisis-hits-Spain-and-Portugal.html

Fairman, R, Yapp, C, 2004, Compliance with food safety legislation in small and micro-businesses: Enforcement as an external motivator, *Journal of Environmental Health Research* 3, 2, www.cieh.org/jehr/jehr3.aspx?id=11454 and LangType=2057

Fairman, R, Yapp, C, 2005, Enforced self-regulation, prescription, and conceptions of compliance within small businesses: The impact of enforcement, *Law and Policy* 2, 491–519

Farnsworth, K, 2006a, Globalisation, business and British public policy, *Contemporary Politics* 12, 1, 79–93

Farnsworth, K, 2006b, Capital to the rescue? New Labour's business solutions to old welfare problems, *Critical Social Policy* 26, 4, 817–42

Farnsworth, K, 2012, *Social versus corporate welfare: Competing needs and interests within the welfare state*, New York: Palgrave Macmillan

Farnsworth, K, 2013, Public policies for private corporations: The British corporate welfare state, *Renewal. A Journal of Social Democracy* 21, 4, 51–65

Farnsworth, K, Fooks, G, 2015, Corporate taxation, corporate power, and corporate harm, *The Howard Journal of Criminal Justice* 44, 1, 25–41

Farnsworth, K, Holden, C, 2006, The business–social policy nexus: Corporate power and corporate inputs into social policy, *Journal of Social Policy*, 35, 3, 473–94

Fee, E, Brown, TM, 2005, *The Public Health Act of 1848: Bulletin of the World Health Organization* 83, 11, 866–7

Finch, J, 2009, Walker report a 'crashing disappointment', *Guardian*, 26 November

Fisher, M, 2009, *Capitalist realism: Is there really no alternative?*, Winchester: Zero Books

Fleming, P, Jones, M, 2013, *The end of corporate social responsibility: Crisis and critique*, London: Sage

Flyvbjerg, B, 2006, Five misunderstandings about case-study research, *Qualitative Inquiry* 12, 2, 219–45

Fooks, G, 1999, *The serious fraud office: A police force of the city or a police force for the city?*, British Society of Criminology Conference, 15 July, Liverpool: Liverpool John Moores University

Forbes, N, Dore, J, Anderson, J, 2012, Spending cuts will create social unrest in our cities, *Observer*, 30 December, www.theguardian.com/theobserver/2012/dec/29/letters-coalition-cuts-threaten-cities.

Fox Piven, F, 2012, Beating back the corporate attack, *New Political Science* 34, 1, 81–90

Frederick, W, 2006, *Corporation, be good! The story of corporate social responsibility*, Indianapolis, IN: Dog Ear

Frank, T, 2001, *One nation under God: Extreme capitalism, market populism and the end of market democracy*, London: Secker & Warburg

French, M, Phillips, J, 2000, *Cheated not poisoned? Food regulation in the United* Kingdom, 1875–1938, Manchester: Manchester University Press

Frerichs, S, 2013, From credit to crisis: Max Weber, Karl Polanyi, and the other side of the coin, *Journal of Law and Society. Special Issue: Towards an Economic Sociology of Law* 40, 7–26

Friedman, M, 1970, The social responsibility of business is to make profits, *The New York Times Magazine*, September 13, 32–3, 122–6

Friedrichs, D, 2011, Occupy Wall Street does have a clear message. Commentary: A call to recognize the crimes of High Finance, *Marketwatch*, 24 October, www.marketwatch.com/story/occupy-wall-street-does-have-a-clear-message–2011-10-24

Froud, J, Nilsson, A, Moran, M, Williams, K, 2012, Stories and interests in finance: Agendas of governance before and after the financial crisis, *Governance: An International Journal of Policy, Administration and Institutions* 25, 1, January, 35–59

Fryzel, B, 2011, *Building stakeholder relationships and corporate social responsibility*, Basingstoke: Palgrave

FSA (Food Standards Agency), 2006, *Food Law enforcement by local authorities: The New Vision*, PRO 06/10/02 Agenda Item 4.2, 12 October, http://tna. europarchive.org/20110116113217/www.food.gov.uk/multimedia/pdfs/pro061002a.pdf

FSA, 2009, *INFO 09/02/01: UK local authority food law enforcement – April 2007 to March 2008*, 10 February, http://tna.europarchive.org/20120419000433/www.food.gov.uk/multimedia/pdfs/board/info090201.pdf

FSA, 2010, *FSA 10/03/09: UK local authority food law enforcement 1 April 2008 to 31 March 2009*, 10 March, www.food.gov.uk/sites/default/files/multimedia/pdfs/board/fsa100309v3.pdf

FSA, 2012, *Annual report of the Chief Scientist, Food Standards Agency*, www.food.gov.uk/multimedia/pdfs/publication/csar1112.pdf

FSA, 2015, *Campylobacter survey: Cumulative results from the full 12 months (Q1–Q4)*, www.food.gov.uk/news-updates/news/2015/14003/campylobacter-survey-results-12months

FSA, (nd) *The second study of infectious intestinal disease in the community (IID2 Study)*, www.foodbase.org.uk/results.php?f_report_id=711

Furness, H, 2012, Regulating the banks: What politicians used to say about the City, *Telegraph*, 4 July, www.telegraph.co.uk/news/politics/9376534/Regulating-the-banks-what-politicians-used-to-say-about-the-City.html

Galtung, J, 1969, Violence, peace, and peace research, *Journal of Peace Research* 6, 3, 167–91

Galtung, J, Hoivik, T, 1971, Structural and direct violence: A note on operationalization, *Journal of Peace Research* 8, 1, 73–6

Gamble, A, 2009, *The spectre at the feast: Capitalist crisis and the politics of recession*, Basingstoke: Palgrave Macmillan

Gamble, A, 2015, Austerity as statecraft, *Parliamentary Affairs* 68, 1, 42–57

Garfinkel, H, 1956, Conditions of successful degradation ceremonies, *American Journal of Sociology* 61, 420–4

Garrett, P, 2012, Adjusting 'our notions of the nature of the state': A political reading of Ireland's child protection crisis, *Capital and Class* 362, 263–81

Garside, R, 2013, Addressing social harm: Better regulation versus social transformation, *Revista Crítica Penal y Poder*, Special Issue: Redefining the Criminal Matter, 5, 247–65

Garsten, C, Jacobsson, K, 2013, Post-political regulation: Soft power and post-political visions in global governance, *Critical Sociology* 39, 3, 421–37

Garwood, C, 2004, Green crusaders or captives of industry? The British alkali inspectorate and the ethics of environmental decision making, 1864–95, *Annals of Science* 61, 1, 99–117

Geras, N, 1972, Marx and the critique of political economy, in R Blackburn, R (ed) *Ideology in social science: Readings in critical social theory*, pp 284–305, London: Fontana

Giddens, A, 1998, *The Third Way: The renewal of social democracy*, Cambridge: Polity

Gigliotti, M, 2013, The compensation of top managers and the performance of Italian firms, *International Journal of Human Resource Management* 24, 4, 889–903

Gill, S, Law, D, 1993, Global hegemony and the structural power of capital, in S Gill (ed) *Gramsci, historical materialism and international relations*, pp 93–124, Cambridge: Cambridge University Press

Giroux, H, 2008, *Against the terror of neoliberalism: Politics beyond the age of greed*, Boulder, CO: Paradigm Publishers

Giroux, H, 2014, *The violence of organized forgetting: Thinking beyond America's disimagination machine*, Sac Francisco, CA: City Lights Books

Glasbeek, HJ, 1988, The corporate social responsibility movement: The latest in the Maginot Lines to save capitalism, *Dalhousie Law Journal* 11, 2, 363–402

Glasbeek, H, 2002, *Wealth by stealth: Corporate crime, corporate law and the perversion of democracy*, Toronto: Between the Lines

Goffman, E, 1963, *Stigma*, New York: Simon and Schuster

Gold, T, 2011, The deification of Steve Jobs is Apple's greatest marketing triumph to date, *Guardian*, 21 October

Gorman, T (ed), 2000, *Clydebank. Asbestos: The unwanted legacy*, Clydebank: Clydebank Asbestos Partnership

Grabosky, P, Shover, N, 2010, Editorial conclusion. Forestalling the next epidemic of white-collar crime: Linking policy to theory, *Criminology and Public Policy. Special Issue: The Global Economy, Economic Crisis, and White-Collar Crime* 9, 641–54

Graham, A, 1997, The UK 1979–95: Myths and realities of Conservative capitalism, in C Crouch, W Streeck (eds) *Political economy of modern capitalism: Mapping convergence and diversity*, pp 117–33, London: Sage

Gramsci, A, 1971, *Selections from the Prison Notebooks*, London: Lawrence and Wishart, 1996

Grayson, D, Hodges, A, 2004, *Corporate social opportunity! Seven steps to make corporate social responsibility work for your business*, Sheffield: Greenleaf Publishing

Greater Manchester Air Quality Steering Group, 2002, *Greater Manchester air quality action plan* (draft), Manchester: Association of Greater Manchester Authorities

Green, J, Lavery, S, 2015, The regressive recovery: Distribution, inequality and state power in Britain's post-crisis political economy, *New Political Economy*, doi:10.1080/13563467.2015.1041478

Green, P, Ward, T, 2009, Violence and the state, in R Coleman, J Sim, S Tombs, D Whyte (eds) *State, power, crime*, pp 116–28, London: Sage

Grigg-Spall, I, Ireland, P (eds), 1992, *The critical lawyers' handbook*, London: Pluto

Guardian, 2012, Financial crisis, five years on: Trust in banking hits new low, 9 August, www.guardian.co.uk/business/2012/aug/09/financial-crisis-anniversary-trust-in-banks

Guardian, 2013, How Britain changed under Margaret Thatcher, www.theguardian.com/politics/datablog/2013/apr/08/britain-changed-margaret-thatcher-charts#economy

Gunningham, N, Grabosky, P, 1998, *Smart regulation: Designing environmental policy*, Oxford: Clarendon

Gunningham, N, Johnstone, R, 1999, *Regulating workplace safety: Systems and sanctions*, Oxford: Oxford University Press

Haines, F, 2011, *The paradox of regulation: What regulation can achieve and what it cannot*, Cheltenham: Edward Elgar

Haiven, M, 2014, *Crises of imagination, crises of power: Capitalism, creativity and the commons*, London: Zed Books

Hall, S, 1988, *The hard road to renewal: Thatcherism and the crisis of the Left*, London: Verso

Hall, Steve, 2012, *Theorising crime and deviance: A new perspective*, London: Sage

Hall, Stuart, 2012, The neoliberal revolution, in J Rutherord, S Davison (eds) *The neoliberal crisis*, pp 8–26, London: Soundings

Hall, S, Winlow, S, 2012, What is an 'ethics committee'? Academic governance in an epoch of belief and incredulity, *British Journal of Criminology* 52, 400–16

Hall, S, Critcher, C, Jefferson, T, Clarke, J, Roberts, B, 1978, *Policing the crisis: Mugging, the State, and law and order*, Basingstoke: Macmillan

Hämäläinen, P, Saarela, K, Takala, J, 2009, Global trend according to estimated number of occupational accidents and fatal work-related diseases at region and country level, *Journal of Safety Research* 40, 125–39

Hamlin, C, Sheard, S, 1998, Revolutions in public health: 1848, and 1998?, *British Medical Journal* 317, 29 August, 587–91

Hampton, P, 2005, *Reducing administrative burdens: Effective inspection and enforcement*, London: HM Treasury/HMSO

Hanlon, G, Fleming, P, 2009, Updating the critical perspective on corporate social responsibility, *Sociology Compass* 3 , 6, 937–48

Hansen, P, 2014, From finance capitalism to financialization: A cultural and narrative perspective on 150 years of financial history, *Enterprise and* Society 15, 4, 605–42

Harcourt, B, 2010, Neoliberal penality: A brief genealogy, *Theoretical Criminology* 14, 1, 74–92

Hargreaves, B, 1975, *The company and its responsibilities*, London: Foundation for Business Responsibilities

Harris, D, 1983, The development of socio-legal studies in the United Kingdom, *Legal Studies* 3, 3, 315–33

Harris, J, 2012a, Emma Harrison: Nice work if you can get it, *Guardian G2*, 22 February

Harris, J, 2012b, Credit crunch: Elusive ghosts of the financial feast lurk in the shadows, *Guardian*, 7 August, www.guardian.co.uk/business/2012/aug/06/credit-crunch-elusive-ghosts-shadows

Harris, R, Milkis, S, 1989, *The politics of regulatory change: A tale of two agencies*, Oxford: Oxford University Press

Hartley McMaster Ltd, 2003, *Local pollution control statistical survey: Management summary*, http://collections.europarchive.org/tna/20031220221853/www.defra.gov.uk/environment/airquality/lapc/survey0203/default.htm

Hartley McMaster Ltd, 2005, *Local pollution control statistical survey: Management summary*, http://collections.europarchive.org/tna/20050301192907/www.defra.gov.uk/environment/airquality/lapc/survey0304/index.htm

Hartley McMaster Ltd, 2006, *Local pollution control statistical survey: Management summary*, http://collections.europarchive.org/tna/20060213205513/www.defra.gov.uk/environment/airquality/lapc/survey0405/index.htm

Hartley McMaster Ltd, 2007, *Local pollution control statistical survey: Management summary*, http://collections.europarchive.org/tna/20070101084356/www.defra.gov.uk/environment/airquality/lapc/survey0506/index.htm

Hartley McMaster Ltd, 2008, *Local pollution control statistical survey: Management summary*, http://collections.europarchive.org/tna/20080108002802/www.defra.gov.uk/environment/ppc/localauth/pubs/reports/index.htm#stats0607

Hartley McMaster Ltd, 2009, *Local pollution control statistical survey: Management summary*, http://collections.europarchive.org/tna/20090104192617/www.defra.gov.uk/environment/ppc/localauth/pubs/reports/index.htm#stats0607

Hartley McMaster Ltd, 2010, *Local pollution control statistical survey: Management summary*, http://collections.europarchive.org/tna/20100304151012/www.defra.gov.uk/environment/quality/pollution/ppc/localauth/pubs/reports/index.htm#stats0809

Hartley McMaster Ltd, 2011, *Local pollution control statistical survey: Management summary*, http://collections.europarchive.org/tna/20110108201415/http://ww2.defra.gov.uk/environment/quality/industrial/las-regulations/reports-surveys-reviews-newsletters/

Hartley McMaster Ltd, 2012, *Local pollution control statistical survey: Management summary*, http://collections.europarchive.org/tna/20120104121013/www.defra.gov.uk/environment/quality/industrial/las-regulations/reports-surveys-reviews-newsletters/

Harvey, D, 2009, Is this really the end of neoliberalism?, *Counterpunch* 14–15 March, www.counterpunch.org/2009/03/13/is-this-really-the-end-of-neoliberalism/

Hastings, A, Bailey, N, Besemer, K, Bramley, G, Gannon, M, Watkins, D, 2013, *Coping with the cuts? Local government and poorer communities*, York: The Joseph Rowntree Foundation

Hawkes, S, Pascoe-Watson, G, 2009, Scumbag millionaires: As 2,300 RBS staff lose their jobs, shamed bank bosses 'sorry' for crisis, *The Sun*, 11 February

Hawkins, K, 1984, *Environment and enforcement*, Oxford: Clarendon

Hawkins, K, 1990, Compliance strategy, prosecution policy and Aunt Sally: A comment on Pearce and Tombs, *British Journal of Criminology* 30, 444–66

Hawkins, K, 1991, Enforcing regulation: More of the same from Pearce and Tombs, *British Journal of Criminology* 31, 427–30

Hawkins, K, 2002, *Law as a last resort: Prosecution decision making in a regulatory authority*, Oxford: Oxford University Press

Hay, C, 2004, The normalizing role of rationalist assumptions in the institutional embedding of neoliberalism, *Economy and Society* 33, 4, 500–27

Hay, C, Watson, M, 1998, The discourse of globalisation and the logic of no alternative: Rendering the contingent necessary in the downsizing of New Labour's aspirations for government, in A Dobson and J Stanyer (eds) *Contemporary political studies 1998*, Volume II, pp 812–22, Nottingham: Political Studies Association

Health Protection Agency, 2012, Analysis of general foodborne outbreaks shows campylobacter as the leading cause in England and Wales in 2011, *News Archives* 6, 18, 4 May, www.hpa.org.uk/hpr/archives/2012/news1812.htm#efoss

Heffer, S, 2004, Postperson Pat and his ethnically diverse cat!, *Daily Mail*, 21 July

Helleiner, E, Thistlethwaite, J, 2013, Subprime catalyst: Financial regulatory reform and the strengthening of US carbon market governance, *Regulation and governance. Regulating finance after the crisis: Unveiling the different dynamics of the regulatory process* 7, 496–511

Helm, D, 2012, Top officials in Newcastle, Liverpool and Sheffield call for halt to 'unfair' measures and say North–South divide will widen, *Observer*, 30 December, www.theguardian.com/politics/2012/dec/29/cuts-councils-newcastle-liverpool-sheffield

Helms, M, Vastrup, P, Gerner-Smidt, P, Molbak, K, 2003, Short and long term mortality associated with foodborne bacterial gastrointestinal infections: Registry based study, *British Medical Journal* 15 February, 326, 357–60

Henriksen, L, 2013, Economic models as devices of policy change: Policy paradigms, paradigm shift, and performativity, *Regulation and governance. Regulating finance after the crisis: Unveiling the different dynamics of the regulatory process*, 7, 481–95

High Pay Commission, 2011a, *More for Less: What has happened to pay at the top and does it matter?*, May, http://highpaycommission.co.uk/wp-content/uploads/2011/09/HPC-IR.pdf

High Pay Commission, 2011b, *Cheques with balances: Why tackling high pay is in the national interest. Final report of the High Pay Commission*, November, http://highpaycentre.org/files/Cheques_with_Balances.pdf

HM Government, 2010a, *Reducing regulation made simple: Less regulation, better regulation and regulation as a last resort*, London: BIS (Department for Business, Innovation and Skills), www.gov.uk/government/uploads/system/uploads/attachment_data/file/31626/10-1155-reducing-regulation-made-simple.pdf

HM Government, 2010b, Independent regulatory policy committee remit strengthened for external scrutiny role of new regulatory proposals, Press release, 6 August, www.gov.uk/government/uploads/system/uploads/attachment_data/file/251225/August-8–2010-press-release.pdf

HM Government, 2011, *Sunsetting regulations: Guidance*, London: BIS (Department for Business, Innovation and Skills)

HM Treasury, 2004, *Chancellor of the Exchequer's budget statement*, http://webarchive.nationalarchives.gov.uk/20061009151550/http://hm-treasury.gov.uk/budget/budget_04/bud_bud04_speech.cfm

HM Treasury, 2006, *Implementing Hampton: From enforcement to compliance*, London: HM Treasury

Holden, C, 1999, Globalization: Social exclusion and Labour's new work ethic, *Critical Social Policy* 19, 4, 529–38

Holloway, J, 1994, Global capital and the nation-state, *Capital and Class* 52, Spring, 23–49

Hope, C, 2010, Health and Safety rules should be removed from offices, says David Cameron adviser, *Telegraph*, 14 June, www.telegraph.co.uk/news/politics/7826183/Health-and-safety-rules-should-be-removed-from-offices-says-David-Cameron-adviser.html

Hope, C, 2013, Health and Safety rules stopping children getting work experience in companies, says David Cameron, *Telegraph*, 3 January, www.telegraph.co.uk/news/politics/9778959/Health-and-safety-rules-stopping-children-getting-work-experience-in-companies-says-David-Cameron.html.

Horton, T, 2010, Vince Cable is a neoliberal democrat, *Guardian*, 4 June, www.guardian.co.uk/commentisfree/2010/jun/04/vince-cable-tory-songbook

House of Commons Environment, Food and Rural Affairs Committee, 2006a, *The Environment Agency: Seventh report of Session 2005–06. Volume I: Report, together with formal minutes and lists of oral and written evidence*, HC 780-I, London: The Stationery Office

House of Commons Environment, Food and Rural Affairs Committee, 2006b, *The Environment Agency: Seventh report of Session 2005–06. Volume II: Oral and written evidence*, HC 780-II, London: The Stationery Office

House of Commons Environmental Audit Committee, 2010. *Fifth report, Air quality*, www.publications.parliament.uk/pa/cm200910/cmselect/cmenvaud/229/229i.pdf

House of Commons Environmental Audit Committee, 2011. *Ninth report, Air quality: A follow up report*, www.publications.parliament.uk/pa/cm201012/cmselect/cmenvaud/1024/102402.htm

House of Commons Treasury Committee, 2008, Treasury committee outlines terms of reference for inquiry into the banking crisis and calls for evidence, Press notice, 25 November, www.parliament.uk/business/committees/committees-archive/treasury-committee/tc0708pn85/

House of Commons Treasury Committee, 2009a, *Banking crisis: The impact of the failure of the Icelandic banks. Fifth report of Session 2008–09*, London: The Stationery Office Limited, www.publications.parliament.uk/pa/cm200809/cmselect/cmtreasy/402/402.pdf

House of Commons Treasury Committee, 2009b, *Banking crisis: Dealing with the failure of the UK banks. Seventh report of Session 2008–09*, London: The Stationery Office Limited, www.publications.parliament.uk/pa/cm200809/cmselect/cmtreasy/416/416.pdf

House of Commons Treasury Committee, 2009c, *Banking crisis: Reforming corporate governance and pay in the City. Ninth report of Session 2008–09*, London: The Stationery Office Limited, www.publications.parliament.uk/pa/cm200809/cmselect/cmtreasy/519/519.pdf

House of Commons Treasury Committee, 2009d, *Banking crisis: Regulation and supervision. Fourteenth report of Session 2008–09*, London: The Stationery Office Limited, www.publications.parliament.uk/pa/cm200809/cmselect/cmtreasy/767/767.pdf

House of Lords and House of Commons, 2013, *Changing banking for good: Report of the Parliamentary Commission on Banking Standards. Volume I: Summary, and conclusions and recommendations*, HL Paper 27-I, HC 175-I, London: The Stationery Office Limited

HSC (Health and Safety Commission), 2005, *Health and Safety Commission annual report and the Health and Safety Commission/Executive Accounts 2004/05*, London: The Stationery Office

HSE (Health and Safety Executive), 2005, We need a common sense approach to risk management – Hunt, Press release E094:05 13 July, www.hse.gov.uk/press/2005/e05094.htm

HSE, 2011, Public urged to 'restore sanity' to Health and Safety Rulebook, Press release, 27 June, www.hse.gov.uk/press/2011/hse-redtape challenge.htm

HSE, 2012a, *Prosecutions (2011/12p). Enforcement action taken by HSE, local authorities and, in Scotland, the Crown Office and Procurator Fiscal Service (2011/12p)*, www.hse.gov.uk/statistics/prosecutions.pdf,

HSE, 2012b, *Health and safety statistics, 2011/12*, London: The Stationery Office

HSE, 2014a, *Health and safety statistics 2013/14*, London: HSE

HSE, 2014b, *Statistics on fatal injuries in the workplace in Great Britain 2014: Full-year details and technical notes*, www.hse.gov.uk/statistics/pdf/fatalinjuries.pdf

HSE, 2014c, *The Health and Safety Executive annual report and accounts 2013/14*, HC228, London: Her Majesty's Stationery Office

HSE, LACORS, 2006, *HSE LACORS working together: Annual report 2006*, www.hse.gov.uk/lau/pdfs/lacors06.pdf

HSE, LACORS, 2008, *HSE LACORS working together: Partnership annual report 2007*, www.hse.gov.uk/lau/pdfs/lacors07ar.pdf

HSE, LACORS (nd) *Annual report 2005: LAs and HSE working together*, www.hse.gov.uk/lau/pdfs/worktog2005.pdf

HSE, Local Authority Enforcement Liaison Committee, 2013, HELA inspection/visit data collection from local authorities, Paper by Julie Sharman (LAU), Paper H14/01, HELA Board Meeting 17 January, www.hse.gov.uk/aboutus/meetings/committees/hela/170113/h14-01.pdf

HSE, Local Government Group, 2011, *Joint guidance for reduced proactive inspections*, www.hse.gov.uk/lau/pdfs/reduced-proactive-inspections.pdf

HSE, Local Government Regulation, 2010, *HSE LA annual partnership report 2009/10*, Sudbury: HSE

Huisman, W, 2012/2013, White-collar crime and the economic crisis, *ESC Newsletter*, 8–12, www.escnewsletter.org

Hutter, B, 1988, *The reasonable arm of the law? The law enforcement procedures of Environmental Health officers*, Oxford: Clarendon

Hutter, B, 2001, *Regulation and risk: Occupational health and safety on the railways*, Oxford: Oxford University Press

Hutter, B, 2005, The attractions of risk-based regulation: Accounting for the emergence of risk ideas in regulation, *Centre for Analysis of Risk and Regulation (CARR) discussion paper* 33, London: CARR, London School of Economics and Political Science

Hutter, B, 2006, The role of non-state actors in regulation, *Centre for Analysis of Risk and Regulation (CARR) discussion paper* 37, London: CARR, London School of Economics and Political Science

Hutter, B, 2011a, *Managing food safety and hygiene: Governance and regulation as risk management*, Cheltenham: Edward Elgar

Hutter, B, 2011b, Understanding the new regulatory governance: Business perspectives, *Law and Policy* 33, 4, 459–76

Hutter, B, Amodu, T, 2008, *Risk regulation and compliance: Food safety in the UK*, London: London School of Economics and Political Science

Hutter, B, Dodd, N, 2008, Social systems failure? Trust and the credit crunch, in *CARR on crisis: Risk and regulation*, December, 4–5, London: Centre for Analysis of Risk and Regulation (CARR), London School of Economics and Political Science

Hutter, B, Jones, C, 2006, *Business risk management practices: The influence of state regulatory agencies and non-state sources*, London: Centre for Analysis of Risk and Regulation (CARR), London School of Economics and Political Science

Hutton, W, 1995, *The state we're in*, London: Jonathan Cape

IFS (Institute for Fiscal Studies), 2015, This government has delivered substantial spending cuts: Big differences in parties' plans for next parliament, http://election2015.ifs.org.uk/public-spending

Illman, J, 2011a, Authorities forced into biggest reserves raid for a decade, *Local Government Chronicle*, 7 April

Illman, J, 2011b, Councils forced to live on financial brink, *Local Government Chronicle*, 17 November

Ingham, G.K, 1984, *Capitalism divided? The city and industry in British social development*, Basingstoke: Macmillan

Ireland, P, Pillay, R, 2009, Corporate social responsibility in a neoliberal age, in P Utting, J Marques (eds) *Corporate social responsibility and regulatory governance*, pp 77-104, Basingstoke: Palgrave Macmillan

Ireland, P, 2009, Financialization and corporate governance, *Northern Ireland Legal Quarterly* 60, 1, 1–34

Jackson, W, 2011, Liberal intellectuals and the politics of security, in M Neocleous, G Rigakos (eds) *Anti-security*, pp 165-89, Ottawa: Red Quill Books

Jackson, W, 2013, The desocialising of economic theory, *International Journal of Social Economics* 40, 9, 809–25

Jacoby, R, 2005, *Picture imperfect: Utopian thought for an anti-Utopian age*, New York: Columbia University Press

Jacobzone, S, Bounds, G, Choi, C-W, Miguet, C, 2007, Regulatory management systems across OECD countries: Indicators of recent achievements and challenges, *OECD Working Papers on Public Governance* 9, Paris: OECD

James, P, Walters, D, 2002, Worker representation in health and safety: Options for regulatory reform, *Industrial Relations Journal* 33, 2, 141–56

James, P, Tombs, S, Whyte, D, 2013, An independent review of British health and safety regulation? From common-sense to non-sense, *Policy and Politics* 34, 1, 36–52

Jenkins, S, 2009, Name, shame, blame the bankers, if you like: But they're the wrong target, *Guardian*, 26 November

Jessop, B, 2013, Putting neoliberalism in its time and place: A response to the debate, *Social Anthropology/Anthropologie Sociale* 21, 1, 65–74

Jessop, B, 2014, The free economy and the sovereign state, *Renewal* 22, 3, 5, www.renewal.org.uk/articles/the-limits-of-neo-liberalism

Job, J, Stout, A, Smith, R, 2007, Culture change in three taxation administrations: From command-and-control to responsive regulation, *Law and Policy* 29, 1, 84–101

Johnson, S, 2009, The quiet coup, *The Atlantic*, May, www.theatlantic.com/magazine/archive/2009/05/the-quiet-coup/7364/2/?single_page=true

Jones, C, Spicer, A, 2009, *Unmasking the entrepreneur*, Cheltenham, UK: Edward Elgar

Kagan, R, Scholz, J, 1984, The criminology of the corporation and regulatory enforcement strategies, in K Hawkins, J Thomas (eds) *Enforcing Regulation*, pp 67–95, Boston: Kluwer-Nijhoff

Kanter, J, 2013, Europe's finance chiefs reject British move to ease caps on bank bonuses, *New York Times*, 5 March, www.nytimes.com/2013/03/06/business/global/britain-isolated-as-european-colleagues-support-bonus-caps.html

Keeling, R, 2013a, Reserves raided as cuts bite, *Local Government Chronicle*, 1 August, www.lgcplus.com/news/reserves-raided-as-cuts-bite/5061850.article

Keeling, R, 2013b, Early figures reveal cuts of 16% for some councils, *Local Government Chronicle*, 8 August

Kelly, L, Boyle, R, 2010, Business on television: Continuity, change and risk in the development of television's 'business entertainment format', *Television and New Media*, http://eprints.gla.ac.uk/32248/

Kelman, J, 1992, A note on the war being waged by the state against the victims of asbestos, in J Kelman (ed) *Some recent attacks: Essays cultural and political*, pp 59–63, Stirling: AK Press

Kelsey, D, 2014, The myth of the City trickster: Storytelling, bankers and ideology in the Mail Online, *Journal of Political Ideologies* 19, 3, 307–30

Kettle, M, 2011, The banks needed Scarman's cold eye, but Vickers blinked, *Guardian*, 14 April, www.guardian.co.uk/commentisfree/2011/apr/14/vickers-look-banking-crisis-eye?INTCMP=SRCH0

Klein, N, 2000, *No logo*, New York: Picador

Klonoski, R. J, 1991, Foundational considerations in the corporate social responsibility debate, *Business Horizons*, 34, 4 (July/August), 9–18

Kolko, G, 1963, *The triumph of conservatism: A reinterpretation of American History, 1900–1916*, New York: The Free Press

Konzelmann, S, 2014, The political economics of austerity, *Cambridge Journal of Economics* 38, 701–41

KPMG, 2013, *Moving on: The scope for better regulation*, London: KPMG

Kramer, RC, 1989, Criminologists and the social movement against corporate crime, *Social Justice* 16, 2, 146-64

Labour Party, 2010, *The Labour Party manifesto: A future fair for all*, London: The Labour Party

Lakoff, G, 2002, *Moral politics*, Chicago, IL: Chicago University Press

Lakoff, G, Halpin, J, 2005, Framing Katrina, *American Prospect*, 7 October, http://prospect.org/article/framing-katrina-0

Lambie, G, 2013, Globalisation before the crash: The City of London and UK economic strategy, *Contemporary Politics* 19, 3, 339–60

Lansley, S, 2012, *The cost of inequality: Why economic equality is better for recovery*, London: Gibson Square

Lansley, S, Mack, J, 2015, *Breadline Britain: The rise of mass poverty*, London: Oneworld Publications

Lapavitsas, C, 2011, Support the campaign to audit Europe's public debt, *Guardian*, 3 March, www.theguardian.com/commentisfree/2011/mar/03/audit-europe-public-debt

Lapavitsas, C, 2014a, Finance's hold on our everyday life must be broken, *Guardian*, 2 January, www.theguardian.com/commentisfree/2014/jan/01/finance-hold-everyday-life-broken-capitalism

Lapavitsas, C, 2014b, Interview with CJ Polychroniou, *Truthout*, 26 January, www.truth-out.org/news/item/21383-costas-lapavitsas-discusses-the-financialization-of-capitalism

Lawrence, F, Wasley, A, Ciorniciuc, R, 2014, Revealed: The dirty secret of the UK's poultry industry, *Guardian*, 23 July, www.theguardian.com/world/2014/jul/23/-sp-revealed-dirty-secret-uk-poultry-industry-chicken-campylobacter

Lea, R, 2006, Personal view: Labour doesn't see that 'better regulation' is an oxymoron, *Telegraph*, 12 June, www.telegraph.co.uk/finance/2940847/Personal-view-Labour-doesnt-see-that-better-regulation-is-an-oxymoron.html

Legislative and Regulatory Reform Act 2006, Chapter 51, www.legislation.gov.uk/ukpga/2006/51/pdfs/ukpga_20060051_en.pdf

Levi, M, 2009, Suite revenge? The shaping of folk devils and moral panics about white-collar crimes, *British Journal of Criminology* 49, 1, 48–67

Leys, C, 2001, *Market-driven politics*, London: Verso

Linebaugh, P, 2001, Plenary. Does History Matter?, *Writing on the Wall*, Liverpool, 21 June.

Lippert, R, Williams, J, 2012, 'Taking exception: The cases of financial and urban governance', *Social and Legal Studies*, 21, 51-72

Liverpool City Council, 2014, *Liverpool economic briefing 2014. A monitor of jobs, business and economic growth*, http://liverpool.gov.uk/media/800053/Liverpool-economic-briefing–2014.pdf

LBRO (Local Better Regulation Office), 2009, *Primary authority guidance: Regulatory Enforcement and Sanctions Act 2008*, Birmingham: LBRO

LBRO (Local Better Regulation Office), 2011, *Priority regulatory outcomes: A new approach to refreshing the national enforcement priorities for local authority regulatory services. Final report*, London: LBRO

Local Government Association, 2013a, *Future funding outlook for councils from 2010/11 to 2019/20*, London: Local Government Association

Local Government Association, 2013b, *Local government finance: Briefing for leaders, lead members and chief executives*, 13 July 2013, www.local.gov.uk/c/document_library/get_file?uuid=9b8997c2-64cf-4e56-889b-03a03b4dd730 and groupId=10180

Local Government Lawyer, 2012, *Parliament approves creation of Better Regulation Delivery Office as successor to LBRO*, 8 February, www.localgovernmentlawyer.co.uk/index.php?option=com_content and view=article and id=9295:parliament-approves-creation-of-better-regulation-delivery-office-as-successor-to-lbro and catid=1:latest-stories

Lodge, M, 2008, Towards a new age of regulation, *CARR on Crisis: Risk and Regulation*, December, 12–13

Löfstedt, R, 2011, *Reclaiming health and safety for all: An independent review of health and safety legislation*, Cmnd 8219, London: HMSO, www.dwp.gov.uk/docs/lofstedt-report.pdf

Lukes, S, 1974, *Power: A radical view*, Basingstoke: Macmillan

Lupton, R, Fitzgerald, A, Fenton, A, 2013, The distribution of local government finance by local authority-level deprivation, *Social Policy in a Cold Climate. Research Note Series RN005*, London: London School of Economics and Political Science

Lynch, M, 2015, The classlessness state of criminology and why criminology without class is rather meaningless, *Crime, Law and Social Change* 63, 65–90

McBarnet, D, 2007, The new corporate accountability: Corporate social responsibility beyond law, through law, for law, in D McBarnet, A Voiculescu, T Campbell (eds) *The new corporate accountability: Corporate social responsibility and the law*, pp 9–57, Cambridge: Cambridge University Press

McBride, S, Whiteside, H, 2011, Austerity for whom?, *Socialist Studies/Études socialistes* 7, 1/2 (Spring/Fall), 42–64

McGurrin, D, 2013a, Theft of a nation symposium: Introduction, *Western Criminology Review*, 1 August, www.readperiodicals.com/201308/3118452791.html

McGurrin, D, 2013b, White collar crime representation in the criminological literature revisited, 2001–2010, *Western Criminology Review*, 1 August, www.readperiodicals.com/201308/3118452781.html

McGurrin, D, Friedrichs, DO, 2010, Victims of economic crime – on a grand scale, *Journal International de Victimologie* 23, www.jidv.com/njidv/index.php/archives/par-numero/jidv-23/150-jidv-23/428-victims-of-economic-crime-on-a-grand-scale

McKenzie, D, 2011, *Economic contribution of UK financial services 2010*, London: TheCityUK Research Centre

McLean, B, Nocera, J, 2011, *All the devils are here: The hidden history of the financial crisis*, New York: Portfolio/Penguin

MacLeod, R, 1965, The Alkali Acts administration, 1863–84: The emergence of the civil scientist, *Victorian Studies* 9, 2, 85–112

Maer, L, 2011, Quangoes, *Standard Note* SN/PC/05609, London: Parliament and Constitution Centre

Mahon, R, 1977, Canadian public policy: The unequal structure of representation, in L Panitch (ed) *The Canadian state: Political economy and political power*, pp 165-98, Toronto: University of Toronto Press

Mahon, R, 1979, Regulatory agencies: Captive agents or hegemonic apparatuses?, *Studies in Political Economy* 1, 1, 154–68

Mail Online, 2008, Sir John Harvey-Jones, TV's original troubleshooter, dies at 83, 11 January, www.dailymail.co.uk/news/article-507465/Sir-John-Harvey-Jones-TVs-original-troubleshooter-dies-83.html

Marshall, A, 2013, Environment Agency job cuts bigger and quicker than expected, *theENDSreport*, 25 October, www.endsreport.com/41255/environment-agency-job-cuts-bigger-and-quicker-than-expected

Marx, K, 1867/1976, *Capital: Volume 1*, Harmondsworth: Penguin

Mason, R, 2012, Nick Clegg plans a 'John Lewis economy', *Telegraph*, 15 January, www.telegraph.co.uk/news/politics/nick-clegg/9016800/Nick-Clegg-plans-a-John-Lewis-economy.html

Massey, D, 2012, Ideology and economics in the present moment, in J Rutherord, S Davison (eds) *The neoliberal crisis*, pp 97-107, London: Soundings

Mathiasen, N, 2011, Hedge funds, financiers and private equity make up 27% of Tory funding, *The Bureau of Investigative Journalism*, 30 September, www.thebureauinvestigates.com/2011/09/30/hedge-funds-financiers-and-private-equity-tycoons-make-up-27-of-tory-funding/.

Mathiesen, T, 2004, *Silently silenced*, Winchester: Waterside Press

May, P, Burby, R, 1998, Making sense out of regulatory enforcement, *Law and Policy* 20, 157–82

Meek, J, 2014, Sale of the century: The privatisation scam, *Guardian*, 22 August, www.theguardian.com/politics/2014/aug/22/sale-of-century-privatisation-scam

Meek, J, 2015, *Private island: Why Britain now belongs to someone else*, Revised edition, London: Verso

Michalowksi, R, Kramer, R, 1987, The space between laws: The problem of corporate crime in a transnational context, *Social Problems* 34, 1 (February), 34-53

Miliband, E, 2011a, Business, finance and politics are out of touch with people, *Observer*, 6 November, www.guardian.co.uk/commentisfree/2011/nov/05/ed-miliband-business-finance-politics

Miliband, E, 2011b, *Keynote speech on the economy by the Rt Hon Ed Miliband*, 24 November, www.ippr.org/images/media/files/event/2011/11/events-speech-miliband-111124.pdf

Miliband, E, 2012, *Labour will deliver fairness when there's less money around, only Labour can*, 10 January, www.labour.org.uk/labour-will-deliver-fairness

Miliband, R, 1973, *The state in capitalist society: An analysis of the western system of power*, London: Quartet

Miller, C, 1997, Regulation of UK industrial air pollution in the 1990s: Continuity and change. Case Law Analysis, *Journal of Environmental Law* 9, 2, 303–20

Mirowski, P, 2014, *Never let a serious crisis go to waste?*, London: Verso

Monbiot, G, 2000, *Captive state: The corporate takeover of Britain*, Basingstoke: Macmillan

Mooney, G, Miller, D, 2010, Introduction to the themed issue. Corporate power: Agency, communication, influence and social policy, *Critical Social Policy* 30, 4, 459–71

Morag-Levine, M, 2011, Is precautionary regulation a civil law instrument? Lessons from the history of the Alkali Act, *Journal of Environmental Law* 23, 1, 1–43

Moran, M, 2010, Regulation and the financial crisis, Keynote address, *European Consortium for Political Research Standing Group on Regulatory Governance*, University College Dublin, 18 June, www.irisheconomy.ie/index.php/2010/06/23/regulation-and-the-financial-crisis/

Morgan, G, 2012, Supporting the City: Economic patriotism in financial markets, *Journal of European Public Policy* 19, 3, 373–87

Morris, P, 1991, Freeing the spirit of enterprise: The genesis and development of the concept of the enterprise culture, in R Keat, N Abercrombie (eds) *Enterprise Culture*, pp 21–37, London: Routledge

Moschella, M, Tsingou, E, 2013, Regulating finance after the crisis: Unveiling the different dynamics of the regulatory process, *Regulation and governance. Regulating finance after the crisis: Unveiling the different dynamics of the regulatory process* 7, 407–16

Murphy, R, 2010, *Green bricks in the wall: Making quantitative easing Green*, Downham Market: Finance for the Future

Myners, P, 2010, The Bankers' Moral Hazard, *Guardian*, 9 March, www.theguardian.com/commentisfree/2010/mar/08/bankers-moral-hazard-discipline-punish

NAO (National Audit Office), 2007, *The Financial Services Authority: A review under section 12 of the Financial Services and Markets Act 2000. Report by The Comptroller and Auditor General*, HC 500 Session 2006–2007, London: The Stationery Office

NAO, 2008a, *Regulatory quality: How regulators are implementing the Hampton vision*, London: NAO

NAO, 2008b, *Effective inspection and enforcement: Implementing the Hampton vision in the Environment Agency*, London: NAO

NAO, 2008c, *Effective inspection and enforcement: Implementing the Hampton vision in the FSA*, London: NAO

NAO, 2008d, *Effective inspection and enforcement: Implementing the Hampton vision in the Health and Safety Executive*, London: NAO

NAO, 2008e, *Effective inspection and enforcement: Implementing the Hampton vision in the OFT*, London: NAO

NAO, 2008f, *Effective inspection and enforcement. Implementing the Hampton vision in the Financial Services Authority*, London: NAO

NAO, 2009a, *Animal health: A Hampton implementation review report*, London: Better Regulation Executive

NAO 2009b, *Gambling commission: A Hampton implementation review report*, London: Better Regulation Executive

NAO, 2009c, *Gangmasters Licensing Authority: A Hampton implementation review report*, London: Better Regulation Executive

NAO, 2009d, *Medicines and healthcare products regulatory agency: A Hampton implementation review report*, London: Better Regulation Executive

NAO, 2009e, *Maintaining financial stability across the United Kingdom's banking system*, www.nao.org.uk/report/maintaining-financial-stability-across-the-united-kingdoms-banking-system/

NAO, 2011, *Lessons from PFI and other projects: Report by the comptroller and auditor general*, HC 920 Session 2010–2012, 28 April, *Executive Summary*, www.nao.org.uk/wp-content/uploads/2011/04/1012920es.pdf

NAO, 2013, *Memorandum for Parliament: Government contracting. The role of major contractors in the delivery of public services*, Norwich: The Stationery Office

Navarro, V, 1983, The determinants of social policy, a case study: Regulating health and safety at the workplace in Sweden, *International Journal of Health Services* 13, 4, 517–61

Neocleous, M, 2003, *Imagining the state*, Maidenhead: Open University Press

Nielsen, V, Parker, C, 2009, Testing responsive regulation in regulatory enforcement, *Regulation and Governance* 3, 376–99

O'Hara, M, 2014, *Austerity bites: A journey to the sharp end of cuts in 2014*, Bristol: Policy Press

O'Neill, R, 2011, Low life: How the government has put a low price on your life, *Hazards Magazine*, January, www.hazards.org/votetodie/lowlife.htm

O'Neill, R, Pickvance, S, Watterson, A, 2007, Burying the evidence: How Great Britain is prolonging the occupational cancer epidemic, *International Journal of Occupational and Environmental Health* 4, 428–36

OECD, 2010, *Better regulation in Europe: United Kingdom*, Paris: OECD

OECD, 2013, *Public consultation on best practice principles for improving regulatory enforcement and inspections*, Draft report submitted to the public for comments, www.oecd.org/gov/regulatory-policy/enforcement-inspections.htm

OECD, 2014, *Regulatory enforcement and inspections: OECD best practice principles for regulatory policy*, Paris: OECD

OECD, nd, Chapter 2: The automobile industry in and beyond the crisis, www.oecd.org/economy/outlook/44089863.pdf

OECD Regulatory Policy Committee, 2009, *Indicators of regulatory management systems*, Report, Paris: OECD

Ojo, M, 2009, Responsive regulation: Achieving the right balance between persuasion and penalisation, *Munich Personal RePEc Archive Paper* 14170, at http://mpra.ub.uni-muenchen.de/14170/

ONS (Office for National Statistics), 2013, *Business demography 2012*, www.ons.gov.uk/ons/publications/re-reference-tables.html?edition=tcm%3A77-329345

Osborne, A, 2014, G4S Wins first central government contract since tagging scandal, *Telegraph*, 15 April, www.telegraph.co.uk/finance/newsbysector/supportservices/10768641/G4S-wins-first-central-Government-contract-since-tagging-scandal.html

Osborne, G, 2010a, Budget 2010: Full text of George Osborne's statement, *Telegraph*, 22 June, www.telegraph.co.uk/finance/budget/7846849/Budget-2010-Full-text-of-George-Osbornes-statement.html

Osborne, G, 2010b, Our tough but fair approach to welfare, Speech to the Conservative Party Annual Conference, 4, October, www.conservatives.com/News/Speeches/2010/10/George_Osborne_Our_tough_but_fair_approach_to_welfare.aspx

Osler, D, 2002, *Labour Party PLC: New Labour as a party of business*, Edinburgh: Mainstream

Palast, G, 2003, *The best democracy money can buy*, London: Robinson

Palmer, H, 2008, The whole story, *Safety and Health Practitioner*, www.shponline.co.uk/article.asp?article_id=8265 and viewcomment=1

Pantazis, C, Pemberton, S, 2012, Reconfiguring security and liberty: Political discourses and public opinion in the new century, *British Journal of Criminology* 52, 651–67

Parker, C, 2013, Twenty years of responsive regulation: An appreciation and appraisal, *Regulation and Governance, Special Issue: Twenty Years of Responsive Regulation* 7, 1, 2–13

Parker, D, 2004, The UK's privatisation experiment: The passage of time permits a sober assessment, *CESifo Working Paper* 1126, www.cesifo.de/pls/guestci/download/CESifo+Working+Papers+2004/CESifo+Working+Papers+February+2004/cesifo1_wp1126.pdf

Parliamentary News, 2010, *Early deaths from air pollution shame UK, says report*, 22 March, www.parliament.uk/business/news/2010/03/early-deaths-from-air-pollution-shame-uk-says-report/

Parliamentary News, 2011, *Environmental Audit Committee publishes report on air quality*, 14 November, www.parliament.uk/business/committees/committees-a-z/commons-select/environmental-audit-committee/news/air-quality-a-follow-up-report/

Paulus, I, 1974, *The search for pure food: A sociology of legislation in Britain*, London: Martin Robertson

Peacock, L, 2013, A4e's Emma Harrison paid £1.5m dividend despite pre-tax loss, *Telegraph*, 9 January, www.telegraph.co.uk/finance/jobs/9788801/A4es-Emma-Harrison-paid-1.5m-dividend-despite-pre-tax-loss.html

Pearce, F, 1976, *Crimes of the powerful*, London: Pluto

Pearce, F, 1993, Corporate rationality as corporate crime, *Studies in Political Economy* 40, 135–62

Pearce, F, Tombs, S, 1990, Ideology, hegemony and empiricism: Compliance theories of regulation, *British Journal of Criminology* 30, 423–43

Pearce, F, Tombs, S, 1991, Policing corporate 'skid rows': Safety, compliance, and hegemony, *British Journal of Criminology* 31, 415–26

Pearce, F, Tombs, S, 1997, Hazards, law and class: Contextualising the regulation of corporate crime, *Social and Legal Studies* 6, 1, 107–36

Pearce, F, Tombs, S, 1998, *Toxic capitalism: Corporate crime and the chemical industry*, Aldershot: Ashgate

Pearson, G, 1975, *The deviant imagination: Psychiatry, social work and social change*, Basingstoke: Macmillan

Peck, J, 2012, *Constructions of neo-liberal reason*, Oxford: Oxford University Press

Pemberton, S, 2015, *Harmful societies: Understanding social harm*, Bristol: Policy Press

Pemberton, S, Tombs, S, with Chan, M, Seal, L, 2012, Whistleblowing, organisational harm and the self-regulating organisation, *Policy and Politics* 40, 2 (April), 263–79

Pennington, H, 2009, *The Public Inquiry into the September 2005 outbreak of E.coli O157 in South Wales*, Cardiff: Welsh Assembly Government

Perren, L, Dannreuther, C, 2013, *Political signification of the entrepreneur: Temporal analysis of constructs, agency and reification, International Small Business Journal* 31, 6, 603–28

Peston, R, 2011, Bank break-up law by 2015, *BBC News Online*, 18 December, www.bbc.co.uk/news/business-16237692

Petras, J, 2012, *The two faces of a police state: Sheltering tax evaders, financial swindlers and money launderers while policing the citizens*, 8 May, http://petras.lahaine. org/?p=1905

Pettifor, A, 2012, Delusional economics and the economic consequences of Mr Osborne: Mis-measurement of health and wealth, Radical Statistics Annual Conference, London, 24 February

Pludwin, S, 2011, Rogue traders, suspect citizens and the invisible hand: Crisis in the theater of responsibility, *New Political Science* 33, 4, 465–77

Polanyi, K, 1971/1944, *The great transformation*, Boston, MA: Beacon Press

politics.co.uk, 2012, David Cameron pro-business speech in full, 23 February 2012, www.politics.co.uk/comment-analysis/2012/02/23/david-cameron-business-in-the-community-speech-in-full

Pollock, A, 2011, *Evidence submitted to the Treasury Committee inquiry into the future of the Private Finance Initiative*, www.allysonpollock.co.uk/ administrator/components/com_article/attach/2011-06-26/AP_2011_Pollock_ TreasuryCtteePFI.pdf

Pontell, H, Black, W, 2012, White-collar criminology and the Occupy Wall Street movement, *The Criminologist* 30, 1, 3–6

Pontell, H, Geis, G, 2014, The trajectory of white-collar crime following the great economic meltdown, *Special Issue, Journal of Contemporary Criminal Justice* 30, February, 29–40

Pontin, B, 2007, Integrated pollution control in Victorian Britain: Rethinking progress within the history of environmental law, *Journal of Environmental Law* 19, 2, 173–99

Poulantzas, N, 1970, *Fascism and dictatorship*, London: New Left Books

Pratley, N, 2012a, Cameron is coming for the crony capitalists – Whoever they are, *Guardian*, 19 January

Pratley, N, 2012b, Vickers report: Banking reforms won't work if they are watered down, *Guardian*, 14 June, www.guardian.co.uk/business/2012/jun/14/vickers-report-banking-reforms-dilution

Prieg, L, Greenham, T, Simms, A, Potts, R, 2011, *Subverting safer finance: How the UK holds back global financial regulation*, London: New Economics Foundation

Priest, M, 2008, Financial crisis: The tsunami will hit European banks harder, *Telegraph*, 1 October, www.telegraph.co.uk/finance/breakingviewscom/3117263/ Financial-crisis-The-tsunami-will-hit-European-banks-harder.html

Prime Minister's Office, 2010, Your freedom, *News Story*, 1 July, www.gov.uk/government/news/your-freedom--6

Prime Minister's Office, 10 Downing Street, BIS (Department for Business, Innovation and Skills), 2014, Supporting business: David Cameron announces new plans, *News Story*, 27 January, www.gov.uk/government/news/supporting-business-david-cameron-announces-new-plans

Prosser, T, 1997, Law *and the regulators*, Oxford: Clarendon Press

Prosser, T, 2010, *The regulatory enterprise: Government, regulation and legitimacy*, Oxford: Oxford University Press

Prosser, T, 2011, 'An opportunity to take a more fundamental look at the role of government in society': The Spending Review as regulation, *Public Law* 3, July, 596–616

QAA (Quality Assurance Agency), 2014, *Subject benchmark statement: Criminology*, Gloucester: QAA

Radaelli, C, 2007, Towards better research on better regulation, Paper delivered to the Advanced Colloquium on Better Regulation, Centre for Regulatory Governance, University of Exeter, 25–26 January

Radice, H, 2011, Cutting government deficits: Economic science or class war?, *Capital and Class* 35, 1, 125–37

Radice, H, 2013, *Why neoliberalism still rules despite the global crisis: Ideology after the crash*, University of Leeds, 27 November

Rankin, J, 2013, How TV Apprentice Yasmina Siadatan became start-ups' friend, *Guardian*, 8 November, www.theguardian.com/business/2013/nov/08/apprentice-winner-yasmina-siadatan-start-up-loans-company

Reed, H, 2012, Credit card maxed out? How UK debt statistics have been misrepresented, Mis-measurement of health and wealth, Radical Statistics Annual Conference, London, 24 February

Regulatory Policy Committee, 2011, *Challenging regulation: An independent report on the analysis supporting regulatory proposals*, September–December 2010, London: Regulatory Policy Committee

Regulatory Reform Act, 2001, Chapter 6, www.legislation.gov.uk/ukpga/2001/6/pdfs/ukpga_20010006_en.pdf

Reilly, B, Pace, P, Hall, P, 1995, Unions, safety committees and workplace injuries, *British Journal of Industrial Relations* 33, 2, 273-88

Reuben, A, 2014, Headline numbers: Public spending heads to 80-year low, *BBC News Online*, 3 December, www.bbc.co.uk/news/business-30318870

Rhodes, A, 2012, *UK local authority food law enforcement: 1 April 2011 to 31 March 2012,* Report by Andrew Rhodes, Director of Operations, Food Standards Agency, FSA 12/11/06 Open Board – 13 November 2012, www.food.gov.uk/sites/default/files/multimedia/pdfs/board/fsa121106.pdf

Richardson, G, with Ogus, A, Burrows, P, 1983, *Policing pollution*, Oxford: Clarendon

Rixen, T, 2013, Why reregulation after the crisis is feeble: Shadow banking, offshore financial centers, and jurisdictional competition, *Regulation and governance. regulating finance after the crisis: Unveiling the different dynamics of the regulatory process* 7, 435–59

Robins, N, 2006, *The corporation that changed the world: How the East India company shaped the modern multinational*, London: Pluto

Robinson, M, 2012, Austerity blues, *Guardian, Saturday Review*, 17 March, www.guardian.co.uk/books/2012/mar/16/culture-credit-crunch-marilynne-robinson

Rogers, P, 2007, *National enforcement priorities for local authority regulatory services*, Norwich: HMSO

Rogers, S, 2011a, News of the World circulation data: Who read it and how many bought it?, *Guardian Datablog*, www.guardian.co.uk/news/datablog/2011/jul/08/news-of-the-world-circulation-data#data

Rogers, S, 2011b, Mortality statistics: Every cause of death in England and Wales, visualised, *Guardian*, 28 October, www.guardian.co.uk/news/datablog/2011/oct/28/mortality-statistics-causes-death-england-wales–2010

Rothstein, H, Huber, M, Gaskell, G, 2006, A theory of risk colonisation: The spiralling regulatory logics of societal and institutional risk, *Economy and Society* 35, 91–112

Rowell, A, 1996, *Green backlash: Global subversion of the environmental movement*, London: Routledge

Ruane, S, 2010, Corporate and political strategy in relation to the private finance initiative in the UK, *Critical Social Policy* 30, 4, 519–40

Ruggiero, V, 2000, *Crime and markets: Essays in anti-criminology*, Oxford: Oxford University Press

Rutter, T, Gil, N, 2014, Which private companies get the most UK government money?, *Guardian Professional*, 26 June, www.theguardian.com/public-leaders-network/2014/jun/26/top–20-suppliers-central-local-government-data

Sassen, S, 2013, The logics of finance: Abuse of power and systemic crisis, in Will, S, Handelman, S, Brotherton, DC, eds, *How they got away with it. White collar criminals and the financial meltdown*, New York: Columbia University Press, pp 26-44.

Sayer, A, 1995, *Radical political economy: A critique*, Oxford: Blackwell

Sayer, A, 2007, Moral economy as critique, *New Political Economy* 12, 2, 261–70

Sayer, A, 2015, *Why we can't afford the rich*, Bristol: Policy Press

Schmidt, V, Thatcher, M (eds), 2013a, *Resilient liberalism in Europe's political economy*, Cambridge: Cambridge University Press

Schmidt, V, Thatcher, M, 2013b, Theorizing ideational continuity: The resilience of neo-liberal idea in Europe, in V Schmidt, M Thatcher (eds) *Resilient liberalism in Europe's political economy*, pp 1–50, Cambridge: Cambridge University Press

Shamir, R, 2004a, The de-radicalization of corporate social responsibility, *Critical Sociology* 33 , 3, 669–89

Shamir, R, 2004b, Between self-regulation and the Alien Tort Claims Act: On the contested concept of corporate social responsibility, *Law and Society Review* 38, 4, 635–64

Shapiro, S, 1984, *Wayward capitalists*, New Haven, CT: Yale University Press

Sharman, J, 2013, HELA inspection/visit: Data collection from local authorities, Paper H14/01, www.hse.gov.uk/aboutus/meetings/committees/hela/170113/h14-01.pdf

Shaxson, N, 2012, *Treasure islands: Tax havens and the men who stole the world*, London: Vintage

Shorthose, J, 2011, Economic conscience and public discourse, *Capital and Class* 35, 1, 107–24

Showstack-Sassoon, A, 2000, *Gramsci and contemporary politics: Beyond pessimism of the intellect*, London: Routledge

SHP (Safety and Health Practitioner) Online, 2012, PM's approach to health and safety not helpful, says Prof Löfstedt, *Safety and Health Practitioner*, 6 March, www.shponline.co.uk/pm-s-approach-to-health-and-safety-not-helpful-says-prof-lofstedt/?cid=searchresult

Sikka, P, 2012, Banks are serially corrupt: But Vince Cable's shareholder plan won't work, *Guardian*, 2 July, www.guardian.co.uk/commentisfree/2012/jul/02/banks-corrupt-vince-cable-shareholder-plan?INTCMP=SRC

Simms, A, Greenham, T, 2010, *Where did our money go? Building a banking system fit for purpose*, London: New Economics Foundation

Simpkins, E, 2004, Serco Profits from Crime, 11 July, *Telegraph*, www.telegraph.co.uk/finance/2889930/Serco-profits-from-crime.html

Simpson, C, 1998, Universities, empire and the production of knowledge: An introduction, in C Simpson (ed) *Universities and empire: Money and politics in the social sciences during the cold war*, pp xi-xxxiv, New York: The New Press

Simpson S, 2002, *Corporate crime, law and social control*, Cambridge: Cambridge University Press

Sinclair, T, 2010, Round up the usual suspects: Blame and the subprime crisis, *New Political Economy* 15, 1, 91–107

Sinfield, A, 2011, Credit, crunch, inequality and social policy, in K Farnsworth, Z Irving (eds) *Social policy in challenging times: Economic crisis and welfare systems*, pp 65-80, Bristol: Policy Press

Sklair, L, Miller, D, 2010, Capitalist globalization, corporate social responsibility and social policy, *Critical Social Policy* 30, 4, 472–95

Slapper, G, Tombs, S, 1999, *Corporate crime*, London: Longman

Smith, D, Ternes, B, Ordner, J, Schloemer, R, Moran, G, Goode, C, Homan, J, Kern, A, Keefer, L, Moser, N, McCannon, K, Byers, K, Sullivan, D, Craft, R, 2011, Mapping the great recession: A reader's guide to the first crisis of 21st century capitalism, *New Political Science* 33, 4, 577–601

Smith, KE, Fooks, GJ, Gilmore, A, Collin, J, Weishaar, H, 2015, Corporate coalitions and policy making in the European Union: How and why British American Tobacco promoted 'better regulation', *Journal of Health Politics, Policy and Law* 40, 2, 325–72

Smulian, M, 2013, Court clears way for Barnet outsourcing, *Public Finance*, 8 August, www.publicfinance.co.uk/news/2013/08/court-clears-way-for-barnet-outsourcing/

Snider, L, 1987, Towards a political economy of reform, regulation and corporate crime, *Law and Policy* 9, 1, 37–68

Snider, L, 1991, The regulatory dance: Understanding reform processes in corporate crime, *International Journal of the Sociology of Law* 19, 2, 209-36

Snider, L, 1993, *Bad business: Corporate crime in Canada*, Toronto: Nelson

Snider, L, 2000, The sociology of corporate crime: An obituary (Or: Whose knowledge claims have legs?), *Theoretical Criminology* 4, 2, 169–206

Snider, L, 2003, Captured by neo-liberalism: Regulation and risk in Walkerton, Ontario, *Risk Management* 5, 2, 17–27

Snider, L, 2009, Accommodating power: The 'common sense' of regulators, *Social and Legal Studies* 18, 179–97

Snider, L, Bittle, S, 2010, The challenges of regulating powerful economic actors, in J Gobert, AM Pascal (eds) *European developments in corporate criminal liability*, pp 53-69, London: Routledge

Social Enterprise UK, 2012, *The shadow state: A report about outsourcing of public services*, London: Social Enterprise UK

Soederberg, S, 2008, Deconstructing the official treatment for 'Enronitis': The Sarbanes-Oxley Act and the neoliberal governance of corporate America, *Critical Sociology* 34, 5, 657–80

Sparrow, A, 2014, Councils in poorest areas suffering biggest budget cuts, Labour says, *Guardian*, 25 August, www.theguardian.com/society/2014/aug/25/councils-poorest-areas-biggest-cuts-labour-says

Sparrow, M, 2000, *The regulatory craft: Controlling risks, solving problems, and managing compliance*, Washington, DC: The Brookings Institute

Spear, S, 2013, Barnet outsourcing deal sealed, *Environmental Health News Online*, 7 August, www.ehn-online.com/news/article.aspx?id=9634

Stanley, E, 2012, *Scumbag millionaires: The rhetorical construction and resistance of stigma during the financial crisis*, PhD thesis, London: Birkbeck, University of London

Strange, S, 1997, *Casino capitalism*, Manchester: Manchester University Press

Straw, W, 2011, Lib Dem, Tory and Labour all in this together on financial regulation, *Left foot forward,* 24 January, www.leftfootforward. org/2011/01/lib-dem-tory-labour-all-in-this-together-on-financial-regulation/

Streeck, W, 2014, How will capitalism end?, *New Left Review* 87, May–June, 35–64

Supiot, A, 2013, Grandeur and misery of the social state, *New Left Review* 82, July–August, 99–113

Sutherland, E, 1983, *White collar crime: The uncut version,* New Haven, CT: Yale University Press

Syal, R, 2012, Coalition cuts fraud investigators as private welfare contracts grow, *Guardian,* 31 March

Szasz, A, 1984, Industrial resistance to occupational safety and health legislation, 1971–1981, *Social Problems* 32, 2, 103–16

Tabb, W, 2012, *The restructuring of capitalism in our time,* New York: Columbia University Press.

Tam, C, Rodrigues, L, Viviani, L et al, 2011, Longitudinal study of infectious intestinal disease in the UK (IID2 Study): Incidence in the community and presenting to general practice, *Gut,* 5 July, http://gut.bmj.com/content/early/2011/06/26/gut.2011.238386.full.pdf

Taylor-Gooby, P, 2012, Root and branch restructuring to achieve major cuts: The social policy programme of the 2010 UK Coalition government, *Social Policy and Administration* 46, 1 (February), 61–82

Temple, M, 2014, *Triennial review report: Health and Safety Executive. An independent review of the function, form and governance of the Health and Safety Executive (HSE),* London: Department for Work and Pensions

The Howard League for Penal Reform, 2014, *Corporate crime? A dossier on the failure of privatisation in the criminal justice system,* London: The Howard League for Penal Reform

The Independent Commission on Banking, 2011, *Final report: Recommendations,* London: The Independent Commission on Banking, http://webarchive. nationalarchives.gov.uk/20131003105424/https:/hmt-sanctions.s3.amazonaws. com/ICB%20final%20report/ICB%2520Final%2520Report%5B1%5D.pdf

TheCityUK, 2013, *Key facts about UK financial and professional services,* London: TheCityUK

TheCityUK, 2014, *Key facts about UK financial and related professional services,* London: TheCityUK

Therborn, G, 2013, *The killing fields of inequality,* Cambridge: Polity

Thompson, EP, 1971, The moral economy of the English crowd in the eighteenth century, *Past and Present,* 50, February, 76–136

Thompson, G, 2009, How the financial crisis is being packaged for public consumption, 4 May, www.open.ac.uk/ccig/dialogues/blogs/how-the-financial-crisis-is-being-packaged-for-public-consumption

Tilly, C, 1985, War making and state making as organized crime, in P Evans, D Rueschemeyer, T. Skocpol (eds) *Bringing the state back in,* Cambridge: Cambridge University Press, pp 164–91

Tombs, S, 1995, Law, resistance and reform: 'Regulating' safety crimes in the UK, *Social and Legal Studies* 4, 3, 343–65

Tombs, S, 1996, Injury, death and the deregulation fetish: The politics of occupational safety regulation in UK manufacturing, *International Journal of Health Services* 26, 2, 327–47

Tombs, S, 2001, Thinking about 'white-collar' crime, in S-Å Lindgren (ed) *White-collar crime research: Old views and future potentials. Lectures and papers from a Scandinavian seminar. BRÅ-Rapport 2001:1,* pp 13–34, Stockholm: Brottsförebyggande rådet/Fritzes

Tombs, S, 2002, Understanding regulation?, *Social and Legal Studies* 11, 111–31

Tombs, S, 2007, Globalisation, neoliberalism and the trajectories of public policy: Closing (and reopening?) political possibilities, *International Journal of Management Concepts and Philosophy* 2, 4, 299–316

Tombs, S, 2013, Corporate theft and fraud: Business as usual, *Criminal Justice Matters* 94, 1, 14-15

Tombs, S, 2015a, Crisis, what crisis? Regulation and the academic orthodoxy, *Special Issue, The Howard Journal of Criminal Justice*, 54, 1, February, 57-72

Tombs, S, 2015b, Corporate theft and fraud: Crime and impunity in the retail financial services sector, in D Whyte (ed) *How corrupt is Britain?*, pp 57-72, London: Pluto

Tombs, S, Whyte, D, 1998, Capital fights back: Risk, regulation and profit in the UK offshore oil industry, *Studies in Political Economy* 57, 73–102

Tombs, S, Whyte, D, 2003, Researching the powerful: Contemporary political economy and critical social science, in S Tombs, D Whyte (eds) *Unmasking the crimes of the powerful: Scrutinising states and corporations*, pp 3–45, New York: Peter Lang

Tombs, S, Whyte, D, 2006, Work and risk, in G Mythen, S Walklate (eds) *Beyond the risk society*, pp 169-93, London: McGraw Hill

Tombs, S, Whyte, D, 2007, *Safety crimes*, Collumpton: Willan

Tombs, S, Whyte, D, 2008, *A crisis of enforcement: The decriminalisation of death and injury at work*, London: Centre for Crime and Justice Studies

Tombs, S, Whyte, D, 2009, Corporate crime? Theft, violence and harm, in J Muncie, D Talbot, R Walters (eds) *Crime: Local and global*, pp 137–72, Cullompton: Willan/Open University Press

Tombs, S, Whyte, D, 2010a, A deadly consensus: Worker safety and regulatory degradation under New Labour, *British Journal of Criminology* 50, 1, 46–65

Tombs, S, Whyte, D, 2010b, *Regulatory surrender: Death, injury and the non-enforcement of law*, London: Institute of Employment Rights

Tombs, S, Whyte, D, 2012, Better regulation: Critical lessons from the reshaping of health and safety law enforcement, in L Dickens (ed) *Making employment rights effective*, pp 67-86, Oxford: Hart

Tombs, S, Whyte, D, 2013a, Transcending the deregulation debate? Regulation, risk and the enforcement of health and safety law in the UK, *Regulation and Governance*, 7, 1, March, 61-79

Tombs, S, Whyte, D, 2013b, *Triennial review of the Health and Safety Executive submission to the Department for Work and Pensions. An IER response*, Liverpool: Institute for Employment Rights, July, www.ier.org.uk/sites/ier.org.uk/files/A%20Response%20to%20DWP%20Triennial%20Review%2013%20July.pdf

Tombs, S, Whyte, D, 2014, Toxic capital everywhere: Mapping the co-ordinates of regulatory tolerance, *Social Justice, Special Issue: Bhopal and after: The Chemical Industry as Toxic Capitalism* 41, 1/2 (December), 28–48

Tombs, S, Whyte, D, 2015, *The corporate criminal: Why corporations must be abolished*, London: Routledge

Trades Union Congress, 2012, *Banking after Vickers*, www.tuc.org.uk/economy/tuc–20572-f0.pdf

Trades Union Congress and the New Economics Foundation, 2015, *Outsourcing public services*, London: Trades Union Congress

Trading Standards Institute, Local Better Regulation Office, Better Regulation Executive, Chartered Institute of Environmental Health, 2012, *Local authority regulatory services budgets 2011–12*, www.lbro.org.uk/resources/docs/lars-budgets–2011-12-overview.pdf

Treanor, J, 2011, Bob Diamond stands firm against MPs' calls he forgo his bonus, *Guardian*, 11 January, www.guardian.co.uk/business/2011/jan/11/bob-diamond-stands-firm-mp-bonus

Treanor, J, 2012a, Standard chartered shares rise as US regulator drops licence threat, *Guardian*, 15 August, www.guardian.co.uk/business/2012/aug/15/standard-chartered-shares-rise-licence-threat

Treanor, J, 2012b, Barclays: From Libor to PPI, the charges in full, *Guardian*, 31 October, www.guardian.co.uk/business/2012/oct/31/barclays-the-full-charges-libor-ppi

Treanor, J, 2012c, John Vickers says George Osborne's banking reforms don't go far enough, *Guardian*, 14 June, www.guardian.co.uk/business/2012/jun/14/vickers-george-osborne-banking-reforms

Treanor, J, 2012d, HSBC warns money-laundering fines could top $1.5bn, *Guardian*, 5 November, www.guardian.co.uk/business/2012/nov/05/hsbc-warns-money-laundering-fines

Treanor, J, 2013a, Barclays closes controversial tax avoidance unit, *Observer*, 9 February, www.guardian.co.uk/business/2013/feb/09/barclays-closes-tax-avoidance-unit

Treanor, J, 2013b, More than 2,400 UK bankers paid €1m-plus, EU regulator says, *Guardian*, 15 July, www.guardian.co.uk/business/2013/jul/15/uk-bankers-pay-european-banking-authority

Treanor, J, Finch, J, 2009, Sir David Walker: 'I'm a man of the people, not a City grandee', The multi-millionaire banker defends his much-criticised blueprint for an accountable financial sector, *Guardian*, 26 November

Tsavalos, A, 2014, HELA data collection – analysis of LAE1 2013/14 data from local authorities, Paper H17/01, www.hse.gov.uk/aboutus/meetings/committees/hela/310714/data-collection–analysis.pdf

Tucker, E, 1990, *Administering danger in the workplace: The law and politics of occupational health and safety legislation in Ontario*, 1850–1914, Toronto: University of Toronto Press.

Tweedale, G, 2000, *Magic mineral to killer dust: Turner and Newall and the asbestos hazard*, Oxford: Oxford University Press

UK Parliament, 2006, Scrutiny of Regulatory Impact Assessments: Briefing note, www.parliament.uk/documents/commons/Scrutiny/RIA%20briefing%20note.pdf

UKSA (UK Shareholders' Association), 2005, *UK stock market statistics*, www.uksa.org.uk/Uk_stock_market.htm

UK Trade and Investment, 2012, *Financial services*, 3 December, www.ukti.gov.uk/investintheuk/sectoropportunities/financialprofessional services.html

UNISON, 2012a, *The damage. Environmental Health: How cuts are putting individuals and communities at risk and damaging local businesses and economies*, London: UNISON

Urry, J, 2014, *Offshoring*, Cambridge: Polity

Van Oosterhout, J, Heugens, P, 2008, Much ado about nothing: A conceptual critique of corporate social responsibility, in A Crane, A Mcwiliams, D Matten, J Moon, D Siegel (eds) *The Oxford handbook of corporate social responsibility*, pp 197–225, Oxford: Oxford University Press

Verbruggen, P, 2013, Gorillas in the closet? Public and private actors in the enforcement of transnational private regulation, *Regulation and Governance. Regulating Finance After the Crisis: Unveiling the Different Dynamics of the Regulatory Process* 7, 512–32

Vickers, I, 2008, Better regulation and enterprise: The case of environmental health risk regulation in Britain, *Policy Studies* 29, 2, 215–32

Vogel, S, 1996, *Freer markets, more rules: Regulatory reform in advanced industrial countries*, Ithaca, NY: Cornell University Press

Walker, D, 2009, *A review of corporate governance in UK banks and other financial industry entities: Final recommendations*, http://webarchive.nationalarchives.gov.uk/+/http:/www.hm-treasury.gov.uk/d/walker_review_261109.pdf

Walklate, S, 2009, Victims and the state, in R Coleman, J Sim, S Tombs, D Whyte (eds) *State, Power, Crime*, pp 174–84, London: Sage

Wall, T, 2011, EHOs hit by 'above average' cuts, *Environmental Health News*, 5 October

Wall, T, 2012a, Councils get £2.2bn for public health, *Environmental Health News*, 1 February

Wall, T, 2012b, EHOs are facing redundancies, *Environmental Health News*, 14 March

Walters, S, 2009, Take big cabinet jobs away from politicians, urges business guru Lord Digby Jones, *Mail Online*, 20 July, www.dailymail.co.uk/debate/article-1200643/Take-big-Cabinet-jobs-away-politicians-urges-business-guru-Lord-Digby-Jones.html

Waters, M, 1970, *Rosa Luxemburg speaks*, New York: Pathfinder Press

Webber, F, 2012, Perverse failure to prosecute G4S over Jimmy Mubenga's death, *Guardian Letters*, 18 July, www.theguardian.com/uk/2012/jul/18/failure-prosecute-g4s-jimmy-mubenga

Weber, M, 1905/1978, *The Protestant ethic and the spirit of capitalism*, London: George Allen & Unwin

Weissman, R, Donahue, J, 2009, *Sold out: How Wall Street and Washington betrayed America*, Washington, DC/Studio city, CA: Essential Information/Consumer Education Foundation, http://www.wallstreetwatch.org/reports/sold_out.pdf

Werdigier, J, 2011, It's time to stop criticizing bankers, Barclays chief says, *DealBook: New York Times*, 11 January, http://dealbook.nytimes.com/2011/01/11/time-to-stop-bashing-bankers-diamond-says/

White, J, 2013, Left and right in the economic crisis, *Journal of Political Ideologies* 18, 2, 150–70

Whitfield, D, 2006, *A typology of privatisation and marketisation*, Tralee: European Services Strategy Unit

Whittle, A, Mueller, F, 2012, Bankers in the dock: Moral storytelling in action, *Human Relations* 65, 1, 111–39

Whyte, D, 2004, Regulation and corporate crime, in J Muncie, D Wilson (eds) *Student handbook of criminal justice*, pp 134–48, London: Cavendish

Whyte, D, 2008, Market patriotism and the 'war on terror', *Social Justice* 35, 2–3, 111–31

Whyte, D, 2013, Market patriotism: Liberal Democracy unmasked, in R Fisher (ed) *Managing democracy, managing dissent*, London: Corporate Watch, pp 42–62

Whyte, D, 2015, Policing for whom?, *The Howard Journal of Criminal Justice* 54, 1, 73–90

Wiegratz, J, 2013, The neoliberal harvest: The proliferation and normalisation of economic fraud in a market society, in S Winlow, R Atkinson (eds) *New directions in crime and deviancy*, Abingdon: Routledge, pp 55–70

Wiener, J, 2006, Better regulation in Europe, *Duke Law School Legal Studies Research Pa*per series, *Research Paper* 130, October

Wilkins, LT, 1964, *Social deviance: Social policy, action and research*, London: Routledge

Wilkinson, R, Pickett, K, 2009, *The spirit level: Why equality is better for everyone*, London: Penguin

Wilks, S, 2013, *The political power of the business corporation*, Cheltenham: Edward Elgar

Will, S, Handelman, S, Brotherton, D (eds), 2011, *How they got away with it: Lessons from the financial meltdown*, New York: Columbia University Press

Will, S, 2013, America's Ponzi culture, in S Will, S Handelman, DC Brotherton (eds) *How they got away with it: White collar criminals and the financial meltdown*, pp 45–67, New York: Columbia University Press

Williams, C, 2012a, Councils' public health money 'not enough', *Environmental Health News*, 16 February

Williams, C, 2012b, Council cuts one in three EHOs, *Environmental Health News*, 3 May

Williams, C, 2012c, Regulation spending cut by a third, *Environmental Health News*, 31 October

Williams, C, 2012d, Council food safety staffing down 7%, *Environmental Health News*, 7 November

Williams, C, 2013, Tesco gave green light to prosecution, *Environmental Health News online*, 10 April, www.ehn-online.com/news/article.aspx?id=8790

Wilson, B, 2009, *Swindled: From poison sweets to counterfeit coffee – the dark history of the food cheats*, London: John Murray

Winlow, S, 2013, Is It OK to talk about capitalism again?, in S Winlow, R Atkinson (eds) *New directions in crime and deviancy*, Abingdon: Routledge, pp 21–39

Winlow, S, Hall, S, 2013, *Rethinking social exclusion: The end of the social?*, London: Sage

Winnett, R, 2011, Stop hounding small firms, says Nick Clegg, *Telegraph*, 25 October, www.telegraph.co.uk/news/politics/nick-clegg/8847340/Stop-hounding-small-firms-says-Nick-Clegg.html

Wintour, P, 2012, David Cameron condemns rhetoric of anti-business snobbery, *Guardian*, 22 February, www.guardian.co.uk/politics/2012/feb/22/david-cameron-condemns-anti-business-snobbery

Wood, C, Ivec, M, Job, J, Braithwaite, V, 2010, Applications of responsive regulatory theory in Australia and overseas, *Regulatory Institutions Network Occasional Paper* 15, Canberra: Regulatory Institutions Network, Australian National University

Wood, T, 2010, Editorial: Good riddance to New Labour, *New Left Review*, 62 (March/April), 5–28

Woodiwiss, M, Hobbs, D, 2009, Organized evil and the Atlantic Alliance: Moral panics and the rhetoric of organized crime policing in America and Britain, *British Journal of Criminology* 49, 106–28

Woods, N, 2009, Recession risks financial 'tsunami', *BBC News Online*, 20 March, http://news.bbc.co.uk/1/mobile/business/7947017.stm

Woolfson, C, Beck, M, Foster, J, 1996, *Paying for the piper: Capital and labour in Britain's offshore oil industry*, London: Mansell

Wright, J, Head, B, 2009, Reconsidering regulation and governance theory: A learning approach, *Law and Policy*, 31, 2, 192–216

Xenakis, S, Cheliotis, L, 2013, Crime and economic downturn: The complexity of crime and crime politics in Greece since 2009, *British Journal of Criminology* 53, 719–45

Young, D, 2010, *Common sense, common safety*, London: The Cabinet Office, www.number10.gov.uk/wp-content/uploads/402906_CommonSense_acc.pdf

Young, K, 2013, Financial industry groups' adaptation to the post-crisis regulatory environment: Changing approaches to the policy cycle, *Regulation and Governance. Regulating Finance After the Crisis: Unveiling the Different Dynamics of the Regulatory Process* 7, 460–80

Žižek, S, 2008, Use your illusions, *London Review of Books*, 14 November, www.lrb.co.uk/2008/11/14/slavoj-zizek/use-your-illusions

Žižek, S, 2009a, *First as tragedy, then as farce*, London: Verso

Žižek, S, 2009b, *Violence: Six sideways reflections*, London: Profile Books

Index